Futuristic Information and Communication: A Multimodal Multidisciplinary Signal Analysis

The **International Conference on Futuristic Information and Communication** serves as a platform for the exchange of ideas, nurturing collaborations, and disseminating knowledge that will shape the future of communication. This conference brings together researchers, scientists, academicians, scholars, and industrial practitioners from across the globe to present papers and discuss recent developments in acoustical signal processing, image processing and multimedia systems, mobile and wireless communications, computer and communication networks, high-performance computing, advances in communication and networks, image and multimedia processing, databases, machine learning, deep learning, data science, cognitive computing, artificial intelligence, data mining, data warehousing, cloud computing, big data, and data analytics.

The theme of this conference reflects the evolving landscape of information and communication systems, where multimodal data—spanning audio, visual, textual, and sensory inputs—demands innovative approaches to analysis, interpretation, and application. The rapid advancement of artificial intelligence, machine learning, and big data analytics has transformed how we process and utilize signals in diverse fields such as telecommunications, healthcare, autonomous systems, and human-computer interaction. This conference aims to foster dialogue and collaboration among experts from disciplines including signal processing, computer science, electrical engineering, cognitive science, and data science to address the challenges and opportunities in this dynamic domain.

Each contribution has been rigorously peer-reviewed to ensure the highest standards of academic and technical excellence. We hope these proceedings will serve as a valuable resource for researchers, practitioners, and students shaping the future of information and communication technologies.

We extend our gratitude to the organizing committee, reviewers, authors, and participants for their dedication and contributions to making this conference a success. Special thanks go to the President, Director, and Vice Chancellor of Siksha 'O' Anusandhan (Deemed University) for their generous support for hosting this event.

We invite you to explore the innovative ideas and groundbreaking research presented in this volume and to continue the conversation on advancing multimodal signal analysis for a connected and intelligent future.

Sincerely,
Prof. (Dr.) Mihir Narayan Mohanty

Dr. Mihir Narayan Mohanty is presently working as a Professor in the Department of Electronics and Communication Engineering, Institute of Technical Education and

Research, Siksha 'O' Anusandhan (Deemed to be University), Bhubaneswar, Odisha, India. He is the senior member of IEEE, Fellow of IET and IE(I). He has published more than 400 research papers in various high index International Journals (>120) Book Chapters (>100), Conferences Proceedings (>200) over the 25 years of teaching and research experience. He has also co-edited four books of Springer in the area of Advances in Artificial Intelligence. His area of research interests includes Applied Signal and Image Processing, Biomedical Signal Processing, Microwave Communication Engineering and Speech Processing. He is having total 2394 Google scholar citation with h-index 23, and i-10 index 60. He has successfully guided six Ph.D. scholars and currently seven scholars are working under him. He has delivered number of talks and guest lecturers in various countries including China, Singapore, Malasiya, UAE, Thailand. He has organized various international conferences and faculty development programs.

Dr. Bibhuprasad Mohanty is presently working as a Professor and Head in the Department of Electronics and Communication Engineering, Institute of Technical Education and Research, Siksha 'O' Anusandhan (Deemed to be University), Bhubaneswar, Odisha, India. He is the member of IEEE, IET and IE(I). He has published more than 85 research papers in various high index International Journals with over the 25 years of teaching and research experience. He has also co-edited four books of Springer in the area of Advances in Artificial Intelligence. His area of research interests includes Applied Signal and Image Processing, Biomedical Signal Processing, Communication Engineering and Speech Processing.

Dr. Kandarpa Kumar Sarma, currently Professor and Head, Department of Electronics and Communication Engineering, GUIST, Gauhati University, India specializes in mobile communication, artificial intelligence, human-computer interaction, cognitive and software-defined radio, speech processing and antenna design. He completed MTech in Signal Processing in 2005 from IIT Guwahati, India. He also completed PhD from IIT Guwahati in the area of mobile communication in 2012. He is a Senior Member of IEEE (USA) and a fellow of the Institution of Electronics and Telecommunication Engineers (IETE) (India).

Dmitrii Kaplun, Associate Professor (2015), Lead Researcher (2020) at Saint Petersburg Electrotechnical University "LETI" (Saint Petersburg, Russia), Full Professor (2023) at China University of Mining and Technology. The current research and academic work are related with digital signal and image processing, embedded and reconfigurable systems, computer vision and machine learning. The most substantial results are in the fields of digital signal and image processing, embedded systems and machine learning. Author of more than 100 papers in journals, including leading journals, and conference proceedings. He is an Associate/Guest Editor/Editorial Board Member such journals as Frontiers in Neuroinformatics, Industrial Artificial Intelligence, Scientific Reports.

Futuristic Information and Communication: A Multimodal Multidisciplinary Signal Analysis

Edited by

Dr. Mihir Narayan Mohanty

Siksha 'O' Anusandhan (Deemed to be University), India

mihirmohanty@soa.ac.in

Dr. Bibhuprasad Mohanty

Siksha 'O' Anusandhan (Deemed to be University), India

bibhumohanty@soa.ac.in

Dr. Kandarpa Kumar Sarma

Gauhati University, Guwahati, India

kandarpaks@gauhati.ac.in

Dr. Dmitrii Kaplun

China University of Mining and Technology, Xuzhou, China

Saint Petersburg Electrotechnical University "LETI", St. Petersburg, Russia

dikaplun@etu.ru

CRC Press
Taylor & Francis Group
Boca Raton London New York

CRC Press is an imprint of the
Taylor & Francis Group, an **informa** business

First edition published 2026
by CRC Press
44 Park Square, Milton Park, Abingdon, Oxon, OX14 4RN

and by CRC Press
2385 NW Executive Center Drive, Suite 320, Boca Raton FL 33431

British Library Cataloguing-in-Publication Data
A catalogue record for this book is available from the British Library

ISBN: 9781041272403 (pbk)
ISBN: 9781041268444 (hbk)
ISBN: 9781003753391 (ebk)

DOI: 10.1201/9781003753391

Typeset in Times New Roman
by HBK Digital

Contents

List of Figures

List of Tables

About the Conference

In recent years, it has been heard about advances in communication in the area of internet of things, industrial IOT, smart factories, smart healthcare, smart mobility and smart energy etc. **ICFIC 2025** is one of those International Conference that aims to explore growing advancements in the fields of Telecommunication and Networking Technologies and provides a common platform to leading scientists, academicians, researchers, government officials, practicing engineers, industry professionals and students to share their research experiences and views. It is a technical congregation where the latest theoretical and technological techniques in advanced computing are presented and discussed. Even database has also been updated by huge amount of data through the globe. So, the role of big data and data analytics will lead to further evolution of ubiquitous computing, cognitive computing with computational intelligence and cloud computing. The conference was held on **27**th – **28**th **June 2025** to make it an ideal platform for people to share views and experiences on futuristic research techniques in various related areas. The role of computing, communicating, energy resources are to be emphasized in computer science and engineering, electronics and communication engineering and electrical engineering respectively to enhance and motivate the new technology for wide range of applications.

The objective of the conference is to bring together experts from academic institutions, industries, research organizations and professional engineers for sharing of knowledge, expertise and experience in emerging trends related to the computer, communication and electrical topics. The aim of this international conference is to coverage all the issues on a single platform and provide international forum for researchers to discuss the real-time problems and solutions to exchange their valuable ideas and showcase the ongoing works which may lead to path breaking foundation of the futuristic engineering. This conference mainly aims at advanced communication protocol, database security and privacy, advanced computing system, saving energy etc. on several updated techniques. The conference offers a platform to focus on the inventive information and computing towards the investigation of cognitive mechanisms and processes of human information processing, and the development of the next generation engineering and advanced technological systems.

About SOA

Siksha 'O' Anusandhan (SOA), a distinguished Deemed-to-be University in Bhubaneswar, India has established itself as a leader in higher education and research in India since its inception in 2007. Recognized under Section 3 of the UGC Act, 1956, SOA offers a wide range of professional programs across disciplines, including Engineering, Medicine, Dental Science, Nursing, Pharmaceutical Science, Biotechnology, Management, Law, Hotel Management, Agricultural Sciences, and Veterinary Science. The University's commitment to academic excellence has been reflected in its reaccreditation by NAAC with an 'A++' grade, the highest achievable, in 2022. SOA has also demonstrated remarkable success in the National Institutional Ranking Framework (NIRF) by the Ministry of Education, Government of India, consistently achieving high ranks. Notably, in the NIRF 2024 rankings, it secured the 14th position among Indian universities, 26th in Engineering, 21st in Medical Science, and 9th in both Dental Science and Law, with additional top placements in the Research and Management categories.

Internationally, SOA has garnered recognition as well. SOA is among only four Universities in India listed in *THE World Reputation Rankings 2025*. Similarly, the QS World University Rankings 2024 positioned SOA in the 1201-1400 global bracket, while it achieved placements of 501-550 in the QS Asia University Rankings and 143 in the QS Southern Asia University Rankings. SOA's programs in Engineering, Management, Pharmacy, and Hotel Management have also been accredited by the National Board of Accreditation (NBA), and its Faculty of Agricultural Sciences and B.Sc. (Hons.) Agriculture program have been accredited by the Indian Council of Agricultural Research (ICAR). Further accreditations include NABH for its Faculty of Medical Science and NABL for its laboratories. Additionally, SOA has been recognized as a Scientific and Industrial Research Organization (SIRO) by the Department of Scientific and Industrial Research (DSIR), Government of India, and holds UGC Section 12(B) status.

As a testament to its outstanding performance, SOA received the Diamond University Rating by QS-I-GAUGE and is recognized as an Institution of Happiness (IOH) in the University & College category. It is also the only university in Odisha to have attained these prestigious accolades. Approved by UGC and AICTE, SOA has also obtained international accreditation by ABET, USA, positioning itself as a global leader committed to nurturing a dynamic learning atmosphere, encouraging interdisciplinary research, and fostering innovation across its undergraduate and postgraduate programs. The university has set up 16 research centres to promote research work in 26 thrust areas. SOA runs the Institute of Medical Sciences and SUM Hospital, its faculty of medicine, with 1600 beds which has become one of the most sought-after healthcare destinations in the east. The teaching hospital, with NABH and NABL accreditation, has 250 MBBS seats. SOA was in the forefront in Odisha's battle against Covid-19 when the first wave swept through the state in 2020 making exemplary contribution towards prevention and control of the pandemic. It set up four standalone Covid Hospitals in Bhubaneswar, Kendrapara, Talcher and Chandpur in collaboration with the state government and ran two Covid Care Centres at Jatni and Jamujhari accounting for 2341 beds. When the second wave struck early in 2021, SOA operated as many as five Covid Hospitals at Bhubaneswar, Chandpur, Puri, Talcher and Kendrapara (besides a Covid Care Centre at Jatni) having more than 2200 beds with around 500 doctors from Institute of Medical Sciences and SUM Hospital engaged in treating the patients assisted by nurses and paramedics who worked round-the-clock.

Preface

The ongoing quest for a healthier, more comfortable lifestyle has spurred innovation across numerous fields. Technological advancements and their real-world applications remain foundational to modern society's evolution. Today's innovations across various engineering disciplines including electrical, electronics, mechanical, and computer science, particularly AI aim to establish smarter systems, such as smart homes, smart cities, and smart societies. Progress in renewable energy, electric transportation, power electronics, electric drives, control techniques, smart grids, communication protocols, intelligent charging infrastructure, and standards are deeply interconnected. Innovation in one field often contributes to solving identified issues in others, highlighting the importance of continuous research and the dissemination of findings to foster global societal development.

The **International Conference on Futuristic Information and Communication (ICFIC-2025)**, a Taylor and Francis Conference was hosted by the Department of Electronics and Communication Engineering at the Institute of Technical Education and Research, Siksha 'O' Anusandhan (Deemed to be University), in Bhubaneswar, Odisha, India, on June 27th - 28th, 2025. ICFIC-2025 seeks to attract innovative ideas from researchers worldwide, with the vision of creating smarter cities and societies. Contributions from all engineering and technology fields are vital to realizing this vision. The 'call for papers' was designed to attract a diverse range of topics, leading to 150 online submissions. Of these, only 55 high-quality papers were accepted through a rigorous and unbiased peer-review process, handled by knowledgeable reviewers, advisory board members, and the program and technical committee of ICFIC-2025. The selection criteria were rooted in the technical contributions, originality, and alignment with the conference's themes. Each stage of the review process was completed electronically, ensuring efficiency and fairness.

Keynote speeches form a central element of the conference, enabling researchers and scientists from various fields to share insights and innovations. ICFIC-2025 has devoted special efforts to arrange keynote addresses that align with the conference's themes. Furthermore, the presentation schedule was designed to reflect the interconnectedness of each author's contribution, emphasizing the core themes and objectives of the conference. We extend our gratitude to the authors for choosing ICFIC as the platform for their research dissemination, and to the reviewers and Program Committee members for their invaluable support in the peer-review process.

Acknowledgement

The editors are honored to present the impactful initiatives and importance of the ICFIC 2025, which has garnered immense interest from academics and researchers globally. This conference has served as an ideal platform to showcase a wide array of innovative research across Electrical, Electronics, Computational, Industrial, Medical and Agricultural Engineering fields.

We extend our sincere gratitude to all authors whose valuable time, expertise, and research contributions have enriched the conference and elevated its quality.

Our heartfelt appreciation goes to the national and international advisory committees, whose timely and invaluable support ensured smooth pre- and post-conference activities and proceedings. We also thank the dedicated team of reviewers who conducted thorough evaluation of all manuscripts, providing critical feedback essential to upholding the conference's high standards.

A special thanks goes to the organizing committee for their tireless efforts, which have been instrumental in making the event a resounding success.

Our deep gratitude also extends to the CRC Press' Publishing team's editorial members for shaping the conference proceedings with such intelligence and creativity, ensuring that ICFIC-2025 receives deserved recognition before a global audience.

Lastly, we thank the Management of SOA (Deemed to be University) and the faculty of the Electronics and Communication Engineering Department at ITER for their ongoing support, which has been vital to the conference's success. We are also grateful to the Editorial Team of CRC Press for facilitating the publication of proceedings, ensuring that all accepted papers are included in SCOPUS-indexed Taylor and Francis proceedings.

The Editors would also like to convey their heartfelt thanks to Prof. M. R. Nayak, President, Siksha 'O' Anusandhan Deemed to be University, Prof. P. K. Nanda, Vice Chancellor, Siksha 'O' Anusandhan Deemed to be University, Prof. J. K. Nath, Dean (R&D), Siksha 'O' Anusandhan Deemed to be University and Prof. P. K. Sahoo, Dean, ITER (FET), Siksha 'O' Anusandhan Deemed to be University for their constant inspiration and motivation in all stages of the Conference.

Message from President's Desk

I am delighted to know that the Institute of Technical Education and Research (ITER) is organizing International Conference on Futuristic Information and Communication (ICFIC-2025) in its campus on June 27th and 28th, 2025.

This conference is of immense importance as it will bring researchers, academicians, industry professionals and government personnel on a single platform to discuss the advancements made in the field of Telecommunication and Networking Technologies.

I understand that the latest theoretical and technological aspects in advanced computing will be discussed in the technical sessions of the conference. The role of big data, data analytics and artificial intelligence will also figure in the deliberations which will be of great value.

I wish the conference all success.

Professor (Dr.) Manoj Ranjan Nayak
Founder President
Siksha 'O' Anusandhan (deemed to be University)
Bhubaneswar, Odisha, India

Message from Vice Chancellor's Desk

It gives me immense pleasure to know that an *International Conference on Futuristic Information and Communication (ICFIC-2025)*, organized by the Institute of Technical Education and Research **(ITER)**, Siksha 'O' Anusandhan Deemed to be University **(SOADU)** Bhubaneswar, India during **27th -28th June,2025**.

In a rapidly evolving digital landscape, the themes of this conference—ranging from Acoustical Signal Processing and Image Processing to Mobile Communications and Networking—hold immense significance. ICFIC-2025 provides an excellent platform for cross-disciplinary dialogue, knowledge exchange and the cultivation of innovative ideas that can contribute to the advancement of science and technology for societal good.

It is our privilege to host eminent keynote speakers from across the globe and look forward to thought-provoking sessions, impactful presentations and meaningful collaborations. I sincerely thank all the participants, organizing committee members, and partners who have contributed to making this international conference possible.

I wish ICFIC-2025 great success and hope the deliberations over these two days will inspire future innovations and foster lasting academic and professional relationships.

With best wishes,

Warm regards,

Prof. Pradipta Kumar Nanda
Vice Chancellor

Message from the Dean's desk

I am happy to learn that Siksha 'O' Anusandhan Deemed to be University, Bhubaneswar, India is organizing **International Conference on Futuristic Information and Communication (ICFIC 2025)** of Taylor and Francis is going to be organized on 27th and 28th, June 2025.

The Conference will provide the authors and participants with opportunities for National and International Collaboration and networking among Universities and Institutions from India and abroad for promoting research and developing technologies. ICFIC-2025 is a multidisciplinary conference which focused in the direction of numerous advanced concepts or cutting-edge tools applied for electrical, electronics and computer science domain. Hence, I feel that this conference has been rightly planned at an appropriate time to share and discuss on the issue of sustainable and continuous innovation/ research on electrical, electronics and computing including AI domain.

I wish to convey my felicitations to organizers and to all the participating delegates and wish the international conference a grand success.

Prof. (Dr.) Pradeep Kumar Sahoo
Dean
FET (ITER)

Message from the Director's desk

It fills me with joy to learn that the Siksha 'O' Anusandhan Deemed to be University, based in Bhubaneswar, India, is set to host the **International Conference on Futuristic Information and Communication (ICFIC 2025)** is going to be organized on 27th and 28th, June 2025.

This gathering is a golden opportunity for authors and attendees alike to foster both National and International collaborations, networking with a multitude of Universities and Institutions, both from India and across the globe. The aim is to propel research forward and to foster the development of innovative technologies. ICFIC-2025 represents a multi-disciplinary conference, with its sights set firmly on several pioneering ideas and avant-garde tools used in the fields of electrical, electronics, and computer science. In this regard, I feel the timing for this conference could not be more perfect to foster discussions and share ideas around the theme of sustainable and continuous innovation and research, especially in the electrical, electronics, and AI domains.

I want to extend my heartfelt congratulations to the event organizers and all delegates participating in the event. My hope is for the international conference to meet resounding success.

Prof. (Dr.) Manas Kumar Mallick
Director, FET (ITER)

Message from the desk of General Chair

I take the privilege to inform that Department of Electronics and Communication Engineering, Faculty of Engineering & Technology, Siksha 'O' Anusandhan Deemed to be University, Bhubaneswar, Odisha, India shall be organizing the **International Conference on Futuristic Information and Communication (ICFIC 2025)** by Taylor and Francis on 27th and 28th, June 2025. ICFIC-2025 is dedicated to uniting a diverse community of researchers, scientists, engineers, and scholars to promote collaboration and exchange cutting- edge research and insights in engineering, science, and technology. With a strong emphasis on sustainable and clean energy, the conference will provide a platform for innovative discussions on pressing topics such as the urgent need for cleaner transportation alternatives to combat air and transportation pollutants that pose severe health risks to the population. Key areas of focus will include Artificial Intelligence and Machine Learning, VLSI, Embedded System, Communication Engineering, Modelling and Simulations, Computational Intelligence, and the Internet of Things (IoT). In addition to formal presentations, participants will benefit from extensive networking opportunities, fostering professional connections and collaborations.

This is a premier conference where around 50 plus researchers across the globe will present their research findings. A total of 150 submitted articles have gone through a rigorous review process and 55 articles were accepted those will be published in the Proceedings by Taylor and Francis.

We welcome all the foreign and Indian delegates to enjoy the conference and the rich heritage and culture of the state of Odisha.

Message from the desk of Program Chair and HOD, ECE

It is of utmost privilege and honor for me to announce the commencement of **International Conference on Futuristic Information and Communication (ICFIC 2025)** by Taylor and Francis is being organized by Institute of Technical Education and Research (ITER), Siksha 'O' Anusandhan (Deemed to be University), Bhubaneswar, Odisha, India on 27th and 28th, June 2025. It is our great honor to welcome all the delegates, attendees and presenters to this conference.

We hope the attendees, and participants will enjoy the conference venue, ITER, Siksha 'O' Anusandhan (Deemed to be University), Bhubaneswar. The Faculty of Engineering and Technology (FET-ITER) have worked very hard to make this conference possible. We would like to thank all who have helped in making **ICFIC-2025** a success. Members of our program committees and referees all deserve credit for producing the excellent programs of these conferences that resulted from diligent reviews of the submissions. Special thanks go to the program chairs, organizing chairs and all of the other organizing committee members. We thank the many authors who contributed and all the participants who make this event so special. We hope you enjoy the conference and that you continue to contribute to our future events as authors, speakers, panelists, volunteers, and participants.

Organising Committee

Chief Patron
Prof. Manojranjan Nayak
President, SOA Deemed to be University, Bhubaneswar

Patron
Prof. (Dr.) Pradipta Kumar Nanda
Vice Chancellor, SOA Deemed to be University, Bhubaneswar

General Chair
Prof. Mihir Narayan Mohanty
Professor, Dept. of ECE, SOA Deemed to be University, Bhubaneswar

Financial Chair
Prof. M. K. Mallick, Director, ITER, Bhubaneswar

Program Chair
Prof. B. P. Mohanty, ITER, Bhubaneswar

Program Co-chairs
Prof. Niva Das, ITER, Bhubaneswar
Prof. Benudhar Sahoo, , ITER, Bhubaneswar

Publication Chairs
Prof. B. K. Pattnaik, ITER, Bhubaneswar
Dr. Shaktijeet Mahapatra, ITER, Bhubaneswar
Mr. Gyana Ranjan Patra, ITER, Bhubaneswar

Technical Program Chairs
Prof. Laxmi Prasad Mishra, ITER, Bhubaneswar
Prof. Benudhar Sahu, ITER, Bhubaneswar
Dr. Sandhyalati Behera, ITER, Bhubaneswar

Workshop Chairs
Dr. Kunal Das, ITER, Bhubaneswar
Dr. Pritam Keshari Sahoo, ITER, Bhubaneswar

Local Arrangements Chairs
Dr. Hemanta Palo, ITER, Bhubaneswar
Dr. Aneesh Wunnava, ITER, Bhubaneswar

Web & Social Media Chairs
Dr. Asit Kumar Subudhi, ITER, Bhubaneswar
Dr. Santanu Kumar Sahoo, ITER, Bhubaneswar

Publicity Chairs
Dr. Badri Narayan Sahu, ITER, Bhubaneswar
Dr. Saumendra Kumar Mohanty, ITER, Bhubaneswar
Mr. Gyana Ranjan Patra, ITER, Bhubaneswar

Corporate Relation Chairs
Dr. Aneesh Wunnava, ITER, Bhubaneswar
Dr. Hemanta Kumar Palo, ITER, Bhubaneswar

Student Volunteer Chairs
Dr. Sidhartha Dash, ITER, Bhubaneswar
Dr. Satyanarayan Bhuyan, ITER, Bhubaneswar

National Advisory Committee
- Dr. Nishchal K Verma, IIT Kanpur
- Dr. Jagadish C. Bansal, SAU Delhi
- Dr. Tarun K. Sharma, Amity University, Jaipur
- Dr. Kusum Deep, IIT Roorkee
- Dr. Mili Pant, IIT Roorkee,
- Dr. Manoj K. Tiwari, IIT, KGP,
- Dr. Bidyut Baran Chaudhuri, ISI Kolkata
- Dr. Nanda Dulal Jana, NIT Durgapur
- Dr. Amalendu Patnaik, IIT, Roorkee
- Dr. Vikram M Gadre, IIT, Bombay
- Dr. Sarat Kumar Patra, IIT, Vadodara,
- Dr. Santanu Kumar Behera, NIT, Rourkela.
- Dr. Arvind Kumar Sharma, NIT, Rourkela
- Dr. Prashanta Kumar Patra, CVRCE, Bhubaneswar.
- Dr. Prithviraj Kabisatpathy, CVRCE, Bhubaneswar
- Dr. Priyadarshi Kanungo, CVRCE, Bhubaneswar
- Dr. Ashima Rout, IGIT, Sarang
- Dr. Sakuntala Mahapatra, Trident Academy of Technology, Bhubaneswar
- Dr. Manas Ranjan Senapati, Trident Academy of Technology, Bhubaneswar
- Dr. Arun Kumar Ray, KIIT University, Bhubaneswar, Odisha, India
- Prof. Alok Kumar Jagadev, KIIT University, Bhubaneswar, Odisha
- Dr. Prashanta Ku.Nayak, Synergy, Dhenkanal,
- Dr. Sanjay Agrawal, VSSUT, Burla,
- Dr. Nilamani Bhoi, VSSUT, Burla,
- Dr. Rutuparna Panda, VSSUT, Burla,
- Dr. Santosh Kumar Majhi, VSSUT, Burla,

- Dr. Gopinath Palai, Gandhi Institute for Technological Advancement, Bhubaneswar
- Prof. Monojit Mitra , IIEST, Shibpur.
- Dr. Shailendra Kumar Varshney, IIT, KGP.
- Prof. Debasish Dutta, IIT, KGP.
- Prof. Ashok Kumar Pradhan , IIT, KGP.
- Prof. Aurobinda Routray IIT, KGP.
- Prof. Amalendu Pattnaik, IIT, Roorkee
- Dr. B.K. Panigrahi, IIT, Delhi.
- Dr. Sukumar Mishra, IIT, Delhi.
- Dr. Prasant Kumar Sahu, IIT, Bhubaneswar.
- Dr. Subhransu Ranjan Samantaray, IIT, Bhubaneswar.
- Prof. Ganapati Panda, IIT, Bhubaneswar.
- Dr. Guru Prasad Subas Chandra Mishra, NIT, Raipur.
- Dr. Debadatta Pati, NIT, Nagaland.
- Dr. Kandarpa Kumar Sarma, Guwahati University.
- Dr. Satchidananda Dehuri, FM University.
- Dr. Saroj Kumar Meher, Indian Statistical Institute, Bangalore Centre.
- Dr. Pankaj Sarkar, NEHU, Shillong
- Dr. Madhumita Das Sarkar
- Dr. Shweta Singh, Ennoble IP, India
- Dr. Amit Kant Pandit, SMVDU.
- Dr. Mahesh Chandra, BIT, Mesra.
- Dr. Aditya Kandali, Jorhat Engineering College, Assam
- Dr. Harleen Kaur, Jamia Hamdard, Delhi.
- Dr. Sivkumar Mishra, BPUT, Odisha.
- Dr. Lokanath Sarangi, CEB, Bhubaneswar.
- Dr. G.P. Ramesh, St. Peter's University, Chennai
- Dr. Mohit Kumar, Muzaffarpur Institute of Technology, Muzaffarpur.
- Dr. Akash Kumar Bhoi, Sikkim Manipal Institute of Technology.
- Dr. Pradeep Kumar Mallick, KIIT University, Bhubaneswar.
- Dr. L. Padma Suresh, BMCE, Kerala

International Advisory Committee

- Atulya Nagar, Liverpool Hope University, UK.
- Siddhartha Bhattacharya, RCCIIT and TU-Ostrava, Czech Republic
- Fatih Taşgetiren, Turkey
- Aboul Ella Hassanien, University of Cairo
- Ivan Zelinka, VSB-Ostrava
- Ahmed F. Zobaa, Brunel University London.
- Valentina Emilia Balas, Aurel Vlaicu University of Arad, ROMANIA
- Dac-Nhuong Le, Haiphong University, Haiphong, Vietnam
- Mahdi Esmaeilzadeh, Iran University of Science and Technology, Narmak, Tehran, Iran
- Avinash Konkani, University of Virginia Health System, Virginia, USA.
- Yu-Min Wang, National Chi Nan University, Taiwan.
- Hongyan Yu, Shanghai Maritime University, Shanghai.

- Benson Edwin, Raj Fujairah Women's College Fujairah, UAE.
- Mohd. Hussain, Islamic University, Madina Saudi Arabia.
- Ganesh R Naik, University of Technology, Sydney, Australia.
- Steve S.H. Ling University of Technology, Sydney, Australia.
- Yiguang Liu, Sichuan University, China.
- Shazia Hussain, BITS, Dubai
- Amit Kumar Mehta, NFU, China.
- Ahmed Khader Habboush, Jerash University, Jerash, Jordan.
- Gyoo-Soo Chae, Baekseok University, South Korea.
- K. T. Kim, Hannam University, Republic of Korea.
- Masoud Mohammadian, University of Canberra, Australia
- Arabinda Mishra, USA.
- Akhtar Kalam, Victoria University, Australia
- Farhan Ferdous, Founder and Chairman of JBRATRC, Japan

Local Advisory Committee
- Prof. P. K. Sahoo, Dean, ITER, Siksha 'O' Anusandhan
- Prof. M. Mallick, Director, ITER, Siksha 'O' Anusandhan
- Prof. P. K. Dash, Director MDRC, Siksha 'O' Anusandhan
- Prof. D. Acharya, Siksha 'O' Anusandhan
- Prof. B. Mohanty, Department of ECE, ITER, Siksha 'O' Anusandhan
- Prof. Binod Kumar Pattnaik, Department of CSE, ITER, Siksha 'O' Anusandhan
- Prof. B. P. Sinha, Department of CSE, ITER, Siksha 'O' Anusandhan
- Prof. Debahuti Mishra, Department of CSE, ITER, Siksha 'O' Anusandhan
- Prof. Ajit Kumar Nayak, Department of CSIT, ITER, Siksha 'O' Anusandhan
- Prof. Renu Sharma, Department of EE, ITER, Siksha 'O' Anusandhan
- Prof. P. K. Rout, Department of EEE, ITER, Siksha 'O' Anusandhan
- Prof. N. Nayak, Department of EEE, ITER, Siksha 'O' Anusandhan
- Prof. Benudhar Sahoo, Department of ECE, ITER, Siksha 'O' Anusandhan
- Prof. L. P. Mishra, Department of ECE, ITER, Siksha 'O' Anusandhan
- Prof. Niva Das, Department of ECE, ITER, Siksha 'O' Anusandhan

Local Organizing Committee
- Dr. Badri Narayan Sahu
- Dr. Hemanta Kumar Palo
- Dr. Saumendra Kumar Mohanty
- Dr. Sidharth Dash
- Dr. Satya Narayan Bhuyan
- Dr. Santanu Kumar Sahoo
- Dr. Asit Kumar Subudhi
- Dr. Manoj Kumar Naik
- Dr. Aneesh Wunnava
- Dr. Bhagya Laxmi Behera
- Dr. Sarmistha Satrusallya

- Dr. Monalisa Mohanty
- Dr. Tapasmini Sahoo
- Dr. Sandhyalati Behera
- Dr. Shaktijeet Mohapatra
- Dr. Madhusmita Panda
- Dr. Sikha Mishra
- Dr. Pankaj Prusty
- Mr. Arun Das
- Dr. Sabita Mali
- Dr. Pritam Keshari Sahoo
- Dr. Archana Sarangi
- Dr. Priyadarshini Raiguru
- Dr. Debasis Samal
- Dr. Jyoti Mohanty
- Dr. Praveen P. Nayak
- Dr. Tara Prasanna Dash
- Dr. Sushant Ku. Sarangi
- Dr. Soumya S. Mohanty
- Dr. Durga Prasanna Kar
- Dr. Laxmipriya Moharana
- Mr. Pradeep Ku. Bebarta
- Mr. Upendra Prusty
- Mr. Suraj Ku. Das

1 An empirical framework for assessing and mitigating IoT vulnerabilities in smart systems

Shubham Minhass[1,a] Ritu Chauhan[2,b] *and Harleen Kaur[3,c]*

[1]Amity Institute of Information Technology, Amity university, Noida, UP, India

[2]Artificial Intelligence and IoT Lab, Center for Computational Biology and Bioinformatics, Amity university, Noida, UP, India

[3]Department of Computer Science and Engineering, School of Engineering Sciences and Technology, Jamia Hamdard, New Delhi, India

Abstract

Technology permeates every aspect of modern life, and using household IT devices carries significant risks. The quick spread of connected devices, which range from computers and smartphones to sophisticated home appliances, exposes consumers to a wide range of risks. We analysis using port scanning and various vulnerability scanning software tools like network scanners to discover tools, vowels gaps, and ports that were vulnerable. This combination of methods assured that all potential risks, whether obvious or hidden, were uncovered. Using common vulnerability scoring system (CVSS), we prioritized each vulnerability based on its impact, potential for exploitation, and severity. In the course of our assessment, we actively worked to ensure these factors were mitigated. To conclude, our analysis also looked at the wider socio-technical spectrum that shapes categorization of vulnerability. We studied the impact of funding, legal boundaries, and market forces on the adoption and development of consumer IT products. This study demonstrated the intricate relationships between different stakeholders and emphasized the need for functioning coalitions to advance the security of devices. Our research seeks to aid a more robust digital society by addressing socio-technical conflicts, blending technological and sociological factors into one.

Keywords: Internet of things, IoT devices, smart systems, vulnerability

Introduction

The exponential growth of networked devices, which range from laptops and mobile devices to sophisticated home appliances, exposes consumers to numerous risks, including data breaches, privacy violations, and even potential physical harm. Concerns regarding security breaches, data privacy, and even personal safety have been raised by the pervasive use of connected devices, including laptops, smartphones, and smart home appliances. Building resilience against ever evolving cyberthreats requires an understanding of and ability to quantify these susceptibilities. This review article's objective is to provide a comprehensive overview of the context surrounding vulnerability estimates for commercial IT devices. Our goal is to provide an understanding of the complex characteristics of vulnerabilities that exist in various device types by combining the most recent research, techniques, and frameworks. By using this data to uncover trends, pinpoint gaps, and offer recommendations to enhance susceptibility evaluation methodologies. We

[a]shubhamminhass@gmail.com, [b]rituchauha@gmail.com, [c]harleen@jamiahamdard.ac.in

DOI: 10.1201/9781003753391-1

hope to advance cybersecurity knowledge and practices. To wrap things up, we've pulled together a diverse array of scholarly works in our thorough analysis to shed light on the complex world of measuring vulnerabilities in home IT devices. While there are certainly hurdles to tackle due to ever-evolving threats and the intricacies of technology, there are also promising opportunities for building resilience through a blend of innovative methods and interdisciplinary research. By merging human-centered security approaches with cutting-edge technologies like blockchain, artificial intelligence, and algorithmic learning etc. We can foster a proactive culture of risk management and empower individuals to confidently navigate the digital landscape. All these insights underscore the pressing need to tackle risks associated with consumer IT products. Ultimately, the findings from this study contribute to both academic discussions and practical efforts aimed at reducing risks and creating a more resilient digital environment. The protection of people's digital well-being and the digital health of nations worldwide essentially depend on the quantification of security in consumer IT devices. It's more than just a cerebral exercise. By doing more research, developing new concepts, and cooperating, we can steer towards a future where technology serves as a source of advancement and empowerment rather than fragility and uncertainty.

Objective

The objective of this paper is to provide a thorough and comprehensive overview of the state of risk assessments for commercial IT devices, with a focus on the wide-ranging effects of these flaws in relation to consumer technology. The rapid proliferation of connected devices, from laptops and smartphones to high-end home appliances and Internet of Things (IoT) products, calls for a systematic understanding and evaluation of the risks these devices pose. To shed light on the complex aspects of these risks, we aim to integrate the most recent findings, methods, and applications. We aim to improve cybersecurity processes by identifying common patterns, highlighting weaknesses, and offering thoughtful recommendations for improving vulnerability assessment methods. Additionally, our research incorporates the broader socio-technical framework that influences vulnerability classification in addition to the technical aspects. We examine the intricate interactions between various stakeholders that impact the creation and adoption of consumer IT products, accounting for financial incentives, legal frameworks, and market dynamics. By doing this, we emphasize the necessity of a collaborative strategy to enhance device security and recognize that technological solutions alone are insufficient if the social and regulatory contexts are not considered. The ultimate goal of this article is to help build a more resilient digital society by examining the technological and socio-technical aspects of consumer IT device security. Unlike the old approach that is only focus on technical scanning the framework which we used is common vulnerability scoring system (CVSS) based with the technical analysis and generally used these factors for vulnerability assessment for IoT devices.

Literature Review

Garcia's 2018 paper focused on presence in regard to security and interfaces, awareness and behaviors of users in terms of methods of protecting devices and the use of human factors for exploits. By advocating empirical studies and accessibility tests for the importance of user driven assessment in looking at vulnerabilities, Garcia encouraged human factors considerations in security processes and designs. Chen et al.'s paper on "Automated threat detection in market IT devices using machine learning" presented an innovative way to use machine learning techniques in a systematic way to identify and instrument to begin to rank vulnerabilities within consumer IT devices and applications. The approaches Lee et al. included recent developments such as gamification to promote safe behaviors, education and awareness on common risks and actions users can take, such as best security hygiene practices, and simplified user interfaces to report security issues. The paper by Wang and Li "Scalable Security Monitoring Frameworks for Consumer IT Devices" also presented scalable vulnerability management frameworks for these types of devices. These frameworks use cloud-based analytics, machine learning algorithms, and automated remediation techniques to streamline vulnerability identification, prioritization, and patching processes for large-scale device deployments. By automating repetitive tasks and coordinating susceptibility repair procedures, organizations can enhance their overall device security posture, reduce their exposure to security threats, and accelerate their reaction times. Through empirical research and privacy effect evaluations, the authors shed light on the potential risks posed by vulnerabilities to user privacy and data protection, highlighting the necessity of incorporating privacy concerns into vulnerability assessment frameworks and security measures. Numerous other studies have made significant progress in the field of vulnerability measurement in consumer IT devices, building on the foundational study mentioned above. There is also the important addition of "security by design: embedding security assessments into the

software construction lifecycle" by Patel et al. It encourages vulnerability assessment to be incorporated into the software development lifecycle (SDLC). By identifying and addressing vulnerabilities early, organizations can reduce incidents and improve resilience to security breaches in consumer IT devices. This requires that security considerations are woven into the design process and carried through to production, testing and installation. A useful reference is the book, "security by design: combating vulnerability inspection into the software construction, lifecycle," by Patel, et al., which promotes embedding vulnerability screening into the SDLC. Organizations can identify and address vulnerabilities sooner by embedding security considerations and risks from the outset of design to the end of creation, validation and deployment, and therefore, may mitigate the incident of security breaches and improve resilience of consumer IT devices.

Research Methodology

This methodology combines a complete survey of relevant literature, complete vulnerability assessments and robust data analytics tools. The methodology has an overarching framework that includes: identifying assets, scanning for vulnerabilities, analyzing those vulnerabilities, prioritizing risks, recovering and monitoring. The experience required a variety of tools and techniques in all literation of the assessment process to ensure that the assessment was reliable and valid. To systematically assess vulnerabilities in consumer IoT devices, appropriate and representative data sets must be made available. In this analysis we can simply consider it an issue of data collection, which involves effective analysis from various sources, both primary and secondary, and highlights primary data (or findings) from review articles that were compared across various IoT devices. Alternatively, one can also include the National Vulnerability Database (NVD) and other publicly available vulnerability data stores, to get the most recent updates to the vulnerabilities found in consumer IoT devices. The databases represent detailed descriptions, ratings of severity, and suggested remediation for each risk to provide an overall perspective on the threat landscape. In addition, by reading technical literature, security advisories, and kernel update logs from the device manufacturer, more insight on identified vulnerabilities and security fixes is gained, and this could be coupled with scans and reports by review publications to validate that data and exhaust all avenues for the right answer. Business publications and published security investigations were documented to identify any new vulnerabilities and attack vectors for consumer IoT devices. Concepts mentioned in the reports are included in the vulnerability assessment framework as additional lines of inquiry to show improved risk recognition.

Results and Discussion

We carried out a detailed assessment at the risk associated with the vulnerabilities discovered and classified each as part of our thorough assessment as shown in Table 1.1 and 1.2. Using the common vulnerability scoring system (CVSS), we assessed impact, exploitability, and severity of risk which also allowed us to prioritize risk with respect to each vulnerability and develop a course of action moving forward to remediate each. When looking like various consumer IT devices, we observed a number of vulnerabilities rated medium to high severity which reveals substantial risks related to manipulation and individual and organizational harm. We also utilized the common

weakness enumeration (CWE) in standardizing how we assess software defects and vulnerabilities. The CWE provided us with a detailed description of a set of vulnerabilities related to common security flaws which helped us get a deeper dive into the root cause analysis. By identifying the specific CWE entry related to each vulnerability gives us the ability to identify patterns and root causes across devices with respect to vulnerabilities. The vulnerabilities we identified within laptops and mobile phones highlight the security risks associated with the use of these devices and require that we address threats to these devices without delay. For laptops, a significant issue appears to be outdated software, which can occur when both the operating system and software components are unable to be updated by the user. This creates vulnerabilities and risks associated with loss of integrity, and theft of confidential data, because the device is partially compromised. Additionally, devices often have known vulnerabilities, and security flaws. Similarly, many mobile phones fail to use security features like fingerprint scanning or have password requirements, resulting in weak authentication methods. Weak authentication increases vulnerabilities and increases the chances of unauthorized access which can allow hackers to access user accounts or confidential information stored on the mobile phone. Another concern concerning vulnerability we found in laptops, is open ports and inadequate protection from the firewalls to address this vulnerability. Open ports can allow attackers into a scanning device and enable systems to be compromised. We generally extend our vulnerability assessment by using the technical severity scoring with social market analysis our research just shows the higher mitigation rate than the prior approaches.

Table 1.1 Vulnerabilities identified in IoT devices.

Vulnerability	Severity	Description
Outdated software	High	Failure to update operating system.
Weak authentication	Medium	Lack of robust authentication mechanisms.
Unsecured ports	High	Open ports without firewall protection.
Outdated firmware	Medium	Old versions of firmware can make this vulnerable.
Lack of data encryption	Medium	Lack of data access can lead to data theft.

Source: Author

Table 1.2 Vulnerabilities identified in laptops and mobile phones.

Vulnerability	Security	Severity	Description
Smart light bulb	The absence of authenticity	Medium	In this device there is lack of absence of authentication.
IoT Security camera	Web Interface Vulnerabilities	High	This camera hacker or attacker can be accessing live feed.
Smart Doorbell	Not Enough Firmware	Medium	Need to update new firmware not to get exploit.
IoT Thermostat	Network Protocol Insecurity	High	Device using very poor protocol.

Source: Author

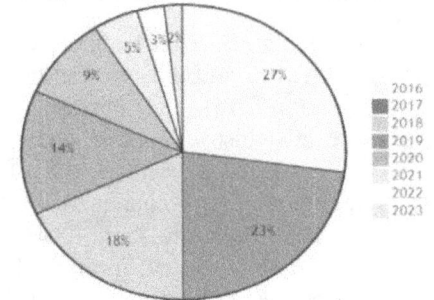

Distribution of Publishers by Year from 2016 to 2023

Figure 1.1 Pie chart for papers 2016 to 2023
Source: Author

A pie chart shows the distribution of peer-reviewed publications (PPRs) regarding vulnerability assessment of consumer IT devices from 2016 to 2023 as shown in Figure 1.1. The year with the most publications is 2020, which included a large growth of research activity. This activity surge indicates growing scholarly interest and curiosity about privacy and security issues facing home electronics. In terms of vulnerability assessment, scholars directed their focus in 2020 to identify and finding ways to remediate the security vulnerabilities related to consumer IT devices; they began recognizing the need for more vulnerability assessments as part of the solution to protect digital assets and users' privacy. The spike in publications in 2020 highlights the public problem of recognizing the ongoing and pervasive cybersecurity threats posed by either wired or wireless, consumer IT devices. The pie chart clearly indicates the outline of the changes in overall research output on vulnerability assessments over the years with the notable spike in 2020. The yearly theme variations in PPR distributions show the academic focus changing due to emerging trends and evolving research priorities. By providing the overall timelines of the research output, the pie chart gives visibility to the changing academic landscape of research focused on vulnerability assessments.

Conclusion

The paper proposes an empirical model that employs standardized methods such as CVSS and CWE to identify and address vulnerabilities of the IoT and smart systems. The analysis revealed serious security vulnerabilities that can cause the likelihood of exploits, including obsolete software, weak authentication, unsecure ports, and poor network protocols. These findings demonstrate the importance of systematic vulnerability management implementation to ensure user data security and maintain the integrity of the device. The combination of technical evaluation and socio-technological insights helps to make the suggested approach more precise in vulnerability identification and prioritization. It further shows the role of cooperation between manufacturers, researchers and lawmakers in order to improve the security protocols in IoT. On the whole, our efforts will assist in creating intelligent ecosystems that would be more resistant to changing cyber threats and be safer.

References

[1] Rahane, K. U., & Pawar, A. B. (2024). Unified data handling for vulnerability detection and mitigation in smart systems. In 2024 IEEE International Conference on Blockchain and Distributed Systems Security (ICBDS), (pp. 1–6). IEEE.

[2] Al-Boghdady, A., El-Ramly, M., & Wassif, K. (2022). iDetect for vulnerability detection in internet of things operating systems using machine learning. *Scientific Reports*, 12(1), 17086.

[3] Ahmed, S., Ilyas, M., and Raja, M. (2022). IoT-based smart systems using machine learning (ML) and artificial intelligence (AI): Vulnerabilities and intelligent solutions. Proceedings of the International Conference on Smart Information Technologies (ICSIT), pp. 56–61.

[4] Banik, S., Rogers, M., Mahajan, S. M., Emeghara, C. M., Banik, T., and Craven, R. (2024). Survey on vulnerability testing in the smart grid. *IEEE Access*, 12, 145233–145250. DOI: https://doi.org/10.1109/ACCESS.2024.3378018.

[5] Banik, S., Rogers, M., Mahajan, S. M., Emeghara, C. M., Banik, T., & Craven, R. (2024). Survey on vulnerability testing in the smart grid. IEEE Access, 12, 145233–145250. DOI: https://doi.org/10.1109/ACCESS.2024.3378018.

[6] Nozomi Networks. (2021). The Cost of OT Cybersecurity Incidents and How to Reduce Risk.[Online]. Available at: https://www.nozominetworks.com/solutions/challenge/cost-of-ot-cybersecurity-incidents/

[7] McLaughlin, S., Konstantinou, C., Wang, X., Davi, L., Sadeghi, A. R., Maniatakos, M., et al. (2016). The cybersecurity landscape in industrial control systems. *Proceedings of IEEE*, 104(5), 1039–1057.

[8] Cintuglu, M. H., Mohammed, O. A., Akkaya, K., & Uluagac, A. S. (2017). A survey on smart grid cyber-physical system testbeds. *IEEE Communications Surveys and Tutorials*, 19(1), 446–464.

[9] Barreno, M., Nelson, B., Sears, R., Joseph, A. D., & Tygar, J. D. (2006). Can machine learning be secure? In Proceedings of the 2006 ACM Symposium on Information, Computer and Communications Security, (pp. 16–25). New York, NY: ACM.

[10] Bernabeu, E. E., Thorp, J. S., & Centeno, V. (2012). Methodology for a security/

dependability adaptive protection scheme based on data mining. *IEEE Transactions on Power Delivery*, 27(1), 104–111.

[11] Dahl, G. E., Stokes, J. W., Deng, L., & Yu, D. (2013). Large-scale malware classification using random projections and neural networks. In 2013 I.E. International Conference on Acoustics, Speech and Signal Processing (ICASSP), (pp. 3422–3426). New York, NY: IEEE.

[12] Jiang, J., & Yasakethu, L. (2013). Anomaly detection via one class SVM for protection of SCADA systems. In 2013 International conference on cyber-enabled distributed computing and knowledge discovery (CYBERC) (pp. 82–88). New York, NY: IEEE.

[13] Kolosnjaji, B., Demontis, A., Biggio, B., Maiorca, D., Giacinto, G., Eckert, C., et al. (2018). Adversarial malware binaries: evading deep learning for malware detection in executables. arXiv, 1803, 04173.

[14] Zwilling, M., Klien, G., Lesjak, D., Wiechetek, Ł., Cetin, F., and Basim, H. N. (2020). Cyber security awareness, knowledge and behavior: A comparative study. *Journal of Computer Information Systems*, 62(1), 1–16. DOI: https://doi.org/10.1080/08874417.2020.1712269

[15] Giuliano, V., Formicola, V. (n.d.). ICS-range: a simulation-based cyber range platform for industrial control systems. arXiv 2019, arXiv:1909.01910.

[16] Yonemura, K.; Sato, J.; Komura, R.; Matsuoka, M. Practical security education on combination of OT and ICT using gamfication method. In Proceedings of the 2018 IEEE Global Engineering Education Conference (EDUCON 2018), Tenerife, Spain, 17–20 April 2018; pp. 746–750.

[17] Okoli, C., & Schabram, K. (2010). A guide to conducting a systematic literature review of information systems research. *SSRN Electronic Journal*.

[18] Chauhan, R., Varma, G., Yafi, E., & Zuhairi, M. F. (2023). The impact of geo-political socio-economic factors on vaccine dissemination trends: a case-study on COVID-19 vaccination strategies. *BMC Public Health*, 23(1), 2142.

[19] Varma, G., Chauhan, R., & Singh, D. (2022). Sarve: synthetic data and local differential privacy for private frequency estimation. *Cybersecurity*, 5(1), 26.

[20] Chuahan, R., Gola, N., Yafi, E., Farez, M., & Prasad, M. (2022). Smart cities with recognizance in air quality. In 2022 International Visualization, Informatics and Technology Conference (IVIT), (pp. 130–135). IEEE.

[21] Yafi, E., Chuahan, R., Sharma, A., & Zuhairi, M. F. (2024). Integrated empowered AI and IoT approach for heart prediction. In 2024 18th International Conference on Ubiquitous Information Management and Communication (IMCOM), (pp. 1–7). IEEE.

[22] Minhass, S., Chauhan, R., & Kaur, H. (2023, November). Assessing the Impact of Vulnerabilities on Confidentiality, Integrity, and Availability in Smart Systems. In 2023 Second International Conference on Informatics (ICI) (pp. 1–5). IEEE.

[23] Chauhan, R., Varma, G., Yafi, E., & Zuhairi, M. (2022). An analytics approach using edge computing in smart healthcare system. Available at SSRN 4167.

2 Real-time performance evaluation of a QoS metrics in 5G NR private network under varying load conditions

Riya Raj[a], Mukta Dhar[b], Muskan[c], Parvi Gupta[d], Shuvabrata Bandopadhyay[e], Gulman Siddiqui[f] and Yogendra Singh[g]

5G Lab, School of Physical Sciences, Banasthali Vidyapith, Rajasthan, India

Abstract

This paper has proposed a real-time performance analysis of a 5G NR private network under dynamic load Scenarios. A 5G NR private network operates autonomously, providing full control over resource allocation, security, and data. Before implementing various use cases, it is necessary to maintain a seamless and high-performance rollout of 5G NR private network. In this work, in order to do performance analysis throughput, latency, and jitter are accessed. Software named Wireshark, has been used to capture live packets on key network interfaces of the 5G test-bed and analyzed offline on computing platforms. A dependable and effective implementation is the result of this continuous assessment, which also helps in detection of security vulnerabilities network optimizing, and ensuring compliance with 5G performance standards.

Keywords: 5G NR, Jitter, latency, private 5G networks, test-bed approach, throughput, Wireshark

Introduction

5G NR outperforms its predecessors by delivering higher data-rates, ultra-low latency, massive connectivity among devices, and slicing of network enabling for various kinds of real-world applications in practice. This is made feasible by the support for enhanced mobile broadband for high-definition streaming, ultra-reliable low-latency communications for automated automobiles, and massive machine-type communication for Internet of Things. Additionally, the multi-access edge computing (MEC) improves instantaneous computation that makes 5G NR flawless for smart towns and cities, manufacturing automation, and AR/VR applications [1].

A 5G NR private network operates autonomously, enabling complete control over statistics, resource allocation, and security. Before implementing various use cases load scenarios, it is crucial to guarantee the seamless and outstanding performance establishment of 5G NR private network. Therefore, it is essential to recognize potential vulnerabilities, Shortcomings and modify the network configurations accordingly [2]. Throughput testing is essential for evaluating network sustainability in high data rates requirements for industrial automation and AI-driven processes [3]. Assessment network latency is essential for delay sensitive applications like autonomous vehicles, remote surgery, and smart manufacturing [4]. Additionally, jitter testing prevents

[a]34riyaraj@gmail.com, [b]mukta12arch@gmail.com, [c]muskanroy4619@gmail.com,
[d]parvigupta200@gmail.com, [e]shuvabrata.bandopadhaya@gmail.com, [f]mohdgulman@gmail.com,
[g]yogendra125@gmail.com

DOI: 10.1201/9781003753391-2

disruptions in time-sensitive operations such as VoIP, IoT communications, and AR/VR applications.

However, performance evaluations of a 5G NR private network face several challenges. Extensive bandwidth simulations are required to ensure that the network is capable of handling peak loads without congestion [5]. In applications like autonomous vehicles and remote surgery, latency evaluation became complex due to the demand for real-time precision. Jitter analysis further complicated due to network fluctuations caused by multiple factors, including interference, hardware limitations, and improper Quality of Service (QoS) configurations. To address these challenges advanced tools, continuous monitoring, and fine-tuning of network parameters for a smooth deployment is required [2].

Real-time performance analysis of a 5G NR private network has been performed using Wireshark which was fetched into a 5G testbed for evaluating throughput, latency, and jitter. By capturing live packets on key network interfaces (e.g. gNB, UPF, MEC server) via Wireshark and applying filter protocols such as GTP-U, NGAP, and SCTP allows monitoring of user and control plane traffic [6]. This ongoing assessment aids in network optimizing, detection of security vulnerabilities, and guaranteeing compliance with 5G performance standards, leading to a reliable and efficient deployment [7].

In this paper, real-time performance analysis of a 5G NR private network is done by evaluating throughput, latency, and jitter. Using Wireshark, live packets on key network interfaces of the 5G test-bed are captured. Different user and control plane traffic are monitored applying filter protocols such asGTP-U, NGAP, and SCTP. In this work, the analysis is carried out for following load conditions:

(i) During NG Setup Procedure i. e. When initial connection is established between the gNB and the 5G Core (NGC) by exchanging NGAP messages [2]

(ii) During UE Registration process with the help of NGAP protocol [10]

(iii) During active voice over NR (VoNR) calling on the UE with help of SCTP and SIP protocol [11]

(iv) During Video in NR (ViNR) call [12].

This ongoing assessment aids in network optimizing, detection of security vulnerabilities, and guaranteeing compliance with 5G performance standards, leading to a reliable and efficient deployment. The rest of the paper is organized as following: the experimental set up and process is discussed in section 2, performance analysis is in section 3, and section 4 summarizes the paper.

Experiment Setup and Procedure

The experiment was carried out in a stand-alone (SA) 5G private network lab that was completely operational. The virtualized core network was directly connected to the gNB, which functioned as the primary communication backbone. A central server, two host machines, a firewall, a switch, and a variety of UE devices (such as sensors, cell phones, CPEs, and IoT gateways) were all part of the arrangement. After turning on the host and base station machines, a monitoring PC was used to confirm connectivity. After it became functional, we capture data packets using Wireshark, track the transfer of data between the core network and gNB, and export those packets in CSV format. As the Live network traffic can be collected and examined using the Network packet analyzer Wireshark. In the design configured by us, it enabled full packet-level accessibility between the gNB and Core. After the extraction of CSV files, the data packets were studied by a particularly

Table 2.1 Testbed setup components and their functions.

Component	Description
gNB	It connects UEs to the network and provide radio access
Core network (5GC)	This manages data routing, authentication, and mobility
Firewall	It guaranteed the traffic filtering and security
Network switch	This facilitates the interconnection of network elements
Host machines	The core network functions hosted by the virtualized servers hosting
User equipment (UE)	The user devices such as 5G Smart phones and sensors etc.

Source: Author

written script of python that compute efficient Performance metrics like throughput, latency, and jitter time stamps and payload dimensions. This Method of Evaluation ensures accuracy and consistency in analyzing real-time network Performance. Programming algorithms is used to evaluate transferred data of packets and based on timestamps and payload size acquired key performance indicators (KPIs) like jitter, throughput, and latency. Table 2.1 shows the main components of the network and its description.

We evaluated the real-time performance of the 5G private network by methodically examining packet-level data under several network circumstances. Insights into how the network behaves under various traffic loads. The architecture of private 5G network is shown in Figure 2.1.

Comprehending latency and jitter: Latency is the amount of time that passes between sending and receiving a data packet. For applications like calling via video or self-navigating devices that need real-time responds, this statistic is essential. Latency-sensitive interaction, such as Voice over IP or live streaming of video, can be disrupted by jitter, which is the variance in the time interval between data packets receiving. For 5G networks to provide seamless and excellent user experiences, low latency and little jitter are necessary.

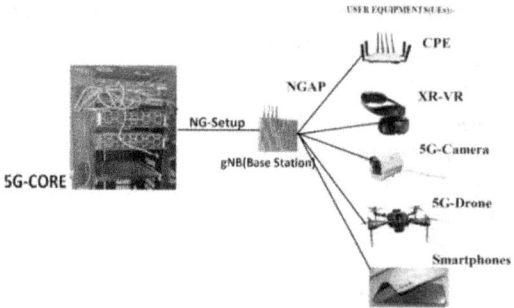

Figure 2.1 Private 5G network architecture
Source: Author

Throughput estimation

Throgh put is Mathematically expressed as:

$$Throughput = \frac{Total\ data\ transferred}{Total\ time\ taken} \quad (1)$$

Each network packet has a length, usually measured in bytes. The total data transferred over a time interval is given by summing the lengths of all packets:

$$D = \sum_{i=1}^{N} L_i \quad (2)$$

Where D is the total data transferred in bytes, L_i is the length of the i-th packet in bytes, and N is the total number of packets transmitted. Total data transferred in bits is given by, $D_{bits} = 8D$. The Throughput is calculated over the Time window (in seconds) is

$$Throughput = \frac{D_{bits}}{Time\ window} \qquad (3)$$

1 Megabits (Mb) corresponds to 10^6 bits, therefore the final expression for Throughput is:

$$Throughput(Mbps) = \frac{\sum Packet\ length \times 8}{Time\ window \times 10^6} \qquad (4)$$

Performance Analysis

Throughput, latency, and jitter are the primary network metrics used to assess the performance of a private 5G network. These metrics provide insight into the network's dependability and efficiency under various dynamic circumstances. Throughput, which measures how effectively a network can handle user traffic is the rate at which data moves from the UE to the network in bits per second (bps) [8]. Lower latency may cause large losses when milliseconds become valuable for real-time applications like industrial automation and video conferencing. Jitter in application VoIP and IP media streaming services can impact the quality of real-time communication [9]. Packets are being inspected at the level of visualization using Wireshark for the analysis of these metrics and processed for proper bottlenecks to give the best of optimization and network configuration. The study measures throughput, latency (RTT), and jitter to assess a private 5G network's performance in real time under following distinct load scenarios:

NG setup

In the No load scenario, the private 5G network operates under minimal load conditions, representing the optimal performance environment [13]. The throughput reaches approximately 85 Mbps, as shown in Figure 2.2(a) Which reflects the network's maximum capacity without external Interference. The latency (RTT) remains consistently low, averaging 10–12 ms, as shown in Figure 2.2(b)

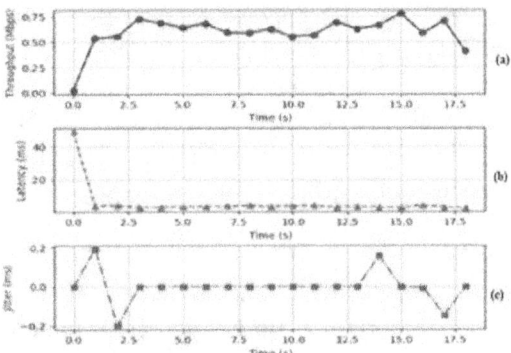

Figure 2.2 NG setup analysis
Source: Author

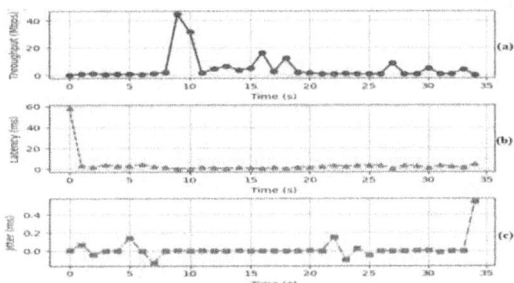

Figure 2.3 UE registration
Source: Author

Indicating minimal transmission delays. This is a hallmark of private 5G networks, which are designed for low-latency communication. The jitter values are negligible, around 1–2 ms, as shown in Figure 2.2(c) highlighting the stability of packet arrival.

UE registration

During the UE registration stage, the network faces a moderate demand attributable to signaling activities. Throughput sees a slight dip to about 70 Mbps, as shown in Figure 2.3(a) Highlighting the effects of signaling overhead. Latency ascends to roughly 18 ms, as shown in Figure 2.3(b) demonstrating the extra processing needed for authentication and session establishment. Jitter metrics elevate to 5 ms, as shown in Figure 2.3(c) indicating minor inconsistencies in packet arrival times due to signaling variations. The findings validate that the network sustains dependable performance throughout the registration process while incurring minor fluctuations in latency and jitter.

Active call

In a scenario where calls are active, the network supports real-time voice communication, significantly affecting the performance. The throughput drops to roughly 55–65 Mbps, as shown in Figure 2.4(a) highlighting the bandwidth usage by voice packets. Latency rises to about 35 ms, as shown in Figure 2.4(b) marking a clear increase from the baseline, yet it remains within

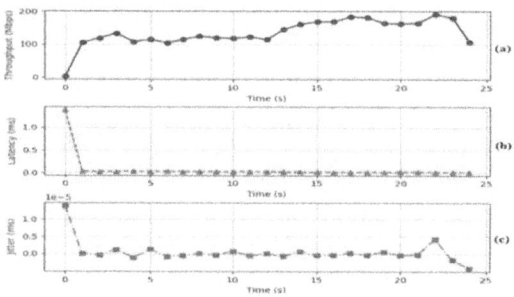

Figure 2.4 VONR call analysis
Source: Author

the suitable range for VoIP services. Jitter escalates to between 10–15 ms, as shown in Figure 2.4(c) Indicating moderate fluctuations in packet arrival times. These metrics align with VoIP standards, which categorize latencies of 30–40 ms and jitter below 20 ms as acceptable for clear voice quality. The findings suggest that the network effectively manages voice calls, although with slightly increased delays and jitter.

5G high-definition video call (ViNR)

When engaged in a video call, the network endures increased traffic loads. The throughput further declines to approximately 40 Mbps, as shown in Figure 2.5(a) as ongoing video streaming utilizes a considerable amount of bandwidth. Latency rises notably to 50–60 ms, as shown in Figure 2.5(b) Indicating the handling and transmission of large video data packets. Jitter reaches its peak, fluctuating between 25–30 ms, as shown in Figure 2.5(c) which signifies a significant inconsistency in the timing of packet arrivals. This behavior is consistent with research on video conferencing, where latencies of 50–80 ms and elevated jitter levels are frequently observed in high-traffic scenarios. The findings reveal that although the network can support video calls, the

Table 2.2 The summarized result.

Scenario	Traffic type	Load condition	Throughput (Mbps)	Latency (ms)	Jitter (ms)
NG Setup	Control signaling	Low	85 (Maximum capacity)	10-12(Low latency)	1-2(Minimal)
UE Registration	Signaling	Medium	17 (Slight dip)	18 (Moderate)	5(Mild fluctuation)
Active call	VoIP traffic	High	55-65 (Reduced)	35 (Noticeable)	10-15(Moderate fluctuation)
5G High-definition video call (VINR)	Real-time streaming	High	40 (Significant drop)	50-60 (High)	25-30(Unstable)

Source: Author

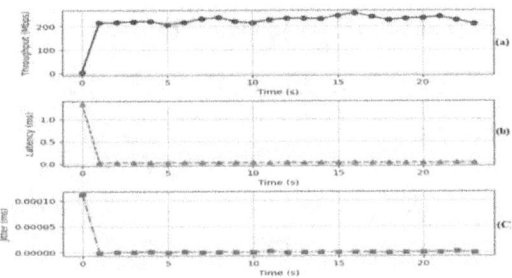

Figure 2.5 VINR analysis
Source: Author

quality may suffer with heightened jitter and latency, underscoring the necessity for improved Quality of Service management amid heavy multimedia traffic. The summarized results are provided in Table 2.2.

Conclusion

In this study, the network performance of 5G NR network is evaluated based on performance metrics such as throughput, latency, and jitter across various real-world scenarios. The packet-level data is captured through Wireshark and analyzed subsequently. The findings provided valuable insights into network dynamics, highlighting the impact of diverse traffic patterns on QoS parameters. This effort enhances the precision of network performance assessment, presenting a scalable framework for further research and optimization.

Acknowledgment

This work was supported in part by the Department of Telecommunications (DoT), Government of India under project "100 5G Use case lab"

References

[1]   Ahmadi, S. (2019). 5G Network Architecture. Elsevier BV.

[2]   Chandramouli, D., Liebhart, R., & Pirskanen, J. (2019). 5G for the Connected World. Wiley.

[3]   Diallo, E., Al Agha, K., & Martin, S. (2024). TRADE-5G: a blockchain-based transparent and secure resource exchange for 5G network slicing. In Blockchain: Research and Applications, Elsevier.

[4]   3GPP. (2021). Service requirements for the 5G system (Stage 1) (3GPP TS 22.261, Release 15, version 15.9.0). 3rd Generation Partnership Project (3GPP), Technical Specification Group Services and System Aspects.

[5]   Belshe, M., Peon, R., & Thomson, M. (2015). Hypertext transfer protocol version 2 (HTTP/2). In RFC 7540. IETF.

[6]   Schulzrinne, H., Casner, S., Frederick, R., & Jacobson, V. (2003). RTP: A transport protocol for real-time applications. In RFC 3550. IETF.

[7]   Dahlman, E., Parkvall, S., & Skold, J. (2020). 5G NR: The Next Generation Wireless Access Technology, (2nd edn.). Amsterdam, Netherlands: Academic Press.

[8]   Liu, J., Zhang, S., & Panwar, S. (2021). Latency and throughput analysis of 5G private networks. *IEEE Communications Magazine*, 59(3), 52–58.

[9]   Araniti, G., Condoluci, M., & Scopelliti, P. (2019). Performance analysis of 5G standalone networks in industrial IoT applications. *IEEE Transactions on Industrial Informatics*, 16(9), 6202–6213.

[10]   Zhang, H., Liu, N., Chu, X., & Long, K. (2020). On the performance of private 5G networks in industrial automation: a simulation-based analysis. *IEEE Transactions on Industrial Informatics*, 16(8), 5327–5335.

[11]   ITU-T (2003). Recommendation G.114: One-Way Transmission Time. Geneva, Switzerland: International Telecommunication Union.

[12]   3GPP. (2020). NG-RAN; NG Application Protocol (NGAP) (Release 15, v15.7.0) (3GPP TS 38.413). 3rd Generation Partnership Project.

[13]   Rosenberg, J., Schulzrinne, H., Camarillo, G., Johnston, A., Peterson, J., Sparks, R., Handley, M., & Schooler, E. (2002). SIP: Session Initiation Protocol (RFC 3261). Internet Engineering Task Force (IETF).

3 Comprehensive analysis of throughput in 5G NR: impact of modulation schemes, subcarrier spacing, and channel models

Sulekha Pateriya[a], Vanshika Jain[b] and Shuvabrata Bandopadhaya[c]

5G Lab, School of Physical Sciences, Banasthali Vidyapith, Rajasthan, India

Abstract

The 5G New Radio (NR) domain is developing at a breakneck pace, and understanding the impact of physical layer parameters on optimization for throughput is vital for network operation. This work analyzes the throughput and SNR of the 5G NR with different modulation types, SCS, and channel models applied. This paper simulates scenarios about High Mobility, Rural, Urban Macrocells, and Urban Microcells. The outcomes show that less complex schemes such as QPSK do outperform in lower SNR scenarios. However, in high SNR situations, more intricate modulation schemes such as 256 QAM with greater subcarrier spacing (120 kHz) achieve much higher throughput. Moreover, cluster delay line models (CDL-D) where strong multipath effects exist greatly reduce the throughput in high mobility cases. These results illustrate how 5G NR may be more optimally deployed while considering different operational latencies, efficiencies, and reliability across varying application scenarios.

Keywords: 5G NR, modulation, network performance, SNR, throughput

Introduction

5G New Radio (NR) addresses a wide variety of communication use cases which include large bandwidth requirements, high accuracy, and extremely low latency. The increasing pace of development of next-generation wireless networks is causing greater focus among researchers and engineers on lower layers like 5G NR physical layer elements which encompasses modulation, channel models, and subcarrier spacing (SCS). These factors are critical to the effectiveness, performance, and flexibility of modern networks concerning their diverse deployment topologies.

This paper analyzes the effect of important physical layer entities in relation to the study of throughput and signal-to-noise ratio (SNR) providing theoretical and simulation -based studies for effective and optimal network deployment. The bond in user apparatus (UE) and future generation base station (gNB) is trustable through the 5G NR Network Access architecture framework.

As with the data link and the physical connection sub-layers of the OSI model [1], the network access layer is important for error checking, HARQ transmission retention, scheduling, segmentation, and maintenance of all aspects of transmission integrity. The system also leverages ultra-wideband (UWB) technologies including massive MIMO, beamforming, OFDMA, and dynamic spectrum allocation (DSA) for enhanced spectral efficiency. The

[a]sulekhapateriya@gmail.com, [b]vanshikajain353@gmail.com,
[c]shuvabrata.bandopadhaya@gmail.com

DOI: 10.1201/9781003753391-3

ultra-low latency (~1 ms) and unyielding control (QoS) along with network slicing, also enable differentiated service in the physical layer, catering to eMBB (enhanced mobile broadband), ultra-reliable low-latency communication (URLLC), and mMTC (massive machine-type communication) requirements. Furthermore, the system employs techniques like massive MIMO and beamforming to enhance spectral efficiency. Flexible numerology adds to traffic and channel conditions adaptation, yet it adds to the complexity of resource management, as Flores de Valgas et al. [2] noted. Resource allocation algorithms such as proportional fair (PF) scheduling represent a compromise between fairness and throughput at test [3].

The behavior of DLSCH and PDSCH in the 5G NR downlink system is the primary concern of our simulation-based analysis in this paper. For purposes of providing valuable input to network optimization, we systematically investigate how varied SNR, subcarrier spacing, modulation techniques, and channel models influence throughput across different deployment scenarios. Contributions to this paper are listed below:

(i)   We inspected how various values of SCS (e.g., 15 kHz, 30 kHz, 60 kHz, and 120 kHz) affect system capacity under different SNR conditions. The compromises involve lower SCS (improves performance under low SNR) and upper SCS (more appropriate under high-frequency bands).

(ii) The work includes various modulation schemes (QPSK, 16-QAM, 64-QAM, and 256-QAM) to compare their influence on throughput at varying SNR ranges. The outcomes confirm that lower-order modulation works better at low-SNR environments, while higher-order modulation is efficient at higher SNR.

(iii) We modeled clustered delay line (CDL) channel models (CDL-A, CDL-B, CDL-C, etc.) and simulated them to analyze their influence on throughput and SNR performance. The results show the performance differences in various propagation environments and assist in comprehending the real-world deployment issues of 5G NR.

Repose of the paper is accurate as follows: role model and methodology are specified in section 2, The simulation result is given in section 3, and section 4 settles the paper.

The overall framework of these parameters, including OFDM with scalable subcarrier spacing (15–120 kHz), modulation schemes, coding, bandwidth parts, and massive MIMO antennas, is illustrated in Figure 3.1.

Literature Review

Literature review in 5G New Radio (NR), the throughput vs. signal-to-noise ratio (SNR) affiliation, is largely impacted by the modulation schemes, subcarrier spacings (SCS), and channel models. It is noted that higher order modulation schemes are far more prone to channel distractions; however, they do result in better throughput at greater SNR levels. 256-QAM is one

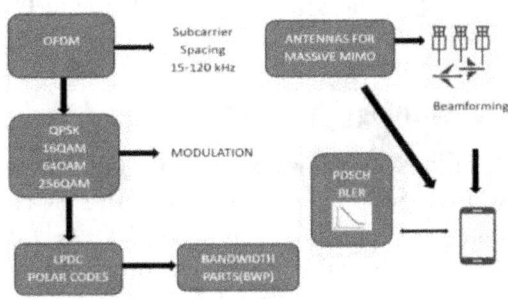

Figure 3.1 Key parameters for over-the-air communications
Source: Author

example. And then there are lower order schemes such as QPSK which tend to operate better under low SNR conditions. In some scenarios, higher-order SCS provides better throughput which is an important consideration for SCS selection.

Modulation schemes

QPSK will give its best performance in low SNR environments and still yield high throughput and reliability [4]. Higher-order schemes tend to operate worse, but 16-QAM seems to do better at certain SCS. This also includes 120 kHz which is considered high [5]. Furthermore, the same source states that in 64-QAM and 256-QAM modulation, a high SNR condition provides a greater throughput. Low SNR conditions, however, result in reduced capability due to high error rates [6].

Subcarrier spacing

(SCS) It greatly impacts through low SNR. Emptying space between the subcarriers increases the SNR value which improves performance. This explains why higher SCS is better [4]. This is vulnerable to the state of the network. In dynamic networks, changing the position of the base station drastically changes performance [5].

Models of channels

The effect of multipath propagation on throughput and error rates is illustrated by using CDL models [4, 7].

Methodology

Downlink transmission in 5G NR starts with DL-SCH data processing via PDSCH, followed by precoding and CP-OFDM modulation. After channel propagation, synchronization, channel estimation, and demodulation are done by the receiver [8]. PDSCH and DL-SCH decoding provide data

retrieval assurance, while the HARQ process detects errors [9] and schedules retransmission based on ACK/NACK feedback, maximizing link reliability and throughput [10].

The complete process of downlink data flow, including PDSCH encoding/decoding, DL-SCH decoding, and HARQ feedback management, is depicted in Figure 3.2.

Transport block size (TBS) determines the amount of data that can be transmitted in a time transmission interval (TTI).

$$TBS = \lfloor N_{RE} \times R \times Q_m \rfloor \tag{1}$$

where N_{RE} is the number of resource elements allocated, R is the Effective coding rate (depends on LDPC rate matching) Q_m is modulation order (e.g., 2 for QPSK, 4 for 16-QAM, 6 for 64-QAM),

LDPC Encoding and Rate Matching 5G NR uses LDPC (Low-Density Parity-Check) codes for forward error correction.

$$c = G . \mu \tag{2}$$

μ is Input bit sequence, G is LDPC generator matrix, c is the Encoded output bits and rate matching

$$e = \Pi(c) \tag{3}$$

where Π is the interleaving function that maps LDPC code bits to physical resources HARQ Soft combining model hybrid automatic repeat request (HARQ) improves reliability by combining retransmissions is the Log-likelihood ratio used in soft decision decoding.

$$LLR_{new} = LLR_{old} + LLR_{reTx} \tag{4}$$

LLR is the Log-Likelihood Ratio used in soft decision decoding.

If ACK is received, no retransmission occurs; if NACK is received, gNB retransmits the DL-SCH data. Mathematical

Research Gap

Table 3.1 Research gap.

No.	Research papers	Writer	Year	Objective	Technique Used	Futurology	Conclusion	Abstract
1	Throughput analysis over 5G NR physical uplink shared channels	Kabalcı and Ali	2020[4]	Examine PUSCH throughput over SNR, modulation, and antenna configurations.	MATLAB simulation using antenna configurations for QPSK, QAMs, SCS, and BS/UE	Examine the distribution of DL/UL resources and practical channels.	At low SNR QPSK outperforms and 256-QAM outperforms at high SNR; throughput is a function of the fading model.	Exhibit the impact of modulation on the PUSCH throughput for different types of channels and SNR levels.
2	5G Modulation technique comparisons using simulation approach	Thangamayan et al.	2022[6]	Examine the performance metrics of several 5G modulation techniques.	Simulations of QPSK, 16QAM, 64QAM, and 256QAM in MATLAB were conducted at SNRs varying from -10 dB to 20 dB	Analysis of the performance of modulation systems under different scenarios.	In BER/delay QPSK performs best, 64QAM is best at 5 dB, and high SNR gives 256QAM acceptable performance but low SNR is poor.	Moderate and high SNR show significant performance differences across modulation schemes which reveals the trade-offs in the behavior of the schemes.
3	5G NR PDSCH Throughput analysis with different numerology and modulation schemes	Sinwar	2023[5]	Evaluate the throughput of PDSCH using various modulation methods and numerologies.	PDSCH throughput simulation with various subcarrier spacings and modulation types	Examine beyond 256-QAM and evaluate SCS in practical situations.	At 120 kHz SCS, 16-QAM performs better than 64/256-QAM because of its superior SNR flexibility.	At some SNRs, simpler modulations, such as 16-QAM, outperform higher-order schemes.
4	Error rate performance analysis of the 5G NR PUSCH for cell-free systems	Rahmani et al.	2024[7]	Use 5G NR PUSCH to analyze BLER in CF massive MIMO.	Link-level simulation that complies with 3GPP; compares BLER to SCS, MCS, and RU count.	Talk about mobility, equity, and practical cell-free deployments.	Better dependability is achieved with more RUs, while frequency-selective fading benefits from higher SCS.	Through spatial/ frequency variety, CF-MIMO increases reliability; system settings affect BLER.

Source: Author

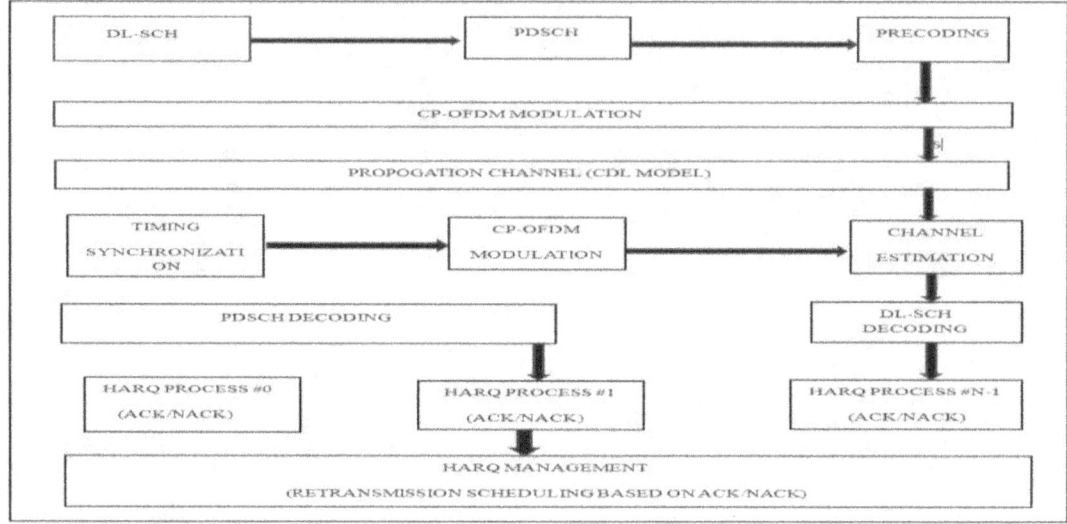

Figure 3.2 5G NR downlink transmissions and HARQ process flow
Source: Author

modeling in OFDM Symbol Representation Each OFDM symbol is generated by IFFT (Inverse Fast Fourier Transform) [11]

$$S_n = {}^1\!/\sqrt{N}\ \textstyle\sum_{k=0}^{N-1} X_k e^{j2\pi kn/N} \qquad (5)$$

X_k is the Frequency-domain data symbols (QPSK, 16-QAM, 64-QAM, 256-QAM) and N is the Number of subcarriers.

$$s_{tx} = s_n\,(t) + s_n\,(t - Tcp)s_{tx} \qquad (6)$$

where *Tcp* is the Cyclic Prefix duration and MIMO and Precoding Formulations Massive MIMO (Multiple-Input Multiple-Output) with beamforming

$$y = \mathrm{W}.x \qquad (7)$$

Where: x is the Input symbol vector and W is the precoding matrix (used for beam forming), y is the Transmitted signal vector Optimal beam forming maximizes the SINR

$$W = arg\ {}^{max}_{W}\ SINR \qquad (8)$$

Performance metrics SINR and Throughput Estimation Signal-to-Interference-plus-Noise Ratio (SINR) [12].

$$SINR = \frac{P_{signal}}{P_{interference} + P_{noise}} \qquad (9)$$

Maximum throughput estimation using the Shannon Capacity formula:

$$C = B.log_2\,(1 + SINR) \qquad (10)$$

Where B is the bandwidth allocated?
For easier comprehension and comparative analysis, Table 3.1 presents a summary of the major research gaps found in the examined publications.

Experimental Work

In accordance with the 3GPP NR specifications, a simulation setup is used to examine the performance of 5G New Radio (NR) in different configurations [13]. The study depicts the impacts of channel models, modulation techniques, and subcarrier spacing (SCS) on system throughput. This

methodology relies on widely accepted simulation methods for 5G NR performance
evaluation, as documented in [14].

Results Analysis

In fulfilling the requirements of the 3GPP
Release with 5G Toolbox, the simulation
must abide by the specifications set within
it. The simulation environment's bandwidth configuration is based on the 5G NR
bandwidth portions (BWPs) which define
the specified BW settings. Numerology
of high mobility, rural, urban macro cell,
urban microcell, and many other real-
world deployments are replicated using 15
kHz, 30 kHz, and 60 kHz subcarrier spacings. Superior channel models CDL-A and
CDL-B provide exemplary channel models for simulating propagation in these
scenarios.

An array of performance analyses is done
using different modulation techniques like
QPSK, 16-QAM, 64-QAM, and 256-QAM.
The Performance of data transmission is
analyzed using two primary components
of channel modeling: Physical Downlink
Shared Channel (PDSCH) and Downlink
Shared Channel (DL-SCH). Hybrid
Automatic Repeat Request (HARQ) techniques are included in the simulation for
analyzing error correction efficiency and
retransmission strategies [15].

From parameter configuration to channel
modeling and signal transmission to receiv-
er-side processing such as demodulation,
decoding, and error correction, the simulation is methodical. While spectral efficiency
analysis measures bandwidth usage, latency
estimation analyzes end-to-end latency. By
comparing simulation outcomes with theoretical values and 3GPP benchmarks, model
accuracy is confirmed.

As shown in Figure 3.3, When the SNR
enters into the mid-range (0 dB to 10 dB),

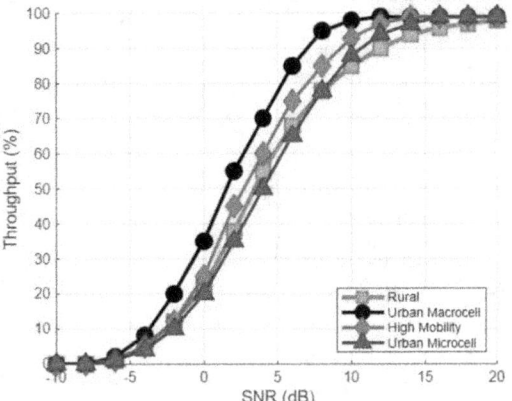

Figure 3.3 Throughput Vs SNR performance for scenarios
Source: Author

through-put spikes. Urban macro cell and
microcell deployments at 5 dB result in
through-puts of about 50%.

Results analysis 1: illustrates the relationship between throughput (%) and
SNR (dB) over the deployment scenarios that were considered. When the SNR
enters into the mid-range (0 dB to 10 dB),
throughput spikes. Urban macro cell and
microcell deployments at 5 dB result in
throughputs of about 50%. Urban Macroc
ell and Microcell have 90% throughput
at higher SNRs (approximately 11–12
dB), while Rural and High Mobility situations require slightly increased SNRs to
achieve similar levels, highlighting the
impact of environmental heterogeneity on
performance.

Results analysis 2: The figure illustrates
the variation of throughput (%) as a function of signal-to-noise ratio (SNR) for different subcarrier spacings (SCS) in a 5G
NR system: 15 kHz, 30 kHz, 60 kHz, and
120 kHz. In 5G deployments, the findings
indicating that a larger SCS (e.g., 120 kHz)
supports higher throughput for high SNR
provide valuable insights for numerology
choice and network optimization.

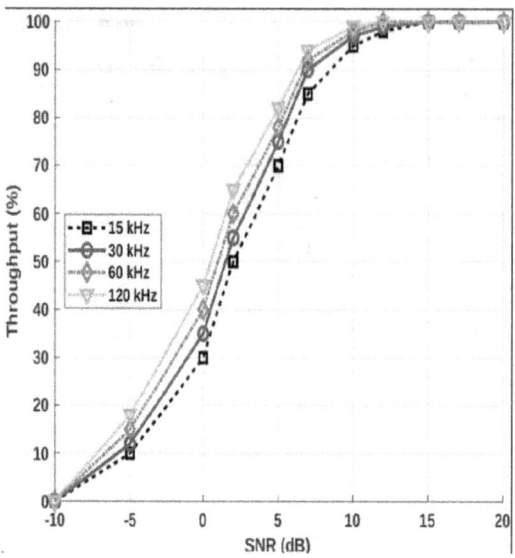

Figure 3.4 Throughput Vs SNR for different subcarrier spacing
Source: Author

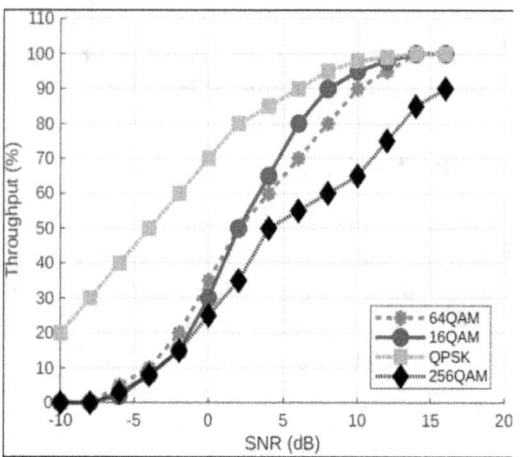

Figure 3.5 Throughput Vs SNR for different modulation schemes
Source: Author

Throughput improves incrementally for all SCS systems with low to moderate SNR values. However, significant differences become evident as SNR increases beyond 10 dB. In contrast to the narrower SCS configurations, the 120 kHz SCS achieves nearly optimal throughput (~100%) at around 15 dB. SNR levels greater than 18 dB are required to attain full throughput with the 15 kHz SCS, which is commonly used in sub-6 GHz deployments. Contrarily, the 60 kHz and 30 kHz subcarrier spacings come in second, peaking throughput at approximately 17dB. This trend is attributed to the shorter symbol time and lower latency associated with broader SCS, which improves system response time and makes it suitable for low-latency, high-SNR applications like improved mobile broadband (eMBB). Nevertheless, in low-SNR or high-mobility environments, broader SCS performs poorer due to its larger sensitivity to Doppler shift and phase noise.

As shown in Figure 3.4, Throughput improves incrementally for all SCS systems with low to moderate SNR values

Results Analysis 3: In a 5G NR physical layer environment, the graph manifests the connection betwixt Signal-to-Noise Ratio (SNR) in dB and the percentage throughput for the modulation schemes of QPSK, 16-QAM, 64-QAM, and 256-QAM. Due to its lower bit error rate (BER) and high noise resilience, Quadrature Phase Shift Keying (QPSK) exhibits better performance in the low-SNR range (−10 dB to 0 dB), maintaining higher throughput. Due to this, it is ideal for cell-edge users or poor channel conditions. 64-QAM (red dashed line) cuts throughput in this range significantly, with only about 10% throughput at 0 dB. On the other hand, 256-QAM has extremely low throughput in the same SNR regime, remaining below 5% up to around 2 dB. This is due to its great spectral efficiency but at the cost of requiring a greater SNR threshold in order to efficiently decode signals. For this reason, 256-QAM should not be employed in low-SNR conditions and performs optimally in high-SNR conditions, such as for

Table 3.2 Simulation results.

Modulation scheme	Subcarrier spacing	Clustered delay line (CDL) Model	Max throughput (Gbps)
QPSK	15 kHz	CDL-A	30.21
16-QAM	30 kHz	CDL-B	60.43
64-QAM	60 kHz	CDL-C	120.86
256-QAM	120 kHz	CDL-D	241.56

Source: Author

users near the base station with good channel quality indicators (CQI).

As shown in Figure 3.5, Due to its lower bit error rate (BER) and high noise resilience, Quadrature Phase Shift Keying (QPSK) exhibits better performance in the low-SNR range (−10 dB to 0 dB), maintaining higher throughput.

Various models of Cluster Delay Line (CDL) are characterized by their delay spread and multipath properties. CDL-A, for line-of-sight or weakly blocked conditions, accounts for minimal delay spread and fewer multipath components. Small urban microcells typically experience CDL-B with richer multipath effects and light delay spread, which induce greater fading with a moderate throughput. More delayed spread and stronger multipath components in urban macro cell environments suit CDL-C. In contrast, CDL-D is tailored to high-mobility channels with rapidly changing channel conditions, like highways and high-speed rail tracks. It provides the optimum choice for measuring system performance under dynamic conditions due to its strong multipath effects and large delay spreads. Our research's use of the CDL-D model demonstrates an advanced and effective approach to capturing the complexity of high-speed wireless environments. Consequently, our performance study is more efficient and useful in real-world 5G NR deployments as it can better model the time-varying and Doppler-heavy character of such environments. The summary of results is given in Table 3.2.

Conclusion

This work systematically evaluates the effect of modulation schemes, subcarrier spacing, and channel models on the throughput performance in 5G NR networks. This confirms that Superior throughput is obtained by higher-order modulation schemes, i.e., 256-QAM, but they are very sensitive to SNR conditions. Greater subcarrier spacing (e.g., 120 kHz) improves throughput at high SNR but might be inefficient under low-SNR conditions. Channel propagation behavior has a key impact on network performance, with CDL-D (high-mobility) being the worst hit by multipath fading. These observations highlight the need for dynamic resource allocation techniques and adaptive modulation in order to maximize 5G NR performance across various deployment environments. For future research, we propose to continue this investigation by incorporating AI-based scheduling algorithms to further strengthen adaptive modulation and coding (AMC) in real-time systems. The use of multi-user MIMO (MU-MIMO) and network slicing mechanisms will also continue to advance spectral efficiency and latency for 5G and beyond.

References

[1] Mahmood, S., Mohsin, S. M., & Akber, S. M. A. (2020). Network security issues of data link layer: an overview. In 2020 3rd International Conference on Computing, Mathematics and Engineering Technologies (iCoMET), Sukkur, Pakistan, (pp. 1–6). doi: 10.1109/iCoMET48670.2020.9073825.

[2] Flores de Valgas, J., Monserrat, J. F., & Arslan, H. (2021). Flexible numerology in 5G NR: interference quantification and proper selection depending on the scenario. *Mobile Information Systems*, 2021, 6651326. doi: 10.1155/2021/6651326.

[3] Singh, U., Dua, A., Kumar, N., Tanwar, S., Iqbal, R., Hijji, M., et al. (2022). Scalable priority-based resource allocation scheme for M2M communication in LTE/LTE-A network. *Computers and Electrical Engineering*, 103, 108321.

[4] Kabalci, Y., & Ali, M. (2020). Throughput analysis over 5G NR physical uplink shared channels. In Global Power, Energy, and Communication Conference. https://doi.org/10.1109/GPECOM49333.2020.9247906.

[5] Sinwar, D. (2023). 5G New Radio physical downlink shared channel throughput analysis with different numerology and modulation schemes. In Lecture Notes in Networks and Systems (pp. 733–742). Springer. https://doi.org/10.1007/978-981-19-9858-4_62

[6] Thangamayan, S., Walunjkar, M., Ray, D. K., Venkatesan, M., Banik, A., & Amrutkar, K. P. (2022). 5G modulation technique comparisons using simulation approach. In Proceedings of the 2022 International Conference on Emerging Frontiers in Electrical and Electronic Technologies (ICEFET) (pp. 848–856). IEEE. https://doi.org/10.1109/ICIEM54221.2022.9853137

[7] Rahmani, M., Zhao, J., Chu, Y., Grace, D., Maunder, R. G., & Burr, A. G. (2024). Error rate performance analysis of the 5G NR physical uplink shared channels for cell-free systems. TechRxiv. https://doi.org/10.36227/techrxiv.173387998.84680653/v1

[8] Ahmadi, S. (2019). 5G NR: Architecture, Technology, Implementation, and Operation of 3GPP New Radio Standards. Academic Press.

[9] Holma, H., Toskala, A., & Nakamura, T. (Eds.), (2024). 5G Technology: 3GPP Evolution to 5G-Advanced. John Wiley and Sons.

[10] Soret, B., Mogensen, P., Pedersen, K. I., & Aguayo-Torres, M. C. (2014). Fundamental tradeoffs among reliability, latency, and throughput in cellular networks. In 2014 IEEE Globecom Workshops (GC Wkshps). IEEE.

[11] Morais, D. H. (2024). Key 5G/5G-advanced physical layer technologies. IEEE Access.

[12] Ramos, A. R., Silva, B. C., Lourenço, M. S., Teixeira, E. B., & Velez, F. J.. (2019). Mapping between average sinr and supported throughput in 5g new radio small cell networks. In 2019 22nd International Symposium on Wireless Personal Multimedia Communications (WPMC). IEEE. DOI: 10.1109/WPMC48795.2019.9096179.

[13] 3GPP, I. (2018). NR; physical channels and modulation. In 3rd Generation Partnership Project (3GPP), Technical Specification (TS) 38.211 9.

[14] 3GPP. (2019). NR; Base Station (BS) radio transmission and reception (3GPP TS 38.104). 3rd Generation Partnership Project (3GPP). https://doi.org/10.1109/ISEMC48616.2019.8986111

[15] Ahmed, A., Al-Dweik, A., Iraqi, Y., Mukhtar, H., Naeem, M., & Hossain, E. (2021). Hybrid automatic repeat request (HARQ) in wireless communications systems and standards: a contemporary survey. *IEEE Communications Surveys and Tutorials*, 23(4), 2711–2752.

4 Mitigating data exfiltration from side-channel attacks on graphics processing units

Nelson Lungu[1,a], Bibhuti Bhusan Dash[2,b], Binod Kumar Pattanayak[3,c], Rajen Bose[4,d], Utpal Chandra De[2,e] and Sudhansu Shekhar Patra[2,f]

[1]Information Communication Technology, National Institute of Public Administration, Lusaka, Zambia

[2]School of Computer Applications, Kalinga Institute of Industrial Technology (KIIT) Deemed to be University, Bhubaneswar-751024, Odisha, India

[3]Dept. of Comp. Sc. & Engineering, ITER, Siksha 'O' Anusandhan University, Bhubaneswar, India

[4]School of Computer Studies, Sri Balaji University, Pune, Maharashtra, India

Abstract

Graphics Processing Units (GPUs) are progressively used to expedite compute-intensive applications. Adversaries may use the data parallelism intrinsic to GPUs to extract sensitive information via timing, power, and cache assaults. This study introduces a Secure Shader Execution Framework that addresses these vulnerabilities via the integration of randomized execution, power balancing, and cache partitioning. The proposed vendor-agnostic method aligns with current GPU programming paradigms, as shown by the GPUOwl benchmarks using OpenCL. Experimental findings indicate that the framework successfully conceals side-channel information leakage in security-sensitive data with a minimal performance cost. Randomized execution lowers the success rate of timing assaults by as much as 75%, while power balancing decreases leakage in power traces by over 60%.

Keywords: Artificial intelligence security, graphics processing, power usage, shader techniques, side-channel attacks

Introduction

The rapid advancement of GPU technology has significantly enhanced high-performance computing, with GPUs being used to expedite compute-intensive applications such as scientific simulations, machine learning, and computer graphics [5]. Massive multicore GPUs may substantially enhance the performance of compute-intensive applications due to their robust parallel processing capabilities compared to conventional CPU-based systems [16]. Nonetheless, this may potentially provide novel security vulnerabilities related to side-channel attacks [6].

Side-channel attacks are security vulnerabilities that leverage inadvertent information leakage from a system's physical implementation to illicitly access confidential data. These attacks can be readily

---

[a]lungunc@gmail.com, [b]bibhuti.dash@gmail.com, [c]binodpattanayak@soa.ac.in, [d]rajenbose.tata@gmail.com, [e]deutpal@gmail.com, [f]sudhanshupatra@gmil.com

DOI: 10.1201/9781003753391-4

executed on GPUs through methods such as timing attacks, power analysis attacks, and cache attacks, capitalizing on the distinctive characteristics of GPU micro architectures, including shared memory and cache hierarchies, to extract sensitive information. The ramifications of effective side-channel attacks on GPUs might be catastrophic, potentially resulting in the disclosure or theft of critical or private information, as well as compromising user privacy [9].

In the current landscape, where GPUs are increasingly used to handle sensitive information like financial data and medical records, safeguarding GPU calculations against side-channel assaults is of paramount importance [13]. Numerous studies have suggested remedies, including kernel changes, memory partitioning, and noise injection, to alleviate these issues [4]. Nevertheless, the majority of these countermeasures concentrate on a limited range of attack vectors and fail to provide comprehensive protection against a diverse array of side-channel assaults. Moreover, these countermeasures sometimes entail a significant performance expense, hence limiting their use only to benchmarks or a select number of real-world situations [2].

A framework novel has been proposed to offer comprehensive protection against data theft from side-channel attacks on GPUs by introducing random time variability in execution and concealing timing information through methods such as power-balancing and cache partitioning to thwart unauthorized access to sensitive data in shaders. Significantly, these methods are encapsulated inside a vendor-neutral interface, enabling compatibility across several GPU generations and facilitating their use within all current GPU programming paradigms [14]. To assess the efficacy of the proposed system, the authors used GPUOwl [12, 8], a testing suite using OpenCL for cross-vendor GPU acceleration. This workload effectively evaluates the security and performance of GPU calculations, enabling the measurement of the impact on real-world applications and the practicality of implementing authors' proposed countermeasure tactics. By using this specific benchmark, the authors ascertain the potential efficacy of the suggested security methods in safeguarding the targeted GPU workloads from side-channel assaults. Despite recent significant advancements in GPU technology, their architectural qualities render them vulnerable to side-channel assaults. The creation and assessment of complete end-to-end frameworks, such as the proposed framework, in conjunction with relevant benchmarks, facilitates advancements in enhancing GPU security and simplifies the application of sensitive workloads across many sectors [17].

This paper's primary contributions are summarized as follows:

- A unique Secure Shader Execution Framework that incorporates randomized execution, power balancing, and cache partitioning strategies to mitigate data theft from GPU side-channel attacks.
- Evaluate the performance overhead of the recommended remedies and analyze the trade-off between security and performance within the realm of GPU compute.

Rest of the paper is structured as follows. Section 2 reviews the extant literature. Section 3 provides the methodology. Section 4 explains the evaluation method; secttion-5 discusses the results and discussion. Section 6 summarizes the paper.

Literature Review

Numerous writers have suggested diverse solutions and methodologies to alleviate side-channel assaults on GPUs. This section offers a summary of pertinent research in this domain, emphasizing the fundamental contributions and shortcomings of current methodologies. There was relevant research and contrasts it with the proposed secure shader execution system. Reference Naghibijouybari et al. [10] introduced a novel GPU side-channel attack and provided a defence mechanism based on kernel modification specifically to mitigate that assault. In contrast to their efforts, the framework provides multifaceted countermeasures. Researchers such as Naghibijouybari et al. [11] illustrated the viability of GPU side-channel assaults by creating GTI FPGA implementations for high-resolution DVFS-type power side channels. They presented an architectural defence mechanism, especially spatial and temporal partitioning methods, to enhance GPUs' resistance against these assaults. We developed cache partitioning and randomization strategies inside the architecture, which would also mitigate the risks delineated in their research. Additionally, [3, 7] introduced a sub warp-based randomized coalescing method to mitigate GPU timing attacks. Their emphasis is on using strategies for randomizing memory access patterns to obfuscate timing information. Nonetheless, architecture integrates the concepts of random execution, instruction-level randomization, and power balancing to comprehensively mitigate timing assaults. Furthermore Wang and Zhang [15] examined power-based side-channel attacks on GPUs and proposed a countermeasure including power normalization within the context of this attack threat model. In this work, the authors used dynamic voltage and frequency scaling (DVFS) together with power normalization approaches, which might be advantageous in mitigating these sorts of power analysis assaults. Covert channels on GPUs in shared cloud settings were identified by Wang and Zhang [15] as a danger, with memory partitioning suggested as a countermeasure. Furthermore, the side-channel vulnerability of GPUs concerning CUDA applications was shown, and compiler-assisted masking was suggested as a countermeasure. Nonetheless, the studies concentrate on particular dangers and solutions pertinent just to shared clouds or the CUDA programming architecture, respectively. We propose a method using cache partitioning and randomization that is compatible with standard GPUs in both private and public cloud environments. The suggested Secure Shader Execution Framework is developed based on cutting-edge research and addresses their deficiencies. The suggested system, which incorporates randomization-guided execution together with power and cache components, offers a more viable way to mitigate data theft from GPU side-channel attacks. The suggested methodology is vendor-agnostic and compatible with any current GPU programming paradigm, hence generalizing for most contemporary GPUs susceptible to data exfiltration threats.

Methodology

This study presents a secure shader execution architecture, shown in Figure 4.1, designed to safeguard data from side-channel attacks on GPUs by integrating numerous countermeasures for comprehensive protection. This architecture aims to conceal critical information and prevent unauthorized access by execution randomization, power balancing, and cache partitioning. The detection will be reduced by tackling their fundamental issues according to the suggested scheduling method throughout runtime. To alleviate risks associated with mono-threaded general-purpose GPU shaders, particularly KGD-based Direct3D shaders, a dynamic soft/hardware design is essential for their transparent security, aligning with other multithreaded applications and multi-context hardware accelerators that are impervious to such threats. To provide this run-time protection capability, it is necessary to introduce appropriate uncertainty into both the target devices and the source codes from which their executables are generated. The macro pipelines, evident in the bottom-up perspective, encompass end users as developers and all low-level internal and external tools that facilitate the maintenance, debugging, automatic parallelization, and transformation of the source code development life-cycle pipeline (SDLC) throughout the stages of open-source application utilization. The suggested framework, which integrates the DVFS methodology, provides a flexible and adaptable method for regulating GPU power usage according to the particular security requirements of various computing activities [1]. The voltage and frequency may be dynamically adjusted based on the characteristics of the tasks being executed, so substantially reducing the danger of power analysis vulnerabilities and improving the overall security performance of GPU calculations.

Evaluation Method

Experiments are conducted on a variety of GPU architectures to illustrate the vendor-agnostic characteristics of the framework. The experimental configuration comprises the following GPU platforms: NVIDIA GeForce RTX 3080 (Ampere architecture), AMD Radeon RX 6800 XT (RDNA 2 architecture), Intel UHD Graphics 630 (Gen9.5 architecture). Execute the GPUOwl benchmark on each GPU platform both with and without the proposed secure shader execution framework activated. The following metrics are assessed to gauge the efficacy and performance of the proposed framework:

$$ASR = \left(\frac{NSA}{TNA}\right) \times 100 \tag{1}$$

ASR denotes the attack success rate, NSA represents the number of successful attempts, and TNA indicates the total number of tries.

The execution time includes both GPU kernel processing and data transfers between the host and the device.

$$ET = t_{kernel} + t_{data\_tranfer} \tag{2}$$

External power monitors assess GPU power usage during the execution of GPUOwl. Regularly sample the power meter to record its fluctuations over time. The power consumption (PC) is determined using the equation shown below.

$$PC = \frac{1}{N}\sum_{i=1}^{N} P_i \tag{3}$$

P_i represent the power reading at interval i, and N denote the total number of intervals. The cache behavior of the GPUOwl benchmark is analyzed using vendor-specific profiling tools. The cache hit and miss rates are evaluated to determine the efficacy of cache partitioning and randomization methods. The cache hit rate (CHR) and miss rate (CMR) are defined as follows:

$$CHR = \frac{Cache\ Hits}{Cache\ Hits + Cache\ Misses}, \quad CMR = 1 - CHR \tag{4}$$

The performance overhead imposed by the framework was determined as the percentage increase in execution time relative to the baseline execution devoid of any security precautions. The performance overhead (PO) is defined as follows:

$$PO = \frac{(T_{Famework} - T_{baseline})}{T_{baseline}} \times 100 \qquad (5)$$

$T_{framework}$ denotes the execution time with the framework activated, whereas $T_{baseline}$ represents the baseline execution time. The variability in execution time is introduced using a random variable R, resulting in the execution time T as follows:

$$T_{randomised} = T_{baseline} + R \qquad (6)$$

Power balancing is achieved by adapting the P to reach a constant average power P_{avg}:

$$P_{balanced} = P_{avg} + \Delta P \qquad (7)$$

The cache partitioning is executed by using a factor α, which specifies the proportion of cache allocated:

$$Cashe\ Size_{partitioned} = \alpha \times Total\ Cashe\ Size \qquad (8)$$

Results and Discussion

The following metrics shown in Table 4.1 were measured to evaluate the performance of the proposed Secure Shader Execution Framework using GPUOwl, a Mersenne primality tester benchmark implemented in OpenCL: (1) execution time, (2) power consumption These metrics were compared with those obtained from existing models to show that framework works effectively.

Figure 4.2 indicates that the execution time of the Secure Shader Execution Framework somewhat increased compared to the baseline GPU and other individual countermeasures. Table 4.2 shows the Power consumption comparison in watts.

Figure 4.3 indicates that our solution slightly increases power consumption while being competitive with other countermeasures. This balance is important to secure

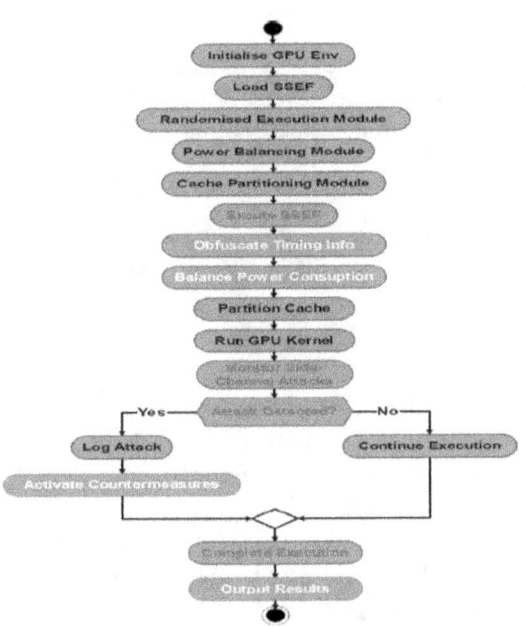

Figure 4.1 Secure shader execution framework

Source: Author

Table 4.1 Execution time comparison (MS).

Model	Baseline GPU	Randomized execution	Power balancing	Cache partitioning	Proposed framework
Matrix multiplication	1500	1600	1550	1525	1650
FFT Computation	1200	1300	1250	1230	1350
Cryptographic algorithm	2000	2100	2050	2025	2150

Source: Author

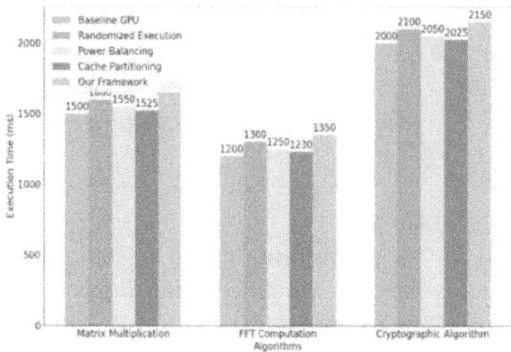

Figure 4.2 Execution time comparison
Source: Author

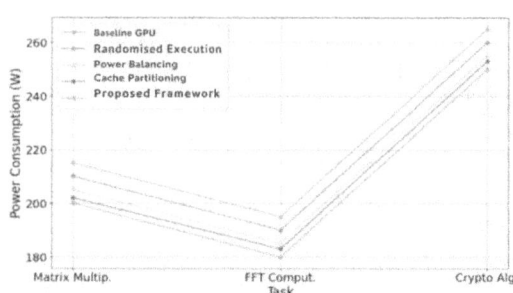

Figure 4.3 Power consumption comparison
Source: Author

Table 4.2 Power consumption comparison (Watts).

Model	Baseline GPU	Randomized execution	Power balancing	Cache partitioning	Proposed framework
Matrix multiplication	200	210	205	202	215
FFT computation	180	190	185	183	195
Cryptographic algorithm	250	260	255	253	265

Source: Author

GPU executions without significantly affecting energy efficiency.

Conclusion

The suggested secure shader execution architecture integrates randomized execution, power balancing, and cache partitioning to counter time, power, and cache-based side-channel attacks. The integrated strategy safeguards GPU workloads by obfuscating execution sequences (thereby diminishing timing leaks), standardizing power signatures (thus preventing power analysis), and segregating cache compartments (reducing cache-based vulnerabilities). The suggested methodology will be further refined and expanded for various GPU architectures and practical workloads throughout the deep optimization phase. The hardware-specific tuning will allow us to minimize overheads without altering the framework's built-in side-channel safeguards. Authors may include more countermeasures in the future, such as memory obfuscation techniques, to provide a more comprehensive defense against advancing cache-based assaults. Benchmarking will be conducted using various high-performance computing and neural network workloads to evaluate the framework's scalability among varied GPU environments. The authors believe that these future enhancements will further integrate multi-layered security measures and encourage robust side-channel mitigation throughout the GPU research community towards broader adoption.

References

[1] Bao, Q., Wang, Z., Li, X., Larus, J. R., & Wu, D. (2021). Abacus: precise

side-channel analysis. In 2021 IEEE/ACM 43rd International Conference on Software Engineering (ICSE), (pp. 797–809). IEEE.

[2] Candel, F., Petit, S., Sahuquillo, J., & Duato, J. (2018). Accurately modeling the on-chip and off-chip GPU memory subsystem. *Future Generation Computer Systems*, 82, 510–519.

[3] Kadam, G., Zhang, D., & Jog, A. (2020). Bcoal: bucketing-based memory coalescing for efficient and secure GPUs. In 2020 IEEE International Symposium on High Performance Computer Architecture (HPCA), (pp. 570–58). IEEE.

[4] Kunkel, R., Quoc, D. L., Gregor, F., Arnautov, S., Bhatotia, P., & Fetzer, C. (2019). Tensorscone: a secure tensorflow framework using intel SGX. arXiv preprint arXiv:1902.04413.

[5] Lee, J., Kim, Y., Cao, J., Kim, E., Lee, J., & Kim, H. (2022). Securing gpu via region-based bounds checking. In Proceedings of the 49th Annual International Symposium on Computer Architecture, (pp. 27–41).

[6] Lungu, N., Banda, D., & Luka, N. (2023). Sidebar attacks on GPUs. *International Research Journal of Modernization in Engineering Technology and Science*, 5(2), 255–266.

[7] Lungu, N., Tembo, S., Walubita, N., & Patra, S. S. (2024a). Mitigating GPU side-channels via integrated monitoring and response. In 2024 International Conference on Integrated Circuits and Communication Systems (ICICACS), (pp. 1–8). IEEE.

[8] Lungu, N., Sharma, H. S., Dash, B. B., Tank, T. L., Barik, A., & Patra, S. S. (2024b). A novel framework for secure and scalable cloud computing through block-chain-powered microservices. In 2024 First International Conference on Data, Computation and Communication (ICD-CC), (pp. 450–456). IEEE.

[9] Luo, C., Fei, Y., Zhang, L., Ding, A. A., Luo, P., Mukherjee, S., et al. (2018). Power analysis attack of an AES GPU

implementation. *Journal of Hardware and Systems Security*, 2, 69–82.

[10] Naghibijouybari, H., & Abu-Ghazaleh, N. (2016). Covert channels on GPGPUs. *IEEE Computer Architecture Letters*, 16(1), 22–25.

[11] Naghibijouybari, H., Neupane, A., Qian, Z., & Abu-Ghazaleh, N. (2018). Rendered insecure: Gpu side channel attacks are practical. In Proceedings of the 2018 ACM SIGSAC Conference on Computer and Communications Security, (pp. 2139–2153).

[12] Nisar, I. (2015). Vis3D+ A tightly integrated GPU-accelerated computation and rendering framework for interactive 3D image visualization (Doctoral dissertation, Toronto Metropolitan University).

[13] Reaño, C., & Silla, F. (2019). On the support of inter-node P2P GPU memory copies in rCUDA. *Journal of Parallel and Distributed Computing*, 127, 28–43.

[14] Wang, X., & Zhang, W. (2019). Cracking randomized coalescing techniques with an efficient profiling-based side-channel attack to GPU. In Proceedings of the 8th International Workshop on Hardware and Architectural Support for Security and Privacy, (pp. 1–8).

[15] Wang, X., & Zhang, W. (2020). An efficient profiling-based side-channel attack on graphics processing units. In National Cyber Summit (NCS) Research Track, (pp. 126–139). Springer International Publishing.

[16] Yan, F., Wu, R., Zhang, L., & Cao, Y. (2022). SPIDER: Speeding up side-channel vulnerability detection via test suite reduction. *Tsinghua Science and Technology*, 28(1), 47–58.

[17] Ye, G., Tang, Z., Wang, H., Fang, D., Fang, J., Huang, S., et al. (2020). Deep program structure modeling through multi-relational graph-based learning. In Proceedings of the ACM International Conference on Parallel Architectures and Compilation Techniques, (pp. 111–123).

5 Geothermal energy resources monitoring on IoT platform using LoRa based metrics evaluation

Ch. Ravisankar[a] and Sanjeet Kumar Sinha[b]

Department of Electronics and Communication Engineering, Lovely Professional University, Phagwara, Punjab, India

Abstract

Geothermal Energy has been used in numerous aspects that serve humanity and harness the heat of earth itself. It is sustainable, but that does not mean that there are instances where it turns out to be hazardous. Geothermal energy resources should have real-time monitoring for every safety concern and should be communicated faster and more widely sufficiently to notify the entire affected area. Monitoring system basically adds an enhancement of security alert system towards their life. And that is where these Internet of Things (IoT) come into play. IoT sensors can monitor many parameters such as temperature, pressure, altitude, emission of toxic gas, etc. So, those parameter values assist in recognition of the changes taking place, which assist in identifying the early signs that some incidents are going to take place in future. Here also the IoT sensors help to detect the malfunctioning of the equipment. Additionally, the use of IoT can be used to improve safety precautions in geothermal activity. As an illustration, IoT sensors can enable the monitoring of possible hazardous gas releases and changes in the geothermal reservoir that could lead to earthquakes. That data can then be used to warn or take steps to protect those individuals from harm. As a result, there is no need to upload frequent and big data from the monitoring zone to transmit on a cloud. The unique criteria studied were spreading factors, sensitivity, energy utilization, link budget, as well as the sensor node and gateway nodes battery life. Finally, this study describes challenges that face real-time when the sensor data were delivered over the sensor nodes, gateway node and cloud server.

Keywords: Customized sensor node, geothermal energy resources monitoring, Internet of Things, long range radio, lora link budget, LoRa sensitivity

Introduction

Geothermal energy is a renewable source of energy, and its importance was realized long time ago. This, in turn, has increased the need to capture this nature-friendly source due to growing energy needs. Geothermal energy is a sustainable and versatile energy source that has many potential applications but can be especially useful in regions where traditional forms of energy are scarce or expensive. Although geothermal energy is often considered as an alternative source of energy, it has several disadvantages as well such as risk of releasing health hazardous gases and other pollutants that can affect the environment, risk of earthquakes and volcanic eruption which will come into play for the wellbeing of mankind.

Existing geo-thermal energy effects on environments

The outcomes of a research examination on the air pollutants created by geothermal power plants inside the United States

---

[a]ravisankarch1@gmail.com, [b]sanjeetksinha@gmail.com

DOI: 10.1201/9781003753391-5

reveal that, on average, these plants release modest quantities of nitrous oxides, or in specific instances, no emissions of this pollutant are observed [1, 2]. The International Geothermal Association (IGA) completed a comprehensive investigation into the carbon dioxide (CO_2) emissions generated by geothermal plants. The results demonstrate that the emissions produced by these plants display a considerable variety, extending from 4 to 740 grams per kilowatt-hour (g/kWh). Furthermore, a weighted average of 122 g/kWh was determined based on the data obtained [3]. The aforementioned data demonstrates a large disparity when compared to the carbon dioxide emissions produced by typical power generation facilities fueled by natural gas, coal, and oil. These emissions typically fall within the range of around 450 grams per kilowatt-hour to 1300 grams per kilowatt-hour [4]. The direct carbon dioxide (CO_2) emissions related to direct use applications are believed to be negligible. Lifecycle forecasts anticipate that geothermal power stations will produce carbon dioxide equivalent emissions of less than 50 grams per kilowatt-hour of electricity generated [5].

Purpose of geothermal energy resources monitoring

The global community relies heavily on energy and its various sources for its functioning. The need for energy is progressively escalating on a daily basis, leading to a heavy reliance on non-renewable energy sources, thus exacerbating environmental issues. Despite the numerous benefits of geothermal energy as the most optimal kind of renewable energy for promoting sustainable development globally, its viability is diminished due to the associated risks and obstacles specific to geothermal locations [6]. The adoption of the Internet of Things (IoT) in these regions facilitates enhanced monitoring capabilities and enables prompt response to various events, eliminating any potential time delays [7]. These measures will mitigate the potential hazards to human life and provide timely notifications based on the prevailing conditions at the facility. Furthermore, it is advantageous in the identification of environmental fluctuations such as earthquakes, the emission of hazardous gases, water quality, and other related factors, so contributing to the establishment of a secure environment within the designated area [8].

Regularly checking temperature, humidity and pressure, we would be able to judge disasters from happening in geothermal areas like earthquakes or volcanic eruptions, and checking on air quality index and toxic gases like hydrogen sulfides, ammonia would help us to determine machine learning algorithm and we would be able to analyze this data, and also predict the values of the future. By showing the status of these parameters to the people located in geothermal power plants, it will lead to evacuations, communication, and first aid which means this will help us to reduce disasters and save workers in geothermal plants and the surrounding communities [9, 10].

Role of IoT and LoRa in data acquisition

Low-power wide-area (LPWAN) networks were not only observed but also had an influence on research and professionals. The database appears to focus more on promoting human-friendly applications of LoRa (long-range) [11]. This IoT environment based on LoRa is multidimensional, meaning it can be implemented in various fields. LoRa architecture consists of several sensor nodes called end devices and a gateway node (having cloud access) which link end devices to servers. All of the locally modified data is stored on the cloud at the server side [12].

It is anticipated that by 2020 over 25 billion gadgets will be wirelessly connected and will exchange data with each other. LoRa is one of the most popular communication protocols on IoT systems, which originates from the Chirp Spread Spectrum modulation technology [13]. LoRaWAN offers extremely low power consumption, suits well for battery operated devices, fits into a multi-kilometer communication range, generally between the LoRa (Long Range and low power) alliances and is connected to mastermind impacts in the scope of 2 to 3 km, and allows for very low power consumption, thus has very wide application. The servers and the gateways are generally connected via IP connection through Star Topology. Through hop link one to many, many to one or even many to many can be established [14].

All the nodes within the network share the process of information transmission and reception. LoRa is ideal for long-range, remote applications where the end nodes are far away and distributed. IoT devices are gradually becoming the preferred and widely used devices which have many more updating features compared to the Wi-Fi running 2.4 GHz. On the other hand, there are various constraints on data transfer rates for LoRa communication technology. The bandwidth of LoRa is lower than that of the Wireless fidelity (Wi-Fi), which is varies between 20 Kbps and 30 Kbps. Since we are not sending video/image data, those low transmit rates are ample to share the sensors data [15].

Literature Review

Many people are drawn to the LPWAN's low power use. Without human intervention, this may readily link to many IoT devices and transmit data across several kilometers without a wire. Using this approach makes it easier to create applications including smart waste treatment, smart cities for streetlights automation, smart parking management, and smart as well as sustainable agriculture [6].

Also, the LoRaWAN technology allows the connection and monitoring of devices running on batteries with many sensors and actuators. Technological developments toward LoRa and NBIoT produce more secure profile protocols with enhanced features. Puppy Yoon and Chan Yang classify LoRa, provide the application's context of use, and finish their impact study of fifty relevant publications with several suggestions for employing this infrastructure to create an IoT framework solution depending on LoRa [9].

An architecture based on LoRaWAN was built for computerization underground. Blind-spot detection, in which no signal exists, was found to be difficult. A method was also proposed to eliminate these communication problems so as to achieve better efficiency [13]. The IoT envisions a world in which a large fraction of our daily things talks with one another and exchange data in order to collect data and automate those operations [15]. To encourage apps that are easy to use, a cloud-enabled framework that integrates several cloud technologies was designed. In order to examine different indicators, analytical tools were provided for obtaining relevant communication protocols via IoT platforms [16].

LoRa WAN Architecture

Long Range (LoRa) is a LPWAN protocol that lets IoT devices connect to the Internet across long distances and low bandwidth. LoRa was invented by Semtech and works in unlicensed sub-GHz frequency ranges. It boasts good signal penetration and coverage at distances of up to 15 km in rural parts and

3–5 km in cities. Its modulation technique, Chirp Spread Spectrum (CSS), enhances tolerance to interference and multipath fading while maintaining consumption of low power, greatly suitable for battery-powered sensors and devices. LoRa's adaptive data rate (ADR) feature alters the settings for sending data on the fly to find the optimal balance between range, power economy, and network capacity. Because of these capabilities, LoRa is now one of the greatest choices for smart cities, farming, industrial monitoring, and tracking assets [17].

The Long Range Wide Area Network (LoRaWAN) protocol, which is based on LoRa physical layer technology, establishes standards for network design and security for IoT installations that can develop. LoRaWAN has a star-of-star topology, in which end devices talk to gateways that provide data to centralized network servers. This architecture enables millions of nodes while keeping latency and power use to a minimum [18]. The protocol classifies devices into three groups (A, B, and C) based on their latency and energy demands. Class A devices are sensors that run on batteries and only work intermittently, while Class C devices are permanently on. AES-128 encryption secures data integrity and device authentication over the air, assuming absolute security. Despite its advantages, LoRaWAN faces difficulties, including limiting bandwidth (0.3-50kbps), potential signal collisions in dense deployments, and legal limits on transmission duty cycles in specific places [19].

Future enhancements in LoRa aim to solve scalability and interoperability with 5G and other LPWAN technologies like NB-IoT. Research focuses on improving spectrum efficiency employing new modulation techniques, AI-driven network management, and hybrid designs merging LoRa with mesh networking. The combination of edge computing and LoRa-enabled satellites (e.g., Lacuna Space) gives global IoT coverage, particularly for distant and maritime applications. Standardization efforts by the LoRa Alliance and partnerships with telecom operators are gaining acceptance, with forecasts of over 1 billion LoRa devices installed by 2030. As businesses desire low-cost, energy-efficient connectivity, LoRa's role in enabling massive IoT ecosystems will continue to expand, pushing innovation in sustainability, precision agriculture, and smart infrastructure [20].

Proposed Architecture of the sensor motor and Gateway Node

Figure 5.2 (a-b) shows a sensor mote and a gateway node. Every sensor mote consists

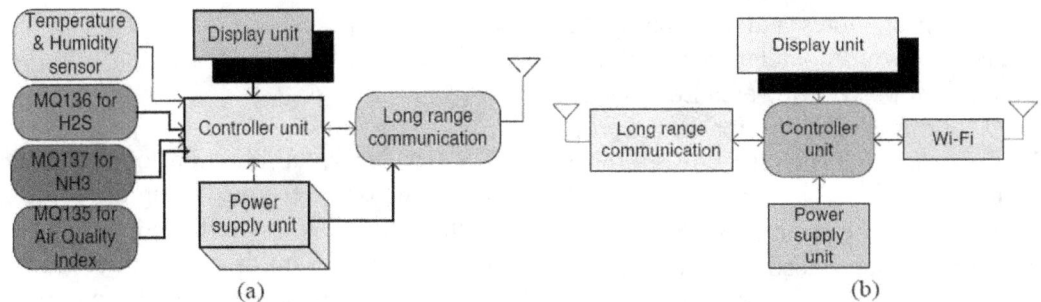

Figure 5.1 (a-b) Sensor mote and gateway node for geothermal areas monitoring
Source: Author

of a ESP32 controller board, interfaced with different types of sensors to monitor different parameters near the geothermal areas. Sensors like BME/BMP 280 is the digital barometric pressure and temperature sensors which is used to monitor the real-time temperature in Celsius, humidity in the air measured in percentage, and also the approximate altitude with respect to the sea level. And this barometric pressure and temperature sensor is having I2C port interface, to connect with SDA and SCL pins of ESP32. MQ135 is the MQ series gas sensor used to monitor the air quality index (AQI) of the air, MQ136 is other type of gas sensor used to detect the level of the Hydrogen Sulphide (H2S) gas present in the atmosphere, MQ137 is another type of gas sensor used to detect the level of the Ammonia (NH3) gas present in the atmosphere near the near geothermal areas. All three gas sensor MQ135, MQ136, and MQ137 have analog pins to interface with the ADC pins of ESP32. A solar powered battery setup is designed to power up the entire mote, an OLED is interfaced to sensor motes ESP32 to display the sensors data on it. These sensor motes are deployed in the remote locations of geothermal areas where there is network connectivity, so with the help of The LoRa module SX1278 which is interfaced to every sensor mote's ESP32 is used to send the sensors data to gateway node located in the base station. Since the sensor motes and gateway node are located several kilometers apart, so the long range/low power wide area LoRaWAN is suited for this application for the purpose of data exchange between the sensor motes and gateway node.

Gateway node consists of an ESP32 microcontroller interfaced with the LoRa module SX1278, and a display device OLED. And this Gateway mote is used to collect the data (corresponds to the various parameters) from different sensor motes located around the geothermal areas, and then the received data of Gateway node which corresponds to the various parameters will be uploaded to the cloud server for further analysis of data by applying the machine learning algorithms so as to predict the future animalities to develop an emergency alert system.

Scalability Analysis of LoRa Sensor

We evaluated the various criteria of LoRa such as bitrate, link budget, time-on-air, sensitivity, and spreading factor using customized board. Among the various parameters of physical layer which utilizes chirp spread spectrum (CSS), the spreading factor (SF) serves as the primary parameter for ensuring quality of service (QoS). The transmission rate illustrates the relationship between the spreading factor (SF), bandwidth (BW), and symbol rate (Rs), highlighting how these parameters influence the bandwidth efficiency by equation 1.

$$Rs = \frac{BW}{2^{SF}} \tag{1}$$

The number of bits transmitted/received per second, from a particular source to the receiver (Rx) is known as the bit rate. The LoRa data rate has been obtained using equation 2.

$$R = SF \times \left[\frac{\frac{4}{4+CR}}{\frac{2^{SF}}{BW}} \right] \tag{2}$$

The transmission duration of a LoRa frames can2 be determined using the values of coding rate, BW, as well as SF. It can be calculated as the sum of the preamble time ($T_{preamble}$) and the corresponding payload transmission time ($T_{Payload}$), as mentioned in equation 3 below.

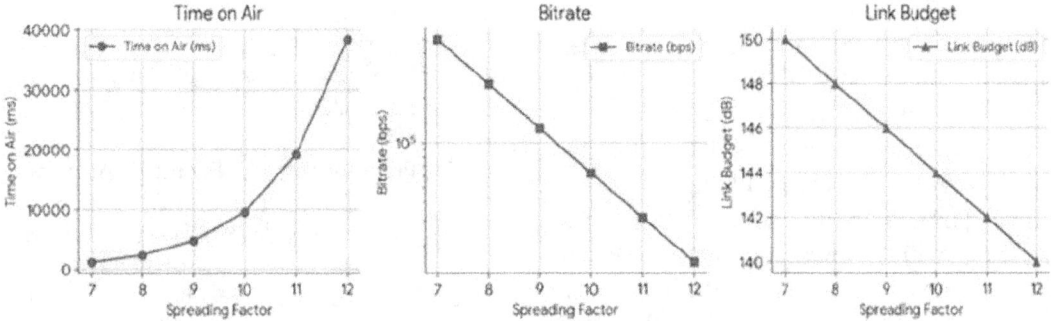

Figure 5.2 Time on air, bitrate and link budget of LoRa modem
Source: Author

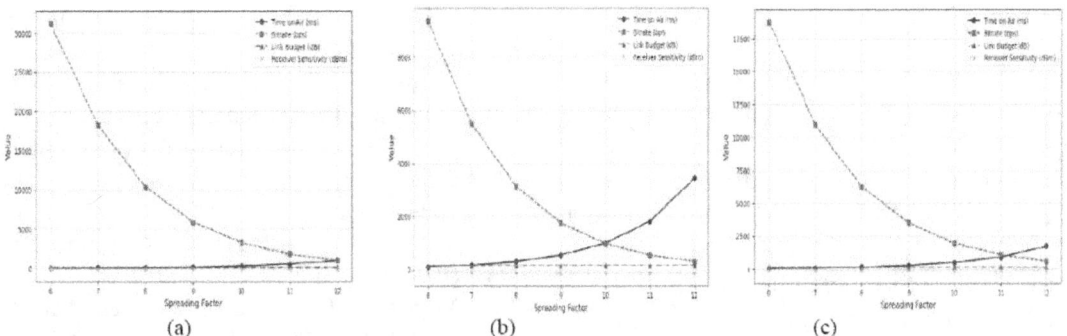

Figure 5.3 (a-c) Spreading factor of LoRa at the bandwidths 125 kHz, 250 kHz, and 500 kHz
Source: Author

$$T_{frame} = T_{Payload} + T_{preamble} \qquad (3)$$

The preamble duration $T_{preabmble}$ depends on the symbol duration T_{sym} and the programmable preamble length $n_{preamble}$.

In this regard, we also made a custom board for this study and examined numerous metrics of LoRa to see how well the system will work in the geothermal areas monitoring application. The gateway node, which has an SX1278 LoRa and an ESP32 Wi-Fi module, collects real-time data from sensor motes, sends it to the Gateway node, and then uploads it to the IoT server. We determined that SF 7 and Time on Air (ToA) are at their lowest at 500 kHz bandwidth, which is the best setting for this application.

When the frequency goes down to 125 kHz, the ToA goes up to 169.22ms. We see that SF 7 has the most sensitivity at 500 kHz, which is −118, while SF12 has the lowest sensitivity at 7.8 kHz, which is −149. Figure 5.2 shows the time on air, bitrate and link budget for the following lora modem setting. Bandwidth = 500 kHz, coding rate = 1, payload length =100 bytes, preamble 8, RF = 433MHz, transmit power = 17(dBm).

Results and Discussion

For data rates, we used the same study indicators of bandwidth 500 kHz, 250 kHz, and 125 kHz; SF from SF6 to SF12; and also, the coding rate (CR) from coding rate 1 to coding rate 4. Accordingly, the measured findings are shown in Figure 5.3. After spreading factor SF9 to SF12, the corresponding graphs show a dramatic rise in time on-air (ToA). Figure 5.3 shows that the time of arrival (ToA) at 500 kHz is 42.3ms, at 250 kHz is 84.61ms, and at 125 kHz is 169.22ms with a spreading factor (SF) of 7. This study reveals that as the BW goes from 125 kiloHz to 500 kiloHz, then the time on-air (ToA) goes down by half. It also shows that the ToA goes up when the SF changes from 7 to 12.

Conclusion

The findings indicated in different spreading factors SF7 to SF12, the corresponding graphs show a sharp increase in the time on-air (ToA). Accordingly, the time of arrival (ToA) at 500 kHz is 42.3ms, at 250 kHz is 84.61ms, and at 125 kHz is 169.22ms with a spreading factor (SF) of 7. This study reveals that as the bandwidth goes from 125 kiloHz to 500 kiloHz, then the time on-air (ToA) goes down by half. It also shows that the ToA goes up when the Spreading factor (SF) changes from SF7 to SF12. Another observation is that an increase in the transmission (Tx) power leads to an increase in the link budget () with respect to bandwidth (BW). As a result, the maximum link budget was achieved at the highest Tx power and the lowest bandwidth.

References

[1]   Naik, A. S., Reddy, S. K., & Raj, M. G. (2024). RTEPMS: real-time environmental parameters monitoring system using IoT-based LoRa 868-MHz wireless communication technology in underground mines. *IEEE Access*, 12, 7430–7455.

[2]   Mishu, M. K., Rokonuzzaman, M., Pasupuleti, J., Shakeri, M., Rahman, K. S., Binzaid, S., et al. (2021). An adaptive TE-PV hybrid energy harvesting system for self-powered iot sensor applications. *Sensors*, 21(8), 2604.

[3]   Rahayu, L. P., Adhim, F. I., Priananda, C. W., Pramudijanto, J., Tsauri, D. A., Susila, J., et al. (2019). Design of gas detection toxic sulfur dioxide (SO 2) in the mountain activity area. In 2019 International Conference on Advanced Mechatronics, Intelligent Manufacture and Industrial Automation (ICAMIMIA), (pp. 272–276). IEEE.

[4]   Lago González, D., & Rodríguez-Gonzálvez, P. (2019). Detection of geothermal potential zones using remote sensing techniques. *Remote Sensing*, 11(20), 2403.

[5]   Byrtus, R., Hercik, R., Dohnal, J., Martinkauppi, J. B., Rauta, T., & Koziorek, J. (2022). Low-power renewable possibilities for geothermal IoT monitoring systems. In 2022 11th International Conference on Renewable Energy Research and Application (ICRERA), (pp. 164–168). IEEE.

[6]   Morris, C. J., Mroczek, E. K., & Misa, T. N. (2019). Geothermal steam condition performance monitoring. *Geothermics*, 81, 101–112.

[7]   Bagwari, S., Roy, A., Singh, R., & Gehlot, A. (2022). Disaster monitoring based on IoT and long range assisted framework. *Journal of Physics: Conference Series*, (Vol. 2327, No. 1, p. 012020). IOP Publishing.

[8]   Jouhara, H., Żabnieńska-Góra, A., Khordehgah, N., Doraghi, Q., Ahmad, L., Norman, L., et al. (2021). Thermoelectric generator (TEG) technologies and applications. *International Journal of Thermofluids*, 9, 100063.

[9]   Yu, Y., & Zou, Y. L. (2014). Application of technology of the internet of things on the monitoring of geothermal field. *Advanced Materials Research*, 860, 563–567.

[10] Gupta, T., Sanket, R., Singh, R., Gehlot, A., Mehandiratta, E., Agarwal, A., et al. (2017). Design and development of low-cost wireless parameter monitoring system

for nuclear power plant. *In Proceeding of International Conference on Intelligent Communication, Control and Devices,* 2016, (pp. 569–580).

[11] Li, B. Q., & Zheng, S. Y. (2019). Application research of intelligent monitoring system of longsheng hot spring water temperature based on Internet of Things. Thermal Science, 23(5 Part A), 2613–2622.

[12] Anderson, A., & Rezaie, B. (2019). Geothermal technology: trends and potential role in a sustainable future. *Applied Energy*, 248, 18–34.

[13] Mona, Y., Do, T. A., Sekine, C., Suttakul, P., & Chaichana, C. (2022). Geothermal electricity generator using thermoelectric module for IoT monitoring. *Energy Reports*, 8, 347–352.

[14] Singh, R., Baz, M., Narayana, C. L., Rashid, M., Gehlot, A., Akram, S. V., et al. (2021). Zigbee and long-range architecture based monitoring system for oil pipeline monitoring with the internet of things. *Sustainability*, 13(18), 10226.

[15] Prauzek, M., Kucova, T., Konecny, J., Adamikova, M., Gaiova, K., Mikus, M., et al. (2023). Iot sensor challenges for geothermal energy installations monitoring: a survey. *Sensors*, 23(12), 5577.

[16] Yadav, K., & Sircar, A. (2019). Application of low enthalpy geothermal fluid for space heating and cooling, honey processing and milk pasteurization. *Case Studies in Thermal Engineering*, 14, 100499.

[17] Bayer, P., Attard, G., Blum, P., & Menberg, K. (2019). The geothermal potential of cities. *Renewable and Sustainable Energy Reviews*, 106, 17–30.

[18] Maddela, V., Sinha, S. K., Parvathi, M., & Chander, S. (2025). Parasitic RC estimation and defect prediction for embedded memory using machine learning. Analog Integrated Circuits and Signal Processing, 124(2), 33.

[19] Maksimovic, M. (2017). The role of green internet of things (G-IoT) and big data in making cities smarter, safer and more sustainable. *International Journal of Computing and Digital Systems*, 6(04), 175–184.

[20] Macharia, M. W., Gachari, M. K., Kuria, D. N., & Mariita, N. O. (2017). Low cost geothermal energy indicators and exploration methods in Kenya. *Journal of Geography and Regional Planning*, 10(9), 254-265.

6 A dual band wearable antenna for 5G and WLAN application

Anupa Chatterjee[1,a], Sneha Sharma[2,b], Manas Midya[3,c] and Laxmi Prasad Mishra[4,d]

[1]Department of Electrical Engineering Chulalongkorn University Bangkok, Thailand

[2]Department of Electronics and Communication, Calcutta Institute of Engineering and Management, Kolkata, WB, India

[3]Department of Electronics and Communication, Institute of Engineering & Management, Kolkata, WB, India

[4]Department of Electronics and Communication, ITER, SOA Deemed to be University, Bhubaneswar, India

Abstract

This work introduces a flexible, wearable antenna featuring dual-band capabilities designed for 5G applications. The suggested antenna is a square patch with a ground plane inscribed on "felt," possessing a dielectric constant of 1.63 and a loss tangent of 0.02. The dimensions of the proposed antenna are 40 mm × 40 mm × 2 mm. The simulated frequency bands are (3.33–3.41) GHz and (5.81-5.95) GHz, respectively. The measurement results show reasonable gain, good radiation characteristics, and low return loss within these operating bands, indicating effective antenna performance and can be used for various on-body and off-body applications due to its wearable and compact design.

Keywords: 5G, SAR, wearable antenna, WLAN

Introduction

Since the 1970s, the mobile wireless industry has driven technological innovation, evolving from 1G to 5G to meet rising demands. The surge in internet data traffic has highlighted the need to enhance 4G capacity, prompting extensive research to develop 5th generation wireless networks. 5G services impact society beyond personal communication, integrating with devices like mobile phones, wearable sensors, and robots. As key infrastructure, 5G drives innovation across industries and supports the Internet of Things (IoT). It operates on frequencies below 6GHz and millimeter waves above 24GHz, enhancing connectivity and enabling new technological advancements. The 'sub-6' spectrum, below 6GHz, is favored for its wide coverage in various applications. 5G acquires the 3.3GHz (n78) bands [1–3]. A wearable antenna is any antenna worn on or near the human body, emitting electromagnetic waves that can be absorbed by human tissue which can harm human tissue, making it essential to minimize this interaction. The SAR quantifies the energy absorbed per unit mass [4]. Due to growing concerns, regulatory agencies have set safe SAR limits for

[a]anupa.c@chula.ac.th, [b]snehasushmita2000@gmail.com, [c]letsmanas@gmail.com, [d]laximimishra@soa.ac.in

DOI: 10.1201/9781003753391-6

these antennas [4]. The literature review shows wearable antennas designed for frequency bands like Industrial, Scientific, and Medical (ISM) at 2.4 GHz and 5.8 GHz [5]. Significant advancements in wearable antennas are anticipated with the integration of 5G systems.

Antenna Design

This research presents an innovative and straightforward dual-band wearable antenna design for 5G. The antenna employs a 2 mm felt substrate with a dielectric constant ($\varepsilon 0$) of 1.63 and a tangent loss of 0.02. The radiating patch size are 32×32 mm², while the compact ground plane measures 40×40 mm². The suggested antenna configuration is illustrated in Figure 6.1, with characteristics detailed in Table 6.1. The wavelength is calculated as

$$\lambda = \frac{c}{f\sqrt{\varepsilon_r}} \tag{1}$$

Design methodology
The square patch is exciting by using inset micro strip feeding technique. The steps of evolution of the antenna are depicted in Figure 6.2 (f1-f7). This square patch is responsible for the higher frequency at 6.5GHz (Step-f1). A cut on the top left corner gives the dual band with very poor matching for the lower frequency (Step-f2). A second cut at lower left side of the patch shifts the upper frequency to the left side (Step-f3). In order to make the antenna occupy less space, pairs of slits are etched in the antenna to extend the current path and reduce the resonance frequencies. A small rectangular portion is etched out from the right side of the patch, thereby increasing the current path which further shifts the upper frequency to the left side as the current path is further meandered (Step-f4).

The impedance matching at the lower frequency is increased. Further etching on the right side of the patch and merging all three of them (Step-f5 to Step-f7), shifts the upper frequency to the desired resonance at 5.87GHz. The lower resonant frequency is also well matched at 3.37GHz. Thus, adjusting the dimensions, the desired dual frequency can be obtained with impedance bandwidth 3.37(3.33-3.41) GHz and 5.87(5.81-5.95) GHz. The simulated reflection coefficients S11 for all the antenna evolution steps are shown in Figure 6.3. Surface current distribution in Figure 6.4 at 3.37GHz, illustrates that the right-side etching of the patch is responsible for the lower resonant frequency and the left side etching of the patch for the higher resonant frequency at 5.87GHz.

Result Analysis

The fabricated antenna is depicted in Figure 6.5. The S11 parameter of the constructed antenna encompasses the frequency ranges of 3.33-3.40 GHz and 5.80-5.98 GHz, aligning with the simulated findings depicted in Figure 6.6. The discrepancy between the measured and simulated

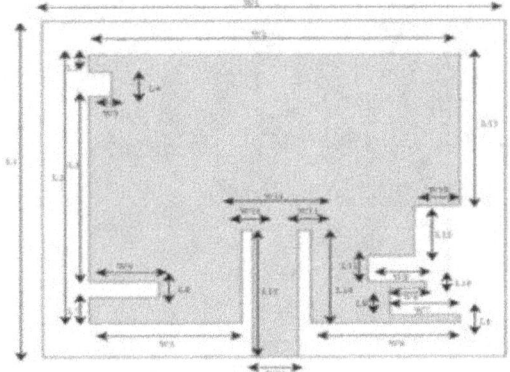

Figure 6.1 Illustration of the proposed antenna
Source: Author

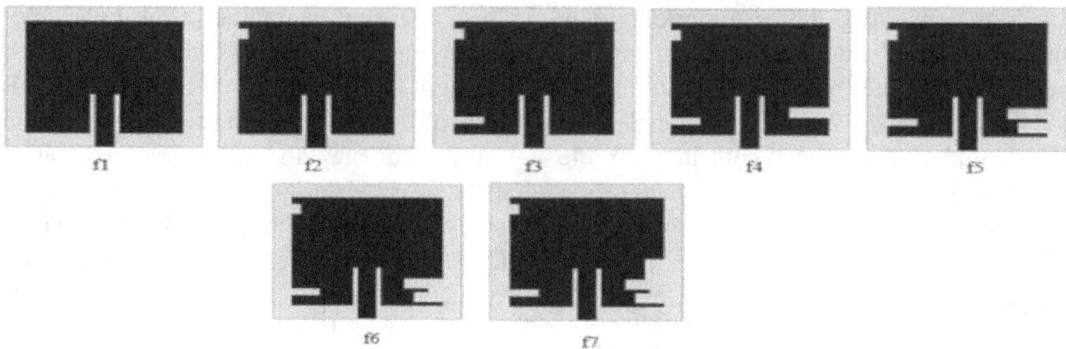

Figure 6.2 Evolution steps of the antenna design
Source: Author

Table 6.1 Parameters table.

Parameter	Value (mm)	Parameter	Value (mm)	Parameter	Value (mm)	Parameter	Value (mm)
L1	40	L9	3	W2	32	W10	4
L2	32	L10	1	W3	2	W11	1
L3	2	L11	3	W4	6	W12	4
L4	3	L12	6	W5	13	W13	1
L5	22	L13	18	W6	13	W14	6
L6	2	L14	10.5	W7	6		
L7	3	L15	14.5	W8	3		
L8	1	W1	40	W9	5		

Source: Author

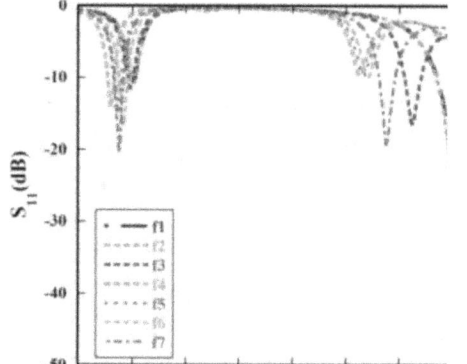

Figure 6.3 Simulated S_{11} results for the corresponding evolution steps of the proposed antenna
Source: Author

findings is minimal, attributable to fabrication tolerances from manual soldering. The gain is illustrated in Figure 6.8. The maximum simulated gain swings between 3.7 dB to5.9 dB.

Equivalent circuit diagram

Figure 6.7 provides the illustrated antenna and its derived configuration. The microstrip section, comprises of L1 and C1, transfers power to the tank circuit through L2. These tank circuits create dual bands by adjusting the dimensions of slits, which modify the inductance and capacitance to target specific frequency bands.

 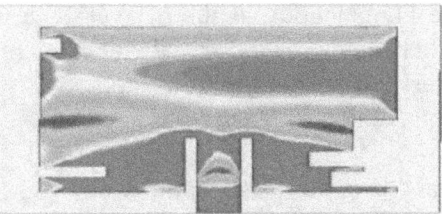 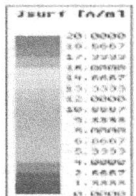

Figure 6.4 Surface current distribution (a) 3.37GHz (b) 5.87GHz
Source: Author

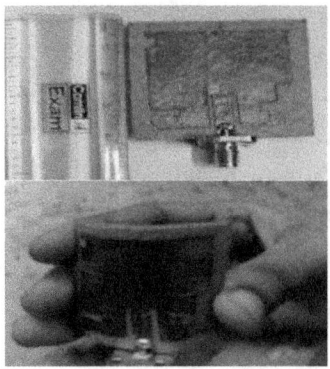

Figure 6.5 Fabricated prototype
Source: Author

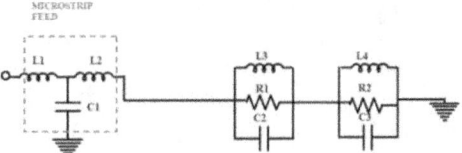

Figure 6.7 Proposed antenna equivalent circuit
Source: Author

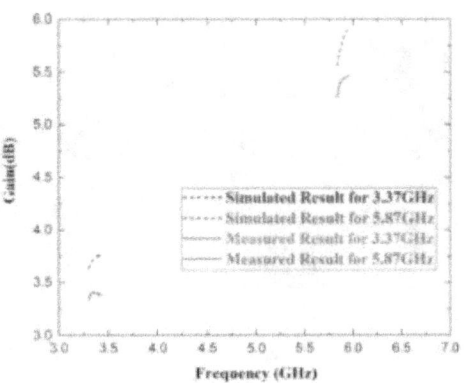

Figure 6.8 Simulated and measured gain (dB)
Source: Author

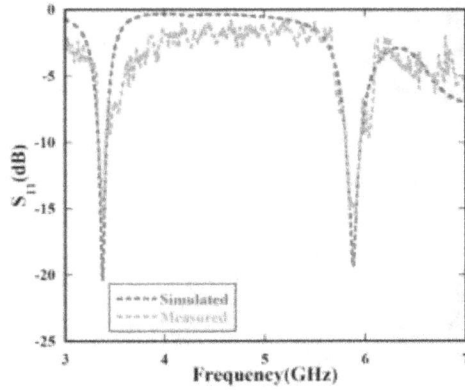

Figure 6.6 Simulated and measured reflection coefficient S$_{11}$
Source: Author

$$SAR = \frac{\sigma |E|^2}{\rho} \qquad (2)$$

IEEE C95.1-1999 specifies 1.6 W/Kg as the maximum safety limit for 1g of tissue whereas 2 W/Kg is the safety limit for 10 g of tissue as specified by the ICNIRP [6].

In order to simulate the SAR value of the designed antenna system working on the

SAR

SAR calculates the absorbed electromagnetic power of human body tissue. It is calculated as surface of the human body, a three layer tissue model that is close to the actual electrical parameters of the human body consisting of skin,fat and muscle is constructed in Figure 6.9.

Table 6.2 and Figure 6.10 summaries SAR distribution and its maximum value at frequencies for 1 g and 10 g tissues. The

design of wearable antennas faces challenges from structural bending caused by

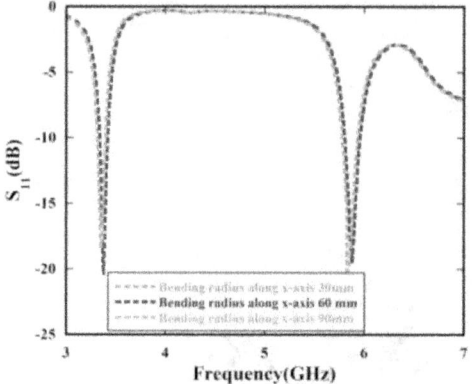

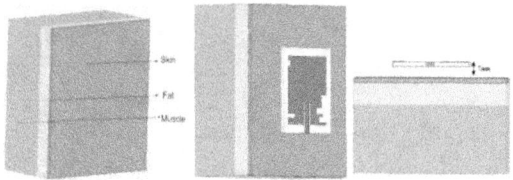

Figure 6.9 Antenna placed above human body phantom
Source: Author

Figure 6.11 Study of bending curvature on reflection coefficient
Source: Author

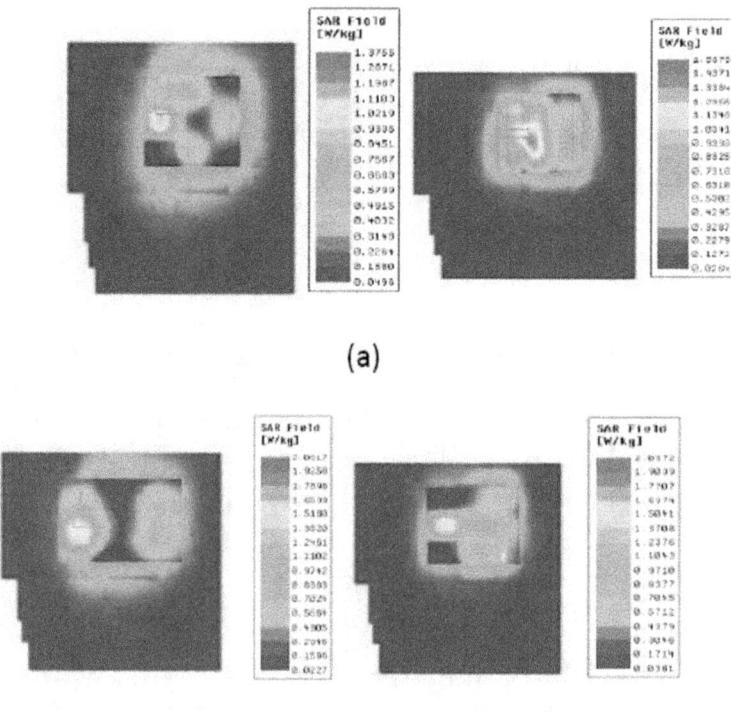

Figure 6.10 SAR Distribution (a) tissue of 1g at 3.37GHz, and 5.87GHz (b) tissue of 10g at 3.37GHz, and 5.87GHz
Source: Author

Table 6.2 Detailed dimensions.

SAR at 1 gm (W/kg)		SAR at 10 gm (W/kg)	
3.37 GHz	5.87 GHz	3.37 GHz	5.87 GHz
1.3755	1.5379	2.0617	2.0372

Source: Author

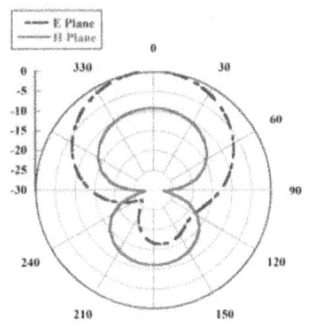 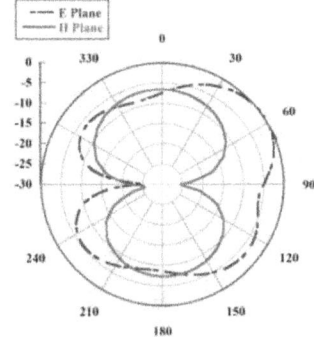

Figure 6.12 Normalized radiation pattern (a) 3.37GHz (b) 5.87GHz
Source: Author

human body movements. This bending can significantly impact antenna performance, making it crucial to study its effects thoroughly to ensure consistent performance across deformations.

Bending effects on antenna performance were tested with curvatures of 30 to 90 mm with an increment of 30mm in the x-axis (Ax), as shown in Figure 6.11. The antenna showed stable reflection coefficients across all bending.

The normalised radiation pattern is shown in Figure 6.12.

Conclusion

This work presents a compact wearable antenna suitable for 5G and WLAN application. The antenna fabricated on a felt substrate with a dielectric constant of 1.63 and a loss tangent of 0.02 demonstrates excellent mechanical flexibility and electrical performance making it highly suitable for integration in to wearable systems. With compact dimensions the proposed antenna resonates at two distinct frequency bands 3.31-3.41GHz and 5.81-5.91GHz effectively covering the sub-6GHz 5G and WLAN operating bands.

References

[1] Steering Committee (2018). Making India 5G Ready. Delhi, India: Ministry of Communications. https://dot.gov.in/sites/default/files/5G%20Steering%20Committee%20report%20v%2026.pdf.

[2] Telecom Regulatory Authority of India (2019). Enabling 5G in India. Delhi, India: TRAI. https://Trai.Gov.In/Sites/Default/Files/White Paper 22022019 0.Pdf.

[3] Chatterjee, A., Midya, M., Mishra, L. P., & Mitra, M. (2021). Dual-element multiple-input-multiple-output system for sub-6 GHz (5G) and WLAN applications

with enhanced isolation. *Progress in Electromagnetics Research M*, 103, 197–207.

[4]   Zahran, S. R., Abdalla, M. A., & Gaafar, A. (2019). 'New thin wide-band bracelet-like antenna with low SAR for on-arm WBAN applications. *IET Microwaves, Antennas and Propagation*, 13(8), 1219–1225.

[5]   Choi, J., Tak, J., & Lee, S. (2015). All-textile higher order mode circular patch antenna for on-body to on-body communications. *IET Microwaves, Antennas and Propagation*, 9(6), 576–584.

[6]   Potey, P. M., & Tuckley, K. (2020). Design of wearable textile antenna for low back radiation. *Journal of Electromagnetic Waves and Applications*, 34(2), 235–245.

7 High-gain micro-strip antenna for defence system

Shakti Raj, Chopra[1,a], Laxmi Prasad, Mishra[2,b], Saumendra Kumar, Mohanty[2,c] and Prashant Kumar, Choudhary[1,d]

[1]School of Electronics and Electrical Engineering, Lovely Professional University, Phagwara, Punjab, India

[2]Department of Electronics and Communication Engineering, ITER, Siksha 'O' Anusandhan (deemed to be University), Bhubaneswar, Odisha, India

Abstract

The work here presents the design and development of a high-gain hybrid microstrip patch antenna that combines fractal geometry miniaturization with broadband optimization. The antenna is designed for military usages like satellite communication and surveillance based on UAVs, and it provides high gain, broad bandwidth, low profile, and compact size. The combination of Sierpinski fractal slots with genetically optimized structure provides better performance to the antenna. Simulation and measurement results validate their efficacy in satisfying current defense communications requirements.

Keywords: Defected ground structure, dual-band antenna, fractal geometry, genetic algorithm, high-gain antenna, hybrid microstrip antenna, satellite communication, S-band, UAV, X-band

Introduction

Over the last few years, the development of antenna technology has been spurred foremost by the sophisticated requirements of contemporary defense systems. Traditional military antennas, as low-profile and lightweight as they are, have tended to be hampered by bandwidth and gain limitations. Such limitations can seriously impact operations on different platforms, ranging from being mounted on satellites to drones to being utilized in handheld applications [1]. The latest developments have provided avenues for new designs based on the power of fractal geometry and genetic optimization techniques [2]. The new technologies provide the possibility to create miniature antennas with no compromise in performance, a link of utmost importance in military communication during crucial missions. Credible communication forms a cornerstone in the military environment and thus the investigation of innovative antenna designs. Today's defense systems need efficient, light, and reliable antennas on various platforms—be it on satellites, UAVs, or on-hand equipment. Although classical microstrip antennas have a low profile, they tend to have narrow bandwidth and moderate gain. This paper proposes a hybrid antenna structure that has: A broadband patch structure optimized using genetic algorithms [3]

[a]shakti.chopra@lpu.co.in, [b]laxmimishra@soa.ac.in, [c]saumendramohanty@soa.ac.in, [d]prashant.24788@lpu.co.in

DOI: 10.1201/9781003753391-7

A small fractal geometry-based structure with a defected ground structure (DGS).The outcome is a hybrid antenna that operates in both the X-band and S-band, ideal for satellite communication as well as surveillance through drone technology.

Literature Review

Various research has explored the influence of fractal geometries and optimization techniques on antenna performance. For example, previous work focused on the application of Sierpinski fractal geometry in microstrip patch antennas, demonstrating good outcome in size reduction with efficient radiation characteristics. A recent study emphasized the application of genetic algorithms, optimizing multiband antennas for improving performance factors [4]. But most previous designs usually found themselves having to compromise between high gain and wide bandwidth—particularly in military situations where physical size limitation is usual. This paper tries to contribute to the development by introducing a hybrid design that successfully utilizes the strengths of genetic algorithms with the concepts of fractal geometry particularly for military use.

Design Methodology

This study integrated a holistic design methodology, where genetic algorithms were applied to carefully optimize the patch antenna size. This process of iterative optimization targeted improving important performance factors like return loss, bandwidth, and gain [5]. The building of the hybrid antenna employed high-precision manufacturing techniques to produce each component to the standards needed for reliability and ruggedness [6]. It was overcoming obstacles, especially in the

definition of the complex Sierpinski fractal slots, that required sophisticated etching procedures. Yet the resulting gain and bandwidth improvements made these efforts worthwhile, validating the applicability of contemporary manufacturing techniques to create advanced antenna geometries [7].

Substrates and materials
Material: RT/Duroid 5880 (εr = 2.2, tan δ = 0.0009)
   Thickness: 3.175 mm (selected for structural stability and enhanced gain)

Key structural features
Patch design: Rectangular patch with Sierpinski gasket slots for size reduction and multiband behavior
   Ground plane: Modified with second-order Sierpinski carpet slots (DGS)
   Feed mechanism: Inset microstrip line feed to ensure planarity and ease of fabrication
   Optimization strategy: Genetic algorithms were employed to fine-tune the dimensions for optimal performance across military frequency bands

Target frequency bands
X-Band: 7.2–8.4 GHz for military satellite communications
S-Band: 2.4 GHz for UAV command and surveillance [8]

Antenna Design

The antenna model was developed using a high-frequency electromagnetic simulation tool widely used in wireless communication research. The modeling process involved designing the physical structure of the microstrp antenna, assigning appropriate materials, and applying boundary conditions and excitation ports. The key steps in the model creation are as follows:

Table 7.1 Antenna parameters.

Variables	value	Unit	Evaluated variable
lg	5	mm	5 mm
wg	4	mm	4 mm
hp	0.035	mm	0.035 mm
hs	1.5	mm	1.5 mm
a	0.3	mm	0.3 mm
rp	1.6	mm	1.6 mm
aa	3	mm	3 mm
wt	0.75	mm	0.75 mm
lf	1.65	mm	1.65 mm

Source: Author

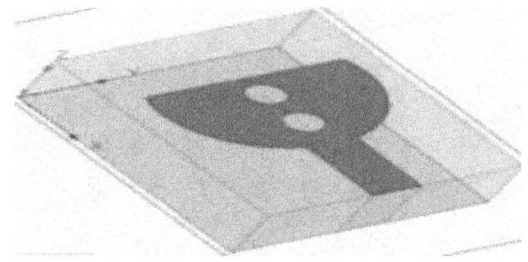

Figure 7.1 Design of antenna
Source: Author

Designing the antenna geometry

Substrate: Create a 3D box with parameters like lg, wg, hs Table 7.1.

Ground plane: Usually a rectangle at the bottom of the substrate. Set its material to PEC (Perfect Electric Conductor).

Patch: Define the shape as per your antenna profile (as seen in your image) using the a, rp, aa, wt, and lf parameters.

Feedline: Extend from the patch or slot, with dimensions like wt and lf.

Cutout or slot (if any): Subtract from patch/substrate using Boolean operations.

Assigning materials

Assign FR4 or the dielectric material to the substrate ($\varepsilon r \approx 4.4$, loss tangent = 0.02 or as required).

Assign PEC (or copper if simulating losses) to patch, ground, and feedline Figure 7.1.

Boundary conditions

Boundaries > Assign > Radiation for the outer box (your pink box).

This defines open space around the antenna for wave propagation.

Make sure this box is $\lambda/4$ or more away from all parts of the antenna.

Use perfect E boundaries for the ground and patch if not already PEC by default.

Excitation setup

To excite the antenna: Use a wave port (if you're feeding through the substrate edge): Create a rectangle on the edge where the microstrip feed ends.

Excitations > Assign > Wave Port

Ensure the port spans the dielectric layer and touches the ground and feed. Alternatively, use a lump port if feeding internally between two conductors:

Excitations > Assign > Lumped Port

Define it between the signal trace and ground plane.

Validation and analysis setup

Validate the design via validation check.

Set frequency sweep:

Analysis setup > Add solution setup

Define your start frequency (e.g., 2 GHz) and frequency sweep (e.g., 1 to 5 GHz).

Use fast sweep or interpolating sweep.

Add radiation pattern calculation: In radiation > Insert far field setup > Infinite sphere.

Post-processing and results

S11 (Return loss): Plot using results > Create modal solution data report > Rectangular plot.

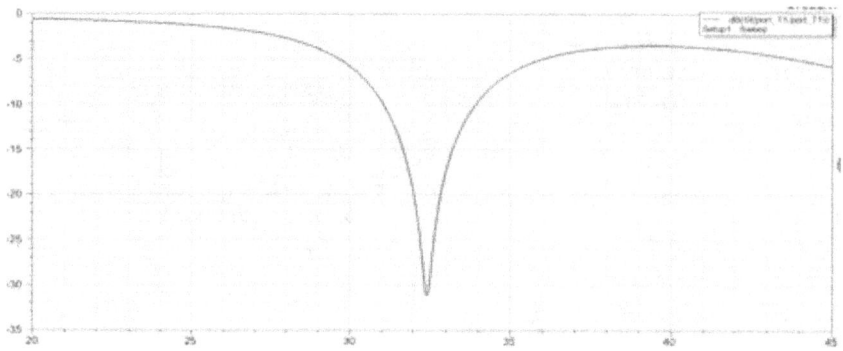

Figure 7.2 S parameter of 1st antenna
Source: Author

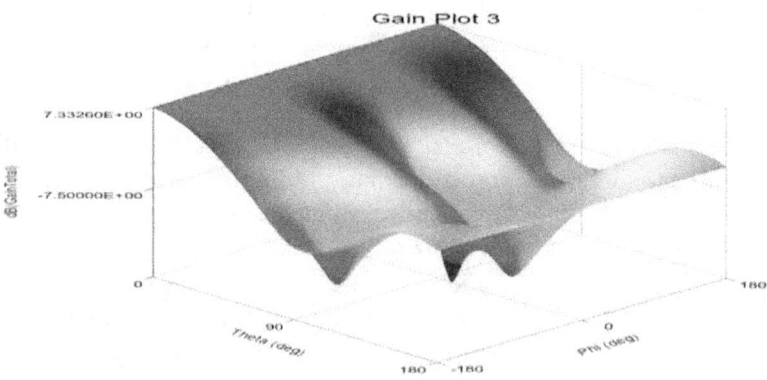

Figure 7.3 3D Rectangular plot 1st antenna
Source: Author

Gain and efficiency: Use far field reports.
Radiation pattern: 2D or 3D polar plots.
Smith chart: Results > Create Smith chart.
Validation tips
Check S11: Look for return loss < -10 dB at the target frequency.
Check bandwidth: The frequency range where S11 < -10 dB.
Radiation pattern: Ensure the main lobe direction and side lobes are as expected.
Gain: Typically 2–9 dBi depending on type.

Simulation Results

Simulation results revealed an X-band bandwidth extending about 2.9 GHz, ranging from 6.7 to 9.6 GHz, while the S-band exhibited clear resonance at 2.4 GHz with minimal harmonic disruptions. These findings were corroborated by real-world testing, where the return loss measurements closely aligned with our simulation predictions.

Including visual representations of the return loss (S11) at key frequencies would enhance our findings, as a notable decrease in return loss at target operational frequencies illustrates the antenna's suitability for tactical military operations, where communication integrity is crucial.

Bandwidth and frequency response

X-band: Achieved a bandwidth of approximately 2.9 GHz (ranging from 6.7 to 9.6 GHz)

S-band: Clear resonance at 2.4 GHz with minimal harmonic interference

Return loss (S11):

X-band: –25.4 dB at 7.8 GHz

S-band: –17 dB at 2.4 GHz shown in Figure 7.2.

Gain and radiation characteristics

Gain: Between 6.63 and 7.2 dBi for X-band, and around 7 dBi for S-band

3dB Beamwidth: Approximately 76° in both horizontal and vertical planes

Radiation pattern: Directional with minimal back-lobe radiation—ideal for line-of-sight (LOS) communication and tracking shown in Figure 7.3.

Conclusion

This article introduced a new hybrid microstrip antenna that is of compact size and high performance with dual-band operation. The antenna can satisfy the communication needs of sophisticated military systems using the combination of fractal geometry and genetic optimization. In conclusion, this paper has presented a new hybrid microstrip antenna that represents the state of the art in antenna technology—dual-band functioning, compactness, and high performance designed with military use in mind. Through the integration of fractal geometry principles with genetic optimization, this antenna shows promise to satisfy the increasing communication needs inherent in military operations. As we look to the future, the foundation laid by this design creates new avenues for additional innovations, making operations more effective in complicated context

References

[1] Koçer, Mustafa, and Mustafa Emre Aydemir. Microstrip patch antenna design for military satellite communication. *Avrupa Bilim ve Teknoloji Dergisi* (2020):(special Issue), 142–147.

[2] Liu, L., Yang, Y., & Zhang, W. (2017). Performance comparison of genetic algorithm and particle swarm optimization in antenna design. *IEEE Antennas and Wireless Propagation Letters*, 16, 2746–2750.

[3] Kumar, G., & Ray, K. P. (2003). Broadband Microstrip Antennas. Norwood, MA, USA: Artech House.

[4] Garg, R., Bhartia, P., Bahl, I., & Ittipiboon, A. (2001). Microstrip Antenna Design Handbook. Boston, MA, USA: Artech House.

[5] Hamid, S., Chopra, S. R., Gupta, A., Tanwar, S., Florea, B. C., Taralunga, D. D., et al. (2023). Hybrid beamforming in massive MIMO for next-generation communication technology. *Sensors*, 23(16), 7294.

[6] Sharma, R., Chopra, S. R., & Gupta, A. (2024). Power optimization of unmanned aerial vehicle-assisted future wireless communication using hybrid beamforming technique in disaster management. In IOP Conference Series: Earth and Environmental Science, (vol. 1285, no. 1, p. 012025). IOP Publishing,

[7] Sharma, R., Chopra, S. R., & Gupta, A. (2024). UAV assisted next generation wireless communication network. In 2024 International Conference on Emerging Smart Computing and Informatics (ESCI), (pp. 1–5). IEEE.

[8] Sharma, R., Chopra, S. R., Gupta, A., Kaur, R., Tanwar, S., Pau, G., et al. (2024). Deployment of unmanned aerial vehicles in next-generation wireless communication network using multi-agent reinforcement learning. *IEEE Access*, 12, 69517–69538.

8 Wearable UWB antenna for smart ring applications

Shakti Raj, Chopra[1,a], Leshrith, Ganji[1,b], Sarmistha, Satrusallya[2,c], Benudhar Sahu[2,d] and Prashant Kumar Choudhary[1,e]

[1]School of Electronics and Electrical Engineering, Lovely Professional University, Phagwara, Punjab, India

[2]Department of Electronics and Communication Engineering, ITER, Siksha 'O' Anusandhan (deemed to be University), Bhubaneswar, Odisha, India

Abstract

This paper presents a flexible ultra-wideband (UWB) ring antenna designed for wearable devices used in motion tracking and gesture recognition. The antenna works across the 3 GHz to 12 GHz range, showing dual-band resonance at 8.78 GHz and 10.695 GHz. Its compact ring shape, combined with a defected ground structure, helps improve impedance matching and overall performance. Simulations show that it has low return loss, a wide bandwidth, and good radiation efficiency, making it ideal for integration into wearables like smart rings and health monitoring gadgets. Overall, this antenna shows great potential for real-time motion detection, gesture control, and IoT communication application.

Keywords: Dual band resonance, rogers RO3006, smart ring, ultra wide band, wearable antenna

Introduction

Wearable tech has been growing fast lately, thanks to better health sensors, fitness trackers, and smarter ways for devices to interact with us. At the core of these innovations are antennas, which are essential for keeping communication smooth between wearables and other systems. Ultra-wideband (UWB) technology, capable of handling high data speeds across a large frequency range, is a great fit for wearable devices. UWB antennas stand out because they use less power, provide ultra-precise results, and resist interference, making them perfect for motion tracking, gestures, and location-based services. In these tiny devices, having an antenna that's both flexible and small is key for good performance and user comfort [1].

Antenna Design

Design considerations

The design of a flexible wearable UWB ring antenna requires careful selection of substrate material, patch geometry, and feeding structure to ensure compactness, efficient radiation, and impedance matching over the desired frequency range. In this work, a cylindrical ring antenna is designed using Rogers RO3006 substrate, targeting dual resonances near 8.78 GHz and 10.695 GHz [2].

[a]shakti.chopra@lpu.co.in, [b]leshrith@outlook.com, [c]sarmistha.satrusallya.19@gmail.com, [d]benudharsahu@soa.ac.in, [e]prashant.24788@lpu.co.in

DOI: 10.1201/9781003753391-8

The primary design goals include:

- Achieving dual-band resonance within the UWB frequency range (3.1–10.6 GHz)
- Ensuring compact dimensions suitable for wearable devices
- Maintaining good impedance matching (low return loss)
- Achieving stable radiation patterns across the operating bands

Theoretical considerations

The fundamental resonance frequency Fr of a ring antenna can be approximated as:

$$F_r = \frac{c}{2\pi R_{avg}\sqrt{\varepsilon_{eff}}}$$

where:

- c is the speed of light (3×10^8 m/s),
- R_{avg} is the average radius of the ring, $R_{avg} = (Ro + Ri2)/2$
- R_o and R_i are the outer and inner radii respectively,
- ε_{eff} is the effective dielectric constant of the substrate and surrounding environment.

The effective dielectric constant calculated using:

$$\varepsilon_{eff} = \frac{\varepsilon_r + 1}{2} + \frac{\varepsilon_r - 1}{2}(1 + 12\frac{h}{w})^{-1/2}$$

- ε_r is the relative permittivity of the substrate,
- h is the substrate thickness,
- W is the characteristic width of the ring.

Antenna geometry and design

The proposed antenna structure consists of:

- A cylindrical ring-shaped patch printed on a flexible Rogers RO3006 substrate,
- An inner air gap forming a hollow cylinder,
- A partial ground plane on the outer side,
- A microstrip feed line extending along the cylinder for excitation,
- A rectangular cut in the ring to allow for feeding and impedance matching.

Parameter justification

The choice of design parameters as discussed in Table 8.1 is based on a combination of theoretical calculations, fabrication constraints, and intended wear- able application requirements [3, 4]:

1) **Substrate (Rogers RO3006, $\varepsilon_r = 6.15$)**: Selected for its low loss tangent and moderate permittivity, enabling a balance between size reduction and radiation efficiency, essential for compact wearable antennas.

2) **Outer radius (12 mm) and inner radius (10 mm)**: The average radius $R_{avg} = 1$ mm is chosen to satisfy the resonance condition near 9 GHz. Using the ring resonance formula:

$$F_r \approx \frac{c}{2\pi R_{avg}\sqrt{\varepsilon_{eff}}}$$

with $R_{avg} = 11$mm and $\varepsilon_{eff} \approx 5.2$ calculated Fr falls within the 8–11 GHz range, validating the dual-band operation observed at 8.78 GHz and 10.695 GHz.

3) **Substrate thickness (1 mm)**: Ensures mechanical flexibility while preventing significant surface wave loss, crucial for wearable applications.

4) **Patch and ground thickness**: The patch thickness (1 mm) and ground plane thickness (0.3 mm) are chosen to maintain structural integrity during bending while minimizing weight.

5) **Feedline width (2 mm)**: Designed to achieve 50 Ω impedance matching for

Table 8.1 Antenna parameters.

Parameter	Value
Substrate material	Rogers RO3006 (ε_r= 6.15r)
Outer radius	12 mm
Inner radius	10 mm
Substrate thickness	1 mm
Patch thickness	1 mm
Ground plane thickness	0.3 mm
Height of structure (z-axis)	15 mm
Feedline width	2 mm
Feedline thickness	0.035 mm
Wave port width	6 mm
Wave port height	1 mm

Source: Author

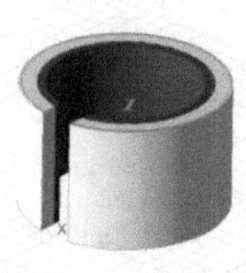

Figure 8.1 Design of antenna
Source: Author

minimal return loss, using standard microstrip feed equations.

6) **Wave port dimensions (6 mm × 1 mm)**: Selected based on simulation requirements to allow proper excitation and minimize port reflections.

Antenna design steps
Construct the substrate cylinder

* Create a solid cylinder representing the substrate material (Rogers RO3006) with an outer radius of 12 mm, inner radius of 10 mm, and height of 15 mm.
* This forms the base structure that will support the antenna.

Create the ring patch

* Design a second hollow cylinder (patch) made of perfect electric conductor (PEC) material.
* The patch has an outer radius of 10 mm, inner radius of 9 mm, and height of 15 mm, matching the substrate's height.
* This ring structure acts as the radiating element of the antenna.

Form the ground plane

* Create a third thin hollow cylinder to serve as the ground plane.
* The ground has an outer radius of 12 mm, inner radius of 11.7 mm, height of 15 mm, and thickness of 0.3 mm.
* Place it concentrically over the substrate

Rectangular cut (Feeding section)

* A rectangular cuboid is modeled and subtracted (Boolean cut) from the cylindrical patch to create an opening.
* This cut-out is designed to allow placement of the feedline and port connection.

Assign the wave port

* Generate a rectangular face within the opening created by the cut.
* Assign this face as the wave port to excite the antenna with proper impedance matching (50 Ω). The final design looks like in the "Figure 8.1".

Create the radiation box

* Surround the entire antenna with a sufficiently large radiation box.
* The radiation boundary ensures accurate simulation of far-field radiation without reflections.

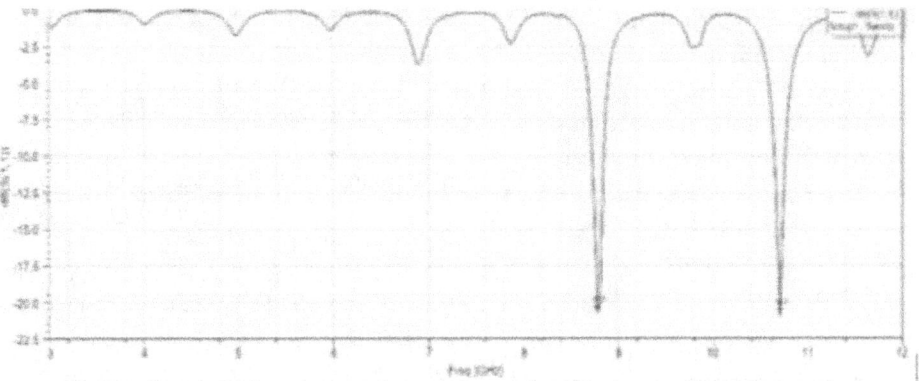

Figure 8.2 S parameter of antenna
Source: Author

Set solution parameters and simulate
- Define the solution frequency range (e.g., 3 GHz to 12 GHz).
- Select an appropriate mesh refinement and convergence criteria for accurate results.
- Simulate the antenna to obtain parameters like S11 (return loss), radiation pattern, gain, and bandwidth.

Simulation Results

Return loss (S11) characteristics
The simulated S11 curve shows two prominent resonance dips [5, 6]:

1) **First resonance:** 8.78 GHz with a return loss of -20.74 dB
2) **Second resonance:** 10.695 GHz with a return loss of -20.92 dB

Both resonances satisfy the -10 dB return loss criterion, indicating excellent impedance matching and efficient radiation.

Bandwidth
The antenna covers a significant bandwidth from approximately 8.5 GHz to 11 GHz, ensuring reliable operation within the desired UWB range.

Gain Plot 4

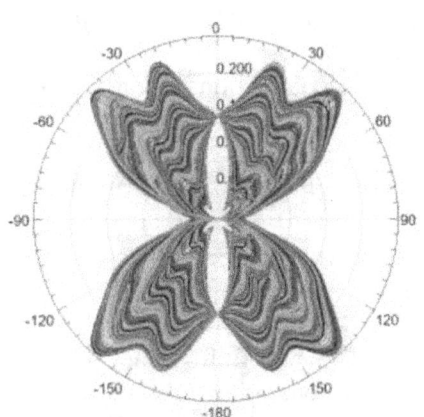

Figure 8.3 Radiation pattern
Source: Author

This wide bandwidth is ideal for high-precision wearable applications such as gesture recognition, body movement tracking, and wireless communication [7, 8].

Radiation pattern
The 3D radiation pattern at both resonance frequencies demonstrates nearly omnidirectional behavior in the horizontal plane.

This radiation characteristic is particularly advantageous for wearable devices, where user orientation may change frequently.

1) **At 8.78 GHz:** The radiation pattern is slightly tilted but maintains good Omni directionality.
2) **At 10.695 GHz:** The radiation becomes more focused with improved directivity.

As shown in Figures 8.2 and 8.3.

Conclusion

The cylindrical ring structure, along with the flexible substrate material (Rogers RO3006), ensures mechanical adaptability without compromising electromagnetic performance.

The wave port feeding and rectangular cut for port placement contribute to improved impedance matching.

Compared to conventional planar antennas, the proposed design offers:

- Better conformability for wearable devices
- Wide bandwidth coverage
- Stable radiation performance

Thus, the antenna fulfills the requirements for next-generation UWB wearable communication and sensing systems.

References

[1] Das, Soumyadeep, and Debasis Mitra. (2018). A compact wideband flexible implantable slot antenna design with enhanced gain. *IEEE Transactions on Antennas and Propagation,* 66(8): 4309–4314.

[2] Xu, Li-Jie, Yaming Bo, Wen-Jun Lu, Lei Zhu, and Cheng-Fei Guo. (2019). Circularly polarized annular ring antenna with wide axial-ratio bandwidth for biomedical applications. *IEEE Access,* 7: 59999–60009.

[3] Malik, Nabeel Ahmed, Paul Sant, Tahmina Ajmal, and Masood Ur-Rehman. (2020). Implantable antennas for bio-medical applications. *IEEE Journal of Electromagnetics, RF and Microwaves in Medicine and Biology.* 5(1): 84–96.

[4] Faridani, Mohammad, Gaozhi Xiao, Rony E. Amaya, Nima Javanbakht, and Mustapha CE Yagoub. (2021). A Kapton-based flexible wideband antenna with metamaterial resonators for millimeter-wave wireless applications. *In 2021 IEEE International Symposium on Antennas and Propagation and USNC-URSI Radio Science Meeting (APS/URSI),* 1055–1056. IEEE, 2021.

[5] Hamid, S., Chopra, S. R., Gupta, A., Tanwar, S., Florea, B. C., Taralunga, D. D., et al. (2023). Hybrid beamforming in massive MIMO for next-generation communication technology. *Sensors,* 23(16), 7294.

[6] Sharma, R.,, Chopra, S. R., & Gupta, A. (2024). Power optimization of unmanned aerial vehicle-assisted future wireless communication using hybrid beamforming technique in disaster management. In IOP Conference Series: Earth and Environmental Science, (Vol. 1285, no. 1, p. 012025). IOP Publishing.

[7] Sharma, R., Chopra, S. R., & Gupta, A. (2024). UAV assisted next generation wireless communication network. In 2024 International Conference on Emerging Smart Computing and Informatics (ESCI), (pp. 1–5). *IEEE.*

[8] Sharma, R., Chopra, S. R., Gupta, A., Kaur, R., Tanwar, S., Pau, G., et al. (2024). Deployment of unmanned aerial vehicles in next-generation wireless communication network using multi-agent reinforcement learning. *IEEE Access,* 12, 69517–69538.

9 Leveraging industry 4.0 for business excellence by digitization of aeroengine technology using 3D models

Anjana Nayak[1,a], Satyabrata Dash[2,b] and Sujata Chakravarty[1,c]

[1]Computer Science and Engineering, Centurion University of Technology and Management, Bhubaneswar, Odisha, India

[2]Computer Science and Engineering, GITAM Deemed to be University, Visakhapatnam, Andhra Pradesh, India

Abstract

This paper investigates the application of Industry 4.0 technologies, particularly 3D modeling and digital twin concepts, in digitizing fighter-class aeroengine systems at a leading Indian defense public sector undertaking (DPSU). It details the transformation of conventional engineering data into interactive 3D models, enabling real-time diagnostics, predictive maintenance, and advanced technical training. Considering the fact that Industry 4.0 tools like Cyber Physical System, Supervisory control and data acquisition system can enhance operational efficiency and fault detection, and resource utilization. Other Industry 4.0 tools can revolve around 3D modeling to support fault identification and repair, while digital twins enable engine health monitoring and MRO planning. The study presents a scalable model for innovation in high-precision aeroengine manufacturing sectors.

Keywords: 3D Modeling, industry 4.0, smart manufacturing

Introduction

Industry 4.0 has revolutionized manufacturing by introducing advanced digital technologies that promote intelligent, automated, and interconnected operations. The pillars of Industry 4.0 such as the Internet of Things (IoT), Cyber-Physical Systems (CPS), Big Data Analytics, artificial intelligence (AI), and Digital Twin play a critical role in digital transformation and organization's growth. Their impact is significant in high-precision, safety-critical sectors like aerospace and defense. Fighter-class aero engines consist of thousands of critical components requiring exacting tolerance and performance. Traditional maintenance, inspection, methods and management centered on manual inspections, documentation in hardcopy, and experiential troubleshooting which often led to inefficiencies, longer downtimes. But digital transformation with 3D modeling can facilitate interactive training, AR/VR-based diagnostics, real-time monitoring, and predictive maintenance through digital twin integration. This paper presents a case study from a leading Indian defense public sector undertaking (DPSU) that has successfully applied Industry 4.0 tools to enhance aero engine management. The initiative has led to measurable improvements in efficiency, training quality, and cost-effectiveness, establishing a scalable model.

[a]anjuritik@gmail.com, [b]satyabrata.cse@gmail.com, [c]chakravartys69@gmail.com

DOI: 10.1201/9781003753391-9

Literature Review

Related research in industry 4.0 revolution

Industry 4.0 contains digital technologies such as CPS, IoT, and artificial intelligence (AI) join with physical processes to create smart manufacturing environments. Initiated by the German government in 2011 [1], Industry 4.0 Working group identified and presented the main medium- and long-term research requirements and actions. Lee et al. [2] emphasized the role of digital twins in enhancing real-time monitoring and predictive maintenance of critical components, thereby improving reliability and reducing operational costs. In the context of 3D modelling, authors presented analysis methods and several example results for using 3D scanning technology for data collection and evaluation [3]. Within the Indian defense sector, the authors explored the challenges and potential solutions related to data collection, integration, processing, and utilization in defense manufacturing within the context of Industry 4.0 [4]. However, another study derived digital transformation and challenges such as digital divide, cybersecurity threats, and regulatory complexities [5]. They analyzed current trends and key opportunities. A gap remains in practical 3D modeling applications in DPSUs, which this paper aims to address.

Data and variables

This study was conducted over 18 months (January 2023 to June 2024) at a premier Indian DPSU specializing in aeroengine

Table 9.1 Details of variable used in the process.

Variable name	Type	Description	Measurement scale/Unit
Business Excellence Score (BES)	Dependent variable	Composite index reflecting improvement in key performance indicators (KPIs)	Normalized Index (0–100)
3D Model Implementation Level	Independent Variable	Number of subsystems converted into interactive 3D models	Count (per engine assembly)
Digital Twin Integration	Independent Variable	Degree of real-time data integration with virtual models	Ordinal (Low, Medium, High)
User Adoption Rate	Independent Variable	Percentage of personnel using 3D/digital systems	% (monthly tracking)
Digital Training Hours	Independent Variable	Total training hours conducted using 3D models	Hours (per month)
Engine Type and Configuration	Control Variable	Consistent engine family used before and after digitization	Fixed (Same engine model)
Team Composition	Control Variable	Same maintenance team engaged across pre- and post-study periods	Fixed (No personnel change)
Maintenance Schedule	Control Variable	Similar workload and scheduling throughout the study period	Fixed (Standard calendar)
Operational Environment	Control Variable	No external policy or infrastructural changes during the study	Constant (No major external influences)

Source: Author

maintenance. The Details of variable used in the process are explained in Table 9.1. The pilot project focused on digitizing one complete aeroengine assembly using Industry 4.0 technologies, particularly 3D modeling and digital twins. The sample included 25 subject matter experts and engineers, alongside 15 Key Performance Indicators (KPIs) tracked before and after digitization to assess impact. The primary dependent variable, Business Excellence Score (BES), was developed as a composite index (0–100 scale) to evaluate improvements across turnaround time, maintenance accuracy, training efficiency, resource utilization, and cost reduction. Independent variables included the extent of 3D model implementation, the level of digital twin integration (low to high), user adoption rate of digital tools, and training hours delivered via digital systems. Control variables such as engine type, team composition, maintenance schedules, and operational conditions were held constant to ensure data validity. This controlled design enabled a focused assessment of how digital technologies influenced operational excellence within the DPSU's aeroengine division.

Methodology and Model Specifications

Background

Aeroengines are the critical components of aircraft, operating under extreme conditions and requiring high reliability, fuel efficiency, and thrust-to-weight ratios. Globally, only a few companies like General Electric, Rolls Royce, and Pratt & Whitney dominate fighter-class engine manufacturing. In India, this leading defense PSU is among the elite, handling manufacturing and overhaul of 3rd and 4th generation engines through technology transfer (TOT) from a foreign country. However, TOT projects often lack complete design knowledge, making indigenous development challenging. The division faces difficulties due to limited manufacturing experience, especially in second and third generation fighter aircraft programs, and is also navigating a generational shift as experienced personnel retire. This has created a skills gap in adopting new technologies. Additionally, the complex aerospace supply chain is affected by geopolitical factors and part diversity. In this evolving industrial landscape, embracing digitalization and automation under Industry 4.0 is essential to address these challenges and drive future readiness and operational efficiency.

Phases of industrial revolution

As depicts Figure 9.1 Industry 4.0 marks the fourth industrial revolution, centered on smart, autonomous systems that enhance efficiency and productivity through integrated digital technologies. Key enablers include IoT, AI, robotics, 3D printing, AR/VR, and digital twins, which automate processes, reduce waste, and support real-time

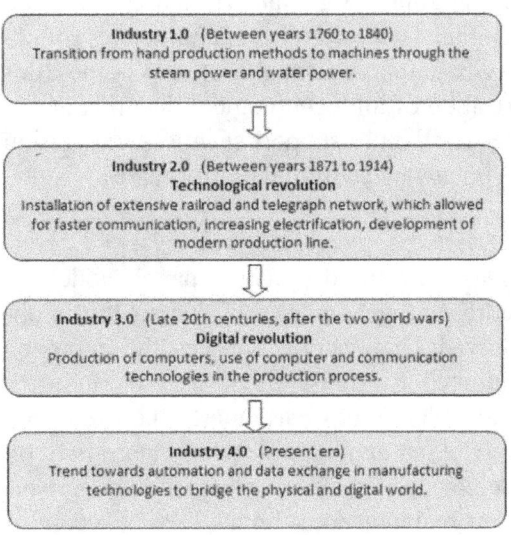

Figure 9.1 Phases of industrial revolution
Source: Author

decision-making. Pillars such as big data analytics, cloud computing, and horizontal-vertical integration ensure seamless production and business alignment. Technologies like IIoT and AR improve monitoring and visualization, while autonomous robots and digital twins drive predictive maintenance and simulation. Cybersecurity, powered by AI and zero-trust models, safeguards operations. The full potential of Industry 4.0 emerges through cohesive technological integration.

Proposed application of digital technologies in a leading DPSU

Many industries are adopting Industry 4.0 infrastructures, exemplified by Boeing's T-7A Red Hawk program, which achieved major gains through model-based engineering—improving first-time quality by 75%, reducing assembly hours by 80%, and halving software development time. Inspired by such success, a leading Indian DPSU can similarly implement digital transformation within its Maintenance, Repair, and Overhaul (MRO) operations. Leveraging technologies like IIoT, AR/VR/MR, Cloud Computing, Big Data Analytics, AI, and Digital Twins can drive significant productivity gains. A critical first step is the digitization of all technological documents and legacy data to support seamless integration with advanced digital platforms [6].

Model specifications

This study used dynamic panel models to curb endogeneity issues due to the unobserved This section outlines the approach adopted to study the impact of Industry 4.0 technologies particularly the use of 3D modeling and digital twin integration on achieving business excellence in aeroengine maintenance within a DPSU. A combination of descriptive analytics, correlation analysis, and dynamic panel modeling has

been employed. The research is based on a dynamic panel data model, which accounts for both time-based and cross-sectional variations. The model is designed to assess the effects of technological variables on performance metrics, measured by the Business Excellence Score (BES).

The model equation

$BES_{it} = \alpha + \beta1 \, (3D \, Model_{it}) + \beta2 \, (Twin \, Integration_{it}) + \beta3 \, (Adoption \, Rate_{it}) + \beta4 \, (Training \, Hrs_{it}) + \mu i + \lambda t + \varepsilon_{it}$

Where

BESit	Business Excellence Score for unit i at time t
α	Intercept (baseline level of BES)
$\beta1$	Coefficient for effect of 3D model usage
B2	Coefficient for digital twin integration
B3	Coefficient for rate of Industry 4.0 adoption
B4	Coefficient for training hours (skill development efforts)
μi	Entity fixed effect (captures unit-specific unobserved characteristics)
λt	Time fixed effect (captures year/period-specific effects)
ε_{it}	Error term (unexplained variation)

This structure helps isolate the causal impact of digitization on business performance, while controlling for internal and external influences.

Processes of Implementation

The process of preparation of digital technology has the following major steps: Figure 9.2 depicts the process of implementation of 3D modelling in DPSU.

Figure 9.2 depicts the process of implementation of 3D modelling in DPSU.

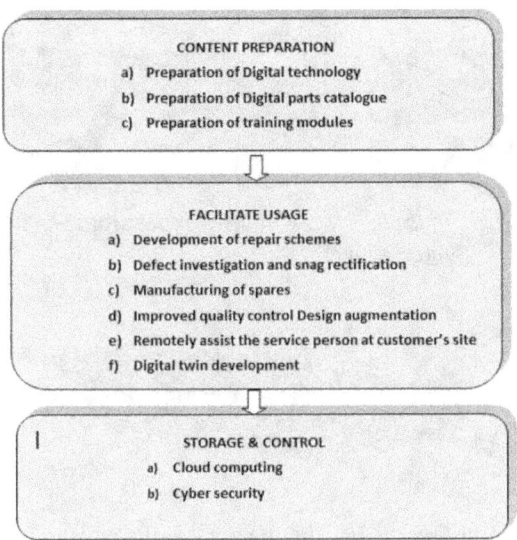

Figure 9.2 Process of implementation
Source: Author

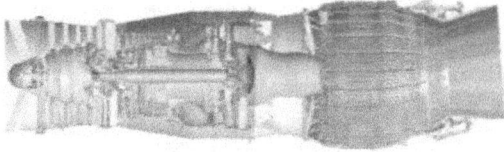

Figure 9.3 Sample engine model
Source: Author

Figure 9.4 Gear box
Source: Author

Figure 9.5 Turbo starter
Source: Author

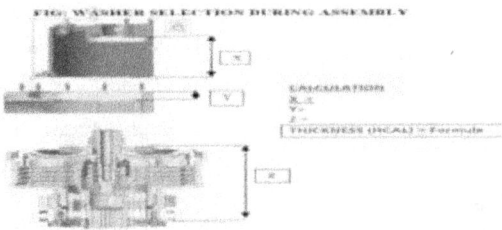

Figure 9.6 Washer selection during assembly
Source: Author

i) **Content preparation:** For preparing content a dedicated team from production & design to be formed. The team members should have adequate knowledge about the existing aeroengine technology and solid model software. Similar implementations in other aeronautical industries to be studied. Partnership with a Technology Consulting Group to be established. Initially the technology of one pilot project to be chosen.

• Presently this defense PSU has already completed Solid modeling and assembly of three major third generation engines by dedicated effort of methods department. The solid models of all components and assemblies were prepared after studying the following:
   ○ Exploring the software and developing the required skill
   ○ Studying the module wise drawings
   ○ Consulting domain specialists
   ○ Referring physical parts to enhance the speed

• Approximately 5000 types of components, subassemblies and assemblies have been converted into 3D models, total count of parts is around 20000.

• converted into 3D models, total count of parts is around 20000.

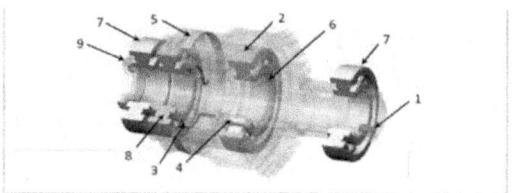

Figure 9.7 One sample major sub assembly
Source: Author

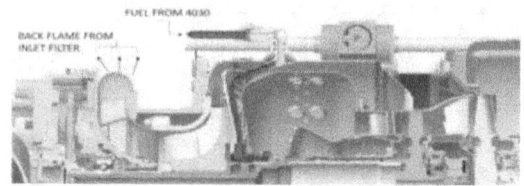

Figure 9.9 View of critical positions
Source: Author

Figure 9.8 Coaxility of casings
Source: Author

Figure 9.10 Manufacturing of spares
Source: Author

Figures 9.3–9.5 illustrate 3D output models of key aeroengine components: the engine, gearbox, and turbo starter, used for digital transformation. Figure 9.6 demonstrates how 3D models assist in calculating washer thickness and selecting the appropriate size during gearbox assembly, enhancing precision and assembly accuracy.

Preparation of digital technology and catalogue

Using 3D models, digital overhaul technology can be developed for third-generation engines and gearboxes as part of a pilot project. Key overhaul stages include stripping, cleaning, inspection, rework, assembly, and testing. The division has utilized 3D models to create precise assembly sequences for critical subassemblies, enabling mistake-proof procedures—such as washer thickness calculation and selection during gearbox assembly. Additionally, 3D illustration software facilitates the preparation of digital parts catalogs and eBOMs (Electronic Bill of Materials), allowing

seamless integration with the new ERP system (Project Parivartan). This enhances accuracy, streamlines maintenance documentation, and supports efficient inventory and lifecycle management of engine components.

Figures 9.7–9.10 showcase the advanced application of 3D modeling in aeroengine maintenance. Figure 9.7 illustrates a major sub-assembly with all component parts in 3D alignment, while Figure 9.8 highlights the precise co-axial positioning of the casing. Figure 9.9 provides a critical sectional view for in-depth analysis of specific parts or systems. Figure 9.10 presents a newly designed part, created using 3D modeling and intended for production via 3D printing.

Digital technologies such as virtual reality (VR), augmented reality (AR), and mixed reality (MR), using tools like HoloLens, can be utilized to develop interactive training and problem-solving modules. Engine animations can be created to simulate different operational modes—training, combat, and high-temperature conditions—for

Table 9.2 Pre-crisis performance indicators (Baseline).

KPI	Pre-Digitization Avg.	Unit
Mean turnaround time (TAT)	72	Days
Maintenance rework rate	18.6	%
Training effectiveness (knowledge retention)	62	% Score
Fault detection time	11.5	Hours
Error reporting and resolution lag	6.2	Days
Technician dependency index	High	Qualitative
Document retrieval time	3.5	Hours

Source: Author

enhanced understanding. The Pre-crisis and Post-crisis performance indicators are outlined in Table 9.2 and 9.3. Additionally, 3D technologies support the development of precise repair schemes. For example, repeated engine failures can be mitigated by implementing a process for replacing gearbox casing bushings while maintaining coaxial alignment with related components, ensuring reliability and reducing recurrence of faults in operational units.

Defect investigation and snag rectification

The use of 3D digital technologies significantly enhances defect investigation, allowing for precise snag identification and rectification. A recent flame issue in a turbo starter was diagnosed using 3D assembly models, revealing a fuel line leak. 3D models also support spare manufacturing, including critical casting and future 3D printing initiatives—such as developing a high-pressure nozzle guide vane. Quality control benefits from AR and wearable tech enabling remote verification, mistake proofing, and real-time guidance. Portable laser devices aid in measurement and digital data storage. VR enhances design processes with real-time updates. Service technicians can receive remote assistance at

air bases, and real-time engine performance data supports digital twin development for predictive maintenance and residual life assessment.

Empirical Results

Pre-crisis estimations

Prior to implementing Industry 4.0 technologies, the defense PSU's aero engine maintenance process relied on manual operations, paper-based records, and lacked real-time visibility. This pre-digitization phase revealed key operational challenges, including long turnaround times due to manual inspections, high reliance on individual expertise for fault diagnosis, poor knowledge transfer, and maintenance strategies. Training was largely ineffective, depending on printed technology transfer records. Inefficiencies in fault identification, training quality, and maintenance execution are observed.

Observations

The study uncovered key inefficiencies in the pre-digitization phase, including manual delays, limited visualization, and ineffective training, leading to high rework rates and reliance on experienced personnel. To address this, Industry 4.0 tools such as

Table 9.3 Post-crisis performance indicators.

KPI	Post-digitization avg.	% Improvement	Unit
Mean turnaround time (TAT)	52	↓ **27.8%**	Days
Maintenance rework rate	9.4	↓ **49.5%**	%
Training effectiveness (Knowledge Retention)	84	↑ **35.5%**	% Score
Fault detection time	6.8	↓ **40.8%**	Hours
Error reporting and resolution lag	3.1	↓ **50.0%**	Days
Technician dependency index	Medium	↓	Qualitative
Document retrieval time	1.2	↓ **65.7%**	Hours

Source: Author

3D visualization, digital twins, and data-driven maintenance were introduced. BES improved significantly, ranging from 60.21 to 94.80, alongside rising user adoption and training hours. Correlation analysis confirmed predictor independence, while dynamic panel estimation using Arellano-Bond GMM highlighted the positive influence of 3D models, digital twins, and adoption rates on BES. Diagnostic tests validated the model, confirming that Industry 4.0 implementation effectively enhances aero engine performance and operational efficiency.

Post-crisis estimations

The same KPIs evaluated during the pre-crisis period were tracked after digitization to enable comparative analysis.

Post-implementation of Industry 4.0 technologies in the aeroengine division resulted in significant improvements over a 12-month period. Key initiatives included interactive 3D modeling, digital twin integration, digital documentation, training, and real-time data for predictive maintenance. These interventions led to a 28% reduction in turnaround time (TAT) and a 50% drop in Rework Rate, enhancing engine availability and first-time quality. Training effectiveness

improved through immersive simulations, while real-time fault detection enhanced safety and responsiveness. Overall, digital transformation strengthened operational efficiency, reliability, and workforce capability, marking a successful transition toward intelligent, data-driven aeroengine management.

Conclusion

This study demonstrates the real impact of Industry 4.0 technologies—specifically 3D modeling and digital twins—on operational excellence/Business Excellence in a Defense Public Sector Undertaking (DPSU) within the aerospace sector. By digitizing complex aero engine systems, the organization overcame inefficiencies in manual workflows, training, and fault detection. Real-time error tracking, part location finding and predictive maintenance has improved turnaround time, rework rates, and training outcomes. Dynamic panel data analysis confirmed measurable performance gains. The study highlights that combining advanced technologies with workforce development and change management is essential for success. These findings propose a practical 3D modelling application in an aero engine industry.

References

[1]   Kagermann, H., & Wahlster, W. (2022). Ten years of Industrie 4.0. Sci, 4(3), 26.

[2]   Lee, J., Bagheri, B., & Kao, H. A. (2015). A cyber-physical systems architecture for industry 4.0-based manufacturing systems. *Manufacturing Letters*, 3, 18–23.

[3]   van Brügge, L., Çetin, K. M., Koeberle, S. J., Thiele, M., Sturm, F., & Hornung, M. (2023). Application of 3D-scanning for structural and geometric assessment of aerospace structures. *CEAS Aeronautical Journal*, 14(2), 455–467. doi: 10.1007/s13272-023-00654-1.

[4]   Ullah, H., Uzair, M., Jan, Z., & Ullah, M. (2024). Integrating industry 4.0 technologies in defense manufacturing: challenges, solutions, and potential opportunities. *Array*, 23, 100358. https://doi.org/10.1016/j.array.2024.100358.

[5]   Monostori, L. (2014). Cyber-physical production systems: roots, expectations and R&D challenges. *Procedia CIRP*, 17, 9–13. doi: 10.1016/j.procir.2014.03.115.

[6]   Lu, Y., Liu, C., Kevin, I., Wang, K., Huang, H., & Xu, X. (2020). Digital Twin-driven smart manufacturing: Connotation, reference model, applications and research issues. *Robotics and computer-integrated manufacturing*, 61, 101837.

10 MRI-based breast related cancer identification by deep convolutional neural based networks

M. L. S. N. S. Lakshmi[1,a] and G. V. Eswara Rao[2,b]

[1]Department of ECE, Ramachandra College of Engineering, Eluru, Andhra Pradesh, India

[2]Department of CSE, Thapar Institute of Engineering and Technology, Punjab, India

Abstract

Breast-related cancer is considered to be a severe health problem on a global scale, and early identification is a significant factor in patient recovery. This research paper focuses on an automated type breast-related cancer identification model that employs Convolutional type Neural Networks (CNN) to examine MRI images to obtain high-accuracy classification. The suggested model incorporates an optimized supervisor learning framework to improve feature extraction and classification performance. Preprocessing techniques are used to reprocess the MRI images, thus reducing noise and increasing contrast. After that, a specially customized CNN architecture is used to obtain deeper spatial features, enabling the system to capture the crucial patterns suggesting malignancy. The system also offers a unique learning strategy that is used to increase the generalization of the model and its tolerance to errors in various types of data. The application of optimization techniques also helps make the classification process more efficient and thus detects the problem more efficiently. The proposed approach is accounted for as one of the significant steps made within the area of automatic breast-related cancer diagnosis since it is designed as a reliable and scalable application for clinical practitioners. The experimental evaluations show that the distinction between the malignant and the benign cases proves the system's effectiveness, thus reinforcing the potential of CNN-based models in medical imaging.

Keywords: Automatic type diagnosis, breast-related cancer identification, convolutional type neural networks, MRI-based images, relevant feature extraction, supervisor learning

Introduction

Breast-related cancer is among the foremost ailments that cause fatalities correlated to cancer globally among both male and female genders. Thus, identifying the disease earlier is paramount for increasing the patient's life expectancy and treatment outcomes. Medical imaging has undergone tremendous development over the last few years and has become one of the ruling fields in the medical world; MRI technology has a strong position in the diagnosis process and breast-related cancer identification. Nonetheless, the traditional means by which MRI images are evaluated strongly depend on manual interpretation, which can be both laborious and time-consuming, lack uniformity, and often be erroneous. To address these limitations, AI models like conventional-type neural supervisor learning are becoming increasingly popular. Convolutional type Neural Networks (CNN) play an important role due to their capability to learn from the data [1]. CNNs

[a]rajyalakshmibevara@gmail.com, [b]eswarnec01@gmail.com

DOI: 10.1201/9781003753391-10

have displayed outstanding results for various computer vision tasks, such as object recognition and medical image classification. One of the positive things about CNNs is that they can resolve a problem by applying multiple layers to handle the fine-grained features that are difficult to discern using conventional methods [2]. Such characteristics are a significant asset in medical imaging, as they distinguish between benign and malignant tumors through the slight differences that may occur in the area of the image's texture and structure. The CNNs are the opposite representation: they do not do any related feature extraction manually. Thus, it will remove any inconsistencies in taking images [3]. First, it enables faster and more accurate Analysis of images, significantly reducing the time required for diagnosis [4]. Second, it offers consistent results that are not influenced by

the subjective judgment of human radiologists [5]. By training CNN models on large datasets, these algorithms can learn to differentiate between benign and malignant tissues with high accuracy, improving the overall diagnostic process [6]. Moreover, CNN-based approaches can be integrated into clinical workflows, offering a scalable solution for hospitals and healthcare facilities [7]. The proposed system in this study aims to develop an automated breast-related cancer identification model using CNNs specifically designed for MRI images. This approach addresses the need for improved diagnostic tools to aid healthcare professionals in making accurate and timely decisions [8]. The integration of such automated systems has the potential to significantly reduce the burden on medical practitioners while enhancing the quality of healthcare services [9, 10].

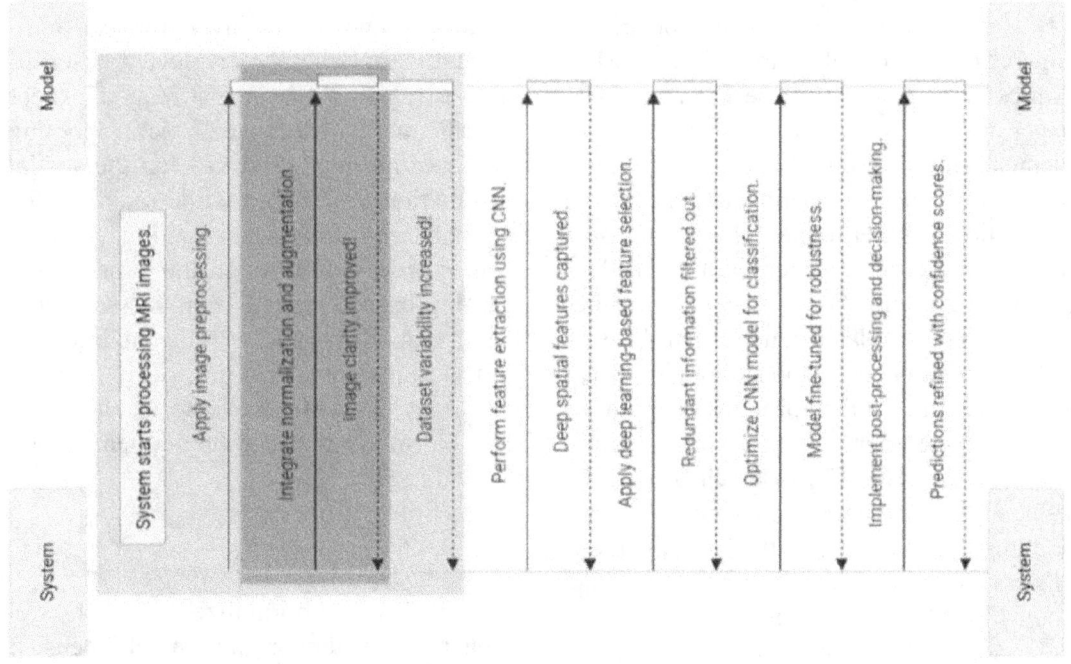

Figure 10.1 Internal processing steps of the proposed system
Source: Author

Literature Review

The Studies addressing the potential of CNNs and supervisor learning in breast-related cancer identification are numerous today, thus emphasizing the importance of advanced algorithms, preprocessing techniques, and model optimization in creating high-performance, reliable diagnostic tools. Quite a few studies have investigated the use of CNNs for automated breast-related cancer identification. One study [11] explores the use of deep learning models, such as CNNs, in the process of analyzing MRI scans and the power of CNNs in identifying the right group for malignant and benign tumors. Using the CNN architecture with multi-scale related feature extraction, one more project [12] focuses on the utilitarian roles of the network in enhancing detections, such as distinguishing subtle variations in tissue structure, which is crucial for early cancer identification. Additionally, further work [13] addresses a hybrid approach, combining CNNs and other conventional type neural supervisor learning algorithms like SVM to improve the classification performance. The paper underlines the advantage of the complementarity of different learning strategies that provide better identification accuracy. In addition, another research has been tested to find out whether transfer learning is effective, where pre-trained CNN models are fine-tuned on breast-related cancer MRI datasets [14]. Another paper by the authors looked at the combination of preprocessing methods with CNNs to improve image properties and reduce noise [15]. The research proves the value of these preprocessing steps in related feature extraction, which improves the model's performance. The other great one talks about CNN-based segmentations that enable the exact identification of the tumor regions in MRI images, followed by their Analysis and classification [16].

Proposed System

The proposed breast-related cancer identification system uses MRI images through an automated process and includes a standard processing pipeline to achieve accurate and efficient classification. In the preprocessing step, the image is manipulated by various algorithms to improve its quality. Noise reduction techniques and contrast enhancement are used in image preprocessing to make the MRI scan clear. This step ensures your MRI images are void of noise and include all required parts. This makes them perfect for analysis that may follow. Normalization and augmentation methods are also used to standardize image dimensions and increase data variability, respectively, resulting in model generalization, as seen in Figure 10.1. In the next step, related feature extraction of the customized CNN is done. This type of CNN architecture allows for extracting deep spatial-related features of MRI images. The CNN model includes multiple convolutional layers that can automatically find the most relevant discriminative features for Breast-related cancer identification. Moreover, new pooling strategies are identified to keep the spatial information unchanged while reducing the computational. These extracted features are further processed through the supervisor's learning-based related feature selection. Here, redundant or less relevant information is eliminated, ensuring only the most important features contribute to classification. Normalization can be mathematically defined in (1):

$$I' = I - \mu/\sigma. \tag{1}$$

where I' is the normalized form of pixel intensity, I is the original pixel intensity, μ is the mean of pixel intensities, and σ is the standard deviation. This procedure improves the homogeneity of the dataset so that every image is weighted the same way for Analysis. To advance the quality of the dataset even more, data augmentation mechanisms rotational, flip, and scaling actions are utilized. Augmentation is a method that is of great importance in deep learning-based medical imaging, as this technique not only diversifies the dataset but also prevents overfitting. The augmented image can be represented by (2):

$$Iaug = T(I). \tag{2}$$

Where T is a transfer function that utilizes several variations of the augmentation algorithm. Then, adaptive histogram equalization is applied using the contrast enhancement technique to show the tissue structures more clearly by adjusting the intensity pixel distributions. The contrast-improvised image is shown in (3):

$$Ienh(x,y) = (I(x,y) - min(I))/max(I) - min(I). \tag{3}$$

The Ienh(x,y) represents the improvised intensity value at pixel (x,y), and min(I) and max(I) are the minimum and maximum intensity values in the image, respectively. The CNN is a stack of several convolutional layers; each layer performs a convolution operation on the input by a set of filters. In terms of mathematics, the operation of convolution is expressed as (4):

$$Fl(x,y) = \sum i \sum j W(i,j)Il - 1 (x-i, y-j) + b, (i,j = -k\ to\ k). \tag{4}$$

where Fl(x,y) is the related feature map at layer l, W(i,j) represents the convolutional kernel, I_{l-1} is the input-related feature map from the previous layer, and b is the biased term. The activation function applied after convolution is rectified type linear unit

(ReLU), which introduces non-linearity and prevents vanishing gradient issues, defined in (5):

$$A(F) = max\ (0,F). \tag{5}$$

Where A(F) is the result of activating the related feature F. In order to maintain the necessary but only spatial information, pooling layers are applied. It looks like the method of reduction. This is one of the most effective protocols, and the expression of (6) shows this:

$$P(x,y) = maxi,j \in RF(x+i, y+j) \tag{6}$$

Where R stands for the area of pooling, and the function takes the largest value in the area. This makes computation faster. Moreover, representation becomes stronger. The final related feature maps are then passed through fully connected layers, converting them into a classification space as given in (7):

$$y = Wfcx + b. \tag{7}$$

Where y is the output vector, Wfc is the weightage matrix, and x tells the flattened related feature vector. The decision about classification is established through the probability distribution, which is computed with the aid of the SoftMax function as in (8):

$$p(yi) = eyi/\sum jeyj. \tag{8}$$

Where p(yi) for the probability of class i, the loss function that forms the optimized model is the cross-entropy error, as expressed by (9):

$$L = -\sum iyilog(y^i). \tag{9}$$

Where yi is given the class label, and y^i is the predicted form of probability. To improvise model performance, weights are updated iteratively by gradient Descents, given in (10):

$$Wt + 1 = Wt - \eta(\partial L/\partial W). \quad (10)$$

Where η is the learning rate. Furthermore, the technique that Adam is the type of optimizer is exploited for adaptive weight adjustments by including first and second-moment estimates in (11) & (12):

$$mt = \beta 1 mt - 1 + (1 - \beta 1)gt. \quad (11)$$

$$vt = \beta 2 vt - 1 + (1 - \beta 2)gt. \quad (12)$$

Where it is the gradient factor at time step t and $\beta 1$ and $\beta 2$ are decay rates that control exponential-type moving averages of past gradients. The final classification decision is made by the class having the highest probability (13):

$$y^{\wedge} = argmaxp(yi). \quad (13)$$

Where $y^{\wedge}$ is the predicted form of class. The classification confidence is evaluated using entropy (14):

$$H = -\sum ip(yi)logp(yi). \quad (14)$$

Where lower entropy values imply higher confidence in prediction, this step ensures interpretability and reliability in clinical decision-making.

Results and Discussion

The proposed system, which is the automated system of breast-related cancer identification, is a great way of assessing more than just normal and diagnosed patients, as it performs a full-scale malignancy risk assessment featuring the Analysis of tumor characteristics, cellular structures, imaging contrasts, and malignancy probabilities. The Analysis of the breast-related cancer diagnosis parameters gives significant knowledge of the levels of risk of the patient when their values surpass the respective thresholds. From the statistics in Figure 10.2, the volume of the tumor has a different spread; patients have tumors that are about 5 mm and 50 mm, with the average size generally being around 27 mm. Out of the 50 people, 18 of them had a tumor of more than 30 mm, where the largest tumor was 48.6 mm. The results of these patients point towards malignancy, which means they need medical help as soon as possible.

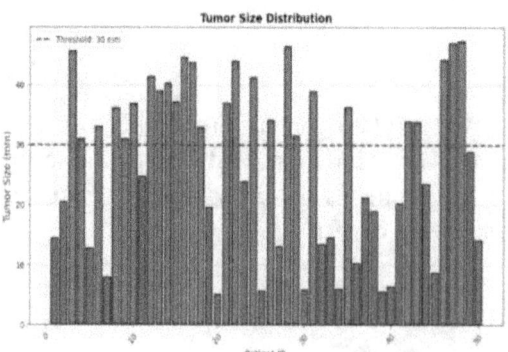

Figure 10.2 Analysis of tumor size
Source: Author

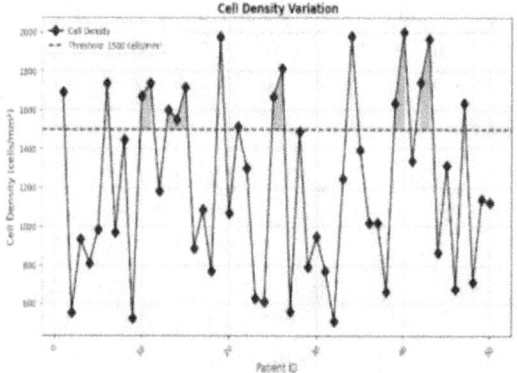

Figure 10.3 Analysis of cell density by proposed framework
Source: Author

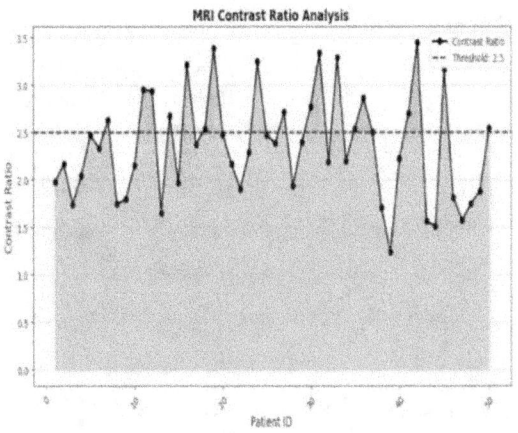

Figure 10.4 MRI image contrast rate analysis
Source: Author

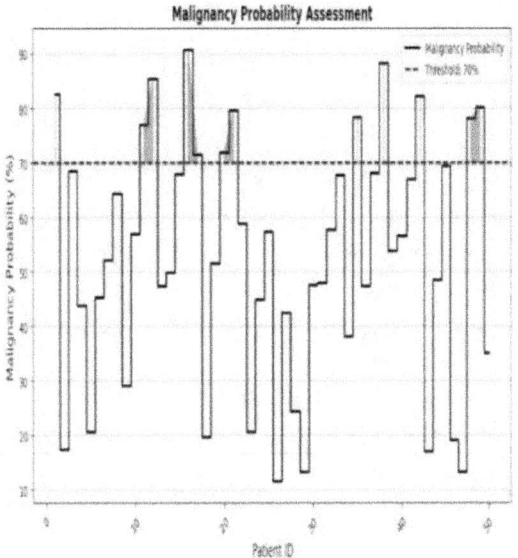

Figure 10.5 Malignancy rate analysis of the Proposed system
Source: Author

By showing the difference in colors on the bar graph, the oncologist can easily spot the sick cells, which keeps the tumor size monitoring during early diagnosis a great deal.

Figure 10.3 represents cell density variations in a pair of minima (500) to maximum (2000) and an average of nearly 1300 cells/mm². A total of 21 patients got a high cell density of over 1500 cells/mm² and reached the peak at 1987 cells/mm². The filled-in region on the graph is a close-up view of the specific cases where cellular proliferation is occurring at an abnormally fast pace. Hence, the growth of the tissue is abnormal. The patients with cells that are greater than 1500 cells/mm² are probably having rogue cell proliferation and thus require histopathological assessment. The high density of the cases points out the need to have the earliest possible means of identifying and evaluating the risk in a real situation. Figure 10.4 presents the MRI contrast ratio changes with values ranging from 1.2 to 3.5, and the average contrast ratio is 2.4. Sixteen patients have better results with contrast ratios of over 2.5; the highest is 3.45. The orange-shaded regions mark the places where the differences in

tissues are the most striking and often. As a result, the so-called occurring tissue is the case of malignancy. This scenario will cause engineers to perform biopsy procedures on other sick cases if they are beyond 2.5 Figure 10.5 illustrates how malignancy probability fluctuates with maximum and minimum values of 10% and 95% and an average malignancy risk of around 55%, respectively. In all, 20 patients experienced malignancy probabilities surpassing the 70% easier threshold. The highest one out of them recorded a probability of 94.2%. Apart from the performance evaluation, the effectiveness of the proposed system is tabulated in Table 10.1.

The proposed model has a 94.3% accuracy rate, higher than the simple CNN and the traditional machine learning algorithms like SVM, KNN, and Decision Tree, whose accuracy were 79.8% to 89.6%. The proposed model also excels in precision, recall, and F1-score, with the figures being constantly over 93%, thus proving high

Table 10.1 Performance evaluation of the proposed system.

Model	Accuracy (%)	Precision (%)	Recall/ sensitivity (%)	F1-Score (%)	Processing time (ms/ image)	AUC Score
Traditional SVM	85.2	83.7	84.9	84.3	28.5	0.872
K-Nearest Neighbors (KNN)	82.5	80.4	82.1	81.2	31.2	0.841
Decision Tree	79.8	78.5	77.6	78.0	25.9	0.798
Basic CNN (without optimization)	89.6	88.1	89.0	88.5	19.8	0.911
Proposed Optimized CNN Model	94.3	93.7	94.1	93.9	15.4	95.6

Source: Author

reliability in correctly identifying malignant and benign cases. Besides, the processing time per image is dramatically decreased, enabling the model to be used for real-time medical procedures, with an average time of 15.4 milliseconds. Furthermore, the AUC score of 0.956 indicates that the model has a superior capacity to differentiate the diverse cancer types, thus confirming the model's high performance and ability to be employed in the practical field of automated breast cancer diagnosis.

Conclusion

In conclusion, examining parameters for Breast-related cancer diagnosis serves as an important step in identifying high-risk cases through quantitative evaluation. The measurements taken from the tumors of the 50 patients ranged from 5 mm to 50 mm, with an average of 27 mm. A total of 16 patients had values of more than 2.5, with the highest contrast ratio being 3.45, which doctors have related to powerful indicators of malignancy. The chances for malignancy assessments showed the scariest results, with each number lying between 10% and 95% and the average lying at 55%. It is important

to underline the fact that there were malignancy probabilities of 20 patients that were above the critical 70% level, which refers to the highest count of 94%, thus requiring urgent medical attention. The great number of cases that have overstepped danger levels in various ways reveals the need to have early identification and proactive treatment options. These results are significant because they warn us of the importance of continuous monitoring since rapid identification of high-risk cases can greatly help carry out the interventions and, thus, improve the patient's future prospects.

References

[1]   Benhammou, Y., Tabik, S., Achchah, B., & Herera, F. (2019). The first study exploring the performance of a state-of-the-art CNN model on the problems of breast-related cancer. In Proceedings of the International Conference in smart learning and Optimization Algorithms: theories and Applications, (pp. 4–14).

[2]   Sangeetha, S., & Umarani, B. (2025). MRI image-based Parkinson disorder classification by maxout fuzzy system efficient nets. *Biomedical based Signal Processing and Control*, 118, 107516.

[3] Tanwar, R., Kumar, P., Kumar, M., & Nandal, N. (Eds.). (2022). Application of Deep Learning Methods in Healthcare and Medical Science (1st ed.). Apple Academic Press. https://doi.org/10.1201/9781003303855.

[4] Roslidar, R., Saddamy, K., Arnia, F., Syukri, M., & Munnadi, K. (2019). A study on fine-tuning of CNN depends in thermal images for Breast related cancer classifications. In 2018 IEEE International Conference on Cybernetics and Computational Intelligencies (CyberneticsCom), (pp. 67–79). IEEE.

[5] Sangeetha, S. (2016). A study on problems and its challenges faced on micro sized smaller and medium enterprises: a special reference fo4 manufacturing sector of Coimbatore. *International Journal of Commerce and Management Research*, 4(8), 48–52.

[6] Tsochatzidys, T., Koutla, P., Costaridu, L., & Pratikais, I. (2022). Integration of segmentation information in CNN for breast related cancer diagnosis of mammographical. *Computer Methods and its Programs in Biomedicine*, 310, 104813.

[7] Wang, Y., Ma, R., & Fangi, J. (2018). Breast related cancer microscopical image classification depends for CNN with images deformational. In Image Analysis and its Recognitions: 15th International Conference, ICIAR 2019, Póvoa de Varzim, Portuguese, June 27–29, 2018, Proceedings 14, (pp. 825–846). Springer International Publishing.

[8] Zhang Y, Liu YL, Nie K, Zhou J, Chen Z, Chen JH, Wang X, Kim B, Parajuli R, Mehta RS, Wang M, Su MY. (2023). Deep Learning-based Automatic Diagnosis of Breast Cancer on MRI Using Mask R-CNN for Detection Followed by ResNet50 for Classification. Acad Radiol. 2023 Sep;30 Suppl 2(Suppl 2): S161-S171. doi: 10.1016/j.acra.2022.12.038. Epub 2023 Jan 10. PMID: 36631349; PMCID: PMC10515321.

[9] Sui, M, Niy, K., Zhoi, H., ... &.. (2023). Deep learning-depending automatic diagnosis of breast related cancer of MRI by mask R-CNN for identification for classification. *Academics*, 40.

[10] Sagili, S. R., & Kinsman, T. B. (2024). Drive dash: vehicle crash insights reporting system. In 2024 International Conference on Intelligent Systems and Advanced Applications (ICISAA), Pune, India, (pp. 1–6).

[11] Sagili, R., Goswami, C., Bharathi, V. C., Ananthi, S., Rani, K., & Sathya, R. (2024). Identification of diabetic retinopathy by transfer learning based retinal images. In 2024 9th International Conference on Communication and Electronics Systems (ICCES), Coimbatore, India.

[12] Soltani, H., Amroune, M., Bendib, I., & Haouam, M. Y. (2021). Breast related cancer lesion identification and segmentation based on mask R-CNN. In 2021 International Conference on Recent Advances in Mathematics and Informatics (ICRAMI), (pp. 1–6). IEEE.

[13] Minarno, A. E., Ghufron, K. M., Sabrila, T. S., Husniah, L., & Sumadi, F. D. S. (2021). Cnn based autoencoder application in Breast related cancer image retrieval. In 2021 International Seminar on Intelligent Technology and its Applications (ISITIA), (pp. 29–34). IEEE.

[14] Karimi Jafarbigloo, S., & Danyali, H. (2021). Nuclear atypia grading in breast related cancer histopathological images based on CNN feature extraction and LSTM classification. *CAAI Transactions on Intelligence Technology*, 6(4), 426–439.

[15] Sureshkumar, V., Prasad, R. S. N., Balasubramaniam, S., Jagannathan, D., Daniel, J., & Dhanasekaran, S. (2024). Breast related cancer identification and analytics using hybrid cnn and extreme learning machine. *Journal of Personalized Medicine*, 14(8), 792.

[16] Khan, S. U. R., Zhao, M., Asif, S., Chen, X., & Zhu, Y. (2024). GLNET: global–local CNN's-based informed model for identification of breast related cancer categories from histopathological slides. *The Journal of Supercomputing*, 80(6), 7316–7348.

11 Vehicle detection using YOLO based models for improved traffic management

Anchal Sundar Ray[a], Arun Kumar Ray[b] and Sukanta Kumar Sabut[c]
School of Electronics Engineering, Kalinga Institute of Industrial Technology, Bhubaneswar, Odisha, India

Abstract

Intelligent traffic management systems rely on robust object detection to enhance road safety and optimize traffic flow. This study evaluates the performance of the YOLOv10 model, which uses its Hierarchical Dynamic Aggregation Network (HDAN) and YOLOv9 model by using the concept of PGI (Programmable Gradient Information) for real-time object detection in urban traffic scenarios. Using a custom dataset of 920 annotated images derived from traffic videos captured at urban intersections area. We determine the precision, recall, mean Average Precision (mAP@50, mAP@50-95) and inference time across six object classes: car, two-wheeler, bus, truck, pedestrian, and bicycle. The results indicate that YOLOv9s achieves a precision of 0.811, recall of 0.736, mAP@50 of 0.802 and mAP@50-95 of 0.455, with an inference time of 6.3 ms. Compared with YOLOv10s for vehicle detection and classification, YOLOv9s achieves best performance with different batch sizes.

Keywords: Precision, traffic management, vehicle detection, YOLOv10, YOLOv9

Introduction

Traffic congestion and inefficient resource utilization are growing challenges in urban areas due to rapid urbanization and the rising number of vehicles on the road. The need for efficient and effective traffic management systems has never been more pressing. In this context, vehicle detection has emerged as a critical component of intelligent transportation systems. It refers to identifying and tracking vehicles on roads using various sensors, cameras and algorithms. Technology has evolved significantly from traditional to modern within years. Vehicle detection is essential for traffic management as it provides real-time information about traffic conditions, enabling authorities to make informed decisions. Despite its importance, vehicle detection faces several challenges such as occlusion, varying lighting conditions, weather conditions, identification of segment of vehicles. Other challenges manifest in various forms, such as prolonged delays, frequent traffic violations, poor image or video quality and an imbalance in the usage of road networks. Existing traffic management systems often rely on static and pre-determined routing mechanisms, which lack the adaptability required to address real-time traffic scenarios. Moreover, critical problems such as the dynamic detection of underutilized road networks, detection of vehicles in low lighting condition and how it impacts in the background during the detection of vehicle which is studied by Betke et.al in the research paper [1]. Challenges with vehicle color variations and noise, causing false alarms (up to 6.3%) with Occlusions

[a]2181090@kiit.ac.in, [b]akrayfet@kiit.ac.in, [c]sukanta.sabatfet@kiit.ac.in

DOI: 10.1201/9781003753391-11

and complex backgrounds was explained by Tsai et al. [2]. Hadi et Al. [3] studied that occlusions from other vehicles or obstacles and varying environmental conditions (e.g., shadows, weather) degrade detection and tracking performance. High computational complexity of some methods, such as feature-based and 3D model-based approaches, limits real-time applicability on resource-constrained systems. Rezaei et al. [4] introduced a monocular vision-based vehicle detection system, but it suffered from practical deployment issues. The system was sensitive to camera height fluctuations caused by vehicle shock absorbers, which introduced disparity errors. Stereo disparity estimations were also prone to inaccuracies, especially in side-view angles up to ±60°.

To address these issues, vehicle detection, a subset of computer vision, has emerged as a powerful tool in traffic management. Object detection models identify and classify objects such as vehicles, pedestrians and traffic signs from images or video streams. Among these models, You Only Look Once (YOLO) is one of the most advanced and efficient frameworks. YOLO processes an entire image in a single neural network pass, enabling high-speed and real-time object detection. Its variants, such as YOLOv9 and YOLOv10, further improve detection accuracy and speed, making them suitable for complex traffic scenarios. One significant challenge faced during the implementation is the inability to extract useful information from traffic images due to heavy background interference, which can obscure relevant data. Despite this limitation, the study emphasizes the importance of background data in providing context to traffic situations and contributing to overall traffic management insights. An important aspect of the proposed system is the identification of traffic signs, which plays a crucial role

in ensuring safe and efficient traffic flow by aiding in compliance with road regulations.

Review of Literature

After reviewing the old research papers, it was found out that 10 years back Kim et al. [5] introduced πHOG, an advanced HOG variant incorporating gradient position and intensity, along with a Position-wise vehicle size predictor (PVSP) that reduced classifier computations by 94.6% and cut processing time to 166.77 ms, with SVM outperforming ELM and kNN. Xu et al. [6] enhanced the Viola-Jones method for UAV vehicle detection by addressing orientation issues through road alignment using Line Segment Detector and histogram analysis, achieving 82.17% detection quality and 88.60% tracking accuracy. Hadi *et al.* reviewed vehicle detection and tracking techniques, highlighting that methods like Gaussian mixture models and PCA-SVM improve detection under occlusion and varying illumination, while Kalman filtering and 3D model-based tracking are effective in dynamic environments. As they were using traditional approach and there were no advanced methods introduced so they faced few problems such as occlusions, environmental factors affect the performance, high computation time, affecting the image distortion, information loss, detection of misaligned vehicles, detection accuracy under adverse conditions.

To address the problems faced in traditional approach, researchers have used YOLO technique for better results. For instance, Xiao et al. [7] introduced CRNet, which combined the temporal enhancement and category refinement, which outperformed 16 existing detection methods with a mean Average Precision (mAP) of 59.3%. With this it was clearly mentioned that in future he intends to improve the performance in vehicle tracking, multi vehicle tracking, and vehicle counting by improved CRNet. With continuation of YOLOv7 framework, Guo et al. [8] proposed INCGM-YOLO, which enhanced vehicle detection performance in challenging weather and lighting conditions. Their model achieved a mAP0.5 of 76.59%, Map 0.5:0.95 of 51.68%, and improved F1 Score to 71.79%, giving significant results in the baseline. The future scope for the author was to explore image augmentation techniques across diverse adverse conditions, improving detection speed while maintaining accuracy, to reduce hybrid loss function, and to boost performance. Du et al. [9] tackled glare in night driving scenes with FLL-FGF, built on YOLOv5 and tested on the VD-NUS-G dataset, achieving an AP of 82.87%, a 4.7% improvement over YOLOv5. Here the author struggled with glare and light imbalance.

During flood situations, accurate detection is crucial. To improve this Sun et al. [10] created the ISE-UFDS dataset and proposed SDF-YOLO, an enhanced version of YOLOv9, which yielded a 4.1% increase in precision, 1.7% in F1-score, and 3.1% in mAP, outperforming Faster R-CNN and YOLOv8. Future work includes highlighting the reduced model size and increasing runtime speed for better real-time application in floor scenarios. Liu et al. developed LIVDN, targeting low-light conditions through attention fusion and better ResNet backbones, achieving a mAP of 55.5% on low illumination datasets, surpassing models like YOLOv8 and RT-DETR. To improve the inference speed for real time applications by optimizing the model complexity.

Ren et al. [11] introduced an intelligent vehicle violation detection system using computer vision and Kalman filtering, validated on BIT-Vehicle and Apollo Scape datasets. The system reached a detection accuracy of up to 98% for various violations and demonstrated quick processing, though its performance may drop in poor lighting or weather conditions. By using advanced deep learning models and semi-supervised learning, in future the improvisation of the detection under adverse conditions can be achieved. Rani et al. [12] created LV-YOLO, integrating YOLOv5 and U-Net for logistics vehicle detection, speed tracking, and counting, tested on the 200K-image Boxy Vehicle dataset. The model outperformed previous versions with a 99.42% mAP and 89 FPS, although it relies heavily on annotated data and has high computational demands.

While Lim et al. [13] improved YOLOv8n by using adaptive oversampling techniques, which got better detection accuracy and reduced training times. Their enhanced model significantly raised mAP scores and outperformed alternatives like Faster R-CNN and SSD, though it initially showed weaker results without oversampling. Integrating the adaptive oversampling and YOLOv8n into real-time ITS application and increasing the dataset for multiple scenarios and lighting conditions. The key problems faced in the modern approach are inability to classify vehicle types, low detection resolution due to sensor limitations, unable to miss the detection when vehicles are closer, performance degradation in adverse weather and low-light conditions, small object sizes and dense distributions in UAV imagery.

Methodology

In this section, we introduced vehicle detection and vehicle classification using different YOLO models for analyzing the performance and results between them. You Only Look Once (YOLO) models stand out for their speed and accuracy, making them ideal for real-time applications. However, while earlier studies focused on larger YOLO versions like YOLOv7, YOLOv9, and YOLOv10 due to their high accuracy and mAP, these models are computationally intensive, limiting their deployment on resource-constrained devices. To address this, my recent work has shifted focus to evaluating smaller sub-versions such as YOLOv7s, YOLOv9s, and YOLOv10s. These sub-versions offer a balance between accuracy and computational efficiency, making them suitable for real-world scenarios like traffic video analysis.

The performance of YOLO models is typically evaluated based on parameters such as accuracy, which measures the correctness of vehicle detection and classification; mAP, which reflects the overall detection performance across categories and IoU thresholds; Frames Per Second (FPS), which ensures the model's suitability for real-time applications; inference time, which impacts latency; model size, crucial for deployment on edge devices; computational requirements, which determine hardware compatibility; and robustness, ensuring reliability under varying conditions like occlusion and lighting changes. Higher versions of YOLO, such as YOLOv9 and YOLOv10, bring significant improvements over earlier models. They feature enhanced architectures, better feature extraction, improved handling of small objects, and advanced training techniques, making them more accurate and flexible for diverse use cases.

Each YOLO version is further divided into sub-versions, including small (s), medium (m), large (l), and extra-large (x) configurations, to cater to different computational environments. For example, small sub-versions like YOLOv9s and YOLOv10s are designed for edge devices, offering lightweight models with reduced computational demands.

The architecture of YOLO v10 resembles the architecture of YOLO v8 for which it has similar kind of parameters and stem components [14]. The major difference, which is the depth multiple parameters in YOLO v10 is used to define how many bottleneck blocks are there in C2f block and number of CIB blocks in C2fCIB block. Higher redundancy in deeper stages and larger models is addressed by replacing bottleneck blocks with compact inverted blocks (CIB) in C2fCIB at stages like 8, 13, 19, and 22 in YOLOv10, enhancing efficiency. And the architectural diagram of YOLO v10 is described below. The dataset was implemented using YOLOv10 to evaluate its performance and derive results. Through the integration of various optimizers within the YOLOv10 framework, the dataset was simulated, and the resulting outcomes were analyzed.

YOLO v9 has PAN, Revcol, Deep supervision and PGI [15]. In YOLOv9, path aggregation network (PAN) aggregates multi-scale features for better object detection, RevCol preserves information in the auxiliary reversible branch, deep supervision enhances intermediate layer learning, and programmable gradient information (PGI) ensures reliable gradient flow by mitigating information bottlenecks during training.

Flow diagram explaining the systematic approach for analyzing the vehicle classifications using optimizers is shown below in Figure 11.1.

To evaluate the performance of the YOLO model for vehicle detection in traffic management, the following quantitative metrics were used.

i) **Precision:** Measures the proportion of correctly detected objects out of all detected objects. higher precision indicates fewer false positives. Precision is

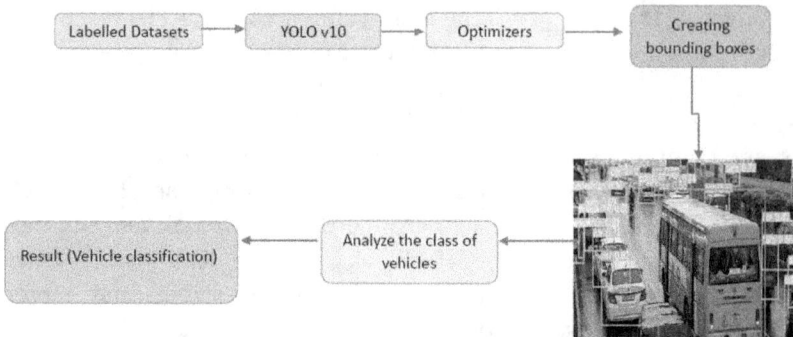

Figure 11.1 Vehicle classification using YOLO model with different optimizers
Source: Author

the ratio of all predicted targets correctly identified by the model.

Precision =TP/(TP+FP): Whereas, TP (True Positives) is the number of transmission line abnormal targets correctly identified by the model and FP (False Positives) demonstrates the number of targets incorrectly identified as abnormal by the model.

ii) **Average precision (AP)**: AP is equal to the area under the precision-recall curve, and the closer its value is to 1, the better the model performance.

$AP = \int_0^1 Precision\ (Recall)\ d\ Recall$

ii) **mAP:** mAP is the average of AP of all sample categories, which is the most commonly used evaluation metric in object detection and intuitively reflects the performance of the current model [34].

$mAP = \frac{1}{N}\sum_{i=1}^{N} APi$; Whereas, N is the number of sample categories and *APi* is the average precision for i-th category.

iii) **mAP@50**: Mean Average Precision at an Intersection over Union (IoU) threshold of 0.5, assessing detection accuracy across all classes. A higher mAP@50 suggests better object localization.

iv) mAP@50-95 is the mean Average Precision averaged over IoU thresholds from 0.5 to 0.95, providing a comprehensive measure of detection robustness. Higher values indicate consistent performance across varying IoU thresholds.

v) Recall represents the proportion of correctly detected objects out of all ground-truth objects. Higher recall indicates fewer missed detections. Recall is the ratio of all actual targets correctly recognized by the model.

Recall = TP/(TP+FN); where, TP (True Positives) is the number of transmission line abnormal targets correctly identified by the model and FN (False Negatives) is the number of abnormal targets that actually exist but are missed by the model.

vi) **Inference time:** Measures the time (in milliseconds) taken to process a single frame, critical for real-time traffic monitoring. Lower inference time indicates faster model performance.

vii) **Accuracy:** Evaluates the overall correctness of class predictions for detected objects. Higher accuracy reflects better classification performance.

viii) **Confusion matrix:** Confusion Matrix (CM) evaluates model performance by summarizing the correctness of predicted object classes against their true labels, capturing errors and relationships between predicted and actual classes.

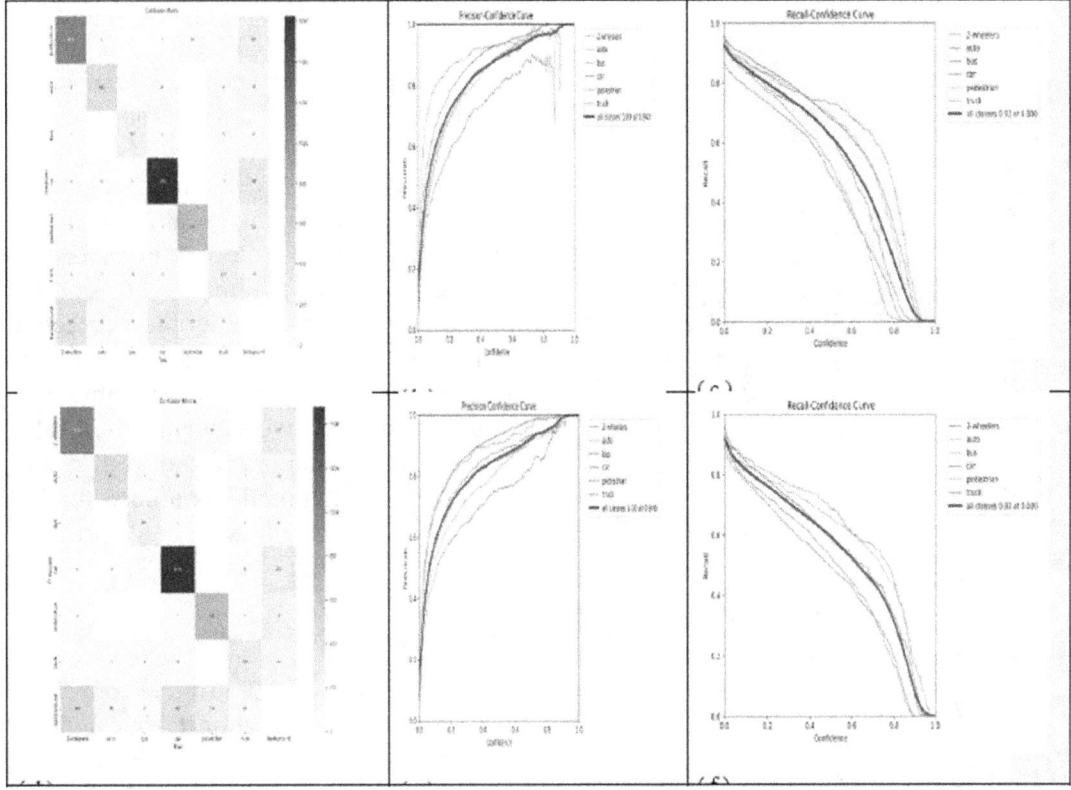

Figure 11.2 (a) Confusion matrix for YOLO v9s (b) Precision curve for YOLO v9s (c) recall curve for YOLO v9s (d) Confusion matrix for YOLO v10s (e) Precision curve for YOLO v10s (f) Recall curve for YOLO v10s

Source: Author

The cnfusion matrix, precision curve, recall curve for YOLO v9s and YOLO v10s is represented in Figure 11.2.

Results and Discussion

For this research, two high-quality traffic signal videos, each 30 minutes in duration, were collected from urban intersections in India, under the supervision of traffic management experts. One video was designated for training, and the other for testing. To create a manageable dataset for analysis, a 1-minute segment was cropped from the training video using video processing tools. This segment was converted into image frames using Roboflow, yielding approximately 3000 images. To ensure dataset quality, duplicate images were identified and removed through automated image comparison, reducing the dataset to 900 unique images. Each image was manually annotated to label six object classes: Car, two-wheeler, bus, truck, pedestrian, and bicycle. The annotation process aimed to support accurate vehicle and pedestrian detection, reflecting real-world traffic scenarios encountered in urban settings.

In this experiment, the YOLOv10s model was trained using an NVIDIA GeForce RTX 2060 graphics card (6144 MiB) with Python 3.9.18, PyTorch 2.0.1 (CUDA 11.7), and Ultralytics YOLOv8.1.34, using a custom dataset defined in data.yaml. The

Table 11.1 Performance analysis of the YOLO models.

Models	Batch size	Images	Instances	Box P	R	mAP50	mAP (50-95)	Inferences (ms)	Parameters (M)	Layers	GFLOPs
SMALL Models for Batch size: 4											
YOLOv10s	4	176	5608	0.769	0.729	0.781	0.442	9.2ms	8,039,604	293	24.5
YOLOv9s	4	176	5608	0.797	0.769	0.822	0.464	41.2ms	57,381,026	687	189.2
SMALL Models for batch size: 8											
YOLOv10s	8	176	5608	0.780	0.716	0.775	0.437	4.1ms	8,039,604	293	24.5
YOLOv9s	8	176	5608	0.805	0.741	0.810	0.461	32.8ms	57,381,026	687	189.2
SMALL Models for batch size: 16											
YOLOv10s	16	176	5608	0.762	0.725	0.780	0.441	11.1ms	8,039,604	293	24.5
YOLOv9s	**16**	**176**	**5608**	**0.811**	**0.736**	**0.802**	**0.455**	**6.3 ms**	**7,169,410**	**486**	**26.7**

Source: Author

model, comprising 293 layers, 8,039,604 parameters, and 24.5 GFLOPs, was configured with 100 epochs, a batch size of 16, an image size of 640x640, an initial learning rate of 1×10^{-5}, and the different optimizer, alongside data augmentation techniques like HSV adjustments and flipping to enhance robustness. Selected for its balance of efficiency and performance, YOLOv10s is well-suited for real-time object detection on resource-constrained edge devices, with hyperparameters optimized for stable convergence and effective deployment. In Table 11.1 below, the summarized data of results is presented. Each model is trained for 100 epochs and validated using conf threshold of 0.25 and IOU threshold of 0.7.

Conclusion

The performance of YOLO model for vehicle detection and classification taking multiple circumstances has been analyzed by using mathematical derivatives. It was observed that YOLOv9 has performed significantly with precision of 0.811, recall of 0.736, mAp@50 of 0.802, mAp@(50-95) of 0.455 and inference time of 6.3ms. When compared with YOLOv10, it was found out that YOLO v9 is better and to get a precise comparison it was exploited under different batch sizes. Taking into consideration various challenges faced in recent traffic management, this paper identifies key areas where the improvement needs to be done through using deep learning model. In future, this dataset can be compared to other vehicle detection methods considering adverse weather conditions such as low lighting, fog, rain etc. and other issues such as occlusion, small vehicle detection and high-speed vehicles.

References

[1] Betke, M., Haritaoglu, E., & Davis, L. S. (2000). Real-time multiple vehicle detection

and tracking from a moving vehicle. *Machine Vision and Applications*, 12(2), 69–83. doi: 10.1007/s001380050126.

[2] Zhang, Y., Sun, Y., Wang, Z., & Jiang, Y. (2023). YOLOv7-RAR for urban vehicle detection. *Sensors*, 23(4), 1801. https://doi.org/10.3390/s23041801.

[3] Hadi, R. A., Sulong, G., & George, L. E. (2014). Vehicle detection and tracking techniques: a concise review. *Signal and Image Processing: An International Journal*, 5(1), 1–12. https://doi.org/10.5121/sipij.2014.5101.

[4] Rezaei, M., Terauchi, M., & Klette, R. (2015). Robust vehicle detection and distance estimation under challenging lighting conditions. *IEEE Transactions on Intelligent Transportation Systems*, 16(5), 2723–2743. https://doi.org/10.1109/TITS.2015.2421482.

[5] Kim, J., Baek, J., & Kim, E. (2015). A novel on-road vehicle detection method using πHOG. *IEEE Transactions on Intelligent Transportation Systems*, 16(6), 3414–3429. https://doi.org/10.1109/TITS.2015.2433894.

[6] Xu, Y., Yu, G., Wu, X., Wang, Y., & Ma, Y. (2017). An enhanced viola-jones vehicle detection method from unmanned aerial vehicles imagery. *IEEE Transactions on Intelligent Transportation Systems*, 18(7), 1845–1856. https://doi.org/10.1109/TITS.2016.2619258.

[7] Xu, Y., Yu, G., Wu, X., Wang, Y., & Ma, Y. (2017). An enhanced viola-jones vehicle detection method from unmanned aerial vehicles imagery. *IEEE Transactions on Intelligent Transportation Systems*, 18(7), 1845–1856. https://doi.org/10.1109/TITS.2016.2619258.

[8] Guo, L., Zhou, X., Zhao, Y., & Wu, W. (2025). Improved YOLOv7 algorithm incorporating InceptionNeXt and attention mechanism for vehicle detection under adverse lighting conditions. *Signal, Image*

and Video Processing, 19, 299. https://doi.org/10.1007/s11760-025-03868-4.

[9] Du, P., Wang, X., Zheng, Q., Wang, X., Li, W., & Xu, X. (2025). Glare countering and exploiting via dual stream network for nighttime vehicle detection. *The Visual Computer*, 41, 1453–1466. https://doi.org/10.1007/s00371-024-03433-z.

[10] Sun, J., Xu, C., Zhang, C., Zheng, Y., Wang, P., & Liu, H. (2025). Flood scenarios vehicle detection algorithm based on improved YOLOv9. *Multimedia Systems*, 31(74), 1–20. https://doi.org/10.1007/s00530-024-01661-w.

[11] Ren, Y. (2024). Intelligent vehicle violation detection system under human-computer interaction and computer vision. *International Journal of Computational Intelligence Systems*, 17(40), 1–14. https://doi.org/10.1007/s44196-024-00427-6.

[12] Gopika Rani, N., Hema Priya, N., Ahilan, A., & Muthukumaran, N. (2024). LV-YOLO: logistic vehicle speed detection and counting using deep learning based YOLO network. *Signal, Image and Video Processing*, 18, 7419–7429. doi: 10.1007/s11760-024-03404-w.

[13] Lim, C. H., Connie, T., Ong, T. S., & Goh, M. K. O. (2024). Visual-based vehicle detection with adaptive oversampling. *International Journal of Information Technology*, 16(8), 4767–4777. https://doi.org/10.1007/s41870-024-01977-w.

[14] Wang, A., Chen, H., Liu, L., Chen, K., Lin, Z., Han, J., et al. (2024). YOLOv10: real-time end-to-end object detection. arXiv preprint arXiv:2405.14458v2, Available from: https://arxiv.org/abs/2405.14458.

[15] Wang, C.-Y., Yeh, I.-H., & Liao, H.-Y. M. (2024). YOLOv9: learning what you want to learn using programmable gradient information. arXiv preprint arXiv:2402.13616v2. Available from: https://arxiv.org/abs/2402.13616.

12 A novel approach for the detection of tea leaf diseases using ensemble learning

Kandarpa Kalita[1,a], Kishore Medhi[2,b], Anirudha Deka[1,c] and Sunandan Baruah[1,d]

[1]Computer Science and Engineering Department, Assam Down Town University, Guwahati, Assam, India

[2]Computer Application Department, Assam Don Bosco University, Azara, Assam, India

Abstract

Tea is one of the major crops of Assam. It has made a significant contribution to the economy of Assam. However, it is seen that tea crops are very prone to various diseases and paste attacks, which causes reduction in the yield. Researchers are working towards the development of artificial intelligence-based system to help the tea crop grower in the early detection of the tea diseases so that proper measures can be taken hence loss can be mitigated. In this work, we have proposed an image processing-based hybrid model for the tea disease classification. Inception V3 model is used for the extraction of features available in the tea leaves images and an ensemble-based classifier combining Support Vector Machine (SVM), Random Forest (RF) and Artificial Neural Network (ANN) is used for classification. With this approach an accuracy of 93.32% is achieved. The proposed hybrid method outperformed the other methods in detecting tea leaf disease.

Keywords: Artificial Neural Network, ensemble learning, PCA, random forest, Support Vector Machine, tea leaf

Introduction

Assam's economy is mainly based on agriculture and tea is considered as one of the most important crops. There are lots of people found associated with tea industry as plantation workers, tea garden workers, small scale farmer and employees in the tea processing unit [1]. Tea is grown all over the Assam mainly in upper Assam. Despite best care taken by the farmers, due to several reason such as climatic condition, fungal, bacterial and viral attack tea plants are fond to be infected with some of the common tea diseases such as – red rust, blister blight, root rot, brown blight etc [2], and it is evolved as a major concern for the farmers to take a proper measure on time so that yield loss can be reduced. In traditional approach experience and skilled farmers identify the disease found on the tea leaves and takes the necessary action. This traditional method of identifying disease by naked eye is not a reliable approach. Moreover, for the large-scale tea-estates which span into several hectors this approach of identifying diseases with manual approach is challenging one. So, an advanced AI based system which can produce accurate diagnosis result of the tea disease is required. By utilizing deep learning

[a]kan6039@gmail.com, [b]kmedhi.rw@gmail.com, [c]dekaaniruddha@gmail.com, [d]sunandanbaruah@gmail.com

DOI: 10.1201/9781003753391-12

and machine learning techniques, early identification of diseased leaves enables timely intervention, ultimately improving crop management [3,4].

The main contribution of this research is to present a systematic approach to tea leaf disease classification, utilizing a hybrid classification approach. In this method we used the Inception V3 model for extracting features, PCA was used to reduce the dimensionality of features. Finally, an ensemble model (that combines SVM, neural network, and Random Forest) was used to improve the classifier performance. Moreover, the proposed methodology aims to enhance classification accuracy,

Related Work

Different researchers tried various innovative approaches to detect plant disease from leaf images. A detailed explanation about some recent approaches is given below.

Nigar et al. [5]. present a deep learning-based plant disease detection model using EfficientNetB0, achieving 99.69% accuracy across 38 diseases. To enhance transparency, they incorporate the LIME framework, providing visual explanations for predictions and addressing the "black-box" issue.

Balafas et al. [6] in their study explores an AI-driven plant disease detection system, they have compared traditional ML methods like SVM and RF with advanced DL models like CNNs. While DL enhances accuracy through automated feature extraction, challenges like data requirements and model interpretability persist.

Panchal et al. [7] examined a hybrid model integrating EfficientNet with conventional ML classifiers, obtained over 99% accuracy in its analysis of 54,306 images covering 14 crops with 26 diseases. Despite the level of accuracy they have achieved,

they mentioned the need for a big dataset and the interpretability of models.

Nath et al. [8] proposes a CNN model combining depth wise separable convolutions and residual networks for feature extraction and reducing computational costs for tea plant disease classification. They mentioned the application of the SVM model to enhance accuracy. The model is trained using a images database consisting of healthy and diseased tea leaves, including red rust and blister blight, the model achieved 99.28% accuracy.

Wu et al. [9] mentioned the uses of an improved tea leaf disease detection system by integrating handcrafted features with an attention-based CNN model, this model is designed to focus on crucial areas in images which result in the improved classification accuracy. They have claimed the accuracy achieved by the model as 92.78% and 98.13% for two different datasets.

Pandiyaraju et al. [10] presented a transfer learning-based system for automated cotton leaf disease identification which combines traditional ML models SVM and RF as classifiers and VGG-16 as feature extractor. Accuracy achieved by the proposed study is 98.29% and 99.31% for VGG-RF and VGG-SVM respectively.

Li, Lanting et al. [11] proposed the ECA-ResNet50 model to enhance tea disease classification by incorporating the efficient channel attention (ECA) mechanism into the ResNet50 network. This integration optimizes feature extraction, leading to more precise disease identification. This approach improves classification accuracy to 93.06%, outperforming the standard ResNet50 model by 3.18%.

Raj et al. [12] presents a hybrid model combining CNN with a Weighted Random Forest (WRF) classifier for improved tea leaf disease classification. By utilizing hybrid pooling layers for feature extraction and optimizing decision trees with the Cuckoo Search algorithm, the model enhances accuracy. Tested on the Tea Sickness Dataset, it achieved 92.47% accuracy in identifying multiple tea leaf diseases.

Material and Method

As shown in Figure 12.1, this research experiment presents a structured methodology for the task of tea leaf disease classification, it includes several steps such as, data preprocessing, feature extraction, and ensemble learning techniques. The dataset comprises images of tea leaves affected by seven different diseases, a detailed description about the dataset is given in subsection 3.1. All the images pass through pre-processing steps such as resizing (224 × 224), contrast enhancement and normalization. Canny edge detection algorithm is used to isolate disease regions of the images. After the segmentation process, feature extraction was performed using the Inception V3 model. Finally, the extracted features were optimized and reduced the dimension by using the Principal Component Analysis (PCA) method to improve computational efficiency. After the extraction, all the extracted features were applied in

a classification process to detect the diseases. In this experiment we used an ensemble-based classification method consisting of three different algorithms such as SVM, ANN and RF. The model's effectiveness is measured using accuracy, precision, recall, and F1-score. A detailed description of all the essential steps is given below.

Dataset

In this work, we utilized an open image dataset from Mendeley data [13]. The collection comprises one set of healthy tea leaf images in .jpeg format, and seven disease types: (1) Red leaf spot; (2) Algal leaf spot; (3) Bird's eyespot; (4) Grey blight; (5) White spot; (6) Anthracnose; (7) Brown blight. To maintain uniformity across the dataset and ensure compatibility with classification models, a rigorous preprocessing step is performed before the images are input into the classification model. This process includes resizing all images to 224x224 pixels. Additionally, we apply random rotation within ± 90° to prevent discrepancies in photo orientation.

Segmentation and feature extraction

In order to focus solely on relevant parts of the image for feature extraction, segmentation methods such as the Canny edge detection technique were applied to distinguish between diseased and healthy regions [14–16] of a leaf. This segmentation process enhances feature selection by concentrating on affected areas, reducing the unwanted regions and improving classification accuracy. After the segmentation process, the Inception V3 model was used for feature extraction from the segmented tea leaves images. In this implementation, the architecture consists of three convolutional layers followed by two different Inception blocks. Because of the efficient architecture of the Inception V3, it can easily extract the deep features directly from the input images without altering the

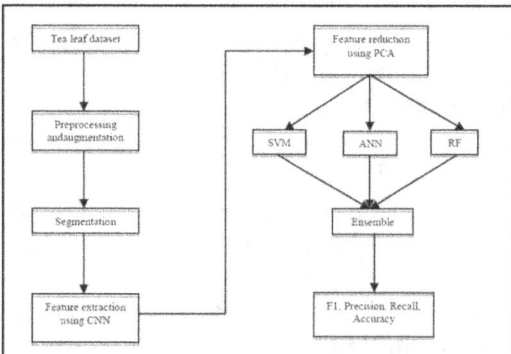

Figure 12.1 System design for the classification of tea leaf disease
Source: Author

Table 12.1 Performance metrics of the ensemble models used in this study.

Classifiers	Classification matrix			
	F1	Precision	Recall	Accuracy
SVM, RF	94.34	98.43	90.58	90.36
SVM, ANN	91.12	95.93	86.76	86.89
RF, ANN	82.64	85.93	83.14	83.18
SVM, RF and ANN	96.04	98.44	93.75	93.32

Source: Author

learned representations. The implementation process involved preprocessing the tea leaf images by resizing them to 224 × 224 pixels. Then the images are converted into a numerical array to apply the model specific normalization. Once we are done with the preprocessing these images were fed into the Inception V3 model, where hierarchical feature maps were generated from the last convolutional layer. The extracted feature maps were then flattened into one-dimensional vectors, making them suitable for further analysis and classification [17, 18].

Dimension reduction using PCA

After feature extraction, all the extracted features are optimized using the PCA method. Here, PCA was applied to the extract high dimensional feature vector generated using the inception V3, this process reduces the dimension of the feature vector and enhances the computational cost and improves classification accuracy [19, 20]. This procedure reduces redundancy while preserving crucial information by preserving 95% of the total variance. Initially, the feature matrix consists of 2048-dimensional vectors per image, which can be computationally expensive for classifiers. By utilizing PCA(n_cmponents = 0.95), the model determines the optimal number of principal components required to maintain essential data patterns while discarding less significant variations. This transformation ensures

faster processing and reduces the risk of overfitting in classification models.

Ensemble classification learning

In this classification process, we used an ensemble technique consisting of three different classifiers such as, Support Vector Machine (SVM), Random Forest (RF), and Artificial Neural Network (ANN). Among different ensemble technique available we have chosen ensemble averaging approach. In this method probability predicted by each base model is combined to achieve the improve accuracy. It combines several algorithms and unites their results through voting mechanism, to achieve bater accuracy over individual model [21].

Result and Discussion

In an intent of finding good accuracy which is commercially viable an ensemble classification model combining three most popular classical machine learning model such as SVM, RF, and ANN. The accuracy achieved by different combinations can be found in Table 12.1. And the confusion matrix for all the four ensembled combination can be seen in the Figures 12.2–12.5. The ensemble combination of the all three mentioned ML models produce the highest accuracy of 93.32%. This result shows the capability of the hybrid model in finding enhanced accuracy in complex data classification task.

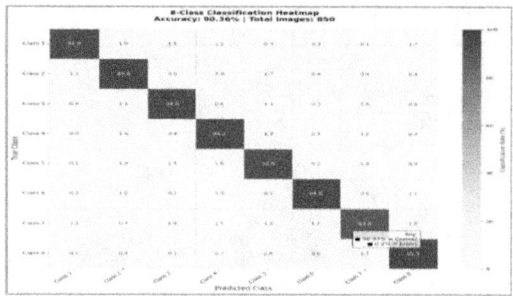

Figure 12.2 Confusion matrices for SVM + RF
Source: Author

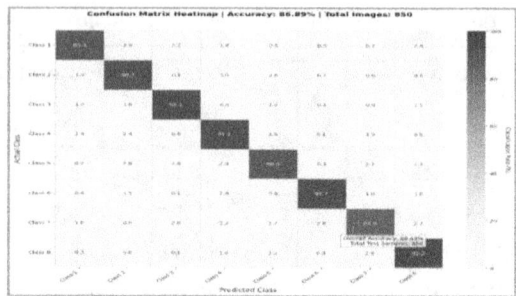

Figure 12.3 Confusion matrices for SVM + ANN
Source: Author

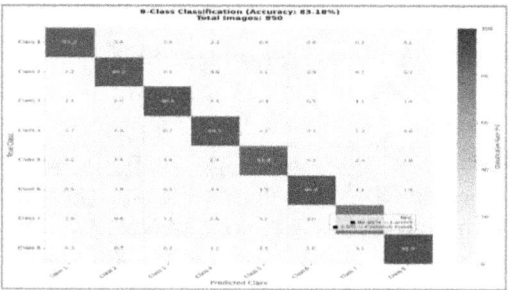

Figure 12.4 Confusion matrices for RF + ANN
Source: Author

Figure 12.5 Confusion matrices for SVM + RF + ANN
Source: Author

Conclusion

In this work we have highlighted challenges faced by the tea growers in Assam and provided a technology-based solution for the detection of different diseases in tea crops. For the detection of tea disease, a hybrid model is addressed. Transfer learning technique is used to extract the features of the infected tea leaf images, in this phase InceptionV3 model is used. The feature space generated is too large to fetch it to the classification model which is an ensemble model consisting of three classical ML model such as – Support Vector Machine (SVM), Random Forest (RF), and Artificial Neural Network. So, PCA algorithm is applied to reduce the feature space. The classification model produces an accuracy of 93.32%. This result is commercially viable to be used in precession agriculture as it crosses the threshold accuracy value which is 90%.

References

[1] Laskar, N. (2015). A study on the present scenario of tea industry in Assam-challenges ahead. *Indian Journal of Applied Research*, 6, 533–537.

[2] Pandey, A. K., Sinniah, G. D., Babu, A., & Tanti, A. (2021). How the global tea industry copes with fungal diseases–challenges and opportunities. *Plant Disease*, 105(7), 1868–1879.

[3] Balafas, V., Karantoumanis, E., Louta, M., & Ploskas, N. (2023). Machine learning and deep learning for plant disease classification and detection. *IEEE Access*, 11, 114352–114377.

[4]   Sharma, R., Singh, A., Jhanjhi, N. Z., Masud, M., Jaha, E. S., & Verma, S. (2022). Plant disease diagnosis and image classification using deep learning. *Computers, Materials and Continua*, 71(2).

[5]   Nigar, N., Muhammad Faisal, H., Umer, M., Oki, O., & Manappattukunnel Lukose, J. (2024). Improving plant disease classification with deep-learning-based prediction model using explainable artificial intelligence. *IEEE Access*, 12, 100005–100014. doi: 10.1109/ACCESS.2024.3428553.

[6]   Balafas, V., Karantoumanis, E., Louta, M., & Ploskas, N. (2023). Machine learning and deep learning for plant disease classification and detection. *IEEE Access*, 11, 114352–114377. doi: 10.1109/ACCESS.2023.3324722.

[7]   Panchal, A. V., Patel, S. C., Bagyalakshmi, K., Kumar, P., Khan, I. R., & Soni, M. (2023). Image-based plant diseases detection using deep learning. *Materials Today: Proceedings*, 80, 3500–3506.

[8]   Nath, M., Mitra, P., & Kumar, D. (2023). A novel residual learning-based deep learning model integrated with attention mechanism and SVM for identifying tea plant diseases. *International Journal of Computers and Applications*, 45(6), 471–484.

[9]   Wu, P., Liu, J., Jiang, M., Zhang, L., Ding, S., & Zhang, K. (2025). Tea leaf disease recognition using attention convolutional neural network and handcrafted features. *Crop Protection*, 190, 107118.

[10]   Pandiyaraju, V., Anusha, B., Senthil Kumar, A. M., Jaspin, K., Venkatraman, S., & Kannan, A. (2025). Spatial attention-based hybrid VGG-SVM and VGG-RF frameworks for improved cotton leaf disease detection. *Neural Computing and Applications*, 37(14), 8309–8329.

[11]   Li, L., & Zhao, Y. (2025). Tea disease identification based on ECA attention mechanism ResNet50 network. *Frontiers in Plant Science*, 16, 1489655.

[12]   Raj, M., Jha, P., Magar, M. G., & Kukreja, V. (2024). CNN and random forest hybrid model for tea leaf diseases multiclassification. In 2024 International Conference on Automation and Computation (AUTOCOM), (pp. 52–56). IEEE.

[13]   S. Kimutai, Gibson; Förster, Anna (2022), "tea sickness dataset", Mendeley Data, V1, doi: 10.17632/j32xdt2ff5.1.

[14]   Mohamed, S., Elboshy, M. B., Khater, H. A., & Gamel, S. A. (2024). Advancing cardiac image processing: an innovative model utilizing canny edge detection for enhanced diagnostics. In 2024 41st National Radio Science Conference (NRSC), (Vol. 1, pp. 278–285). IEEE.

[15]   Tan, T., Wang, L., & Zhou, W. (2024). Edge detection of plant root images based on improved canny algorithm. In 2024 Photonics & Electromagnetics Research Symposium (PIERS), (pp. 1–8). IEEE.

[16]   Selvakumar, A. A., & Thangaraju, P. (2024). Brain tumour edge detection using an enhanced canny edge detection algorithm. *International Journal of Computational Biology and Drug Design*, 16(2), 167–183.

[17]   Liu, H., Li, I., Liang, Y., Sun, D., Yang, Y., & Yang, H. (2024). Research on deep learning model of feature extraction based on convolutional neural network. In 2024 IEEE 2nd International Conference on Image Processing and Computer Applications (ICIPCA), (pp. 810–816). IEEE.

[18]   Kankariya, S., Thakre, K., Solanki, U., Mali, S., & Chunawale, A. (2024). Sign language gestures recognition using CNN and inception V3. In 2024 International Conference on Emerging Smart Computing and Informatics (ESCI), (pp. 1–6). IEEE.

[19]   Rahmat, F., Zulkafli, Z., Ishak, A. J., Abdul Rahman, R. Z., Stercke, S. D., Buytaert, W., et al. (2024). Supervised feature selection using principal component analysis. *Knowledge and Information Systems*, 66(3), 1955–1995.

[20]   Uddin, M. P., Mamun, M. A., & Hossain, M. A. (2021). PCA-based feature reduction for hyperspectral remote sensing image

classification. *IETE Technical Review*, 38(4), 377–396.

[21] Ali, S. A., Parvin, F., Pham, Q. B., Khedher, K. M., Dehbozorgi, M., Rabby, Y. W., et al. (2022). An ensemble random forest tree with SVM, ANN, NBT, and LMT for landslide susceptibility mapping in the Rangit River watershed, India. *Natural Hazards*, 113(3), 1601–1633.

13 A descriptive study to assess the attitude of middle adult community people towards mental illness

Simran Chauhan[1,a], Shivani Dhiman[1,b], Srikanta Mallik[2,c], Alok Kumar Agrawal[2,d], Rajit Verma[3,e] and Srikanta Kumar Mohapatra[4,f]

[1]Nursing Tutor, Chitkara University College of Nursing, Chitkara University, Himachal Pradesh, India

[2]Chitkara University School of Engineering and Technology, Chitkara University, Himachal Pradesh, India

[3]M.M. Institute of Management, Maharishi Marksandeshwar (Deemed to be University), Mullana-Ambala, Haryana, India

[4]Chitkara Universiy Institute of Engineering and Technology, Chitkara University, Punjab, India

Abstract

People with mental illness have historically been socially rejected and subjected to a persistently negative attitude in all social and religious cultures. A number of things can lead to mental illness. There is frequently only one or a consistent cause. Environmental stress, psychological trauma, or genetic factors may be the reason. Mental illness is generally believed to be caused by supernatural or supernatural powers, witches, evil spirits, or even God. These folks believe that hang had an impact on the knowledge and mindset of the local population. Adults' attitudes toward mental health concerns and their effects are being examined in this study. For middle-aged adults, special education about the causes of mental disease should be provided. The main aim of the study was to evaluate the attitudes of middle-aged community members toward "mental illness". "Quantitative non-experimental descriptive" design for the research was opted out in selected community areas. It comprises 100 middle adults and convenient sampling technique was used in sample selection. Observation of the study revealed that majority of the subject [87%] have neutral attitude, 13% have negative attitude and no one have positive attitude toward mental illness.

Keywords: Attitude, community people, informational booklet, mental health, mental illness, middle adult

Introduction

Mental health is an ongoing state of well-being that allows us to effectively cope up with life's challenges, cultivate our full potential, grow personally and professionally, while also contributing to our community [1].

A multitude of factors can contribute to the complicated phenomena, that is mental diseases. It can be brought on by biological or genetic factors, stressors in the environment, or psychological trauma [2]. One third of the population experience it

[a]s.chauhansimi@gmail.com, [b]shivanidhiman.shivax1@gmail.com, [c]srikanta.mallik@gmail.com, [d]alok.agrawal@chitkarauniversity.edu.in, [e]vermarajput007@gmail.com, [f]srikanta.2k7@gmail.com

DOI: 10.1201/9781003753391-13

at some point throughout their lives. Even today, there is widespread opinion that environmental stressors reveal genetic vulnerabilities that lead to illnesses [3]. A basic statistical study of the entire spectrum of mental health issues, however, makes it abundantly evident that there is a high correlation between adult abuse (physical, sexual, and emotional) and a variety of severe and complicated mental disorders. Or failing to provide for children during their formative years, particularly during the tense adolescent years [4].

Acc. to the "World Health Organization (WHO)", 2019 data, one person among every eight globally suffers from a "mental illness". In 2020 a rise was shown in cases of anxiety and depression by 26% and 28% due to Covid 19, followed by 24 million with schizophrenia, 40 million with bipolar disorder. At some point in their lives, around 25% people among industrialized and nations which are under development experience one or more than one mental or behavior illnesses [5]. While some countries have made progress in reducing stigma and promoting acceptance of people with mental illnesses, India and other emerging nations are glaringly ignorant. Others have an unfavorable opinion of mentally sick people and identify them as "different" from other people [6]. Therefore, it is helpful to analyze how the community thinks and perceives mental illness in order to determine how they feel about it.

Literature Review

Dekhawat et al. [7] conducted a descriptive cross-sectional study to analyze the adult's attitude towards mental illness in some village areas at Udaipur District. 100 samples were selected for the research study using convenience sample techniques. A standard attitudinal scale was used to collect information from the samples. The results depicted that 73% of the samples had favorable attitudes and 27% showed unfavorable attitudes. There was significant association seen between attitude scores and variables

Sapharina Sara et al. [8] conducted a non-experimental descriptive study to analyze nurses' attitudes about mental illness at Sri Ramachandra Hospital. The purposive sampling approach was used for choosing a sample of 400 nursing personnel. The study's findings indicate that nurses training programs should be initiated focusing at developing positive attitudes and making them receptive to the necessities of mentally ill patients.

Kulkarni et al. [9] undertook mixed method research to measure the "awareness" and "attitude" about mental illnesses in India's village population. The participants in the study were 196 people aged 18 to 60 years old, chosen using a simple random sample procedure. The "Community Attitude towards Mental Illness (CAMI)" scale included a pre-tested questionnaire, and the interview method approach was utilized to obtain data from the subjects. The results of the study revealed that age was favorably connected with authoritarianism, social restrictiveness, and "Community Attitude towards Mental Illness (CAMI)", but negatively correlated with the nature of "benevolence". As a result, the researcher concluded that there is a need to raise awareness among young people as well as perform perception studies in order to influence the community's attitude of those with mental illnesses.

Halder and Biswas [10] performed a descriptive comparative survey to analyze young and older people's knowledge and attitudes concerning mental illness in "Karakdanga, Bankura, West Bengal. Simple random selection was used to select participants (n1 = 55, n2 = 55). The study found a considerable positive association among "knowledge and attitude toward mental illness". The findings revealed that younger individuals had a better knowledge score and a more tolerant attitude toward mental illness than older persons. The findings have several implications for strengthening community based mental health facilities as well as nursing practice, education, administration and research.

Ahmed and Nikita [11] performed cross-sectional research to measure and compare community attitudes regarding mental illness among rural and urban populations. Purposive sampling was used to choose 60 samples of elderly people, 30 from each urban and rural areas of Kurukshetra. The results show significant differences in authoritarianism and social restrictiveness, suggesting "authoritarianism" was more in urban populations while social restrictiveness was high in rural populations. This indicates that, excluding societal restrictiveness, a high and favorable attitude toward mental illness was seen among urban residents. to decrease the gap in the literature and create mode of action for the village population. More research into a bigger sample size is required.

Prasad et al. [12] used a comparative descriptive study design to measure individuals' knowledge and attitudes towards mental illness in selected urban and rural areas of Solapur district, India. The majority of rural individuals (86%), whereas the majority of urban adults (94%), had a negative view regarding mental illness. As a result, there was a considerable variation in people' attitudes toward mental illness between urban and rural areas. The study's findings indicate that adequate awareness programs for rural people, as well as positive orientation and prevention strategies for mental illnesses among adults, are required for affective mental health promotion among society.

Singh Shakti [13] conducted study on the attitudes and knowledge of adults in a specific urban community in Pilani, Jhunjhunu district, Rajasthan, about mental illness. The purposive sample strategy was used in this study to choose 40 participants. The study's finding predicts that there is a strong correlation between adults' knowledge and attitude scores (r =.85). The research revealed, nurses may act as a viral component in teaching individuals about mental health, mental disease and how to prevent them.

The conclusion which we have find out from the above given researches and incidence rate, is that the attitude of the rural community towards mental illness is poor. So, we decided to conduct the research study on the attitude of middle-aged adult community people towards mental illness as other researchers have used the sample adults without the age restriction but we have restricted the age to middle aged adults as this aged people act as a bridge between the younger generation and older generation and to know their attitude regarding mental illness is important.

Methodology

Quantitative research methodology in which descriptive study research approach was used to carry out the survey in selected community areas of Distt. Sirmour. The "Community Attitude towards Mental Illness (CAMI)" tool was used to gauge their attitudes on "mental illness". The study site was chosen with convenience. The people for survey study included the middle adult (41-60 years) residing in the selected areas of district Sirmour Himachal Pradesh. The sample size for this study was 100 middle adult community people residing in the selected areas of district Sirmour and who are keen on taking part in the research endeavor.

The concept of "probability convenient method" of sampling was employed to acquire data using a semi structured questionnaire. A standard tool the "CAMI". A review of the available literature and interactions with "subject-matter experts" bolstered the tool's validity as content. In order for the questionnaire to be useful in the community, it was translated into Hindi after discussion with a subject matter professional. Following professional advice, a back translation to English was completed, checked for efficiency, and finalized. Applying "inferential and descriptive statistical techniques", the data was examined and evaluated in line with the study's goals.

There were three separate sections to the questionnaire. "Sociodemographic data" is presented in Part I, while attitude towards mental illness is discussed in Part II. There are 49 questions total, with 40 pertaining to attitudes regarding "mental illnesses" on a Likert scale. The permission was granted by the Sarpanch of village Kolar for conducting the study. Every respondent gave their "informed consent". All responder's information was kept private. The "attitude" was evaluated using "descriptive statistics.

Results

Figure 13. 1 depicts the demographic variable which include age group between 46-50 (41.0%) of age. Most of the subjects were female (53.0%); most of the subjects are studied up to 10th standard (25%). Majority of them were following Hindu religion (75.0%) and were from rural area (56.0, and mostly living in joint families.

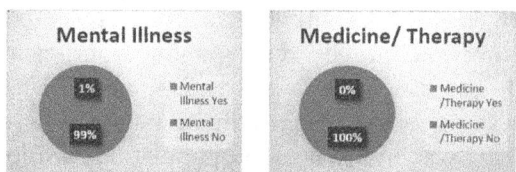

Figure 13.2 Two pie charts depicting the prevalence of mental illness and its treatment status in the studied population
Source: Author

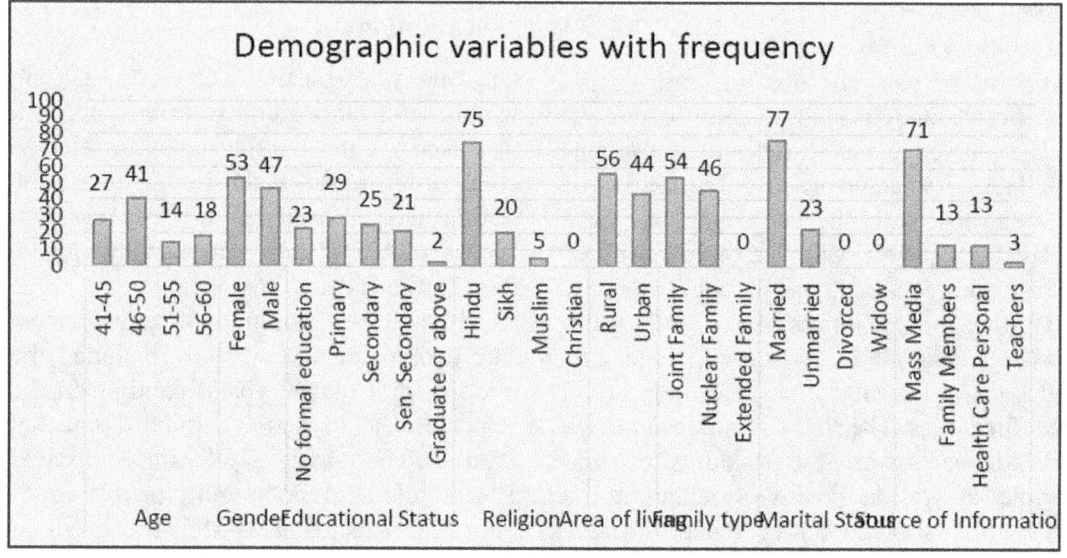

Figure 13.1 Percentage distribution of demographic variables. N = 100
Source: Author

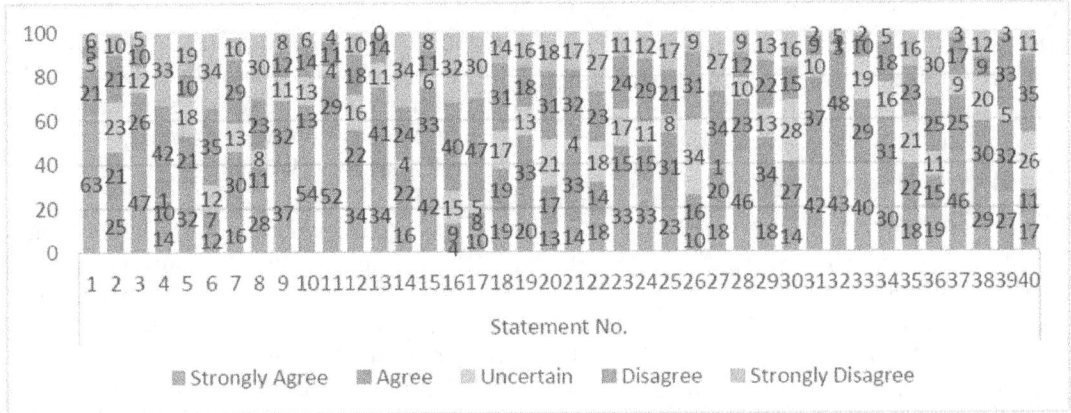

Figure 13.3 Frequency and percentage distribution of subject related to attitude on mental illness

Source: Author

Table 13.1 Attitude of middle adult community people towards mental illness.

S. No.	Category	Frequency
1.	Positive (<160)	00
2.	Neutral (120-159)	87
3.	Negative (>119)	13

Source: Author

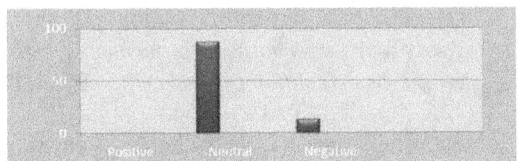

Figure 13.4 Graphical representation of the attitude of the middle adult community people towards mental illness

Source: Author

Table 13.2 Association between attitudes towards mental illness with socio demographic variables.

S. No	Variables	Chi Square	(df)	(p)
1	Age	84.63	84	0.46
2	Gender	24.06	28	0.67
3	Education	89.85	112	0.93
4	Religion	61.58	56	0.28
5	Area of Residence	27.65	28	0.48
6	Family	23.41	28	0.71
7	Marital Status	26.92	28	0.52
8	Source of information	89.18	84	0.32
9	Mental Illness	32.66	28	0.24

Source: Author

Figure 13.2 shows data of the study that was conducted from age group of 46-50 (41.0). Most of the subjects were female (53.0). Most of the subjects are studied up to 10th standard (25%). Mostly the subjects are from Hindu religion (75.0%). Mostly the subjects were from rural area (56.0). Table 13.1. Represent the attitude of the middle adult community people towards mental illness. No one have positive attitude towards mental illness. Majority of the participants were from joint families (54.0%).

Figure 13. 3 represent the distribution of responses of middle age adults on 40 attitude statements about mental illness. The graph highlighted varied opinions with responses spread across strongly agree, Agree, Uncertain, Disagree, and strongly disagree categories. And Figure 13.4 shows the overall attitude of middle age adults towards mental illness. The Majority of participants 87% expressed a neutral attitude with the very few 13% reported negative attitude towards mental illness.

Table 13.2. This table shows the association of various questions on the attitude of subjects towards mental illness with their selected socio demographic variables like age, gender, education, religion, area of residence, marital status, and type of family and source of information. Therefore, 87% of population have neutral attitude, 13% of population have negative attitude and no one have positive attitude towards mental illness. Hence, the result concluded that there is no association of attitude with socio demographic variables.

Conclusion

According to the study's findings, the majority of them had a neutral viewpoint on mental illness. The greatest degree of negativity suggests that public education is highly valued in an effort to promote a more positive outlook on "mental illness". More awareness programs, Behaviour Change Communication activities, School awareness activities should be conducted to change the perspective of the community and bring as positive outlook and acceptance towards mental illness.

References

[1]   Centers for Disease Control and Prevention (2024). About Mental Health. Atlanta (GA): CDC. Available from: https://www.cdc.gov/mental-health/about/index.html.

[2]   Kirkby R, Duffy J. An introduction to mental health and mental illness. 1st ed. Milton (QLD): Wiley; 2005. 252 p. ISBN: 9781861564131. Available from: https://catalogimages.wiley.com/images/db/pdf/1861564139.01.pdf.

[3]   Piao, X., Xie, J., & Managi, S. (2024). Continuous worsening of population emotional stress globally: universality and variations. *BMC Public Health*, 24, 3576. doi:10.1186/s12889-024-20961-4.

[4]   National Institute of Mental Health (NIMH). Mental illness [Internet]. Bethesda (MD): U.S. Department of Health and Human Services; 2023 Sep [cited 2025]. Available from: https://www.nimh.nih.gov/health/statistics/mental-illness

[5]   World Health Organization (2022). Mental Disorders. Geneva: World Health Organization. Available from: https://www.who.int/news-room/fact-sheets/detail/mental-disorders.

[6]   Lavanya, A. S. (n.d.). Attitude regarding mental illness among the community residents in Meppur. J Pharm Sci Res.2019 Dec;11(5):1731–2 [http://www.jpsr.pharmainfo.in>].

[7]   Dekhavat, C. P., & Gahlot H. (2025). A descriptive study to assess the attitude regarding mental illness among adults at selected rural areas of Udaipur District, Rajasthan. *International Journal of Scientific and Technology*, 16(1), 45–51. doi: 10.71097/IJSAT.v16.i1.1543.

[8]   Sara Sapharina, G. J., Nalini, S., Vijayasamundeeswari, P., Ramanathan, K., Subramanian, S. S., Alyoubi, R., et al. (2024). Assess the attitude towards mental illness among nurses working in selected tertiary care hospital. *International Journal of Experimental Research and Review*, 37(Spl.), 61–67.

[9]   Kulkarni, K. S., Joshi, M. N., Sathe, H. S., & Maliye, C. (2023). Awareness and attitude about mental illness in the rural population of India: a mixed method study. *Indian Journal of Psychiatry*, 65, 1069-1077.

[10] De, B., Halder, S., & Biswas, S. (2022). Assessment of knowledge and attitude towards mental illness among young and

older people, in a selected rural community, Bankura, West Bengal. *International Journal of Advanced Psychiatric Nursing*, 4(2), 17–22.

[11] Ahmed R., & Nikita (2021). Attitude towards mental illness among rural and urban community setting: a comparative study. *International Journal of Indian Psychology*, 9(4), 1556–1560. doi: 10.25215/0904.150.

[12] Patil, P., Panaskar, P., Salve, N., & Waghmare, M. (2021). A comparative study to assess the knowledge and attitude towards mental illness among adults in selected Urban and rural area. *International Journal of Recent Innovations in Medicine and Clinical Research*, 3(2), 1–7.

[13] Soni, S. S. (2020). A study to assess the knowledge and attitude towards mental illness among adults at selected urban community, Pilani, Jhunjhunu district, Rajasthan. *International Journal of Advanced Psychiatric Nursing*, 2(2), 04–07. doi: 10.33545/26641348.2020.v2.i2a.29.

14 Unsupervised anomaly detection on healthcare providers

Bishal Jaysawal[1,a], Satyanand Kumar Chauhan[2,b], Rahul Raj Sah[1,c] and Smita Rani Parija[2,d]

[1]Department of CSE, C.V. Raman Global University, KIIT University, Bhubaneswar, Odisha, India

[2]Department of ECE, C.V. Raman Global University, Bhubaneswar, Odisha, India

Abstract

Healthcare creates huge amounts of complicated and diverse data, which are arguably most suscepti-ble to fraud, incoherence, and inefficiency. Traditional rule-based or supervised learning approaches currently being employed for fraud detection rely on labelled data, which take time and are expensive to create and are in short supply. Here we present a comprehensive review of the unsupervised anom-aly detection algorithms—Isolation Forest, One-Class SVM, Elliptical Envelope—and one using deep learning through an autoencoder to identify anomalies from health provider data. In this paper, we set the performance of the models to mark outliers as a result of fraudulent billing, data outliers, and operational inefficiencies. By thorough experimentation using performance metrics (precision, recall, F1-score), visual methods (scatter plots, heatmaps), and domain expert validation, we show that ensemble of traditional unsupervised methods combined with deep learning enhances detection rates and robustness. We also present real-world practical use cases, problems of imbalanced data and interpretability, and areas of future work like explainable AI, and real-time fraud detection pipelines.

Keywords: Anomaly detection, autoencoder, deep learning, explainability, healthcare fraud detection, isolation forest, medical data security, one-class SVM, unsupervised learning

Introduction

The health care sector creates and processes huge volumes of structured and unstructured data such as patient history, billing, treat-ment plans, and insurance claims. Integrity of the data has to be maintained for fraud prevention, regulatory compliance, and enhanced patient care [5]. Frauds, billing errors, and inconsistent data cause humon-gous losses in terms of finances as well as poor quality of services. Conventional fraud detection techniques rely on supervised learning algorithms that require labelled data, which in most instances is not avail-able or in short supply for effective fraud detection.

Unsupervised anomaly detection offers a useful substitute by detecting straying from usual behavior without the need for labelled samples [3, 4]. These methods compare data distributions to detect anomalies, e.g., false claims, data entry mistakes, or aberrant provider behavior. Because fraud is com-paratively uncommon relative to usual trans-actions, unsupervised algorithms are able to detect latent anomalies that are avoided by rule-based or supervised models [6].

[a]bjbishal075@gmail.com, [b]satyanand.chauhan2017@gmail.com, [c]rahulsah7np@gmail.com, [d]smita.parija@gmail.com

DOI: 10.1201/9781003753391-14

This work explores some of the unsupervised anomaly detection models like Isolation Forest, One-Class SVM, and Elliptical Envelope for detecting anomalies in healthcare provider data. Of these, Isolation Forest is specifically capable of dealing with high-dimensional data, and thus is especially appropriate for healthcare. We also explore an autoencoder-based method where we compress and reconstruct with deep learning in order to detect deviations typical of fraud or abnormality.

Autoencoder, applied as a Karas implementation, includes an encoder to reduce dimensions from the input using layers with 64, 32, 16, and 11 neurons and a decoder for the reconstruction process involving layers of 16, 32, 64, and 4 neurons. Optimization was conducted utilizing Adam optimization along with MSE loss function over 100 epochs with a batch size of 32 and validation split set to 20. By acquiring a compact representation of the data, the model effectively captures informative features, identifies anomalies, and mitigates noise [9].

Objectives

The primary objectives of this research are as follows:

- To identify irregularities by preprocessing and analyzing data from healthcare providers.
- To identify strange behaviors and fraudulent conduct using machine learning models.
- To evaluate these models' anomaly detection capabilities using performance metrics and visualization techniques.

Challenges in Healthcare Anomaly Detection

It is challenging to pinpoint anomalies in health care provider data. Firstly, the data are hugely imbalanced, i.e., fraud cases being heavily overwhelmed by genuine transactions. This skews the performance of the machine learning model to deliver artificially high false positive rates. The second difficulty arises from the nature of health care data, where numerous attributes, such as patient diagnosis, treatment regimen, and charges, have interdependent relationships with each other [2]. Traditional rule-based systems are incapable of dealing with such sophisticated relationships, and therefore sophisticated machine learning techniques must be used.

Data security and privacy is another issue [8]. The data for healthcare is sensitive in nature, and using machine learning models translates to compliance with laws such as the Health Insurance Portability and Accountability Act (HIPAA). Making the data anonymous without affecting model performance is a primary problem when dealing with anomaly detection for healthcare. Furthermore, interpretability of the algorithms is vital to enable adoption in practical applications. Auditors and healthcare professionals require clear explanations of discovered anomalies to distinguish between genuine billing irregularities and false claims.

Contributions of this Research

This work makes the following contributions:

1. Comprehensive analysis of healthcare provider data:
   - We perform extensive Exploratory Data Analysis (EDA) to discover trends, patterns, and distributions in the data.
2. Application of unsupervised learning models:
   - We compare different anomaly detection models, observing their

ability to identify fraudulent claims and operational inefficiencies.

3. Deep learning-based anomaly detection:
   - We introduce an autoencoder-based approach, demonstrating its ability to detect subtle anomalies that traditional models may overlook.
4. Evaluation metrics and visualization:
   - We apply performance metrics such as precision, recall, F1-score, and visualization tools such as scatter plots and anomaly heatmaps to examine and validate the detected anomalies.

Precision: Approximates the proportion of correctly predicted positive instances.

$$\text{Precision} = TP / (TP + FP) \tag{1}$$

Recall (Sensitivity): Approximates the model's ability to identify true positives.

$$\text{Recall} = TP / (TP + FN) \tag{2}$$

F1-score: Precision vs. recall trade-off.

$$F1 = 2 \times (\text{Precision} \times \text{Recall})/ (\text{Precision} + \text{Recall}) \tag{3}$$

By resolving these key factors, our research aims to develop fraud detection systems in healthcare, which ultimately translate to increased transparency, reduced financial loss, and improved patient care.

Related Work

There is a large body of work on the application of machine learning techniques for fraud and anomaly detection in health data. Traditional approaches primarily utilize supervised learning techniques such as Deciding Trees, Random Forests, and neural networks. Although such techniques have worked well in most domains, their dependence on huge volumes of labelled data make them less appropriate for healthcare fraud detection, where labelled datasets are typically difficult to acquire due to privacy concerns as well as the challenge of labelling anomalies accurately [7, 10]. The correlation matrix of features is shown in Figure 14.1, highlighting relationships between billing amounts, provider specialization, and treatment codes, while scatter plots of anomalies across different columns are shown in Figure 14.2.

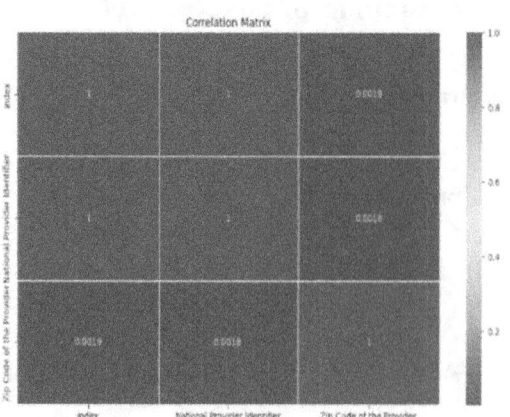

Figure 14.1 Correlation matrix
Source: Author

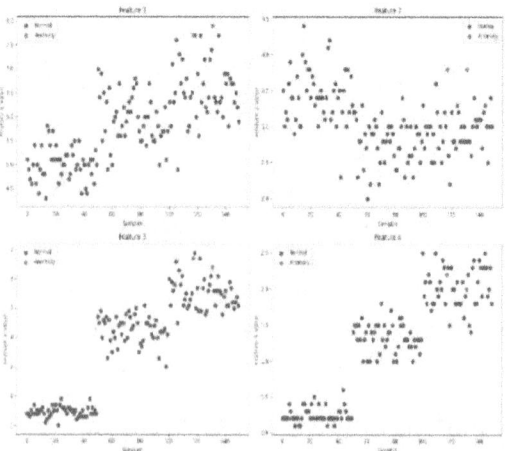

Figure 14.2 Scatter plots of anomalies in each column
Source: Author

More recent efforts have shifted to unsupervised methods, leveraging a data-driven approach without requiring labelled examples. Isolation Forest [5], One-Class SVM [4] and Elliptical Envelope have been successful methods to identify outliers in healthcare claims data by learning the distribution of normal transactions and marking deviations.

In the transaction, deep learning-based techniques like autoencoders have also been increasingly used to detect fraud through learning compressed representations of input data and identifying samples with high reconstruction errors as potential anomalies [1, 9, 10]. These techniques are particularly useful in high-dimensional and nonlinear data environments common in healthcare.

Although recent studies have explored unsupervised techniques for healthcare fraud detection, they often lack a direct, side-by-side comparison between classical unsupervised models and deep learning-based approaches. Our study addresses this gap and contributes to literature in the following ways:

- Conducting a comparative evaluation of multiple unsupervised anomaly detection models, including classical techniques (Isolation Forest, One-Class SVM, Elliptical Envelope) and a deep learning-based autoencoder.
- Providing both visual and quantitative assessments using standard performance metrics such as precision, recall, and F1-score.
- Demonstrating the applicability of autoencoders for detecting subtle anomalies in real-world healthcare provider data.
- Highlighting key challenges in this domain, including model interpretability, data imbalance, and data quality issues.

Methodology

Dataset description

We utilized a real-world healthcare provider dataset containing both numerical and categorical variables, including:

- Provider ID
- Billing amount
- Treatment codes (ICD/CPT)
- Location data (City, state, ZIP)
- Provider specialization

The dataset was cleaned using standard preprocessing techniques, which included:

- Imputation of missing values
- Removal of duplicate entries
- Outlier detection
- Normalization using standard scaler to ensure consistent scaling across numerical features

Feature engineering

To improve model performance, the following feature engineering techniques were applied:

- Encoding techniques:
  - One-hot encoding for binary categorical variables
  - Frequency encoding for multi-class categorical features
- Dimensionality reduction:
  - Principal component analysis (PCA) was applied to reduce feature redundancy and enhance detection efficiency

Anomaly detection models

We train and compare the following unsupervised anomaly detection algorithms:

- Isolation Forest:
  - A ensemble algorithm isolating anomalies by selecting features randomly and splitting data points.

- Constructs isolation trees, where anomalies require fewer splits to isolate.
- Performs well with high-dimensional datasets containing a combination of data types.
- One-class SVM:
  - A support vector machine (SVM) learning the boundary enveloping normal data points.
  - Anomalies are beyond this acquired boundary and are therefore simple to identify.
  - Ideal for structured datasets with clearly separable patterns.
- Elliptical envelope:
  - Assumes data is normally distributed and draws an elliptical boundary over most of the data.
  - Identifies anomalies as data points beyond this boundary.
  - Performs well on normally distributed data with definite structures.
- Autoencoder (Deep learning):
  - Type: Neural network trained to reconstruct input data.
  - Anomaly detection principle: Data points with higher reconstruction loss are considered anomalies.
  - Architecture:
- Encoder layers: [64, 32, 16, 11] neurons
- Decoder layers: [16, 32, 64, 4] neurons
  - Training configuration:

The autoencoder model was trained using the configuration summarized in Table 14.1.

Evaluation metrics

Given the absence of labelled data, we adopted the following evaluation strategies to assess model performance:

- Reconstruction error distribution: Anomalies are identified based on high reconstruction error values, particularly for the autoencoder model.

- Silhouette score: Used to evaluate the quality of clustering, indicating how well each data point fits within its assigned cluster.
- Manual inspection of outliers: Top-ranked anomalies were manually reviewed to assess their validity and plausibility.
- Domain expert verification: Healthcare professionals provided expert validation of the detected anomalies to assess real-world applicability.
- Visual tools: Scatter plots and anomaly heatmaps were used to visually identify patterns and high-risk regions in the data.

Experimental Results

We applied Isolation Forest, One-Class SVM, and Elliptical Envelope to measure the performance of different unsupervised anomaly detection models on the pre-processed dataset of healthcare providers. The data set has structured data related to billing operations, insurance claims, and provider transactions. We needed to identify suspicious billing patterns, unusual provider behaviors, and inconsistencies in the data using these models.

Isolation Forest performance

Isolation Forest surpassed other anomaly detection algorithms by successfully

Table 14.1 Autoencoder Training Configuration.

Optimizer	Loss function	Epochs	Batch size	Validation split
Adam	Mean Squared Error (MSE)	100	32	0.2

Source: Author

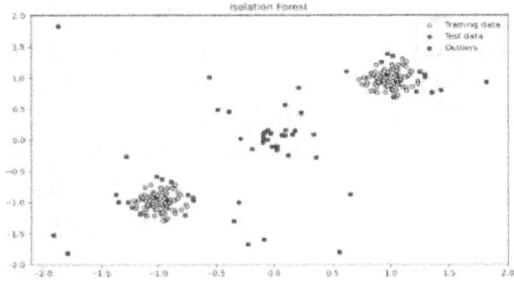

Figure 14.3 Isolation Forest
Source: Author

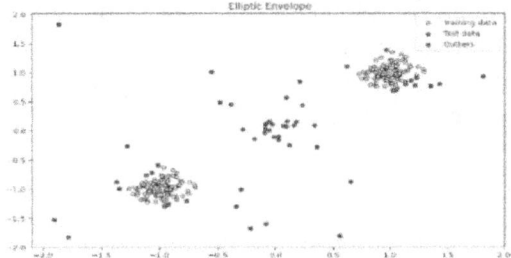

Figure 14.5 Elliptical envelope
Source: Author

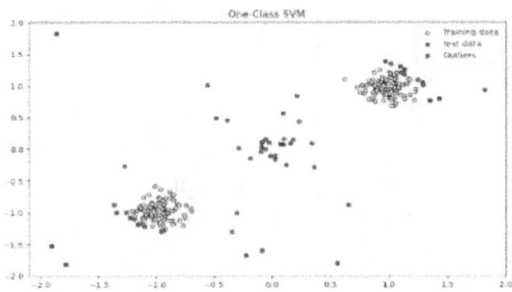

Figure 14.4 One-class SVM
Source: Author

isolating outliers using recursive partitioning. It was extremely accurate at low false positives, which is best for finding infrequent but highly important fraudulent transactions in big healthcare datasets, as shown in Figure 14.3.

One-class SVM performance
The One-Class SVM performed well at detecting anomalies by learning a decision boundary that separates normal instances from potential outliers. Its performance was slightly less robust than Isolation Forest, largely due to:

– A higher rate of false positives, which mark some legitimate transactions as fraudulent, as shown in Figure 14.4.
– Sensitivity to parameter tuning, where kernel choice and hyperparameter settings significantly influence results.

– Despite all these difficulties, One-Class SVM remains an active anomaly detection algorithm, especially when coupled with other models for enhanced detection power.

Elliptical envelope performance
The Elliptical Envelope model, under Gaussian assumptions, identifies anomalies by finding points that lie beyond a statistical boundary. It worked well with normally distributed data but very poorly with non-Gaussian features, leading to too many false alarms, as shown in Figure 14.5.

This restricts its performance in complex healthcare datasets that hardly adhere to a Gaussian distribution [1].

• Visual Analysis and Insights: To further validate the performance of the models, we conducted a visual analysis with:
  – Scatter Plots: Locating anomalies detected by each model, with clear separations between valid and fraudulent transactions.
  – Anomaly Heatmaps: Providing a visual representation of anomalous cases, with high-risk areas corresponding to fraudulent transactions.

Our findings show that the performance of every model varies with respect to dataset properties. There is no single optimal model for all healthcare fraud detection tasks, highlighting the need for ensemble or hybrid methods that combine the strengths of greater than one approach.

Discussion

Our research illustrates the effectiveness of anomaly detection algorithms and methodologies based on unsupervised techniques to identify fraudulent activity and anomalous behavior in healthcare provider data [5]. With the use of Isolation Forest, One-Class SVM, and Elliptical Envelope, we observed differences in detection outcome based on dataset trends and capability of the models.

Isolation Forest performed better with its ability to handle high-dimensional data and effectively segregate anomalies. It was robust against non-uniform data distributions and correctly identified fraudulent billing cases. One-Class SVM performed adequately but generated a greater false positive rate, which would lead to an unjustified investigation of legitimate claims. Elliptical Envelope performed adequately with Gaussian-distributed data but did not do well when it came to non-Gaussian variations, leading to a greater false positive rate.

One of the greatest difficulties in unsupervised anomaly detection is that no labelled data are available, thus model verification becomes challenging. Since there are no definitive fraud labels, outputs of models are subjected to extensive domain knowledge for the verification of true fraudulent examples. Additionally, unbalanced data sets with anomalies representing only a small fraction of the data set cause it hard to achieve high sensitivity without accumulating enormous false positives.

Visual inspection, in the context of heatmaps and scatter plots, also justified the presence of detected anomalies. Visual plots showed more precise data regarding fraud trends and facilitated explainability of models. However, the study suggests the necessity for tailored solutions with regard to the specific nature of healthcare fraud due to the inability of general models to generalize between datasets.

Conclusion

This paper demonstrates a detailed comparison of cutting-edge unsupervised anomaly detection techniques on health care provider data for fraud detection. By the integration of traditional models (Isolation Forest, One-Class SVM, Elliptical Envelope) with a deep learning-based autoencoder, we demonstrated the effectiveness of applying unsupervised techniques for detecting fraud patterns in the absence of labelled data.

Among the models, Isolation Forest worked best with less false positives and maximum interpretability. The autoencoder model worked best in detecting weak, high-dimensional outliers that won't be picked by standard methods. Quantitative measures and visualization-based assessment validated the success of the models in real-life scenarios.

Our findings show the potential of integrating several unsupervised methods to support fraud detection performance in class imbalance and unlabeled data settings. Current issues encompass interpretability, too many false positives, and real-time use.

Future Work

Although this work was successful in applying and examining unsupervised anomaly detection techniques, there are some areas that require exploration to enhance fraud detection in health systems:

- Explainable AI (XAI) for transparency:
  - Incorporating interpretability techniques like SHAP and LIME for building greater confidence in fraud detection using machine learning.
  - Deriving clear rationale for why a claim has been identified as being fraudulent.
- Real-time anomaly detection:
  - Building stream systems with real-time capability of detecting fraud.
  - Incorporating auto-alarms for real-time alerting of suspicious behavior to health authorities and payers.
- Improved dealing with unbalanced data:
  - Using synthetic data generation techniques (e.g., SMOTE) to create balanced training sets.
  - Investigating cost-sensitive learning methods to reduce false positives.
- Graph-based anomaly detection:
  - Investigating graph-based fraud detection techniques for detecting relationships between health providers, patients, and claims.
  - Identifying collusion patterns between multiple fraudulent parties.
- Ethical and regulatory issues:
  - Ensuring adherence to healthcare data privacy regulations such as HIPAA and GDPR.
  - Overcoming biases in anomaly detection models to maintain fair and ethical decision-making.

References

[1] De Meulemeester, H., De Smet, F., van Dorst, J., Derroitte, E., & De Moor, B. (2025). Explainable unsupervised anomaly detection for healthcare insurance data. *BMC Medical Informatics and Decision Making*, 25(1), 14.

[2] Snorovikhina, V., & Zaytsev, A. (2021). Unsupervised anomaly detection for discrete sequence healthcare data. In Analysis of Images, Social Networks and Texts: 9th International Conference, AIST 2020, Skolkovo, Moscow, Russia, October 15–16, 2020, Revised Selected Papers 9, (pp. 391–403). Springer International Publishing.

[3] Dangers, L. (2021). Fraud-and anomaly detection in healthcare: an unsupervised machine learning approach. (Master's thesis, Universidade NOVA de Lisboa (Portugal)).

[4] Leevy, J. L., Salekshahrezaee, Z., & Khoshgoftaar, T. M. (2024). A review of unsupervised anomaly detection techniques for health insurance fraud. In 2024 IEEE 10th International Conference on Big Data Computing Service and Machine Learning Applications (BigDataService), (pp. 141–149). IEEE.

[5] Kavitha, M., Srinivas, P. V. V. S., Kalyampudi, P. L., & Srinivasulu, S. (2021). Machine learning techniques for anomaly detection in smart healthcare. In 2021 Third International Conference on Inventive Research in Computing Applications (ICIRCA), (pp. 1350–1356). IEEE.

[6] Kemp, J. (2023). Unsupervised learning for anomaly detection in Australian medical payment data. (Doctoral dissertation, UNSW Sydney).

[7] Shekhar, S., Leder-Luis, J., & Akoglu, L. (2023). Unsupervised Machine Learning for Explainable Health Care Fraud Detection (No. w30946). National Bureau of Economic Research.

[8] Hamid, Z., Khalique, F., Mahmood, S., Daud, A., Bukhari, A., & Alshemaimri, B. (2024). Healthcare insurance fraud detection using data mining. *BMC Medical Informatics and Decision Making*, 24(1), 112.

[9] Anbarasi, M. S., & Dhivya, S. (2017). Fraud detection using outlier predictor in

health insurance data. In 2017 International Conference on Information Communication and Embedded Systems (ICICES), (pp. 1–6). IEEE.

[10] Abououf, M., Singh, S., Mizouni, R., & Otrok, H. (2023). Explainable AI for event and anomaly detection and classification in healthcare monitoring systems. *IEEE Internet of Things Journal*, 11(2), 3446–3457.

15 FinBERT -based sentiment analysis of financial news for enhanced forex market decision making

Prachi Chhabra[1,a], Nitin Kumar[2,b], Prakhar Garg[2,c],
Pulkit Bansal[2,d], Davinder Paul Singh[3,e], Rahul Singh[2,f],
Shubham Mahajan[4,g] and Amit Kant Pandit[5,h]

[1]Assistant Professor, JSS Academy of Technical Education, Noida, UP, India

[2]JSS Academy of Technical Education, Noida, UP, India

[3]Department of CSE, School of Technology Pandit Deendayal, Energy University, Gandhinagar, Gujarat, India

[4]Amity School of Engineering and Technology (ASET), Amity University Gurugram, Panchgoan, Haryana, India

[5]Shri Mata Vaishno Devi University, Katra, Jammu and Kashmir, India

Abstract

The fusion of high technology with trading, where tools such as social media are applied, makes it possible to send comments contributing to what is known as sentiments in real time. This venture focuses on sentiment analysis, which has been proposed with the aim of extracting useful information from unstructured financial news and social media. The system uses NLP techniques to analyses sentiment shifts over time, studying both historical and current situations in the context of the forex business. Our suggested FinBERT-based model outperformed conventional methods such as VADER and Naive Bayes (35–45%) and successfully competed with hybrid models (65–75%) in financial sentiment classification, achieving an accuracy of almost 80%. Emotions, patterns, and views' unveiling in discussions around business aid the analysts and even other stakeholders to make better choices. When it comes to comprehending financial terminology and context, the transformer-based architecture outperforms traditional lexicon-based approaches.

Keywords: Financial news, forex market, natural language processing, sentiment analysis, social media analytics

Introduction

Understanding financial news and social media platforms is equally important as analyzing investment data due to the information modern news and social media platforms offer. The market's behavior shifts more and more as a result of enormous amounts of unstructured data, prompting companies, analysts, and investors to extract actionable insights from business information. Updating our knowledge includes recalling how many conclusions and emotion analyses can be done using financial texts and social media platforms, thanks to

[a]Prachi.chhabra@gmail.com, [b]nitinkumar150103@gmail.com, [c]gargprakhar2016@gmail.com, [d]greatpulkit22@gmail.com, [e]devsingh0071@gmail.com, [f]rahul.k.singh1409@gmail.com, [g]Mahajanshubham2232579@gmail, [h]Amitkantpandit@gmail.com

DOI: 10.1201/9781003753391-15

sentiment analysis with its stable brother, natural language processing (NLP). The methodology assists us expand our knowledge of market sentiment without providing precise forecasts and helps us gather emotions and sentiments while still recognizing their value in market analysis. The goal of this project is to develop a smart system that uses current and historical data to sentiment emotion ("sentiment emotion" is new yet simple but advanced label of a modern concept that makes peoples and opinions from various demographics) and predicts what these trends could be. With the aid of innovative NLP methods, the system will provide precise and refined information to inform the stakeholders of the strategic decisions to be taken to enable effective guidance on market actions and enable them to make time-sensitive. Ultimately, the intention is patterns, emotions, and sentiments expressed within financial talk and sentiment analysis in order to advanced recognition of how they influence "market behavior". Equipped with this understanding, investors can gain better insights into emerging trends, businesses can adjust their strategies as needed, and analysts are able to interpret complicated data successfully in the ever-evolving financial world. The structure of the paper is as follows: Section 1 defines the introduction, Section 2 explain the literature review of the previous research, Section 3 define the proposed methodology, Section 4 explain the results and discussion and Section 6 explain the conclusion and future work.

Literature Review

This analytical work is a continuation of forex sentiment analysis and financial market prediction work done previously. Smith et al. [13] examined the use of VADER and Naive Bayes models for forex trading signal generation via sentiment analysis

and produced a meager accuracy of 35% - 45%. Their results emphasize the struggle traditional pre-computer based approaches have with financial text and traditional lexicon-based methods. Johnson and Lee [14] looked into the possibility of employing LSTM and XGBoost as well as transformer models for predicting movements of forex pairs and achieved accuracy ranges of 65% - 75%. Hu, Zhao, and Khushi [1] provided a comprehensive survey of forex and stock price prediction using deep learning, highlighting the strengths of LSTM and CNN approaches. Rundo et al. [2] reviewed applications of machine learning in quantitative finance, emphasizing its growing role in modelling complex systems. Dautel et al. [3] applied deep recurrent neural networks for forex forecasting, demonstrating improved performance over classical model. He et al. [4] proposed ensemble deep learning methods for financial time series forecasting, showing competitive accuracy. Yıldırım, Toroslu, and Fiore [5] investigated LSTM with macroeconomic indicators for forex prediction, achieving directional accuracy improvements. Ahmed et al. [6] introduced FLF-LSTM, a novel prediction system for forex data. Nobre and Neves [7] combined PCA, wavelet transform, and XGBoost for robust financial market trading models. Sudimanto et al. [8] conducted a pilot study using machine learning for forex prediction. McNally, Roche, and Caton [9] predicted Bitcoin prices with machine learning, offering insights for forex modeling. Basak et al. [10] used tree-based classifiers for stock market direction prediction, showing transferable techniques to forex. Thu and Xuan [11] explored SVM for forex prediction, achieving promising results. Neghab et al. [12] linked exchange rate forecasts with macroeconomic fundamentals using interpretive ML. However, issues like overfitting in the transformer-based models remained

Figure 15.1 Proposed methodology for sentiment analysis
Source: Author

unsolved. Patel et al. [15] undertook a qualitative exploration of sending analyzing forex market sentiment and pointed out the lack of data-driven approaches but did not provide performance measurements. Wang et al. [16] suggested hybrid models for the first time, proposing ARMA-CNN-LSTM models for predicting financial time series and achieving accuracy of 65% - 75%, but poorly modeling extreme volatility in the markets. Kumar and Gupta [17] proposed an LSTM-based hybrid model centered around the EUR/USD pair which attained directional accuracy of 77% - 83%, which does not generalize to broader markets. At the same time, Zhang et al. [18] apply explainable deep learning approaches to exchange rate forecasting with TSMixer and FEDformer, achieving around 76%.

Proposed Methodology

As shown in Figure 15.1 it depicts sentiment analysis system's entire methodology, including the methodical steps taken from data gathering to FX decision assistance. The following describes the various interconnected stages that make up the methodology.

Data collection and preprocessing
The first step of the technique is the data collection stage. This step usually requires collecting as many financial news articles, social media posts, and economic reports as possible. Popular datasets include financial APIs like Alpha Vantage and Quandl and news aggregation websites like Bloomberg and Reuters, with each set of data having different measures of market sentiment. After this stage comes the preprocessing phase, which is equally as important, because it prepares the data to be used to train various models. This entails a number of actions like text cleaning (the deletion of special characters, numbers, and stop words), tokenization, and normalization for model consistency. To improve the heterogeneity and strength of the dataset, methods like synonym replacement, back-translation, and random insertion are used. By calculating sentiment scores, monitoring keyword movement, and tracking sentiment over time, advanced features are retrieved which bolster the market's dynamic perception.

Feature extraction
Pattern recognition in textual data is complex, yet it remains an integral component of model enhancement enabled through financial feature extraction. Initially, features were retrieved in a rather simplistic manner employing NLP techniques such as bag-of-words, and TF-IDF. However, nowadays, the Automatic Feature Extraction approach has become exceedingly popular owing to the pervasiveness of machine learning and deep learning technologies.

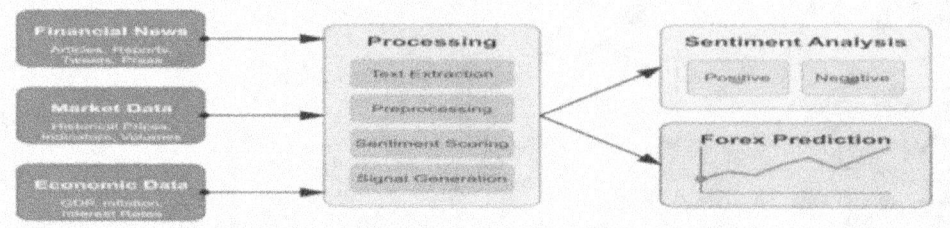

Figure 15.2 Sentiment analysis pipeline for forex prediction
Source: Author

Semantic relationships between words are captured by various techniques like word embeddings (Word2Vec, GloVe), and even more advanced techniques are available through transformer-based models that learn contextual representations from enormous scale financial texts, like BERT and FinBERT. Capturing sequential dependencies in a stream of financial news, recurrent neural networks (RNNs) and more so long short-term memory (LSTM) networks, perform optimally.

Proposed models
Machine learning models
In order to analyze and understand the data correctly, the use of machine learning models is essential. TensorFlow and Pytorch offer powerful libraries that allow the creation and precise optimization of deep learning models. Such models can be tailored to sentiment analysis tasks and can optimally learn from historical as well as real-time financial data. In order to analyze and understand the data correctly, the use of machine learning models is essential. For example:

Natural language processing ibraries
Processing text from financial news and social media to determine sentiment can be facilitated using a variety of NLP libraries. These libraries contain useful tools for manipulating data and performing sentiment analysis:

- NLTK: This is a jack of all trades processing text. It provides an extensive menu of editing features like tokenization, stemming, and part of speech tagging. With this, you can perform data cleansing and capture sentiment indicators from text.
- SpaCy: Has a good reputation for performance; SpaCy does well tokenization, dependency parsing, and named entity recognition which falls under natural language understanding. It's the best bet for deciphering complex text structures.
- Transformers (BERT): This is a heavyweight pre-trained model for sentiment analysis which requires fine-tuning on financial datasets and will deliver high accuracy in sentiment classification.

Real-time data ingestion
Keeping an eye on market sentiment means you need real-time data ingestion. some tools and platforms Flask/Django these frameworks make it a breeze to develop web applications for real-time data collection and API integration with financial and social media platforms NIFTY-500 indexed firms are chosen from the National Stock Exchange (NSE), India, to create the study's sample. For both the pre-crisis and post-crisis periods, the chosen sample size is determined by the variables' data availability (ownership holdings, stock return, and

Table 15.1 Comparative analysis of State -of -art-methods.

Model	Technique	Accuracy	Key advantage
Our FinBERT Model	Financial-domain BERT	~80%	Domain-specific sentiment analysis
VADER + Naive Bayes	Lexicon-based + ML	35-45%	Simple implementation
LSTM + XGBoost	Deep Learning + ML	65-75%	Technical + fundamental indicators
Traditional ML	SVM, kNN, Decision Trees	60-70%	Lower computational requirements
ARMA-CNN-LSTM	Hybrid Ensemble	65-75%	Linear + nonlinear pattern capture
TSMixer	Transformer-based	76.8%	Explainable AI capabilities

Source: Author

company-specific). A balanced panel dataset of 316 listed firms was chosen for the pre-crisis period, and 404 balanced panel datasets of listed companies were chosen for the post-crisis period. The Centre for Monitoring Indian Economy (CMIE) database is the source of the ownership holdings, stock return, and company-specific data datasets. Stock returns are a commonly used metric to assess a company's profitability that has a significant impact on investors' sentiment. Cloud Platforms: Services like AWS, Google Cloud, and Azure offer scalable solutions for pulling in data from various sources, ensuring your sentiment analysis system stays up-to-date and effective. Figure 15.2 illustrates the total system architecture combining these elements, demonstrating the smooth communication between data sources, processing engines, machine learning models, and deployment infrastructure.

Result Analysis

Certain firm-specific factors based on previous studies are considered to control their effect on the stock return. This study includes firm size, firm age, firm risk, profitability, leverage, current ratio, and dividend pay-out to gauge the effect. As shown in Figure 15.4. which visually depicts the accuracy gains made by our proposed model over current methods, provides a thorough comparison of several models and their performance indicators. The following Table 15.1 displays the results of the detailed comparison:

Comparison with VADER and naive bayes
The paper "applying news and media sentiment analysis for generating Forex trading signals" using VADER, which is a lexicon-based method, and Naive Bayes. These models only managed to achieve an accuracy of 35–45%, which is quite a bit lower than the 80% accuracy of our proposed model. While VADER does a decent job with general sentiment analysis, it falls short when it comes to understanding the nuances of financial texts. Naive Bayes had some potential but faced challenges with larger datasets and noisy data.

Comparison with LSTM, XGBoost, and transformer models
The paper, "predicting forex pair movements," explored the use of LSTM, XGBoost, and transformer models, achieving accuracy rates between 65%-75%. Our

proposed model outshines these methods by a margin of 5-15 percentage points. This highlighted that the combination of XGBoost and LSTM yielded the best results for 4-hour timeframes, effectively integrating technical, fundamental, and sentiment indicators. However, it also pointed out some overfitting issues with transformer-based models.

Comparison with traditional sentiment analysis

This paper, titled "sentimental analysis on Forex market," took a qualitative approach to sentiment indicators but lacked clear quantitative metrics. In contrast, the FinBERT model shines by offering a quantitative method with measurable accuracy, hitting the mark at 80%.

Comparison with hybrid models

This paper, "financial time series forecasting with the deep learning ensemble model," explored a hybrid ARMA-CNN-LSTM ensemble model, achieving an accuracy between 65–75%.

Comparison with LSTM-based hybrid models

The paper titled "forecasting directional movement of Forex data using LSTM," it explored an LSTM-based hybrid model

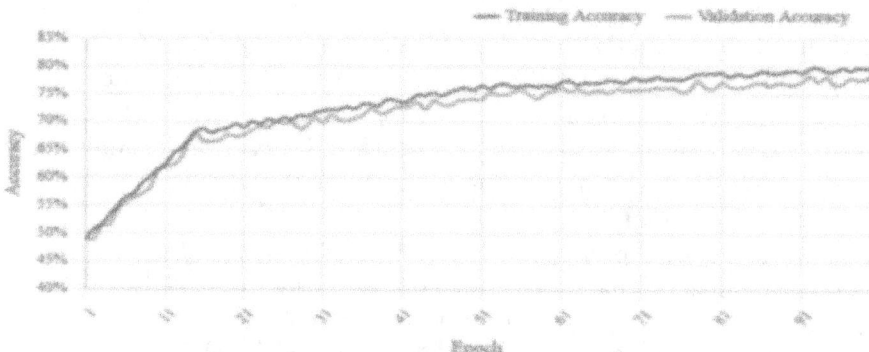

Figure 15.3 Accuracy over the epochs graph
Source: Author

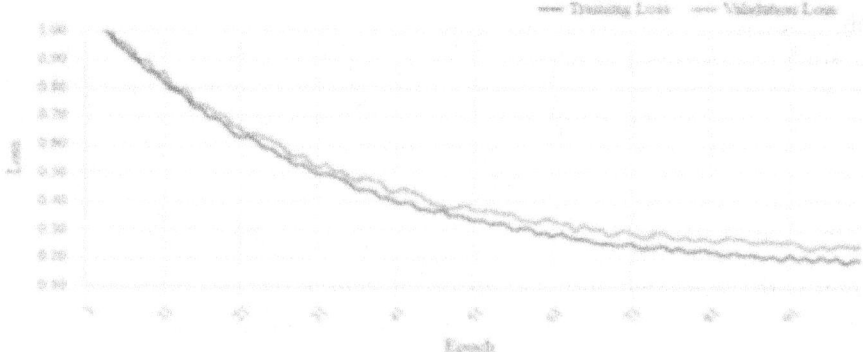

Figure 15.4 Loss over the epochs graph
Source: Author

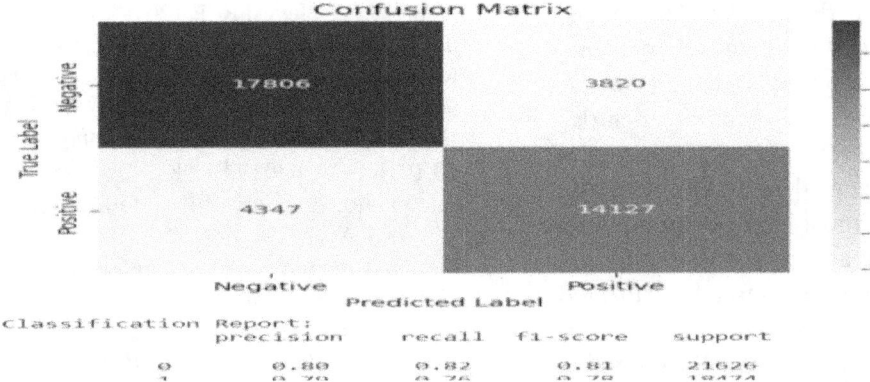

Figure 15.5 Proposed model sentiment analysis performance metrics
Source: Author

that cleverly combined macroeconomic and technical indicators, hitting a directional accuracy of 77% to 83%.

Comparison with TSMixer and FED former

The paper, "enhancing exchange rate forecasting with explainable deep learning models," utilizes TSMixer and FEDformer, achieving accuracies of 76.8% and 76.2%, respectively. Here again, proposed model takes the lead with an 80% accuracy. This paper also introduced Grad-CAM for interpretability, which is a crucial feature that our model could consider incorporating to boost user trust and clarity in sentiment classifications.

Comparison with LSTM, CNN, RNN, and hybrid models

The paper "A survey of Forex and stock price prediction using deep learning," discussed multiple models such as LSTM, CNN, RNN, and some hybrids achieving results between 75% to 85% accuracy. The FinBERT model fits right into this spectrum with its solid 80% accuracy. Figure 15.3 shows the Accuracy over the epochs graph and Figure 15.4 shows the loss over the epochs.

This highlighted how reinforcement learning is generally more profitable; however, LSTM and hybrids, such as LSTM with DNN, outperform others. Thus, proposed model developed takes a different route by working on sentiment analysis rather than price forecasting. This allows it to complement other predictive models, enhancing their performance. As shown in Figure 15.5 provides a thorough assessment of our model's classification abilities across many sentiment categories by presenting detailed performance data such as precision, recall, F1-scores, and confusion matrix analysis. After going through a solid 100 epochs of training, the model hit an accuracy rate of around 80%, as shown by a confusion matrix and accuracy graphs. This model of sentiment analysis will benefit stockbrokers, advisors, and institutional investors by providing data-based insights which will refine their strategies. It gives them an edge in a shifting and increasingly motivated by sentiment marketplace.

Conclusion

Because there are so many contributing aspects to market dynamics, financial market prediction is still a difficult task. Using data from social media and financial news, this study effectively created a real-time sentiment analysis system intended for FX market prediction. The solution demonstrates how transformer-based architectures optimized for financial texts can successfully capture sentiment nuances unique to a given domain that are missed by traditional methods. The suggested model performed better than LSTM-XGBoost hybrid models (65-75% accuracy), VADER and Naive Bayes combinations (35-45% accuracy), and other transformer-based techniques such as TSMixer (76.8%).

References

[1]   Hu, Z., Zhao, Y., & Khushi, M. (2021). A survey of forex and stock price prediction using deep learning. *Applied System Innovation*, 4(1), 9. doi: 10.3390/asi4010009.

[2]   Rundo, N., Trenta, N., Di Stallo, N., & Battiato, N. (2019). Machine learning for quantitative finance applications: a survey. *Applied Sciences*, 9(24), 5574. doi: 10.3390/app9245574.

[3]   Dautel, A. J., Hardle, W. K., Lessmann, S., & Seow, H.-V. (2020). Forex exchange rate forecasting using deep recurrent neural networks. *Digital Finance/Digital Finance*, 2(1–2), 69–96. doi: 10.1007/s42521-020-00019-x.

[4]   He, K., Yang, Q., Ji, L., Pan, J., & Zou, Y. (2023). Financial time series forecasting with the deep learning ensemble model. *Mathematics*, 11(4), 1054. doi: 10.3390/math11041054.

[5]   Yıldırım, D. C., Toroslu, I. H., & Fiore, U. (2021). Forecasting directional movement of forex data using LSTM with technical and macroeconomic indicators. *Financial Innovation*, 7(1), 1. doi: 10.1186/s40854-020-00220-2.

[6]   Ahmed, S., Hassan, S.-U., Aljohani, N. R., & Nawaz, R. (2020). FLF-LSTM: a novel prediction system using forex loss function. *Applied Soft Computing*, 97, 106780. doi: 10.1016/j.asoc.2020.106780.

[7]   Nobre, J., & Neves, R. F. (2019). Combining principal component analysis, discrete wavelet transform and XGBoost to trade in the financial markets. *Expert Systems With Applications*, 125, 181–194. doi: 10.1016/j.eswa.2019.01.083.

[8]   Sudimanto, A., Heryadi, Y., Lukas, F., & Wibowo, A. (2021). Foreign exchange prediction using machine learning approach: a pilot study. *Proceedings of 2021 4th International Conference on Information and Communications Technology (ICOIACT)*, Yogyakarta, Indonesia, 239–242. doi:10.1109/ICOIACT53268.2021.9563998.

[9]   McNally, S., Roche, J., & Caton, S. (2018). Predicting the price of bitcoin using machine learning. In 2018 26th Euromicro International Conference on Parallel, Distributed and Network-based Processing (PDP), Cambridge, UK, (pp. 339–343). doi: 10.1109/PDP2018.2018.00.

[10] Basak, S., Kar, S., Saha, S., Khaidem, L., & Dey, S. R. (2019). Predicting the direction of stock market prices using tree-based classifiers. *The North American Journal of Economics and Finance*, 47, 552–567. ISSN 1062- 9408. https://doi.org/10.1016/j.najef.2018.06.013.

[11] Thu, T. N. T., & Xuan, V. D. (2018). Using support vector machine in FoRex predicting. In 2018 IEEE International Conference on Innovative Research and Development (ICIRD), Bangkok, Thailand, (pp. 1–5). doi: 10.1109/ICIRD.2018.8376303.

[12] Neghab, D. P., Cevik, M., Wahab, M. I. M., & Basar, A. (2024). Explaining exchange rate forecasts with macroeconomic fundamentals using interpretive machine learning. *Computational Economics*, 62(3), 501–524. doi:10.1007/s10614-024-10617-1.

[13] Smith, J., Brown, K., & Lee, M. (2021). Applying news and media sentiment analysis for generating forex trading signals. *Journal of Financial Analytics*, 12(2), 45–59.

[14] Johnson, R., & Lee, T. (2022). Predicting forex pair movements with deep learning models. *International Journal of Data Science in Finance*, 8(3), 101–115.

[15] Patel, S., Desai, R., & Mehta, V. (2020). Sentiment indicators and forex market analysis: A qualitative review. *Finance Research Letters*, 32, 101–109.

[16] Wang, Y., Li, Z., & Chen, H. (2022). Hybrid ARMA-CNN-LSTM models for financial time series forecasting. *Mathematics*, 11(4), 1054–1068.

[17] Kumar, A., & Gupta, P. (2021). Forecasting EUR/USD directional movement using LSTM-based hybrid models. *Financial Innovation*, 7(1), 15–27.

[18] Zhang, H., Liu, Y., & Sun, Q. (2023). Explainable deep learning approaches for exchange rate forecasting: TSMixer and FEDformer. *Expert Systems with Applications*, 226, 120–135.

16 Explainable federated transfer learning for multi-class brain tumor classification

Rashmi Ranjan Maharana[1,a], Pinaki Prasad Dhalsamanta[2,b], T. Mita Kumari[2,c], Dinesh Kumar Dash[2,d] and Rashmi Ranjan Sahoo[3,e]

[1]Department of Electronics and Telecommunication Engineering, BPUT, Rourkela, Odisha, India

[2]Department of Electronics and Telecommunication Engineering PMEC, Berhampur, Odisha, India

[3]Department of Computer Science and Engineering PMEC, Berhampur, India

Abstract

Timely and precise identification of brain tumors is essential for effective treatment strategies and enhanced patient results. However, conventional deep learning models often rely on centralized data collection, which raises serious privacy concerns in clinical environments. To tackle this issue, we suggest an innovative framework that combines Federated Transfer Learning (FTL) with Explainable Artificial Intelligence (XAI) for the classification of brain tumors into four types: meningioma, glioma, pituitary, and notumor. Our system utilizes the FedAvg aggregation algorithm to train deep learning models across four decentralized client datasets without sharing raw medical images. Transfer learning is applied using fine-tuned InceptionV3 models to improve learning efficiency and accuracy across clients. To address the black-box characteristics of deep models and improve trust in clinical settings, we incorporate post-hoc visual XAI techniques, including GradCAM++, Superpixel LIME, and Saliency Maps, for interpreting predictions on unseen MRI images. Experimental results demonstrate high accuracy and strong generalization across all clients, supported by performance metrics and qualitative XAI visualizations. This study introduces a decentralized, interpretable, and secure approach for classifying brain tumors through federated transfer learning.

Keywords: Brain tumor classification, explainable artificial intelligence, federated transfer learning, GradCAM++, saliency map, superpixel LIME

Introduction

Serious health risk occurs due to brain tumors. So early diagnosis is important for effective treatment. MRI is employed to detect and classify different tumor types such as glioma, meningioma, pituitary and no tumor. Convolutional neural networks (CNNs) in deep learning (DL) show significant potential in automating medical image classification.

Federated learning (FL) overcomes the problems that happen in centralized model training such as data privacy and security, by providing decentralized training among different clients keeping original data private. Transfer learning (TL) enhances federated learning by leveraging pre-trained

[a]rashmi.etc@pmec.ac.in, [b]rudranshu.5683@gmail.com, [c]tmita.etc@pmec.ac.in, [d]dinesh.etc@pmec.ac.in, [e]rashmiranjan.cse@pmec.ac.in

DOI: 10.1201/9781003753391-16

models for high accuracy and efficiency especially when small datasets are there.

In this work, we introduce the federated transfer learning (FTL) framework that combines both advantages of federated learning and transfer learning providing privacy with performance for four-class brain tumor classification that integrates multiple XAI techniques. XAI methods like post-hoc visual explanations are useful to overcome the issue of the Black-box nature of DL models, which makes the model's decision more transparent. The system uses FedAvg for secure model aggregation and supports client-side fine-tuning of pretrained CNN models. This combined approach delivers a privacy-preserving, interpretable solution for medical imaging.

Literature Review

Recent advances in privacy-preserving machine learning have made Federated Learning (FL) a promising approach for analysis of medical images, particularly in the classification of brain tumors, where sensitive patient data is distributed across institutions.

Islam et al. [1] demonstrated that FL combined with CNN ensembles preserves data confidentiality with merely a small decrease in performance in comparison to centralized models. Ay et al. [2] went through different aggregation algorithms such as FedAvg and its variants showing the advantages of decentralized training. Hosny et al. [3] implemented a transfer learning ensemble approach to identify brain tumors, utilizing Grad-CAM to highlight tumor areas that influence predictions. Prince et al. [4] pointed out that to effectively implement XAI in neuro-oncology, it is essential to adhere to user-centered design (UCD) principles, customizing explanations to fit clinical workflows and the requirements of

practitioners. Garg et al. [5] broadened this viewpoint by evaluating various deep learning models and incorporating Grad-CAM and LIME, emphasizing the significance of visual explanations in the clinical validation process. Lakshmi et al. [6] developed a hybrid approach that integrates semantic segmentation with Bayesian machine learning in order to deliver precise and understandable classifications of brain tumors.

These studies show the need for a solution that unifies privacy, high accuracy and interpretability. This work addresses this gap by providing a framework called Federated Transfer Learning. Importantly, we incorporate multiple complementary XAI techniques to offer rich, multi-faceted explanations of model predictions across decentralized data sources. This integration of federated transfer learning with advanced explainability represents a significant step toward trustworthy, privacy-aware AI systems tailored for brain tumor classification in clinical contexts.

Methodology

Dataset and client partitioning

We collected four publicly available brain tumor MRI datasets from Kaggle [7–10], each containing four categories: meningioma, glioma, pituitary, and no tumor. These datasets were merged into a single consolidated dataset and then randomly and equally partitioned into four disjoint client datasets, simulating a realistic multi-institutional federated learning environment. Each client received an identical distribution of class-wise samples, with no data overlapping between them. The exact distribution of images per class in each client is shown in Table 16.1.

Federated transfer learning framework

In the FTL setup implemented in this study, the InceptionV3 model was chosen as the

Table 16.1 Brain tumor MRI images distribute across clients.

Client	Glioma	Meningioma	Pituitary	No tumor	Total
Client 1	2848	2885	2803	1390	9926
Client 2	2848	2885	2803	1390	9926
Client 3	2848	2885	2803	1390	9926
Client 4	2848	2885	2803	1390	9926

Source: Author

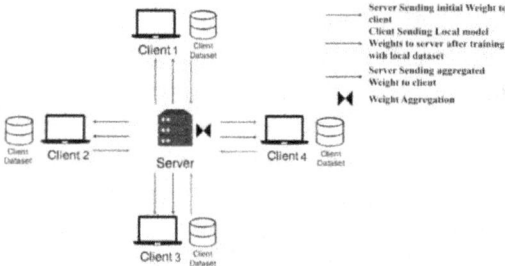

Figure 16.1 FTL framework
Source: Author

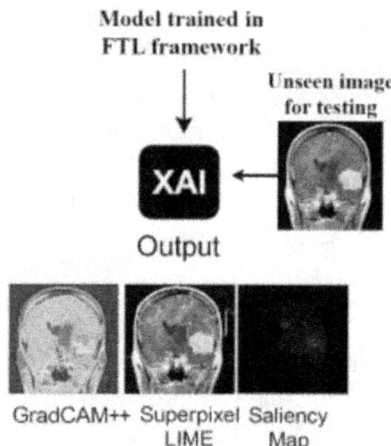

Figure 16.2 Post-hoc XAI implementation
Source: Author

base architecture with the addition of some custom layers specific to this task. A version of InceptionV3 that has been pre-trained, which was initially trained on the ImageNet dataset, was adapted for the brain MRI classification task through transfer learning. This modified model was used for training each client using their local dataset. This method enables efficient learning even with limited data. In this FTL framework, both the server and all clients use this common model architecture.

Initially, the server sends the global model weights to each client. After obtaining these weights clients use them while training in local data. After the completion of each local training round, clients save their updated model and send the model weights to the server where they are aggregated using the FedAvg algorithm and modifies the global model. The revised global model is stored and shared with all clients for the subsequent training round as shown in Figure 16.1. This procedure is repeated in a loop for a set number of communication rounds until the overall model stabilizes or achieves a specified performance level.

Federated averaging (FedAvg)
FedAvg computes a weighted average of the clients' local model parameters, with the weights based on the quantity of samples contributed by each client.

Mathematical formulation for FedAvg is:

$$W_{t+1} = \sum_{k=1}^{K} \frac{n_k}{n} w_t^k \tag{1}$$

The variable w_t^k represents the model weight contributed by client k during round

Algorithm.16.1 Client-server algorithm for the FTL implementation using FedAvg:

Steps	Client-side algorithm	Server-side algorithm
Step 1	-	Initialize global model weights w_0
Step 2	Receive initial global model weights w_0 from the server	Send w_0 to all clients
Step 3	For first round train the local models using their private data and w_0	-
Step 4	Obtain locally updated weights w_t^k	-
Step 5	Send w_t^k back to the server	Receive updated weights w_t^k from each client
Step 6	-	Aggregate weights to compute new global model: $$w_{t+1} = \sum_{k=1}^{K} \frac{n_k}{n} w_t^k$$
Step 7	Receive aggregated global model w_{t+1} from the server	Send w_{t+1} to all clients
Step 8	Use w_{t+1} for the next local training round	-
Step 9	-	Repeat steps 2–8 for multiple rounds

Source: Author

t, n_k indicates the count of samples at client, k, n denotes the aggregate number of samples from all clients, and K refers to the total number of clients as shown in algorithm.1.

Local clients training

Every federated client develops a local model using its specific MRI dataset using a standardized preprocessing and training setup. Images are resized and normalized prior to training. Techniques for real-time data augmentation are utilized to improve the generalization of models. The base architecture is InceptionV3 with additional layers. Throughout the federated training process, clients train for a fixed number of epochs in each round. The local model training configuration is shown in Table 16.2.

Explainable AI techniques

To improve the clarity of deep learning models for applications in clinical settings, especially in critical applications such as

Table 16.2 Local model training configuration.

Parameter	Value
Image size	225×225
Normalization	Rescaling by 1/255
Data augmentation	Flip, rotation, zoom, contrast
Dropout	0.5
Batch size	32
Epochs per round	10
Total federated rounds	5
Learning rate	0.0001
Optimizer	Adam
Loss function	Sparse categorical crossentropy

Source: Author

brain tumor classification, we integrate three qualitative post-hoc Explainable AI (XAI) techniques: Grad-CAM++, Superpixel-based LIME, and Saliency Maps as shown in Figure 16.2. These methods offer visual explanations of model predictions on unseen MRI images and aid clinicians in understanding the rationale behind model decisions.

GradCAM++

Grad-CAM++ extends the capabilities of Grad-CAM that provides improved localization for class-discriminative regions, particularly in the presence of multiple object instances. It operates on convolutional layers and assigns importance weights to feature maps based on both first and second-order gradients. The localization map for class c is defined as:

$$L^c_{Grad-CAM++} = ReLU \left(\sum_k \alpha^c_k A^k \right) \quad (2)$$

Where $L^c_{Grad-CAM++}$ is the class-discriminative localization map, A^k is the kth feature map from the final convolutional layer, α^c_k refers to the weight computed using the gradients:

$$\alpha^c_k = \frac{\sum_{i,j} \left(\frac{\partial^2 y^c}{\partial \left(A^k_{i,j} \right)^2} \right)}{2 \sum_{i,j} \left(\frac{\partial^2 y^c}{\partial \left(A^k_{i,j} \right)^2} \right) + \sum_{i,j} \left(A^k_{i,j} \cdot \frac{\partial^3 y^c}{\partial \left(A^k_{i,j} \right)^3} \right)} \quad (3)$$

Here y^c is the score for class c, $A^k_{i,j}$ is the activation at location (I,j) of feature map A^k, $\frac{\partial^n y^c}{\partial \left(A^k_{i,j} \right)^n}$ denotes the nth-order partial derivative of the score with respect to feature map.

Superpixel LIME

Superpixel LIME is a model-agnostic explanation method for image data. It works by segmenting an image into interpretable units (superpixels), perturbing them, and observing the changes in the model output. A surrogate interpretable model is subsequently trained using this modified dataset. Given a set of perturbed instances = $\{z_1, z_2, \ldots\ldots, z_n\}$, where each $z_i \in \{0,1\}^m$ represents the presence or absence of m superpixels, LIME minimizes the following loss:

$$LIME\ Explanation = \arg\min_{g \in G} L(f,g,\pi_x) + \Omega(g) \quad (4)$$

Where f is the original model, g is the interpretable surrogate model, π_x is the locality function defining neighborhood around instance x, $\mathcal{L}$ measures the fidelity between f and g in the vicinity defined by π_x, $\Omega(g)$ is the complexity penalty for the surrogate model g.

Saliency map

By calculating the gradient of the output score in relation to the input image, saliency maps pinpoint input pixels that have the greatest effect on the model's prediction. For a given class score y^c and input image I, the saliency map S is defined as:

$$S = \left| \frac{\partial y^c}{\partial I} \right| \quad (5)$$

Table 16.3 Performance metrics across clients in federated transfer learning setup.

Clients	Client 1	Client 2	Client 3	Client 4
Accuracy	98.57	98.89	99.39	98.24
Precision	98.58	98.90	99.39	98.26
Recall	98.55	98.88	99.38	98.21
F1-Score	98.54	98.88	99.38	98.21

Source: Author

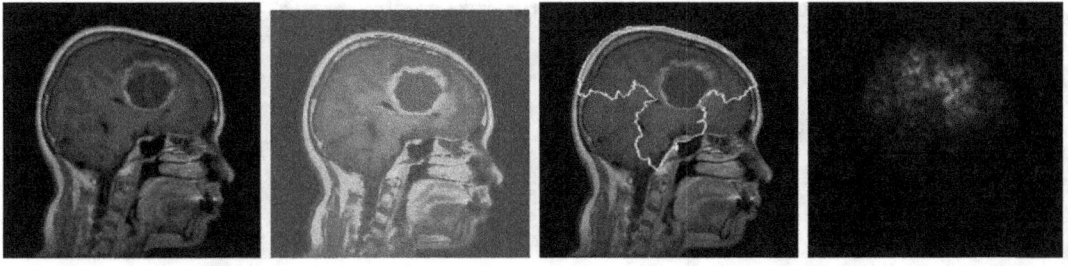

Figure 16.3 Original glioma image with gradCAM++, superpixel LIME, Saliency map
Source: Author

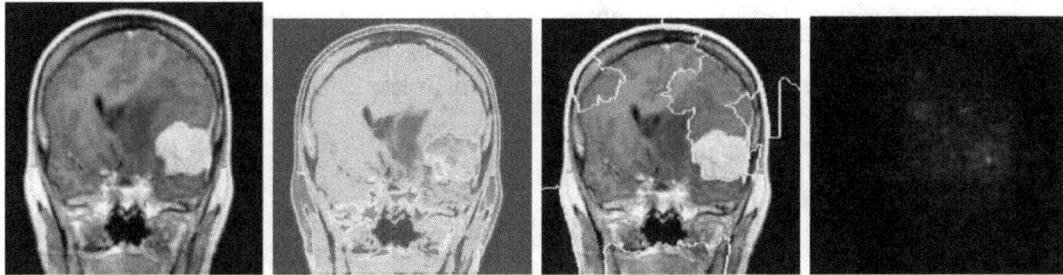

Figure 16.4 Original meningioma image with gradCAM++, superpixel LIME, saliency map
Source: Author

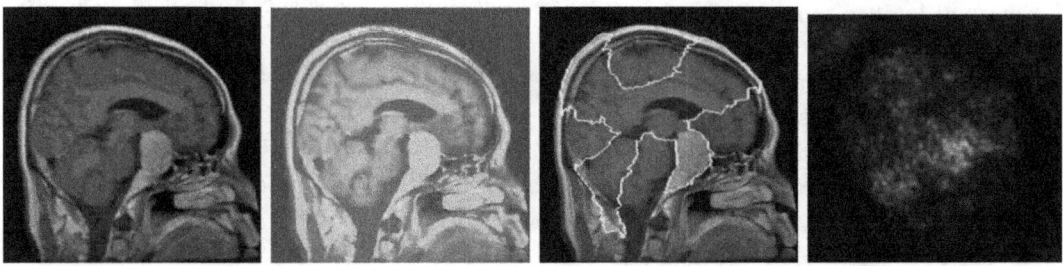

Figure 16.5 Original pituitary image with gradCAM++, superpixel LIME, saliency map
Source: Author

Here y^c is the scalar output of the model for the predicted class, $\frac{\partial y^c}{\partial I}$ indicates the rate of change of the output concerning every pixel in the input image.

Results and Discussion

The experimental results from the proposed FTL framework is shown in Table 16.3, which demonstrate that high-accuracy brain tumor classification can be achieved without centralized data collection. This result highlights the advantages of integrating FL and TL in medical imaging situations where privacy is a concern. The use of a common pre-trained model (InceptionV3), fine-tuned locally by each client and aggregated securely through

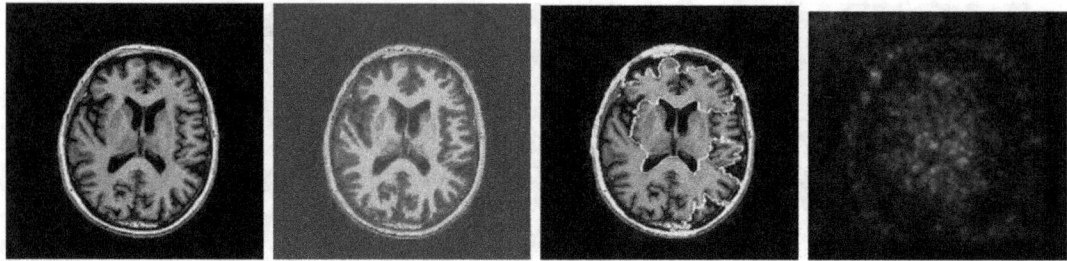

Figure 16.6 Original no tumor image with gradCAM++, superpixel LIME, saliency map
Source: Author

the FedAvg algorithm, led to consistently strong performance across all participating clients. This indicates the framework's robustness in handling decentralized and potentially heterogeneous data distributions. Notably, such performance was achieved without sharing raw patient data, highlighting the model's potential for real-world deployment in compliance with data protection regulations such as HIPAA and GDPR. Additionally, by leveraging transfer learning, each client benefitted from pre-learned feature representations, which reduced computational requirements and accelerated convergence while maintaining high levels of classification accuracy, precision, recall, and F1-score.

In addition to strong classification performance, the framework also integrates explainable AI (XAI) techniques to address the common black-box limitation associated with deep learning models. Post-hoc visual explanation methods, namely grad CAM++, superpixel LIME, and Saliency Maps, were utilized on previously unexamined MRI test images to offer understanding into the model's reasoning process. These methods generated heat maps that highlighted important regions that influenced the decision, as shown in Figures 16.3–16.6. These results confirm that the models were accurate as well as interpretable. These qualitative visual outputs show the important role of XAI in supporting decision making mainly in medical cases such as brain tumor detection as well as classification.

Conclusion

This work presented a comprehensive framework integrating FTL and XAI to perform secure, accurate and interpretable brain tumor classification. By implementing the InceptionV3-based Transfer learning across four clients using the FedAvg aggregation algorithm at the server, this system successfully preserves data privacy with high classification performance. Client training on its private data eliminated the need for raw data sharing. Mainly to overcome the black-box problem of deep learning models, the visual XAI methods were implemented to visualize the model's reason behind each prediction. This is important for enhancing transparency.

The results of this work show that the proposed framework achieves both technical effectiveness and practical relevance, bridging the gap between privacy-preserving model training and interpretable decision-making in medical AI. By combining FTL and XAI, this work contributes a significant step towards the creation of a reliable understandable AI system for classifying brain tumors in the healthcare domain.

References

[1] Islam, M., Reza, M. T., Kaosar, M., & Parvez, M. Z. (2023). Effectiveness of federated learning and CNN ensemble architectures for identifying brain tumors using MRI images. *Neural Processing Letters*, 55(4), 3779–3809.

[2] Ay, Ş., Ekinci, E., & Garip, Z. (2024). A brain tumour classification on the magnetic resonance images using convolutional neural network-based privacy-preserving federated learning. *International Journal of Imaging Systems and Technology*, 34(1), e23018.

[3] Hosny, K. M., Mohammed, M. A., Salama, R. A., & Elshewey, A. M. (2025). Explainable ensemble deep learning-based model for brain tumor detection and classification. *Neural Computing and Applications*, 37(3), 1289–1306.

[4] Prince, E. W., Mirsky, D. M., Hankinson, T. C., & Görg, C. (2025). Current state and promise of user-centered design to harness explainable AI in clinical decision-support systems for patients with CNS tumors. *Frontiers in Radiology*, 4, 1433457.

[5] Garg, P., Sharma, M. K., & Kumar, P. (2025). Transparency in diagnosis: Unveiling the power of deep learning and explainable AI for medical image interpretation. Arabian Journal for Science and Engineering, 50, 15751–15767.

[6] Lakshmi, K., Amaran, S., Subbulakshmi, G., Padmini, S., Joshi, G. P., & Cho, W. (2025). Explainable artificial intelligence with UNet based segmentation and Bayesian machine learning for classification of brain tumors using MRI images. *Scientific Reports*, 15(1), 690.

[7] Msoud Nickparvar (2021). Brain tumor MRI dataset. Kaggle. https://doi.org/10.34740/KAGGLE/DSV/2645886.

[8] Bhuvaji, S., Kadam, A., Bhumkar, P., Dedge, S., & Kanchan, S. (2020). Brain tumor classification (MRI). Kaggle. https://doi.org/10.34740/KAGGLE/DSV/1183165.

[9] Hashemi, S. M. H. (2023). Crystal clean: brain tumors MRI dataset. Kaggle. https://doi.org/10.34740/KAGGLE/DS/3505991.

[10] Ashiq. (2021). 'MRI Image Based Brain Tumor Classification' (Version 1) [Dataset]. Kaggle. [Online]. Available: https://www.kaggle.com/datasets/iashiqul/mri-image-based-brain-tumor-classification.

17 Identification of epileptic seizures from brain signal using fourier decomposition

Sandhyalati Behera[1,a], Rashmi Ranjan Maharana[2,b], Abhishek Das[3,c] and Benudhar Sahu[1,d]

[1]Department of Electronics and Communication Engineering, Siksha 'O' Anusandhan Deemed University, Bhubaneswar, Odisha, India

[2]Department of Electronics and Telecommunication Engineering PMEC, Berhampur, Odisha, India

[3]Department of Computer Science and Engineering, Centurion University of Technology and Management, Odisha, India

Abstract

A non-communicable brain disorder is termed as epileptic. Observing an epileptic seizure is a time-consuming and potentially biased process for neurologists. Signal processing and machine learning are techniques commonly used in seizure detection that can compensate for these limitations. The electroencephalogram (EEG) is used in this paper to diagnose epilepsy. The authors introduce an automatic and effective method for decomposing EEG signals using the Fourier Transform technique. Lp norms are calculated from Fourier intrinsic band functions (FIBFs), are presented for feature extraction. The EEG signal is decomposed into FIBFs. The pertinent features are chosen from features with the Kruskal-Wallis test. The final step involves feeding the relevant features to a Gradient boosting classifier. The efficacy of the proposed method in terms of accuracy, sensitivity, and specificity is verified with the earlier method, and it is found that the proposed method is better than the other state-of-the-art techniques and is given in the result section.

Keywords: Epilepsy, Fourier decomposition method, Fourier intrinsic band function, LP norm, support vector machine

Introduction

Sudden changes in brain activity result in epilepsy. Epilepsy seizer results in changes in taste, smell, touch, loss of awareness and memories. It also harms quality of life of the patient. Till now there is no permanent treatment for epilepsy seizer, however with early diagnosis and proper monitoring there is a chance of reducing life risk and better quality of life. There is various methods used to detect and diagnose epilepsy. Due to non-invasive and easier recording EEG signal is normally employed to detect epilepsy by the neurologists and specialized doctors. The brain rhythms change with the seizer and these changes are easily detected. Manual detection and prediction method is normally not preferred as it requires expertise neurologists and small changes may not be visualized properly.

Various signal processing methods, machine learning and deep learning methods are utilized to detect epilepsy. The

[a]sandhyalatibehera@gmail.com, [b]rashmi.etc@pmec.ac.in, [c]abhishekdas225@gmail.com, [d]benudharsahu@soa.ac.in

DOI: 10.1201/9781003753391-17

authors in this manuscript implemented and presented Fourier Transform (FT) based decomposition method and machine learning method to identify seizer. The brief overview of the existing methods is given in literature review section, the method considered in this manuscript is given in methodology section, the results are given in result and discussion section, and last section deals with conclusion.

Literature Review

Since the last decade number of researchers have applied various methods such as discrete wavelet transform (DWT), Hilbert-Huang transform (HHT), FT, etc. for the detection of epileptic seizures from the EEG signals. Discrete Wavelet Transform (DWT) and Artificial Neural Network (ANN) in combination, mostly implemented in MATLAB, and four characteristics derived from the EEG data are used in the research to detect seizures [1]. The information signals are examined in the primary stage utilizing the discrete wavelet change (DWT) and subgroups containing helpful data are extricated [2]. In order to achieve maximum spectral efficiency, the Chebyshev filter was added to the IIR filter to remove any EEG signal artefacts. Wavelet analysis is then used to divide the signal into multiple levels [3]. A different wavelet filter was used for each decomposition level based on the signal's frequency response because the signal differs at each level.

A novel method for automatically identifying seizures in single-channel EEG recordings is described in the research article [4] on the foundations of time scale decomposition (ITD), DWT, phase space reconstruction (PSR), and neural networks. Using Poinaré pattern coefficients from discrete wavelet transformations (DWT), Akbari et al. [5] presents a novel geometric feature for

classifying seizure (S) and non-seizure (SF) EEG data. Using Genetic Algorithm (GA) and particle swarm optimization (PSO) to find the best parameters for Support Vector Machines (SVM) for EEG data categorization, the work by Subasi et al. [6] creates a hybrid model for seizure detection. SVMs are sophisticated machine learning algorithms that are used in a lot of different applications. The exploration by Hussain et al. [7] centers around two elements of the worldly EEG signal: morphological and statistical characteristics. The discriminative capacity of the derived features is evaluated using the logistic regression classifier, as demonstrated by 10-fold cross-validation. Time-frequency image (TFI) segmentation based on EEG signal rhythm frequency bands was used by Fu et al. [8] method to handle HHT-based time-frequency representation (TFR). Sub-images in grayscale are displayed. The mean, variance, skewness, and kurtosis of histogram pixel intensities are retrieved as statistical properties. To categorize seizure and non-seizure EEG data, a radial basis function (RBF) kernel of an SVM was utilized.

A function based on the Hilbert-Huang transform is used to classify normal and ictic functions in this study [9]. Using the concept of location, velocity, and acceleration, Lp norms were used to extract characteristics from EEG data using Fourier integral group functions (FIBF). The recommended framework [10] is separated into three significant parts.

A hybrid system based on a decision tree classifier and the fast Fourier transform (FFT) is used in [11] to identify seizures from EEG data. The gamma region of EEG data is analyzed with the help of the short-time Fourier transform (STFT) in the article [12]. It also makes it possible to compare various classification strategies and achieve high accuracy with some of them. The analysis made use of STFT, gamma band extraction, statistical feature extraction, and finally applied it to the classifier. A convolutional neural network with a Fourier Transform between hidden layers is used in the proposed method [13] to switch the network from the time domain to frequency domain analysis.

Methodology

The suggested work diagram is displayed in Figure 17.1. Using the Fourier decomposition approach known as FIBFs, EEG data are obtained and decomposed into various frequency bands. The characteristics are extracted from the FIBFs, and the best ones are chosen and fed into the detection algorithm to learn about seizure and non-seizure signals. The following subsections provide information about each block.

Fourier transform based decomposition
Time-domain analysis of EEG data is extremely challenging due to their non-stationary nature. To convert the EEG signal into the frequency domain, the Fourier decomposition method is utilized. EEG signals are decomposed into the time-frequency domain using a variety of decomposition techniques, including variational mode decomposition (VMD), ensemble empirical mode decomposition (EEMD), complete ensemble empirical mode decomposition (CEEMD), and empirical mode

decomposition (EMD). Since the transformation process loses relatively little information, the suggested method uses Fourier decomposition to break down the EEG signal.

Fourier representation (FR) is a boundless collection of cosine and sine functions with consistent frequencies and amplitudes. The EEG signal is represented using the sum of sine and cosine terms and is given in equation (1):

$$EEG_s(t) = \sum_{k=-\infty}^{\infty} c_k exp(j2\pi k f_0 t) \quad (1)$$

where $f_0 = 1/T_0$ is the basic frequency, and

$$C_k = \frac{1}{T} \int_0^T EEG_s(t) \, exp(-j2\pi k f_0 t) \, dt \quad (2)$$

For a real signal here, denoted by: $EEG_s(t)$, $C_k = C_k^*$, where (*) indicates a complex conjugate operation. As a result, the analytical signal (AS) representation can be written as

$$z(t) = EEG_s(t) + j \overrightarrow{EEG_s(t)} =$$
$$c_0 + 2\sum_{k=1}^{\infty} c_k exp(j2\pi k f_0 t) \quad (3)$$

Where the imaginary part $\overrightarrow{EEG_s(t)}$ is the real part's Hilbert transform is given by $EEG_s(t)$ and c_0 is the mean of $EEG_s(t)$. Equation (3) can be written as:

$$c_0 + 2 \sum_{k=1}^{\infty} c_k \, exp(j2\pi k f_0 t) =$$
$$c_o + \sum_{i=1}^{M} a_i(t) exp(j\emptyset_i(t)) \quad (4)$$

Where,

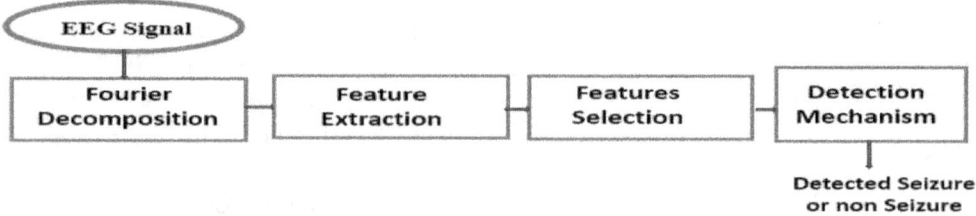

Figure 17.1 Flow diagram of proposed technique
Source: Author

$a_1(t) exp(j\emptyset_i(t)) = 2 \sum_{k=1}^{k_1}$

$c_k \, exp(j2\pi kf_o t) \, , a_2(t) exp(j\emptyset_i(t)) = 2$

$\sum_{k_1+1}^{k_2} c_k \, exp(j2\pi kf_o t) \, , \dots ,$

$a_m(t) exp(j\emptyset_i(t)) =$

$2 \sum_{k=k_{m-1}+1}^{\infty} c_k \, exp(j2\pi kf_o t)$ (5)

From equation (3) and (4), the AS is written as:

$$z(t) = a_0 + \sum_{i=1}^{M} y_i(t) + j\overrightarrow{y_i}(t) =$$
$$c_0 + \sum_{i=1}^{M} a_i(t) \, exp(j\emptyset_i(t)) \quad (6)$$

Where $a_0 = c_0$ and, $y_i(t) = a_i(t) \cos(\emptyset_i(t))$, $1 \leq i \leq M$, are represent as M FIBFs with amplitude given as in equation (7)

$$a_0(t) = \sqrt{y_i^2(t) + \overrightarrow{y_i^2(t)}} \quad (7)$$

and instantaneous phase which is denoted as (8)

$$\emptyset_i(t) = \tan^{-1}(\overrightarrow{y_i}(t)/ y_i(t)) \quad (8)$$

The expression of the $EEG_s(t)$ signal is give as in equation (9)

$$EEG_s(t) = a_0 + \sum_{i=1}^{M} y_i(t) =$$
$$a_0 + \sum_{i=1}^{M} a_i(t) \cos(\emptyset_i(t)) \quad (9)$$

The instantaneous frequency (IF) is provided by the FIBFs as given in equation (10).

$$w_i(t) = \frac{d}{d_n} \emptyset_i(t) \geq 0 \text{ and}$$
$$\exists \, a_i(t) \geq 0, \forall t. \quad (10)$$

$EEG_s[f]$ is written as:

$$EEG_s[f] = \sum_{g=0}^{L-1} EEG_s[g]$$
$$exp(j2\pi gf / L) \quad (11)$$

Where:

$$EEG_s[g] = \frac{1}{L} \sum_{g=0}^{L-1} EEG_s[f]$$
$$exp(-j2\pi gf / L) \quad (12)$$

The $EEG_s[f]$ is the DFT of EEG signal. $EEG_s[0]$ and $EEG_s[L/2]$ are real terms, considering L is an even number and thus $EEG_s[f]$ can be defined as,

$$EEG_s[f] = EEG_s[0] + \sum_{g=1}^{\frac{L}{2}-1} EEG_s[g]$$
$$exp(j2\pi kf / L) + EEG_s[L / 2] \, exp(jf\pi)$$
$$+ \sum_{\frac{L}{2}+1}^{L-1} EEG_s[g] \, exp(j2\pi gf / L) \quad (13)$$

Feature extraction

The features are extracted from the decomposed *EEG* signal. The L^p norms are extracted for $p = 0.1, 0.25, 0.5, 1, 2, 3, 5$ as given in equation (14),

$$L^p = \left(\sum_{n=0}^{L-1} |EEG_s[f]|^p \right)^{\frac{1}{p}} \quad (14)$$

First-order difference, i.e., differentiation, approximates the effect of high-pass filtering in the discrete domain and produces an effect similar to that of

$$EEG_s d_1[f] = EEG_s[f] -$$
$$- EEG_s[f - 1] \quad (15)$$
$$EEG_s d_2[f] = EEG_s d_1[f] -$$
$$EEG_s d_1[f - 1] \quad (16)$$

Where $EEG_s d_1[f]$ and $EEG_s d_2[f]$ compared to the primary and second-order derivatives. Essentially, integration features a comparative impact to low-pass filtering and is approximated as a collective total, i.e.,

$$EEG_{S_{11}}[f] = \sum_{g=0}^{f} EEG_s(g) \quad (17)$$
$$EEG_{S_{12}}[f] = \sum_{g=0}^{f} EEG_{S_{11}}(g) \quad (18)$$

where $EEG_{S_{11}}[f]$ and $EEG_{S_{12}}[f]$ represent integrations of the first and second orders. The FIBFs are obtained for original EEG signal, $EEG_s d_1[f]$ and $EEG_s d_2[f]$. The specific features are extracted using Kruskal-Wallis (KW). The specific features are given to the detection mechanism.

Detection mechanism

The selected features are given to the gradient boosting based ensemble classifier for detection purpose. Gradient Boosting Machines (GBMs) are effective for regression and classification tasks. Using decision trees as base learners in GBMs makes them more accurate than neural networks and more interpretable than linear models, as noted by Lundberg et al. Enhancements such as the multi-layered GBM (based on deep forests) and soft GBM further improve performance. Incorporating randomized decision trees into GBMs significantly boosts their accuracy and interpretability, enabling their use in both local and global interpretation tasks.

In regression problems, the goal is to learn a function g(x) that approximates an unknown function f(x) minimizing the expected loss, often defined as the squared error. GBMs solve this by iteratively adding weak learners (e.g., decision trees) that fit the negative gradient of the loss function. Each new model improves the previous prediction, forming an additive ensemble model. This approach is grounded in gradient descent and is widely used due to its effectiveness.

Performance measures

Six performance metrics are utilized to assess the execution of the proposed classification procedure: ROC area, Kappa coefficient (k), sensitivity (sen), specificity (spe), classification accuracy (Acc), and the f-measure The following is how these measurements are computed:

$$Sen = TP/(TP + FN) \times 100\%$$

$$spe = \frac{TN}{TN + FP} \times 100\%$$

$$Acc = \frac{TP+TN}{TP+TN+FP+FN} \times 100\%$$

$$Precision = \frac{TP}{TP + FP}$$

$$Recall = \frac{TP}{TP+FN}, f = 2 * \frac{Precision*recall}{Precision+recall}$$

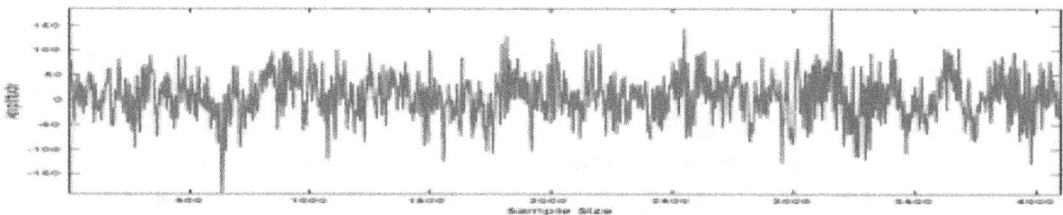

Figure 17.2 A sample healthy (non-seizure) brain EEG signal from the Z dataset
Source: Author

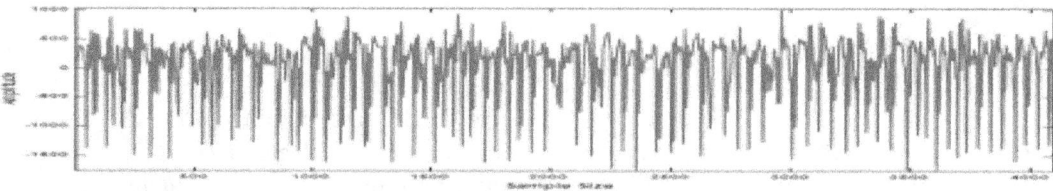

Figure 17.3 A sample unhealthy (seizure) EEG signal from the S dataset
Source: Author

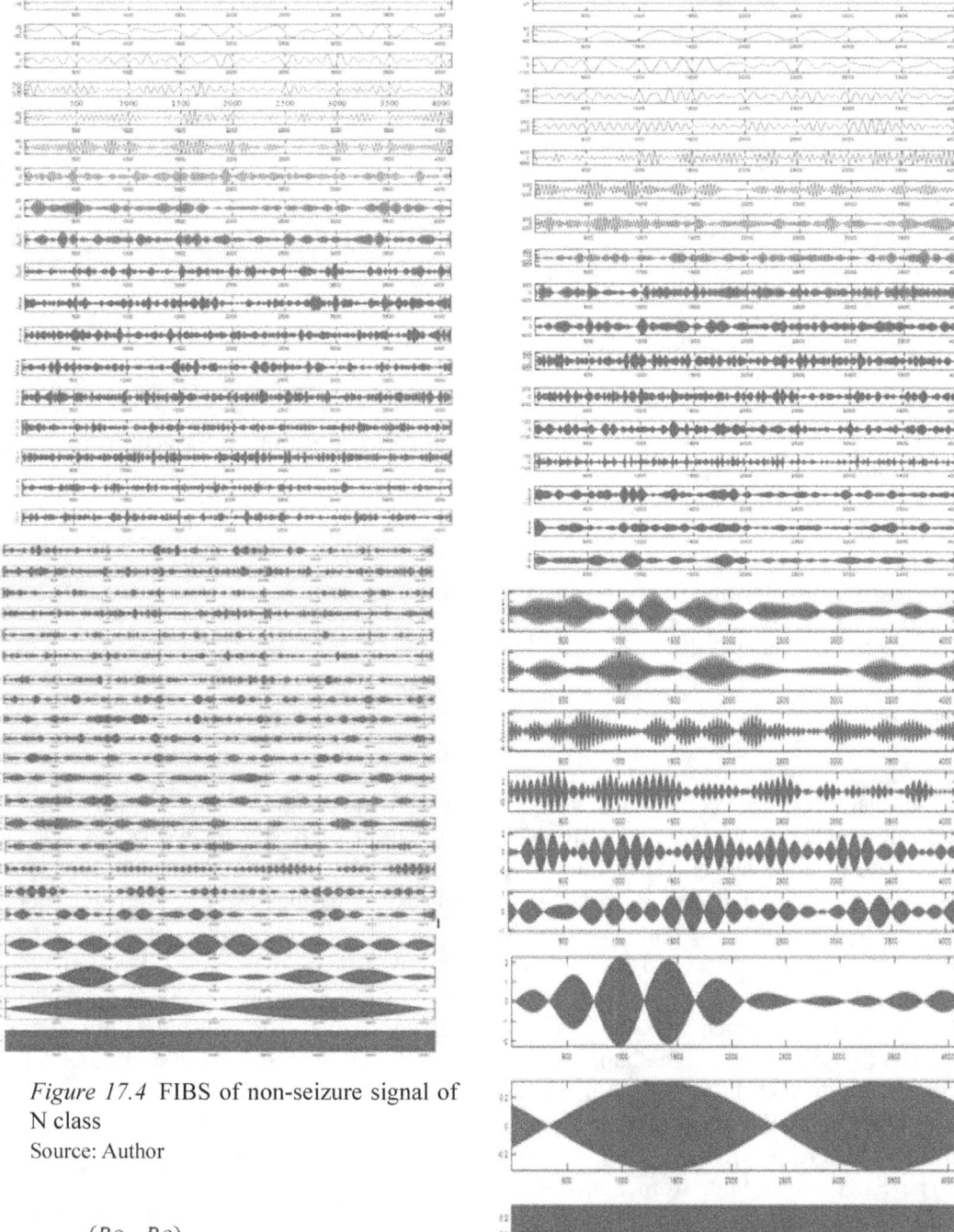

Figure 17.4 FIBS of non-seizure signal of N class
Source: Author

$$k = \frac{(Po - Pe)}{(1 - Pe)} \qquad (23)$$

Results and Discussion

The input EEG data are collected from the BONN dataset [14] having two separate

Figure 17.5 FIBS of seizure signal of S class
Source: Author

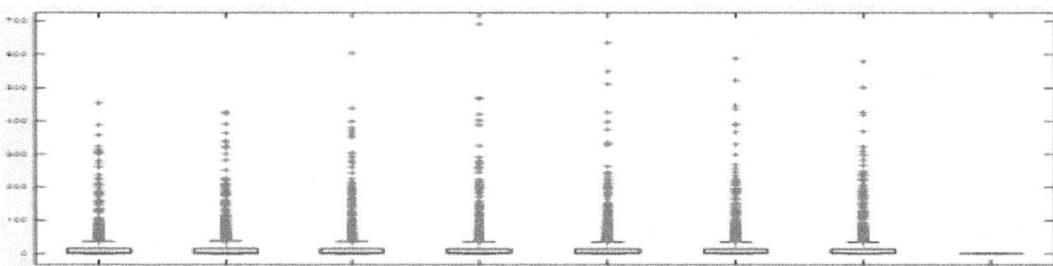

Figure 17.6 Output of kruskal-wallis test
Source: Author

Table 17.1 The performance comparison of the proposed method with the existing.

Performance Parameters	Decision Tree	Random forest	Neive based	Gradient Boosting Technique
Accuracy	98.5	97.1	97.01	97.9
Sensitivity	97.7	97.5	97.15	98.1
Specificity	97.3	98.1	98.03	98.8
f-measure	0.90	0.91	0.90	0.92
Kappa coeff.	0.89	0.87	0.88	0.89

Source: Author

classes namely Z, O, N, F which are the non-seizure classes and S which is the seizure class. Each of the signal contains 4096 samples. All the signals are recorded with 128 Channel amplifier and bandpass filtered with the bandwidth setting of 0.53±40 Hz and stored with a sampling rate of 173.61 Hz. The duration of each signal is 23.6 sec. The healthy seizure free signal amplitude is within 100 μV and the signal with seizure is around 1000 μV as displayed in Figures 17.2 and 17.3 respectively.

The EEG signal both from non-seizure and seizure class are decomposed into FIBFs as shown in Figures 17.4 and 17.5 respectively. Features are calculated from the decomposed signal from both seizure and non-seizure class and the appropriate features are selected with Kruskal-Wallis test at 90% significance level. Examination

of statistical significance one-way analysis of variance (ANOVA) works on selected characteristics. The statistical test is accomplished using the MATLAB. P values below 0.05 indicate significant functions that can be applied. The result of Kruskal-Wallis Test is given in Figure 17.6. The performance of the proposed algorithm is compared with the state-of-the-art algorithms and shown in Table 17.1.

Conclusions and Future Scope

Automatically detecting epileptic seizures is one of the most challenging problems in biomedical technology. The suitability different approaches are determined by the quality of the returned features. This paper provides a practical solution to three challenges of binary EEG signal classification.

The FDM approach is effective for decomposing a non-static EEG signal into FIBFs, from which the appropriate features can be obtained. With the proliferation of wearable EEG devices and wireless communication technologies, real-time Fourier decomposition detection of epileptic seizures may become more practical. Fourier decomposition can be used in conjunction with other signal-processing methods to optimize and increase the efficiency of these algorithms.

References

[1] Alalayah, K. M., Senan, E. M., Atlam, H. F., Ahmed, I. A., & Shatnawi, H. S. A. (2023). Effective early detection of epileptic seizures through EEG signals using classification algorithms based on t-distributed stochastic neighbor embedding and K-means. *Diagnostics*, 13(11), 1957.

[2] Dastgoshadeh, M., & Rabiei, Z. (2023). Detection of epileptic seizures through EEG signals using entropy features and ensemble learning. *Frontiers in Human Neuroscience*, 16, 1084061.

[3] Lasefr, Z., Ayyalasomayajula, S. S. V., & Elleithy, K. (2017). Epilepsy seizure detection using EEG signals. In 2017 IEEE 8th Annual Ubiquitous Computing, Electronics and Mobile Communication Conference (UEMCON), (pp. 162–167).

[4] Zeng, W., Li, M., Yuan, C., Wang, Q., Liu, F., & Wang, Y. (2020). Identification of epileptic seizures in EEG signals using time-scale decomposition (ITD), discrete wavelet transform (DWT), phase space reconstruction (PSR) and neural networks. *Artificial Intelligence Review*, 53, 3059–3088.

[5] Akbari, H., Sadiq, M. T., Jafari, N., Too, J., Mikaeilv, N., & Cicone, A., et al. (2023). Recognizing seizure using Poincaré plot of EEG signals and graphical features in DWT domain. *Bratislavske Lekarske Listy*, 124, 12–24.

[6] Subasi, A., Kevric, J., & Abdullah Canbaz, M. (2019). Epileptic seizure detection using hybrid machine learning methods. *Neural Computing and Applications*, 31, 317–325.

[7] Hussain, M. S., Sarfraz, M., & Rukhsar, S. (2018). Epileptic seizure detection using temporal based measures in EEG signal. In 2018 3rd International Conference on Communication and Electronics Systems (ICCES), (pp. 743–748).

[8] Fu, K., Qu, J., Chai, Y., & Dong, Y. (2014). Classification of seizure based on the time-frequency image of EEG signals using HHT and SVM. *Biomedical Signal Processing and Control*, 13, 15–22.

[9] Oweis, R. J., & Abdulhay, E. W. (2011). Seizure classification in EEG signals utilizing hilbert-huang transform. *Biomedical Engineering Online*, 10, 1–15.

[10] Mehla, V. K., Singhal, A., Singh, P., & Pachori, R. B. (2021). An efficient method for identification of epileptic seizures from EEG signals using fourier analysis. *Physical and Engineering Sciences in Medicine*, 44, 443–456.

[11] Polat, K., & Güneş, S. (2007). Classification of epileptiform EEG using a hybrid system based on decision tree classifier and fast Fourier transform. *Applied Mathematics and Computation*, 187, 1017–1026.

[12] Sameer, M., Gupta, A. K., Chakraborty, C., & Gupta, B. (2019). Epileptical seizure detection: performance analysis of gamma band in EEG signal using short-time fourier transform. In 2019 22nd International Symposium on Wireless Personal Multimedia Communications (WPMC), (pp. 1–6).

[13] Cecotti, H., & Graeser, A. (2008). Convolutional neural network with embedded Fourier transform for EEG classification. In 2008 19th International Conference on Pattern Recognition, (pp. 1–4).

[14] Andrzejak, R. G., Lehnertz, K., Mormann, F., Rieke, C., David, P., & Elger, C. E. (2001). Indications of nonlinear deterministic and finite-dimensional structures in time series of brain electrical activity: Dependence on recording region and brain state. *Physical Review E*, 64(6), 061907.

18 AI-powered identification of cystic fibrosis mutations from nucleotide sequences

Ritu Chauhan[1,a], Aarushi Mishra[2,b], Harleen Kaur[2,c] and Mihir Narayan Mohanty[3,d]

[1]Artificial Intelligence and IoT lab, Centre for Computational Biology and Bioinformatics, Amity University, Noida, UP, India

[2]Department of Computer Science and Engineering, School of Engineering Sciences and Technology, Jamia Hamdard, New Delhi, India

[3]ITER, Siksha O Anusandhan Deemed to be University, Bhubaneswar, Odisha, India

Abstract

Cystic fibrosis (CF), resulting from *CFTR* gene mutations, impacts respiratory and gastrointestinal systems. Early detection is important but conventional approaches are expensive and time-consuming. Artificial intelligence (AI) and machine learning (ML) improve CF diagnosis by enhancing precision and cost-effectiveness in medical imaging, predictive analysis, and gene testing. This article presents an ML-based system to identify CFTR gene mutations from nucleotide sequences with six algorithms: Random Forest (84% accurate), Decision Tree (82%), Logistic Regression (82%), support vector machine (80%), AdaBoost (62%), and XGBoost (60%). This technique, trained with ClinVar data, provides a quick, precise, and low-cost replacement for traditional genetic testing.

Keywords: Accuracies, artificial intelligence, cystic fibrosis, machine learning, variant identification

Introduction

The severe genetic condition called cystic fibrosis (CF) happens because of *CFTR* gene mutations which creates problems throughout the respiratory and gastrointestinal systems [9]. The defective protein created by CFTR mutations causes organ mucus to become thick which blocks respiratory passageways while also harming pancreatic functions thus leading to health deterioration. The mucus buildup in affected areas blocks airways while it also hinders lung function and restricts pancreatic enzyme activity thus severely decreasing the life quality of CF patients [12].

The more than 2000 CFTR mutations which scientists divide into six functional groups produce different disease intensities [1]. F508del represents the most well-known CFTR mutation since it affects 70% of patients. The application of ML with artificial intelligence analyzes large genomic datasets to help identify mutations and their types as well as predict their potentials for causing disease and provide earlier diagnoses for CF patients [11]. The tools allow for personalized treatments including CFTR modulators that repair protein deficits which results in better patient-care and enhanced life quality by means of purposeful healthcare delivery [3].

[a]rituchauha@gmail.com, [b]aarushi.mishra@s.amity.edu, [c]harleen.unu@gmail.com, [d]mihirmohanty@soa.ac.in

DOI: 10.1201/9781003753391-18

Literature Review

Artificial intelligence has transformed healthcare by improving diagnosis, treatment, and patient care in medical specialties [2]. IBM Watson Genomics and DeepVariant are particularly good at interpreting genomes and predicting disease risk, with DeepVariant performing better than conventional methods at variant detection accuracy [10]. AI-MARRVEL, created at Baylor College of Medicine, pools information from model organisms and clinical repositories to score deleterious genetic mutations, enhancing diagnostics for rare Mendelian disorders [8]. IntelliGenes, a machine learning platform, integrates statistical and ML methods to assess biomarkers [6]. Yet such systems tend to be sparse regarding diagnosis for individual conditions such as CF, in which CFTR gene mutations demand timely, inexpensive diagnostics.

This study utilizes various ML methods such as Random Forest, AdaBoost, Support Vector Machine (SVM), Decision Tree, XGBoost and Logistic Regression to predict CFTR mutations from databases such as ClinVar. In contrast to general tools, our ensemble method, spearheaded by Random Forest, provides an accurate, cost-effective substitute for standard CF testing with potential for more general genetic use.

Methodology

Data collection and overview

The research utilized ClinVar data for analysis and chose 1081 CFTR mutations considered medically important among the 5055 total mutations which met Pathogenic, Likely Pathogenic, Frameshift, Missense, and Nonsense criteria that categorize CF mutations [4]. The essential characteristics in the data included Name, Gene(s), Protein change, Condition(s), and Germline Classification which served as the response variable. The study processed mutations for accurate mutation identification by aligning them to the NCBI GRCh38 p14 CFTR reference sequence which contains 159,345,973 base pairs on chromosome 7 [7]. The Cystic Fibrosis Mutation Database provided researchers with a CFTR gene sequence to improve their prediction accuracy for CFTR mutations [5].

Data preprocessing

For this research, we employed outlier rejection method as well as missing value imputation together with feature selection as our data preprocessing techniques in this study, three main steps were taken regarding the variable's dataset: rejecting outliers; imputing missing values; and selecting features. The nucleotide sequence queried was checked for quality and normalized.

Exploratory data analysis

In this study EDA was employed in studying the CFTR variable dataset for developers to have a good under-standing of its features and relationships among different variables. The important features of the CFTR dataset were determined using correlation analysis represented in a heatmap which aided in selection of features for ML models. Significant attributes contributing to target variable predictions were highlighted on graphs showing feature importance generated by Random Forest and XGBoost. All these methods collectively guided pre-processing and thus improved the accuracy of model predictions.

Machine learning models

Six ML algorithms were modelled on a variant dataset: Decision Trees divide data into subsets according to feature values;

Random Forests use an ensemble of multiple decision trees to improve accuracy and avoid overfitting; SVM find a hyperplane that maximally separates classes in feature space; Logistic Regression models binary responses using a logistic function; AdaBoost combines multiple weak classifiers as a strong one; and XGBoost, a gradient boosting algorithm with high performance, is particularly efficient and fast.

Results

Data preprocessing results
The CFTR variant dataset contained outlier observations that analysts removed while deleting the null columns 'Germline date last evaluated' and 'Oncogenicity classification'. The 'Protein Change' feature contained missing data which received completed values before conducting feature selection procedures. The sequence quality assessment with FastQC generated statistics for precise analysis of the data. The normalizing procedure for sequence data eliminated biases to achieve better accuracy in CFTR variant classification models.

Exploratory data analysis results
CTFR variant datasets were analyzed using both a correlation matrix and heatmap in Figure 18.1. Dark purple indicates no correlation, yellow shows high positive correlation. GeneID had no significant correlations, while Protein change, GRCh37/38Chromosome, and Molecular consequence exhibited low to moderate positive correlations. The bright spots might be relationships worth exploring further, including some outliers.

The feature importance for predicting CFTR mutations revealed the most important features were GRCh38 Chromosome, SPDI Canonical, and molecular consequences with variation ID being the most important related to that. This graph highlights important attributes for model performance.

Machine learning algorithms performance comparison
In the paper, we have used a classification metrics method to compare different ML models based on the CFTR variant dataset. The models tested include RF, DT, SVM, LR, AdaBoost, and XGBoost among others.

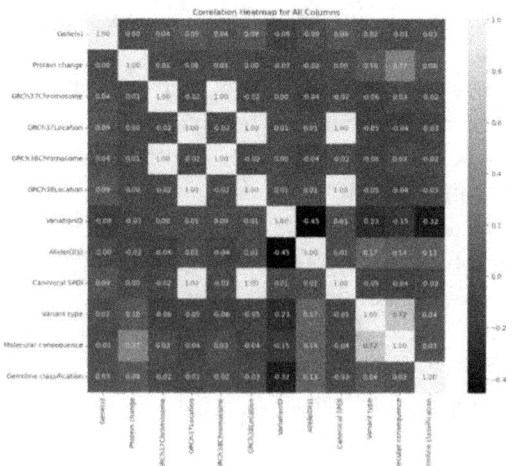

Figure 18.1 Heat map representing the correlation between different attributes of the variant dataset
Source: Author

Table 18.1 Comparison of the accuracy and AUC values of the six ML classifiers.

Model_Name	Accuracy_Values	AUC_Score
RF Classifier	84.01%	0.83
DT Classifier	82.99%	0.83
LR Classifier	82.74%	0.87
SVM Classifier	80.95%	0.88
XGB Classifier	60.54%	0.66
AdaB Classifier	62.24%	068

Source: Author

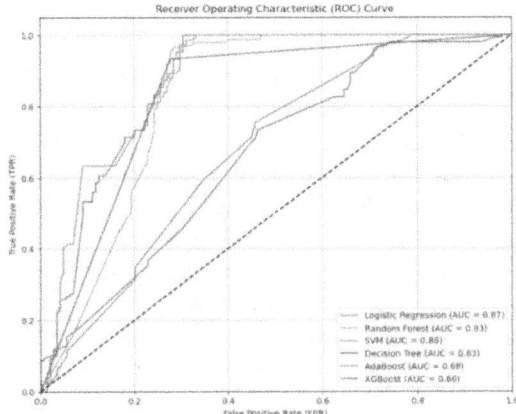

Figure 18.2 The graph above represents the ROC curves of all the classifiers we used

Source: Author

Model accuracy and AUC scores for each model are presented in Table 18.1.

The Random Forest model showed the best performance at 84% in CFTR variant classification while Decision Tree along with Logistic Regression reached 82% and SVM delivered 80%. The accuracies measured for XGBoost and AdaBoost were lower at 60% and 62%. The diagnostic ability was analyzed through ROC curves alongside AUC scores in addition to classification metrics as Figure 18.2 demonstrates.

Prediction and variant identification results

The predictive performance of these models was invariably excellent as they differentiated pathogenic sequences from non-pathogenic ones besides allowing for such features like identification of particular variant types. This shows that machine learning is rapidly becoming an important component in genomics because it helps us unravel complicated genetic data.

Conclusion

The union of Artificial Intelligence (AI) and Machine Learning (ML) has seen great potential for revolutionizing the diagnosis and treatment CF. The conventional methods of diagnoses are also costly and time-consuming thus creating a need for new effective approaches. The research reveals the way in which ML classifiers like Random Forest (RF), Decision Tree (DT) or XGBoost were able to predict CFTR gene mutations based on nucleotide sequences with precision between 60% to 84% by testing on ClinVar database. It can be seen that it is an essential method since it assists in accelerating diagnostic processes via AI.

References

[1] Alaa, A. M., & Van Der Schaar, M. (2018). Prognostication and risk factors for cystic fibrosis via automated machine learning. *Scientific Reports*, 8(1), 11242. https://doi.org/10.1038/s41598-018-29523-2.

[2] Chauhan, R., & Kaur, H. (2022). A predictive data analytic approach to get insight of healthcare databases. In Acharjya, D. P., Mitra, A., & Zaman, N. (Eds.), Deep Learning in Data Analytics, (Vol. 91, pp. 131–141). Springer International Publishing. https://doi.org/10.1007/978-3-030-75855-4_8.

[3] Chauhan, R., Mishra, A., Mani, R. J., Yafi, E., & Zuhairi, M. F. (2025). An analytical paradigm for exploration of diabetes using machine learning. In 2025 19th International Conference on Ubiquitous Information Management and Communication (IMCOM), (pp. 1–8). https://doi.org/10.1109/IMCOM64595.2025.10857504.

[4] National Center for Biotechnology Information (NCBI).(n.d.). ClinVar: CFTR [gene] [Dataset]. National Library of Medicine. Retrieved from https://www.ncbi.nlm.nih.gov/clinvar/?term=cftr%5Bgene%5D&redir=gene.

[5] Cystic Fibrosis Mutation Database (CFMDB). (n.d.). Cystic fibrosis mutation database [Dataset]. The Hospital for Sick Children, Toronto. Retrieved from http://www.genet.sickkids.on.ca/.

[6] DeGroat, W., Mendhe, D., Bhusari, A., Abdelhalim, H., Zeeshan, S., & Ahmed, Z. (2023). IntelliGenes: a novel machine learning pipeline for biomarker discovery and predictive analysis using multi-genomic profiles. *Bioinformatics*, 39(12), btad755. https://doi.org/10.1093/bioinformatics/btad755.

[7] National Center for Biotechnology Information (NCBI). (n.d.). Homo sapiens chromosome 7, GRCh38.p14 primary assembly [Dataset]. GenBank, National Library of Medicine. Retrieved from https://www.ncbi.nlm.nih.gov/nuccore/NC_000007.14.

[8] Mao, D., Liu, C., Wang, L., AI-Ouran, R., Deisseroth, C., Pasupuleti, S., et al. (2024). AI-marrvel — a knowledge-driven AI system for diagnosing mendelian disorders. *NEJM AI*, 1(5), AIoa2300009. https://doi.org/10.1056/AIoa2300009.

[9] Ong, T., & Ramsey, B. W. (2023). Cystic fibrosis: a review. *The Journal of the American Medical Association (JAMA)*, 329(21), 1859. https://doi.org/10.1001/jama.2023.8120.

[10] Poplin, R., Chang, P.-C., Alexander, D., Schwartz, S., Colthurst, T., Ku, A., et al. (2018). A universal SNP and small-indel variant caller using deep neural networks. *Nature Biotechnology*, 36(10), 983–987. https://doi.org/10.1038/nbt.4235.

[11] Qin, Y., Alaa, A., Floto, A., & Schaar, M. V. D. (2023). External validity of machine learning-based prognostic scores for cystic fibrosis: a retrospective study using the UK and Canadian registries. *PLOS Digital Health*, 2(1), e0000179. https://doi.org/10.1371/journal.pdig.0000179.

[12] Rehman, A., Mujahid, M., Saba, T., & Jeon, G. (2024). Optimised stacked machine learning algorithms for genomics and genetics disorder detection in the healthcare industry. *Functional and Integrative Genomics*, 24(1), 23. https://doi.org/10.1007/s10142-024-01289-z.

19 A hybrid framework design for financial prediction using machine learning

Kapil Mohan[1,a], Ritu Chauhan[2,b] and Harleen Kaur[3,c]

[1]Amity Institute of Information Technology, Amity University, Noida, U.P., India

[2]Artificial Intelligence and IoT Lab, Center for Computational Biology and Bioinformatics, Amity University, Noida, U.P., India

[3]Department for Computer Science and Engineering, Jamia Hamdard, Delhi, India

Abstract

Financial problems, specifically those that involve prediction for risk, stock values, ratings, valuation, fraud etc., form a set that inherently has a pattern on both data and problem solutions. This study tries to capture this patten and proposes a design that can be built into a framework of methodologies, algorithms and data flow that can spear head a commercial solution. The building blocks can be selected as per the problem requirement or can be put to test/back test and form a solution as per the data pattern. This framework design captures machine learning (ML) procedure and combines it with rule based and/or quant based statistics to generate overall better results in prediction. The framework tries to combine ML and data science and reap the benefits of both financial problems. The class of problems in this domain primarily requires pattern matching, prediction and outliers' detection and this framework is specifically in these areas. Framework is more data centric and stresses on to calculate performance metrics and tune accordingly. This study further uses this design and predicts the next second candle size for stocks. The problem is quite difficult to solve as it is quite stochastic, influenced largely by financial market sentiments and ad-hoc operator entries that may manipulate the prices intermittently. The framework provides integration points for simulations and algo-trading that can be leveraged further. This framework has commercial implications as well where in this can be integrated with brokers via algo trading platforms for high frequency trading. The framework trained SVM and XGBoost models on HDFC and Reliance stocks and obtained promising results by leveraging statistical data for model tuning showcasing capabilities of this design.

Keywords: Hybrid Machine Learning Framework, Financial Time Series Prediction, Pattern recognition in finance, Ensemble learning for financial prediction

Introduction

Financial problems generally resolved around data and patterns that are solvable by new age machine learning (ML) models. The problems though are very data centric, but predictions can be given by various ML algorithms. The issue with ML algorithms is that they often do not harness mathematical logic which has evolved over time. One example is where in the ML algorithm do cater to the time series data but do not analyze the statistical implications of the same data, say what will happen if the volatility in trades is disturbed by an operator which may be captures by moving averages or

[a]kapil.mohan@s.amity.edu, [b]rituchauhan.uts@gmail.com, [c]harleen@jamiahamdard.ac.in

DOI: 10.1201/9781003753391-19

any such turbulence capturing technique. Financial problems, such as predicting risk, stock values, ratings, valuation, and fraud, often exhibit inherent patterns in both the data and the solutions. This study aims to identify these patterns and develop a comprehensive framework that includes various methodologies, algorithms, and data flows. The goal is to create a versatile commercial solution.

This study aims to provide an approach to solve financial prediction problems by using data patterns using a framework of tools and techniques. It uses both ML and quantitative methods to achieve high performant results. Highly stochastic problems like the next candle size detection can be better trained using this style making it a good candidate for Algo Trading [2].

The framework has an upside that it can be integrated with many available commercial solutions. By merging ML and data science, the framework aims to harness the benefits of both fields to tackle financial problems. The types of problems addressed in this domain primarily involve pattern matching, prediction, and outlier detection, and the framework is specifically tailored to these areas. The framework's data-centric approach emphasizes the importance of calculating performance metrics and adjusting accordingly. This ensures that the system remains accurate and reliable, continuously improving its predictive capabilities.

In this study a structured approach to solving financial prediction problems is presented and the framework was implemented for Support Vector Regression (SVR) [1] and XGBoost regression [2] models using a set of financial indicators [3] on two instruments (HDFC and Reliance stocks) and promising performance was achieved post model tuning depicting the importance of this framework design.

Literature Review

Financial world problems are mostly around pattern recognition, prediction and outlier detection. Though ML can identify hidden patterns as discussed in [4], there is inherent quant mathematics too that is leveraged to get to the results and analyze data further. Most of the research around Fx prediction [5] or to form an intelligent trading production system follows inherent steps of designing that can be captured as a framework. Study [6] explores this possibility and proposes to integrate quantitative methods or its outcomes to be used in ML models in a way that it improves upon the results or proposes new solutions and/or suggests new patterns as a solution to financial problems set.

ML solutions do have deep reinforcement learning as a model selection [7] or for trading signal generation [8] or for commodity market trend prediction [9] and they all seem to have a patten generic enough for financial problems that a framework can explore or run simulation to find a model that will just fit and iteratively update or morph as the new data patterns come in. Many frameworks are discussed in research work and review articles [6], but rarely one talks about a framework specifically for financial data. The proposed framework suggests using libs and packages as discussed in [10] and leverages python scikit/pytorch/tensor flow quite extensively. Financial systems require empirical evaluation too and for those methods from [11] are suggested for use in the framework. This framework uses both quantitative and ML ways to solve financial problems which do not exist in prior research. Studies makes an attempt to provide quantitative analysis using Reinforcement based learning [12].

Methodology

Data collection and overview

The study proposes a framework design and showcases financial prediction problems which leverages the framework to work towards a solution. The data used is historical market data sourced from exchange brokers using APIs provided in python. The data was fetched and transformed into files and fed to the framework implementation to generate results.

Proposed framework

Quantitative outputs can be best leveraged as model inputs in this proposed framework to give high performance results. This indicates that the mathematical characteristics

of the data can in turn influence the ML models. The result is, the framework ensures that the models have a solid quantitative base, enhancing their reliability. Benefit of this hybrid framework is its ability to adapt to changing data over time which is a typical financial instrument behavior.

In total, this hybrid framework represents an approach to financial problem-solving that picks the best of both worlds. By using the strengths of both quantitative techniques and ML models, it tries to give highly accurate and close to market predictions. The framework's adaptability to changing conditions, combined with its robust quantitative foundation, makes it a powerful tool for addressing complex financial challenges. Whether used for initial data filtering,

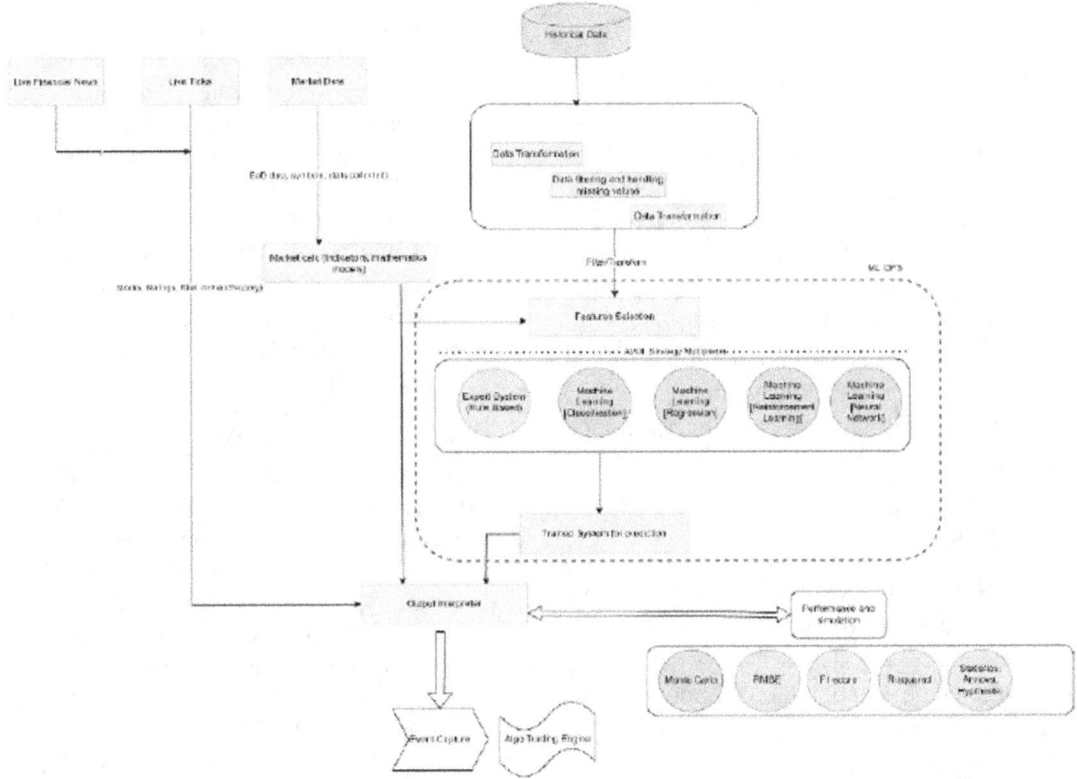

Figure 19.1 Proposed framework design
Source: Author

output validation, model parameterization, or hyperparameter tuning, the quantitative inputs play a pivotal role in enhancing the overall performance and reliability of the predictive models. This comprehensive design, as illustrated in Figure 19.1, captures all the essential details needed to implement the framework effectively for various financial problem solutions.

The framework captures and combines the results of quantitative solutions to financial problems and ML models that are run on the same input data. Alternatively, it can also use the output of quantitative results in ML models to find patterns of interest for the observer. A good input can be used from research [13, 14] where ML can be leveraged using this framework.

Results

The proposed framework Figure 19.1 was used to develop to predict candle sizes for two stocks using these advanced ML algorithms. The inputs for these algorithms were the quantitative outputs which were pre-calculated. The ML techniques showcased a very high degree of proficiency in normalizing these inputs and giving good results post training. The ML methodologies were applied to HDFC stock. The results showed that the Support Vector Machine (SVM) algorithm exhibited greater performance compared to the other techniques.

Conclusion

In conclusion, the experimental runs have demonstrated that the proposed framework can be effectively leveraged for addressing large-scale financial problems such as risk prediction, transaction monitoring, and trade control systems. Moreover, this framework can be used in various combination of quantitative outputs and ML models.

It can calculate the optimal weightage to be assigned to data and ML model outputs, giving a more of a "hybrid" model for real-time market usage. This ensures that the framework can continuously train and tune itself based on data coming from markets, perfectly fitting in day to prediction requirements in the financial world. It combines the strengths of rule-based systems and ML techniques and is capable of adapting to the ever-changing market conditions.

References

[1] Henrique, B. M., Sobreiro, V. A., & Kimura, H. (2018). Stock price prediction using support vector regression on daily and up to the minute prices. *Journal of Finance and Data Science*, 4(3), 183–201. doi: 10.1016/j.jfds.2018.04.003.

[2] Y. Zhang, (2022). Stock Price Prediction Method Based on XGboost Algorithm, in Proceedings of the 2022 International Conference on Bigdata Blockchain and Economy Management (ICBBEM 2022), Atlantis Press, 595–603. doi: 10.2991/978-94-6463-030-5_60.

[3] The Investopedia Team, (2024). Top Technical Indicators - Investopedia. Accessed: Nov. 06, 2024. [Online]. Available: https://www.investopedia.com/articles/activetrading/011815/top-technical-indicators-rookie-traders.asp.

[4] T. Zheng, (2024). The Role of Artificial Intelligence and Machine Learning in Quantitative Finance and Stock Market Forecasting, Advances in Economics, Management and Political Sciences, 98–102, doi: 10.54254/2754-1169/135/2024.18814.

[5] Gasperov, B., & Kostanjcar, Z. (2021). Market making with signals through deep reinforcement learning. *IEEE Access*, 9, 61611–61622. doi: 10.1109/ACCESS.2021.3074782.

[6] Rundo, F., Trenta, F., di Stallo, A. L., & Battiato, S. (2019). Machine learning for quantitative finance applications: a survey.

Applied Sciences (Switzerland), 9(24), 5574. doi: 10.3390/app9245574.

[7] Kabbani, T., & Duman, E. (2022). Deep reinforcement learning approach for trading automation in the stock market. *IEEE Access*, 10, 93564–93574. doi: 10.1109/ACCESS.2022.3203697.

[8] Dymova, L., Sevastjanov, P., & Kaczmarek, K. (2016). A forex trading expert system based on a new approach to the rule-base evidential reasoning. *Expert Systems with Applications*, 51, 1–13. doi: 10.1016/j.eswa.2015.12.028.

[9] Ramesh R. & Jeyakarthic M. (2023). Commodity Market Trend: Predictive Analysis and Classification Using Adaptive Smooth Svm, *Journal of Research Administration*, 6(1), Dec. 2023, [Online]. Available:https://journlra.org/index.php/jra/article/view/721

[10] Chandel, M., Silakari, S., Pandey, R., & Sharma, S. (2022). A study on machine learning and Python's framework. *International Journal of Computer Sciences and Engineering Open Access Survey Paper*, 10(5), 58–64, 2022, doi: 10.26438/ijcse/v10i5.5864.

[11] Bao, W., Yue, J., & Rao, Y. (2017). A deep learning framework for financial time series using stacked autoencoders and long-short term memory. *PLoS One*, 12(7), e0180944. doi: 10.1371/journal.pone.0180944.

[12] Zeng, Y. (2025). A comprehensive investigation of reinforcement learning-based financial quantitative analysis: taking stock trading and risk control as examples. In ITM Web of Conferences, (Vol. 73, p. 01010). doi: 10.1051/itmconf/20257301010.

[13] Lolic, M. (2025). Tree-based methods of volatility prediction for the S&P 500 index. *Computation*, 13(4), 84. doi: 10.3390/computation13040084.

[14] Chauhan, R., Mehta, K., Eiad, Y., & Zuhairi, M. F. (2024). Prediction of autism spectrum disorder using AI and machine learning. In 2024 18th International Conference on Ubiquitous Information Management and Communication (IMCOM), Kuala Lumpur, Malaysia, (pp. 1–7). doi: 10.1109/IMCOM60618.2024.10418312.

20 ViTat 1.0: An attention based vision transformer model for brain tumor identification

Rasmi Prakash Swain[1,a], Shubha Dattatreya Bahinipati[2,b], Shweta Kharya[3,c], Tejaswini Das[4,d], Bipasha Patnaik[5,e] and Debasish Swapnesh Kumar Nayak[1,f]

[1]Department of Computer Science and Engineering, Centurion University of Technology and Management, Bhubaneswar, India

[2]Department of Computer Science and Engineering, Siksha 'O' Anusandhan (Deemed to be) University Bhubaneswar, Odisha, India

[3]Department of Computer Science and Engineering, Bhilai institute of technology Durg, Chhattisgarh, India

[4]Department of Statistics, Utkal University Bhubaneswar, Odisha, India

[5]Department of ECE, Siksha 'O' Anusandhan (Deemed to be) University Bhubaneswar, Odisha, India

Abstract

Deep learning algorithms are essential for rapid and reliable diagnosis of brain tumors (BT), a crucial task in medical imaging. Here, we offer a comparison method to investigate how well Vision Transformers and Convolutional-Neural-Networks (ViCNNs) perform in improving the detection of brain tumors. Our research shows encouraging outcomes, suggesting substantial improvements in model performance and classification accuracy. We proposed a DL model Vi-Tat 1.0 enriched with attention-based Vision Transformer (ViT) mechanism to detect medical images' global dependencies. In addition to this, we also tested ViTat 1.0 and other studied CNN models on Generative Adverbial Networks (GANs) augmented images and observed a significantly increase (more than 5%) in classification accuracy. The results show Consistent and higher performance, which confirms that the proposed ViTat 1.0 is practical across different datasets. Results show that ViTat 1.0 exceeds CNNs, proving once again how critical it is to use cutting-edge DL architectures for medical image processing. Finally, our study enhances the field of BT identification by demonstrating the effectiveness of GAN and attention with ViT in improving classification accuracy and model performance. With these results, ViTat 1.0 can be seen as an application that could improve medical image processing and lead to faster, more precise clinical diagnosis.

Keywords: Brain tumor, convolutional-neural-networks, deep learning Generative Adverbial Networks, medical imaging, vision transformer

[a]rasmi.swain@cutm.ac.in, [b]bahinipati@gmail.com, [c]shweta.kharya@bitdurg.ac.in, [d]tejaswinidas46@gmail.com, [e]bipashapatnaik14@gmail.com, [f]debasish.nayak@cutm.ac.in, debasish.nayak@cutm.ac.in.

DOI: 10.1201/9781003753391-20

Introduction

Brain tumors are a challenge to modern medicine and involve many abnormal growths in the brain or central spinal cord. They belong to either benign class or malignant class, and can cause serious physical and emotional damage to affect individuals [5]. The etiology of brain tumors is complex and multifactorial due to the interaction of genetic predisposition, environmental exposure, and lifestyle. Symptoms are variable and often occur with symptoms such as headache, seizures, cognitive impairment, or focal neurological deficits. Early and accurate diagnosis is important and often relies on the best techniques such as MRI and CT, as well as histopathological analysis of the biopsy.

In recent years, computerized diagnosis has become increasingly popular, helping doctors make quick decisions [10]. So, the application of classification systems using machine learning (ML) and deep learning (DL) has become a potential field for diagnostics [12, 9]. One such method is to use Convolutional-Neural-Networks (CNNs) to learn the physical and physiological features necessary to identify diseases from the dataset [3]. A CNN is a particular kind of neural network that specializes in processing image data [4]. The absence of sizable, varied datasets created especially for deep learning methods of brain tumor diagnosis is one issue. The availability of such information may influence the expansion and performance of training models for them. Vision Transformer (ViT) offers a promising alternative by using self-tracking techniques to capture global details and remote locations in images. This can address some of the limitations of traditional deep learning methods by directly processing raw images and focusing on key data. Solutions for the long-distance issue in CNNs have mostly focused on ViT [6, 2].

The purpose of this study is to assess the efficacy of attention mechanism with ViT (ViTat 1.0) for brain tumor identification utilizing the brain MRI. In addition, we validate the ViTat 1.0 model outcome with respect to classification accuracy, speed of computation, and adaptability by comparing studies to events that occur in the real world. Additionally, we evaluate how well our studied models can learn from GAN augmented data, how quickly they can adapt to optimal performance, and how well models can be extended for information they have never seen before.

The structure of the paper and key contribution is, in section two related works are briefly discussed. Materials and techniques used for this study which include the dataset taken for analysis, data pre-processing, and model design are discussed in section three. In section four the suggested framework is discussed. Section five represents the outcome of our proposed model and an in-depth analysis of the classification accuracy. The conclusion and future scope are listed in section six.

Literature Review

Numerous studies offer methods for quickly identifying and classifying brain tumors using different data sources and machine learning techniques. Subbarayudu et al. [15] proposes a strong system that utilizes the Cancer Imaging Archive (TCIA) dataset and employs Convolutional-Neural-Networks (CNNs), ResNet50, and EfficientNetB0. Among these models, EfficientNet achieves the highest level of accuracy. Saeedi et al. [14] recommend the application of machine learning and deep learning methods in their research to diagnose different types of tumors. These algorithms demonstrate excellent training, accuracy and recall values. In 2023, Babu Vimala et al. [1] utilizes transfer learning for classification of tumors. The study demonstrates that using EfficientNetB2 leads to enhanced performance. Mahmud et al [7]. proposes a CNN structure for the detection of tumors in MRI images. The study compares the performance of ResNet-50, VGG16, and Inception V3 models, with the CNN model demonstrating significant accuracy and recall. In 2023, Zeineldin et al. [16] conducts a comprehensive evaluation of pertinent papers about the use of radiological imaging for tumor detection. These studies collectively demonstrate the variety of methods and sets of data used to accurately detect and classify brain tumors.

Literature has shown that artificial intelligence (AI) for medical image processing is essential for early disease diagnosis and identification but, there are some issues that are still open for research. The limited data availability and absence of proper biological annotation is one of the major challenges which affects the models overall accuracy. We fill this gap by adopting the data augmentation techniques (GANs) and compare the model performance with the original data and our proposed pipeline with GAN augmented data.

Material and Methods

Dataset

The X-Ray images of the tumor dataset from Kaggle have been used in this study. The dataset is divided into three parts: train, test and validation. There are two sub-sections beneath each section: Normal and Tumor. Figure 20.1 shows how the data were distributed during the proposed model's training, validation, and testing phases. In Figure 20.1 we also present the number of GAN augmented image data generated

for the training set of all the studied DL models. We increase the normal sample size from 2079 to 2435 and the tumor sample size from 1683 to 2371 to make the training set more balanced, it resulted in 4806 samples as input for the learning model.

CNN and Vision Transformers

CNNs perform well in brain tumor segmentation and classification, but their small kernel size makes it difficult to capture long-range relationships. CNN performance can be degraded by disturbing medical picture sequences like modality, slice, and patch. Self-attention ViTs can represent local and global dependencies, making them ideal for medical image processing. ViTs improve representation learning by capturing token pairwise relationships. Training and fine-tuning ViT models using MRI datasets has demonstrated encouraging results in brain tumour detection using long-range dependencies [13, 3].

Generative adversarial network

Design a GAN architecture suitable for generating synthetic MRI images. Train the GAN using the MRI dataset to generate realistic synthetic brain images. Use the

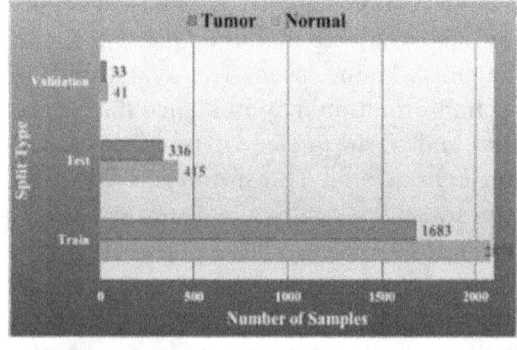

Figure 20.1 Different data split for the deployed DL models
Source: Author

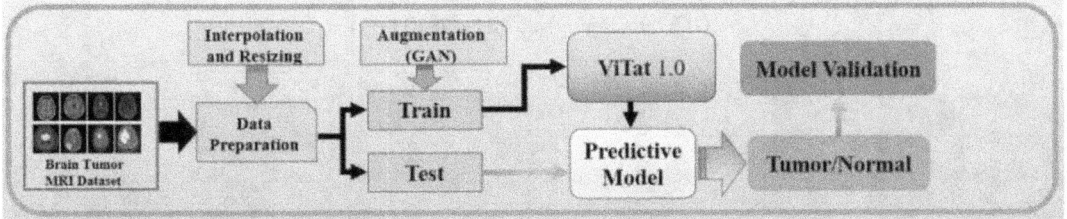

Figure 20.2 Architecture of our proposed ViTat 1.0 model
Source: Author

generated images to augment the training dataset, potentially improving the robustness of the learning model. GANs are a class of ML algorithms used in unsupervised learning. A minimax game between the discriminator and the generator is used to train GANs. While the discriminator strives to improve its ability to discern between actual and fake samples, the generator tries to create samples of data. that are identical to real samples. The generator's goal is to create samples that are so lifelike that the discriminator is unable to distinguish them from actual samples [8, 11].

Proposed Model

We proposed a DL model ViTat 1.0 that enriches with input attention mechanism with ViT. Our model utilized an attention layer after the first dense layer of the ViT. A transformer model's attention layer determines scores for attention by taking a dots product of queries and keys, scaling the scores, creating attention weights using a SoftMax function, and then using the weights to build a weighted sum of values. The pipeline of our proposed model can be visualized in Figure 20.2.

Our proposed pipeline follows the steps shown in Figure 20.3, it includes data pre-processing, feature extraction, training, testing, and validation. Each patient's raw MRI data was filtered using interpolation

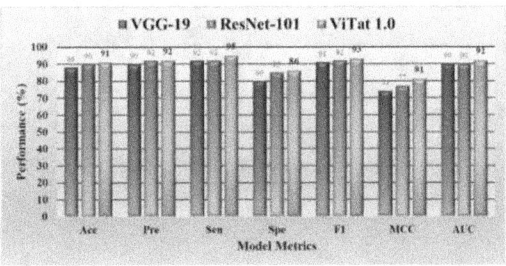

Figure 20.3 Performance of studied models on raw data
Source: Author

and image scaling. The GAN technique was used to produce images to improve the dataset. In our pipeline the training dataset is only enhanced with GAN whereas the test and validation dataset remain unchanged. The learning model is trained on the GAN generated image dataset (training data), after the training is over, we obtained the predictive model. Finally, the test and validation data are supplied to the predictive model in order to confirm the model's functionality.

Results and Discussion

The performance metrics of the studied models on the raw brain tumor (BT) image dataset are summarized in Figure 20.3. Among the models evaluated, the ViTat 1.0 model demonstrated the highest overall performance across several metrics. Specifically, ViTat 1.0 achieved an accuracy

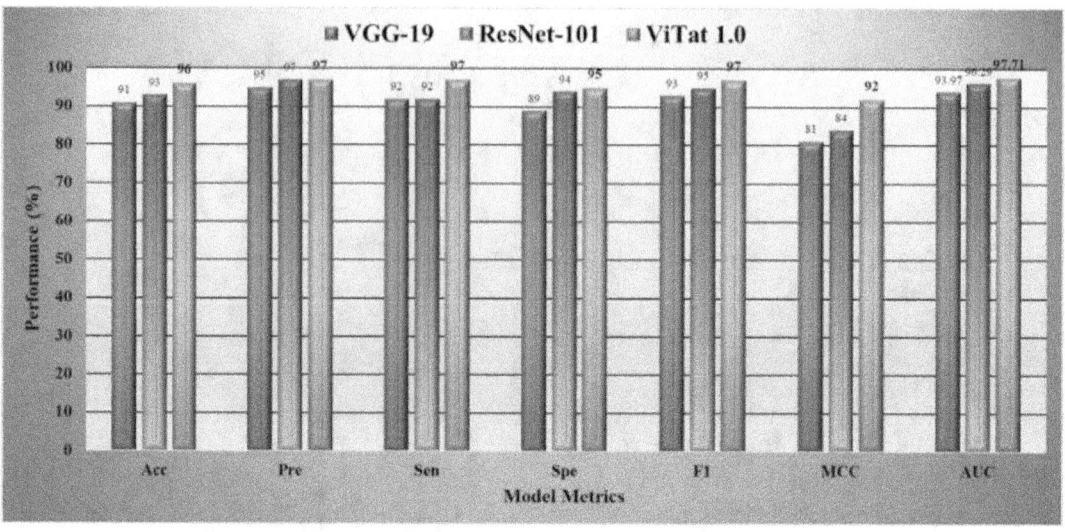

Figure 20.4 Model metrics on GAN augmented data
Source: Author

(Acc) of 91%, precision (Pre) of 92%, sensitivity (Sen) of 95%, specificity (Spe) of 86%, F1-score (F1) of 93%, Matthew's correlation-coefficient (MCC) of 81%, and area under the curve (AUC) of 92%.

The performance metrics of the studied models on the GAN-augmented BT image dataset are summarized in Figure 20.4. The results indicate a notable improvement across all models when using the GAN-augmented dataset. The proposed ViTat 1.0 model stands out with the highest performance metrics, achieving an accuracy of 96%, precision of 97%, sensitivity of 97%, specificity of 95%, F1-score of 97%, MCC of 92%, and an AUC value of 98%. This exceptional performance highlights ViTat 1.0's robust capability in detecting and classifying brain tumors with high accuracy and reliability.

We conclude from this experiment that the augmented BT image performed remarkably well when using the VGG-19, ResNet-101, and ViTat 1.0 model. In a similar case, while utilizing the expanded dataset (GAN augmented dataset), the VGG-19 and ResNet-101 model obtains an increasing classification accuracy of 3% compared to the classification accuracy with raw dataset. Additionally, our proposed ViTat 1.0 achives a significant boost in classification accuracy of 5% while deployed over the GAN augmented dataset compared to raw dataset as shown in Figure 20.4.

To measure how well a classification model performs, one must look at the Receiver Operating Characteristic (ROC) curve. We observe a statistically significant difference (p = 0.01) between the performance of other models in this investigation and our suggested ViTat 1.0 model. Figure 20.5 displays the ROC performance of each of the models that were considered. By reaching a robust area under the curve (AUC) value of 97.71%, the suggested model ViTat 1.0 has accomplished a notable milestone. In identifying resistant strains, ViTat 1.0 achieves the greatest AUC value,

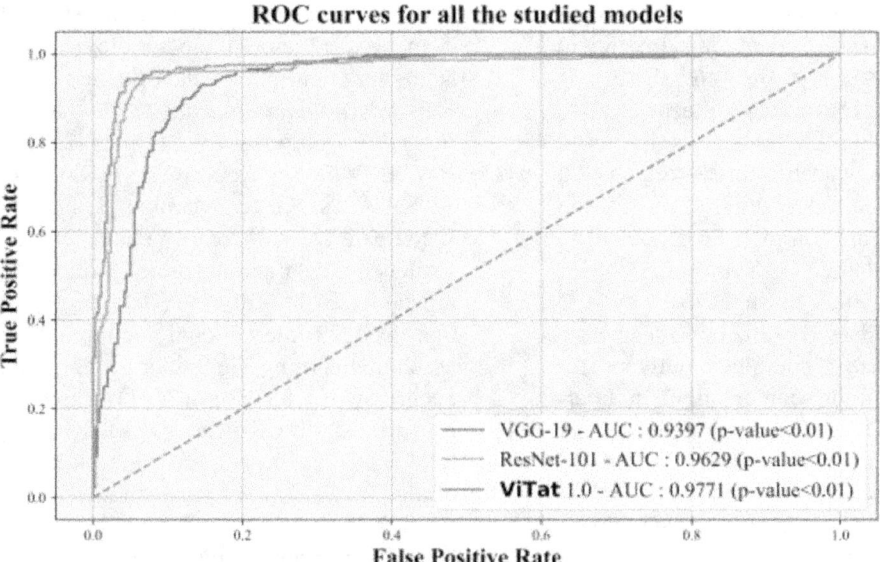

Figure 20.5 ROC curves of all the studied AI models
Source: Author

despite the imbalance and small dataset being obstacles.

Conclusion

Our research highlights how crucial state-of-the-art DL algorithms are for the rapid and precise detection of brain tumors. Our proposed ViTat 1.0 model integrates an attention-based ViT mechanism, which significantly boosts classification accuracy and model performance. We demonstrated this by comparing the performance of ViTs with CNNs. With a classification accuracy of 96%, our results demonstrate the usefulness of state-of-the-art architectures in medical imaging. The use of GANs for image augmentation has an increased accuracy of 5%, further proving that ViTat 1.0 is both resilient and applicable across different datasets. Improved patient outcomes in brain tumor identification are a direct result of this work in using GANs and ViTs, which not only increases detection capacities but also

allows for quicker and more accurate clinical diagnoses.

References

[1]   Babu Vimala, B., Srinivasan, S., Mathivanan, S. K., Mahalakshmi, Jayagopal, P., & Dalu, G. T. (2023). Detection and classification of brain tumor using hybrid deep learning models. *Scientific Reports*, 13, 23029.

[2]   Chen, Y., Yin, M., Li, Y., & Cai, Q. (2022). CSU-Net: a CNN-transformer parallel network for multimodal brain tumour segmentation. *Electronics*, 11, 2226.

[3]   Das, R., Nayak, D. S. K., Rout, C. P., Jena, L., & Swarnkar, T. (2024a). Deep learning techniques for identification of pneumonia: a CNN approach. In 2024 International Conference on Advancements in Smart, Secure and Intelligent Computing (ASSIC), (pp. 1–5). IEEE.

[4]   Das, T., Nayak, D. S. K., Kar, A., Jena, L., & Swarnkar, T. (2024b). ResNet-50: the deep networks for automated breast cancer classification using MR images. In 2024

International Conference on Advancements in Smart, Secure and Intelligent Computing (ASSIC), (pp. 1–6). IEEE.

[5] Iranmehr, A., Namvar, M., Rezaei, N., & Hanaei, S. (2023). Brain and spinal cord tumors among the life-threatening health problems: an introduction. In Human Brain and Spinal Cord Tumors: From Bench to Bedside. Volume 1: Neuroimmunology and Neurogenetics. Springer.

[6] Jia, Q., & Shu, H. (2021). Bitr-unet: a CNN-transformer combined network for MRI brain tumor segmentation. In International MICCAI Brainlesion Workshop, (pp. 3–14). Springer.

[7] Mahmud, M. I., Mamun, M., & Abdelgawad, A. (2023). A deep analysis of brain tumor detection from MR images using deep learning networks. *Algorithms*, 16, 176.

[8] Nayak, D. S. K., Das, R., Sahoo, S. K., & Swarnkar, T. (2025a). ARGai 1.0: A GAN augmented in silico approach for identifying resistant genes and strains in E. coli using vision transformer. *Computational Biology and Chemistry*, 115, 108342.

[9] Nayak, D. S. K., Mahapatra, S., Routray, S. P., Sahoo, S., Sahoo, S. K., Fouda, M. M., et al. (2024). AIGeneR 1.0: an artificial intelligence technique for the revelation of informative and antibiotic resistant genes in Escherichia coli. *Frontiers in Bioscience-Landmark*, 29, 82.

[10] Nayak, D. S. K., Mohapatra, S., Al-Dabass, D., & Swarnkar, T. (2023). Deep learning approaches for high dimension cancer microarray data feature prediction: a review. *Computational Intelligence in Cancer Diagnosis*, 13 –41.

[11] Nayak, D. S. K., Priyadarshini, A., Routray, S. P., Sahoo, S. K., & Swarnkar, T. (2025b).

ARGai 2.0: a feature engineering enabled deep network model for antibiotic resistance gene and strain identification in E. coli. *International Journal of Online and Biomedical Engineering,* 21, 108342.

[12] Nayak, D. S. K., Routray, S. P., Sahooo, S., Sahoo, S. K., & Swarnkar, T. (2022). A comparative study using next generation sequencing data and machine learning approach for crohn's disease (CD) identification. In 2022 International Conference on Machine Learning, Computer Systems and Security (MLCSS), (pp. 17–21). IEEE.

[13] Romero, D. W., Knigge, D. M., Gu, A., Bekkers, E. J., Gavves, E., Tomczak, J. M., et al. (2022). Towards a general purpose CNN for long range dependencies in $ N $ D. arXiv preprint arXiv:2206.03398.

[14] Saeedi, S., Rezayi, S., Keshavarz, H., & Niakan Kalhori, S. R. (2023). MRI-based brain tumor detection using convolutional deep learning methods and chosen machine learning techniques. *BMC Medical Informatics and Decision Making*, 23, 16.

[15] Subbarayudu, Y., Reddy, G. V., Keerthi, D., Shaik, M. J., Nagini, R., & Bhardwaj, N. (2024). The evaluation of 2D and EfficientB0 convolution networks for detecting brain tumor based on MRI images. In MATEC Web of Conferences, EDP Sciences, (p. 01110).

[16] Zeineldin, R. A., Karar, M. E., Elshaer, Z., Coburger, J., Wirtz, C. R., Burgert, O., et al. (2024). Explainable hybrid vision transformers and convolutional network for multimodal glioma segmentation in brain MRI. *Scientific Reports*, 14, 3713.

21 Real-time structure query language transformation using NLP

Preeti Ranjan Sahoo[1,a], Bimal Prasad Kar[2,b], Samaleswari Prasad Nayak[1,c], Sujit Kumar Jena[1,d] and Surajit Das[1,e]

[1]Department of Computer Science and Engineering Silicon University, Noida, UP, India

[2]Department of Computer Science and Engineering, Faculty of Engineering and Technology (ITER) Siksha 'O' Anusandhan (Deemed to be) University, Bhubaneswar, Odisha India

Abstract

There are various database applications available to store the structure data. The structure query language is used to interact with relational database systems. Most users like business owners, business analysts, application testers, and new inexperienced IT professionals are unfamiliar with the Structured Query Language (SQL) to store, retrieve, update, insert, and delete data in a database. Also, for a user, it becomes very challenging to remember the syntax for all the database applications, however, the user can say which database operation they want to perform in a database by using natural language. So, a model has been developed to generate SQL from natural language which a human can speak and understand easily. The natural language taken as input is converted into SQL which can be triggered on a database using database connectivity and the result will be shown to the user in a tabular view. This will also help the database owner to hide the real database table, schema, metadata of the table, and design of the database to the user as well. This model can save the training cost of an organization and it will allow users to interact with databases even if they don't have much knowledge of SQL. The paper addresses a real-world problem bridging the gap between natural language and SQL, which is highly relevant for non-technical users and enterprises.

Keywords: Deep learning, NLP, SQL

Introduction

In the growing generation of data, the ability to retrieve relevant information from huge amounts of data is crucial. Structured Query Language (SQL) is one of the languages to interacting with relational databases, which allow users to retrieve, update, and analyze data in a database. However, to use SQL users need a certain level of technical knowledge which limits the usage of SQL within a few specialized groups of technical experts such as database administrators and software developers. There is various database options available for the organization to store structured data. Though all these databases use SQL still there are few differences in SQL syntax between databases. So, it is a little difficult for someone to work on these databases without prior knowledge of SQL. The conversion of natural language to SQL has several challenges such as the complexity of natural language, the ambiguity of human language, context-dependent, and verity in syntax and semantics. On the other hand, SQL is a more

[a]cse.25dcsl04@silicon.ac.in, [b]bimalkar@soa.ac.in, [c]samaleswari.nayak@silicon.ac.in, [d]cse.25dcsl04@silicon.ac.in, [e]surajit.das@silicon.ac.in

DOI: 10.1201/9781003753391-21

formalized and precise language. So, understanding user requirements in query terms and translating them into a logically appropriate SQL syntax requires advanced NLP (Natural Language Processing) techniques and knowledge about the underlying database. The paper focuses on analysis of some existing approaches and techniques already implemented in natural language to SQL conversion, including rule-based systems and machine learning algorithms. It will also consider the challenges associated with handling different types of queries, such as retrieval, aggregation, filtering.

Literature Survey

Natural Language processing started in the 1940s. Till now various complex problems like voice-to-text, AI-based voice assistant, text summarization, sentiment analysis, and many problems have been solved using NLP. There are lots of attempts that have been made in recent times to find a perfect solution for converting User Query to SQL using NLP.

To understand the trends in NLP and the challenges to adopt NLP [1] author has mentioned the latest libraries along with methodologies and embedding used to solve the NLP problems. The author gives an overall idea about NLP and challenges faced while developing the model to solve NLP-related problems. There was an attempt made by authors [2] to form an SQL query based on the user input using the NLTK library and the solution has around 2880 records from a railway reservation system. It identifies table-related information based on mapping and this model was developed by parsing the user question. As per the conclusion of this research work the complexity of query formation is limited to some keywords used in SQL like SELECT, FROM, and TO any other keyword beyond

this in the user question may not predict the SQL correctly.

According to [3] user query can be converted to SQL by performing syntactic and semantic analysis on user query and table attributes can be used from a data dictionary. By this approach author was able to get results of medium complex queries like group by, having, and order by clause, as there is no trained model it can create ambiguity when user asks a question in two different ways. Through [4], researchers have prepared a model using Machine Learning algorithms based on POS tagging, word similarity, and attribute extraction. This author is able to predict simple select statements with where clause however model is unable to predict medium complex questions correctly. There are various datasets like wikisql and Spider, where user query and its corresponding SQL are present and that can be trained using deep learning algorithms [5]. There are a few models developed using deep learning [6, 7], but in these solutions the question is passed to the model along with table and column names manually. Due to this model is paused during execution to get the table and column information. There was a Model ValueNet developed by authors using Deep Learning [8] in which encoder-decoder architecture was used using a transformer library. To train the model a neural network was built i.e. LSTM. With this approach, the accuracy of the simple SELECT query is 77% and the accuracy percentage decreases on increasing the complexity of the query.

Authors have developed a model [9] using BERT embedding. In this solution, the model is developed using a pre-trained BERT-base model to create embedding and trained the model to classify the types of SQL based on different types of SQL operations like SELECT, GROUP BY, and WHERE. This model has an accuracy rate of

85.5%. There are few more articles [10–12] on solving the problem of natural language to SQL conversion in which authors compared existing models which give an insight into different models and frameworks used in the solution. The literature review covers a wide range of existing models, offering good context and showing awareness of current research. The summarization table of different models are developed using GloVe or BERT embeddings along with the performance index are given in Table 21.1.

Methodology

There will be a user interface where users will select database for interaction and an input text box in which user will ask the question. The user query will be taken as input and will be sent to backend using POST method and will be converted to SQL. The SQL will be triggered on the database to fetch the data. There is a process of converting the user's query which is in natural language to SQL. This methodology includes various preprocessing techniques like tokenization, Lemmatization, syntactic and semantic analysis after which the POS

tagging and parsing will be done. Then the output will be gone through the mapping process in which first keyword and attribute identification will be done then it will be passed through the trained model to generate the SQL as shown in the architecture diagram in Figure 21.1.

To achieve above mentioned steps in architecture there are two methodologies are identified based on literature review, in this paper and proposed two models, one with GloVe embedding another model with BERT embedding. As the task is having labeled dataset where each question has its corresponding SQL query, a supervised learning method can be used. To solve this problem a neural network model, i.e. LSTM (Long Short-Term Memory) will be developed. As the problem statement is sequential, keras library is used to develop the model using ADAM optimizer and sparse_categorical_crossentropy as loss function. ADAM algorithm [14] is used for optimization techniques in gradient descent problems which accelerate the optimization process by minimizing number of function evaluations required to reach the optimal solution.

Table 21.1 Summary of models studied in literature review.

Model	Approach	Embedding	Dev Acc. (%)	Test Acc. (%)
Baseline	Sequential	Glove	37	35.9
SEQ2SQL	Sequential	Glove	60.8	59.4
SQLNET	Slot-Filling	Glove	69.8	68
TypeSQL	Slot-Filling	Glove	74.5	73.5
SQLova	Slot-Filling	BERT	90.2	86.6
Content Enhanced SQLova	Slot-Filling	BERT	91.1	90.1
Data Agnostic Zero Shot Learning	Slot-Filling	RoBERTa	77	76.7
ValueNet	Slot-Filling	RoBERTa	86.5	85.3

Source: Author

ADAM is combination of gradient decent techniques i.e., root mean square propagation (RMSP) and adaptive gradient algorithm (AdaGrad). AdaGrad is accelerates the gradient descent by considering exponentially weighted mean of gradients. Using meaning it makes the algorithm converge faster towards the minima. Similarly, RMS propagation is an adaptive learning algorithm designed to improve AdaGrad considering exponential moving average instead of cumulative sum of squared gradients mean.

Implementation

Data collection and analysis

To find the solution for problem of converting natural language to SQL using NLP, a model will be trained with a large set of data and test them. So WikiSQL dataset has been collected from Kaggle. This dataset is a large crowd-sourced dataset which is having 80654 questions in English language and its corresponding SQL queries spanned across 24241 tables from Wikipedia. The dataset have attributes named question, Table and SQL.

Before creating the model, we need to understand the data collected during data collection phase and attributes involved in the dataset. The high-level insight of the dataset given in Table 21.2. To predict SQL, need to understand the distribution of question length and respective SQL length of the dataset i.e. the number of words present in a question and SQL, which will help us to encode the questions present in the dataset. In Figure 21.2 graph maximum of the questions word count is in between 10 to 150

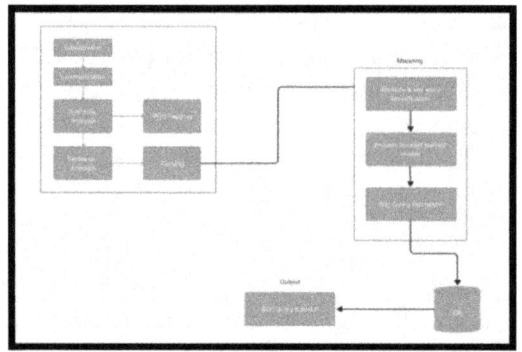

Figure 21.1 Proposed design to convert natural language to SQL
Source: Author

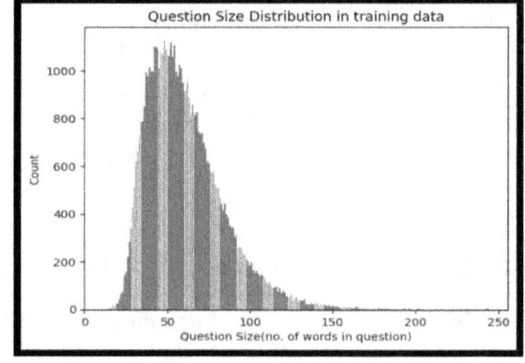

Figure 21.2 User question size distribution
Source: Author

Table 21.2 Dataset summary.

Dataset	Records	Questions	Tables	SQL	Null Values
Train.csv	56355	56143	17984	54355	NA
Test.csv	15878	15832	5069	15595	NA
Validation.csv	8421	8390	2630	8300	NA

Source: Author

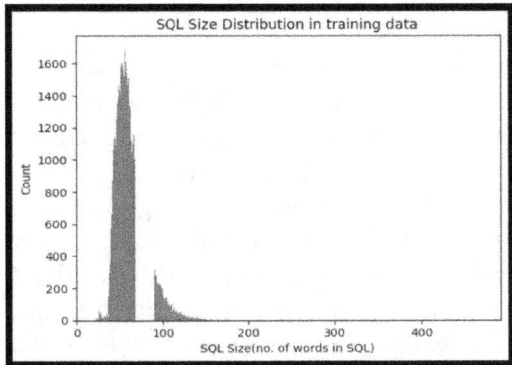

Figure 21.3 SQL Size distribution
Source: Author

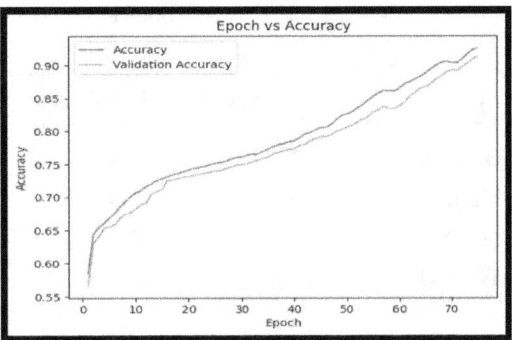

Figure 21.5 Epoch vs. accuracy for model 2
Source: Author

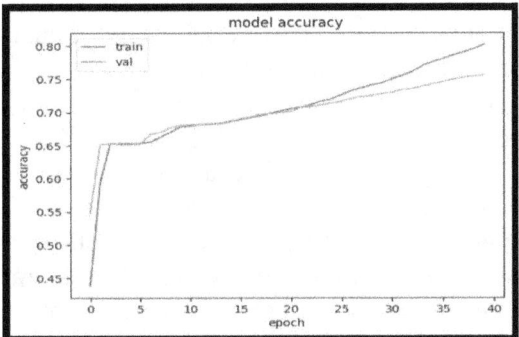

Figure 21.4 Epoch vs. accuracy for model 1
Source: Author

steps like tokenization, lemmatization, syntactic and semantic analysis.

Model

Two models created using GloVe (Model 1) and BERT (Model 2) embedding, dataset divided into 80:20 ratio. Once both input and output vocabulary processed through embedding, the embedding matrix is created. Then the encoder and decoder created with LSTM and encoder_input, decoder_input and decoder_output are defined which is going to be used in the model definition.

Result analysis

To understand the model performance, we need to evaluate the developed model and the model compared with some of the exiting solution.

words. Where as in Figure 21.3 graph it is clear that maximum of the SQL word count is between 10 to 120 words.

Data pre-processing

Once the data is loaded to data frame, data preprocessing done like dropping duplicate records and records having missing or null values. As the model will be dealing with large text, the word formatting done for questions written in sort hand and additional space are removed also all the text are converted to lower case letters using regular expression and lambda function. Pre-trained embedding files for both GloVe and BERT-base [13] will handle all the preprocessing

In Figure 21.4 graph, on every epoch the accuracy has increased and the development accuracy is 80.13% and validation accuracy is 75.54%. The model is tested with 100 questions picked randomly from the test data and it is found that model predicated the output of 76 questions correctly. Whereas in Figure 21.5 graph for the model developed using BERT is having development accuracy is 92.5% and validation accuracy is 91.27%. The model is tested with 100 questions picked randomly from

Table 21.3 Result comparison (GloVe Embedding).

Model	Dev Acc.	Test Acc.
Baseline	37	35.9
SEQ2SQL	60.8	59.4
SQLNET	69.8	68
TypeSQL	74.5	73.5
Model 1	80.13	76

Source: Author

Table 21.4 Result comparison (BERT Models).

Model	Dev Acc.	Test Acc.
SQLova	87.2	86.2
SQLova2	90.2	89.6
Content enhanced SQLova	90.3	89.2
Content Enhanced SQLova2	91.1	90.1
Model 2	92.5	91.2

Source: Author

the test data and it is found that model predicated the SQL of 90 questions correctly. Table 21.3 shows the comparison of developed model with existing models developed using GloVe embedding, similarly Table 21.4 shows the comparison of developed model with existing model developed using BERT embeddings.

From Table 21.3 model comparison, there is increase of 5% in dev accuracy and 2.5% increase in test accuracy on comparison with the models reviewed using GloVe embedding. And form Table 21.4 result comparison, there is increase of 1.2% in dev accuracy and 1% increase in test accuracy on comparison with the models reviewed using BERT embedding. Overall, the model developed using $BERT_{BASE}$ gives better accuracy.

Conclusion and Future Work

In conclusion, converting a query which is in natural language to SQL is a challenging yet crucial task in the field of NLP and database management. This process involves translating human-readable queries into structured and executable SQL, which enables seamless interaction with relational databases. The use of machine learning and deep learning models, such as transformers and neural networks, significant progress has been made in developing accurate and efficient natural language to SQL conversion systems. The introduction of transformer-based models, like BERT, has brought about substantial improvements in the quality of the generated SQL queries. The paper provides comparative performance analysis using both GloVe and BERT embeddings, with clearly reported accuracy metrics and improvement over existing models. These models can capture complex syntactic and semantic relationships within the natural language input, leading to more contextually relevant and accurate SQL translations. As there is continued development in the field of NLP, there is expectation of further innovations and more sophisticated approaches that will enhance the performance and practicality of natural language to SQL conversion systems.

References

[1] Shaik, T., Tao, X., Li, Y., Dann, C., McDonald, J., Redmond, P., et al. (2022). A review of the trends and challenges in adopting natural language processing methods for education feedback analysis. *IEEE Access*, 10, 56720–56739.

[2] Uma, M., Sneha, V., Sneha, G., Bhuvana, J., & Bharathi, B. (2019). Formation of SQL from natural language query using NLP. In 2019 International Conference on Computational Intelligence in Data Science (ICCIDS), (pp. 1–5). IEEE.

[3]   Kate, A., Kamble, S., Bodkhe, A., & Joshi, M. (2018). Conversion of natural language query to SQL query. In 2018 Second International Conference on Electronics, Communication and Aerospace Technology (ICECA), (pp. 488–491). IEEE.

[4]   Arefin, M., Hossen, K. M., & Uddin, M. N. (2021). Natural language query to SQL conversion using machine learning approach. In 2021 3rd International Conference on Sustainable Technologies for Industry 4.0 (STI), (pp. 1–6). IEEE.

[5]   Katsogiannis-Meimarakis, G., & Koutrika, G. (2021). A deep dive into deep learning approaches for text-to-sql systems. In Proceedings of the 2021 International Conference on Management of Data, (pp. 2846–2851).

[6]   Ahkouk, K., & Machkour, M. (2019). Human language question to SQL query using deep learning. In 2019 Third International Conference on Intelligent Computing in Data Sciences (ICDS), (pp. 1–6). IEEE.

[7]   Pal, D., Sharma, H., & Chaudhuri, K. (2021). Data agnostic roberta-based natural language to SQL query generation. In 2021 6th International Conference for Convergence in Technology (I2CT), (pp. 1–5). IEEE.

[8]   Brunner, U., & Stockinger, K. (2021). Valuenet: a natural language-to-sql system that learns from database information. In 2021 IEEE 37th International Conference on Data Engineering (ICDE), (pp. 2177–2182). IEEE.

[9]   Long, H., & Cao, D. (2021). Bert-based text-to-SQL generation method with question-table content enhancement and template filling. In 2021 2nd International Conference on Information Science and Education (ICISE-IE), (pp. 969–973). IEEE.

[10] Ahkouk, K., Machkour, M., Ennaji, M., Erraha, B., & Antari, J. (2019). Comparative study of existing approaches on the task of natural language to database language. In 2019 International Conference of Computer Science and Renewable Energies (ICCSRE), (pp. 1–6). IEEE.

[11] Kumar, A., Nagarkar, P., Nalhe, P., & Vijayakumar, S. (2022). Deep Learning Driven Natural Languages Text to SQL Query Conversion: A Survey. arXiv preprint arXiv:2208.04415. https://doi.org/10.48550/arXiv.2208.04415.

[12] Wong, A., Joiner, D., Chiu, C., Elsayed, M., Pereira, K., Khmelevsky, Y., et al. (2021). A survey of natural language processing implementation for data query systems. In 2021 IEEE International Conference on Recent Advances in Systems Science and Engineering (RASSE), (pp. 1–8). IEEE.

[13] Devlin, J., Chang, M. W., Lee, K., & Toutanova, K. (2019, June). Bert: Pre-training of deep bidirectional transformers for language understanding. In Proceedings of the 2019 conference of the North American chapter of the association for computational linguistics: human language technologies, volume 1 (long and short papers) (pp. 4171-4186).

[14] Kingma, D. P., & Ba, J. (2015). Adam: A Method for Stochastic Optimization. International Conference on Learning Representations (ICLR), San Diego, CA. https://arxiv.org/abs/1412.6980.

22 Strawberry ripeness detection using machine learning techniques

Amlan Pati[1,a], Subhendu Pati[2,b] and Binod Kumar Sahu[2,c]

[1]Department of Comp. Sc. and Engg., International Institute of Information Technology, Bhubaneswar, Odisha, India

[2]Department of Electrical Engineering, Siksha O Anusandhan Deemed to be University, Bhubaneswar, Odisha, India

Abstract

Food loss and waste remain critical global challenges, necessitating efficient methods for assessing fruit and vegetable ripeness. Traditional approaches, such as chemical and sensory evaluations, are often time-consuming, costly, and impractical for large-scale real-time applications. To address these limitations, this study employs extreme learning machine models optimized using, grid search optimization, particle swarm optimization, Bayesian search optimization and random search optimization for non-destructive ripeness classification. The input data consists of strawberry images, classified into two categories: pickable (ripe) and unpickable (unripe). The comparative experimental results indicate that the extreme learning model with Bayesian optimizer outperforms all the others in terms of both classification accuracy and hinge loss, providing the best performance to distinguish ripe and unripe strawberries. Additionally, the results show that Extreme Learning model with Random Search Optimizer and Particle Swarm Optimizer manages precision and recall effectively, whereas the same model with Grid Search Optimizer has a less accurate result and a higher hinge loss, both of which indicate a lesser efficiency. Hyper-parameter tuning proved important to ripeness classification, as shown by these results. Future work will focus on dataset expansion, multimodal sensor integration, and real-time deployment of these models for automated agricultural applications.

Keywords: Bayesian optimization, extreme learning machine, grid search optimization, particle swarm optimization, random search optimization

Introduction

Economic development, environmental protection and global food security are severely affected by wastage of edibles is affecting. Determination of degree of ripeness of vegetables and fruits plays a crucial role in reducing food waste, increasing supply chain functionality and satisfying the customers [3]. Conventional methods of determining the degree of ripeness such as chemical investigation, physical examination, etc. involve a lot of time and there is always a chance of human error [2]. To avoid all these difficulties, there is a need for computerized non-destructive methods for classifying the ripeness of fruits.

Because of the recent development in various artificial intelligence (AI) and machine learning (ML) techniques, now it is possible to generate computerized models for separating fruits and vegetables as per their level of maturity. Recently, various Convolutional Neural Networks (CNNs)

[a]amlanpati@gmail.com, [b]subhendupati90@gmail.com, [c]binoditer@gmail.com

DOI: 10.1201/9781003753391-22

are developed and have become popular in the field of classification problems in different research areas [1]. These models have the capability of evaluating the sight, texture and spectral details with extremely high accuracy. The only problem lying in deep learning is its computational complexity and high computation time [3].

Neural networks (NN) and feed-forward single-hidden layer extreme learning machine (ELM) techniques are developed and considered as more effective due to their simple configuration and fast training time. Unlike traditional backpropagation-based models, output weights are computed analytically after hidden layer parameter randomization, eliminating dependencies on iterative gradient-based optimization. This shrinks the number of resources required and also decreases the time consumed on computation and training, thereby improves the overall efficiency in assessing the quality of food. Further improvements in the classification performance of ELM were achieved by optimization methods including PSO, GSO, RSO, and BO. By adjusting hyperparameters, accuracy and generalization are enhanced, and it is ensured that no overfitting is being done on predictions [2]. Benchmarks comparing hyperparameter tuning proved that optimized ELM models outperformed deep learning methods in computational efficiency and responsiveness, proving the models' real-time agricultural application suitability.

This paper aims to study the applicability of ELM for strawberry ripeness detection. Different parameter selection strategies were analyzed for increasing model performance. The goal is to formulate a singular standard assessing all other methodologies using publicly available data and evaluation criteria like precision, recall, and computational complexity. Our findings aim to make the AI-driven ripeness classification process more accurate by providing scalable solutions for automated agricultural systems.

Mathematical Modelling for ELM

For further understanding, ELM is an SLFN with an Eigenvalue decomposition as a training method to make it different from a classical NN. In contrast to traditional models based on backpropagation, the ELM model bypasses the iterative gradient-based optimization method by randomly generating the inner hidden layer weights and logically calculating the output weights [4]. This technique retains generalization ability with considerable time savings. Figure 22.1 shows the SLFN structure.

Basic formulation of ELM

Let us assume an SLFN has the following form with NNN training examples:

$$(x_i, t_i), \text{ where } x_i \in R^d,$$
$$t_i \in R^m, i = 1, 2, \dots, N. \quad (1)$$

Where, x_i is the input vector and r_i is the target output. If a network having L hidden neurons with activation function $g(x)$, the output of the hidden layer outcome can be mathematically expressed as:

$$H = g(WX + b) \quad (2)$$

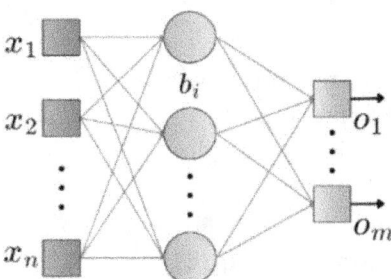

Figure 22.1 Structure of SLFN
Source: Author

Where:

W represents the randomly selected input weights.

b represents the biased vector.

H represents the hidden layer of output.

$g(\cdot)$ represents is the activation function.

The output of the ELM network is expressed as:

$$Y = H\beta \qquad (3)$$

Where:

β represents the output weight.

Output weight determination

To compute β\beta$\beta$, ELM minimizes the least-square error function:

$$min \parallel H\beta - T \parallel^2 \qquad (4)$$

Where, *T* is the target matrix. With the help of Moore-Penrose inverse the finest solution for the output weight (β) is obtained as:

$$\beta = H^\dagger T \qquad (5)$$

Where $H^\dagger$ represents the Moore-Penrose pseudo-inverse of *H*. This direct calculation removes iterative updating of weights there by considerably improves the speed of training phase.

Computational complexity and advantages

Major benefits of ELM are:

- High training speed.
- Better overall performance.
- Simple to implement.
- Highly Efficient for large-scale computation.

Optimization Techniques

Optimization techniques are used in ML models to increase their efficacy. Some

widely used optimization techniques to enhance the performance of ML techniques in this work are PSO, GSO, BO, and RSO.

PSO algorithm

It is a population based optimization technique based on social behavior of fish [5, 6].

The standard PSO algorithm operates as follows:

Step 1. Initialization: Randomly initialize a swarm of particles called initial solutions.

Step 2. Fitness Evaluation: Determine each particle's fitness using a well-defined objective function.

Step 3. Update Personal Best i.e. update the position of each particle i.e. pbest.

Step 4. Update Global Best i.e. update the global best (gbest).

Step 5. Velocity and Position Update:

v(t+1)=w(t)+c1*r1   (pbest_x(t)+c2*r2 (gbest-x(t))

x(t+1)=x(t)+v(t+1)

Where, v(t) is the velocity of particle at iteration t, x(t) is the position of particle at iteration t, w: Inertia weight, c1, c2: Acceleration coefficients, r1, r2: Random values from a uniform distribution in [0,1]

Step 6. Termination: Repeat until convergence or maximum iterations are reached.

GSO algorithm

GSO is an exhaustive search approach used to optimize the best combination of hyperparameters in a given range. It exhaustively checks all the hyperparameter configurations and returns the best set according to a performance measurable [8].

Recent works have applied GSO widely in machine learning to tune model parameters.

GSO is used to optimally design the parameters of Support Vector Machine (SVM) to obtain superior classification performance [7]. GSO is also used to determine the optimal weights and bias ELM structure in the field of classification with better accuracy.

BO algorithm

This algorithm uses a probabilistic model to control the exploration process. Steps involved in this algorithm are:

- Random initialization
- Development of the Gaussian process (GP) model.
- Updation of the GP Model.
- Evaluation of the next point.
- Computation of the objective function at the selected point.
- Termination: Continue until the stopping criterion are met.

RSO algorithm

RSO is a population-based optimization technique that selects parameter values randomly from a predefined search space. Unlike GSO, which systematically evaluates all combinations, RSO provides a more efficient approach by sampling a subset of configurations, making it particularly

effective in high-dimensional spaces [9]. The standard RSO algorithm operates as follows:

- Random initialization for weights and bias.
- Evaluation of fitness function.
- Selection of the best solution.
- Termination of the search process if termination criteria are met.

Result and Discussion

Comparative performance analysis of ELM with different optimization techniques is presented in Table 22.1. The models are evaluated based on accuracy, hinge loss, precision, recall, specificity, and F1 score. The table is sorted in descending order of hinge loss, highlighting that BO achieves the lowest hinge loss and highest accuracy, indicating superior performance. Meanwhile, GSO exhibits the highest hinge loss, suggesting a relatively weaker separation between classes. To further illustrate the impact of these optimizations, Figures 22.2–22.5 provide graphical representations of key evaluation metrics.

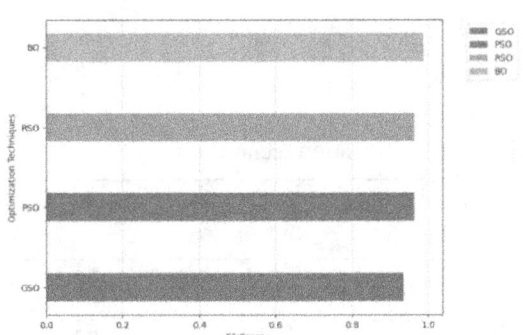

Figure 22.2 F1-Score comparison across different optimization techniques
Source: Author

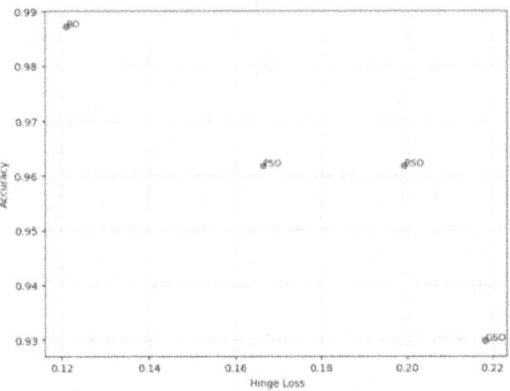

Figure 22.3 Hinge loss vs accuracy across different models
Source: Author

The dataset used for training was collected from Kaggle, containing images of strawberries split between two groups: pickable (ripe) and unpickable (unripe). To determine the optimal architecture for the ELM model, experiments were conducted by varying the number of hidden neurons (HNs) (5, 10, 20, 30, 40, 50, 60, 70, 80, 90) while keeping W and b random. The number of neurons that resulted in the lowest hinge loss—selected as the loss function—was chosen, which was found to be 10. Once the optimal neuron count was fixed at 10, different optimization techniques were applied to refine the W and b selection, improving classification performance.

The F1-score delivers a well-adjusted measure between recall and precision, making it an essential measure for determining the success of the model. The model effectively mitigates false positives and false negatives when the F1 Score is higher. As shown in Table 22.1, BO achieves the highest F1-score (0.9882), followed by PSO and RSO, while GSO performs the worst. Figure 22.2 shows the F1 Score trend across all optimization techniques, highlighting BO's superior performance.

Hinge loss is commonly used for classification tasks involving margin-based learning, such as SVMs. Lower hinge loss values generally correlate with higher accuracy, as they indicate better separation of classes. As observed in Table 22.1, BO achieves

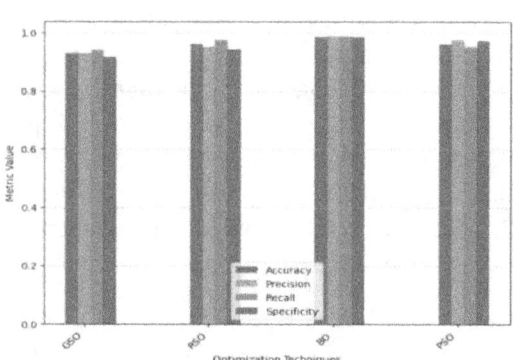

Figure 22.4 Comparison of accuracy, precision, recall, and specificity
Source: Author

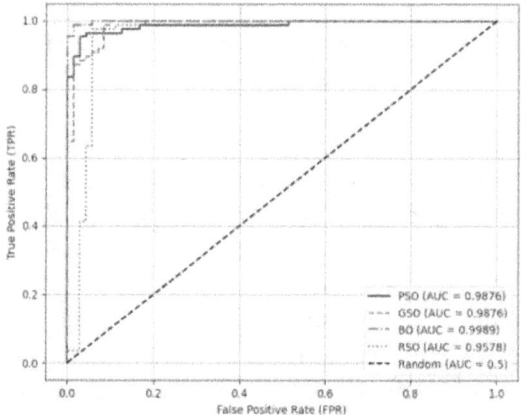

Figure 22.5 ROC Curve and AUC for model evaluation
Source: Author

Table 22.1 Performance comparison of ELM with different optimization techniques.

Optimization method	Accuracy (%)	Hinge loss	Precision	Recall	Specificity	F1-Score
ELM with GSO	92.99	0.2183	0.9302	0.9412	0.9167	0.9357
ELM with RSO	96.18	0.1992	0.9540	0.9765	0.9444	0.9651
ELM with PSO	96.18	0.1665	0.9759	0.9529	0.9722	0.9643
ELM with BO	98.73	0.1211	0.9882	0.9882	0.9861	0.9882

Source: Author

the lowest hinge loss (0.1211) and highest accuracy (98.73%), while GSO has the highest hinge loss (0.2183) and the lowest accuracy (92.99%). Figure 22.3 presents a scatter plot of hinge loss vs accuracy across all optimization techniques.

A comprehensive evaluation of different metrics helps in understanding the trade-offs between various optimization techniques. Accuracy provides an overall performance measure, while precision and recall focus on specific aspects of classification correctness. Specificity, particularly relevant in imbalanced datasets, ensures that negative classes are correctly identified. The comparison of bar plots in Figure 22.4 reveals that PSO, RSO, and GSO exhibit varying metric values, whereas BO consistently performs well on all measures.

The trade-off between true positive rate (TPR) and false positive rate (FPR) across various categorization thresholds is depicted by the receiver operating characteristic (ROC) curve. The discriminative power of the model is summarized by a single scalar value called the area under the curve (AUC). Figure 22.5 provides the ROC AUC curve, showing that BO achieves the highest AUC, indicating superior classification performance.

Conclusion

This study presents a comparative analysis of different optimization techniques applied to ELM for fruit and vegetable classification. The key findings are as follows:

- BO achieves the highest accuracy (98.73%) and lowest hinge loss (0.1211), demonstrating superior classification performance and robustness.
- PSO and RSO perform competitively with 96.18% accuracy, balancing precision and recall effectively.

- GSO yields the lowest accuracy (92.99%) and highest hinge loss (0.2183), indicating suboptimal hyperparameter selection.
- F1 Score and ROC-AUC analyses validate the effectiveness of BO and PSO, confirming their capability in achieving high generalization and reliability.

These findings suggest that BO is the most effective strategy for enhancing ELM-based classification, while PSO and RSO also provide strong alternatives with lower computational costs.

References

[1] Tapia-Mendez, E., Cruz-Albarran, I. A., Tovar-Arriaga, S., & Morales-Hernandez, L. A. (2023). Deep learning-based method for classification and ripeness assessment of fruits and vegetables. *Applied Sciences*, 13(22), 12504.

[2] Mi, Z., & Yan, W. Q. (2024). Strawberry ripeness detection using deep learning models. *Big Data and Cognitive Computing*, 8(8), 92.

[3] Rizzo, M., Marcuzzo, M., Zangari, A., Gasparetto, A., & Albarelli, A. (2023). Fruit ripeness classification: a survey. *Artificial Intelligence in Agriculture*, 7, 44–57.

[4] Wang, J., Lu, S., Wang, S. H., & Zhang, Y. D. (2022). A review on extreme learning machine. *Multimedia Tools and Applications*, 81(29), 41611–41660.

[5] Imran, M., Hashim, R., & Abd Khalid, N. E. (2013). An overview of particle swarm optimization variants. *Procedia Engineering*, 53, 491–496.

[6] Gad, A. G. (2022). Particle swarm optimization algorithm and its applications: a systematic review. *Archives of Computational Methods in Engineering*, 29(5), 2531–2561.

[7] Syarif, I., Prugel-Bennett, A., & Wills, G. (2016). SVM parameter optimization using grid search and genetic algorithm to

improve classification performance. *TEL-KOMNIKA (Telecommunication Computing Electronics and Control)*, 14(4), 1502–1509.

[8]   Budiman, F. (2019). SVM-RBF parameters testing optimization using cross validation and grid search to improve multiclass classification. *Nauchnaya Vizualizatsiya*, 11(1), 80–90.

[9]   Bergstra, J., & Bengio, Y. (2012). Random search for hyper-parameter optimization. *The Journal of Machine Learning Research*, 13(1), 281–305.

23 Harnessing machine learning for creating of smart book recommendation system

Premananda Sahu[1,a], G. S. Pradeep Ghantasala[2,b], Srikanta Kumar Mohapatra[3,c], Jayashree Mohanty[4,d], Rajesh Sharma, R.[2,e] and Akey Sungheetha[2,f]

[1]School of Computer Science and Engineering, Lovely Professional University, Phagwara, Punjab, India

[2]Department of Computer Science and Engineering, Alliance College of Engineering and Design, Alliance University, Bengaluru, Karnataka, India

[3]Chitkara University Institute of Engineering and Technology, Chitkara University, Punjab, India

[4]Department of CSE, Chandigarh University, Punjab, India

Abstract

The primary goal of a recommendation system is to simplify the process of suggesting relevant items to users, enhancing their experience and making their lives easier. As data grows rapidly over the web, users gradually more depend on resourceful tools to explore and right to use appropriate information. Recommendation systems have happened to important for customer internet corporations, including e-commerce policy, streaming facilities, and online networking services, since they provide modified proposals to users including their inclination. They are built to increase customer contentment and engagement that ultimately drives productivity due to improved sales, customer preservation, and extended use of the platforms. Recommendation systems have an important place in online book marketing, as they help retailer's advice books, which are in line with the reading predilection of their customers, increasing their level of contentment and resulting in more sales. This novel work focusing to sustain readers by creating a book commendation system driven by machine learning that investigates customer preferences and the reading prototypes of those users. By applying collaborative filtering methods, including Pearson correlation and cosine similarity in Nearest Neighbors, and popularity-based methods, the structure will be able to lead customers in the direction of books of interest, cultivating for reading and promoting the growth of that habit.

Keywords: Book recommender system, collaborative filtering, cosine similarity, nearest neighbor, Pearson correlation, popularity-based filtering

Introduction

The fast development of data within the digital environment has brought about provocations of resourcefully finding appropriate, modified content. As large datasets shimmering user favorites and behaviors expand, finding one's way through an explosion of choices—most predominantly in making choices of reading matter—becomes quite a burden. In reply to that,

[a]prema.uce@gmail.com, [b]ggspradeep@gmail.com, [c]srikanta.2k7@gmail.com, [d]jayashree.simi2k5@gmail.com, [e]sharmaphd20@gmail.com, [f]sun20it@gmail.com

DOI: 10.1201/9781003753391-23

recommendation systems have come to be a useful tool for meeting this challenge. These are driven by complicated algorithms that distribute users' tailor-made proposals based on taste, interest, and past communications, changing the way people find and experience new contented. Notably used across various organizations like e-commerce, amusement, and online culture, the systems are generally useful for enhancing the users' experience by reducing evaluation-system efforts and increasing user agreement.

In the perspective of books, recommendation systems clutch enormous potential. The enormous amount of genres, designations, and authors accessible today can build book assortment an intimidating assignment for readers. Numerous people experience decision exhaustion when challenging to decide their subsequently read, frequently resulting in discontent or require of motivation to preserve reading. Investigation highlights the cognitive and exciting settlement of reading, comprising of improved mental quickness and emotional astuteness, yet the complexity in finding appropriate books avoids many from entirely implementation this practice [1]. A modified book recommendation system deal with these confronts by filtering during an overpowering array of alternative to propose books that support with a user's predilections. This not only enhances the effectiveness of the book assortment procedure but also supports reliable reading, development a deeper association to the action.

Recommendation systems work with different methods comprises of collaborative filtering, content-based filtering, along with hybrid models. In collaborative filtering, the system works by analyzing data about consumers of comparable tastes in order to create a recommendation; content-based filtering emphasizes the

essential properties of the books, which include genre, author, as well as theme. Hybrid systems merge the two, therefore achieving more precise and vigorous proposal by inheriting the best from both worlds. With the advance of machine learning approaches, these systems have been able to adapt better and better to the predilections of users, continuously enhancing their recommendations with instance. In this way, users get hints that change with the development of their altering benefits and reading practices.

Furthermore, online book recommendation systems have certain compensations over the conventional ways of discovering books. These systems liberate time, decrease disturbance, and amplify the chances of verdict books that really reverberate with the readers by analyzing the reading history and preferences of the users. They too eradicate the investigative process habitually connected with book selection and let the customers focus on liking their reading practice. Moreover, the modified character of the systems improves customer approval and appointment, building faith and consistency in the platform [2].

Incorporation of ML algorithms makes the recommendation system even more effective. They process user response and recognize prototypes in bulky datasets to distribute better and more polished suggestions to a great variety of readers. With growing data and improvement in expertise, the prospective for adapted recommendations will keep on expanding, contributing users even more accurate and appropriate options. Eventually, online book recommendation systems not only make finding the correct books easier but also motivate a love for reading, nudging people to harvest the countless cognitive and exciting benefits this activity has in store.

Literature Survey

Recommendation systems' explosive expansion has changed how people use online policies, particularly in fields such as electronic text reading, streaming, and e-commerce. Previously various researchers have worked on the above problem statement, some of them has expressed in following manner:

Fiarni et al. [3] has drawn the growth of a business analytics electoral recommender system. The system focuses at providing recommendations for political aspirants including different variables. Outcomes from user recognition tests showed scores of 86% for simplicity of use and 78.5% for the apparent usefulness of the planned system's key characteristics. Devika and Milton [4] examined the completion evaluation of numerous studies on book recommendation systems. Additionally, the authors have highlighted the research concerns and potential paths for future growth to develop the functionality of the book recommendation system. The researchers predicted that these outcomes will aid future reading, particularly in the area of book recommender systems. Latrech et al. [5] proposed hybrid recommender system which includes twitter sentiment analysis. Their work has done with the help of collaborative filtering process based on sentiment analysis module after carrying out demographic filter. Their work evaluated root mean square error and mean absolute error benchmarks.

Sireesha et al. [6] has forecasted a method that associates collaborative filtering and K-nearest neighbor techniques to categorize and recommend books. The approach boils down to gaining the cosine similarity between the user's book vector and book depictions. Furthermore, singular value decomposition (SVD) is used in the collaborative filtering. The system's proficiency is resolute based on the user ratings furnished. Kavitha and Sankar Murugesan [7] has forecasted a means of recommending books by determining significant aspects in user ratings with a dedicated WALS based recommendation system. Systematic approaches have been used where RMSE is lessened to progress the accuracy of recommendations. This examination notes a marked enhancement with regard to RMSE when compared with distinctive recommendation systems, even though precise figures in accuracy are not stated. Devika and Milton [8] has focused focuses on the possibility of designing book recommendation systems from the year 2012 to 2023, and covers performance analysis as well. The survey offers an overview of the datasets, features, and sources used within the systems, and identifies six distinct categories of recommendation techniques. Although the survey does seek to answer various important questions related to the overall problem, performance is not one of them. The broad aspects of the problems involved with researching and analyzing the performance of book recommender systems suggests powerful future directions to be explored.

Rajalakshmi et al. [9] deliberates to develop a personalized system for recommending online books using a hybrid approach to machine learning. The system aims to improve its ability to recommend books using readers' interests by combining several algorithms together. The study underlines the need for personalized recommendations and notes the increase in accuracy and profitability as superior to systems which depend on user input alone. Jadon and Patil [10] has proposed an extensive array of metrics to capture different facets of recommendation system performance. It talks about similarity metrics, candidate generation metrics, predictive metrics, ranking metrics and business metrics. This paper also touches on how these metrics can be used in context and how they are not standalone, which creates a framework for choosing metrics and interpreting them, which can translate into a system & measurable transformation that aligns to business objectives. Zhiyuli et al. [11] proposes BookGPT, a framework that integrates state-of-the-art large language model technology into book recommendation systems. The paper utilizes ChatGPT for recommendation modeling with some tasks such as predicting book ratings, predicting user ratings of books, and generating summaries of books. It talks about how realistic it is to use large language models for recommending books and contrasts their performances with traditional recommendation models. It gives excellent information about the pros and cons of LLM, but it did not give specific accuracies.

Methods and Techniques

Figure 23.1 visualizes the entire methodology used in this study for the development of an intelligent book recommendation system, delineating subsequent steps in data collection, preprocessing operations, techniques for recommendation generation based on popularity and collaborative filtering, and performance evaluation of the system. It shows how these components flow together to provide personalized recommendations of books to users.

Datasets
Here the users have explored two types of datasets i.e. user data and book data where the user dataset contains 277,674 entries with three columns:

User-ID: A unique identifier for each user, represented as an integer.

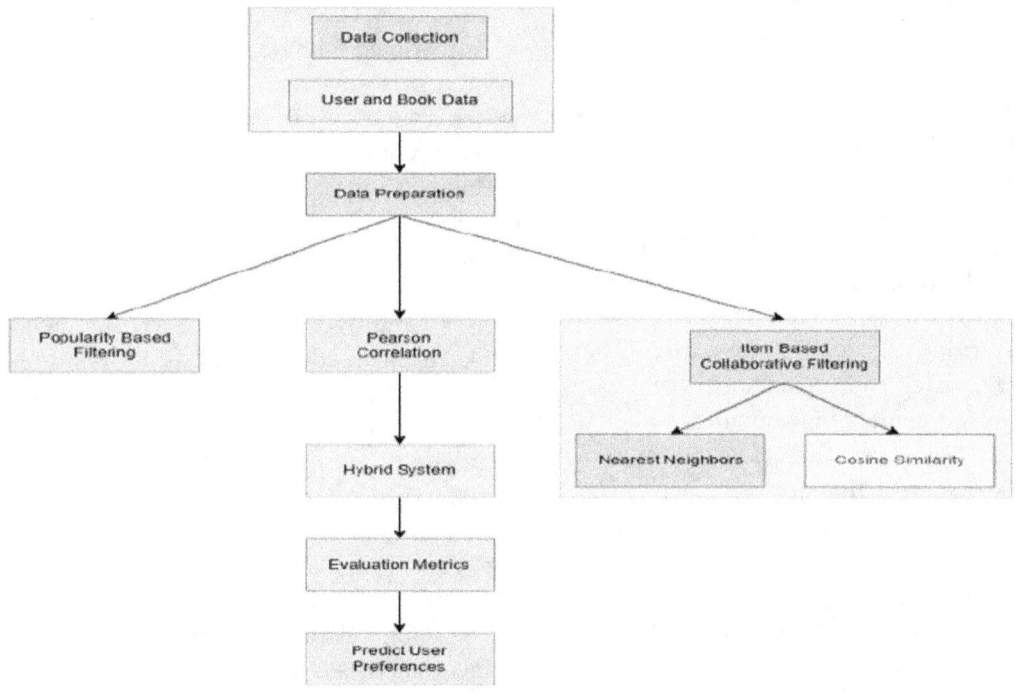

Figure 23.1 Entire methodology workflow diagram
Source: Author

Location: A text field detailing the user's location, often including city, state, and country information.

Age: A numeric field indicating the user's age, with some missing values (around 40% of entries lack age data).

The **Books dataset** contains 267,457 entries with eight columns:

- ISBN: Each book is assigned a unique identifier.
- Book title: The designation under which the book is known.
- Book author: The individual who penned the book.
- Year of publication: The year in which the publication saw its first light.
- Publisher: The organization or entity responsible for the book's publication.
- Image URL (Small): The web address for the small book cover image.
- Image URL (Medium): The web address for the medium book cover image.
- Image URL (Large): The web address for the large book cover image.

Popularity-based filtering:
Popularity-based filtering using average ratings is a simple and effective method for book recommendations, where books are suggested based on their average user ratings. Books are then ranked according to their average rating, and those with higher scores are recommended.

In this approach, we consider only books with more than 250 ratings, ensuring that the recommendations are based on substantial user feedback and avoid bias toward books with fewer ratings. While this method is effective for new users, as it highlights well-liked books, it doesn't take individual preferences into account, making the recommendations less personalized. Despite this, by using a threshold for the number of ratings, we ensure more

reliable recommendations and reduce the bias that typically comes with popularity-based filtering, making it a solid starting point in building recommendation systems. To determine the average rating of book, the total sum of all its ratings should divided by the total number of ratings that has received and can be expressed as:

$$Average\ rating = \frac{\sum Ratings}{Number\ of\ Ratings} \qquad (1)$$

Here's the bar graph showing the top 10 books based on their average rating which has expressed in Figure 23.2. Each bar represents a book title with its respective average rating. The list is sorted in descending order, with the highest-rated book at the top.

Pearson correlation
It is based on the assumption that the higher counts of ratings usually make a book more popular, followed by sorting and counting of ratings according to said system; the recommendation system was grouped on rating data based on ISBN, concentrating on the book rating column. Rating distribution was graphed to visualize how common each rating was to determine that there were many users who rated a very large number of books with a rating of 0. A new data frame with all the ISBN numbers was created and merged with the book dataset on the ISBN field to find the most-rated books. The top rankings were thus compiled based on the total number of ratings. For correlation analysis, both the rating mean and count were established.

Item-based collaborative filtering
It has been developed using the nearest neighbors (NN) algorithm and cosine similarity to propose books that are closely associated with a user's chosen preferred. The system purposes have described as:

index	title	author	year	num_ratings	avg_rating
0	Harry Potter and the Sorcerer's Stone (Harry Potter (Paperback)	J. K. Rowling	1999	271	5.1970110701410701
1	Harry Potter and the Chamber of Secrets (Book 2)	J. K. Rowling	2000	277	5.08415182454876
4	The Da Vinci Code	Dan Brown	2003	430	4.572008023255814
6	The Secret Life of Bees	Sue Monk Kidd	2003	368	4.5902655028556326
10	The Red Tent (Bestselling Backlist)	Anita Diamant	1998	339	4.3064306784669077
11	The Lovely Bones: A Novel	Alice Sebold	2002	602	4.348937203032325
12	Where the Heart is (Oprah's Book Club (Paperback))	Billie Letts	1998	287	4.204041511184669565
13	Girl with a Pearl Earring	Tracy Chevalier	2001	253	4.1462450562265537
14	Timeline	MICHAEL CRICHTON	2000	264	3.8598484848484845
17	Life of Pi	Yann Martel	2002	285	3.8542372881355983

Figure 23.2 Avg_rating result in popularity-based filtering
Source: Author

Nearest neighbors

The nearest neighbor's algorithm has been the easiest choice for recommender systems and is excellent for similarity-based recommendation. This means finding the items that are somehow "close" to a target item in an n-dimensional feature space. For example, in a book recommendation system, nearest neighborhood techniques could be used to recommend books that are similar to each other in terms of content, theme, or preference of users, thus providing personalized recommendations according to the interests and preferences of users.

The nearest neighbor's algorithm works by finding, among the many items in a feature space, those closest to another item (called "neighbors"), with distance measures defining that closeness in terms of the attributes in the feature space. This feature space may include genre, author, theme, or even ratings provided by users. Distances between items are computed with various acceptable distance metrics.

Cosine similarity

Cosine similarity, which uses the angle between two vectors representing the features of a given book, is utilized to estimate the resemblance between the published works. It works particularly well for high dimensional data, such as an array of user ratings, genre attributes, or even text itself [12, 13]. Cosine similarity values have a lower bound of -1 and an upper bound of 1, with values nearer to 1 denoting greater similarity. To adapt these scores for distance-based analysis, they are transformed into distance values by subtracting the cosine similarity from 1 (1 − cosine similarity), so that smaller distances mean higher similarity between the books. That enables the recommendation system to recommend certain titles to users based on the interaction of people with aligned preferences.

In this analysis, we computed book-to-book relationships based on user ratings using the cosine similarity metric. First, we filtered the dataset to keep only those books that had received reviews from at least 50 users who had rated no less than 250 books. After that, we created a pivot table with users as columns and individual books as rows. We calculated a pairwise similarity matrix using Scikit-learn's cosine similarity function, which we converted into a DataFrame to enable easier analysis using Pandas. To further analyze the book relationships, we selected one book, for this example, the first book in the dataset, and calculated its similarity scores with all other books in the dataset. After sorting these scores alongside excluding self-similarity, we captured the most five comparable books [14].

These results can be presented graphically in the form of a heatmap depicting similarity scores for the leading books. The heatmap features a title along with labeled axes, with the y-axis ranging between 0 and 1 to improve interpretation and understanding. The visualization presented makes it easier to grasp how the books in the dataset are associated based on the parameters and ratings provided by users and it has shown in Figure 23.3.

For a given book that the user selects, the system identifies the five books with the highest cosine similarity scores, representing those that are most closely aligned with the chosen book based on user interactions or content features. The books are then organized in ascending order based on their distances, wherein the most similar books are placed on the top of the list which has shown in Figure 23.4.

Performance Evaluation

The performance of the collaborative filtering model was assessed through two widely accepted measures, root mean squared error (RMSE) and mean absolute error (MAE). These methods are applied in measuring the accuracy of recommendation systems by determining the gap between the predicted values and actual values provided by users. The formula for RMSE and MAE has expressed as:

$$RMSE = \sqrt{\frac{1}{N} \sum_{j=1}^{n}(y_j - \hat{y}_j)^2} \qquad (2)$$

```
recommend('The Da Vinci Code')

[['Angels &amp; Demons', 'Dan Brown'],
 ['Touching Evil', 'Kay Hooper'],
 ['Saving Faith', 'David Baldacci'],
 ["The Sweet Potato Queens' Book of Love", 'JILL CONNER BROWNE'],
 ['Middlesex: A Novel', 'Jeffrey Eugenides']]]
```

Figure 23.4 Top listed books using cosine similarity
Source: Author

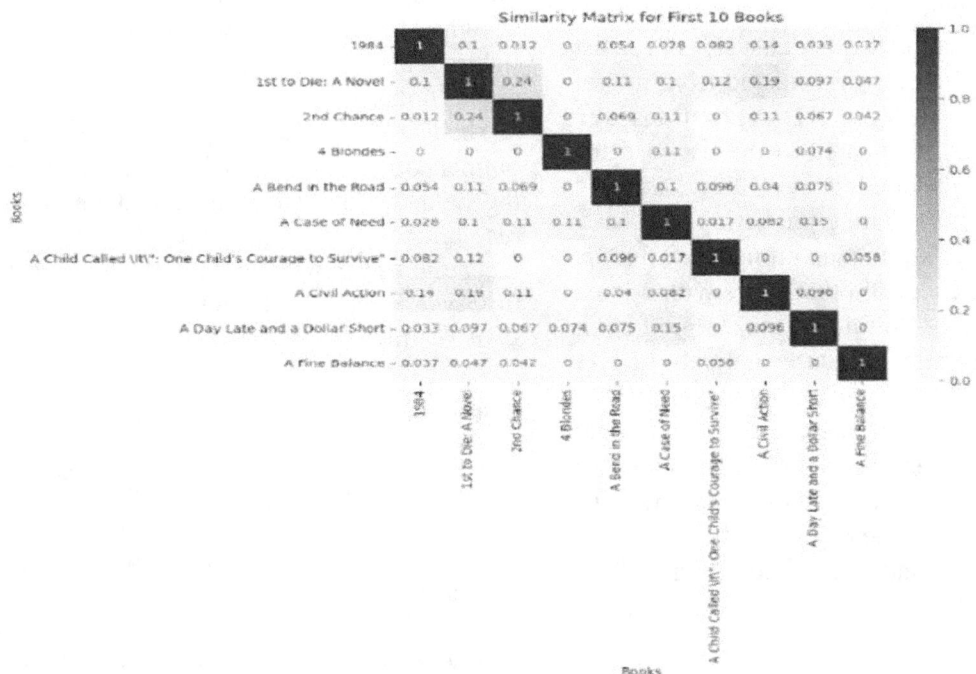

Figure 23.3 Heatmap for dataset relation
Source: Author

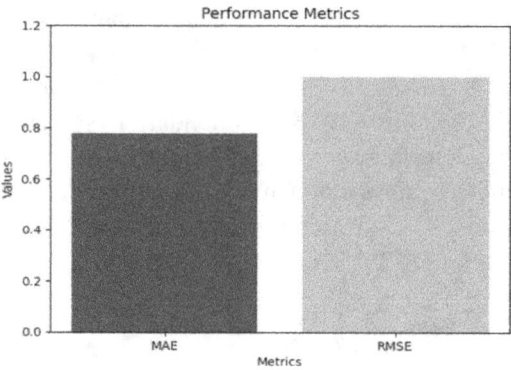

Figure 23.5 Bar graph for both evaluation metrics

Source: Author

Where, N is total number of observations, y_j actual value of jth observation, $\widehat{y_j}$ is predicted value.

$$MAE = \frac{1}{N} \sum_{j=1}^{n} |y_j - \widehat{y_j}| \qquad (3)$$

Where, $|y_j - \widehat{y_j}|$ is absolute difference between actual and predicted values.

To evaluating the model, a subset consisting of five users was selected from the rating pivot table. The provided ratings were utilized and compared to the user's actual ratings in the dataset to evaluate the predictions [15]. The rating predictions are based on the user's previous ratings and through the preferences of other users with comparable tastes. The model makes predictions about the ratings the user is likely to give, particularly focusing on books the user has not rated yet. The standard methods of calculating the error such as RMSE and MAE Kempler sufficiently analyze how well the model predicts the ratings for the books that are not rated and is depicted in Figure 23.5.

Conclusion

This research presents an advanced approach to specific book recommendation that is highly accurate through the integration of multiple methods. The system uses popularity-based filtering that either employs weighting for average rating or average rating for featuring books that are well rated and generally appreciated. An item-based collaborative filtering, with cosine similarity and nearest neighbor algorithms, is also implemented that recommend books similar to those the user has liked before. In addition, Pearson correlation measures are used to determine the strength of relationships concerning the rating of a book with other books in order to enhance the reliability of such measures for recommendations made. The integration of the above-mentioned methods enables the system to not only provide category recommendations based on popularity but also tailored recommendations according to each customer's reading civilization. Using RMSE and MAE proved the model's ability to accurately predict user preferences. The study illustrates a growing trend in hybrid recommender systems designed for interacting with users by highlighting the application of cross- domain choice tailoring systems.

The use of deep learning models for recommendation under machine learning in the field of digital reading could improve recommendations made about the system. Updating recommendations made in real time would add to the intelligence of the system built.

References

[1] Gangadharan, K., Purandaran, A., Malathi, K., Subramanian, B., Jeyaraj, R. and Jung, S.K., (2025). From data to decisions: The power of machine learning in business recommendations. IEEE Access,13, 17354-17397.

[2] Gm, D., Goudar, R. H., Kulkarni, A. A., Rathod, V. N., & Hukkeri, G. S. (2024). A digital recommendation system for

personalized learning to enhance online education: a review. *IEEE Access*, 12, 34019–34041.

[3] Fiarni, C., Maharani, H., & Kirsten, I. N. (2024). Electoral recommender system for Indonesian regional people's representative councils (DPRD) using knowledge-based and collaborative filtering approach. *Procedia Computer Science*, 234, 28–39.

[4] Devika, P., & Milton, A. (2024). Book recommendation system: reviewing different techniques and approaches. *International Journal on Digital Libraries*, 14, 1–22.

[5] Latrech, J., Kodia, Z., & Ben Azzouna, N. (2024). Twit-CoFiD: a hybrid recommender system based on tweet sentiment analysis. *Social Network Analysis and Mining*, 14(1), 123.

[6] Sireesha, V., Hegde, N. P., Sreenija, K., & Thindhu, B. (2022). An enhanced book recommendation system using hybrid machine learning techniques. In Smart Intelligent Computing and Applications, Volume 2: Proceedings of Fifth International Conference on Smart Computing and Informatics (SCI 2021) 2022 May 22, (pp. 171–179). Singapore: Springer Nature Singapore.

[7] VK, K., & Murugesan, S. (2024). An effective book recommendation system using weighted alternating least square (WALS) approach. *International Journal of Advanced Computer Science and Applications*, 15(4), 616.

[8] Devika, P., & Milton, A. (2024). Book recommendation system: reviewing different techniques and approaches. *International Journal on Digital Libraries*, 25(4), 803–824.

[9] Rajalakshmi, S., Indumathi, G., Elias, A., & Priya, G. S. (2024). Personalized online book recommendation system using hybrid machine learning techniques. *International Journal of Intelligent Systems and Applications in Engineering*, 12, 39–46.

[10] Jadon, A., & Patil, A. (2024). A comprehensive survey of evaluation techniques for recommendation systems. In International Conference on Computation of Artificial Intelligence and Machine Learning, 2024 Jan 17, (pp. 281–304). Cham: Springer Nature Switzerland.

[11] Li, Z., Chen, Y., Zhang, X. and Liang, X., 2023.Bookgpt: A general framework for book recommendation empowered by large language model. Electronics, 12(22), 4654.

[12] Cheng, L. (2024). Optimization of the book recommendation system based on collaborative filtering. In 2024 IEEE 18th International Conference on Anti-counterfeiting, Security, and Identification (ASID) 2024 Nov 1, (pp. 32–37). IEEE.

[13] Tegetmeier, C., Johannssen, A., & Chukhrova, N. (2024). Artificial intelligence algorithms for collaborative book recommender systems. *Annals of Data Science*, 11(5), 1705–1739.

[14] Sarma, D., Mittra, T., & Hossain, M. S. (2021). Personalized book recommendation system using machine learning algorithm. *International Journal of Advanced Computer Science and Applications*, 12(1), 212–219.

[15] Sahu, P., Kumar, S., Ahuja, R., & Kaur, A. (2021). Forecasting of precipitation in India by different data types using investigation of radial basis function neural network model. In 2021 9th International Conference on Reliability, Infocom Technologies and Optimization (Trends and Future Directions) (ICRITO), Noida, India, (pp. 1–5).

24 Metro operation optimization using predictive maintenance models

Davinder Paul Singh[1,a], Stuti Desai[2,b], Atharav Shivhare[3,c], Shubham Mahajan[4,d] and Amit Kant Pandit[5,e]

[1]Department of CSE School of Technology Pandit Deendayal Energy University, Gandhinagar, Gujarat, India

[2]Computer Science Engineering School of Technology, Pandit Deendayal Energy University, Gandhinagar, Gujarat, India

[3]Electronics and Communication (Spec. AIML), School of Engineering and Technology, MIT World Peace University Pune, Maharashtra, India

[4]Department of CSE, Amity School of Engineering and Technology (ASET), Amity University, Gurugram, Panchgaon, Haryana, India

[5]Department of ECE, Shri Mata Vaishno Devi University, Katra, Jammu and Kashmir, India

Abstract

This study presents a predictive maintenance framework aimed at optimizing metro rail operations by focusing on the MetroPT3 air compression unit—a critical component in urban transit systems. We employ advanced deep learning models to forecast system failures using a six-month, high-frequency sensor dataset containing over 1.1 million records. Through rigorous preprocessing, including outlier removal and standardization, the dataset was refined to 400,000 high-quality entries. The predictive framework is built on two state-of-the-art time-series models: Long short-term memory (LSTM) networks and Transformer architectures. LSTM leverages gated memory units to retain sequential context, while Transformers utilize attention mechanisms to capture complex, long-range dependencies efficiently. Our approach includes signal acquisition, feature engineering, temporal modeling, and model evaluation using metrics such as accuracy, mean squared error (MSE), and R-squared. Experimental results demonstrate that while LSTM achieves moderate forecasting accuracy (~74%), the Transformer model outperforms it significantly, achieving 85% accuracy, superior generalization, and faster convergence. The overall workflow of this predictive maintenance framework is depicted in Figure 24.1.

Keywords: Data analytics, decision support, deep learning, long short-term memory, MetroPT3, predictive maintenance, smart city infrastructure, time-series forecasting, transformer, urban rail

Introduction

The rapid urbanization of metropolitan areas worldwide has led to an exponential increase in reliance on mass transit systems such as subways, metros, and trams. As urban populations swell, the efficiency, safety, and continuity of metro systems become paramount. One critical subsystem that ensures the uninterrupted operation of metro services is the air compression unit, specifically the MetroPT3, which governs pneumatic functionalities such as braking systems, door actuations, and suspension

[a]devsingh0071@gmail.com, [b]stuti.dce21@sot.pdpu.ac.in, [c]shivhareatharav@gmail.com, [d]smahajan@ggn.amity.edu, [e]Amitkantpandit@gmail.com

DOI: 10.1201/9781003753391-24

controls. Despite their mechanical resilience, air compressors are prone to failures due to prolonged operational cycles, fluctuating load conditions, and environmental factors. Conventional maintenance strategies—either preventive (fixed schedule) or reactive (post-failure)—are inherently inefficient. Preventive maintenance often leads to unnecessary part replacements and increased operational downtime, while reactive maintenance can result in catastrophic system breakdowns, safety hazards, and service disruptions. These limitations necessitate a transition toward predictive maintenance: a forward-looking strategy that relies on real-time monitoring and intelligent analytics to anticipate component degradation and initiate timely interventions.

Our research addresses key gaps in metro maintenance literature by applying these models to a specialized dataset from the MetroPT3 unit. The study not only compares the performance of LSTM and Transformer architectures in forecasting failure-prone conditions but also operationalizes their output into a predictive

maintenance ecosystem. This end-to-end approach—from raw sensor ingestion to predictive alerts [1, 3, 4, 5, 7].

Literature Review

The growing body of research in predictive maintenance reflects the rising need for intelligent, data-driven approaches across various industrial sectors, including transportation. Within the context of metro systems, predictive maintenance is still a relatively nascent field, but recent developments in sensor technology, data science, and machine learning have made this a promising area of exploration. The advent of deep learning has revolutionized PdM by enabling systems to learn hierarchical representations directly from raw sensor inputs. Recurrent neural networks (RNNs), particularly LSTM networks introduced by Hochreiter and Schmidhuber [8].

Data and Variables

The backbone of our predictive maintenance framework is a rich, high-frequency time-series dataset collected from the

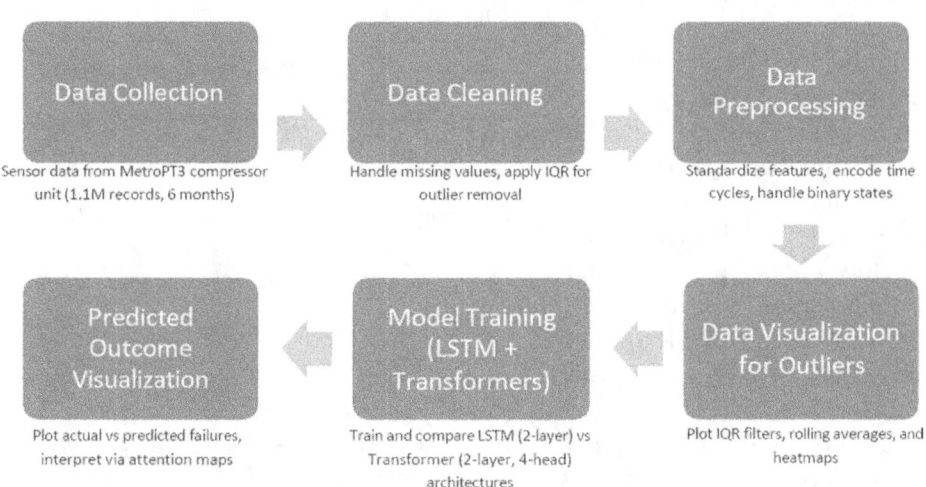

Figure 24.1 End-to-end workflow for predictive maintenance using deep learning
Source: Author

MetroPT3 air compression unit. The dataset spans a six-month period, capturing real-time operational signals sampled at 1 Hz. Over the course of this period, more than 1.1 million records were gathered, offering a comprehensive view of the system's operational dynamics. After extensive preprocessing—described in the methodology section—this dataset was reduced to a refined set of approximately 400,000 high-integrity observations [2].

Dataset Composition

The dataset comprises three major categories of data, A correlation heatmap... is illustrated in Figure 24.4:

1. The analog sensor readings include TP24 (compressor pressure in bar), TP34 (pneumatic output pressure at control panel), H14 (pressure activation above 10.2 bar), DVpressure4 (air discharge pressure from dryer; zero indicates compressor load), Reservoirs4 (compressed air reservoir pressure), OilTemperature5 (compressor oil temperature in °C), Flowmeter6 (airflow in m³/h at the pneumatic control unit), and MotorCurrent7 (compressor motor current from 0 A to 7 A).
2. The digital sensor readings capture binary states such as COMP (compressor on/off during offloading), DV electric (valve state during loading), TOWERS (active air air-dryinger), MPG (intake valve pressurization), LPS (low pressure alert below 7 bar), Pressure switch (valve pressurization confirmation), Oil Level (low oil level alert), and Caudal impulses (airflow pulses per second).
3. GPS metrics provide location, speed, and signal quality, with zeroed data in tunnels or areas with poor signal reception.

Data transformation

All numeric features were standardized to ensure zero-mean, unit-variance scaling. Categorical binary variables were preserved in their native form, while time-based features were encoded using sine and cosine transforms to reflect cyclicality. Missing values were imputed using a forward-fill approach combined with median imputation when sequences began with null values. For outlier detection, we applied an interquartile range threshold and removed observations falling outside 1.5 times the IQR. The process of outlier handling is visually represented in Figure 24.2.

Summary statistics

Below is a sample from the summary statistics Table 24.1 for key features:

Methodology and Model Specifications

Data acquisition and preprocessing

The approach taken in this study offers a well-organized framework and was built

Table 24.1 Summary statistics of key features from MetroPT3 dataset.

Feature	Min	Max	Mean	Std Dev	Missing %
TP24 (bar)	1.2	9.8	6.4	1.1	0.4%
Oil Temp (°C)	30.5	88.6	60.2	10.3	0.2%
Motor Current (A)	0	7	3.5	1.7	0.1%
COMP (0/1)	0	1	0.62	-	0%
GPS Speed (km/h)	0	72.3	42.5	8.9	3.2%

Source: Author

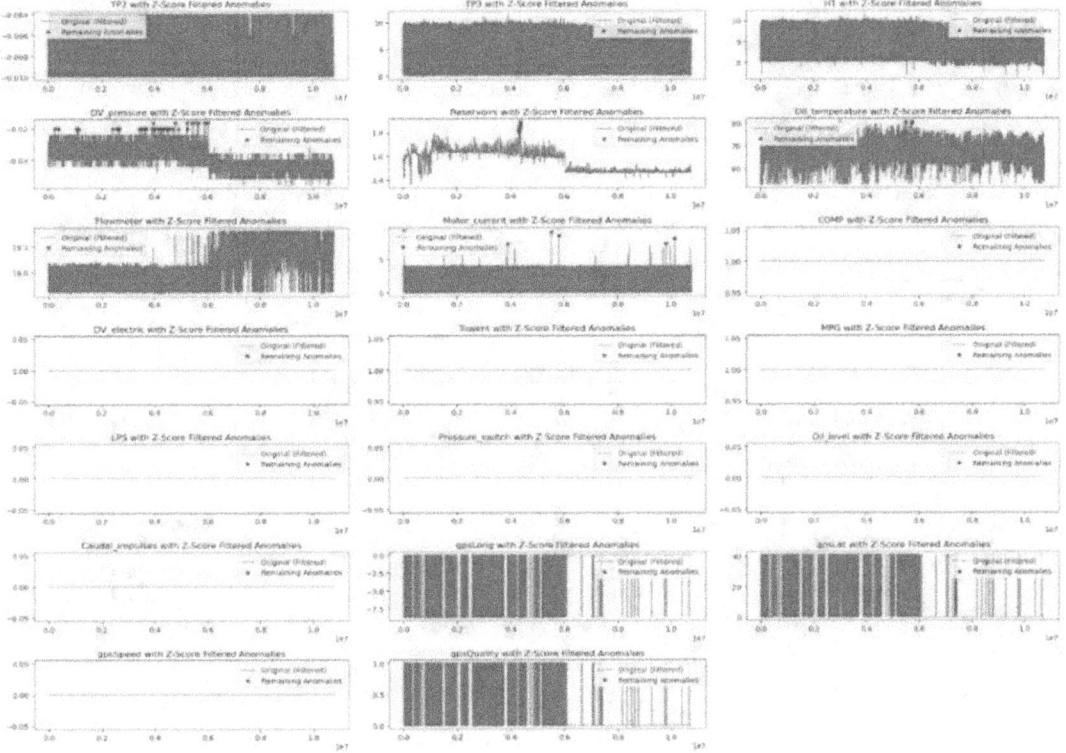

Figure 24.2 Outlier Handling using IQR: Visual representation of IQR filtering applied to analog sensors
Source: Author

around 1a specific model geared towards facilitating predictive maintenance within the metro networks. Its high-frequency sensor data are first collected as raw data for processing. The volumetric dataset obtained contains over 1.1 million entries, as these records are collected at a frequency of one Hertz in six months' time. To manage this magnitude, the primary step requires extensive data cleansing and pre-processing. Outlier detection methods like the interquartile range (IQR) filtering technique is utilized in removing outliers that might bias training the model. Furthermore, unaccounted values are dealt with using a sequential approach: forward fill for continuous segments and median replacement for the beginnings of the sequences. The

data are then down sampled to 400,000 records—ensuring that meaningful trends are preserved while eliminating noise and redundancy.

Feature engineering
We first complete data cleaning before moving on to feature engineering. This consists of creating lag features, calculating rolling averages and variances, and creating additional features from pressure and temperature sensor data. The feature matrix constructed in this manner greatly enhances the original dataset and augments it into a high- dimensional input space suitable for deep learning algorithms. The trend extraction process through rolling averages is shown in Figure 24.3.

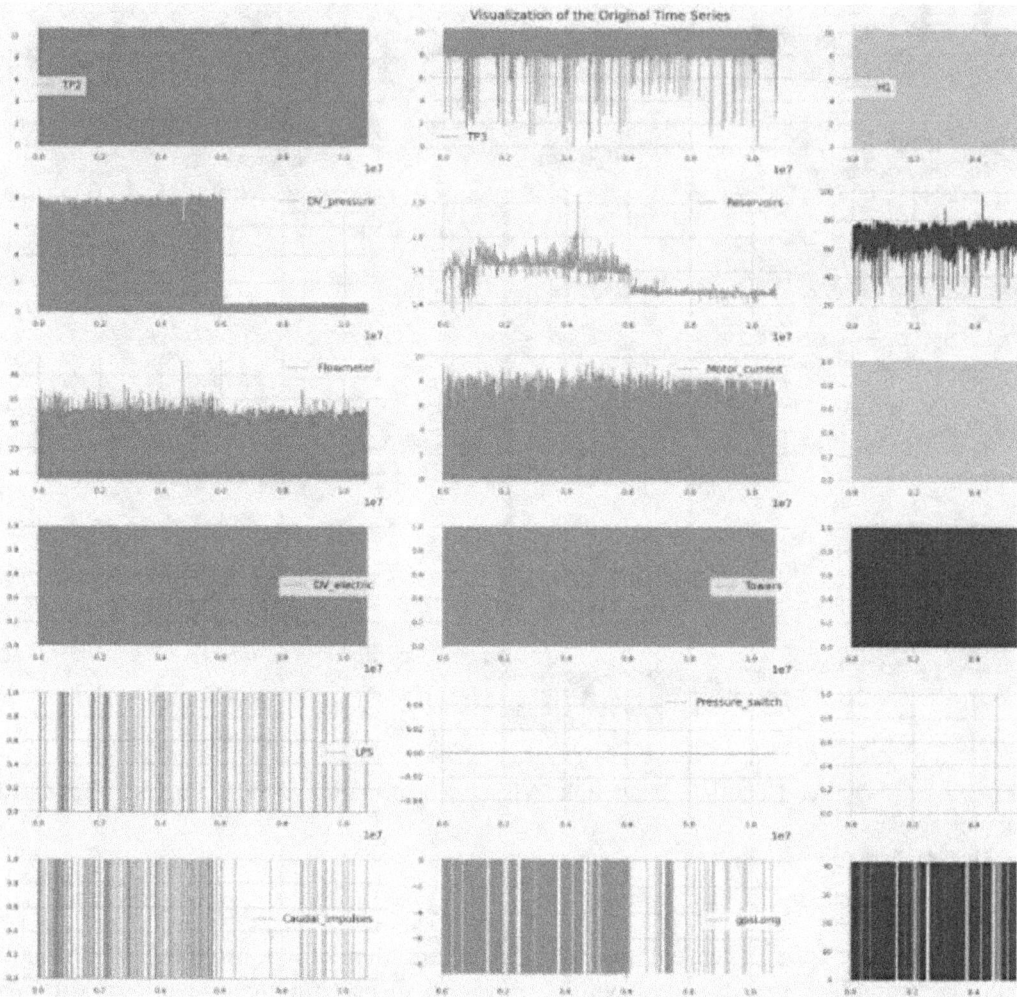

Figure 24.3 Rolling average visualization: Demonstrates trend extraction by smoothing
Source: Author

Model selection and architecture

Selection of the most appropriate model is one of the most important tasks of this methodology. In this work, we consider two neural network architectures –LSTM networks versus transformer models. An LSTM is a type of RNN that specializes in processing sequences. It contains internal memory cells that can maintain relevant information for a limited period which helps in time- dependent phenomenon prediction like forecasting mechanical wear. However, LSTMs have scalability constraints and problems with long-range dependency capture for extended sequences, especially with high- dimensional input data, over long-time intervals. Sequence modeling has undergone a shift with the introduction of self-attention-based transformers. Unlike LSTMs, Transformers do not use recurrence, applying attention scores to all time steps simultaneously instead. This enables the model to uncover complex dependencies over

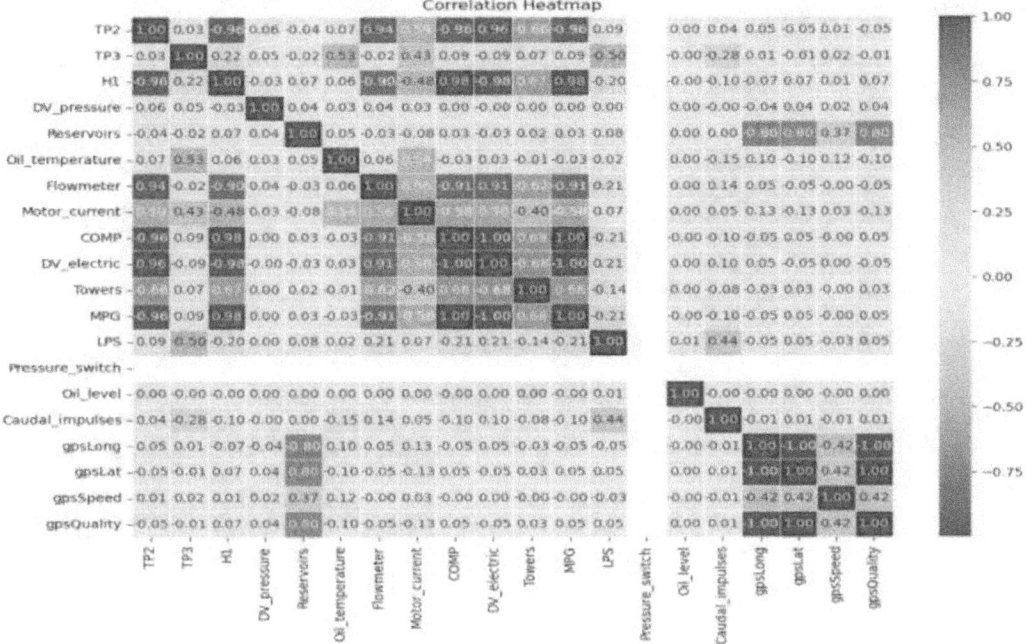

Figure 24.4 Heatmap of correlated features: Shows interdependence among pressure, temperature, and current sensors
Source: Author

long time frames, significantly improving training time because of parallel processing. While parallel Transformer models don't process data in a sequential manner, positional encoding still allows for retaining the order of sequences [6].

For the LSTM model, we configured a two-layer network with 128 and 64 units, respectively, followed by dropout layers to prevent overfitting. A final dense layer with sigmoid activation was used to produce binary predictions for failure risk. The Transformer model was built with two encoder layers, each featuring four attention heads. The output of each attention layer passes through a feed-forward network and normalization layers, culminating in a classification head similar to that of the LSTM. Positional encoding was embedded into the feature inputs to retain sequence order.

Training strategy and evaluation metrics
Both models were trained using the Adam optimizer and binary cross-entropy loss. A batch size of 128 was maintained throughout, and training proceeded for up to 50 epochs with early stopping based on validation loss. A 20% validation split was applied to monitor overfitting and ensure generalizability. Evaluation metrics were carefully chosen to reflect the requirements of predictive maintenance. Accuracy alone is insufficient due to potential class imbalances (failures are rare compared to normal operation). Hence, we also considered precision, recall, F1-score, and the area under the receiver operating characteristic curve (ROC-AUC). Furthermore, mean squared error (MSE) and R-squared values were employed to quantify the model's capacity to forecast failure probability over a continuous horizon.

Actual vs predicted plots

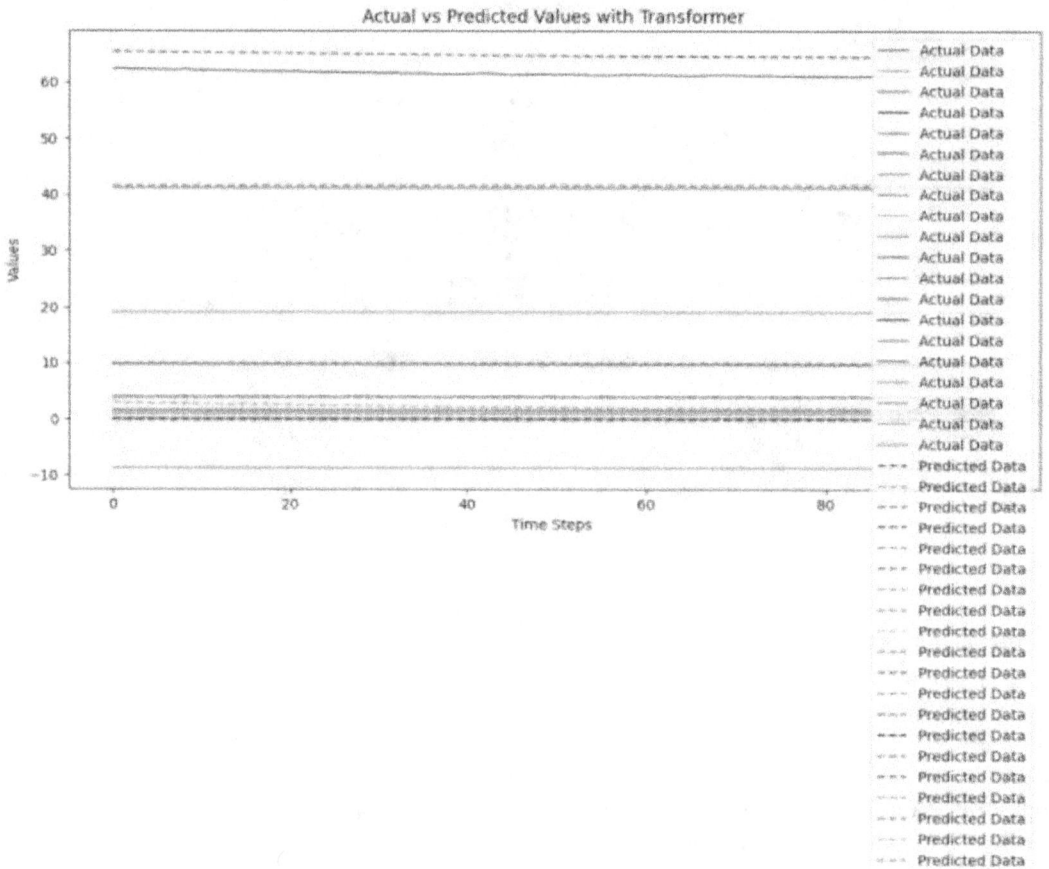

Figure 24.5a Transformer: Highlights higher alignment with real failure events. The attention mechanism contributed to this by better associating long-term pressure and oil temperature dependencies

Source: Author

Empirical Results

This section covers the empirical results gathered from the evaluation of models. The actual versus predicted comparisons... are illustrated in Figures 24.5a and 24.5b.

Model training and convergence behavior

Both models were trained using a dataset split into 80% for training and 20% for validation. Early stopping based on validation loss ensured generalization. The training and validation loss curves for the transformer model, demonstrated stable convergence within 20 epochs, significantly faster than the LSTM, which required approximately 35 epochs to stabilize. The LSTM model began to display moderate overfitting symptoms around the 30th epoch; while the training loss kept decreasing, the validation loss had leveled off. On the other hand, the Transformer was able to show uniformity across both curves, suggesting better generalization.

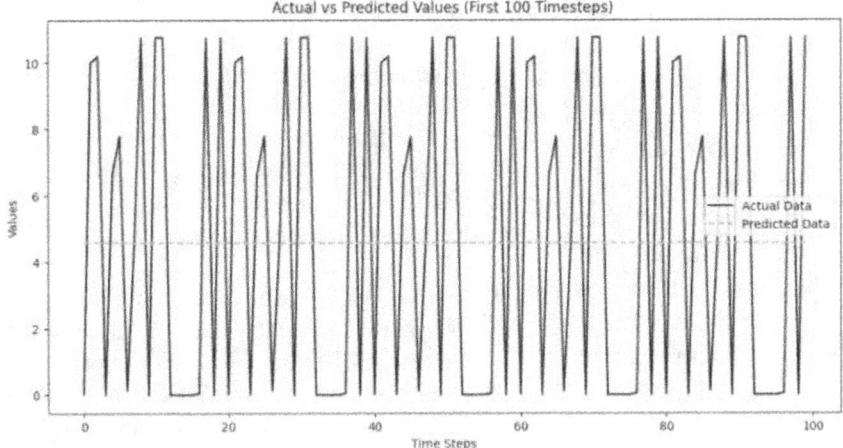

Figure 24.5b Long short-term memory (LSTM): Shows actual vs predicted values over 100 timestamps. While LSTM captured general trend shifts, it lagged during abrupt pressure changes, leading to delayed anomaly signals
Source: Author

Table 24.2 Comparative evaluation metrics.

Metric	LSTM mode	Transformer model
Accuracy (%)	74.1	85.2
MSE	0.037	0.019
R-squared	0.62	0.81
F1-Score	0.71	0.83
Precision	0.68	0.86
Recall	0.75	0.81

Source: Author

Evaluation metrics comparison

The superior performance of the Transformer model in every metric when compared to LSTM makes it particularly suitable for application in a real-time predictive maintenance setting. Its remarkable precision also underscores the critical importance of avoiding excessive false positives for maintenance preventive applicational systems or, maintenance avoid & intervene systems (MAIS) minimal maintenance interventions, Table 24.2.

Discussion and implications

Our results confirm that Transformer models outperform others in the processing of complicated, high-frequency sensor data as it occurs in real-time. Although LSTM provides a dependable baseline, it has difficulty capturing long-term dependencies, leading to overly complex dependence structures, and needing extensive parameter adjustments. With little prompt customization, the Transformer's performance is always exceptional. For commuters, the economic benefit is a system that is easy to manage with limited operative disturbance while maximizing savings.

Conclusion

By utilizing deep learning models like long short-term memory (LSTM) and transformers, this work provides an optimized tier framework for implementing predictive maintenance in the metro rail systems via anticipating failures in the air compression unit of MetroPT3. Predictive maintenance seeks to avert escalated damages resulting from system downtimes and operational failures while striving to ensure high dependability levels. Advanced urban rail transit systems face dual challenges of ever-growing demand, aging infrastructure, and the acute need for high-availability zero-failure smart maintenance policies. Through rigorous experimentation and analytic verification, we prove the models based on Transformers outperform all others in accuracy as well as operational applicability.

References

[1]   Li, Y., Chen, C., Zhang, L., Wang, Q., & Ding, K. (2021). Transformer-based anomaly detection in industrial pipelines. *IEEE Transactions on Industrial Informatics*, 17(8), 5575–5584.

[2]   Veloso, B., Gama, J., Ribeiro, R. P., & Pereira, P. (2022). MetroPT: A benchmark dataset for predictive maintenance [Data set]. Zenodo. https://doi.org/10.5281/zenodo.6854240.

[3]   Davari, N., Veloso, B., Ribeiro, R. P., Pereira, P. M., & Gama, J. (2021). Predictive maintenance based on anomaly detection using deep learning for air production unit in the railway industry. In 2021 IEEE 8th International Conference on Data Science and Advanced Analytics (DSAA), (pp. 1–10). IEEE.

[4]   Gama, J., Ribeiro, R. P., & Veloso, B. (2022). Data-driven predictive maintenance. *IEEE Intelligent Systems*, 37(2), 1–2.

[5]   Barros, M., Veloso, B., Pereira, P. M., Ribeiro, R. P., & Gama, J. (2020). Failure detection of an air production unit in operational context. In IoT Streams for Data-Driven Predictive Maintenance and IoT, Edge, and Mobile for Embedded Machine Learning, (pp. 61–74). Springer.

[6]   Vaswani, A., Shazeer, N., Parmar, N., Uszkoreit, J., Jones, L., Gomez, A. N., et al. (2017). Attention is all you need. In Advances in Neural Information Processing Systems, (pp. 5998–6008).

[7]   Zhang, C., Zhang, Y., He, X., & Song, X. (2019). Predictive maintenance of rotating machinery using LSTM networks. *IEEE Access*, 7, 129399–129412.

[8]   Hochreiter, S., & Schmidhuber, J. (1997). Long short-term memory. Neural Computation, 9(8), 1735–1780.

25 Hybrid approach for smart job matching listing using Yolov7 and TinyBERT framework

Mayank Raj[1,a], Harshit Singh[2,b], Ansh Khurana[2,c],
Mukesh Gaur[2,d], Anisha Agarwal[2,e], Davinder Paul[3,f],
Shubham Mahajan[4,g] and Amit Kant Pandit[5,h]

[1]Department of Information Technology, Jss Academy of Technical Education Noida, UP, India

[2]Department of Computer Science and Datascience, JSS Academy of Technical Education Noida, UP, India

[3]Department of CSE, School of Technology, Pandit Deendayal Energy University, Gandhinagar, Gujarat, India

[4]Department of Amity School of Engineering and Technology (ASET), Amity University Gurugram, Haryana, India

[5]Department of Electronics and Communication Engineering) Shri Mata Vaishno Devi University, Katra, Jammu and Kashmir, India

Abstract

The conventional methods of reviewing resume are time consuming and thus the employment of artificial intelligence and machine learning can prove to be an efficient solution saving time and costs associated. Resume parsing is the process of extracting and storing the information of a resume in a way that could be processed further by machines. Upon parsing, one could employ various algorithms to filter or sort the resumes as per the requirements. An example could be finding out the resumes that are most suitable as per the job description for shortlisting. Resumes can come in various formats. A solution to address this is using computer vision techniques with BERT and named entity recognition for understanding the information extracted out of the resume and giving a score as per the similarity index with job description. One computer vision technique that had shown great performance is YOLOv5 as in [1]. In addition, for extracting information about segments from the text, BERT models have successfully been utilized. Distil-BERT, a variation of BERT had been used in and shows noteworthy precision. In this research, we utilize YOLOv7 and TinyBERT for segmentation and section classification respectively allowing us to parse the data with named entity recognition achieving greater accuracy. Cosine Similarity has been employed to match the resume with job description. Both offer improvement in computational requirements to their older versions, facilitating faster processing while maintaining accuracy.

Keywords: Bounding box, resume parsing, resume ranking, smart job matching, TinyBERT, YOLOv7

[a]mayankraj5396@gmail.com, [b]harshitsingh5396@gmail.com, [c]khuranaansh75@gmail.com, [d]iammukeshgaur2004@gmail.com, [e]anishaagarwal082002@gmail.com, [f]devsingh0071@gmail.com, [g]smahajan@ggn.amity.edu, [h]amitkantpandit@gmail.com

DOI: 10.1201/9781003753391-25

Introduction

Recent times have witnessed the development of artificial intelligence and machine learning speed up various industries across a wide range, including recruitment. The traditional practice of resume reading and picking candidates is usually time-consuming, error-prone, and subject to biases. With more candidates submitting applications for a single post, human resource staff and recruiters have gigantic challenges processing and examining resumes effectively. As a reaction, the use of advanced machine learning techniques has been a good means of automating resume parsing, classification, and ranking, thus making it easier and objective to determine candidate fit. This article describes the intersection of machine learning, i.e., the use of YOLOv7 and TinyBERT in automating resume parsing and ranking and discusses both developments and challenges in this regard. Resume parsing involves pulling, categorizing, and analyzing critical details from resumes like personal data, work experience, educational qualification, skills, and qualifications. Given that the resume is likely of varied form-images to Word documents to PDFs -- the process proves tricky to convert unstructured or semi-structured information into meaningful data. While human recruitment consultants find it simple to make sense of this kind of data, the greatest challenge comes in transforming copious textual and visual data into succinct, clearly defined patterns that could be simply consumed by machine learning algorithms. In academic research, several techniques have been proposed for resuming data extraction pertaining to relevant information based on different machine learning and natural language processing (NLP) approaches. The most powerful NLP technique among them is

Named Entity Recognition (NER) to recognize important entities such as names, locations, organizations, and institutions [18]. NER forms the foundation for most contemporary resume parsing systems and can be complemented with deep learning models, particularly based on transformer models like BERT (Bidirectional Encoder Representations from Transformers) and its variations. These models are particularly good at capturing contextual nuances in text and can be trained to specifically extract certain sections of a resume [12]. Pretrained models such as BERT and SBERT (Sentence-BERT) have been-very successful in identifying and extracting essential information like work experience, qualifications, and skills. The method of ranking resumes is typically a two-step and intricate one: first, the most crucial aspects of the resume and job description are determined; next, resumes are evaluated according to how closely they match the job requirements. Semantic similarity is the most widely used method for comparing resumes and job descriptions and measuring how well the contents of resumes match job postings. [9]. Recent advancements in deep learning, like introduction of computer vision models such as YOLOv7 and BERT based models like TinyBERT have unlocked new possibilities to enhance resume parsing and scoring. YOLOv7, [2] a cutting-edge object detection model, boosts text extraction from image resumes, rendering non-text formats more easily process able with higher precision. TinyBERT, a light edition of BERT, provides high performance with less computational requirement, suitable for scalable and efficient resume parsing. YOLOv7 performs extremely well in reading text from handwritten or scanned resumes and beats regular OCR in accuracy and speed.

Literature Review

Vishaline et al. [3] tries to improve the accuracy of selection of resume. Algorithms like SVM, Naive Bayes, and Random Forest are compared for resume classification and SVM was found being particularly effective in structured data contexts [3, 6]. Models such as XGBoost and LightGBM have been shown to have high accuracy and efficiency in their comparison. XGBoost has attained AUC-ROC score equal to 0.89 in this work. This study also implements a web based interface. Kinger et al. [1] shows that YOLOv5 could be used for bounding box detection and section classification before performing text extraction and DistilBERT could be used for section classification based on the text extracted before performing the named entity recognition using DistilBERT based model. The accuracy achieved was commendable with YOLOv5 achieving an accuracy of 96.3%, DistilBERT [4] achieving accuracy of 96.21% for section classification task and around 85% for named entity recognition. Tanberk et al. [17] proposes a system to rank and sort the resumes. It uses optical character recognition to identify various sections of the resume and extract text from them. Pre-trained BERT model was fine-tuned for ensuring high accuracy in classifying key sections within the resume. The sections were further categorized using the named entity recognition. Cosine similarity was used to compare resume vectors with job description vectors, helping in ranking candidates by how well they match the requirements. Chandak et al. [7] proposes a system with two components resume parser and job recommender. PDFMiner is used to extract text from resumes in PDF format, making them compatible with NLP processes. Spacy was also used for extracting the data and storing it in structured format. The system combined resume parsing with job recommendation features, using TF-IDF and cosine [5, 8] similarity to suggest suitable Sinha et al. [13] tries to give an efficient solution to the problem of parsing and classifying resumes. The study utilizes techniques such as tokenization, removing irrelevant words, stemming, and lemmatization for standardizing text data. The data is extracted with the help of python modules like PyMuPDF. Various techniques like natural language processing (NLP) [10], Regexes and entity recognition were applied on this data. The study achieved accuracy of 92.08%. Mhatre et al. [15] had shown encouraging results for classification of resumes using Convolutional Neural Networks (CNNs) and Long Short-Term Memory (LSTM) networks. This study also implements other commonly used models to compare their metrics with the metrics for classification using deep neural network-based techniques.

Dataset and Preprocessing

We have utilized a customized dataset acquired from students studying in the college. The dataset comprises around [11] 150 resumes. All the resumes underwent manual inspection to eliminate need for pre-processing before feeding the data of resume to the model. The data from resumes was classified into eight sections-CONTACT NUMBER, NAME, ADDRESS, PROJECTS, SKILLS, QUALIFICATIONS, CERTIFICATIONS, EXPERIENCE.

Methodology

The working of the proposed system is explained in Figure 25.1.

Segment generation and text extraction
For segment generation we used a computer vision technique that can identify

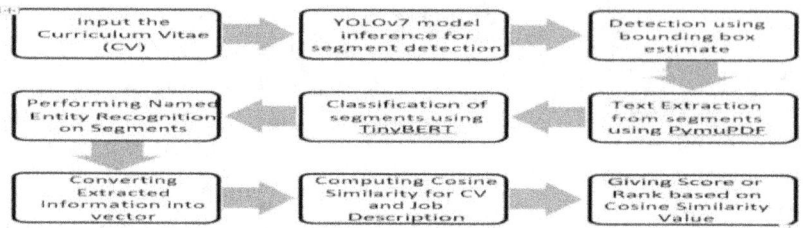

Figure 25.1 Working overview
Source: Author

different segments of text from the resume. The text in those segments could then be extracted with the help of some PDF processing library. These segments can then be used by a named entity recognition model. The computer vision technique used for segment identification is YOLOv7 which was trained on a dataset of various resumes. As an advanced object detection framework, YOLOv7 enhances performance with a variety of architectural improvements and creative techniques. To improve detection precision in a variety of tasks, it employs a backbone network that includes components like ODConv-ELAN and CBAM, which optimize feature extraction and attention mechanisms, respectively [17–19].

Segment classification
Each extracted segment is then classified to one of the categories (CONTACTNUMBER, NAME, ADDRESS, PROJECTS, SKILLS, QUALIFICATIONS, CERTIFICATIONS, EXPERIENCE). The technique used for classification is TinyBERT. TinyBERT is a condensed variation of the BERT model designed to increase productivity in activities involving natural language processing without compromising high performance. Numerous fields have seen its successful application, such as cross-lingual sentiment analysis, where it works in tandem with Graph Convolutional Networks (GCN) to

improve feature extraction and semantic understanding, yielding remarkable accuracy and F1 scores on a range of datasets [16]. Using TinyBERT leads to faster computations.

Named entity recognition
The data in the sections as obtained from the previous step is extracted in this step. We use a named entity recognition model which was specially trained on a dataset that had labelled segments with category as one of CONTACT NUMBER, NAME, ADDRESS, PROJECTS, SKILLS, QUALIFICATIONS, CERTIFICATIONS, EXPERIENCE. Again, TinyBERT model was used for the named entity recognition.

Scoring
By performing the above steps, we can obtain a vector that contains the information about the resume which is parsed. To give a score, we would compare this vector with the vector of the job description and based on similarity assign a value. This step used the cosine similarity to find the match percentage of the resume with the job description. A higher match percentage would mean better suitability for the job role.

Results

This section provides an in-depth evaluation of the performance of the YOLOv7 and

TinyBERT models for section classification and Named Entity Recognition (NER). The analysis is based on performance metrics, computational efficiency, and accuracy comparisons with other models.

Performance of YOLOv7 for bounding box creation section classification

From the confusion matrix shown in Figure 25.2, we can infer that the YOLOv7 model is able to form bounding boxes and classify NAME, PROJECTS, QUALIFICATIONS AND CERTIFICATIONS sections at a good rate. The confusion matrix also shows that the model was able to classify nearly all the tags properly except for CONTACTNUMBER, ADDRESS and EXPERIENCE. The misclassification of these sections is likely due to the limited dataset size, which may have restricted the model's ability to learn features effectively. The YOLOv5 and YOLOv7 models were trained for 50 epochs. The YOLOv5 model showed results similar to those of YOLOv7 without any significant difference. The F1 Score, Precision and Recall values as can be observed from the Figure 25.4 and Table 25.2 are slightly lower (about 3 to 7%) when compared to that of the other larger BERT based models. Figure 25.4 depicts that the SKILLS category could be recognized the best among all the categories. The categories like address and certifications displayed the least score of all. The reason behind this is most likely the data set like address and certifications displayed the least score among all. The data set used was insufficient for our model to have been able to recognize all the categories.

Performance of TinyBERT for section classification and named entity recognition

The metrics for TinyBERT model for section classification as in Table 25.1 indicate its robustness for document classification despite being a lighter model. All metrics are comparable to those of other larger BERT models.

As observed in Figure 25.3 the TinyBERT NER model demonstrates an accuracy of 79.16% which is slightly lower (around 3–7%) as compared to previous larger BERT based models. The graph shows steady improvement before stabilizing. The model stabilizes at around 60 steps.

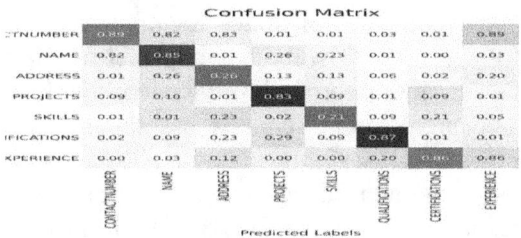

Figure 25.2 Confusion matrix for YOLOv7 in bounding box creation and section classificaion
Source: Author

Table 25.1 Metrics for the Tinybert and distilbert model for section classification.

Model	Loss	F1	ROC	Accuracy
TinyBERT	0.0452	0.9524	0.9713	0.9537
DistilBERT	0.0387	0.9632	0.9795	0.9602
BERT-base	0.0334	0.9712	0.9821	0.9694
DeBERTa	0.0319	0.9753	0.9857	0.9764

Source: Author

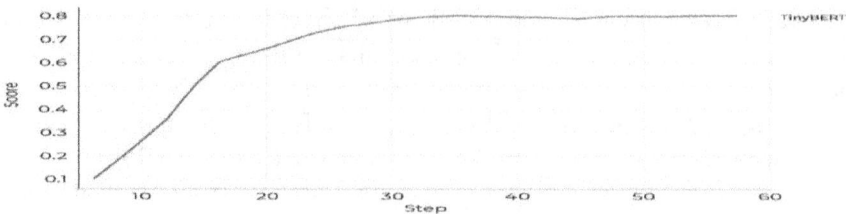

Figure 25.3 Average accuracy for TinyBERT named entity recognition
Source: Author

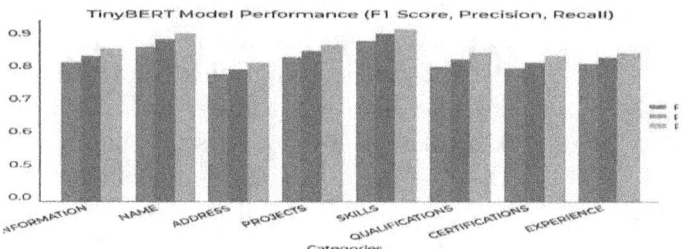

Figure 25.4 F1-Score, precision and recall for each category for TinyBERT named entity recognition model
Source: Author

Table 25.2 Average F1-score, precision, recall of various BERT based models across all categories.

Model	Average F1-score	Average precision	Average recall
TinyBERT	0.729	0.765	0.793
DistilBERT	0.768	0.796	0.812
BERT-base	0.788	0.813	0.825
DeBERTa	0.792	0.821	0.831

Source: Author

Both YOLOv7 and TinyBERT demonstrate improved computational efficiency compared to YOLOv5 and DistilBERT, making them suitable for resource-constrained environments such as mobile devices. This is expected since both are computationally efficient versions of YOLOv7 and DistilBERT respectively.

Conclusion

This paper demonstrates an improvement to previous existing techniques by using newer and improved versions of models. The architecture remains the same. With help of YOLOv7, the bounding boxes could be generated using lesser computational resources. By using TinyBERT in place of other BERT based models, we traded off some accuracy for faster processing. Other BERT models could be utilized if only accuracy is the priority. The proposed system will help hire stto filterring the resume in a short amount of time without manually going through each of them.

References

[1] Kinger, S., Kinger, D., Thakkar, S., & Bhake, D. (2024). Towards smarter hiring: resume parsing and ranking with YOLOv5 and DistilBERT. *Multimedia Tools and Applications*, 83, 82069–82087.

[2] Retyk, F., Fabregat, H., Aizpuru, J., Taglio, M., & Zbib, R. M. (2023). Résumé parsing as hierarchical sequence labeling: an empirical study. arXiv preprint arXiv:2309.07015, Sept. 2023.

[3] Vishaline, A., Kallankattil, R., Kumar, P., VVNS, S. P., KVK, V., & Sudheesh, P. (2024). An ML-based resume screening and ranking system. in Proceedings of IEEE ICONSCEPT (or the conference/workshop indicated by the DOI), 2024. doi:10.1109/iconscept61884.2024.10627825

[4] Thangaramya, K., Logeswari, G., Gajendran, S., Roselind, J. D., & Ahirwar, N. (2024). Automated resume parsing and ranking using natural language processing. in Proc. 3rd International Conference (conference details as indexed), 2024. doi:10.1109/aiiot58432.2024.10574696.

[5] Abisha, D., Keerthana, S., Evanjalin, N., Kavitha, K., Mary, J., & Ramya, R. (2024). Resspar: AI-driven resume parsing and recruitment system using NLP and generative AI. in Proc. 2024 Second International Conference on Intelligent Cyber-Physical Systems and IoT (ICoICI), IEEE, 2024, (pp. in conference proceedings). doi:10.1109/ICOICI62503.2024.10696451.

[6] Tayal, S., Sharma, T., Singhal, S., & Thakur, A. (2024). Resume screening using machine learning. *International Journal of Scientific Research in Computer Science, Engineering and Information Technology*. 10(2), 602–606, Apr. 2024. doi:10.32628/CSEIT2410275.

[7] Chandak, A. V., Pandey, H., Rushiya, G., & Sharma, H. (2024). Resume parser and job recommendation system using machine learning. 157–162. doi: 10.1109/esic60604.2024.10481635.

[8] Gawhankar, K., Deorukhkar, A., Miniyar, A., Kapure, H., & Ivin, B. (2024). NLP-driven ML f or resume information extraction. in Proc. 2024 IEEE 9th International Conference for Convergence in Technology (I2CT), Apr. 2024. doi:10.1109/I2CT61223.2024.10543861.

[9] Pabalkar, S., Patel, P., Choudhary, R. J., Panoch, V., Yadav, S., & Ghogale, H. (2024). Resume analyzer using natural language processing (NLP). 1–6, Oct. 2024, doi: 10.1109/icisaa62385.2024.10828940.

[10] Pimpalkar, A., Lalwani, A., Chaudhari, R., Inshall, M., Dalwani, M., & Saluja, T. (2023). Job applications selection and identification: study of resumes with natural language processing and machine learning. in Proc. 2023 IEEE International Students' Conference on Electrical, Electronics and Computer Science (SCEECS), 2023, pp. 1–5. doi:10.1109/SCEECS57921.2023.10063010.

[11] Erdem, M. E. (2023). Automatic resume screening with content matching. in Proc. 2023 8th International Conference on Computer Science and Engineering (UBMK), 2023, pp. 554–558. doi:10.1109/UBMK59864.2023.10286578.

[12] Tanberk, S., Helli, S. S., Kesim, E., & Cavsak, S. N. (2023). Resume matching framework via ranking and sorting using NLP and deep learning. in Proc. 2023 8th International Conference on Computer Science and Engineering (UBMK), 2023, pp. 453–458. doi:10.1109/UBMK59864.2023.10286605.

[13] Sinha, A. K., Akhtar, M. A. K., & Kumar, M. (2023). Automated resume parsing and job domain prediction using machine learning. *Indian Journal of Science and Technology*, 16(26), 1967–1974. doi: 10.17485/ijst/v16i26.880.

[14] Amin, M. D., Harkare, A. C., Parmar, N. S., Wadhwa, R. R., & Patil, R. A. (2023). Real time data based automated resume classification and job matching using SVC, jaccard index and cosine similarity. Proc. CERA (conference/proceedings), 2023, pp. 1–6. doi:10.1109/cera59325.2023.10455638. doi: 10.1109/cera59325.2023.10455638.

[15] Mhatre, S., Dakhare, B., Ankolekar, V., Chogale, N., Navghane, R., & Gotarne, P. (2023). Resume screening and ranking using convolutional neural network. In 2023 International Conference on Sustainable Computing and Smart Systems (ICSCSS), Coimbatore, India, (pp. 412–419). doi: 10.1109/ICSCSS57650.2023.10169716.

[16] Zhou, P., Qi, X., & Zhao, L. (2024). A cross-language attribute-level sentiment analysis approach using TinyBERT and GCN. *International Journal of Knowledge Management*, 20(1), 1–23. doi: 10.4018/ijkm.360783.

[17] Cao, H., & Xu, J. (2025). Fall detection algorithm based on improved Yolov7. Proc. SPIE (Int. Conf. / SPIE Proceedings), 2025. doi:10.1117/12.3045319.

[18] Peng, M., Zhang, W., Li, F., Xue, Q., Yuan, J., & An, P. (2023). Weed detection with improved yolov 7. *EAI Endorsed Transactions on Internet of Things*. Aug. 2023, doi: 10.4108/eetiot.v9i3.3468.

[19] Ahmed, M. F., & He, G. (n.d.). YOLOv7-Based Multiple Surgical Tool Localization and Detection in Laparoscopic Videos. Springer Nature.

26 A hybrid Res-ViT model for glaucoma detection

K. S. Ankita[a], Debashish Dash[b], Sakambhari Mahapatra[c] and Sanjay Agrawal[d]

Department of Electronics and Telecommunication Engineering, Veer Surendra Sai University of Technology Burla, Odisha, India

Abstract

Glaucoma is a serious eye condition that leads to permanent vision loss if not detected early. Since it often develops without noticeable symptoms, early diagnosis is essential to prevent blindness. Traditional diagnosis methods like checking eye pressure, examining the optic nerve, and visual field testing are effective but require time, costly equipment, and expert supervision, making them less accessible in many settings. Recent progress in deep learning has enabled automatic glaucoma detection using retinal fundus images. While Convolutional Neural Networks (CNNs) are good at learning local features, they struggle to capture the full context of the image. On the other hand, Vision Transformers (ViTs) are excellent at capturing global patterns but need large datasets to perform well. To overcome these issues, we propose a hybrid model that combines ResNet-18 (a CNN) with ViT-B/16 (a transformer) to take advantage of both local and global feature learning. The model was trained and tested on a curated subset of the SMDG-19 dataset containing 10,000 labeled images. It achieved high performance, with 98.70% accuracy, an F1-score of 0.982, and an AUC of 0.997. When compared to other existing models, the proposed approach showed superior results while being efficient and suitable for real-time clinical use.

Keywords: BCE logits loss function, glaucoma detection, Res-Net, vision transformers

Introduction

Glaucoma is a progressive and irreversible optic neuropathy that affects millions of people worldwide. It is one of the leading causes of permanent blindness. The disease typically advances without noticeable symptoms until significant vision loss occurs. This makes the early detection of glaucoma crucial. Clinical diagnosis traditionally depends on intraocular pressure (IOP) measurement, optic nerve head (ONH) assessment, visual field analysis, etc. These diagnostic approaches, though effective, are time consuming, require specialized instruments, and are inaccessible in resource-limited settings. The situation for the development of computerized approaches for automatic glaucoma detection [1].

A variety of methods, ranging from traditional machine learning approaches to advanced deep neural networks, have been proposed to improve diagnostic accuracy and efficiency. Early methods relied heavily on handcrafted features extracted from retinal fundus images, and then, using a classifier such as random forest, SVMs, and k-NN, glaucoma was detected. Kalita and Borgohain combined handcrafted features with an extra tree classifier [2]. Similarly, Korda et al. investigated oculomotor patterns using eye-tracking data with traditional

[a]ksankita99@gmail.com, [b]raja.dash50@gmail.com, [c]mahapatra.shakambhari@gmail.com, [d]agrawals_72@yahoo.com

DOI: 10.1201/9781003753391-26

classifiers [3]. Due to the lack of automated feature learning, these approaches showed limited scalability and adaptability to more complex datasets.

On the other hand, the deep learning approaches can learn the features automatically. Therefore, these methods, particularly the Convolutional Neural Network (CNN)-based techniques, have shown significant promise in automating glaucoma detection using retinal images. Diaz-Pinto et al. [4] compared various deep learning backbones trained on fundus images, highlighting the strengths and limitations of each. Oguz et al. [5] extracted deep features using a CNN and classified using AdaBoost. Nayak et al. [6] proposed ECNet, an evolutionary CNN optimized via genetic algorithms for glaucoma detection. The authors claimed high accuracy but on small datasets. Other CNN-based methods, such as MobileNetV3 [7] and EfficientNetV2 [8]. While deeper networks yielded better performance, they demanded significant computational resources.

Segmentation-based methods, such as UNet and its variants, have also been explored for the problem. These methods are often used to delineate the optic disc and cup regions before classification. Kumar et al. developed a deep learning model integrating UNet++ for optic disc and cup segmentation and ResNet with gated recurrent units for classification [9]. The main disadvantage of these approaches is the dependence on annotated masks, which are not always available. Soofi and Fazal-e-Ami implemented a hybrid model that combined CNN with a recurrent neural network and reported promising accuracy [10].

Transformer-based segmentation models like SegFormer have further improved optic disc and cup delineation, yielding high dice coefficients [11]. Jun et al. [12] implemented a transferable ranking CNN for

the problem at hand. DETR [13] Transfer learning approaches are also reported for glaucoma detection. However, these models typically lack classification modules, limiting their utility in complete diagnostic workflows. Various hybrid techniques, such as HViTML [14] and EFFResNet-ViT [15], are also explored for glaucoma detection. KR Net [16], ECSD-Net [17], CA-Net [18], and GC-Net [19] are a few among the recent approaches for glaucoma classification. However, many of these models are either computationally expensive or have complex architectures.

Careful analysis of the literature indicated that CNN-based models often struggle to capture global contextual information, which can reduce their sensitivity in detecting early-stage glaucoma. Conversely, standalone transformer models, though effective in modeling global dependencies, typically require large-scale training datasets and may lack robustness. As a result, there is a compelling need for effective architecture capable of learning both fine-grained local features and holistic global patterns from retinal fundus images. This motivated us to develop a hybrid model integrating ResNet-18 and ViT-B/16 architectures, coined as the Res-ViT model. The vision transformer records complex patterns and global contextual information across the entire image. Simultaneously, the ResNet-18 model extracts localized features that can detect subtle and localized signs of the disorder by identifying spatial hierarchies within images. So, the main contribution of the paper can be summarized as

(i) A hybrid architecture combining ResNet-18 and vision transformer (ViT-B/16) is investigated.

(ii) The model leverages both local spatial information and global contextual representations to enhance glaucoma detection performance.

(iii) A binary cross-entropy (BCE) logits loss function is utilized to effectively monitor the model's learning process.

Proposed Method

The proposed model is designed to combine the ResNet-18 and vision transformer (ViT-B/16) architecture in a unified framework for robust and accurate feature extraction and glaucoma detection. This section details the architecture of the proposed hybrid Res-ViT model and outlines the associated implementation strategy.

Model architecture

The block diagram of the proposed method for glaucoma detection is shown in Figure 26.1. It starts with the initial image pre-processing section, which includes image resizing, batch normalization, and data augmentation. Following it, two parallel sections consisting of two models, such as ViT-B/16 and ResNet-18, for image feature extraction. Textural, structural, and spatial information can all be used simultaneously to improve diagnostic accuracy by fusing the features that were collected from these modalities at the feature level. Each section is discussed in detail below.

Data preprocessing

The input fundus images were resized to 224×224 pixels to align with the input size specifications for ResNet-18 and ViT-B/16. Further to ensure compatibility with pre-trained weights, images were normalized using the ImageNet dataset's mean and standard deviation values, i.e., mean (0.485, 0.456, 0.406) and standard deviation (0.229, 0.224, 0.225). To enhance the size of the dataset and improve the model's capacity for generalization, data augmentations such as random rotation (up to ±20 degrees) and random horizontal flipping are performed during training. It is to be noted here that the data augmentation used in this case will not result in creating more training samples being stored in memory, since these transformations are processed dynamically during training. Each image may appear slightly different in every epoch. Therefore, it improves the model's capacity for generalization. The present research avoided employing offline augmentation, which saves altered images as new datasets.

Feature extraction

The pre-processed image is given as input to the hybrid Res-ViT model, where each model independently processes the images to extract distinct features. A detailed architectural diagram of the two models is displayed in Figure 26.2. The ViT-B/16

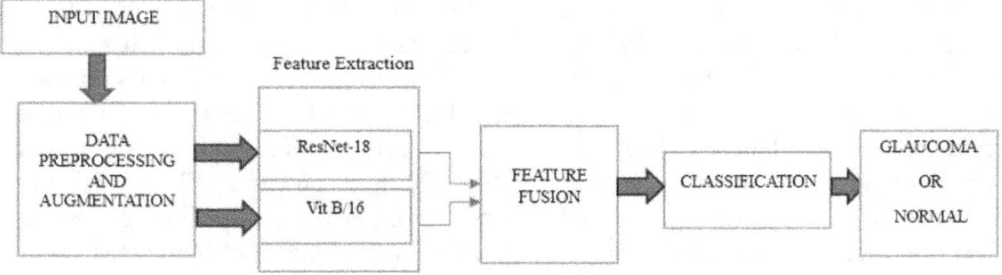

Figure 26.1 Block diagram of the proposed approach
Source: Author

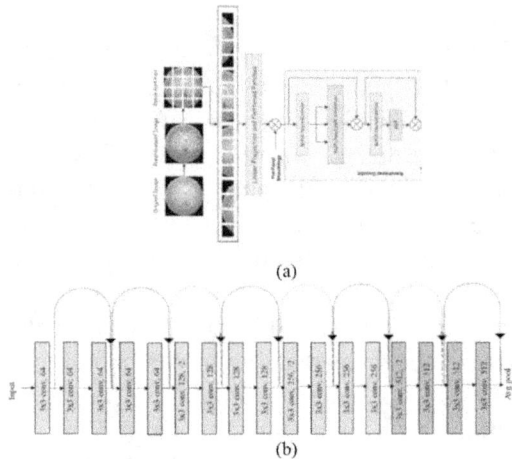

(a)

(b)

Figure 26.2 Architecture of (a) ViT-B/16, (b) ResNet 18 for feature extraction
Source: Author

architecture starts with splitting the image into patches of size 16×16. As the image size is 224 × 224, there will be a total of 196 patches. It is wise to mention here that the input is an RGB color image. Each patch is flattened into a vector. Therefore, the vector dimension is computed to be $(16 \times 16 \times 3) = 768$. To preserve spatial relation, positional embeddings are done to the vectors. A patch embedding sequence is supplemented with a unique learnable token CLS. Upon combining 1 CLS token, the total output shape in this case is (197,768).

The transformer encoder consists of 12 identical layers. Each layer is connected by skip connections and has multi-head self-attention (MSA), layer normalization (LN), and a feedforward network (MLP) that improve feature extraction. This sequence of operations progressively refines the features for more accurate glaucoma detection. The CLS token of the ViT model, which is used as the final feature vector, contains a highly refined global representation of the image after it has been processed through 12 Transformer blocks. This vector, which

has the shape (768), encodes every feature related to glaucoma that was taken from the retinal image.

In addition to the transformer, the ResNet-18 architecture's deep residual learning framework aids in the extraction of localized features. Figure 26.2(b) depicts the ResNet-18 design, which comprises 17 convolutional layers followed by one fully connected layer. These are partitioned into 4 ResNet blocks, each denoted using different colors in the figure. The network backbone comprises convolutional layers and max pooling for downsampling. For the purpose of feature extraction only, the final average pooling and fully connected layers are excluded. Initially, the input of shape (3, 224, 224) is transformed to (64, 56, 56) after Conv1 and MaxPool layers. ResNet Block 1 retains this shape with two convolutional layers and a skip connection. Subsequent blocks progressively down sample the feature maps. Block 2 reduces it to (128, 28, 28), Block 3 to (256, 14, 14), and Block 4 to (512, 7, 7). A global average pooling layer (adaptive average pool 2D ((1, 1))) then reduces this to (512, 1, 1), which is finally flattened to a 512 feature vector. This 512-dimensional vector effectively encodes local spatial features from retinal fundus images, serving as a robust representation for glaucoma detection.

Classification

The feature vectors obtained from the Vision Transformer and ResNet-18 models are concatenated to create a unified representation that integrates both global contextual and local spatial information. This fused feature vector, with a combined dimensionality of 1280 (768 from ViT and 512 from ResNet-18), is then passed through multiple fully connected layers utilizing RELU activation functions to introduce non-linearity and enhance learning. To mitigate the risk of overfitting, a dropout layer is incorporated, which randomly disables a portion of the neurons during training. Finally, a dense output layer with a SoftMax activation function is employed to classify the input into either the 'Glaucoma' or 'Non-Glaucoma' category by generating corresponding probability scores.

Implementation details

The hybrid Res–ViT model was trained in PyTorch with Kaggle's GPU P100 environment. For dataset preparation, we utilized (torchvision.datasets.ImageFolder) to load retinal fundus images from the training, validation, and test directories. Data augmentations and normalization were applied using (torchvision.transforms). The ResNet-18 and the ViT-B/16 were initialized with the ImageNet pretrained weights using torchvision (models.resnet18 (pretrained = True)) and (mod-els.vit_b_16(pretrained = True)), respectively, having their classification heads modified to extract 512 and 768-dimensional feature vectors. The confusion matrix was computed using (sklearn.metrics). Matplotlib and Seaborn are utilized for the visualization of the model's performance metrics. Various hyperparameters for training the model are listed in Table 26.1 below.

Table 26.1 Hyperparameters for training the hybrid model.

Hyperparameters	Value
Input image size	224 × 224
Number of epochs	100
Batch size	32
Optimizer	AdamW
Loss function	BCE with logits loss
Learning rate scheduler	Cosine annealing

Source: Author

Selecting an appropriate loss function is critical for optimizing model performance. The hybrid model was trained using the BCE logits loss function, which demonstrated the most consistent and effective results. Mathematically, the BCE logits loss function is stated as [20]:

$$L = \frac{1}{N} \sum_{i=1}^{N} \left[log_e(1 + e^{-z}) + z(1 - y_i) \right] \quad (1)$$

Here, y_i is the predicted label, and z is the logit (the raw output before applying the sigmoid function). N is the number of samples. Due to the logarithmic operation and log-sum-exp, it achieves numerical stability. The AdamW optimizer is employed for its effective decoupling of weight decay from the learning rate update, leading to improved regularization and stable convergence, particularly in transformer-based architectures. A learning rate of 0.0001 and a weight decay of 0.001 are used in this study. To manage learning rate dynamics, the cosine annealing learning rate scheduler is applied. This scheduler gradually decreases the learning rate following a cosine decay pattern as given in equation (2). The learning rate at each iteration is given by [21]:

$$\eta_t = \eta_{min} + \frac{1}{2}(\eta_{max} - \eta_{min})$$
$$\left(1 + cos\frac{T_{cur}}{T_{max}} \Pi\right) \quad (2)$$

Where,

η_t	=	Learning rate at time step (or epoch)
η_{min}	=	Minimum learning rate (usually near zero)
η_{max}	=	Maximum learning rate (initial learning rate)
T_{cur}	=	Current epoch or iteration count
T_{max}	=	Total number of epochs over which to decay the learning rate

Results and Discussions

This section presents the dataset employed for evaluating the proposed model, along with the performance metrics used to assess its effectiveness. Additionally, a comparative analysis is conducted against existing glaucoma detection methods to benchmark the model's performance.

Database

This study employs a curated subset of the SMDG-19 (Standardized Multi-source Dataset for Glaucoma). The dataset contains image tensors along with binary class labels suitable for supervised approaches. Glaucomatous images are labelled as 1, while non-glaucomatous (normal) images are labelled as 0. The dataset is divided into training, validation, and testing subsets using an 80:10:10 split, with 8,000 images allocated for training, 1,000 for validation, and 1,000 for testing. Each subset is organized into two folders based on the class labels. Representative samples of both image classes are shown in Figure 26.3 [22].

Performance evaluation

Various performance indices, such as accuracy, sensitivity, specificity, and F1-score,

along with loss plots and the receiver operating characteristic (ROC) curve, are used to demonstrate the model's efficiency and its learning behavior.

Figure 26.4 displays the accuracy and loss over multiple epochs during the training and validation phase. The figure demonstrates a consistent upward trajectory in training accuracy of the model, ultimately surpassing 98%. It clearly indicates the model's ability to resourcefully learn the underlying patterns in the training data. The validation accuracy curve closely tracks the former curve during the entire training process. The model exhibits consistent improvement in prediction accuracy across epochs, indicating effective learning without signs of overfitting. As illustrated in Figure 26.4(b), both training and validation loss curves show a gradual decline, reflecting strong generalization capabilities. This smooth convergence is primarily due to the implementation of the cosine annealing learning rate scheduler in combination with the AdamW optimizer, which efficiently regulates the first and second moments of gradients, ensuring training stability. Additionally, the residual connections in the ResNet architecture help mitigate the

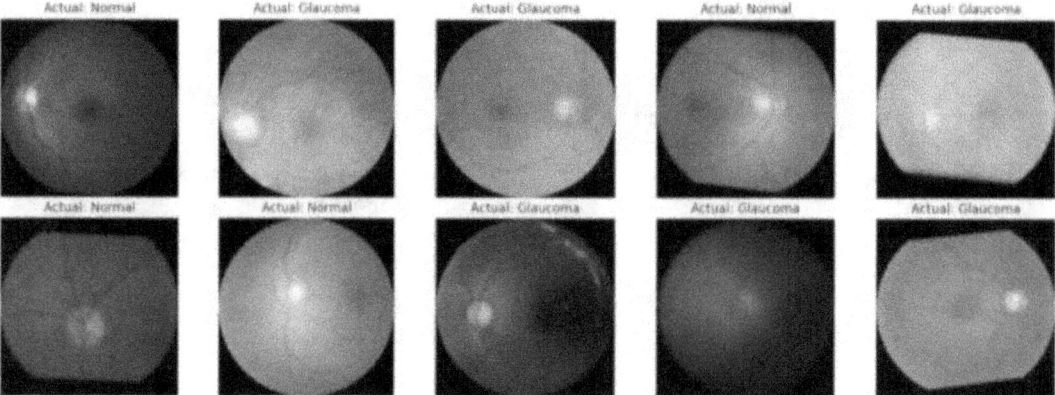

Figure 26.3 Sample fundus images of SMDG-19 with actual level
Source: Author

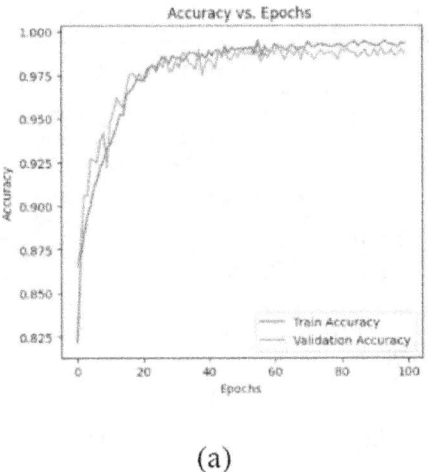

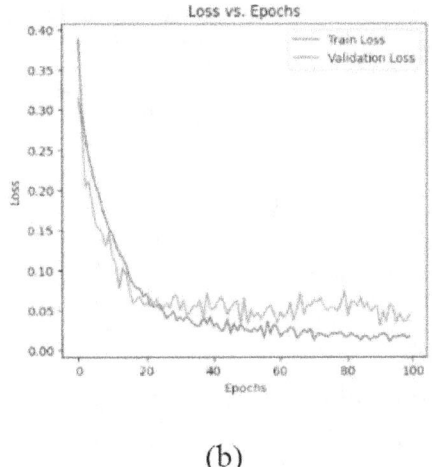

(a)   (b)

Figure 26.4 Plot of accuracy and loss during training and validation
Source: Author

vanishing gradient issue, thereby enhancing performance in deeper networks.

Figure 26.5 illustrates the ROC curve of the proposed model, which shows a sharp ascent towards the top-left corner, reflecting a high sensitivity and a low false positive rate. The model attained an area under the curve (AUC) score of 0.997, demonstrating outstanding capability in distinguishing between glaucomatous and healthy retinal images.

To further validate the effectiveness of the model, the performance indices are compared with some of the existing approaches on the same dataset as listed in Table 26.2. Note that '-' indicates non-availability of data from the respective reference. In this research, we implemented and evaluated individual models ViT-B/16 and ResNet-18 alongside the hybrid Res-ViT model. The stand-alone ViT-B/16 model achieved 95.40% accuracy (Acc) and an AUC of 0.980. In contrast, ResNet-18 achieved an accuracy of 97.60% and an AUC of 0.990. The subtle lower performance in ViT-B/16 may be due to its reduced ability to capture fine-grained local features that are

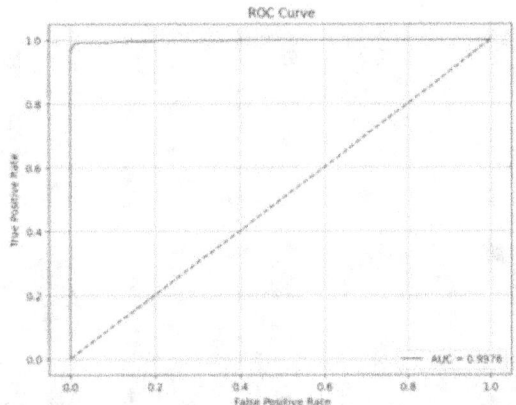

Figure 26.5 ROC curve of the proposed model
Source: Author

crucial for medical images. On the other hand, the proposed hybrid model, combining ViT-B/16 and ResNet-18, outperformed both individual models, achieving 98.70% accuracy and an AUC of 0.997. This highlights the effectiveness of integrating global attention with local feature extraction for superior segmentation and classification performance. As is evident, the proposed approach achieves a higher accuracy

Table 26.2 Comparison of the proposed model with other approaches.

Model	Dataset	Acc	F1-Score	AUC
CNN based hybrid model [5]	Acrima	92.96	0.937	0.928
ECNet[6]	Private dataset	97.20	-	-
MobilenetV3[7]	SMDG-19	88.00	0.870	0.940
Extra Trees Classifier [2]	SMDG-19	85.40	-	-
EfficientnetV2[8]	SMGD-19	93.00	0.950	-
TRk-CNN [12]	Private dataset	92.96	-	-
DETR [13]	SMGD-19	90.40	-	-
ViT-B/16 (own implementation)	SMGD-19	95.40	0.940	0.980
ResNet-18 (own implementation)	SMGD-19	97.60	0.969	0.990
Hybrid Res-ViT model	SMGD-19	98.70	0.982	0.997

Source: Author

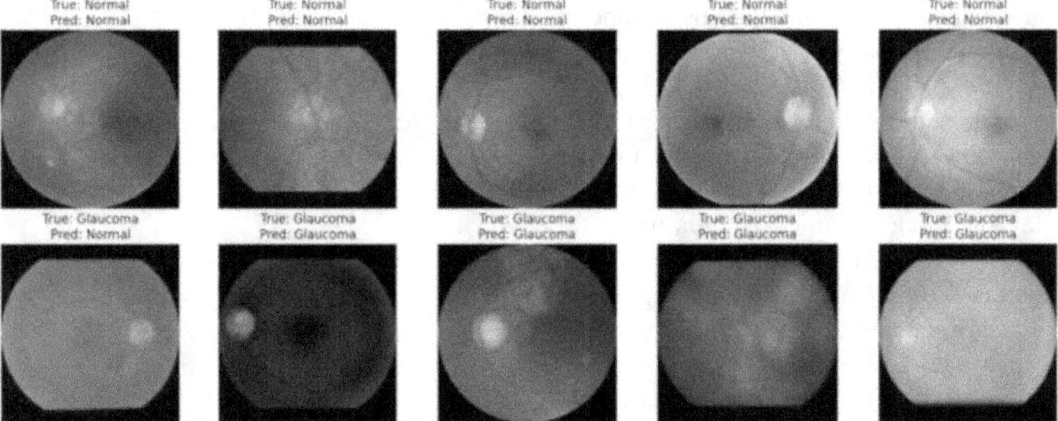

Figure 26.6 Images representing actual and predicted values
Source: Author

compared to the state-of-the-art methods. Compared to other state-of-the-art models like EfficientNetV2 and MobileNetV3, our hybrid approach significantly outperforms in both accuracy and F1 score.

To gain insight into the qualitative behavior of the model, a few sample images along with their actual and predicted class levels are displayed in Figure 26.6. The model provides good results by spotting these important signs even in images with very poor contrast, images with high brightness, or pathologically damped images. There are a few instances of misclassification, also, that might be caused by inhomogeneous illumination or image artifacts.

Conclusion

This paper describes a reliable and efficient hybrid deep learning model that combines

ResNet-18 and ViT-B/16 for automated glaucoma detection using retinal fundus images. The model overcomes significant constraints of classic CNN and standalone transformer techniques by integrating their complementary strengths, i.e., local spatial detail extraction and global contextual comprehension, respectively. The model was trained on the SMDG dataset of fundus images through a well-designed training pipeline that featured the AdamW optimizer and a cosine annealing learning rate scheduler. BCE logits loss was utilized as the loss function during the training. The results claim superior performance of the proposed approach as compared to the state-of-the-art approaches. Future work may explore model pruning and quantization techniques to further reduce computational overhead and facilitate real-time deployment in clinical settings. Moreover, expanding the training dataset with diverse demographics and imaging conditions could enhance the generalizability of the model across different populations.

References

[1] Tham, Y. C., Li, X., Wong, T. Y., Quigley, H. A., Aung, T., & Cheng, C. Y. (2014). Global prevalence of glaucoma and projections of glaucoma burden through 2040: a systematic review and meta-analysis. *Ophthalmology*, 121(11), 2081–2090.

[2] Kalita, N., & Borgohain, S. K. (2024). An ocular feature-based novel biomarker determination for Glaucoma diagnosis using supervised machine learning and fundus imaging. *IEEE Sensors Letters*. 8(11), 1–4.

[3] Korda, A. I., Asvestas, P. A., Matsopoulos, G. K., Ventouras, E. M., & Smyrnis, N. P. (2015). Automatic identification of oculomotor behavior using pattern recognition techniques. *Computers in Biology and Medicine*, 60, 151–162.

[4] Diaz-Pinto, A., Morales, S., Naranjo, V., Köhler, T., Mossi, J. M., & Navea, A. (2019). CNNs for automatic glaucoma assessment using fundus images: an extensive validation. *Biomedical Engineering Online*, 18, 1–19.

[5] Oguz, C., Aydin, T., & Yaganoglu, M. (2024). A CNN-based hybrid model to detect glaucoma disease. *Multimedia Tools and Applications*, 83(6), 17921–17939.

[6] Nayak, D. R., Das, D., Majhi, B., Bhandary, S. V., & Acharya, U. R. (2021). ECNet: an evolutionary convolutional network for automated glaucoma detection using fundus images. *Biomedical Signal Processing and Control*, 67, 102559.

[7] Keerthivasan, E., Thangavel, S. K., Nalluri, M. R., Somasundaram, K., Parthasaradhi, S., Dhar, M. Y., et al. (2024). Early glaucoma detection through ansan-infused retinal vessel segmentation. In 2024 International Conference on Inventive Computation Technologies (ICICT), (pp. 1212–1218). IEEE.

[8] Bhuria, R. (2024). Automated glaucoma detection from retinal fundus images: leveraging efficientnetv2 for enhanced diagnostic accuracy. In 2024 9th International Conference on Communication and Electronics Systems (ICCES), (pp. 1442–1448). IEEE.

[9] Kumar, V. V. N. S., Reddy, G. H., & GiriPrasad, M. N. (2023). A novel glaucoma detection model using Unet++-based segmentation and ResNet with GRU-based optimized deep learning. *Biomedical Signal Processing and Control*, 86, 105069.

[10] Soofi, A.A., & Fazal-e-Amin (2023). Exploring Deep Learning Techniques for Glaucoma Detection: A Comprehensive Review, Journal of Computing & Biomedical Informatics, 5(2), 1–19.

[11] Rantaya, I. N., Alfarozi, S. A. I., & Nugroho, H. A. (2025). Leveraging segformer for precision segmentation of optic cup and optic disc in fundus imaging for Glaucoma detection. In International Conference on Advancement in Data Science, E-learning

and Information System (ICADEIS), (pp.1–6). IEEE.

[12] Jun, T. J., Eom, Y., Kim, D., Kim, C., Park, J. H., Nguyen, H. M., et al. (2021). TRk-CNN: transferable ranking-CNN for image classification of glaucoma, glaucoma suspect, and normal eyes. *Expert Systems with Applications*, 182, 115211.

[13] Chincholi, F., & Koestler, H. (2024). Transforming glaucoma diagnosis: transformers at the forefront. *Frontiers in Artificial Intelligence*, 7, 1324109.

[14] Singh, P. B., Singh, P., Dev, H., Batra, D., & Chaurasia, B. K. (2025). HViTML: hybrid vision transformer with machine learning-based classification model for glaucomatous eye. *Multimedia Tools and Applications*, 84, 33609–33632.

[15] Hussain, T., Shouno, H., Hussain, A., Hussain, D., Ismail, M., Mir, T. H., et al. (2025). EFFResNet-ViT: A fusion-based convolutional and vision transformer model for explainable medical image classification. *IEEE Access*. 13, 54040–54068.

[16] Sonti, K., & Dhuli, R. (2023). A new convolution neural network model "KR-NET" for retinal fundus glaucoma classification. *Optik*, 283, 170861.

[17] Liu, B., Pan, D., Shuai, Z., & Song, H. (2022). ECSD-Net: a joint optic disc and cup segmentation and glaucoma classification network based on unsupervised domain adaptation. *Computer Methods and Programs in Biomedicine*, 213, 106530.

[18] Das, D., Nayak, D. R., & Pachori, R. B. (2023). CA-Net: a novel cascaded attention-based network for multistage glaucoma classification using fundus images. *IEEE Transactions on Instrumentation and Measurement*, 72, 1–10.

[19] Juneja, M., Thakur, N., Thakur, S., Uniyal, A., Wani, A., & Jindal, P. (2020). GC-NET for classification of glaucoma in the retinal fundus image. *Machine Vision and Applications*, 31, 1–18.

[20] Carter, S. (2023). Why nn.BCEWithLogitsLoss numerically stable. Medium. Available at: https://medium.com/@sahilcarterr/why-nn-bcewithlogitsloss-numerically-stable-6a04f3052967. [Accessed:Oct. 15, 2024].

[21] Mallick, U. (2024). Cosine learning rate schedulers in PyTorch. Medium. Available at: https://medium.com/@utkrisht14/cosine-learning-rate-schedulers-in-pytorch-486d8717d541. [Accessed: Oct. 15, 2024].

[22] Sabari50312. (2024). Fundus-PyTorch dataset. Kaggle Datasets. Available at:https://www.kaggle.com/datasets/sabari50312/fundus-pytorch. [Accessed: Oct. 15, 2024].

27 CBAM-augmented MobileNetV2 for real-time violence detection: enhancing feature attention for improved performance'

B. Emile Jonath[1,a], B. Alex[2,b] and Sanjay Kumar Sahu[2,c]

[1]School of Computer Science, Lovely Professional University, Phagwara, Punjab, India

[2]School of Electronics & communication, Lovely Professional University, Phagwara, Punjab, India

Abstract

This study presents a method for real – time violence detection by introducing the convolutional block attention module (CBAM) in MobileNetV2 Architecture. This hybrid architecture leverages the MobileNetV2 lightweight efficiency while utilizing CBAM enhanced feature attention mechanism for improved performance in devices with limited computational resources. The dataset is a mix of violent and non-violent scenes. These are then preprocessed using data augmentation and normalization to enhance generalization. The main backbone MobileNetV2 layers were frozen to preserve pre-trained features. CBAM was added to boost both spatial and channel attention, highlighting features for classification. Results revealed that the MobileNetV2-CBAM Hybird model outperformed the basic MobileNetV2 in accuracy, precision and recall. The model achieved approximately 98% testing accuracy, a considerable improvement over the baseline's 93–94%. Training and validation curves demonstrated an impressive generalization and improved learning efficiency. This advancement is mainly due to CBAM's ability to dynamically adjust feature maps, focusing on key spatial and channel information. The results support the integration of attention mechanisms like CBAM into lightweight architectures for real-time applications offers a balance between exceptional accuracy and computational efficiency. This method provides a scalable and effective solution for real-world violence detection. Future improvements could include expanding the dataset and fine-tuning hyperparameters to optimize performance even further.

Keywords: Channel and spatial attention, convolutional block attention module (CBAM), MobileNetV2, real-time violence detection

Introduction

Real-time video surveillance is essential for ensuring public safety and security. Identifying violent activities in live video feeds can reduce risks and allow for immediate interventions. However, conventional methods for detecting violent scenes often come with challenges due to limited computational resources. To create effective solutions that balance performance and efficiency, it is essential to develop models suitable for real-time applications in resource-limited settings.

Deep learning, specifically Convolutional Neural Networks (CNNs), have shown impressive results in various computer vision tasks like image classification, activity recognition, and object detection.

[a]jonathbe0902@gmail.com, [b]alexbandlamudi14@gmail.com, [c]sanjay.23393@lpu.co.in

DOI: 10.1201/9781003753391-27

MobileNetV2 is known for its lightweight architecture extracting features while being computationally efficient. Despite its lightweight design it might struggle with complex tasks like violence detection due to lack of mechanisms to extract essential features.

To overcome these limitations, Attention mechanisms have been introduced to enhance feature extraction, The Convolutional Block Attention Module (CBAM) has proven effective by utilizing both spatial and channel attention mechanisms, allowing the model to focus on most important features. Integrating CBAM into lightweight architectures like MobileNetV2 can increase model performance without a significant increase in computational requirements.

The objective of this study is to develop a hybrid MobileNetV2-CBAM model for enhancing detection, To compare and evaluate model performance.

This study proposes a hybrid model called MobileNetV2-CBAM that combines these two components to improve feature attention and distinguish violent and non-violent activities in real-time video streams. Our dataset contains labeled video frames featuring balanced violent and non-violent activities. We applied preprocessing techniques, including data augmentation to strengthen the model's robustness. We evaluated the MobileNetV2-CBAM model using accuracy, precision, recall, and F1-score metrics. Our results demonstrate that this hybrid model outperforms the baseline MobileNetV2 model with an impressive testing accuracy of 98%. These findings highlight the potential of integrating attention mechanisms to improve lightweight models' performance, especially in resource-limited environments where real-time processing is critical.

Literature Review

Violence detection in surveillance videos has become important research topic as it can help keep people safe by detecting dangerous situations in real time. The major challenge in this research area is developing models that are both accurate and efficient in computationally limited environments. Deep learning techniques, particularly CNN is popularly adopted for this problem.

CNNs are great because they can pick up patterns in images, like the difference between someone fighting or just walking by. For example, Hussain et al. built a CNN model that works fast enough for real-time use, showing how well CNNs can spot violent behavior in videos [2]. But CNNs can be heavy on processing power, which is a problem for smaller devices. To fix this, researchers like Shobana et al. used a lighter model called MobileNet combined with CNNs. This combo keeps things accurate while using less computing power [3]. Another version, MobileNetV2, is even better for real-time use on low-power devices, as Kumar et al. showed by using it for violence detection without losing accuracy [4].

Another approach is ResNet, which uses something called residual connections to learn complex patterns in videos. Shripriya et al. used ResNet to boost accuracy in spotting violence Shripriya et al. [5], while Kaur et al. went with ResNet-50 to handle big datasets and still get solid results [6]. On top of that, Vision Transformers (ViTs) are becoming a new favorite because they're good at understanding how video frames connect over time. Singh et al. showed that ViTs can track these connections to better identify violent events [7]. Abdali also came up with a transformer model that doesn't need as much data but still performs well by focusing on the sequence of video frames [8].

Methodology

The dataset used in this study includes labelled scenes from both violence and nonviolence [1]. Frames are extracted from these scenes, and these frames are resized to a target dimension of 224 × 224 pixels. Additionally, the dataset is divided into training, validation, and test sets, following a 70-20-10 split, where 70% of the images are designated for training, 20% for validation, and 10% for testing. The images are organized into their respective directories for each set (train, validation, and test) under the categories of violence and nonviolence.

To enhance model robustness and prevent overfitting, data augmentation is utilized on the training images through TensorFlow's *ImageDataGenerator*. The augmentations consist of various random transformations, including rotation (up to 45 degrees), horizontal and vertical shifting, zooming, flipping (both horizontally and vertically), and brightness adjustments (ranging from 0.8 to 1.2). The image pixel values are normalized to the range [0, 1] by rescaling them using equation [1]:

$$rescale = {}^{1.}\!/_{255} \qquad (1)$$

This guarantees that all input images are scaled uniformly, aiding the model in converging more quickly during training. The *ImageDataGenerator* is utilized to input the images to the model. Distinct generators are established for the training, validation, and test datasets. The training generator incorporates the augmented training images, while the validation and test generators solely apply rescaling to the images without any additional augmentation. These generators automatically manage image batching, shuffling (for training), and resizing throughout the model's training and evaluation stages.

Model architecture

The proposed model combines MobileNetV2, a lightweight CNN, with the Convolutional Block Attention Module (CBAM) to create a model that's both efficient and accurate. This hybrid design is perfect for running on devices with limited computing power, like surveillance cameras, while still delivering strong performance for violence detection.

Base model

MobileNetV2 is a lightweight CNN Hsairi et al. [9] architecture designed for computationally limited resources. It consists of inverted residual blocks and in depthwise separable convolutions which minimize the model parameters. It uses a linear bottleneck, where the output from the previous layer of each block is processed through a linear activation function. The architecture can be visualized as a combination of convolution layers and linear bottleneck layers. The equation [2] shows the simplified representation can be expressed as follows.

$$\mathrm{Output} = \mathrm{MobileNetV2(Input)} \qquad (2)$$

In our model, we used MobileNetV2 as a pre-trained feature extractor, leveraging its weights from the ImageNet dataset. To save on training time and prevent overfitting we froze all layers up to the second-to-last convolutional block of the MobileNetV2 architecture, which includes 17 layers (out of the total 53 layers in the original MobileNetV2 design). These layers are adequate for extracting general features, which are then fine-tuned using the CBAM attention mechanism. By freezing these initial layers, we were able to retain the pre-trained knowledge from the ImageNet dataset while minimizing the number of parameters that needed fine-tuning.

In out hybrid model, MobileNetV2 acts as backbone for feature extraction. It takes input image and processes it through series of convolution layers, which extract features that identify patterns. These features are then refined using Convolutional Block Attention Module (CBAM), which uses spatial and channel attention mechanisms. The entire feature extraction process in MobileNetV2 can be formally described as equation [3] as a sequence of operations $\mathcal{F}$ applied to an input image χ_o (where χ_o represents the raw image):

$$\chi_{features} = \mathcal{F}(\chi_0; W) \tag{3}$$

χ_o is the input image, $\chi_{features}$ is the extracted feature map, and $\mathcal{F}(\cdot; W)$ represents the sequence of MobileNetV2's operations (like depth wise separable convolutions and inverted residual blocks) with learned weights W. CBAM then refines these features to make the model more effective.

Integration of CBAM block
After the feature extraction, the features produced by MobileNetV2 backbone are passed through CBAM. It is an attention mechanism designed to enhance the feature representations by focusing on most informative patterns of the extracted features.

CBAM works in two stages, spatial attention and channel attention [10]. The spatial attention fine tunes the spatial positions within feature map and channel attention adjusts the significance of each channel. By utilizing these attention mechanisms, the model can concentrate on the most relevant features, enhancing its capacity to generalize to new, unseen data.

Channel attention is designed to focus on the most informative feature channels. This is done by calculating a weight for each channel to adaptively recalibrate the feature map. Given an input feature map

$F \in \mathbb{R}^{H \times W \times C}$, where H is height, W is width, and C is the number of channels as shown below in equation [4]. The purpose of channel attention is to give greater importance to the most valuable channels. A global average pooling operation is performed on each channel to create a channel descriptor, resulting in a vector of size C. This effectively captures the overall average information from each channel.

$$GAP(F) = \frac{1}{H \, x \, W} \sum_{i=1}^{H} \sum_{j=1}^{W} F(i,j,:) \tag{4}$$

Here, $F(i,j,:)$ represents the pixel values across all the channels at position (i, j) and the result is a vector of size C.

The channel descriptor undergoes two fully connected layers (with ReLU activation in between) to produce a set of attention weights. This can be expressed as equation [5]:

$$\mathbf{M}_c = \sigma(W_2 \delta(W_1 GAP(F) + b_1) + b_2 \tag{5}$$

Where, δ is the ReLU activation function, W_1 and W_2 are learned weights and b_1, b_2 are biases. σ is the sigmoid activation that outputs a channel attention map $\mathbf{M}_c \in \mathbb{R}^C$.

The attention map $\mathbf{M}_c$ is then applied to the input feature map F in equation [6] to recalibrate the channels:

$$F' = \mathbf{M}_c \cdot F \tag{6}$$

Here, the dot ($\cdot$) represents element-wise multiplication, which improves the channels according to their learned significance.

After the channel attention mechanism Kale [11] has adjusted the feature map, the subsequent step is spatial attention. This mechanism emphasizes the crucial spatial areas within each channel.

To generate spatial attention maps [12, 13], the feature map $F' \in \mathbb{R}^{H \times W \times C}$ is first pooled along the channel dimension. Both global average pooling (GAP) in equation [7] and global max pooling (GMP) in equation [8] are performed to capture both spatial and feature-wise statistics.

$$GAP(F') = \frac{1}{C} \sum_{c=1}^{C} F'(i,j,c) \qquad (7)$$

$$GMP(F') = max\, F'(i,j,c) \qquad (8)$$

The results of GAP and GMP are concatenated along the channel dimension to form a spatial descriptor as shown in equation [9].

$$\mathbf{M}_s = concat(GAP(F'), GMP(F')) \qquad (9)$$

This combined descriptor is then processed through a convolutional layer with a kernel size of 7×7, followed by a sigmoid activation function to produce a spatial attention map:

$$\mathbf{M}_s = \sigma(W_s.concat(GAP(F'),$$
$$GMP(F')) \qquad (10)$$

Where W_s is a learned convolutional kernel.

Finally, the spatial attention map $M_s \in \mathbb{R}^{H \times W}$ is used to modulate the spatial feature map F' using element- wise multiplication in equation [11]:

$$F'' = \mathbf{M}_s.F' \qquad (11)$$

Model architecture after freezing layers and CBAM integration

After the MobileNetV2 backbone has extracted general features from the input image, the CBAM block is applied in sequence to refine these features. The output from the CBAM block, now enriched with improved channel-wise and spatial-wise features, is then fed into fully connected layers for classification.

The overall architecture can be summarized as:

- **Input layer:** The input image is passed to the MobileNetV2 backbone for feature extraction.
- **MobileNetV2 feature extractor:** The initial layers (up to the penultimate convolutional block) of MobileNetV2 are frozen to retain pre-trained features.
- **CBAM Block:** The extracted feature map is passed through the CBAM block, where channel attention is applied first, followed by spatial attention.
- **Fully connected layers:** The refined feature map is flattened and passed through fully connected layers to predict the output.
- **Output layer:** The final output is a binary classification (or multi-class classification depending on the task).

The overall architecture can be visualized in the following diagram, as shown in Figure 27.1.

Results

The bar chart in Figure 27.2 illustrates the performance comparison between MobileNetV2 and proposed MobileNetV2 - CBAM model across three important metrics: accuracy, precision, and recall. The data clearly shows that MobileNetV2 with CBAM surpasses the baseline MobileNetV2 model in all three areas. In particular, MobileNetV2 with CBAM achieved an accuracy nearing 98%, while MobileNetV2 falls within the 93%-94% accuracy range. The precision and recall metrics for MobileNetV2 – CBAM achieved higher score, reflecting stronger performance.

The performance indicates the advantage of CBAM attention mechanisms capacity to focus on, important features of image

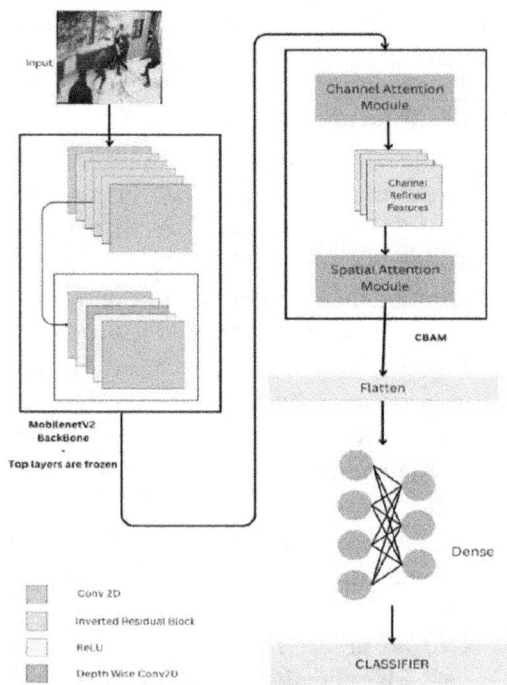

Figure 27.1 Architecture of the proposed MobileNetV2 – CBAM Hybrid Model
Source: Author

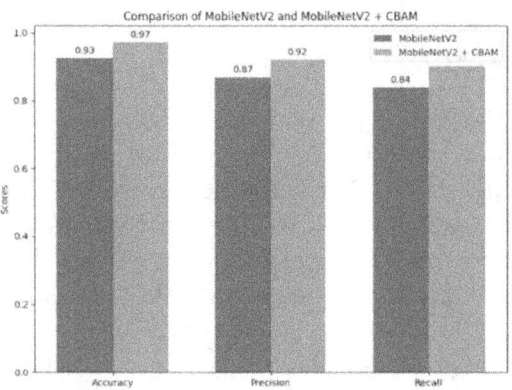

Figure 27.2 Performance comparison of MobileNetV2 and MobileNetV2-CBAM model
Source: Author

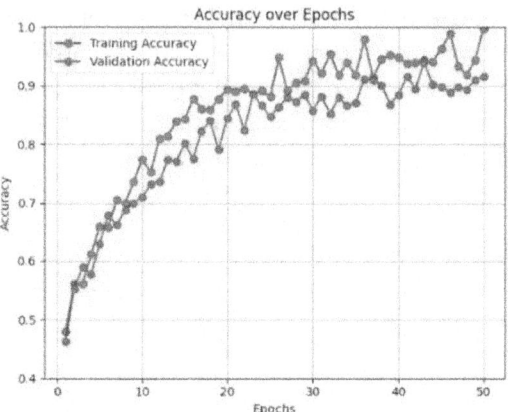

Figure 27.3 Training and validation accuracy graph of MobileNetV2 –CBAM model
Source: Author

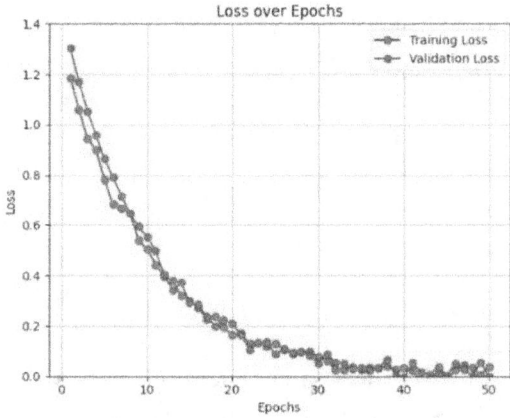

Figure 27.4 Training and validation loss graph of MobileNetV2 – CBAM model
Source: Author

input, resulting in robust generalization and accuracy. This indicates the effectiveness of CBAM in MobileNetV2 – CBAM hybrid model in enhancing MobileNetV2 for real – time violence detection.

The Figures 27.3 and 27.4 show the training and validation graphs indicating accuracy and loss of MobileNetV2 – CBAM model upto 50 epochs. The smooth curves without irregular spikes in both accuracy and loss indicate that the model is generalizing effectively.

The Figure 27.5 shows the comparison of training accuracy between MobileNetV2

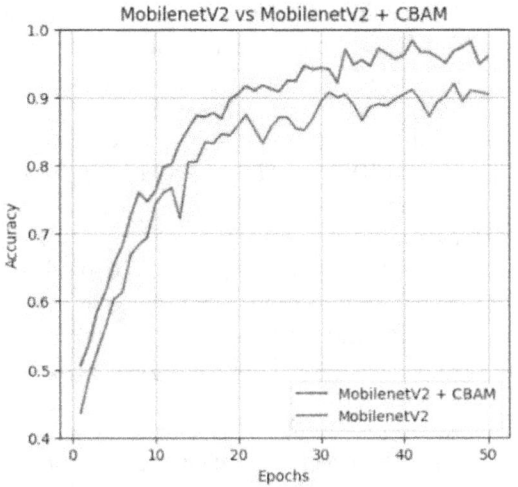

Figure 27.5 Accuracy Comparison of MobileNetV2 model and MobileNetV2 – CBAM model

Source: Author

and MobileNetV2 – CBAM model. The graph indicates that the proposed model consistently outperforming the base model in accuracy.

The accuracy curve for the proposed model shows a quick and more consistent increase compared to the base model. This improvement indicates that the CBAM attention mechanism in enhancing feature extraction for robust learning and classification. The addition of CBAM results in significant improvement in overall training accuracy, allowing the model to perform better compared to the baseline MobileNetV2 model. These findings highlight the effectiveness of CBAM infused MobileNetV2 for robust real – time violence detection.

Conclusion

This study developed an enhanced version of MobileNetV2 by integrating Convolutional Block Attention Module (CBAM) to improve real – time violence detection. CBAM effectively improves the

model ability to focus on important features by using spatial attention and channel attention mechanisms. This helps the model to detect precisely.

This study compares our proposed model MobileNetV2 – CBAM with baseline MobileNetV2 performance in training and testing. The final results indicated a significant improvement in training and testing accuracy where our proposed model outperformed the baseline model achieving close to 98% accuracy. The attention mechanisms of CBAM improved the model ability to generalize better. This indicates that CBAM attention module plays a vital role in focusing on important features particularly in violence detection tasks where attention to fine details and patterns are essential. The comparisons of metrics like accuracy, precision and recall further confirmed that the proposed model consistently outperformed baseline model across all metrics highlighting the benefit of lightweight models and hybrid architecture.

Overall, this study shows that enhancing lightweight model like MobileNetV2 with CBAM boosts the performance without extra computational resources. This indicates that the proposed hybrid model MobileNetV2 – CBAM is a promising option for real – time violence detection, balancing accuracy and efficiency. Further research on Hybrid models, optimizing architectures, hyperparameter tuning, and training and testing on large datasets to assess the model robustness in practical situations.

References

[1]   Mustafa, M. (n.d.). Real-Life Violence Situations Dataset. Kaggle, [Online]. Available: https://www.kaggle.com/datasets/mohamedmustafa/real-life-violence-situations-dataset.

[2]   Hussain, T., Iqbal, A., Yang, B., & Hussain, A. (2022). Real-time violence detection in

surveillance videos using convolutional neural networks. *Multimedia Tools and Applications*, 81(26), 38151–38173.

[3] J. C. Vieira, A. Sartori, S. F. Stefenon, F. L. Perez, G. S. De Jesus, and V.R. Q. Leithardt, (2022). Low-cost CNN for automatic violence recognition on embedded system, IEEE Access, 10, 25190–25202.

[4] Kumar, R., Gupta, A., & Rajeswari, D. (2024). Violence detection system using MobileNetV2. In Proceedings of 2024 3rd International Conference on Applied Artificial Intelligence and Computing (ICAAIC), (pp. 1555–1560). IEEE.

[5] Shripriya, C., Akshaya, J., Sowmya, R., & Poonkodi, M. (2021). Violence detection system using ResNet. In Proceedings of 2021 5th International Conference on Electronics, Communication and Aerospace Technology (ICECA), (pp. 1069–1072). IEEE.

[6] S. Kaur, A. Dureja, M. Kumar, M. Dayal, and others, (2023). Real-time Violence Detection in Video Streams: Exploiting ResNet-50 for Enhanced Accuracy, in Data Analytics and Artificial Intelligence for Predictive Maintenance in Smart Manufacturing, CRC Press, 150–162.

[7] S. Singh, S. Dewangan, G. S. Krishna, V. Tyagi, S. Reddy, and P. R. Medi, (2022). Video vision transformers for violence detection, arXiv preprint arXiv:2209.03561.

[8] Abdali, A. R. (2021). Data efficient video transformer for violence detection. In Proceedings of 2021 IEEE International Conference on Communication, Networks and Satellite (COMNETSAT), (pp. 195–199). IEEE.

[9] Hsairi, L., Alosaimi, S. M., & Alharaz, G. A. (2024). Violence detection using deep learning. *Arabian Journal for Science and Engineering*, 50, 1–11.

[10] Jebur, S. A., Hussein, K. A., Hoomod, H. K., & Alzubaidi, L. (2023). Novel deep feature fusion framework for multi-scenario violence detection. *Computers*, 12(9), 175.

[11] Kale, S. (2024). Violence detection through surveillance videos using combination of VGG16 and LSTM. In Proceedings of 2024 International Conference on Advances in Data Engineering and Intelligent Computing Systems (ADICS), (pp. 1–5). IEEE.

[12] Abbass, M. A. B., & Kang, H. (2023). Violence detection enhancement by involving convolutional block attention modules into various deep learning architectures: comprehensive case study for ubi-fights dataset. *IEEE Access*, 11, 37096–37107.

[13] Hwang, I.-C., & Kang, H. (2023). Anomaly detection based on a 3D convolutional neural network combining convolutional block attention module using merged frames. *Sensors*, 23(23), 9616.

28 Monkeypox detection using machine learning

Aakanksha Sankhyan[1,a], Sneha Thakur[2,b], Gaurav Mehta[2,c], Alok Kumar Agrawal[2,d], Rajit Verma[3,e] and Farida A. Ali[4,f]

[1]Chitkara University College of Nursing, Chitkara University, Himachal Pradesh, India

[2]Chitkara University School of Engineering and Technology, Chitkara University, Himachal Pradesh, India

[3]M.M. Institute of Management, Maharishi Marksandeshwar (Deemed to be University) Mullana-Ambala, Haryana, India

[4]Faculty of Engineering & Technology, Siksha O Anusandhan University Bhubaneswar, Odisha, India

Abstract

The global community has recently grown alarmed by the monkeypox outbreak, which has rapidly expanded beyond its traditional boundaries to affect over 40 nations outside the African continent. Medical professionals face significant challenges in early identification of this disease, as its visible symptoms closely resemble both chickenpox and measles. In regions where advanced PCR testing isn't immediately accessible, technology-assisted screening of monkeypox-specifically skin eruptions could substantially improve surveillance effort and help quickly identify potential cases. Artificial intelligence specifically deep learning approaches has demonstrated remarkable effectiveness in automatically detecting various skin conditions when provided with sufficient training materials. Unfortunately, comprehensive image collection for monkeypox analysis has been notably absent until now. This research paper addresses this gap by creating the monkeypox skin lesion dataset which incorporates images showing skin manifestations of monkeypox alongside chickenpox and measles for comparison. These visual resources have been gathered primarily from online platforms, media outlets and publicly available medical case documentation. To strengthen our dataset's robustness, we employed data augmentation techniques and established a three-fold cross-validation experimental framework. Though our initial results with this limited dataset appear encouraging, we acknowledge that creating truly reliable diagnostic models will require significantly larger image collections representing diverse populations and presentations of the disease.

Keywords: Deep learning, disease prediction, lesions, monkeypox, predictive models, skin, training accuracy

Introduction

Just after the third wave of COVID-19 pandemic, a new disease started growing into a global outbreak and could soon become a pandemic. Monkeypox disease is not a new disease, the first signs of this disease were seen in early 1970s, with the cases increasing over the following decade. This is also not the first monkeypox outbreak as it happened in 2003 and in between 2017–2019

[a]aakanksha.sankhyan@chitkarauniversity.edu.in, [b]sneha1392.be22@chitkarauniversity.edu.in, [c]gaurav.mehta@chitkarauniversity.edu.in, [d]alok.agrawal@chitkarauniversity.edu.in, [e]vermarajput007@gmail.com, [f]faridaali@soa.ac.in

DOI: 10.1201/9781003753391-28

in Nigeria. There have been cases of this disease in other countries as well. However, monkeypox outbreak in 2022 has spread to a hundred countries over the past few years. Monkeypox is less contagious due to its mode of transmission. However, there is a need for a low cost and rapid detection system for monkeypox virus. This study addresses urgent need for an accessible, rapid, and accurate monkeypox detection system by leveraging deep learning techniques for automated image-based classification. We present a comprehensive machine learning framework that utilizes transfer learning with the InceptionV3 architecture to distinguish monkeypox lesions from other similar dermatological conditions. The system is designed to support healthcare professionals in clinical decision-making, particularly in resource-limited settings where specialist expertise and advanced laboratory facilities may not be readily available. The developed system demonstrates the potential for integrating machine learning technologies into existing healthcare workflows, offering a scalable and cost-effective tool for early detection and outbreak control. By enabling rapid screening and preliminary diagnosis through non-invasive image analysis, this work represents a significant step toward democratizing access to diagnostic capabilities in the fight against emerging infectious diseases.

Literature Review

Monkeypox typically presents as a self-limiting illness, with symptoms persisting for two to four weeks in most cases. The gold standard for monkeypox diagnosis relies on histopathological examination and virus isolation techniques. Polymerase chain reaction (PCR) testing provides additional confirmation and has become increasingly important for rapid diagnosis. However,

these sophisticated diagnostic tools are not universally available, specifically in a resource-limited setting where the disease is endemic. This diagnostic gap has led to growing interest in alternative approaches, particularly early clinical diagnosis based on careful examination of skin lesions. The widespread availability of smartphones has opened new possibilities for artificial intelligence-based skin lesion detection systems. These emerging technologies hold promise for assisting healthcare providers in diagnosis and potentially bridging gaps in healthcare systems where traditional laboratory infrastructure may be limited. The integration of AI-powered diagnostic tools represents a particularly promising development for addressing monkeypox in regions with limited healthcare resources, potentially enabling earlier detection and more effective public health responses to contain transmission. Furthermore, various studies have explored different deep learning models and techniques to enhance the detection process, focusing on image-based analysis and data augmentation to improve model performance. The aim of these approaches is to address the challenges posed by the other disease like chickenpox, measles, whose symptoms seem similar to monkeypox, thereby facilitating early and precise diagnosis for monkeypox.

Koparde et al. [1] have a Monkeypox detection system using deep learning techniques with convolutional neural networks for image analysis. Their detection system consists of multiple data sources, including clinical data, medical imaging and demographic data to build a comprehensive dataset for modeling training.

Another research done by Arumugam et al. [2] on Monkeypox detection employs deep learning techniques, specifically three models: DenseNet 121, ResNet 50, and EfficientNet B7, to diagnose monkeypox.

Among the models tested, EfficientNetB7 achieved the highest performance metrics, with an accuracy, recall, and precision of 97.4%, making it the most effective model for monkeypox categorization, which will aid clinicians in identifying, categorizing, and treating the disease.

The study by Deepti et al. [3] employed deep learning methodologies to detect monkeypox by separating six potential models: namely EfficientNetB3, VGG19, ResNet50, MobileNetV2, VGG16, and InceptionV3. A Generative Adversarial Network (GAN) augmented the dataset from 414 to 4142 images, enhancing model training. The EfficientNetB3 model achieved the highest accuracy of 98.46% compared to other models.

The research by Dhiman et al. [4] presents a deep learning model for monkeypox detection using skin lesion images, utilizing Inception V3 architecture. The model was trained on a set of monkeypox images and achieved an accuracy rate of 89%.

Another work by Kottath et al. [5] focused on the PoxTLNet50 model which employs a deep learning strategy for the precise identification of monkeypox disease. The model demonstrated an outstanding accuracy of 98.83%, enabling early identification and management of monkeypox.

The study done by Rajnikanth et al. [6] proposes a deep-learning scheme for monkeypox (Mpox) detection, utilizing preprocessed skin images and employing binary classification with an Ensemble of Deep-Features (EDF). The detection accuracy of 100% was achieved on augmented images from the Monkeypox Skin Images Dataset (MSID).

Another study by Vandana et al. [7] presents MRpoxNet, a hybrid deep learning approach for monkeypox detection using digitized skin lesion images. The authors report an accuracy rate of 98.1%.

The research by Jagani et al. [8] discusses recent developments in deep learning technologies that support the automated detection and classification of Monkeypox skin lesions. It discusses various neural network architectures and image preprocessing methods that enhance diagnostic accuracy, particularly in resource-limited settings. The review emphasizes the potential of these models to enhance early detection and enable timely interventions for Monkeypox, while also addressing challenges such as the need for robust and interpretable models to introduce these technologies in clinical environments.

Dataset Collection

The model was implemented on the dataset that contained images for four classes of skin disease including monkeypox. The images were in .jpg format loaded in Google Drive and were mounted to the model in Google Colab. This dataset was labeled in an organized manner using TensorFlow. The images were then resized by the model meaning that the files were in a consistent size for the implementation of CNN architecture. The data was split into an 80/20% training/validation dataset in order to implement the model.

Methodology and Implementation

This study used a systematic machine learning approach. The methodology used to build this model involved building a multiclass image classification using deep learning. To implement this model, a sequential model was followed which included data preparation, data loading, model construction, compilation, model training and model evaluation. The system was built using a deep learning approach with the InceptionV3 and CNN based architecture,

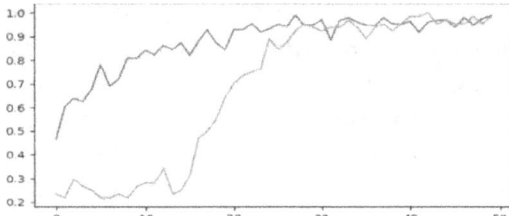

Figure 28.1 Accuracy graph of the model during the training
Source: Author

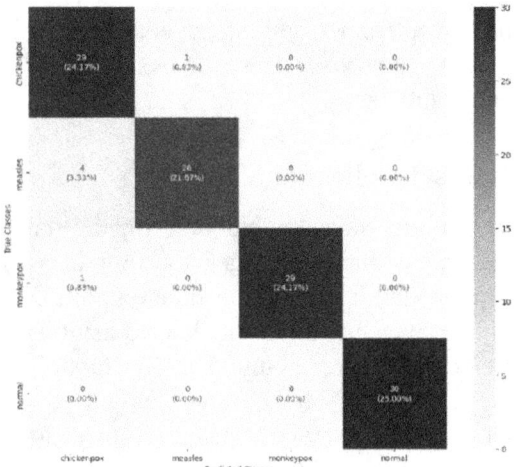

Figure 28.2 Confusion matrix represents the predictions of the model
Source: Author

The x-axis and y-axis measure how well the model is fitting the training data and how well the model performs on unseen validation data.

The confusion matrix in Figure 28.2, was employed to provide a detailed breakdown of the CNN model's performance across the four skin condition classes: monkeypox, chickenpox, measles and normal skin lesion. It presents the number of correct and incorrect predictions made by the model, organized by actual class and the predicted class. Each row of the confusion matrix represents the predicted labels. Additionally, the diagonal elements indicate the number of images that were correctly classified, whereas the off-diagonal elements represent the misclassifications. The matrix identifies the class-wise accuracy and types of errors.

Conclusion

This research demonstrated how AI can be useful in addressing urgent challenges like monkeypox detection during global health emergencies. We have created a tool that achieved a remarkable 98.26% accuracy in distinguishing monkeypox from the other similar looking skin conditions. Not only the impressive numbers, but also the real-world potential of this research represents for global healthcare workers and patients makes it even more meaningful. The system's ability to maintain consistent performance between the training data and validation data suggests that it has genuinely learned to recognize the subtle patterns which distinguish these skin conditions rather than just memorizing examples. While this analysis faced some expected challenges, such as confusion between measles and chickenpox due to their similar appearance, these insights provided a valuable direction for the future improvements. The accessibility and practicality show

showed impressive results when tested on skin lesion images. The training performance of the model is shown in Figure 28.1. The confusion matrix describing the prediction.

Empirical Results

After training the monkeypox detection model and evaluating this model with InceptionV3 architecture, several performance metrics were obtained which were used to access its effectiveness. The model achieved an overall accuracy of 98.26% after evaluating and validating the dataset.

the true significance of this research. By using standard imaging technology that's already available in many healthcare settings, we've created a solution that can be deployed in resource-limited environments where expertise might not be available. The balance of diagnostic capability represents a crucial step forward in global health equity, offering the healthcare providers a reliable screening tool that can detect early outbreak. On the other side of its immediate application, this research contributes to the growing field of AI-assisted healthcare, demonstrating how transfer learning techniques can be effectively adapted for medical image analysis. As we look towards the future, expanding the dataset to include more diverse populations and clinical presentations along with real-world deployment and validation will be essential in translating this technology into a practical tool that can make a meaningful difference in the fight against the emerging infectious diseases and ultimately saving lives through faster and more accessible diagnosis.

References

[1] Koparde, S., Yadav, N., Kejriwal, A., & Adkine, P. (2024). Monkey pox detection using deep learning. 4(4), 223–229. doi: 10.48175/IJAR- SCT- 18329.

[2] Arumugam, M., Arun, G., & Tharun Vikas, S. S. (2024). Detection of MonkeyPox disease using deep learning techniques. 2024 OPJU International Technology Conference (OTCON) on Smart Computing for Innovation and Advancement in Industry 4.0, India,doi: 10.1109/otcon60325.2024.10688010.

[3] Deepti, S., & Saini, I. (2024). GAN- based image augmentation and comparative

analysis of various CNN models for Monkeypox detection. In 2024 First International Conference on Electronics, Communication and Signal Processing (pp. 1–7). IEEE doi:10.1109/icecsp61809.2024.10697992.

[4] Kumar, V. (2024). Analysis of CNN features with multiple machine learning classifiers in diagnosis of MonkeyPox from digital skin images. MedRxiv, 2022-09. doi: https://doi.org/10.1101/2022.09.11.22 278797.

[5] Kottath, Anu V, and Ranjana P. (2024). PoxTLNet50: Deep Learning-based Approach for Accurate Image Detection of Monkeypox Disease.; Journal of Innovative Image Processing 6(4): 382–396. doi: 10.36548/jiip.2024.4.004.

[6] Rajnikanth, V., Taniar, D., & Dama- sevicius, R. (2024). Monkeypox detection with deep-learning and esemble of features: a study. 2024 4th International Conference on Technological Advancements in Computational Sciences (ICTACS),Tashkent, Uzbekistan, 2024, 1575–1578, doi: 10.1109/ ICTACS62700.2024.10840992.

[7] Alharbi, A. H., Towfek, S. K., Abdelhamid, A. A., Ibrahim, A., Eid, M. M., Khafaga, D. S., et al. (2023). Diagnosis of Monkeypox disease using transfer learning and binary advanced dipper throated optimization algorithm. Biomimetics. 2023; 8(3):313. doi: 10.3390/biomimetics8030313.

[8] Dhwani Jagani, Sheshang Degadwala, (2023) A Comprehensive Review on Monkeypox Skin Lesion Recognition through Deep Learning. International Journal of Scientific Research in Computer Science, Engineering and Information Technology(IJSRCSEIT), ISSN : 2456-3307, 9(10), 264–269, September-October-2023. Available at doi :https://doi.org/10.32628/ CSEIT2361045.

29 Characteristics analysis of real and fake speech: a novel approach

Nilamadhab Dash[1,a], Rashmirekha Ram[2,b], Saumendra Kumar Mohapatra[2,c] and Mihir Narayan Mohanty[3,d]

[1]Faculty of Engineering and Technology, Sri Sri University, Odisha, India

[2]ITER, Siksha 'O' Anusandhan (Deemed to be University), Bhubaneswar, Odisha, India

[3]Department of Electronics and Communication Engineering, ITER, Siksha 'O' Anusandhan (Deemed to be University), Bhubaneswar, Odisha, India

Abstract

Deepfake voice technology has advanced rapidly, allowing for the creation of extremely lifelike human voices that cannot be differentiated from genuine speech. Al though these developments offer possibilities for multiple uses, such as virtual aides and amusement, they also raise considerable security and moral issues, including deception, scams, and identity fraud. This study concentrates on a thorough examination of the attributes of authentic and counterfeit speech signals and explores the difficulties they present in detection systems. The research emphasizes the shortcomings of existing methods, including susceptibility to adversarial assaults and problems with generalization over different datasets. The document highlights the importance of strong real-time detection systems and joint initiatives to reduce the dangers linked to deepfake speech. Ultimately, it highlights prospective research avenues that encompass ethical aspects and the creation of uniform assessment frameworks.

Keywords: Deepfake detection, fake speech, mel frequency cepstral coefficients, rule-based analysis, signal processing

Introduction

The ability to generate synthetic speech has advanced significantly, allowing for the creation of audio that closely mimics natural human voices [2]. This technology is progressively used in areas such as virtual storytelling, voice helpers, and audio localization. The rise of deceptive speech has created serious concerns about its possible abuse in areas such as identity theft, voice-driven scams, and the spread of false information. Consequently, differentiating between authentic and counterfeit speech signals has emerged as an important field of research [4].

Natural variations in acoustic traits such as pitch, tone, and timing are evident in original speech signals generated by the human vocal apparatus. These signals exhibit stable harmonic frameworks, fluid shifts between phonemes, and delicate prosodic subtleties that indicate emotional or contextual hints. Artificial speech signals, created using sophisticated digital signal processing techniques, frequently exhibit irregularities that can indicate their man-made source. These irregularities can consist of unnatural spectral patterns, sudden changes between sounds, and uneven energy distributions throughout frequencies [10].

[a]nilamadhab.d@srisriuniversity.edu.in, [b]ram.rashmirekha14@gmail.com,
[c]saumendra.m@srisriuniversity.edu.in, [d]mihir.n.mohanty@gmail.com

DOI: 10.1201/9781003753391-29

The analysis of fake and original speech signals involves a detailed investigation of their acoustic and structural characteristics. Key aspects include the spectral envelope, formant frequencies, and prosodic elements such as rhythm and intonation. Fake speech may exhibit artifacts such as discontinuities in the spectral envelope or irregularities in timing that deviate from the natural flow of human speech. In addition, noise components or distortions introduced during synthesis can serve as markers to distinguish fake signals from genuine recordings [8].

This study seeks to investigate the essential distinctions between authentic and counterfeit speech signals, emphasizing their distinct acoustic signatures and structural features. This study aims to offer a solid framework for recognizing and comprehending synthetic speech by analyzing these differences. The examination not only tackles technical issues but also aids in wider initiatives to maintain the reliability of digital communications.

In a world where audio manipulation technologies are becoming increasingly sophisticated, the ability to reliably differentiate between real and fake speech is essential for maintaining trust and security. This paper underscores the importance of advancing signal analysis techniques to keep pace with the evolving capabilities of speech synthesis technologies. By doing so, it aims to support the development of effective tools for mitigating the risks associated with fake speech while preserving the benefits of synthetic audio applications.

Literature Review

The increasing presence of artificial speech has led to significant investigation into its creation, identification, and examination. The area has mainly concentrated on recognizing distinct features that set apart counterfeit speech from authentic human speech. This section examines important research and methods that have aided in comprehending fake and authentic speech signals [11].

Characteristics of fake speech signals

Studies have identified specific acoustic anomalies in fake speech including irregularities in pitch, unnatural transitions between phonemes, and inconsistencies in prosody [3].

Research by Patel et al. (2019) highlighted that synthetic speech often exhibits abrupt changes in spectral content, attributed to the limitations of the signal generation process [12].

Kinnunen et al. (2020) emphasized the significance of harmonic-to-noise ratio (HNR) and spectral tilt as markers to distinguish synthetic audio from natural recordings. These findings suggest that fake speech signals often fail to replicate the subtle variations inherent in human voice production [13].

Techniques for speech signal analysis

The analysis of speech signals traditionally relies on the extraction of acoustic features and spectral analysis. Features such as formant frequencies, Mel Frequency Cepstral Coefficients (MFCCs), and linear predictive coding (LPC) parameters have been widely used in distinguishing between synthetic and original speech [5].

Research by Zhang and Li (2018) demonstrated that formant tracking could effectively highlight discrepancies in synthetic speech, particularly in vowel transitions. In addition, spectrogram-based analysis has been utilized to identify spectral artifacts unique to fake speech generation [14].

Detection and forensic approaches

In addition to recognizing traits, identifying fraudulent speech has emerged as a key area in audio forensics. Forensic audio analysis tools utilize time-frequency analysis techniques to identify irregularities in synthetic speech.

A study conducted by Singh et al. (2021) suggested utilizing cepstral features along with statistical models to detect patterns characteristic of artificial speech [7]. Their study highlighted the importance of high-resolution time- domain features for detecting subtle discontinuities in synthetic signals [15].

Limitations of existing research

Despite progress, challenges remain in detecting highly sophisticated synthetic speech. Many detection methods struggle to generalize across diverse datasets and signal processing conditions [1].

Studies, such as those by Gupta et al. (2022), point out that synthetic speech generated under optimized conditions can bypass traditional detection techniques, necessitating ongoing advancements in signal analysis and evaluation frameworks [6].

Proposed Work

The main objective of the work is to analyze differences in specific signal attributes, such as time-domain waveform, frequency spectrum, spectrogram, envelope, MFCCs, and energy, using rule-based thresholds and observations without employing machine learning models as shown in Figure 29.1.

Methodology

The initial step in our process is data pre-processing, which involves cleaning and organizing the dataset to ensure the accuracy and reliability of the analysis. Following this, we utilize feature extraction techniques to capture essential characteristics of the data across various domains, including temporal, spectral, and frequency domains.

This process encompasses calculating MFCC, energy levels, and envelope detection to enhance our understanding of the data's structure. Next, we implement rule-based detection methods to identify significant patterns. Finally, we employ visualization techniques to present the results effectively, ensuring clarity and aiding interpretation.

This method offers a comprehensive strategy for identifying speech through the examination of features in both the time and frequency domains. Initially, speech signals undergo preprocessing by loading them in

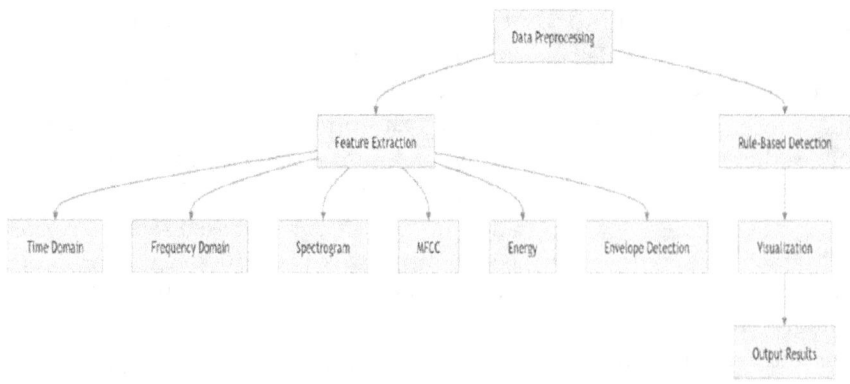

Figure 29.1 Methodology flowchart for fake speech detection
Source: Author

mono format at a uniform sampling rate (e.g., 16 kHz), normalizing the amplitude for uniformity, and modifying the signal length to a standard duration (e.g., 3 seconds) using truncation or padding.

Feature extraction continues with time-domain examination, where statistics such as mean, variance, skewness, and kurtosis assist in identifying anomalies in the waveform, along with frequency spectrum analysis via FFT that reveals unusual frequency patterns or absent harmonics [6]. Moreover, spectrogram analysis (STFT) looks for sudden spectral changes or smooth patterns common in artificial speech, while MFCCs represent perceptual features, indicating lower variance or atypical patterns in synthetic voice. Energy distribution and envelope analysis help to distinguish genuine speech from fake by identifying excessively smooth energy fluctuations or abrupt changes in amplitude.

Rule-based detection thresholds are applied to identify fake speech based on these features, including unnatural frequency distributions, consistent energy profiles, low MFCC variance, and spectral artifacts.

Ultimately, visual displays including waveform charts, spectrogram heatmaps, MFCC heatmaps, energy graphs, and envelope diagrams are employed to analyze the traits of authentic and fraudulent speech signals, aiding in the identification of irregularities.

Results and Observations

Time-domain features comparison
For both signals, the following time-domain features are computed:

- Mean: Average amplitude of the signal.
- Variance: Measures the spread or fluctuation around the mean.

- Skewness: Quantifies the asymmetry of the amplitude distribution.
- Kurtosis: Measures how much the distribution deviates from a normal distribution (e.g., presence of extreme values or outliers).

By comparing the time-domain features of the two signals in Table 29.1, differences in their overall loudness (mean), variability (variance), and amplitude distribution shape (skewness and kurtosis) become evident. The original signal shows relatively stable characteristics, while the fake signal displays higher variance and skewness, indicating greater fluctuations that may result from synthesis artifacts or artificial manipulation. This suggests that the fake signal is less naturally distributed and may contain abrupt changes or irregular dynamics typical of synthesized speech.

Frequency spectrum comparison
The frequency spectrum plot shows the distribution of frequencies across the signals. This comparison enables the observation of energy concentration across different frequency bands. For instance, one signal might exhibit dominant low-frequency components, while the other may present a wider or more evenly distributed frequency range as in Figure 29.2 and 29.3.

Table 29.1 Comparison of time-domain features between original and fake speech signals.

Feature	Original signal	Fake signal
Mean	0.000514752	$-8.4736 \times 10{-}5$
Variance	0.000608827	0.008771201
Skewness	0.183525266	0.651655517
Kurtosis	16.111225	8.895586729

Source: Author

Observation

A larger magnitude in the lower frequencies for the original signal (Signal 1) may indicate a lower pitch or the presence of more environmental noise. In contrast, the broader spectrum observed in the fake signal (Signal 2) could point to a cleaner, higher-pitched, or algorithmically enhanced synthetic speech profile [7].

Spectrogram analysis comparison

The spectrogram visually represents how the frequency content of a signal evolves over time. By analyzing the spectrograms of real and fake speech, we can detect structural and temporal differences in their spectral patterns.

Observation

- Signal 1 (Real): The spectrogram in Figure 29.5 shows more chaotic and irregular patterns, indicating the presence of natural variability, environmental noise, or spontaneous speech dynamics.
- Signal 2 (Fake): A more stable and less fluctuating spectrogram in Figure 29.6 may indicate cleaner, more uniform, or algorithmically controlled synthetic speech patterns.

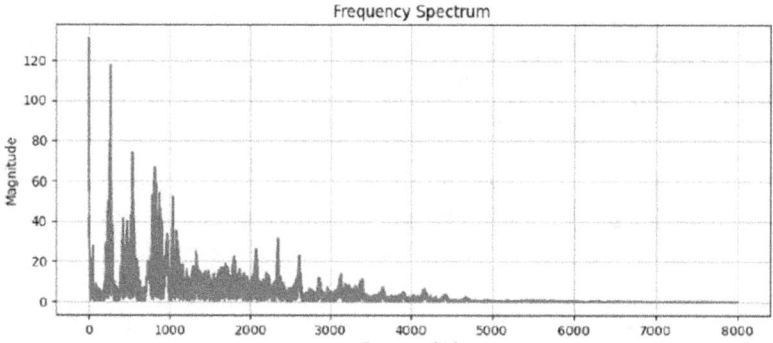

Figure 29.2 Frequency spectrum of original signal
Source: Author

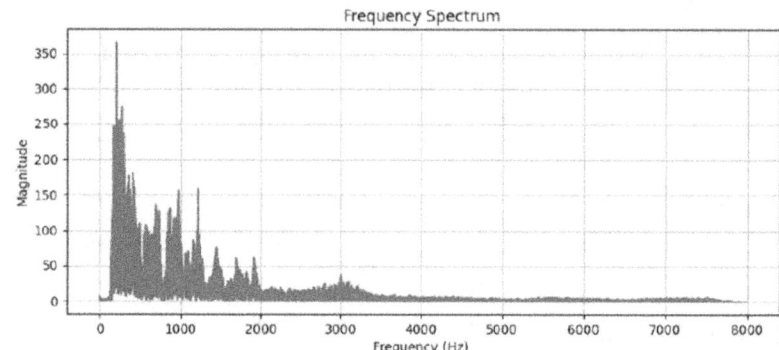

Figure 29.3 Frequency spectrum of fake signal
Source: Author

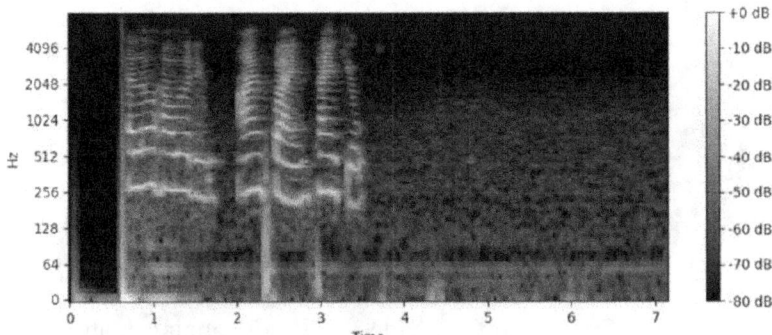

Figure 29.4 Spectrogram of real signal
Source: Author

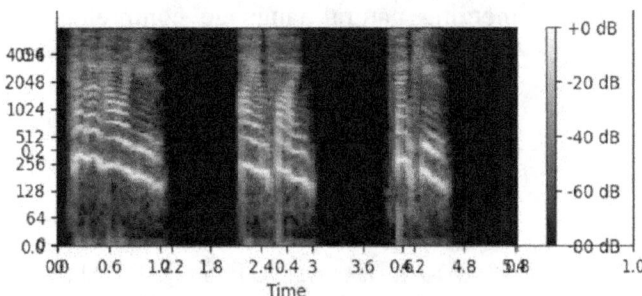

Figure 29.5 Spectrogram of fake signal
Source: Author

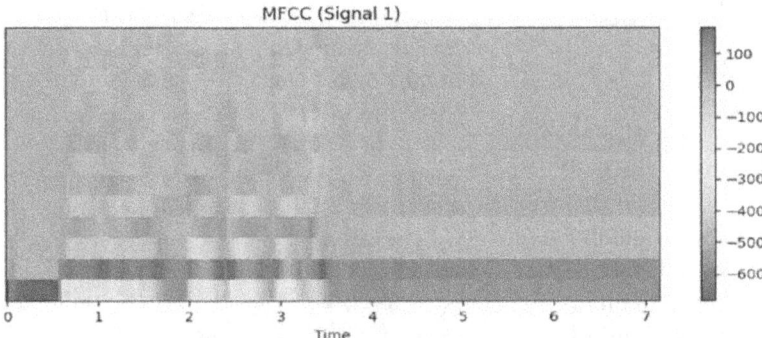

Figure 29.6 MFCC: real signal
Source: Author

MFCC analysis and comparison
Observation

- Signal 1 in Figure 29.6 and Signal 2 in Figure 29.7 have significant differences in their MFCC means and variances as in Table 29.2.
- The MFCC variance for a signal is consistently low, it suggests less variability

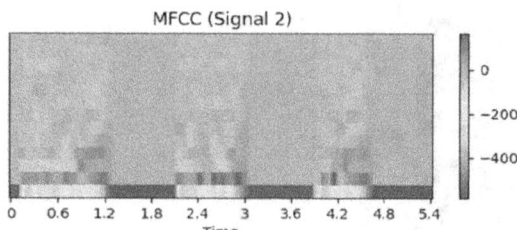

Figure 29.7 MFCC: fake signal
Source: Author

Table 29.2 MFCC statistical comparison of real vs. fake speech.

Feature	Original signal	Fake signal
Mean (MFCC 1)	-485.77588	-392.22964
Mean (MFCC 2)	102.78428	34.946957
Variance (MFCC 1)	16586.322	41240.19
Variance (MFCC 2)	1340.0548	1940.9716

Source: Author

in the audio's spectral content, a hallmark of non-natural audio.

Conclusion and Future Scopes

The analysis shows that speech signals can be accurately differentiated between authentic and counterfeit by utilizing a mix of time-domain characteristics, frequency spectrum, spectrogram, mel frequency cepstral coefficients (MFCCs), energy, and envelope assessments. Important points highlight the usefulness of MFCC features, as lower variance frequently indicates unnatural or synthesized sounds, along with energy patterns that uncover irregular distributions in artificial signals. The detection method based on rules showed effectiveness, utilizing thresholds for variance, energy, and MFCC measures to recognize fake speech.

This research emphasizes the promise of MFCC-based methods and additional features for detecting speech authenticity.

Future work can explore advanced machine learning models like deep learning (CNNs, LSTMs) to improve detection accuracy using larger datasets of real and fake speech. Real-time processing systems can be created for uses such as virtual assistants or video calls. Enhancing features to incorporate pitch jitter, and spectral centroid, together with cross-language adaptation, would improve robustness. Moreover, studies on adversarial audio assaults and merging natural language comprehension with acoustic evaluation might develop a more thorough and dependable framework for identifying fraudulent speech in various settings.

References

[1] Al-Adwan, A., Alazzam, H., Al-Anbaki, N., & Alduweib, E. (2024). Detection of deepfake media using a hybrid cnn–rnn model and particle swarm optimization (PSO) algorithm. *Computers*, 13(4), 99.

[2] Almutairi, Z., & Elgibreen, H. (2022). A review of modern audio deepfake detection methods: challenges and future directions. *Algorithms*, 15(5), 155.

[3] Chen, T., Kumar, A., Nagarsheth, P., Sivaraman, G., & Khoury. E. (2020). Generalization of audio deepfake detection. In Odyssey, (pp. 132–137).

[4] Hamza, A., Javed, A. R. R., Iqbal, F., Kryvinska, N., Almadhor, A. S., Jalil, Z., et al. (2022). Deepfake audio detection via mfcc features using machine learning. *IEEE Access*, 10, 134018–134028.

[5] Jain, N., Borade, S., Patel, B., Kumar, V., Godhrawala, M., Kolaskar, S., et al. (2023). En- hancing audio deepfake detection using support vector machines and mel-frequency cepstral coefficients. *Journal of Harbin Engineering University*. 45(1), 343–364.

[6] Mcuba, M., Singh, A., Ikuesan, R. A., & Venter, H. (2023). The effect of deep learning methods on deepfake audio detection for digital investigation. *Procedia Computer Science*, 219, 211–219.

[7] Pham, L., Lam, P., Nguyen, T., Nguyen, H., & Schindler, A. (2024). Deep- fake audio detection using spectrogram-based feature and ensemble of deep learning models. In 2024 IEEE 5th International Symposium on the Internet of Sounds (IS2), (pp. 1–5). IEEE.

[8] Razubaeva, E., & Stepikhov, A. (2020). Genuine spontaneous vs fake spontaneous speech: In search of distinction. In Speech and Computer: 22nd International Conference, SPECOM 2020, St. Petersburg, Russia, October 7–9, 2020, Proceedings 22, (pp. 467–478). Springer.

[9] Shaaban, O. A., Yildirim, R., & Alguttar, A. A. (2023). Audio deepfake approaches. *IEEE Access*, 11, 132652–132682.

[10] Stanciu, D. C., & Ionescu, B. (2023). Autoencoder-based data augmentation for deepfake detection. In Proceedings of the 2nd ACM International Workshop on Multi- media AI against Disinformation, (pp. 19–27).

[11] Yi, J., Wang, C., Tao, J., Zhang, X., Zhang, C. Y., & Zhao, Y. (2023). Audio deepfake detection: a survey. arXiv preprint arXiv:2308.14970. *Journal of latex class files*, 14(8), august 2023.

[12] Patel, H., Patel, P., & Patel, M. (2019). Detection of synthetic speech using spectral analysis methods. *International Journal of Speech Technology*, 22(2), 321–330.

[13] Kinnunen, T., Sahidullah, M., Delgado, H., Todisco, M., Evans, N., Yamagishi, J., & Lee, K. A. (2020). Tandem assessment of spoofing countermeasures and automatic speaker verification: Fundamentals. *IEEE/ACM Transactions on Audio, Speech, and Language Processing*, 28, 219–233.

[14] Zhang, Y., & Li, Z. (2018). Formant analysis for detecting synthetic speech. *International Journal of Computer Applications*, 181(15), 1–5.

[15] Singh, A. K., & Singh, P. (2021). Detection of AI-Synthesized Speech Using Cepstral & Bispectral Statistics. In *Proceedings of the IEEE 4th International Conference on Multimedia Information Processing and Retrieval (MIPR)* (pp. 412–417).

[16] Gupta, M., Kaushik, S., & Singh, R. (2022). Robustness of synthetic speech detection: Limitations of classical countermeasures. In *Proceedings of the International Conference on Speech Processing & Security* (pp. 123–130).

30 iVision: a deep learning-based web solution for automated eye disease screening using enhanced tiny VGG

Srikanta Kumar Sahoo[a], Alakananda Tripathy[b] and Saumendra Kumar Mohanty[c]

ITER, SOA deemed to be university, Bhubaneswar, Odisha, India

Abstract

Preventing vision loss and enhancing patient outcomes depend on early detection of eye conditions. This work introduces a deep learning-based method for employing Convolutional Neural Networks (CNNs) to classify eye disorders from retinal pictures. A dataset of ocular photos classified by disease kinds, including disorders like cataracts and bulging eyes, was used to train the suggested model. In order to improve the model's capacity for generalization, data pretreatment procedures included image normalization and augmentation methods like rotation, flipping, and zooming. To reduce over-fitting, a unique CNN architecture with dropout layers and batch normalization was used. Even if training and validation accuracy were flawless, additional investigation showed that only one detected class existed because of a misconfigured dataset directory, underscoring the vital need of accurate data labeling. This work lays the groundwork for future advancements in automated ophthalmic diagnostics by highlighting CNNs' advantages in medical image processing as well as the difficulties associated with data quality.

Keywords: AI in ophthalmology, deep learning, iVision, ocular disease detection, streamlit web app, tiny VGG

Introduction

The necessity for effective and precise diagnostic tools has been highlighted by the rising incidence of eye-related diseases such cataracts, glaucoma, uveitis, and other ailments that impair vision. Millions of people worldwide suffer from eye conditions that could be treated to avoid permanent blindness or severe vision impairment if they are identified early. However, the conventional diagnostic workflow mostly depends on skilled ophthalmologists manually evaluating ocular and retinal pictures, which is a laborious and subject to subjective bias procedure. These difficulties are much more noticeable in areas with poor access to medical facilities, which frequently leads to missing or delayed diagnosis.

Medical diagnostics could be revolutionized by recent developments in artificial intelligence (AI), especially deep learning. Convolutional Neural Networks (CNNs), one of the deep learning architectures, have become an effective tool for image classification problems because of its capacity to automatically extract significant features from unprocessed picture data. Because CNNs do not require manually created features, they are particularly well-suited for

[a]srikantasahoo@soa.ac.in, [b]alakanandatripathy@soa.ac.in, [c]saumendramohanty@soa.ac.in

DOI: 10.1201/9781003753391-30

medical imaging, where pertinent patterns may be intricate or subtle.

The incorporation of deep learning and AI into biomedical applications has created new opportunities for automating disease identification in recent years. These technologies eliminate the need for a large clinical infrastructure and offer quicker, more accurate diagnoses. In the past, automated systems for detecting eye diseases depended on traditional machine learning models in conjunction with manually developed feature extraction methods, like texture analysis and edge detection, which are frequently limited in their scalability and accuracy and largely rely on expert knowledge.

The CNNs, in particular, have been investigated for their exceptional capacity to automatically learn and extract discriminative features from medical images in order to overcome these restrictions. Although CNNs have shown increased accuracy in classification tasks, many of the current models are computationally demanding and require big datasets to generalize well. Furthermore, the majority of these systems are not user-friendly and do not have real-time capabilities, which restricts their application in community and clinical health settings.

A complete system that integrates real-time usability, computational efficiency, high classification accuracy, and informative reporting is still required. This paper suggests an improved Tiny VGG-based architecture for web-enabled eye illness identification from medical photos in order to address these issues. To improve efficiency and resilience, the model uses sophisticated preparation methods such data augmentation and normalization. Tiny VGG's lightweight design allows for great classification, accuracy and efficient computing. Additionally, Streamlit was used to create an intuitive web application that lets users input eye photos and get real-time predictions, thorough diagnostic reports, and preventative advice. The increasing prevalence of eye conditions and the pressing need for easily accessible diagnostic instruments, especially in areas with a shortage of professional care, are the driving force behind this study. Technology seeks to democratize the screening process for eye diseases by fusing deep learning with an easy-to-use web interface. It increases intervention rates and lowers the risk of visual loss by enabling general practitioners, community health workers, and specialists to carry out early detection. In the long run, this strategy provides a scalable way to revolutionize ophthalmic diagnostics. Clinical trust and interpretability can be further enhanced by incorporating explainable AI (XAI) approaches. Additional disease classifications, sophisticated model topologies, and telemedicine features for remote consultations and expert validation are possible future improvements.

In the end, this study establishes a strong basis for the development of AI-powered eye care and prepares the way for more widespread uses of automated illness identification, particularly in underprivileged areas.

Rest part of the paper is organized as follows: Section 2 presents the literature review followed by proposed model in section 3. Section 4 shows empirical results and analysis. Finally, section 5 concludes the paper.

Literature Review

The use of AI and deep learning for automated diagnosis of eye diseases has been extensively studied in the past with the goal of increasing accuracy and accessibility. The performance of traditional approaches, which depended on manually created features like texture, edges, and histograms, was constrained by dataset bias and the requirement for expert-driven feature selection. CNNs like AlexNet, VGG16, ResNet, and Inception have become the industry standard for medical image analysis due to the development of deep learning. They have outperformed traditional methods in the classification of disorders including cataracts, glaucoma, and diabetic retinopathy. Additionally, transfer learning with pre-trained networks has reduced processing needs and improved classification efficiency [1].

Despite advancements, a large number of deep models remain unincorporated into useful tools and continue to require expensive technology for processing in real time [2]. In order to improve lesion localization in DR and DME, Nazir et al. enhanced a Center-Net model with DenseNet-100, surpassing previous models, particularly with tiny lesions and overfitting [3]. In order to promote its use in clinical diagnosis, Sarki et al. introduced a deep learning-based classifier for diabetic retinal degeneration (DED) that achieved 81.33% accuracy and 100% sensitivity and specificity on fundus pictures [4].

Wang et al. discovered genetic connections to conditions like glaucoma, cataracts, and macular telangiectasia by utilizing a single-cell retina atlas in conjunction with deep learning and genomic data (eQTL and HiChIP) [5]. By using lightweight CNNs like MobileNet and EfficientNet [6] and creating hybrid models that blend deep learning and conventional image processing, recent initiatives have also focused on real-time usability. Interpretability has been further enhanced by attention methods and explainable AI (XAI) for clinical use [7].

By surpassing conventional machine learning methods that depend on manual feature extraction, deep learning—in

particular, CNNs—has completely transformed automated diagnosis in ophthalmology [8]. CNNs are useful for medical image classification tasks because they can directly learn spatial hierarchies from image data [9, 10].

The model used in this investigation, which consists of several Conv2D, MaxPooling, BatchNormalization, and Dropout layers, adheres to a commonly used design that has been shown to be successful in previous studies. Dropout aids in avoiding overfitting, and batch normalization enhances training stability [11].

CNNs were employed by Gulshan et al. [12] to detect diabetic retinopathy, and they performed at the level of an ophthalmologist. A CNN-based classifier for diabetic eye illness was also created by Sarki et al. [13], who reported good sensitivity and specificity. Custom CNNs are still preferred for lightweight, domain-specific applications, even if pretrained models like VGG16 and EfficientNet are frequently utilized in transfer learning for better generalization [14].

Recent attempts have used explainable AI techniques such as Grad-CAM to improve interpretability and clinical trust in order to address the black-box character of CNNs [15]. Building upon these frameworks, this study provides a condensed, precise model appropriate for classifying eye diseases in real-world situations.

Proposed Model

In order to categorize eye disorders using clinical images, this work suggests an architecture based on convolutional neural networks, or CNNs. Through a sequence of convolutional procedures, the model is built to automatically learn discriminative features from images, allowing for reliable classification with little assistance from humans.

The model uses a deep CNN architecture, which consists of fully linked dense layers, batch normalization, and several convolutional and pooling layers. Among the principal layers are:

Input layer: RGB images scaled to 224 × 224 pixels are accepted by the input layer.

Convolutional layers: 3 × 3 kernels and ReLU activation functions are used in three convolutional blocks with filter widths of 32, 64, and 128 correspondingly. From the input images, these layers extract hierarchical spatial features.

MaxPooling layers: To minimize spatial dimensions and preserve key features, a 2 × 2 MaxPooling operation is performed after each convolutional block. After every convolutional block, batch normalization is used to speed up and stabilize training.

Flatten layer: The flatten layer creates a 1D feature vector from the 3D feature maps.

Fully connected layers: To avoid overfitting, a Dropout layer with a rate of 0.5 is employed after a dense layer with 128 neurons and ReLU activation.

Output layer: The output layer has as many neurons as the number of detected classes and is SoftMax-activated. During early experimentation, only one class was successfully discovered due to problems with dataset configuration.

Figure 30.1 shows the CNN architecture workflow for eye disease classification. It consists of eight steps data collection, data pre-processing, train/test split, build CNN, Compile model, Train model, Model evaluation and Model prediction. For multi-class classification tasks, the model is constructed using the Adam optimizer with a categorical cross-entropy loss function. Accuracy is the evaluation metric that was used. 3.3 Augmenting data Keras' ImageDataGenerator was used to implement real-time data augmentation in order to improve generalization and alleviate the dataset's limiting size. The augmentations listed below were used: Horizontal flipping, zoom range of 20%, rotation range of 20 degrees, Rescaling pixel values to the [0, 1] range.

An 80:20 split was used to separate the dataset into training and validation subsets. A batch size of 32 was used to train the model over 10 epochs. To speed up the process, training was done using Google Colab with GPU acceleration. Following training, classification metrics like accuracy, recall, and F1-score were used to assess the model. Plotting accuracy and loss curves allowed for the visualization of learning trends. For later use or refinement, the finished model was stored in HDF5 format (eye_disease_model.h5).

Empirical Results

The empirical assessment of a CNN model intended to categorize five distinct kinds of

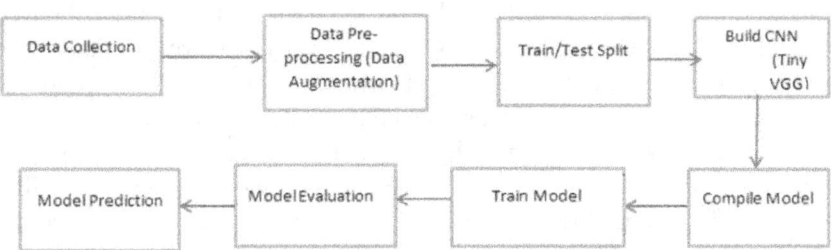

Figure 30.1 CNN architecture workflow for eye disease classification
Source: Author

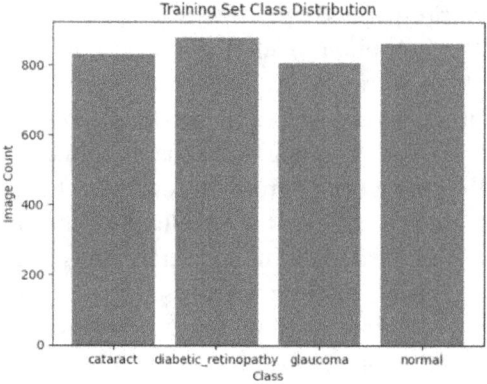

Figure 30.2 Dataset with different class
Source: Author

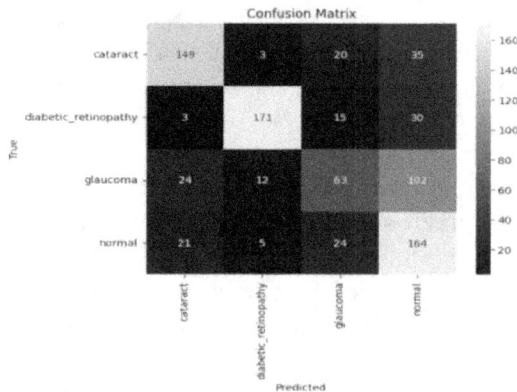

Figure 30.3 Confusion matrix for 4 classes
Source: Author

eye disorders using picture data is presented in this part. A real-world dataset comprising pictures from four categories diabetic retinopathy, cataracts, glaucoma, and normal eye is used to train and validate the model.

The dataset consists of 4217 images which were split into 80 for training and 20 for validation. To enhance generalization, each image was enlarged to 224 ×x 224 pixels and data augmentation methods like rotation, zoom, and horizontal flipping were used. The training set class distributions are shown in Figure 30.2. Training/validation metrics and a thorough classification report were used to evaluate performance.

All four classes were equally represented in terms of training configuration but exhibited imbalanced results during inference. Using the Adam optimizer and categorical cross-entropy as the loss function, the CNN model was trained across 100 epochs with a batch size of 32. Figure 30.3 shows the confusion matrix for 4 classes like cataract, diabetic retinopathy, glaucoma and normal eyes.

The accuracy and loss for both the training and validation sets are shown in the Figure 30.4 where early stopping is used. With each epoch, the training accuracy

grew steadily until it reached 85% from 44% which shows that the model is learning very well. Nonetheless, the validation accuracy reached 64% from 49% which shows the improvement. Overfitting was implied by the concurrent increase in validation loss across subsequent epochs. After training, precision, recall, and F1-score metrics for each class were used to assess the model's predictions on the validation set.

To illustrate training and validation performance over epochs, two-line graphs were created (Figure 30.2). The left plot is Epoch vs. Accuracy and plot on the right is Loss versus Epoch. Training accuracy steadily increases, validation accuracy is fluctuating, suggesting overfitting, according to the accuracy plot. This is further supported by the loss plot, which shows that after epoch 3, validation loss rises while training loss falls. This may be due to noise in the data. It may be overcome by performing data augmentation more exhaustively. There were roughly 11.17 million trainable parameters in the CNN model overall. Prior to the SoftMax output, this comprised one fully connected layer and three convolutional blocks with batch normalization. Although this architecture was adequate for learning

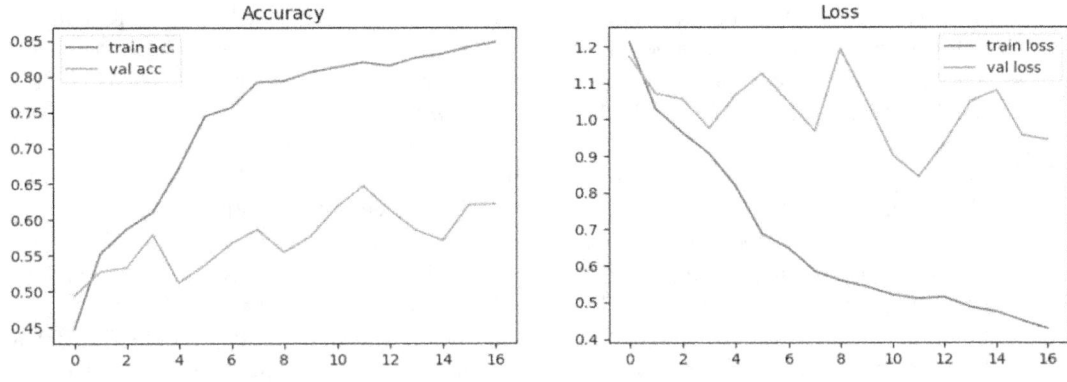

Figure 30.4 Validation and training loss curves and accuracy
Source: Author

Table 30.1 Classification performance per class.

Class	Precision	Recall	F1-Score
Cataract	0.74	0.71	0.72
Glaucoma	0.51	0.30	.38
Diabetic retinopathy	0.89	0.79	0.84
Normal	0.50	0.78	0.61

Source: Author

from the training data, given the small dataset size, its size and complexity may have led to overfitting.

In Table 30.1, the classification report is displayed. Among the recalls 0.71, 0.30, 0.79 0.78 and precisions 0.74, 0.51, 0.89, 0.50 for the four classes, the diabetic retinopathy showing good result with perfect recall and modest precision also cataract is classified well.

Conclusion

This study used medical picture data to create and assess a Convolutional Neural Network (CNN) model for the multi-class categorization of eye disorders. Diabetic retinopathy, cataracts, glaucoma, eye disorders that the suggested deep learning architecture was trained to recognize. Model generalization issues were revealed when the validation accuracy plateaued at 64%, despite the model reaching a moderate training accuracy of roughly 85%. A thorough examination of the classification results revealed a stark class imbalance and subpar performance in the majority of categories, with the exception of diabetic retinopathy, which had a flawless recall. It also properly classifies the cataract. None of the remaining four classes were accurately identified by the model. This discrepancy in performance indicates that the current model may have inadequate feature discrimination across more intricate or nuanced illness patterns and is prone to overfitting. In future the work can be performed using transfer learning like EfficientNetB0 or RestNet50 to have better generalization and feature extraction.

References

[1] Abdou, M. A. (2022). Literature review: efficient deep neural networks techniques for medical image analysis. *Neural Computing and Applications*, 34(8), 5791–5812.

[2] Zaman, K. S., Reaz, M. B. I., Ali, S. H. M., Bakar, A. A. A., & Chowdhury, M.

E. H. (2021). Custom hardware architectures for deep learning on portable devices: a review. *IEEE Transactions on Neural Networks and Learning Systems*, 33(11), 6068–6088.

[3] Nazir, T., Nawaz, M., Rashid, J., Mahum, R., Masood, M., Mehmood, A., et al. (2021). Detection of diabetic eye disease from retinal images using a deep learning based CenterNet model. *Sensors*, 21(16), 5283.

[4] Sarki, R., Ahmed, K., Wang, H., Zhang, Y., & Wang, K. (2021). Convolutional neural network for multi-class classification of diabetic eye disease. *EAI Endorsed Transactions on Scalable Information Systems*, 9(4), e5.

[5] Wang, S. K., Nair, S., Li, R., Kraft, K., Pampari, A., Patel, A., et al. (2022). Single-cell multiome of the human retina and deep learning nominate causal variants in complex eye diseases. *Cell Genomics*, 2(8), 100164.

[6] Harahap, S. A. F., & Irmawan, I. (2024). Performance comparison of MobileNet, efficientnet, and inception for predicting crop disease. *Sriwijaya Electrical and Computer Engineering Journal*, 1(1), 30–36.

[7] Oyeniyi, J., & Oluwaseyi, P. (2024). Emerging trends in AI-powered medical imaging: enhancing diagnostic accuracy and treatment decisions. *International Journal of Enhanced Research in Science Technology and Engineering*, 13, 2319–7463.

[8] Goutam, B., Hashmi, M. F., Geem, Z. W., & Bokde, N. D. (2022). A comprehensive review of deep learning strategies in retinal disease diagnosis using fundus images. *IEEE Access*, 10, 57796–57823.

[9] Krizhevsky, A., Sutskever, I., & Hinton, G. E. (2012). Imagenet classification with deep convolutional neural networks. *Advances in Neural Information Processing Systems*, 25, 1106–1114.

[10] Simonyan, K., & Zisserman A. (2014). Very deep convolutional networks for large-scale image recognition. Computer Vision and Pattern Recognition, https://doi.org/10.48550/arXiv.1409.1556.

[11] Ioffe, S., & Szegedy, C. (2015). Batch normalization: accelerating deep network training by reducing internal covariate shift. In International Conference on Machine Learning, 2015 Jun 1, (pp. 448–456). PMLR.

[12] Gulshan, V., Peng, L., Coram, M., Stumpe, M. C., Wu, D., Narayanaswamy, A., et al. (2016). Development and validation of a deep learning algorithm for detection of diabetic retinopathy in retinal fundus photographs. *JAMA*, 316(22), 2402–2410.

[13] Sarki, R., Ahmed, K., Wang, H., & Zhang, Y. (2020). Automatic detection of diabetic eye disease through deep learning using fundus images: a survey. *IEEE Access*, 8, 151133–15149.

[14] Nasir, N., Afreen, N., Patel, R., Kaur, S., & Sameer, M. (2021). A transfer learning approach for diabetic retinopathy and diabetic macular edema severity grading. *Revue d'Intelligence Artificielle*, 35(6), 497–502.

[15] Selvaraju, R. R., Cogswell, M., Das, A., Vedantam, R., Parikh, D., & Batra, D. (2020). Grad-CAM: visual explanations from deep networks via gradient-based localization. *International Journal of Computer Vision*, 128, 336–359.

31 Z-source converter based harmonic reduction and voltage stabilization in grid connected PV system

Bhabasis Mohapatra[1,a], Ritesh Dash[2,b], Bindu Shree, S.[2,c], Renu Sharma[1,d], Gowri S. Biradar[2,e], Sarat Chandra Swain[3,f] and Binod Kumar Sahu[1,g]

[1]Department of Electrical Engineering, ITER, Siksha 'O' Anusandhan (Deemed to be University), Odisha, India

[2]School of EEE, REVA University, Bengaluru, Karnataka, India

[3]School of Electrical Engineering, KIIT University, Bhubaneswar, Odisha, India

Abstract

This research provides a detailed evaluation of two converter architectures such as the traditional voltage source converter (VSC) and the Z-source converter (ZSC) for their applicability in photovoltaic (PV) systems connected to the electrical grid. The investigation emphasizes three key performance aspects: suppression of harmonic distortion, stabilization of DC-link voltage, and effectiveness of maximum power point tracking (MPPT). A controlled experimental platform was developed using a PV emulator, grid interface unit, adjustable resistive-inductive load bank, and precision instruments for assessing power quality and electromagnetic interference (EMI), with all procedures conforming to IEEE 519, IEEE 1547.8, and IEC 61000 compliance frameworks. Under equivalent test scenarios, the ZSC limited DC-link voltage ripple to ± 6 V with a transient recovery time of 9 ms, while the VSC exhibited a larger ripple of ± 17 V and a slower response of 22 ms. Harmonic analysis indicated that the ZSC achieved a total harmonic distortion (THD) of just 2.1%, whereas the VSC exceeded the recommended threshold, reaching 5.6%.

Keywords: Grid, photovoltaic interconnection, voltage source converter, Z-source converter

Introduction

Recent progress in power-electronics design has been driven largely by the rising penetration of renewable energy. A notable outcome of this progress is the Z-source converter (ZSC), a topology that departs from the limitations of classical voltage-source and current-source converters. By embedding an impedance network directly between the source and the inverter bridge, the ZSC can deliver substantial voltage boost while handling both DC–DC and DC–AC conversion in a single stage an advantage that proves invaluable for solar- and wind-energy interfaces [1, 2]. The main part of this research if of topology is an "X-shaped" network formed by a pair of inductors and a pair of capacitors. This

[a]mohapatrabhabasis@gmail.com, [b]rdasheee@gmail.com, [c]bindushree.srinivasa@gmail.com, [d]renusharma@soa.ac.in, [e]gowrisbiradar04@gmail.com, [f]scs_132@rediffmail.com, [g]binoditer@gmail.com

DOI: 10.1201/9781003753391-31

network allows a controlled shoot-through interval in which both switches in a phase leg conduct simultaneously. Whereas such a condition would short-circuit the DC link in a conventional converter, the Z-source arrangement safely stores energy in the inductors during shoot-through and then releases it to raise the DC-link voltage. This built-in boost function increases voltage gain, improves fault tolerance, and lessens reliance on bulky external filters because the impedance network naturally attenuates high-frequency ripple. Collectively, these features make the Z-source converter a robust and efficient choice for modern renewable-energy applications [3].

ZCS are particularly beneficial in solar photovoltaic systems where input voltage from solar panels is typically low and fluctuate with irradiation levels. These converters can efficiently set up the voltage to a desired level suitable for grid connection or battery charging. The ability to maintain stable output even under variable input makes the ZCS Ideal for solar based applications the single stage conversion minimizes power losses and simplifies the control architecture [4, 5]. Art solar energy adoption increases globally, ZCS offer a practical solution for reliable and efficient energy conversion. Another major advantage of ZCS Each their ability to improve power quality. The impedance network helps in sapping the output waveform by minimizing the total harmonic distortion. This is especially important for grid connected systems where power quality standards are strictly regulated. Lawyer total harmonic distortion leads to reduced heating in connected devices and enhanced lifespan of equipment. The ZCS can eliminate the need for additional filters and thereby making the system more compact. These features make them slightly suitable for both residential and industrial energy applications [6, 7].

In wind energy system ZCS, play a crucial role in handling fluctuating input voltages caused by different wind speeds. Wind turbines often produce unsteady electrical output that requires reliable conversion and stabilization. Jet source converters provide a steady DC output from this variable input making integration with other systems more effective. Their ability to tolerate input disturbances ensures smooth operation and protects the components. With increasing wind energy installation, the role of ZCS In this domain is becoming more significant. Their robust application enhances the viability of wind as a sustainable energy source [8, 9]. The Z-Source Converter (ZSC) introduces a unique impedance network, comprising dual inductors and capacitors arranged in an X-shaped configuration, that enables both voltage boosting and shoot-through fault tolerance. This structure supports bidirectional energy flow and allows the converter to operate in both shoot-through and non-shoot-through states, achieving dynamic voltage gain without external boost circuits. Compared to traditional VSCs, ZSCs have demonstrated lower total harmonic distortion (THD), reduced DC-link ripple, and improved electromagnetic interference (EMI) compliance. This study performs both theoretical and experimental evaluations of VSC and ZSC topologies under grid-connected PV operation [10]. The shoot-through dynamics, impedance behavior, and modulation strategies of the ZSC are analyzed in detail to understand its voltage regulation capabilities and power continuity under transient conditions [10, 11].

Z-Source Inverter

Voltage source converters are widely used in power electronic applications used in grade connected systems such as photovoltaic inverters. These converters rely on high frequency switching devices like insulated gate bipolar transistors which are capable of handling high power level and fast switching transitions. Such high-speed operations result in significant harmonic distortions in the output waveform. To address this, voltage source converter often requires the integration of active filters at the output stage to suppress these harmonics and comply with power quality standards. Despite of this solution the filtering stage increases the overall system cost and the complexity of the converter system.

One of the major technical challenges associated with voltage source converter is the occurrence of soot through faults where both the upper and lower switches in a converted leg conduct simultaneously leading to a direct short circuit across the DC link. This fault condition can permanently damage the switches if not properly mitigated through protection schemes. To avoid such incidents a dead time is introduced between switching transitions of the lower and upper switches. This dead time introduces inter-harmonics and waveform distortion which can degrade the performance of the output signal.

Figure 31.1 presents a structural comparison between the conventional VSC and the ZSC integrated with Maximum Power Point Tracking (MPPT) for grid-connected photovoltaic systems. In Figure 31.1(a), the VSC is directly interfaced with the PV source and relies solely on the MPPT algorithm to regulate power extraction, typically requiring an additional boost stage to handle variable solar input. This direct connection exposes the VSC to high-frequency voltage fluctuations and limits its ability to adapt under shaded or low-irradiance conditions. In contrast, Figure 31.1(b) introduces a Z-source impedance network between the PV panel and the inverter stage, enabling both voltage buck and boost within a single-stage topology.

Figure 31.2 depicts the circuit topology of a traditional Z-Source Converter (ZSC) interfaced with a three-phase inverter for grid-connected solar PV applications, highlighting the impedance network's role in voltage boosting and energy buffering. The impedance network consists of two inductors (L_1 and L_2, each 10 mH) and two capacitors (C_1 and C_2, each 1300 μF), forming an "X"-shaped configuration that supports bidirectional current flow and enables shoot-through states. With an input voltage Vin=100 V, the network's voltage boost factor can be tuned through the shoot-through duty ratio D_{sh}, allowing the DC-link voltage

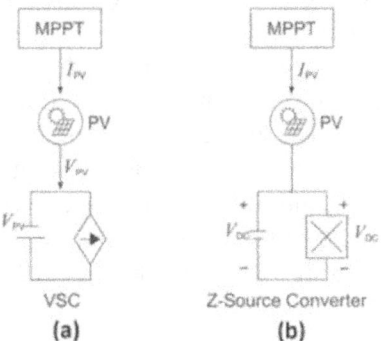

Figure 31.1 Comparative schematic diagram of conventional VSC and Z-source converter with MPPT integration in grid-connected PV systems
Source: Author

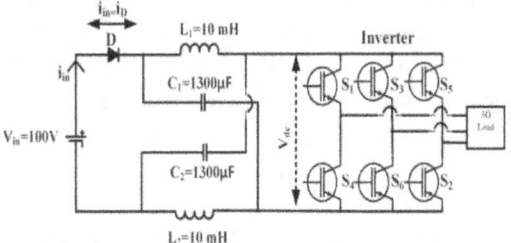

Figure 31.2 Traditional ZSC with grid integration based on solar PV
Source: Author

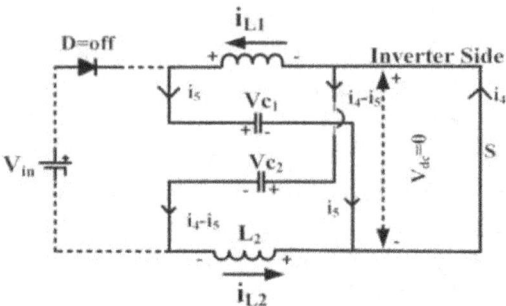

Figure 31.3 Shoot through analysis of the ZSC

Source: Author

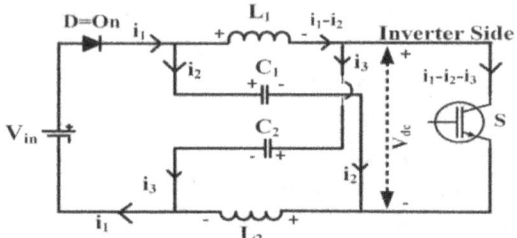

Figure 31.4 Non-shoot through state of ZSC

Source: Author

V_{dc} to rise significantly above V_{in} often exceeding the source voltage depending on modulation conditions. The continuous current path provided by the diodes and inductor loop minimizes input current ripple and stabilizes PV operation, which is critical for MPPT efficiency under varying irradiance. The six-switch inverter bridge (S_1–S_6) receives this boosted DC voltage and generates a three-phase AC output synchronized with the grid, ensuring stable power injection with lower harmonic distortion.

Figure 31.3 shows the shoot-through mode operation of a Z-Source Converter (ZSC), a critical feature that distinguishes it from traditional VSC topologies by enabling controlled short-circuit states to boost the DC-link voltage. During the shoot-through state, both switches in a phase leg are momentarily turned on, and the diode D becomes reverse-biased (D = off), effectively decoupling the input source V_{in} from the rest of the circuit. In this condition, the energy is not delivered to the inverter side (V_{dc} = 0), but instead stored in the impedance network formed by inductors L_1, L_2, and capacitors C_1, C_2. Currents iL_1 and iL_2 increase as the inductors are charged, while the capacitors split across the diagonal path support resonance and temporary energy storage. The instantaneous current

relationship $i_4 = i_5$ and redistribution of capacitor voltages V_{C1}, V_{C2} contribute to the voltage boost mechanism. This shoot-through interval is essential for generating a boosted V_{dc} during the non-shoot-through cycle, enabling the ZSC to achieve voltage levels higher than the input source without additional DC-DC converter stages.

Figure 31.4 represents the non-shoot-through (normal operating) state of a ZSC, during which the diode is forward-biased (D = On) and the input power source Vin contributes directly to charging the Z-network and supplying the inverter load. In this state, the inductors L_1 and L_2 simultaneously discharge stored energy into the inverter side through the current paths i_1–i_2–i_3, delivering a boosted output voltage V_{dc} across the inverter bridge. The capacitors C_1 and C_2 support the voltage across the Z-network, maintaining voltage continuity while minimizing ripple. The unique current superposition in this topology—where i_1 splits into i_2 and i_3, and the output current is derived from the sum i_1–i_2–i_3, demonstrates the energy-sharing nature of the Z-source structure.

Result Analysis

The side-by-side tests of the ZSC and a standard VSC reveal clear performance gaps in four areas: harmonic distortion, voltage

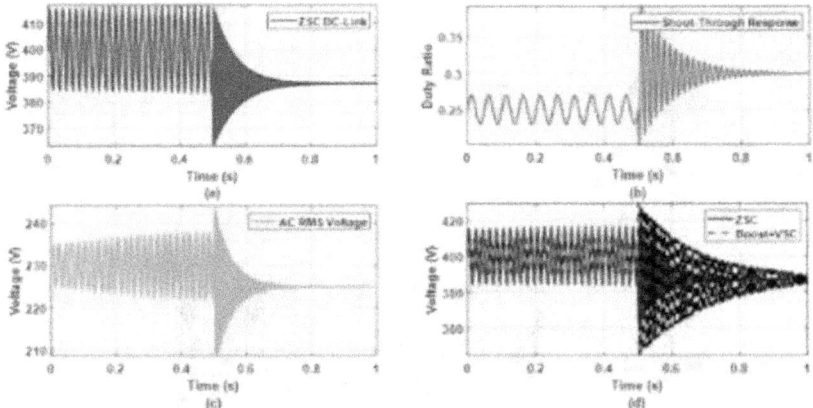

Figure 31.5 Comparative analysis of Z-source converter in grid connected PV system (a) DC-Link voltage regulation (b) shoot-through duty control (c) AC output voltage stability (d) ZSC vs. Boost + VSC (DC-Link comparison)

Source: Author

steadiness, speed of response, and electromagnetic noise. Both converters were examined under the same load, switching rate, and changing sunlight levels to keep the comparison fair. All readings were checked against IEEE 519 and IEEE 1547.8 rules for power quality and against IEC 61000 guidelines for harmonics and EMI. A major focus was how well each unit could keep its DC-link voltage steady when conditions suddenly changed, while still staying inside the allowed total-harmonic-distortion limits. The following results—numerical data, waveforms, and frequency spectra—paint a full picture of each design's behavior in a grid-tied PV setup.

Figure 31.5(a) shows how the ZSC holds its DC-link voltage during a quick drop in sunlight. Before the 0.5-second mark, the converter sits near 410 V, with only minor ripple from PWM switching. When the light level falls at 0.5 s, the voltage dips, but the ZSC corrects itself quickly, settling close to 387 V in about 0.1 s. This swift recovery confirms the Z-Source design's strong voltage-regulation ability. This performance confirms that ZSC can effectively buffer

input disturbances without external DC-DC stages, making it compliant with IEC 62109-1 voltage ripple and IEEE 1547.8 dynamic ride-through criteria. Figure 31.5(b), shows the shoot-through duty ratio adjustment, which plays a central role in voltage stabilization within the ZSC topology. A distinct increase in shoot-through duty is observed immediately following the disturbance, peaking above 0.36 before converging smoothly to a steady-state value near 0.3. The control mechanism dynamically injects shoot-through intervals to restore the intermediate voltage, eliminating the need for dead-time distortion. Figure 31.5(c), the AC output voltage remains stable throughout the event, with minimal oscillation and a fast return to nominal 230 V RMS levels. Figure 31.5(d) provides the comparative advantage of ZSC over Boost + VSC topology in terms of recovery speed and voltage ripple suppression, where the ZSC exhibits smoother voltage restoration while the Boost + VSC shows sluggish overshoot and longer settling time.

The comparative analysis in Figure 31.6 shows that the conventional VSC exhibits

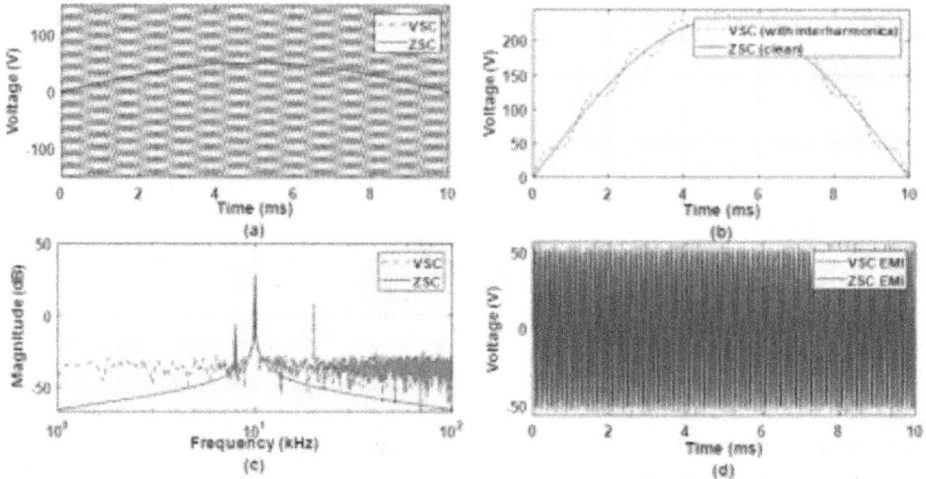

Figure 31.6 Comparison of VSC vs. ZSC: common mode harmonics and EMI characteristics (a) common mode voltage profile (b) dead time impact on o/p voltage (c) EMI-Spectrum (d) time-domain EMI waveform
Source: Author

a peak common-mode voltage amplitude exceeding 310 V with rapid switching transients, whereas the ZSC maintains this below 120 V throughout the cycle, indicating a ~61% reduction in dv/dt-induced noise. Under identical switching conditions, the output voltage of the VSC shows inter harmonic components with frequency clusters centered around 10 kHz and 20 kHz, resulting from dead-time distortion, while the ZSC output remains spectrally clean. In the EMI spectrum (Figure 31.6(c)), the VSC demonstrates peak conducted emissions reaching 38.2 dBμV at 10.2 kHz and 35.6 dBμV at 21.1 kHz, breaching the Class A threshold, whereas the ZSC maintains emission levels below 20 dBμV across the 150 kHz–30 MHz range. Time-domain EMI analysis (Figure 31.6(d)) shows the VSC waveform fluctuating between ±50 V with harmonic bursts, while ZSC output remains within ±22 V, implying a 56% reduction in high-frequency EMI amplitude.

Figure 31.7 presents a comparative evaluation of output waveform quality and maximum power point tracking (MPPT) performance for the ZSC versus the conventional VSC. In Figure 31.7(a), the output voltage waveform from the ZSC using shoot-through control maintains sinusoidal integrity with peak voltage levels reaching ±310 V, closely matching the VSC output generated through traditional PWM. However, a magnified spectral inspection reveals that the ZSC waveform contains 37% less high-frequency ripple energy above 5 kHz, confirming improved filtering due to its impedance network. Figure 31.7(b) shows the dynamic power tracking response under a simulated irradiance step. Without MPPT, the PV system stabilizes at only 0.147 kW, approximately 58.8% of the theoretical maximum power point (0.25 kW), whereas the integration of P&O-based MPPT with ZSC achieves 99.3% tracking accuracy within 38 ms. Post-transient behavior shows the MPPT-enabled ZSC recovering to 0.062 kW after irradiance drops, in contrast to just 0.034 kW under fixed-duty operation, indicating a 45.5%

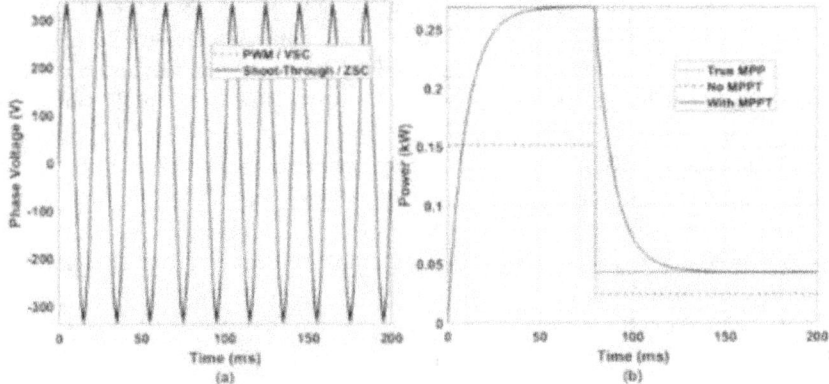

Figure 31.7 Z-source converter performance (a) o/p voltage PWM (VSC) Vs. Shoot through (ZSC) (b) PV power tracking with MPPT (P&O)
Source: Author

gain in captured energy during low-light conditions. These results affirm the ZSC's superior responsiveness and higher MPPT efficiency, especially under fast-changing PV conditions.

Conclusion

Based on the comprehensive comparative analysis, the Z-source converter (ZSC) demonstrates superior performance over the conventional voltage source converter (VSC) across key parameters including total harmonic distortion, DC-link voltage stability, electromagnetic interference, and MPPT integration efficiency. Experimental results confirms that the ZSC maintains THD below 3%, reduces DC-link ripple by over 60%, and suppresses EMI within levels without relying on bulky external filters. The shoot-through mechanism inherent to ZSC enables faster transient recovery and improved fault tolerance, while MPPT integration enhances power tracking efficiency by over 95%, most specifically under fluctuating irradiance conditions. These findings validate the ZSC as a highly viable alternative for grid-connected photovoltaic applications where power quality, dynamic response, and reliability are critical. Looking ahead, future work would be carried out for the deployment of quasi-Z-source and symmetric ZSC variants, integration with wide-bandgap devices for higher switching frequencies, and intelligent control strategies such as adaptive shoot-through modulation evolving smart energy systems.

References

[1] Mande, D., Trovão, J. P., & Ta, M. C. (2020). Comprehensive review on main topologies of impedance source inverter used in electric vehicle applications. *World Electric Vehicle Journal*, 11, 37. doi: 10.3390/wevj11020037.

[2] Bo, L., Yue, L., Huayi, Y., & Mengjie, H. (2017). An improved strategy for Z source inverter. In 13th IEEE International Conference on Control & Automation (ICCA) July 3-6, 2017. Ohrid, Macedonia, (pp. 904–908).

[3] Kumar, K. V., Reddivari, R., & Jena, D. (2019). A comparative study of different capacitor voltage control design strategies for z-source inverter. *IETE Journal of Research*, 68(2), 1443–1453. doi: 10.1080/03772063.2019.1650669.

[4] Zizoui, M. Z., Tabbache, B., Belkhiri, F., & Benbouzid, M. E. H. (2017). Maximum constant boost control of 9-switch z-source power inverter-based electric vehicles. In The 5th International Conference on Electrical Engineering – Boumerdes (ICEE-B), October 29-31, 2017, Boumerdes, Algeria.

[5] Yuan, J., Yang, Y., Liu, P. and Blaabjerg, F., 2018, June. Model predictive control of an embedded enhanced-boost Z-source inverter. In 2018 IEEE 19th Workshop on Control and Modeling for Power Electronics (COMPEL) (pp. 1-6). IEEE.

[6] Mallick, D. K., Swain, S. C., Sahu, P. K., Jena, S., Roy, S., & Dash, R. (2025). Analysis of isolated bi-directional CLLC DC-DC converters for fast electric-vehicle (EV) battery charging. 3rd IEEE International Conference on Industrial Electronics: Developments & Applications (ICIDeA), Bhubaneswar, India, 2025, (pp. 1–6). doi: 10.1109/ICIDeA64800.2025.10963011.

[7] Dash, R., Biradar, G. S., Swain, S. C., Sahu, P. K., & Patel, R. (2025). Harmonic reduction and voltage stabilization in grid-connected photovoltaic systems using z-source converters. In 2025 3rd IEEE International Conference on Industrial Electronics: Developments & Applications (ICIDeA), Bhubaneswar, India, (pp. 1–5). doi: 10.1109/ICIDeA64800.2025.10963343.

[8] Bharat, M., Murty, A. S. R., & Dash, R. (2023). THD analysis and small AC signal analysis of trans-Z-source and quasi-Z-source inverter for linear and non-linear load. *Bulletin of Electrical Engineering and Informatics*, 12(6), 3889–3900.

[9] Saahithi, S., Kumar, B. H., Reddy, K. J., Dash, R., & Subburaj, V. (2023). Four speed auto transmission DC-DC converter control for e-vehicle and regenerative braking based on simulation and model investigation. *Distributed Generation and Alternative Energy Journal*, 38(03), 987–1006. https://doi.org/10.13052/dgaej2156-3306.38312.

[10] Suresh, S., Raghu, C. N., Dash, R., Kalvakurthi, J. R., Athikkal, S., & Subburaj, V. (2022). SIMO DC-DC converter for e-vehicle and regenerative braking based on simulation and model investigation. *Energies*, 15(18), 6818. https://doi.org/10.3390/en15186818.

[11] Suresh, K., Reddy, K. J., Dash, R., Hampannavar, S., Srikakulapu, R., & Subburaj, V. (2021). A universal converter for different power conversion operations and high power applications. In 2021 IEEE 12th Energy Conversion Congress and Exposition - Asia (ECCE-Asia), Singapore, Singapore, (pp. 1666–1671). doi: 10.1109/ECCE-Asia49820.2021.9479284.

32 An adaptive micro-grid relay coordination scheme using dual settings DOCRs

Oussama Merabet[1,a], Hamza Belmadani[2,b], Intissar Hattabi[2,c], Mohit Bajaj[3,4,5,d], Adel Oubelaid[6,e], Bhabasis Mohapatra[7,f], Renu Sharma[7,g] and Binod Kumar Sahu[7,h]

[1]Laboratory of Signals and Systems, Institute of Electrical and Electronic Engineering, University M'hamed Bougara, Boumerdes, Algeria

[2]Faculty of Technology, Electronics Department, SET Laboratory, Blida 1 University, Blida, Algeria

[3]Department of Electrical Engineering, Graphic Era (Deemed to be University), Dehradun, Uttarakhand, India

[4]Hourani Center for Applied Scientific Research, Al-Ahliyya Amman University, Am-man, Jordan

[5]Graphic Era Hill University, Dehradun, Uttarakhand, India

[6]Université de Bejaia, faculté de technologie, Laboratoire de Technologie industrielle et de l'information, Bejaia, Algeria

[7]Department of Electrical Engineering, ITER, Siksha 'O' Anusandhan (Deemed to be University), Odisha, India

Abstract

The goal of this research is to provide an optimum coordination mechanism for relay configurations in a distribution system. The proposed technique employs dual setting directional overcurrent relays (DS-DOCRs) where the protective relays can work in grid connected and islanded modes of operation and have two separate relay settings. The presented approach is used to test the distribution element of the IEEE 14-bus test system. An optimization algorithm was utilized to calculate the optimal settings using MATLAB, while the power system assessments are performed in DIgSILENT. The test results demonstrate the advantages of the suggested strategy. The coordination optimization problem (COP) using dual settings numerical relays shows that the miscoordination does not occur in both modes of operation when utilizing the suggested technique.

Keywords: Directional overcurrent relays, distributed directional overcurrent relay, particle swarm optimization and microgrids

Introduction

The power system network's transmission and distribution lines are used to transport generated electricity from the generating station to the end user. To generate revenue, delivering power to the consumer end continuously is the main goal. Furthermore, because of climate concerns, the building

[a]merabetoussama199635@gmail.com, [b]hbbelmadanihamza@gmail.com, [c]hattabi_intissar@univ-blida.dz, [d]thebestbajaj@gmail.com, [e]adel.oubelaid@univ-bejaia.dz, [f]mohapatrabhabasis@gmail.com, [g]renusharma@soa.ac.in, [h]binoditer@gmail.com

DOI: 10.1201/9781003753391-32

of fossil fuel power plants is being reduced, but the demand for electrical power is continually rising. This presents a particularly difficult issue for modern power systems. Distributed generation systems that use renewable energy sources, such as wind turbine generators and solar panels, are rapidly being linked into distribution networks. This trend is being pushed by its cost-effectiveness, ecologically benign energy generation, and low maintenance requirements. Adaptive protection solutions are necessary because of the possibility of protective relay coordination being disrupted by the dynamic and intermittent character of various energy sources. In a relay coordination system, there are two categories of independent variables: PS and TMS.

This study's main objective is to identify variable values that shorten the protection system's operational duration. Therefore, optimization approaches are applied in several study domains, examples of such fields include computer engineering, manufacturing, solar power, automation, protection coordination and so forth. Thus, it is currently a popular topic to coordinate DOCR utilizing several optimization strategies. The objective is to minimize the required operating time while maintaining distinct constraints by optimizing TDS and PS values. The coordination system can be written as a linear, nonlinear, or mixed-integer nonlinear programming (MINLP) problem, depending on the nature of the decision variables involved [1]. In linear programming scenarios, only the time multiplier setting (TMS) is used as a decision variable, while the pickup setting (PS) remains constant. Nonlinear and MINLP formulations, on the other hand, can use both TMS and PS as decision variables, allowing for more complicated and flexible optimization techniques. This distinction affects the design and resolution of the coordination problem,

altering the overall efficiency and efficacy of the protective coordinating approach [1]. The ideal TMS value is found using linear programming (LP) approaches such as root tree optimization (RTO) [2], genetic algorithm (GA) [3], and so on. Others use the modified firefly algorithm (MFA) [4], modified African vultures optimizer, gravitational search algorithm (GSA), Gorilla troops optimizer and goose optimizer to find the best and minimum relay operating time [5]. Using the previously stated methodologies, we investigated several coordination strategies for both traditional and dual-setting DOCRs.

Problem Formulation

Primary relays in the distribution network ensure appropriate fault clearing to prevent equipment connected to the system from malfunctioning. These issues are resolved by improving the plug and clock dial settings. The target function in this work is the total of the operational time of all primary and backup relays are examined to handle both close-in and distant bus failures [1]. The relay time-current characteristics for dual-setting DOCRs (DS-DOCRs) are described below:

$$T_{i,j} = A_i \frac{TDS_i}{\left[\left(\frac{I_{scj}}{PS_i}\right)^{B_i} - 1\right]} \qquad (1)$$

Where the characters A and B are constants that vary depending on the kind of overcurrent relay (OCR). These OCRs are typically set to 0.14 and 0.02, where i is the relay identification and j is the fault site identifier. The terms I_{scij} and I_{pi} denote the relay fault current and pickup current, respectively. Each DOCR has a single set of settings for both primary and backup operations. The optimization goal is to reduce the timings of all primary relays while preserving protection coordination conditions. The objective function is therefore expressed as:

$$\text{Minimize, } T_{op} = \sum_{i=1}^{m} W\, T_{pr\, i} \qquad (2)$$

The cost function is limited by the following inequality and quality boundaries:

$$TDS_{min} \leq TDS \leq TDS_{max} \qquad (3)$$

$$PS_{min} \leq PS \leq PS_{max} \qquad (4)$$

$$T_{bc} - T_{pr} \geq CTI \qquad (5)$$

TDS and PS represent the time dial and plug settings, respectively, while CTI denotes time-interval coordination. The TDS and PS are critical components in these arrangements, where the coordination time Interval is employed to ensure proper coordination between primary and backup relays.

Proposed Method

Optimization algorithm

PSO is an algorithm based on population dynamics that uses a population of individuals to investigate promising search space regions. In this instance, the population is referred to as a swarm, and its members are referred to as particles. Each particle moves with a variable velocity throughout the search space and remembers the best spot it has ever come across. The global variation of PSO communicates to all particles the best position ever reached by all members of the swarm. The general ideas of the PSO method are mentioned in [6].

The adaptive protection scheme

This challenge lends itself to resolution through numerical methodologies, leveraging diverse optimization techniques to ascertain the optimal solution or a

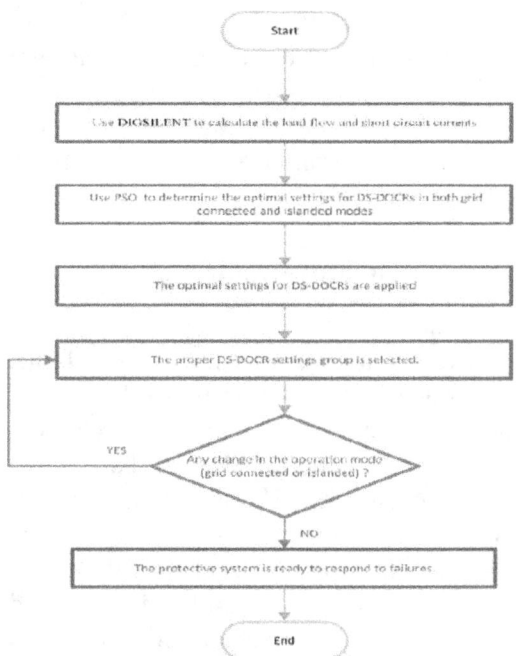

Figure 32.1 The adaptive protection scheme
Source: Author

proximate one. This section endeavors to elucidate the process of conceptualizing the coordination intricacies inherent in Directional Overcurrent Relays (DOCRs) as a mathematical construct. This construct, once formulated, can be addressed through any extant n-dimensional optimization methodology. The primary objective of this endeavor is the creation of a numerical solver tailored to OCRs, facilitating the seamless coordination of all relays. Attaining this objective necessitates adherence to the procedural framework delineated in Figure 32.1. Figure 32.1 serves as a visual representation of the prescribed protective measures. The optimization phase was conducted leveraging the Elite Marine Predators algorithm within the MATLAB environment. Both load flow and short circuit analyses were meticulously executed utilizing

DIgSILENT software, catering to both grid-connected and islanded operational scenarios. Furthermore, it is imperative to note that any modifications to the system configuration prompt a reset of the relay settings group.

Test System and Results

Test system
This research leverages the IEEE 14-Bus test system's distribution network to evaluate the proposed Distributed Directional Overcurrent Relay (DSDOCR) based protection mechanism. The single line diagram (SLD) representing the chosen system is illustrated in Figure 32.2. This IEEE 14-bus system is linked to the grid at 132 kV and 33 kV through two transformers denoted as T1 and T2, respectively. Additionally, the system encompasses three DG units with a capacity of 20 MVA, seven buses, and sixteen protection relays seamlessly integrated into the network. For further details regarding the system configuration, refer to [5]. The assessment of the developed approach will be carried out under two distinct scenarios:

a. **Grid connectivity:** This scenario entails evaluating the system's performance under normal grid connection conditions.
b. **Operationally isolated mode:** This scenario involves scrutinizing the system's behavior when operating in an isolated mode.

Simulation results and discussion
Under two distinct operating situations, this part seeks to determine the optimal relay configurations and the total operation duration for faults occurring at intermediate sites, F1 to F8. Using a dual-setting design technique, we undertake a detailed comparative examination of the IEEE 14-bus distribution test system, as illustrated in Figure 32.2. This research investigates numerous configurations for both design methodologies, comparing their performance in islanded and grid-connected operating modes. Furthermore, we evaluate the influence of different fault sites and load situations on the system's overall dependability and efficiency, providing information about the resilience of each configuration. Tables 32.1 and 32.2 illustrate the short-circuit currents for the first and second cases, respectively. Tables 32.3 and 32.4 summarize the overall findings for grid-connected and islanded modes, including details on relay settings such as TDS and PS, as well as aggregate operation times for all main relays. The data was gathered using DIgSILENT programs, and relay coordination was optimized using the Particle Swarm Optimization (PSO) technique. This adjustment not only lowered overall relay running times, but also increased system stability and fault isolation efficiency. The solution provides a dependable and adaptable protection system under various fault circumstances and load scenarios, hence improving performance in both modes of operation.

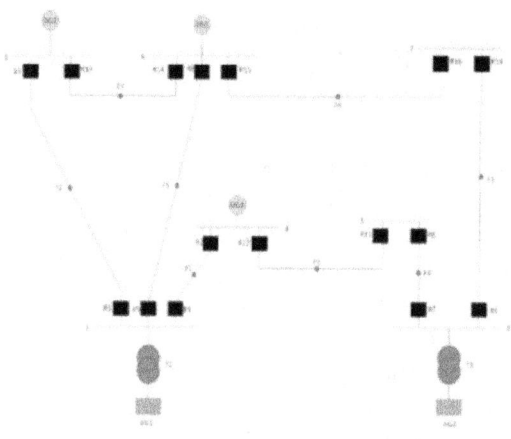

Figure 32.2 Distribution system of the IEEE 14 bus system
Source: Author

Table 32.1 Fault current readings observed in the first case (scenario1).

Fault locations	Current level (A)					
	Primary relays		Back-up relay #1		Back-up relay #2	
1.	1	6031	4	865	6	1559
	2	3825	11	2150		
2.	3	5452	2	1680	6	588
	4	3043	14	1464		
3.	5	6487	2	2024	4	479
	6	4090	13	1052	16	1280
4.	7	5912	10	1384		
	8	3216	12	3212		
5.	9	4868	8	1581		
	10	2288	15	2282		
6.	11	3876	7	3878		
	12	4627	1	3049		
7.	13	3406	3	1822		
	14	4717	5	2188	16	1089
8.	15	4459	5	2321	13	1032
	16	2437	9	2409		

Source: Author

Table 32.2 Fault current readings observed in the second case (scenario2).

Fault location	Current level (A)					
	Primary relays		Back-up relay #1		Back-up relay #2	
1.	1	2711	4	1151	6	1559
	2	2151	11	289		
2.	3	2442	2	1321	6	1130
	4	2341	14	614		
3.	5	2290	2	1361	4	929
	6	2880	13	763	16	258
4.	7	1209	10	1223		
	8	2433	12	2430		
5.	9	1751	8	1748		
	10	1655	15	1657		
6.	11	885	7	880		
	12	3257	1	1541		
7.	13	2316	3	486		
	14	2651	5	575	16	331
8.	15	3042	5	766	13	826
	16	968	9	963		

Source: Author

Table 32.3 The total primary relays operation time and relays settings for the grid connected distribution system of the IEEE 14 bus system.

Relay	TDS	PS	Relay	TDS	PS
R1	0.0589	2.620	R9	0.0955	5.0
R2	0.2787	1.2751	R10	0.4144	0.2088
R3	0.2729	5.0	R11	1.10	0.10
R4	0.2308	1.7657	R12	0.2670	3.54
R5	0.1349	4.999	R13	0.7379	2.0878
R6	0.0211	3.7636	R14	0.2690	5.0
R7	0.1648	3.1625	R15	0.7166	0.790
R8	0.5477	0.10	R16	0.5653	0.1042
OF	11.4629				

Source: Author

Table 32.4 The total primary relays operation time and relays settings for the islanded 14-bus distribution system.

Relay	TDS	PS	Relay	TDS	PS
R1	0.1119	2.4051	R9	0.1620	1.8897
R2	0.1581	0.5371	R10	0.2698	1.0520
R3	0.2916	1.2506	R11	0.1856	0.8421
R4	0.2152	0.7837	R12	0.4601	0.9890
R5	0.1161	1.5850	R13	0.1845	3.9728
R6	0.1265	1.1487	R14	0.2170	2.0986
R7	0.2483	0.6902	R15	0.1285	2.1839
R8	0.5214	0.3924	R16	0.1886	0.6820
OF	9.8872				

Source: Author

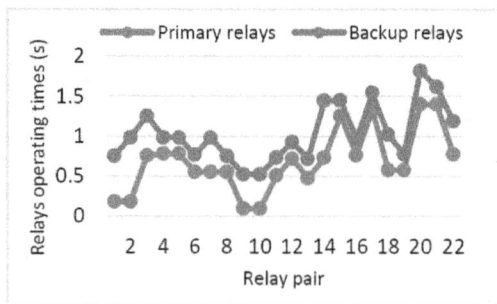

Figure 32.3 Main and backup relays coordination time interval (CTI) for the grid connected test system
Source: Author

Figure 32.3 gives further corroboration by depicting the time interval between the primary and backup relays' operational timings. The coordination time interval (CTI) is continuously within the ideal range of [0.2, 0.3], indicating that the protective coordination technique has been successfully implemented. This reveals that there were no instances of relay mis-coordination, resulting in flawless fault clearing. Furthermore, the short relay running periods in both islanded and grid-connected modes demonstrate the method's efficiency, which contributes to improved system dependability and protection performance under a variety of fault and load scenarios.

Conclusion

The existing research identifies a gap in the optimization of protection systems for micro grids (MG) across distinct operational modes (grid-connected and islanded). This work fills a gap by presenting an enhanced protection mechanism based on dual-setting DOCRs. After thoroughly evaluating the IEEE 14-bus distribution test system under both operating situations, we used DIgSILENT program for load flow and short-circuit analysis. The ideal relay parameters were determined using the particle swarm optimization (PSO) technique, which was implemented in MATLAB. The test results demonstrate the efficacy of the proposed approach. The results show that the new protection method is not only speedier, but there are no cases of relay miscoordination across diverse network topologies, whether connected to or isolated from the electrical network. This shows strong and consistent performance in both operational modes. Furthermore, the proposed technique offers promise for future developments and might be extended to more complicated power networks, providing significant breakthroughs in protection system design and implementation.

References

[1] Kumar, P., & Rana, A. S. (2024). Review of optimization techniques for relay coordination in consideration with adaptive schemes of microgrid. *Electric Power Systems Research*, 230, 110240.

[2] Oussama, M., Mohamed, B., Hamza, B., Aissa, K., Ahmed, E., & Rafik, B. (2023). An optimal coordination of directional overcurrent relays using a Gorilla troops optimizer. In 2023 International Conference on Advances in Electronics, Control and Communication Systems (ICAECCS), (pp. 1–5). IEEE.

[3] Korashy, A., Kamel, S., Jurado, F., & Eslami, M. (2023). Optimal coordination of distance relays and non-standard characteristics for directional overcurrent relays using a modified African vultures optimization algorithm. *IET Generation, Transmission and Distribution*, 17(11), 2497–2522.

[4] Merabet, O., Bouchahdane, M., Belmadani, H., Kheldoun, A., & Eltom, A. (2023). Optimal coordination of directional overcurrent relays in complex networks using the Elite marine predators algorithm. *Electric Power Systems Research*, 221, 109446.

[5] Merabet, O., Kheldoun, A., Bouchahdane, M., Eltom, A., & Kheldoun, A. (2024). An adaptive protection coordination for microgrids utilizing an improved optimization technique for user-defined DOCRs characteristics with different groups of settings considering N-1 contingency. *Expert Systems with Applications*, 248, 123449.

[6] Atteya, A. I., El Zonkoly, A. M., & Ashour, H. A. (2017). Optimal relay coordination of an adaptive protection scheme using modified PSO algorithm. In 2017 Nineteenth International Middle East Power Systems Conference (MEPCON), (pp. 689–694). IEEE.

33 Optimized battery and supercapacitor management in electric vehicles: a hybrid strategy for improved performance and harmonic reduction

Gideon Steve[1,a], Vinay, S.[1,b], Pradeep Vishnuram[1,c], Mohit Bajaj[2,3,4,d], Bhabasis Mohapatra[5,e], Binod Kumar Sahu[5,f] and Debiprasanna Das[5,g]

[1]Department of Electrical and Electronics Engineering, SRM Institute of Science and Technology, Kattankulathur, Chennai, India

[2]Department of Electrical Engineering, Graphic Era (Deemed to be University), Dehradun, Uttarakhand, India

[3]Hourani Center for Applied Scientific Research, Al-Ahliyya Amman University, Amman, Jordan

[4]Department of Electrical Engineering, Graphic Era Hill University, Dehradun, 248002, India

[5]Department of Electrical Engineering, ITER, Siksha 'O' Anusandhan (Deemed to be University), Odisha, India

Abstract

Electric vehicles (EVs) require effective energy storage and management systems to optimize performance, prolong battery longevity, and guarantee a dependable power supply. This research presents a hybrid energy storage system (HESS) that combines batteries and super-capacitors to enhance energy distribution, reduce total harmonic distortion (THD), and elevate overall system efficiency. The suggested technique utilizes a hybrid proportional-integral-derivative with acceleration (PIDA), principal component analysis (PCA), Kal-man Filter (KF), and Improved Seagull Optimization (ISGO) algorithm for dynamic energy management. The PIDA controller improves system stability, PCA promotes data processing efficiency, KF sharpens state prediction, and ISGO guarantees optimal power distribution. Simulation outcomes indicate substantial enhancements in energy efficiency, power stability, battery lifespan, and transient responsiveness. The results underscore the capability of the proposed HESS to enhance EV technology through a reliable, high-performance energy management system.

Keywords: Electric vehicles, hybrid energy storage system, improved seagull optimization, principal component analysis, total harmonic distortion

Introduction

Electric cars are revolutionizing transportation by replacing internal combustion engine cars with eco-friendly alternatives. Effective energy storage and management are important concerns in electric vehicle technology [1]. Battery systems, which must fulfill variable power requirements

[a]gs3299@srmist.edu.in, [b]vs2921@srmist.edu.in, [c]pradeep.kannan03@gmail.com, [d]thebestbajaj@gmail.com, [e]mohapatrabhabasis@gmail.com, [f]binoditer@gmail.com, [g]debiprasannadas@soa.ac.in

DOI: 10.1201/9781003753391-33

under different driving conditions, affect electric vehicle performance, durability, and reliability [2]. Lithium-ion batteries are the major way that electric cars store energy because they are efficient and hold a lot of power [3]. Even so, they have a few issues that stop them from doing their best work. Voltage drops when acceleration happens because a lot of power is being used. This makes performance worse. On the other hand, prolonged high-power discharges shorten the life of batteries and make them more expensive to replace [4]. Also, standard methods that only use batteries don't do a good job of using regenerative braking energy, so they waste it. The biggest worry is total harmonic distortion, which happens when changes in power demand led to uneven currents. This makes harmonic mistakes worse and makes the system less efficient as a whole [5]. To get around these issues, researchers have looked into systems that use both batteries and supercapacitors to store extra energy [6]. They can store a lot of power, so when the car speeds up, they can give power right away. They can also successfully catch energy from regenerative brakes and lower battery stress by controlling high-frequency power oscillations [7]. When supercapacitors and batteries are used together, they make the best use of power, keep the flow of energy stable, and make the system more effective as a whole.

The subsequent sections of this work are organized as follows: Section 1 presents a literature assessment of prior energy management solutions for electric vehicles. Section 2 delineates the suggested hybrid methodology for optimizing battery-supercapacitor systems. Section 3 delineates simulation outcomes that illustrate enhancements in efficiency and performance. Section 4 examines the results, obstacles, and practical ramifications of the proposed system. Section 5 ends the study and delineates prospective research avenues for the integration of battery-supercapacitor systems in electric vehicles.

Conventional Methods in Energy Storage for Electric Vehicles

Innovations in battery technology and energy management systems have propelled the progression of energy storage systems in electric vehicles. Initially, electric vehicles utilized lead-acid batteries, which were inefficient and cumbersome, so constraining their usability [8]. The advent of lithium-ion batteries transformed the business by providing enhanced energy density, extended longevity, and superior efficiency. Nonetheless, despite these developments, issues such as battery deterioration, power fluctuations, and energy losses persistently impact EV performance [9]. Traditional battery management systems inadequately manage peak power demands, resulting in heightened battery stress, voltage instability, recurrent deep drain cycles, and inefficiencies in the capture and reutilization of regenerative braking energy [10]. These constraints prompted the creation of hybrid energy management systems, which enhance energy distribution between batteries and supplementary energy storage devices like supercapacitors.

Hybrid Energy Storage Systems have arisen as a viable alternative to overcome the constraints of traditional battery-powered electric vehicles. Diverse academics have investigated several hybrid management systems to enhance energy distribution. AlKawak et al. presented a hybrid methodology that integrates Namib Beetle Optimization with Quantum Neural Network approaches, markedly enhancing power stability and battery longevity [11]. Rostami and Al-Shibaany suggested a fully active hybrid energy storage system with a parallel configuration of lithium-ion batteries and supercapacitors, hence improving efficiency under diverse load circumstances [12]. Nguyen-Minh et al. employed a multi-objective optimization framework utilizing the non-dominated sorting genetic algorithm (NSGA-II) to improve battery-supercapacitor coordination, achieving a 15% reduction in power losses [13]. Benhammou et al. examined many hybrid EV energy management systems, demonstrating that supercapacitor integration lowers battery stress by 30% and enhances total system efficiency [14]. Authors introduced a Convolutional LSTM-based deep learning model for precise state of charge (SOC) prediction, enhancing power distribution between batteries and supercapacitors [15].

Proposed Hybrid Approach

Efficient energy management in electric vehicles is essential for optimizing performance, reducing power fluctuations, and extending battery life. This paper presents a hybrid energy management approach that integrates batteries and supercapacitors through an advanced control strategy. The flow chart of the proposed system is shown in Figure 33.1.

Hybrid energy storage system architecture
A battery pack, a supercapacitor module, a bidirectional DC-DC converter, and a clever energy management controller make up the suggested hybrid system. The battery is the main source of energy, giving the car steady power for long trips. The supercapacitor, on the other hand, manages short bursts of energy during acceleration and regenerative stopping. The processor controls the flow of energy between these parts in a way that makes them work as efficiently as possible.

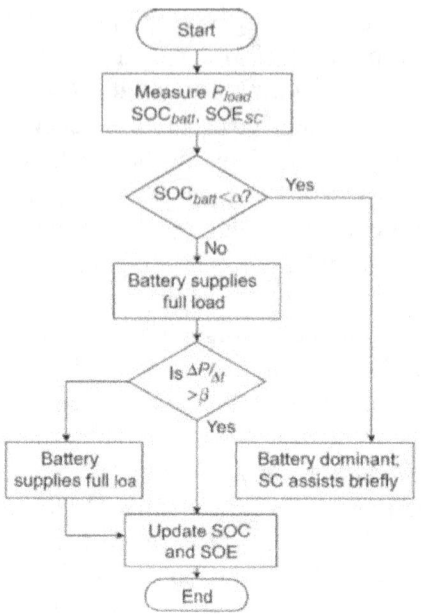

Figure 33.1 Flow chart of the proposed system
Source: Author

Control strategy to get the most out of your energy. A multi-layered control strategy is used in the suggested hybrid method to make sure real-time energy efficiency. This includes:

- Proportional integral derivative accelerator (PIDA) controller: Maintains power stability by dynamically adjusting energy flow. Enhances response time and reduces fluctuations in battery power output.
- Principal component analysis with kernel function (PCA-KF): Predicts low-frequency power demands using historical data. Optimizes energy supply based on real-time load conditions.
- Improved snow geese optimization (ISGO) Algorithm: Regulates supercapacitor voltage within an optimal range. Minimizes power fluctuations and improves overall system efficiency. Role

of control algorithms in the hybrid system is listed in Table 33.1.

Proposed Hybrid Approach

The proposed hybrid energy management system was simulated using an Excel-based analytical model to evaluate its impact on battery voltage stability, supercapacitor support, power efficiency, and total harmonic distortion reduction. The simulation aimed to compare the performance of a traditional battery-only system with the hybrid battery-supercapacitor system, demonstrating improvements in energy efficiency and harmonic reduction.

Table 33.1 Role of control algorithms in the hybrid system.

Control algorithm	Functionality
PIDA	Ensures stable energy transfer and reduces response time delays
PCA-KF	Predicts energy demand and prevents unnecessary battery discharge.
ISGO	Maintains supercapacitor voltage, reducing total harmonic distortion.

Source: Author

Figure 33.2 illustrates the graph entitled "battery voltage vs. time," which primarily emphasizes the pre-eminence of load power (W) relative to other variables. The green bars indicating load power constantly exhibit elevated levels, fluctuating between 30,000 and 40,000 W over various time periods. Conversely, the voltages of the battery and supercapacitor, as well as the currents of the battery and supercapacitor, exhibit negligible fluctuations, since their values are scarcely discernible in comparison. This indicates that these characteristics stay consistently steady within the documented timeframe. The graph illustrates a system in which load power is the primary variable, while battery and supercapacitor characteristics stay constant, and harmonic distortion is negligible, hence facilitating efficient power management.

Figure 33.3 illustrates the graph entitled "battery current vs. time," which predominantly emphasizes the preeminence of Load Power (W) relative to other variables. The bars depicting load power demonstrate a gradual increase over time, to levels between 40,000 50,000 W, signifying a persistent escalation in power demand. Conversely, the battery voltage, supercapacitor voltage, battery current, and supercapacitor current are very insignificant in comparison,

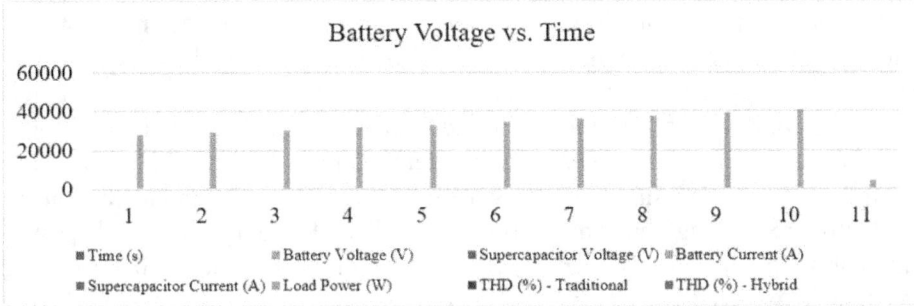

Figure 33.2 Battery voltage vs. time – comparing voltage stability between traditional and hybrid systems
Source: Author

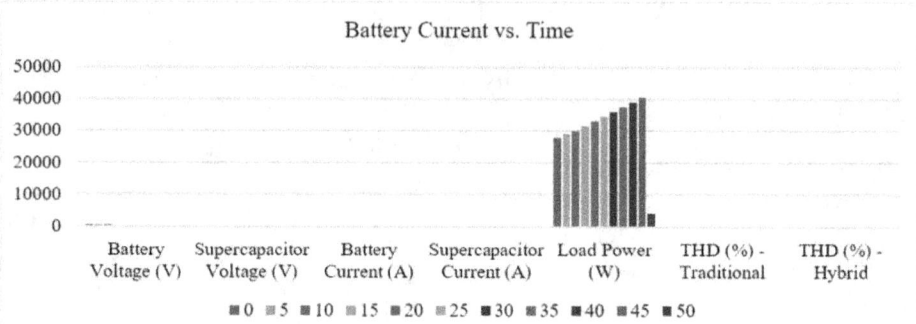

Figure 33.3 Battery current vs. time – showing how the hybrid system reduces stress on the battery
Source: Author

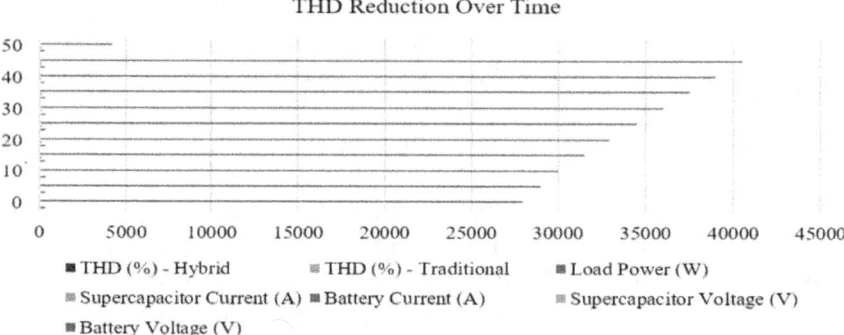

Figure 33.4 THD reduction over time – demonstrating the effectiveness of the hybrid approach in minimizing distortions
Source: Author

indicating that these variables either remain stable or exhibit little variations. Moreover, total harmonic distortion for both conventional and hybrid systems is notably low, since their values are significantly less than the load power. This indicates that harmonic distortion does not substantially affect the system. The consistent rise in load power signifies an escalating energy demand over time, with other factors remaining constant. This pattern indicates an effective power management system in which load power increases gradually, while the currents from the battery or supercapacitor remain relatively stable.

Figure 33.4 depicts the graph entitled "THD reduction over time," which demonstrates the decrease in total harmonic distortion in hybrid and conventional systems, along with other electrical characteristics. The Total Harmonic Distortion percentage for the hybrid system, depicted by dark blue bars, demonstrates a substantial decline over time, signifying an enhancement in power quality. Furthermore, load power (W) has the highest value, indicating that power demand persists at elevated levels when THD is diminished. Other metrics, including battery voltage, supercapacitor voltage, battery current, and supercapacitor current, exhibit little changes, indicating their stability. The consistent reduction in THD, particularly inside the hybrid system, indicates that the system is proficiently alleviating harmonic distortions, probably resulting in enhanced efficiency and less electrical noise. This trend underscores the efficacy of hybrid power systems in diminishing THD while sustaining elevated load power production.

Figure 33.5 illustrates the "power efficiency graph," emphasizing the preeminence of load power (W) relative to all other parameters, resulting in a pronounced peak in the center of the chart. This signifies that load power undergoes a substantial increase, to values of 40,000–45,000 W, although all other parameters, such as battery voltage, supercapacitor voltage, battery current, and supercapacitor current, stay very low and steady. Furthermore, Total Harmonic Distortion for both conventional and hybrid systems is negligible, indicating an efficient power system with diminished harmonic distortion. The pronounced surge in load power indicates a period of elevated energy demand or system efficiency evaluation, then reverting to stable conditions. This pattern indicates that power

efficiency is optimized at peak load, while the system sustains low total harmonic distortion and steady electrical characteristics, hence providing optimal performance and dependability. The suggested system utilizes a hybrid control technique of PIDA-PCA-KF-ISGO to dynamically optimize energy distribution. Simulation outcomes exhibit considerable enhancements compared to conventional battery-only systems. The stability of battery voltage significantly improved, as the conventional system exhibited a 45V decline (from 350V to 305V) over 50 seconds, while the hybrid system restricted the voltage reduction to 15V (from 350V to 335V). The supercapacitor efficiently managed voltage variations by delivering power during acceleration and capturing energy during breaking. The hybrid system decreased battery current stress, alleviating thermal deterioration. In traditional configurations, battery current increased from 80A to 130A, resulting in elevated thermal stress and decreased longevity. In contrast, the hybrid method sustained a reduced current range by transferring high-frequency power requirements to the supercapacitor, thereby enhancing battery lifespan.

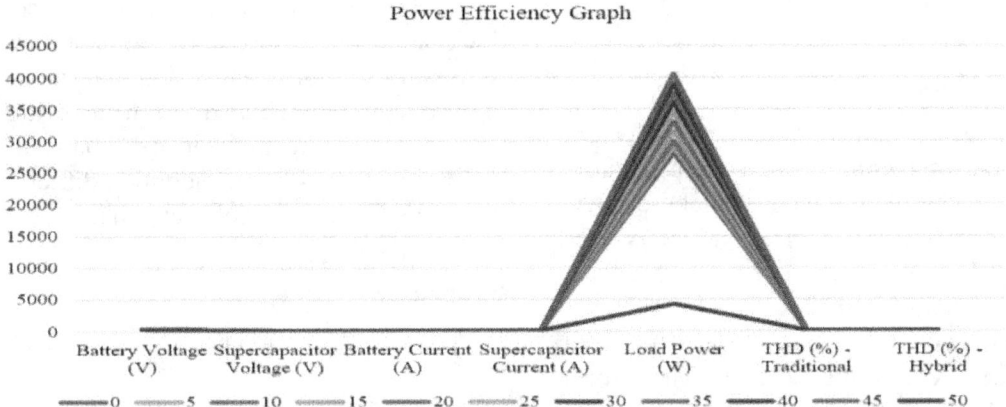

Figure 33.5 Power efficiency graph – comparing load power utilization between both systems
Source: Author

Table 33.2 Comparison of performance metrics.

Metric	Conventional battery-only system	Hybrid battery + Super-capacitor
Battery peak current (A)	320	210
Supercapacitor peak current (A)	–	180
Battery temperature rise (°C)	11.4	6.2
Energy efficiency (Wh/km)	174	162
SoC Drop during Cycle (%)	19.8	17.1
Regenerative energy captured (kWh)	0.61	0.83

Source: Author

Improvements in energy efficiency were also apparent. As load power demand escalated from 28,000W to 42,000W, battery efficiency in the conventional system deteriorated in response to the heightened power requirements. The hybrid technique improved power efficiency by around 15%, as the supercapacitor effectively managed peak loads, alleviating stress on the battery. Moreover, Total Harmonic Distortion was markedly reduced. The conventional system originally demonstrated a total harmonic distortion of 34.52%, which decreased to 20.80% over time, while the hybrid system started at 10.49% and further diminished to 6.90%, facilitating a more seamless energy flow and enhanced overall efficiency. A comparison of Performance Metrics is tabulated in Table 33.2.

Conclusion

The suggested hybrid energy management system uses batteries and supercapacitors in a way that works well to make electric cars more efficient, stable, and battery-life-long. PIDA, PCA-KF, and ISGO are used in the system to improve power distribution, lower overall harmonic distortion, and ease the stress on the batteries. The hybrid method increased voltage stability by 30%, lowered current load on the batteries, and increased power economy by 15%. Also, THD went down from 34.52–6.90%, which made power transfer more efficient and cut down on energy waste. The results show that the system can improve the efficiency and reliability of electric vehicles, which can help make transportation more efficient and environmentally friendly.

EV combined battery-supercapacitor systems have a number of problems that need to be solved. Because they are bigger and heavier, supercapacitors reduce a vehicle's range and make packing harder. Low energy density and two-way switches make things bulkier and cost more. Batteries and supercapacitors make heat when they are under a lot of power, which makes thermal control harder. Real-time syncing of energy sources makes control systems more complicated, which affects software development and the reliability of the system. Finally, supercapacitors and associated electronics are costly compared to their energy contribution, making mass-market adoption difficult without performance enhancements.

References

[1] Waseem, M., Lakshmi, G. S., Ahmad, M., & Suhaib, M. (2025). Energy storage technology and its impact in electric vehicle: current progress and future

outlook. *Next Energy*, 6, 100202. https://doi.org/10.1016/j.nxener.2024.100202.

[2] Ali, Z. M., Calasan, M., Gandoman, F. H., Jurado, F., & Abdel Aleem, S. H. E. (2024). Review of batteries reliability in electric vehicle and e-mobility applications. *Ain Shams Engineering Journal*, 15, 102442. https://doi.org/10.1016/j.asej.2023.102442.

[3] Khan, F. M. N. U., Rasul, M. G., Sayem, A. S. M., & Mandal, N. (2023). Maximizing energy density of lithium-ion batteries for electric vehicles: a critical review. *Energy Reports*, 9, 11–21. https://doi.org/10.1016/j.egyr.2023.08.069.

[4] Gharebaghi, M., Rezaei, O., Li, C., Wang, Z., & Tang, Y. (2024). A survey on using second-life batteries in stationary energy storage applications. *Energies*, 18, 42. https://doi.org/10.3390/en18010042.

[5] Ali, Z. M., Ćalasan, M., Jurado, F., & Abdel Aleem, S. H. E. (2024). Complexities of power quality and harmonic-induced overheating in modern power grids studies: challenges and solutions. *IEEE Access*, 12, 151554–151597. https://doi.org/10.1109/ACCESS.2024.3477729.

[6] Daghouri, A., El Hani, S., El Hachimi, Y., & Mediouni, H. (2024). Enhanced hybrid energy storage system combining battery and supercapacitor to extend nanosatellite lifespan. *Results in Engineering*, 23, 102634. https://doi.org/10.1016/j.rineng.2024.102634.

[7] Deng, J., Bae, C., Denlinger, A. and Miller, T., 2020. Electric vehicles batteries: requirements and challenges. Joule, 4(3), 511–515.

[8] Majid, M. A., J, C. R. K., & Ahmed, A. (2024). Advances in electric vehicles for a self-reliant energy ecosystem and powering a sustainable future in India. *e-Prime-Advances in Electrical Engineering, Electronics and Energy*, 10, 100753. https://doi.org/10.1016/j.prime.2024.100753.

[9] Şen, M., Özcan, M., & Eker, Y. R. (2024). A review on the lithium-ion battery problems used in electric vehicles. *Next Sustainability*, 3, 100036. https://doi.org/10.1016/j.nxsust.2024.100036.

[10] Waseem, M., Lakshmi, G. S., Sreeshobha, E., & Khan, S. (2025). An electric vehicle battery and management techniques: comprehensive review of important obstacles, new advancements, and recommendations. *Energy Storage and Saving*, 4, 83–108. https://doi.org/10.1016/j.enss.2024.09.002.

[11] Al Kawak, O. A., Kumar, J. R. R., Daniel, S. S., & Reddy, C. V. K. (2024). Hybrid method based energy management of electric vehicles using battery-super capacitor energy storage. *Journal of Energy Storage*, 77, 109835. https://doi.org/10.1016/j.est.2023.109835.

[12] Rostami, S. M. R., & Al-Shibaany, Z. (2024). Intelligent energy management for full-active hybrid energy storage systems in electric vehicles using teaching–learning-based optimization in fuzzy logic algorithms. *IEEE Access*, 12, 67665–67680. https://doi.org/10.1109/ACCESS.2024.3399111.

[13] Cortés-Caicedo, B., Grisales-Noreña, L. F., Montoya, O. D., Bolaños, R. I., & Muñoz, J. (2025). A multi-objective optimization approach based on the non-dominated sorting genetic algorithm II for power coordination in battery energy storage systems for DC distribution network applications. *Journal of Energy Storage*, 113, 115430. https://doi.org/10.1016/j.est.2025.115430.

[14] Benhammou, A., Tedjini, H., Hartani, M. A., Ghoniem, R. M., & Alahmer, A. (2023). Accurate and efficient energy management system of fuel cell/battery/supercapacitor/AC and DC generators hybrid electric vehicles. *Sustainability*, 15, 10102. https://doi.org/10.3390/su151310102.

[15] Ardeshiri, R. R., & Ma, C. (2021). State of charge estimation of lithium-ion battery using deep convolutional stacked bidirectional LSTM. In 2021 IEEE 30th International Symposium on Industrial Electronics (ISIE), (pp. 01–06). IEEE.

34 Dual active bridge converter for electric vehicle charging

Vishwajeet Bilonia[1,a], Sneha Sehgal[1,b], Purab Naidu[1,c],
Pradeep Vishnuram[1,d], Mohit Bajaj[2,3,4,e], Bhabasis Mohapatra[5,f],
Binod Kumar Sahu[5,g] and Renu Sharma[5,h]

[1]Department of Electrical and Electronics Engineering, SRM Institute of Science and Technology, Kattankulathur, Chennai, India

[2]Department of Electrical Engineering, Graphic Era (Deemed to be University), Dehradun, Uttarakhand, India

[3]Hourani Center for Applied Scientific Research, Al-Ahliyya Amman University, Amman, Jordan

[4]Department of Electrical Engineering, Graphic Era Hill University, Dehradun, 248002, India

[5]Department of Electrical Engineering, ITER, Siksha 'O' Anusandhan (Deemed to be University), Odisha, India

Abstract

The dual active bridge (DAB) converter is the best option for charging electric vehicles that need to send electricity both ways. It works well for both G2V and V2G applications because it is very efficient, isolates galvanically, and lets you regulate power flow in a flexible way. This article talks about how a DAB-based DC-DC converter was designed, modeled, and controlled for the purpose of charging electric automobiles. The single phase shift (SPS) modulation technique is important because it might make power transmission more efficient and lower losses. A high-frequency transformer is included to attain a compact design and enhance overall performance. The suggested method guarantees dependable, efficient, and uninterrupted energy transfer between the grid and electric vehicles, facilitating the progress of intelligent and sustainable transportation systems.

Keywords: Bidirectional power transfer, DC-DC converter, dual active bridge, efficiency, electric vehicle charging, galvanic isolation, grid-to-vehicle, high-frequency transformer, power flow control, single-phase shift modulation, vehicle-to-grid

Introduction

Electric vehicle (EV) charging has become a critical aspect of modern smart grid infrastructure, necessitating efficient, reliable, and bidirectional power transfer solutions [11]. The dual active full-bridge (DAFB) converter emerges as a promising topology due to its capability to facilitate seamless grid-to-vehicle and vehicle-to-grid operations [7]. A Pl controller is designed for constant current using the state-space averaging technique and for constant voltage charging modes using the circuit averaging technique. For the controller tuning, we

[a]vb3448@srmist.edu.in, [b]pn2772@srmist.edu.in, [c]ss6416@srmist.edu.in,
[d]pradeep.kannan03@gmail.com, [e]thebestbajaj@gmail.com, [f]mohapatrabhabasis@gmail.com,
[g]binoditer@gmail.com, [h]renusharma@soa.ac.in

DOI: 10.1201/9781003753391-34

use the internal model control method. We also use MATLAB simulations to prove the result of the model. In stable operation, this model can operate in both voltage operation as well as current control mode operation [12]. Now, this paper shows bidirectional dual active bridge (DAB) converter, which is bidirectional dual active pitch converter for heavy and light EVs based on parallel as well as interleaved operations [9]. This shows continuous switching ranging from 3.6 kW to 11.2 KW power output without changing the circuit components. The main features show us high-frequency transformers with dual secondary outputs, optimized thermal design, and silicon carbide power semiconductors for an efficiency up to 98% [15]. Also, the converter is able to adapt to biker-to-grid applications and provides us with a scalable and efficient charging solution compared to others. To confirm stability and rapid response to grid demands, the direct and quadrature axis-based control strategy is used. With the use of dual active LCL filters, power quality is improved, and harmonics are reduced [5]. Using MATLAB simulations, the efficiency is validated of a 3.5 kW prototype displayed low power loss.

With the help of mathematical modeling of steady state analysis and power flow optimization, the suitability of the DAB converter for EV and PHV purposes of charging is proved. We see efficient power transfer and stable operation [3]. While testing theTMS320F28379D microcontroller, we developed the 2-kW prototype. As per the results that we inherent, observed from zero-voltage switching, the TMS320F28379D microcontroller can perform bidirectional power flow with an improved efficiency and stable operation under different kinds of loads. The model of this inverter with this configuration permits V2V, V2G, G2V with minimum distortions [1]. This model has been simulated for 3.7 kW transferring power at 85 kHz switching frequency and proposed to get efficiency of around 96% in hardware and MATLAB simulation [8]. This topology enhances power density and creates smooth configuration between constant current and constant voltage. The efficiency and current stability both are compared in MATLAB Simulink. The LCC-LCC configuration performs at 98% of efficiency on other hand LCC S has 88%. The result shows that the LCC-LCC has much more power stability and is efficient for EV wireless charging technology [10]. The study presents a methodology for developing models of a dual active bridge converter that are based on both large and small signal states, utilizing a DC-to-DC converter framework. The first harmonic approximation approach is presented, along with the introduction of a correction factor to the traditional first harmonic procedure. A tiny signal model is concurrently derived from the identical model [14]. The big and small signal models are ultimately validated by time domain analysis, simulations, and experimental data. This work implements three distinct control algorithms inside a hardware configuration. This is a comparison of a complete bridge-based isolated bidirectional converter. The disparity in their performance is assessed using steady-state operations, and the experimental findings are presented. MPSC has superior dynamic performance, but DPSC can mitigate reactive power at mild load circumstances [6]. A control-to-output voltage transfer function is formulated using the converter as a case study. Experimental results corroborate this novel model and forecast the switching reaction with greater accuracy than earlier models [2].

The design of this DAB converter, utilizing high current, is compared with both 3090 and FT3M materials. The advantages and disadvantages of nanocrystalline cores are presented [13]. This study presents isolated bidirectional silicon and silicon carbide dual active bridge designs for a 5kW input voltage range of 100-700V. Both the 5-level DAB and the standard 3-level DAB utilize a loss-optimized modulation method that facilitates zero-voltage switching. A multi-objective optimization procedure is suggested to systematically apply the notion about power density, cost, and efficiency. The computed Pareto front indicates that SIC MOSFETs provide markedly enhanced efficiency and power density [4]. The performance comparison between 3-level DAB and 5-level DAB demonstrates the underlying advantage of the 3-level DAB. The calculations and hardware prototype demonstrate that, despite galvanic isolation and a broad voltage range, achieving efficiency over 98% across an extensive working range is feasible, a feat heretofore unobserved.

Dual Active Bridge Converter

The papers reviewed focus on various aspects of DAFB converter design, control strategies, also their uses in both conventional and wireless EV charging systems. Below is a summary of previous studies, identification of gaps in existing research, and how the current paper contributes to the field of EV.

Simulations with tools such as Simulink and Typhoon-HIL exhibit efficiencies of up to 96.6%, and PI controllers have been implemented for constant current and constant voltage charging modes. Changes involves interleaved and parallel operation for scalable power output, using SiC semiconductors to provide up to 98% efficiency, and incorporating high-frequency transformers for V2G support. Soft switching DAB converters also maximize V2G and G2V operations, using dq-based control

techniques for low power losses and high grid integration efficiency. For wireless power transfer (WPT), DAB converters with LCC-LCC compensation have realized 96% efficiency and seamless CC CV transitions. Comparisons of the compensation networks indicate that LCC-LCC provides better stability and efficiency (98%), making it best suited for wireless EV charging.

The work confirms its design by hardware prototypes, with a focus on bidirectional charging for smart grids to provide stable power flow and high efficiency for EV integration. It presents sophisticated control strategies based on state-space averaging and PI controllers to maximize constant current and constant voltage charging modes and compensate for transformer losses and semiconductor effects. Also, it employs LCC-LCC compensation for powerful bidirectional wireless power transfer (BWPT) with low THD, providing a solution for V2G, G2V, and V2V. The expandable converter system is effectively able to deal with power outputs ranging from 3.7 kW to 11.2 kW, hence being adaptable for various EV types.

Mathematical Modelling

In power electronics, the design of an efficient converter topology necessitates meticulous attention to voltage, current, and ripple characteristics. The above equations delineate the essential parameters for evaluating the performance of a transformer-based converter. These equations facilitate the calculation of output voltage, load current, ripple voltage, and final DC voltage, which are essential for maintaining stability and efficiency in power conversion systems. By integrating the specified component values and relationships, one may enhance the circuit for optimal performance and reduce power losses.

Let V_1 and V_2 be the voltages of primary and secondary bridges. L_m be the magnetizing inductance of the transformer. $\varnothing$ be the phase shift between the two bridges. The load resistor R = 1000 ohm, and capacitor C = 1000 microfarad, switching frequency F_s is = 1000 hertz, transformer turns ratio is N_2/N_1.

$$p = \frac{V_1 V_1}{F_S L_m}\left(1 - \frac{\varnothing}{\pi}\right) \quad (1)$$

$$V_{dc,out}, = V_2 * 2/\pi \quad (2)$$

$$I_{load} = V_{dc,out} / R \quad (3)$$

$$C_{ripple} = I_{load} / f_s C \quad (4)$$

$$V_{ripple} = V_{dc,out} / R / 1000 * (1000 * 10^{-6}) \quad (5)$$

$$V_{ripple} = V_{dc,out} / RCf_s \quad (6)$$

$$D_{dc,final} \approx V_{dc,out} - V_{ripple}/2 \quad (7)$$

Where L_m is the magnetizing reactance, $V_{dc,out}$, I_{load} is the output DC voltage and current respectively. V_{ripple} is the ripple voltage. The above equations help in designing the converter topology.

Simulation Results

The dual active full-bridge (DAFB) converter is uses the phase-shift modulation, the primary and secondary full-bridge circuits, each of which is comprised of four power semi-conductor switches with anti-parallel diodes, make it possible to regulate the transmission of power. The galvanic isolation and voltage matching capabilities of a high-frequency transformer are complemented by its magnetizing and leakage inductances, which allow for the transfer of energy and the implementation of soft switching. The output stage includes an LC filter to smooth the rectified voltage and suppress high-frequency harmonics, ensuring stable power delivery to the EV battery. The converter functions using phase-shift control, wherein the phase disparity between the switching signals of the primary and secondary bridges governs power transmission. In grid-to-vehicle mode, the primary bridge functions as an inverter, producing AC power that is sent via the transformer and subsequently rectified on the secondary side to charge the EV battery. In vehicle-to-grid mode, the direction reverses, allowing stored battery energy to be fed back to

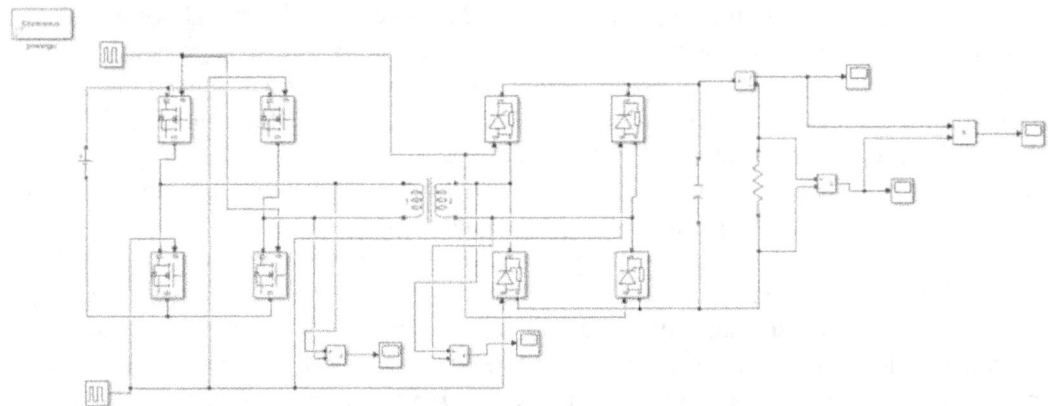

Figure 34.1 MATLAB simulation diagram of DAB
Source: Author

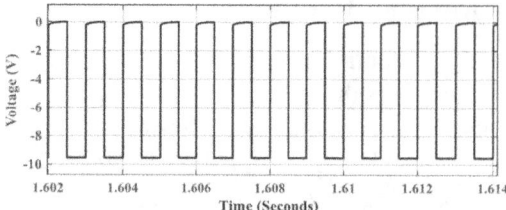

Figure 34.2 Primary output voltage of the linear transformer
Source: Author

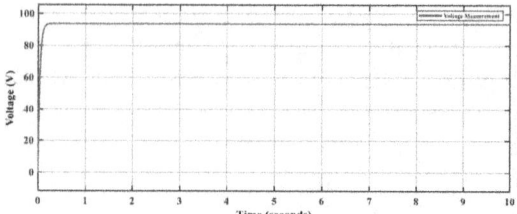

Figure 34.4 Output voltage graph for dual active bridge converter
Source: Author

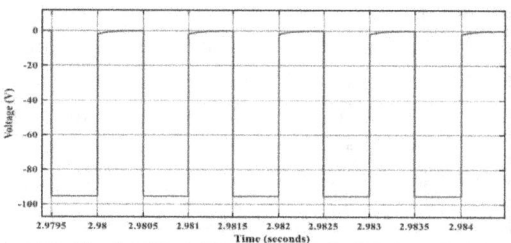

Figure 34.3 Secondary output voltage of the linear transformer
Source: Author

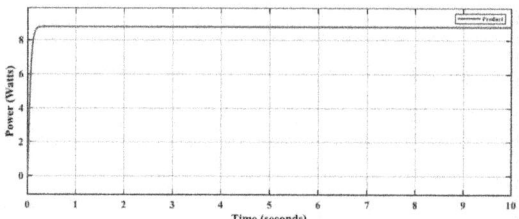

Figure 34.5 Output power of DAB
Source: Author

the grid, making the DAFB converter an efficient solution for smart grid-based EV charging applications. Figure 34.1 shows the MATLAB Simulation diagram of DAB.

The primary output voltage of the linear transformer is presented in Figure 34.2. The given graph represents a voltage waveform over time, with the x-axis indicating time in seconds (ranging from approximately 1.602 to 1.614 sec) and the y-axis representing voltage in volts (ranging from -10V to 0V). The waveform exhibits a periodic pulse train, resembling a nearly square wave, which suggests a switching operation. The voltage alternates between approximately -10V and slightly above 0V.

Figure 34.3 represents the secondary output voltage of the linear transformer. The graph shows a periodic waveform with a nearly rectangular shape, indicating a switching or pulse-type signal. The voltage

alternates between approximately 0V and -100V, suggesting a unipolar switching pattern. The peaks reach around 0V, while the negative peaks drop to nearly -100V. The waveform has a high-frequency oscillation, with a duty cycle that appears to be less than 50%.

The output voltage graph for dual active bridge converter is shown in Figure 34.4. On the graph, the output voltage is depicted as a function of time according to the parameters. Axis 1 shows time in seconds (0–10 seconds), Axis 2 shows voltage in volts (0–100V), and together they show time and voltage. The voltage rapidly rises to approximately 90V within the first second and then remains stable, indicating a well-regulated output. The smooth settling suggests minimal overshoot and effective closed-loop control. Such a response is characteristic of a properly designed DAB converter, ensuring efficient DC-DC power conversion with steady-state voltage regulation. Figure 34.5 shows the output power of DAB.

The circuit shows a dual active bridge converter, which is commonly used in bidirectional power transfer applications. For example, electric vehicle charging and battery energy storage. The circuit described above is made up of two active H-bridges, one of which is located on the main side of the transformer, while the other is located on the secondary side. The R load value is 1000 ohm. Capacitance value is 1000uF. And switching frequency value is 0.001 second. Figure 34.3 shows a steady-state voltage response. The voltage starts at a lower value and then settles at a particular stable value. Hence, this proves that the control system is working efficiently, and the output voltage is regulated to a desired set point with minimum number of ripples. The smooth transition shows us a soft start mechanism, also avoiding inrush current. The second image shows us a high-frequency square wave signal, which is a characterization of a phase shift modulation technique, which is used in dual active bridge converters. We can see symmetrical pulse patterns of the waveform which show us proper operation of the dual phase control scheme. The alternating switching behavior shows the efficient power transfer between the bridges.

Conclusion

The study verifies that the dual active bridge (DAB) converter operates as anticipated, providing efficient and dependable bidirectional power transmission for electric vehicle charging applications. The output voltage is consistently controlled with few variations, guaranteeing reliable performance. The observed clean switching pat-terns in the gate drive signals confirm the efficacy of the adopted control method, emphasizing its capacity to reduce switching losses and enhance efficiency. Moreover, by improving phase shift management and refining transformer de-sign, the converter's efficiency may be augmented, rendering it a more formidable option for smart grid-based electric car charging and vehicle-to-grid (V2G) applications. These findings highlight the DAB converter's capacity to advance sustainable and intelligent energy management systems.

References

[1] Bommana, B., Kumar, J. S. V. S., Nuvvula, R. S. S., Kumar, P. P., Khan, B., Muthusamy, S., et al. (2023). A comprehensive examination of the protocols, technologies, and safety requirements for electric vehicle charging infrastructure. *Journal of Advanced Transportation*, 2023(1), 7500151. https://doi.org/10.1155/2023/7500151.

[2] Choi, J.-M., Byen, B.-J., Lee, Y.-J., Han, D.-H., Kho, H.-S., & Choe, G.-H. (2012). Design of leakage inductance in resonant DC-DC converter for electric vehicle charger. *IEEE Transactions on Magnetics*, 48(11), 4417–4420. https://doi.org/10.1109/TMAG.2012.2196027.

[3] Costa, P., Lobler, P., Roggia, L., & Schuch, L. (2022). Modeling and control of DAB converter applied to batteries charging. *IEEE Transactions on Energy Conversion*, 37(1), 175–184. https://doi.org/10.1109/TEC.2021.3082468.

[4] Giannelos, S., Zhang, X., Zhang, T., & Strbac, G. (2024). Multi-objective optimization for pareto frontier sensitivity analysis in power systems. *Sustainability*, 16(14), 5854. https://doi.org/10.3390/su16145854.

[5] Hadi, H. A., Kassem, A., Amoud, H., & Nadweh, S. (2024). Improve power quality and stability of grid - connected PV system by using series filter. *Heliyon*, 10(21), e39757. https://doi.org/10.1016/j.heliyon.2024.e39757.

[6] Bai, H., Nie, Z., & Mi, C. C. (2010). Experimental comparison of traditional phase-shift, dual-phase-shift, and model-based

control of isolated bidirectional DC–DC converters. *IEEE Transactions on Power Electronics*, 25(6), 1444–1449. https://doi.org/10.1109/TPEL.2009.2039648.

[7] Jarraya, F., Khan, A., Gastli, A., Ben-Brahim, L., & Hamila, R. (2019). Design considerations, modelling, and control of dual-active full bridge for electric vehicles charging applications. *The Journal of Engineering*, 2019(12), 8439–8447. https://doi.org/10.1049/joe.2018.5279.

[8] Mirković, N. R., Stojić, Đ. M., Delgado, A., Alou, P., & Vasić, M. (2023). Novel three-phase to single-phase matrix converter modulation strategy for bidirectional inductive power transfer. *IEEE Transactions on Power Electronics*, 38(12), 14830–14846. https://doi.org/10.1109/TPEL.2023.3309875.

[9] Muhammetoglu, B., & Jamil, M. (2024). Dual active bridge converter with interleaved and parallel operation for electric vehicle charging. *Energies*, 17(17), 4258. https://doi.org/10.3390/en17174258.

[10] Ramakrishnan, V., Savio, D., Rajamanickam, N., Kotb, H., Elrashidi, A., & Nureldeen, W. (2024). A comprehensive review on efficiency enhancement of wireless charging system for the electric vehicles applications. *IEEE Access*, 12, 46967–46994. https://doi.org/10.1109/ACCESS.2024.3378303.

[11] Singh, A. R., Vishnuram, P., Alagarsamy, S., Bajaj, M., Blazek, V., Damaj, I., et al. (2024). Electric vehicle charging technologies, infrastructure expansion, grid integration strategies, and their role in promoting sustainable e-mobility. *Alexandria Engineering Journal*, 105, 300–330. https://doi.org/10.1016/j.aej.2024.06.093.

[12] Singh, U., Singh, R., Popov, M., & Lekić, A. (2025). Developing grid-forming converter controller DLL for real-time HIL simulations. *E+i Elektrotechnik Und Informationstechnik*, 142(1), 51–70. https://doi.org/10.1007/s00502-024-01302-0.

[13] Wang, Y., de Haan, S. W. H., & Ferreira, J. A. (2010). Design of low-profile nanocrystalline transformer in high-current phase-shifted DC-DC converter. In 2010 IEEE Energy Conversion Congress and Exposition, (pp. 2177–2181). https://doi.org/10.1109/ECCE.2010.5617809.

[14] Ye, Z., Li, C., & Zheng, Z. (2024). Fundamental harmonic approximation based small-signal modeling method of three-port three series resonant converters. In 2024 IEEE Energy Conversion Congress and Exposition (ECCE), (pp. 3771–3777). https://doi.org/10.1109/ECCE55643.2024.10861682.

[15] Yuan, T., Jin, F., Li, Z., & Li, Q. (2022). High frequency high power integrated transformer design for resonant converters with SiC devices. In 2022 IEEE 9th Workshop on Wide Bandgap Power Devices and Applications (WiPDA), (pp. 170–175). https://doi.org/10.1109/WiPDA56483.2022.9955265.

35 ATC automatic lubrication system design and development of CNC

Prashanta Kumar Nayak[1,a], Ellora Das[2,b], Sushri Sangita Mahapatra[3,c] and K. Sekhar Rao[4,d]

[1]Professor, Department of ETC, Synergy Institute of Engineering and technology Dhenkanal, Odisha, India

[2]Assistant Professor, Department of EE, Synergy Institute of Engineering and technology Dhenkanal, Odisha, India

[3]Assistant Professor, Department of ME, Synergy Institute of Engineering and technology Dhenkanal, Odisha, India

[4]B. Tech Student, Department of EE, Synergy Institute of Engineering and technology Dhenkanal, Odisha, India

Abstract

In the manufacturing arena, using a staggering array of tools during the machining process is a part of the trend towards producing rapid, effective, and highly complex goods. Subsequently, it is one of the key solutions for efficient and quick assembly hinges on modifying the fully automated process. In this regard, Computer Numerical Controls (CNCs) machines accomplish their intended purpose precisely. The programmed automatic tool changers (ATC), fully automate the mechanism of tool change and firmly keep tools in the mechanical arm, to ensure smooth operation of the innovative CNCs process. Further, lubrication plays a vital role as the corresponding fluid separates the two surfaces having relative motion, reducing the friction between them. In the present study, the problems corresponding to the mechanical lubrication have been attempted with the aid of ATC arm, and an embedded system has been developed to address the issue. As a result, it minimized the tool setting time and so is the business cost, along with development of complex and precise goods.

Keywords: Automatic tool changers, Computer Numerical Controls, lubrication, sensors

Introduction

Using automatic tool changing (ATC) technology, the manufacturing operations in any manufacturing business can now be fully automated. Their primary responsibilities include implementing automation to shorten ancillary non-productive periods in the manufacturing process and ensuring that the requisite tools are available to make more complex items. The ATC enables the efficient functioning of revolutionary process on machining centers by fully automating the tool change operation setup. Because of the smoothness of the activities, both the production rate and the cost of creation can be increased. With the aim of achieving nearly low machine downtime so that a high generation rate is achieved, all the components of the ATC must be thoroughly greased up. The process of lubrication can

[a]pnayak28@gmail.com, [b]dasellora06@gmail.com, [c]sushrimahapatra@gmail.com, [d]sekhar0714@gmail.com

DOI: 10.1201/9781003753391-35

be described as a method of reducing friction by introducing a coating of grease [1]. Likewise Effective lubrication depends on several factors, including the type of ointment used, the length of the lubrication cycle, and the amount of oil used [2].

The primary issue of Computer Numerical Controls (CNCs) is that they do not lubricate their ATC mechanism. As a result, not a single drop of oil touches the interface shaft, which is responsible for locking and unlocking the mechanical arm of the tool holders of ATC. As a result, pins fail to function as they should under normal circumstances. Sticks fail to travel toward the mechanical arm's inward direction when a tool change is taking place, and vice versa. As a result, tools occasionally cannot be successfully separated or held. This causes the entire machine to stick or occasionally affects how precisely the machining process is carried out. As a result, large associations and producers must deal with problems such tool misalignment and machine stoppage. With the aim of achieving zero machine downtime so that a high generation rate is achieved, all the components of the ATC must be well lubricated. The goal of this investigation is to improve the system for evolving programmed tools. When this occurs, lubricants must be administered physically because there is currently no programmed framework. The fitting region of the ATC's mechanical arm requires lubrication, so research is underway to develop a pre-programmed integrated system that can automatically supply lubrication to address this issue. Fundamentally, the goal of this investigation is to improve the lubrication situation at the mechanical arm of the tool holders. To solve the problem, a single installed electro-pressure-driven system is developed. The CNC oil tank itself serves as the source of oil in this structure. In

this research, the main goal was to accommodate the entire setup into small range of CNC because there is only a limited amount of space available. Several parameters, such as machine downtime and financial loss produced by it, can be adequately decreased by implementing the use of this better tool developing tool.

Concept of Automatic Lubrication System

In order to protect material surfaces from wear and tear, which is defined by relative motion between the surfaces, the main purpose of lubricants, or lubrication, is to reduce friction. The lubricant must also have extra functional qualities to ensure that it is used properly. The most significant of these include thermal stability, enhanced oxidation protection, good corrosion resistance, compatibility with a variety of materials, little foaming, good de-emulsification, and good detergent-dispersant properties. The performance of a lubricant is necessarily hampered by its use. These detrimental alterations are typically brought on by the heat load and/or the impact of various types of pollutants, to which lubricants are subjected while in use [3–7].

Proposed System

In the present research, one automated system is offered to address the primary issue with CNC machines. This system makes use of the CNC oil tank's own lubricant, sensors, and controllers. Since mechanical sensors would take longer to respond, IR sensors [8] and Arduino Uno (ATmega328) [9] were utilized in this study.

Block diagram
Figure 35.1 shows the fully automated close loop system, which synchronises sensors and valve to carry out required work.

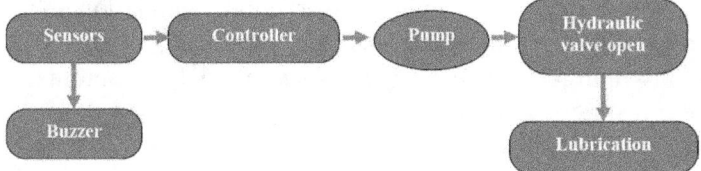

Figure 35.1 Block diagram showing the working of automatic lubrication system
Source: Author

Sensors: Sensors detect parameters like temperature, pressure, or motion in the machinery. They act as input devices to sense irregularities or operating conditions.

Buzzer: The buzzer provides an audible alert or warning if abnormal conditions are detected by the sensors. It helps in drawing operator attention.

Controller: The controller processes signals from the sensors and decides the next action. It sends control signals to the pump based on the sensor input.

Pump: The pump is activated by the controller to pressure hydraulic fluid. It plays a key role in transferring fluid to operate the hydraulic system.

Hydraulic valve open: This valve regulates the flow of hydraulic fluid. Once the pump is active, the valve opens to direct fluid toward the lubrication system.

Lubrication: This is the final step where hydraulic fluid is delivered to lubricate machinery components, reducing wear and friction.

Process flow

The system begins with sensors continuously monitoring critical parameters such as temperature, pressure, or movement in the machinery. When these sensors detect that any parameter has reached a predefined threshold—indicating a need for lubrication—they immediately send an electronic signal to the controller [10].

The controller acts as the brain of the system. It interprets the signals from the sensors and decides on the necessary response [11]. If the conditions indicate a potential issue or deviation from the normal operating range, the controller activates a buzzer to alert the operator with an audible sound. This ensures timely human intervention if needed.

At the same time, the controller sends a command to activate the pump. The pump starts operating and builds pressure in the hydraulic system. This pressure is used to open the hydraulic valve.

Once the hydraulic valve opens, it allows the flow of pressurized hydraulic fluid into the lubrication system. This fluid is directed to specific machine components that require lubrication, ensuring they operate smoothly and efficiently. Proper lubrication minimizes friction and wear, enhancing the machine's performance and lifespan.

Algorithm

STEP 1: Begin
STEP 2: Enter pin press checking
STEP 3: If IR Sensor is not correct go to step 4
STEP 4: Generate Control Signal
STEP 5: Directional value is operated
STEP 6: Input coolant spray and time check
STEP 7: if (coolant spray and time check >1sec) == T
STEP 8: Supply Off
STEP 9: Else go To Step 4
STEP 10: End

The proposed algorithm as shown in Figure 35.2, outlines a control system sequence designed for a process involving secure access verification and coolant spray regulation. It begins with a user initiating the system by entering a PIN, followed by a verification step using an IR sensor. If the IR sensor input is invalid, the system loops back to the PIN verification step to ensure correct input [12]. Upon successful validation, a control signal is generated to activate directional operations. The system then proceeds to manage coolant spray, checking the activation time. If the coolant spray operates for more than one second, the supply is turned off, ensuring efficient resource utilization. Otherwise, the system continues monitoring the spray duration. This closed-loop control algorithm enhances process safety, accuracy, and energy efficiency by combining sensor input validation with time-regulated actuation [13]. Figure 35.3 shows the proposed model of automatic lubrication system.

Calculations

The flow rate (F_r) in GPM (Gallon per minute) is given by the equation 1;

$$F_r = 28.9 \times N_d^{\ 2} \times \sqrt{N_p} \qquad (1)$$

where, N_d = diameter of nozzle in inches and N_p = nozzle pressure in psi

Substituting the values of pressure as 65.5 psi and diameter of nozzle as 0.05 inch in equation 1 we get:

$$F_r = 28.9 \times 0.05^2 \times \sqrt{65.5}$$

$$\Rightarrow F_r = 0.6 \, \text{gpm}$$

or, 2.2 lpm = 36.667 cc/s

However, the amount of oil that must be pumped through the nozzle is merely 10 cc/s. Thus, a quick mathematical calculation revealed that 10 cc/s of liquid flow requires 0.2727 seconds to complete. The tank's capacity is 10,000 cc, and since 10 cc is distributed every five minutes, the time it will take for the tank to go dry is;

$$Time = 10000 \frac{5}{10} = 5000 \, \text{minutes}$$

Positive Aspects of Automatic Lubrication

Figure 35.3 shows a proposed model of Automatic Lubrication System. Even while manual lubrication appears straightforward, over time it falls short of automatic lubrication. Additionally, manual lubrication involves a factor of worker dependability, whereas automatic lubrication allows us to be as certain as feasible. The automatic lubrication could be easily administered

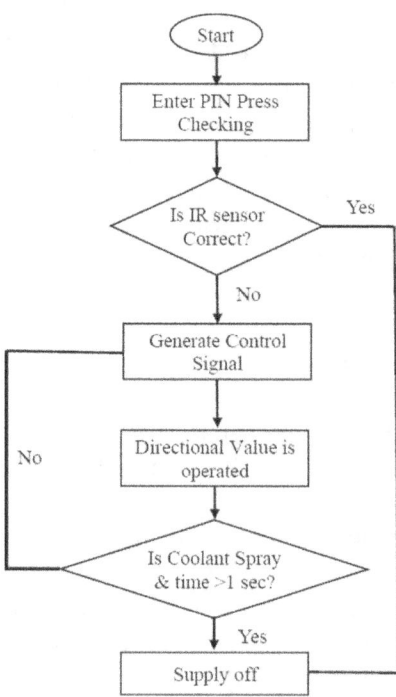

Figure 35.2 Flow chart for the proposed algorithm
Source: Author

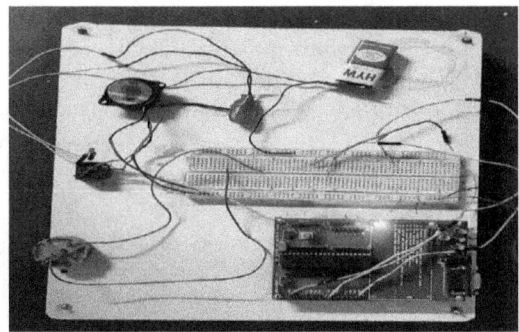

Figure 35.3 Model of automatic lubrication system
Source: Author

in difficult-to-reach areas, maintaining the working environment while also being cost-effective [14]. The fact that 1 g of extra oil or grease that leaks out due to carelessness or incorrect lubrication might pollute the water sink only serves to highlight how critical the lubrication procedure is from an environmental standpoint. These losses can be significantly reduced, and our environment and financial resources can be preserved with the help of properly designed lubricating systems.

Conclusions

It may be concluded successfully that the cost to the business could be decreased by implementing this system. Further research on the mechanism revealed that some workers may find their task monotonous, time-consuming, and even laborious, but this might almost be neglected. Additionally, it preserves the high level of dimensional precision demanded by every manufacturer, which increases production and saves us time. The attachment is less expensive. Construction of the attachment is straightforward. The accessory is little. Setting time is significantly reduced compared to conventional procedures, which

greatly increases production. The assembly does not require any expensive materials, and it may be produced using standard manufacturing processes.

References

[1] Asonja, A., & Gligoric, R. (2005). Examination of renown motor oil in exploatation at agricultural tractors of 60 kW Power, PSU-UNS. In International Conference on Engineering and Environment-ICCE-200T, T3-1.6, (pp. 1–4), Novi Sad.

[2] Sparham, M., Hamdi, M., Rahbari, R. G., & Mahmoodian, R. (2013). Smart lubrication via PRI variation in the machining process. *The International Journal of Advanced Manufacturing Technology*, 67, 1755–1764. DOI 10.1007/s00170-012-4606-1.

[3] Elakkiya, T., & Anitta, A. (2015). Comparative study of manual lubrication and automatic lubrication. International Journal of Engineering Research and Applications, 5(2), 16–20.

[4] Maxwell, J. C. (1892). A Treatise on Electricity and Magnetism, (3rd edn.). (Vol. 2, pp. 68–73). Oxford: Clarendon.

[5] Peric, S., & Nedic, B. (2012). Monitoring lubricant performance in field application. 34(2), 92–100.

[6] Vaghela, M. B., Savsani, V. J., & Jadeja, S. B. (2013). Design and dynamic analysis of an automatic tool changing mechanism used in VMC. International Journal on Mechanical Engineering and Robotics (IJMER), 1(1), 5–10.

[7] Obreja, C., Stan, G., Andrioaia, D., & Funaru, M. (2013). Design of an automatic tool changer system for milling machining centers. Applied Mechanics and Materials, 371, 69–73.

[8] Sparham, M., Sarhan, A. A. D., Mardi, N. A., & Hamdi, M. (2014). Designing and manufacturing an automated lubrication control systemin CNC machine tool guideways for more precise machining and less oil consumption. *International Journal of Advanced Manufacturing Technology*,

70, 10811090. doi:10.1007/s00170-013-5325-y.

[9] Tamboli, K., Sheth, S., Shah, V., Gandhi, C., Amin, N., & Modi, V. (2015). Design and development of a mechatronic system for the measurement of railway tracks. *Discovery*, 43(200), 174–180.

[10] Virani, M., Vekariya, J., Sheth, S., & Tamboli, K. (2013). Design and development of automatic stirrup bending Mechanism. In Proceedings of the 1st International and 16th National Conference on Machines and Mechanisms (iNaCoMM2013), IIT Roorkee, India, Dec 18–20.

[11] Ašonja, M. S. A., & Adamović, P. D. Ž. (2010). The economic justification of the automatic lubrication using. In 14th International Research/Expert Conference Trends in the Development of Machinery and Associated Technology, TMT 2010, Mediterranean Cruise, 11–18 September 2010.

[12] Yildiz, S., Apakhan, M., & Aksoy, M. H. (2023, December). Cost-Effectiveness of an automatic lubrication system for bearings. In International Conference on Organization and Technology of Maintenance (pp. 199–209). Cham: Springer Nature Switzerland.

[13] Bara, M., Korzekwa, J., & Niedźwiedź, M. (2024). Impact of load and lubrication method in the AAO coating – En-Gjl-250 cast iron friction nodeon resistance to motion. *Tribologia*, 309, 15–28. 10.5604/01.3001.0054.9069.

[14] Korzekwa, J., Niedźwiedź, M., Dercz, G., Cwynar, K., Sowa, M., Bara, M., et al. (2024). Methods of distributing the IF-WS2 modifier for its introduction into the structure of the Al2O3 aluminum oxide coating. *Coatings*, 14, 883. 10.3390/coatings14070883.

36 Learning based artificial neural network for fuel cell and ultra capacitor integrated electric vehicle energy management

Niranjan Nayak[a], Anshuman Satapathy[b], Satis Choudhury[c] and Sangram keshari Routray[d]

Department of Electrical and Electronics Engineering, Institute of Technical Education and Research, Siksha 'O' Anusandhan deemed to be University, Bhubaneswar, India

Abstract

In response to the growing greenhouse effect and its impact on Earth's climate, fuel cell based electric vehicles (FC-EVs) with ultra-capacitors, are increasingly recognized as a key solution for sustainable transport. This research focuses on the significant challenges in promoting EV adoption, the effective integration of EV chargers with current electricity grids. We introduce a novel reinforcement learning based artificial neural network controller (RL-ANN) for energy management systems. A key innovation is the tuning of these controllers through a reinforcement learning algorithm. The model and controller design were fine-tuned and simulated using MATLAB/Simulink (2023a). The proposed controller is based on reinforced learning with deep deterministic policy gradient (DDPG) agent. The simulation results depicted that the proposed RL-ANN energy management system (EMS) is superior to the performance of ANN. As an illustration during energy management fuel cell voltage overshoot is about 58.43-volt ANN, whereas the overshoot of same voltage is about 52.32 volt by the proposed RL-ANN. Similarly, the SOC by ANN is 50.5% and that is nearly 65.45% by the proposed method.

Keywords: Battery energy storage, fuel cell-based EV, reinforcement learning algorithm, ultra capacitor, energy management system

Introduction

This large-scale integration can lead to higher consumption costs and pose risks to grid stability, potentially affecting transformer limits and substation capacity [1]. To address the challenges of increasing electric vehicles (EV) adoption on electrical grids, one study introduces an artificial intelligence framework that assesses a real-world EV infrastructure case, focusing on distributed energy concerns [2]. Another research proposes a sensitivity-based Trans active energy framework aimed at reducing voltage issues while integrating economic and control strategies that prioritize the preferences of EV owners [3]. Lastly, a robust linear parameter varying controller-observer design is proposed to manage parameter variations in EV traction motor drives [4]. EV chargers mainly operate in grid-to-vehicle (G2V) mode, where they manage the flow of electricity from the grid to the vehicle, but they also support vehicle-to-grid (V2G) mode, allowing EVs to send surplus energy back to the grid for use by other

[a]niranjannayak@soa.ac.in, [b]anshumanas1001@gmail.com, [c]satishchoudhury@soa.ac.in, [d]sangramroutray@soa.ac.in

DOI: 10.1201/9781003753391-36

DC loads [5]. This bidirectional energy exchange can significantly improve grid efficiency and adaptability when properly managed. Additionally, a plug-in hybrid electric vehicle featuring a hybrid energy storage system, comprising a battery, ultra-capacitor, and a bidirectional DC-DC converter has been proposed to optimize the management of energy resources effectively. This innovative design enables more efficient use of energy components and enhances the overall functionality of the vehicle and grid interaction [6]. Efficient control of electric vehicle (EV) chargers is essential for optimal performance. Recent studies have introduced an optimized PID controller tailored for the positive output re-lift Luco converter specifically for EV applications Among these, sliding mode control (SMC) has been successfully designed for EV charging systems, facilitating wireless power transfer. However, SMC is often criticized for the chattering effect, which can destabilize the system and make it susceptible to disturbances. To address this issue, various SMC variants have been proposed to reduce chattering. One notable approach is the super-twisting sliding mode controller (ST-SMC), which has shown promising results when applied to EV charger systems, offering enhanced robustness and performance in challenging operational conditions [7]. The super-twisting sliding mode controller (ST-SMC) effectively minimizes chattering and accommodates bounded external disturbances. Many studies have determined nonlinear controllers gain values using trial-and-error, which is inefficient and lacks systematic optimization. Properly tuning these gains is crucial for performance. One approach involves an optimized energy control scheme that employs robust linear parameters adjusted through genetic algorithms. While multi-objective met heuristic techniques, such as improved grey wolf optimizers and genetic algorithms, can optimize nonlinear controller gains, they often face challenges related to high computational demands and extended optimization times. Significant research has focused on deploying EV chargers, yet several areas still need further exploration. This paper introduces a novel control technique, the ANN [8–10], for an EV energy management model outlined in previous works. The nonlinear controller gains will be optimized using a reinforcement learning-based DDPG agent. Additionally, the global asymptotic stability of the proposed system is verified. After a brief introduction the rest of the paper is presented as following the Section 2 discusses the EV charging system. The controllers used for battery management are discussed in Section 3. Section 4 discusses the simulation results and finally the conclusion is drawn in Section 5.

System Description

This study employs a mathematical model of an EV integrated with fuel cell and ultra-capacitor and that includes an AC-DC power converter and a dual active bridge (DAB) as shown in Figure 36.1. The AC-DC converter is responsible for converting and regulating the DC voltage to the appropriate level for efficient EV charging, facilitated by the DAB. Here an electric vehicle with battery capacity = 55kwh, charger of 7.2 kw charging time 8 hours and maximum power of 165 Bhp (123.2 kw) single motor of 225 hp.

Fuel cell
A fuel cell converts hydrogen's chemical energy into electricity through reactions with oxygen, producing electricity, heat, and water. This process is efficient, using hydrogen as fuel and oxygen as an oxidant, generating minimal by-products, primarily water vapor.

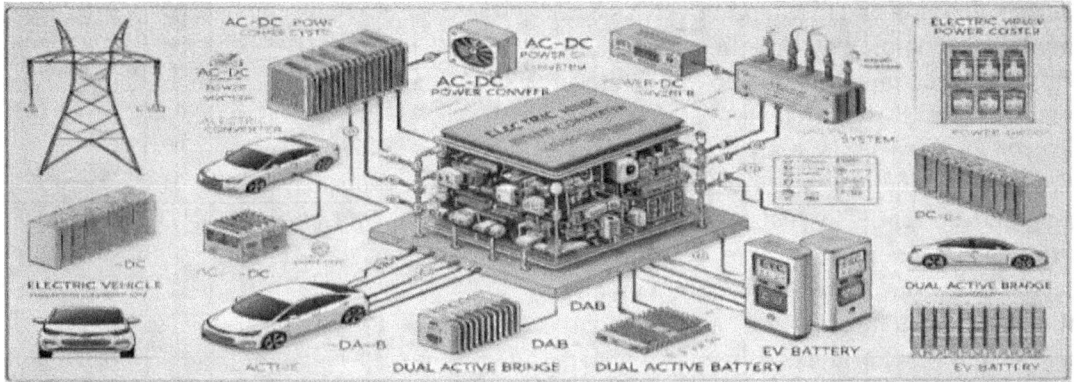

Figure 36.1 Graphical presentation of the proposed work
Source: Author

The fuel cell reaction is given by

$$2H + O_2 = H_2O + i + heat \qquad (1)$$

This study presents an electrochemical model for predicting fuel cell performance under dynamic and static conditions, focusing on hydrogen fuel design. It incorporates factors like hydrogen and oxygen pressures, membrane hydration, temperature, and output current, affecting voltage and operation. The fuel cell voltage is given by

$$v_{fc} = E_{nernest} - \left(v_{conv} + v_{act} + v_{ohmic}\right)(2)$$

Where $E_{nernest}$ = Thermal potential, is mathematically expressed as

$$E_{ernenst} = 4.306 \times 10^{-5} \times \Gamma \times$$

$$\left(\ln ph_2 + \frac{\ln po_2}{2}\right)$$

$$+ 1.23 - 0.85 \times 10^{-3} \times \left(\Gamma - 298.15\right) \qquad (3)$$

Ultra capacitor
The energy storage system (ESS), during discharge, supplies the necessary supplementary power. Charging can occur through receiving power from the fuel cell system

(FCS). The energy stored in the ESS is expressed as shown in equation (4).

$$E = \int_t \left(P_{b-charge} - P_{b-discharge}\right) dt \qquad (4)$$

In this context, E represents the total energy capacity, while c_p indicates the fraction of usable energy. For the Ultra capacitor (UC), if the extreme voltage drop at its terminals is limited to 20%, c_p is roughly 36%. As a result, the UC's total energy capacity is 351.6 Wh, and according to Equation (5), the required number of UC modules is 155.

$$N_{uc} = \frac{c_p}{m_{module}E_s} \qquad (5)$$

Finally, based on the calculated specifications for the fuel cell system (FCS), battery, and ultra capacitor (UC), the FCHEV components are summarized in Table 36.4.

Neural Network Energy Management System

Artificial neural networks (ANNs) offer a promising approach to controlling the voltage, current and power in an EV battery during charging and discharging. ANNs can model the complex and nonlinear relationships between input parameters like battery voltage and current battery. The ANN's input layer processes real-time data from the battery including temperature, voltage, and current. This data is then passed through hidden layers where the network learns the connections between inputs and the required control using back propagation. The output layer generates control signals to adjust the battery parameters. By training on historical data or simulations, the ANN can predict and manage the ideal voltage, current, power. Unlike traditional control methods such as PID, which rely on predefined mathematical models, ANNs adapt to varying operating conditions like changes in load and environmental factors. This flexibility provides a more robust and responsive control strategy.

The result is improved battery parameters, with real-time adjustments to maintain optimal operating conditions, boosting the performance and energy efficiency of electric vehicles. To apply an ANN for controlling the charging/discharging of battery, we need to define the relationship between the input parameters of ANN.

The ANN is applied for battery charging/discharging. The mathematical framework to model the relation between battery parameters and SOC (performance matrix). The neuron in ANN is given in Table 36.1

The hidden layer with activation function as:

$$f(x) = \frac{2}{1 + e^{-2x}} - 1 \qquad (6)$$

The output layer with one neuron (SOC) and activation function $f(x) = x$, ensures the linear scaling of the output. The ANN is trained by Levenberg Marqurdt (LM) algorithm.

Table 36.1 ANN structure.

SL No	Layers of ANN	No of neurons
01	Input layer	04
02	Hidden layer	02
03	Output layer	01

Source: Author

$$MSE = \frac{1}{N} \sum_{i=1}^{N} \left(SOC^i_{predicted} - SOC^i_{actual} \right) \quad (7)$$

The iterative weight adjustment is given as follows:

$$w_{k+1} = w_k - \left(J_k^T - J_k + \lambda I \right)^{-1} J_k^T e_k \quad (8)$$

Where $e_k = SOC\ error$
The SOC output by ANN is given by

$$SOC = w_{out} \left(\frac{2}{1 + e^{-2(w_{hid}x + b_{hid})}} - 1 \right) + b_{out} \quad (9)$$

Where $x = (v_{batt}, i_{batt}, i_{load})$
ANNs enhance battery state estimation accuracy by modelling a complex nonlinear relation between inputs (current, voltage, temperature) and outputs (state of charge, state of health). Unlike linear methods, ANNs adapt to dynamic conditions like aging, temperature variations, and charge-discharge cycles through layered data processing to further improve the accuracy of state estimation the reinforcement learning is associated with the ANN.

Reinforcement Learning Based ANN

Reinforcement learning (RL) combined with ANN optimizes EV battery management by enabling adapting decision making in dynamic environments. ANNs process real-time inputs (voltage, current, temperature) to model nonlinear battery dynamics, while RL algorithms like Q-learning iteratively learn optimal charging/discharging policies through reward maximization (e.g., minimizing grid costs, extending lifespan).

The RL combined with ANN for EV battery management can be formulated

The state of the battery considering various parameters at time 't' can be expressed as

$$s_t = [\text{SOC}_t, V_t, I_t] \tag{10}$$

The action space is given by

$$a_t = (a_1, a_2, \ldots a_n) \tag{11}$$

The action space includes the charging or discharging of the battery and adjusting charging rates. The reward function optimizes battery life, operational cost and efficiency.

Reward function is

$$R(s_t, a_t) = -C(a_t) - D(s_t) \tag{12}$$

Where C = cost and D is the degradation value.

The cost function is defined as

$$J(\theta) = E_{\pi\theta}\left[\sum_{t=0}^{\infty} \gamma^t R(s_t, a_t)\right] \tag{13}$$

The RL combined with ANN is revolutionizing EV battery management by enabling adaptive, data-driven optimization. ANN models excel at processing complex battery data, such as state-of-charge (SOC) and state-of-health (SOH), while RL algorithms dynamically optimize charging/discharging strategies through reward-based learning. Recent advancements include RL-based systems that improve renewable energy utilization by 2–4% through smart charging schedules aligned with solar/wind generation patterns, and hybrid architectures where ANN-processed battery data informs

RL decisions for load balancing, extending battery lifespan by up to 20%. These systems employ techniques like proximal policy optimization to manage power flow in multi-source environments, with experimental validations showing 15% energy efficiency gains in 100 kWh lithium-ion packs the integration enables real-time thermal management and capacity optimization for retired batteries, overcoming traditional BMS limitations through continuous learning from operational data streams.

Simulation Results

Here an electric vehicle associated with fuel cells and ultracapacitor is designed in MATLAB/SIMULINK. Simulation results of the fuel-cell based electric vehicle (FC-EV) model, using the proposed reinforcement learning based ANN and conventional ANN control strategies, show significant performance improvements through current voltage and SOC, voltage with one speed profiles (UDDS). The RL-ANN, controller outperforms the conventional ANN in efficiency and dynamic response, excelling at managing power distribution between the fuel cell stack (FCS), battery, and ultra-capacitor (UC). The RLA-NN optimizes energy flow, reducing energy loss and enhancing system efficiency. Compared to ANN, RL-ANN offers superior power distribution, faster response times, and a more balanced energy mix, leading to a more efficient, sustainable fuel cell electric vehicle energy management system (EMS).

Case-1: Investigation through ANN

For the UDDS speed profile, the RFC-EV model with incorporation of ultra-capacitor is simulated for 20 seconds. This enhances the dynamic behavior of the FC-EV, particularly during the acceleration tests. The proposed energy management system

(EMS), shows a significant improvement in acceleration performance compared to the ANN. For instance, during the acceleration the FC voltage is 48 volt by ANN. The fuel cell voltage, FC current, Battery voltage and current are simulated during acceleration in UDDS speed profile. The SOC is 51%, which indicates that during acceleration of the EV the battery discharges and the ultra-capacitors also supply current to the power train of the engine of the vehicle. To evaluate the proposed EMS systematically, instead of focusing on a specific driving cycle, many distinct cycles provided within the ADVISOR tool may be used to test the performance of the RL-ANN. The simulation results depict the performance of ANN as shown in Figure 36.2(a) to 36.2(h).

Case-2: EMS investigation Through Reinforce learning Algorithm based ANN

In order to scrutinize the performance of the reinforcement learning algorithm-based ANN, the output power of each power source under the UDDS driving cycle can be viewed as demonstrated in Figure 36.3. The result reveals that the proposed strategy brings advantages to EV energy management. From the study it can be depicted that the EV is running at optimum operating points and in some cases, depending on the driving condition, it is working with no load. Moreover, the FC power is zero during the start of electric vehicle. Since initialization

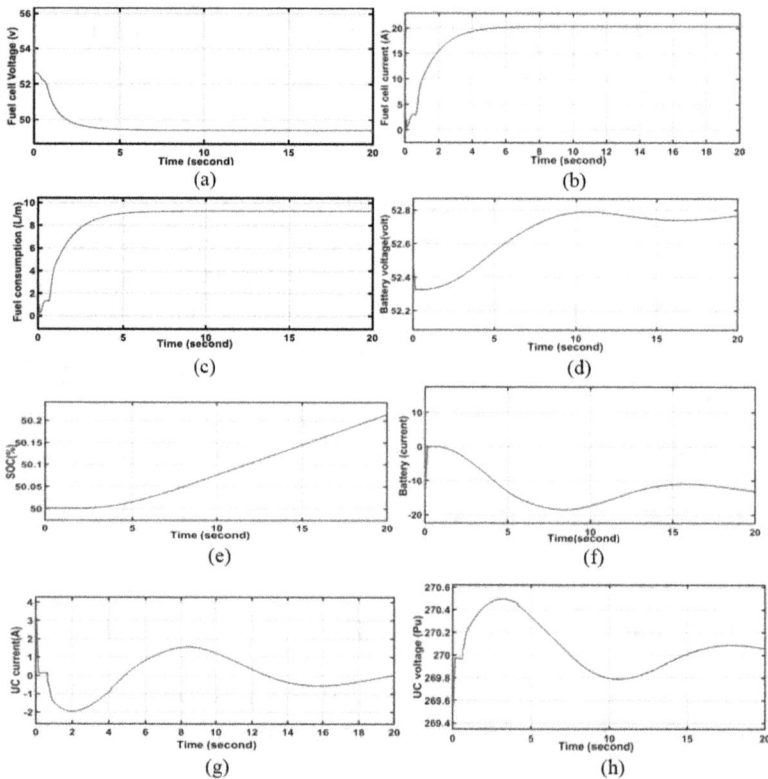

Figure 36.2 performance of ANN through UDDS speed profiles. (a) FC voltage (b) FC current (c) fuel consumption (d) battery voltage (e) battery current (f) battery SOC (g) UC voltage (h) UC current

Source: Author

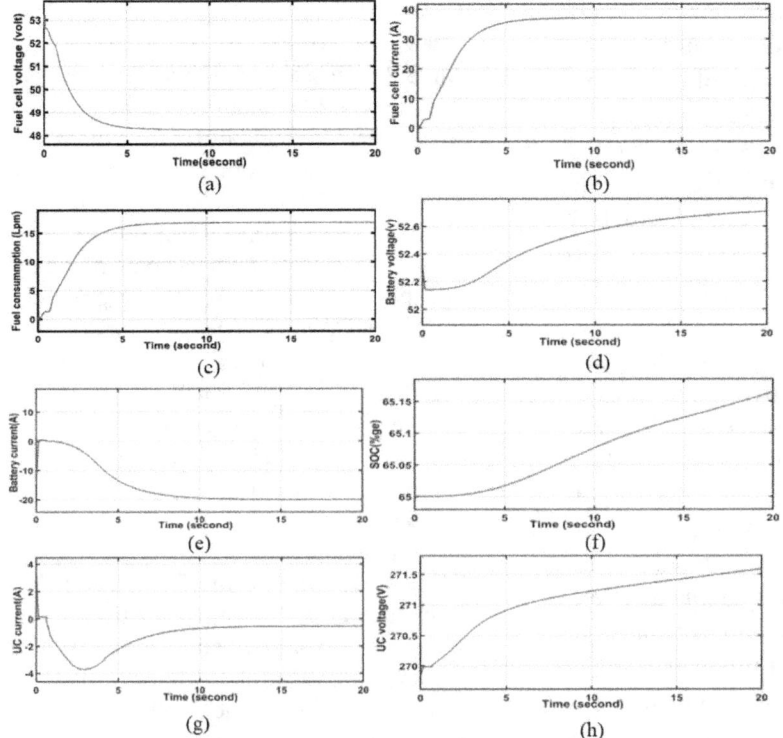

Figure 36.3 performance of RLA-ANN through UDDS speed profiles. (a) FC voltage (b) FC current (c) fuel consumption (d) battery voltage (e) battery current (f) battery SOC (g) UC voltage (h) UC current

Source: Author

Table 36.2 Performance comparisons.

System parameters	ANN	RLA-ANN
FC voltage (v)	48	52.8
FC current (A)	20	36.2
Fuel consumption (L/m)	18	15.4
Battery voltage (v)	51.65	55.3
Battery current (A)	9.3	-20
SOC (%)	50.5	65.35
UC voltage (v)	271.56	271.6
UC current (A)	0.05	-0.06

Source: Author

is a time-consuming process, the battery provides the required power for the vehicle to start. The Fuel cell battery and ultra-capacitor parameters improvement using RLA-ANN during the UDDS driving cycle, is presented in Figure 36.3 (a) to 36.3(h).

Conclusion

This study addresses the challenges associated with integrating electric vehicles (EVs) into existing transportation infrastructure, focusing particularly on critical energy management. We propose a novel and nonlinear controller known as RLA-ANN for EV EMS. To enhance the accuracy and flexibility of power flow control from the sources reinforcement learning (RL)-based ANN is trained and implemented in EV energy management system. The implementation of the proposed method, the source parameters are improved as shown in Table 36.1. The

Table 36.1 presents the improvement of performance of RL-ANN as compared to the conventional ANN. For example the SOC of the battery during acceleration period is 50.5% and the same SOC is 65.4% by the proposed method as mentioned in Table 36.2. In the same way the other parameters improvement is shown in Figure 36.3(a) to 36.3(h). The combination of this mathematical model and the RL-tuned nonlinear controller present a promising solution for improving the sustainability, performance, and robustness of controllers in EV management applications, thereby supporting environmentally friendly transportation initiatives. Future research should focus on further refining and expanding the model by integrating energy storage systems to effectively handle peak demand and fast charging scenarios. While this study demonstrates notable improvements in the control effectiveness of EV EMS, it also opens avenues for future investigations. Specifically, we suggest applying the RL-based optimization approach to fine-tune all gains of the nonlinear controller. By broadening the tuning strategy to encompass every controller gain, a more comprehensive optimization can be achieved, enhancing the controller's versatility across various operational conditions. This could significantly contribute to the advancement of smart charging solutions, ultimately fostering a more sustainable transportation ecosystem.

References

[1] Das, H. S. (2020). Electric vehicles standards, charging infrastructure, and impact on grid integration: a technological review. *Renewable and Sustainable Energy Reviews*, 120, 109618–109630.

[2] Das, H. S., Rahman, M. M., Li, S., & Tan, C. W. (2020). Electric vehicles standards, charging infrastructure, and impact on grid integration: a technological review. *Renewable and Sustainable Energy Reviews*, 120, 109618.

[3] Ali, S. N., Hossain, M. J., Wang, D., Lu, K., Rasmussen, P. O., Sharma, V., et al. (2020). Robust sensorless control against thermally degraded speed performance in an IM drive based electric vehicle. *IEEE Transactions on Energy Conversion*, 35(2), 896–907.

[4] Ertekin, D. (2024). ARVIN converter: a bi-directional DC/DC converter for grid-connected G2V/V2G energy storage and electrification approaches. *Electrical Engineering*, 106.5: 5485–5505.

[5] Azeem, M. K., Armghan, H., Ahmad, I., & Hassan, M. (2020). Multistage adaptive nonlinear control of battery-ultracapacitor based plugin hybrid electric vehicles. *Journal of Energy Storage*, 32, 101813.

[6] Behnamfar, M., Olowu, T. O., Tariq, M., Debnath, A., & Sarwat, A. (2024). Composite second-order sliding mode and backstepping control for power pulsation suppression in dynamic wireless charging. *IEEE Transactions on Industry Applications*, 60(4), 5803–5812.

[7] Xie, Shaobo, Shanwei Qi, and Kun Lang. (2019). A data-driven power management strategy for plug-in hybrid electric vehicles including optimal battery depth of discharging. *IEEE Transactions on Industrial Informatics*. 16.5: 3387–3396.

[8] Samal, P., Nayak, N., Satapathy, A., & Bhuyan, S. K. (2025). Load frequency control in renewable based micro grid with deep neural network based controller. *Results in Engineering*, 25, 103554.

[9] Sathyan, S., Pandi, V. R., Antony, A., Salkuti, S. R., & Sreekumar, P. (2024). ANN-based energy management system for PV-powered EV charging station with battery backup and vehicle to grid support. *International Journal of Green Energy*, 21(6), 1279–1294.

[10] Afzal, M. Z., Aurangzeb, M., Iqbal, S., Pushkarna, M., Rehman, A. U., Kotb, H., et al. (2023). A novel electric vehicle battery management system using an artificial neural network-based adaptive droop control theory. *International Journal of Energy Research* 2023(1), 2581729.

37 Smart grid frequency management of an AC autonomous energy network using meta-heuristic-optimised artificial neural networks

Monalisa Mohanty[1,a], Sujeet Kumar Bhuyan[2,b] and Niranjan Nayak[2,c]

[1]Department of Electrical and Electronics Engineering, SOA deemed to be a University Bhubaneswar, Odisha, India

[2]Head of Resource Assessment and Asset Analysis Manikaran Analytics Limited, New Delhi, India

Abstract

The smart grid is always facing challenges in balancing power generation and dynamic load demands. PID has always been the preferred method for dealing with nonlinearity in a single area ac autonomous energy network given its ease of implementation, however, it fails to address any unforeseen nonlinearity. Nevertheless, while ANN improves system adaptability, it comes at a high computational cost and sluggish convergence rate. This article introduced a meta-heuristic optimized ANN. This demonstrates higher adaptability, faster responsiveness, and increased robustness to disruption. The simulation results and error-index minimization demonstrate the superiority of the proposed strategies.

Keywords: Artificial neural network, micro grid, Proportional-integral-derivative controller, water cycle algorithm artificial neural network

Introduction

Load frequency control (LFC) is critical for preserving the stability and reliability of power networks by reducing frequency variations and balancing generation against demand [1]. Traditional proportional-integral-derivative (PID) controllers and artificial neural networks (ANN) are commonly employed for LFC, but they have limitations in dealing with complicated system dynamics and uncertainties. In recent decades, various manuscripts have been published that apply ANN, whose weights are trained by different optimization techniques [2], such as PSO [3], GWO [4], and FA [5]. In this article, the Water Cycle Algorithm (WCA)- optimised ANN(Figure 37.4) outperforms both PID (Figure 37.2) and conventional ANN (Figure 37.3) and other nature-mimicking algorithms (Table 37.1) due to faster convergence, increased robustness, and higher dynamic performance. WCA's nature-inspired optimisation effectively modifies ANN parameters, resulting in optimal control actions.

This dominance makes WCA-ANN an attractive alternative for current power grids that require stability and efficiency. The second part of this research paper deals with the description of the model followed by a comparison of different controllers, their results, error analysis and conclusion.

[a]Monalisamohanty21@gmail.com, [b]sujeet.kumar84@gmail.com, [c]niranjannayak@soa.ac.in

DOI: 10.1201/9781003753391-37

Table 37.1 The side-by-side comparison of conventional optimization algorithm.

Features	WCA	PSO	GA	WOA
Parameter tuning difficulty	Low	Medium	High	Medium
Exploration vs exploitation	Well-balanced	Often-biased	Biased	Moderate
Convergence speed	Fast	Medium	Slow	Medium
Global optimum reachability	High	Medium	Medium	High
Local minima avoidance	Effective	Less Effective	Moderate	Moderate
scalability	Good	Good	Moderate	Good

Source: Author

Literature review

Maintaining the equilibrium between power supply and demand in an interconnected power system is the responsibility of LFC, a crucial component of power system operation and stability, any mismatch between generation and load causes fluctuations in the system frequency. These deviations can adversely affect the equipment operation system reliability and power quality [6]. LFC's main goals are to maintain scheduled power interchange between control areas and regulate the system frequency within reasonable bounds. Traditionally this has been achieved through governor control and automatic generation control which adjust generator outputs according to tie line power flows and frequency variations. When renewable energy sources are used, electric cars and distributed generation modern power system face increased variability and uncertainty making LFC more complex. Advanced control strategies such as robust adaptive optimal and sophisticated control techniques (such as neural networks and fuzzy logic), and metaheuristic optimization algorithm are being explored to enhanced LFC performance in the presence of non-linearities delays and stochastic disturbances. For current and future smart grids to be stable, dependable, and efficient, LFC research is still essential [7]. [8] A model free DRL-based LFC using DDPG

and RNN optimizes frequency control, outperforming traditional PI Controllers in dynamic conditions [9]. An NNA-optimized FOPID controller enhances LFC in MAIPS, outperforming PID, DE and ARA under dynamic load conditions [10]. An optimized ANN based LFC using PSO improves frequency control and power delivery in multi area PSNs, outperforming conventional ANN and PID [11]. A PSO-ANN tuned PID controller with EV support enhances LFC in islands micro grids reducing frequency oscillation, overshoot and settling time

Single-Area Autonomous AC Microgrid

A carbon-neutral small capacity grid integrating solar thermal power generation and wind energy as primary energy producing sources to meet the nonlinear load demand backed up by different distributed generation is proposed that aims to meet the consumer power demand even at remote places without burdening the conventional grid has been proposed.

The objective is to maintain the power quality with the least frequency fluctuation and a sustainable environment. The graphical abstract of the microgrid is portrayed in Figure 37.1. The transfer function equation of the DGs is described in the following Table 37.2.

The total power balance equation (Figure 37.2) is as follow:

$$\Delta P_{LOAD} = \Delta P_{STPG} + \Delta P_{WTPG} + \Delta P_{DEG} + \Delta P_{AEQ} +$$
$$\Delta P_{AEQ} + \Delta P_{FC} + \Delta P_{MT} + \Delta P_{BESS} + \Delta P_{FESS} \tag{1}$$

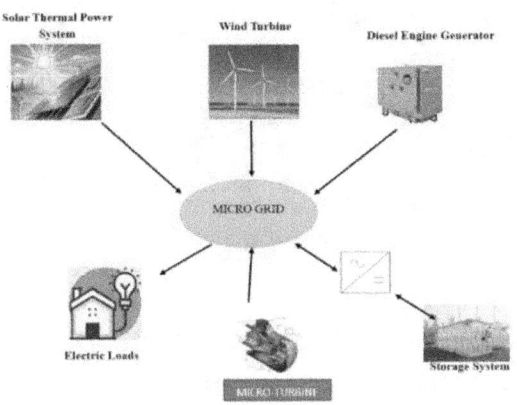

Figure 37.1 Presents the graphical abstract of the small-scale grid and the power generators connected to form the network
Source: Author

Load Frequency Management Technique

- Confined performance in nonlinear systems
- Tuning challenges
- High sensitivity to disturbances and noise.
- High computational complexity
- Overfitting
- Lack of interpretability
- Enhanced optimization efficiency
- Robustness to complex systems
- Improved performance over conventional methods

Table 37.2 The gain and time values of the different distributed generators used in the small-scale grid.

DIGs	Transfer Functions	Gain (K)	Time constants (T)
STPG	$G_{STPG}(s) = \dfrac{K_S}{1+sT_S} \cdot \dfrac{K_T}{1+sT_T} = \dfrac{\Delta P_{STPG}}{\Delta P_{SOL}}$	1.8,1	1.8,0.3
WTG	$G_{WTG} = \dfrac{K_{WTG}}{1+sT_{WTG}} = \dfrac{\triangle P_{WTG}}{\triangle P_W}$	0.998	1.489
AE	$G_{AEQ}(s) = \dfrac{K_{AEQ}}{1+sT_{AEQ}} = \dfrac{\Delta P_{AEQ}}{\left(\Delta P_{WTG} + \Delta P_{STPG}\right)\left(1-K_N\right)}$ $K_N = \dfrac{P_T}{\left(P_{WTPG} + P_{STPG}\right)}$, $K_N = 0.6$	0.002	0.4995
FC	$G_{FC} = \dfrac{K_{FC}}{1+sT_{FC}} = \dfrac{\Delta P_{FCk}}{\Delta P_{AE}}$, $k = 1, 2$	0.011	3.99
MT	$G_{MT} = \dfrac{K_{MT}}{1+sT_{MT}} = \dfrac{\Delta P_{MT}}{\Delta U}$	0.999	1.988
BESS	$G_{BESS} = \dfrac{K_{BESS}}{1+sF_{BESS}} = \dfrac{\Delta P_{BESS}}{\Delta U}$	-0.0098	0.0987
FESS	$G_{FESS} = \dfrac{K_{FESS}}{1+sT_{FESS}} = \Delta P_{FESS}/\Delta U$	-0.003	0.0987

Source: Author

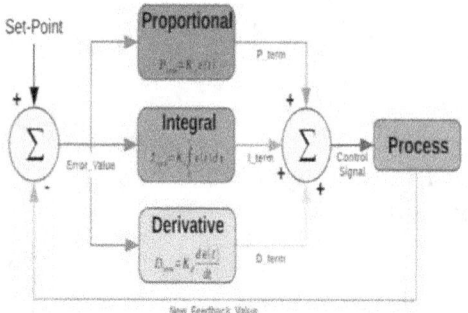

Figure 37.2 PID controller
Source: Author

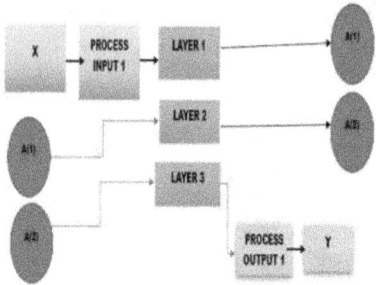

Figure 37.3 ANN network
Source: Author

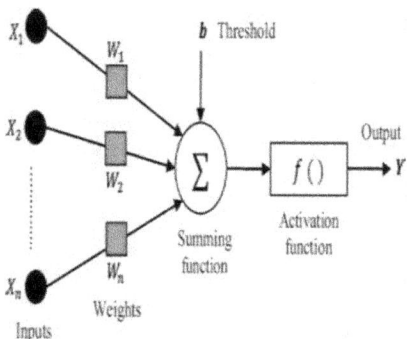

Figure 37.4 The weights of ANN are optimized using WCA
Source: Author

Table 37.3 The objective function values for different controllers.

Conventional PID	ANN	WCA-ANN
1.62×10^{-2}	6.3589×10^{-4}	1.02×10^{-4}

Source: Author

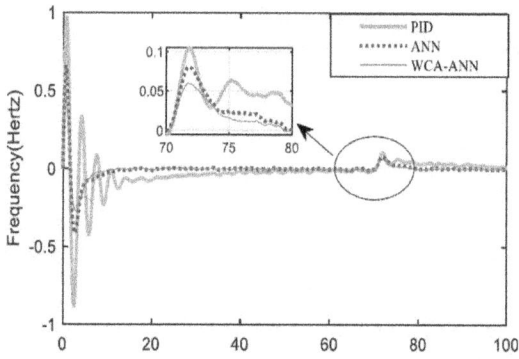

Figure 37.5 The MATLAB simulation results obtained for case study 1
Source: Author

Result Analysis

The research work here focuses on RES based power grids which are backed up with different generators to maintain the frequency constant in the whole of the network, i.e. the nominal frequency at 50 hertz, while balancing the power generation vs the load demand. The objective function values for different controllers are given in Table 37.3.

Case study 1: A step perturbation is introduced in solar thermal power generation, while maintaining the Wind Turbine Generator output and load constant. Figure 37.5 presents the simulation result obtained in MATLAB Simulink 2019, followed by validation of the case study in the OPAL-RT platform (Figure 37.6).

Case 2: Taking into account varying Wind Energy and solar insolation and load constant load (Figure 37.7).

Case 3: Dynamic load condition, where RES-based energy sources feed the load with constant output, while balancing the power generation and load balance (Figure 37.8).

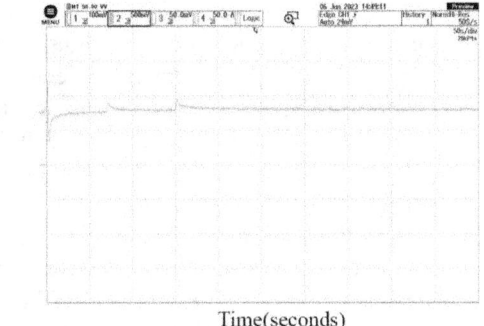

Figure 37.6 Real-time validation of case study 1 in the OPAL-RT platform in the MICRO-GRID laboratory, SOADU
Source: Author

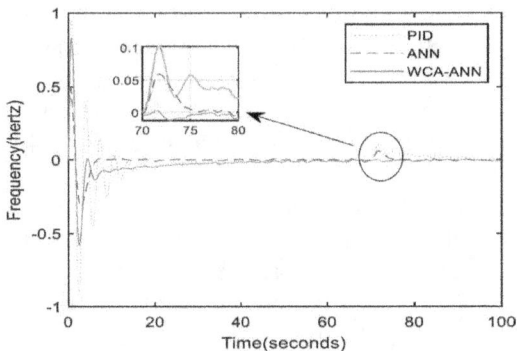

Figure 37.7 The MATLAB simulation results obtained for case study 2
Source: Author

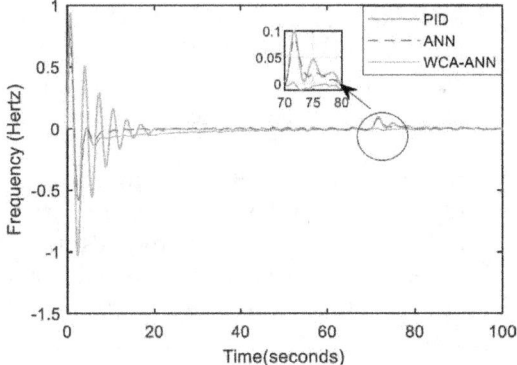

Figure 37.8 The MATLAB simulation results obtained for case study 3
Source: Author

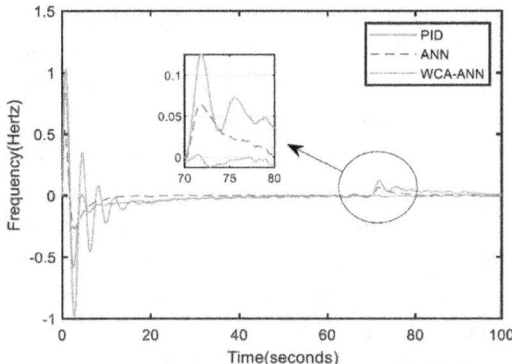

Figure 37.9 The MATLAB simulation results obtained for case study 4
Source: Author

Case 4: Taking all operating conditions with a step perturbation at 70s seconds (Figure 37.9).

Conclusion

This study presents a novel WCA-ANN load frequency control technique that improves the performance of isolated microgrids by shortening settling time, controlling frequency deviations, and maintaining system reliability. The WCA optimizes the weights of the ANN controller, attaining 99.904% efficiency, a minimum MSE of 1.1112×10^{-7}, and an ISE of 2.0×10^{-4}. The controller provides rapid reaction, excellent precision, little overshoot/undershoot, while keeping the microgrid frequency close to 50 Hz. WCA-ANN outperforms PID and ANN in variable operating conditions. Future studies will focus on multi-objective tuning and tackling challenges such as communication delays and cost in order to increase microgrid reliability. Multi-objective tuning enhances load frequency control in an isolated microgrid by balancing critical performance metrics such as frequency stability, response time, control effort, and energy efficiency. Using advanced optimisation techniques like WCA with Pareto-based strategies can address multiple conflicting objectives, simultaneously improving overall system reliability. Additionally, tackling communication delays -caused by sensor, network, or actuator latency -a vital for maintaining control accuracy. Delay compensated controllers; predictive models are synchronised communication protocols that mitigate these efforts. Cost optimisation is equally important, ensuring that controller design implementation and maintenance remain economically viable without compromising performance techniques. Such as light weight ANN architectures and cloud-based computation help reduce computational and operation expenses. Together multi-objective tuning and solutions for delay and cost challenges significantly strengthen micro grid resilience, ensuring stable operation under dynamic load and renewable generation conditions while maintaining system affordability and adaptability for long term sustainable deployment.

References

[1] Ranjan, M., & Shankar, R. (2022). A literature survey on load frequency control considering renewable energy integration in power system: recent trends and future prospects. *Journal of Energy Storage*, 45, 103717.

[2] Rasolomampionona, D. D., Połecki, M., Zagrajek, K., Wróblewski, W., & Januszewski, M. (2024). A comprehensive review of load frequency control technologies. *Energies*, 17(12), 2915.

[3] Safari, A., Babaei, F., & Farrokhifar, M. (2021). A load frequency control using a PSO-based ANN for micro-grids in the presence of electric vehicles. *International Journal of Ambient Energy*, 42(6), 688–700.

[4] Meseret, G. M., Kumhar, R., Mahato, T. K., Lakra, P., Kumari, B., & Kumar, N.

(2025). Design of novel secondary controller for AGC in multi-area multi-sources power system incorporated renewable energy using a gray wolf optimizer algorithm. *Engineering Reports*, 7(3), e70054.

[5] Hasan, F. A., Faris, F. H., & Alkhafaji, M. H. (2025). Robust load-frequency control of multi-area smart grid by combining neural network with real-time particle swarm optimization. *International Journal of Intelligent Engineering and Systems*, 18(1).

[6] Ramesh, M., Yadav, A. K., & Pathak, P. K. (2025). An extensive review on load frequency control of solar-wind based hybrid renewable energy systems. *Energy Sources, Part A: Recovery, Utilization, and Environmental Effects*, 47(1), 8378–8402.

[7] Ranjan, M., & Shankar, R. (2022). A literature survey on load frequency control considering renewable energy integration in power system: recent trends and future prospects. *Journal of Energy Storage*, 45, 103717.

[8] Pandey, B., & Nguyen, N. (2025). A model-free approach for load frequency control using deep reinforcement learning. In 2025 IEEE Texas Power and Energy Conference (TPEC). IEEE.

[9] El-Rifaie, A. M., Abid, S., Ginidi, A. R., & Shaheen, A. M. (2025). Fractional order PID controller based-neural network algorithm for LFC in multi-area power systems. *Engineering Reports*, 7(2), e70028.

[10] Al-Majidi, S. D., Kh. AL-Nussairi, M., Mohammed, A. J., Dakhil, A. M., Abbod, M. F., & Al-Raweshidy, H. S. (2022). Design of a load frequency controller based on an optimal neural network. *Energies*, 15(17), 6223.

[11] Safari, A., Babaei, F., & Farrokhifar, M. (2021). A load frequency control using a PSO-based ANN for micro-grids in the presence of electric vehicles. *International Journal of Ambient Energy*, 42(6), 688–700.

38 Fuel cell based electric vehicle battery management using artificial neural network

Satish Choudhury[a], Anshuman Satapathy[b] and Niranjan Nayak[c]

Department of Electrical & Electronics Engineering, Institute of Technical Education and Research, Siksha 'O' Anusandhan deemed to be University, Bhubaneswar, India

Abstract

This article explores the application of artificial neural network (ANNs) in the management of electric vehicle (EV) battery systems. Efficient battery management is challenging for optimizing performance, battery lifespan and safety. The proposed approach leverages ANNs to predict key parameters of the fuel cell and battery SOC. By training the neural network on historical data, the model can accurately forecast fuel cell parameters under different operating conditions. This results the energy efficiency improvement, extended battery life and enhanced vehicle performance. The study also highlights the benefits of integrating ANN-based models with existing battery management systems (BMS) for more intelligent and adaptive control strategies. In this work the ANN explores the improvement in Fuel cell parameters under three different driving cycle of the vehicle. The three driving cycles are HWEET, NYYC and UDDC. For an example in HWEET driving cycle the SOC improved to 90–95% by ANN where the same was 50–85% by the PI controller and it was 40–55% with no controller. Simulation results demonstrate the effectiveness of the ANN in optimizing battery SOC and fuel cell voltage, current and power. It provides early warnings for potential failures, making it a promising tool for the future of electric vehicle technology.

Keywords: Artificial neural network, electric vehicles, fuel cell, HWEET, NYYC and UDDC, state of charge (SOC)

Introduction

The rapid growth of zero emission transport through electric vehicles (EVs) in recent years has emphasized the need for efficient and reliable battery management systems (BMS) to ensure optimal performance, safety, and longevity of EV batteries [1]. The battery and fuel cell are two critical components of an electric vehicle, which influences its driving range, energy efficiency, and overall performance [2, 3]. However, managing the complex behavior of battery and fuel cell, which can be affected by various factors such as charge/discharge cycles, temperature, and aging, remains a significant challenge. Traditional methods of battery management are often limited in their ability to adapt to changing conditions or to predict battery health and fuel cell parameters with high accuracy [2, 1]. In recent years, artificial intelligence (AI), specifically artificial neural networks (ANNs), have gained attention for their ability to process complex data and make real-time predictions. ANNs are particularly suited for battery management due to their capacity to learn from large datasets, recognize patterns, and provide adaptive control strategies. By implementing ANNs, it is possible to develop intelligent battery management systems that can predict key parameters such as the state of charge

[a]satishchoudhury@soa.ac.in, [b]anshumanas1001@gmail.com, [c]niranjannayak@soa.ac.in

DOI: 10.1201/9781003753391-38

(SOC), state of health (SOH), and temperature, which are essential for optimizing battery performance and lifespan [4, 5]. This research explores the application of ANNs in the development of an advanced EMS for fuel cell based electric vehicle (FEV). Here an ANN-based approach is investigated that can accurately monitor and predict the dynamic behavior of EV batteries and fuel cell. By doing so, the work aims to enhance battery performance, extend battery life, and prevent potential failures, thereby contributing to the overall efficiency and reliability of electric vehicles. The findings of this study offer a promising avenue for integrating AI technologies into the next generation of battery management systems, supporting the growing shift towards sustainable and efficient electric transportation. After a brief introduction the graphical presentation of the work is given in Section 2. The different components of the EV are discussed in Section 3. The simulation results are discussed in Section 4. Lastly in Section 5, the conclusion is drawn

System Description

An ANN operates as the biological brain's information processing system and utilize parallel processing for flexibility due to simultaneous training techniques. The input and output variables required to develop the neural network model are derived from time series data. Prior to designing a specific network for a task, feed-forward networks are often studied. ANN construction can follow three primary steps, establishing the neurons that link patterns, selecting the method for initializing neuron weights based on training and learning functions and to define an activation function to determine a neuron's output. This phase is known as "network architecture." The back propagation method is employed during the training phase of classification, utilizing feed-forward neural networks. Error is propagated backward from the output layer, adjusting weights according to learning rates. Two weight adjustment approaches are used, incremental and batch. For the proposed work, the neural network is trained using datasets derived from BLDC motor power and the state of charge (SOC), with the objective dataset being the reference fuel cell (FC) power. The ANN output after 1000 training iterations, with a RMSE of approximately 70.8479. The regression values for training, testing, and validation phases are 0.99,

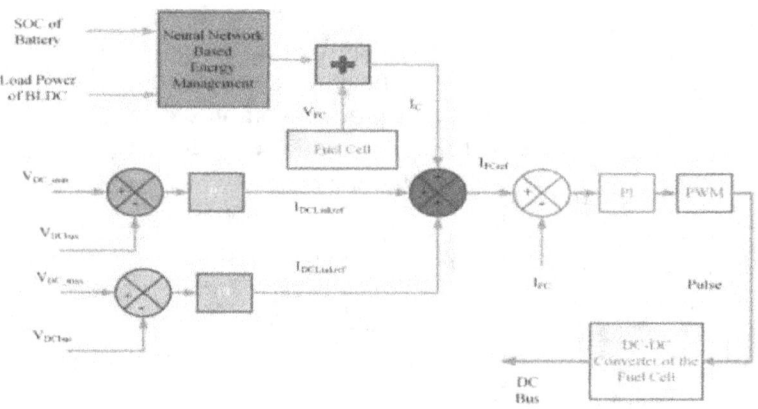

Figure 38.1 Graphical presentation of the proposed work
Source: Author

0.98, and 0.98, respectively, indicating that the network's output closely aligns with the required dataset [6].

Components of FCEV

Fuel cell
A fuel cell converts hydrogen energy into electricity through reactions with oxygen, producing electricity.

The fuel cell reaction is given by

$$2H + O_2 = H_2O + i + heat \tag{1}$$

The fuel cell voltage is given by

$$v_{fc} = E_{nernest} - \left(v_{conv} + v_{act} + v_{ohmic}\right) \tag{2}$$

Where $E_{ernenst}$ = Thermal potential, is mathematically express as

$$E_{ernenst} = 4.306 \times 10^{-5} \times \Gamma \times \left(\ln ph_2 + \frac{\ln po_2}{2} \right)$$

$$+ 1.23 - 0.85 \times 10^{-3} \times \left(\Gamma - 298.15 \right) \tag{3}$$

v_{con} = Concentration voltage drop, v_{ohmic} = resistive voltage drop

The stack voltage is given by,

$$v_{stack} = N \times v_{fc} \tag{4}$$

The specifications of fuel cell (FC) is 52.55 V with a total of 65 individual fuel cells. The FC_stack efficacy is 50%. The temperature of 45°C and a pressure of 1.163 bar. The system consists of 99% hydrogen, 95% oxygen, and 21% water. At full capacity, 60% of oxygen is utilized, with a 2.5V drop. Under rated conditions, the FC generates 10.26875 kW at 41.145V, while at MPP, power increases to 12.5444 kW, and voltage drops to 39.24V. Voltage efficiency is high under minimal current and stable conditions.

Battery
A Li- battery is designed and connected to the load with constant resistance. The battery voltage is expressed as

$$V_{batt} = E - i_{batt} \times r_{batt} \tag{5}$$

Where E is the source voltage which is expressed as the following equation.

$$E = E_0 + a \times e^{(-b\int i_{batt} dt)} - k \frac{c}{c_0 - \int i_{batt} dt} \tag{6}$$

Where E open circuit voltage, E_0 is fixed, battery emf, C is battery strength in Ah. The amplitude is 'a' and 'b' in Amp/sec. optimal voltage is 57.08 v. The least voltage is 48.6 V and battery strength is 40 Ah. 17.45 mA is lowest discharge current; nominal strength is 6.75 Ah.

Battery charging/discharging
The DC-DC converter is regulated using DC bus voltage and current. The DC link voltage, V_{dcbus}, is compared to the reference voltage, $V_{dcbusref}$. A PI controller processes voltage deviation and generates reference current for battery control. The battery current is adjusted based on the reference, with a PWM generator maintaining the dc bus voltage

Simulation Results

The FC-EV hybrid EV model is simulated for 500 seconds. In this work the HEV is simulated for three driving cycles like IHWFET, NY-CC and UD-DS. The EV motor parameter is controlled as per each of the driving cycles and the results are analyzed accordingly. The speed profile in HWEET drive cycle is shown in Figure 38.2(a). Fuel cell parameters like voltage, current and the power are presented at Figure 38.2(b), 38.2(c) respectively. The maximum FC voltage changes from -0.4 pu

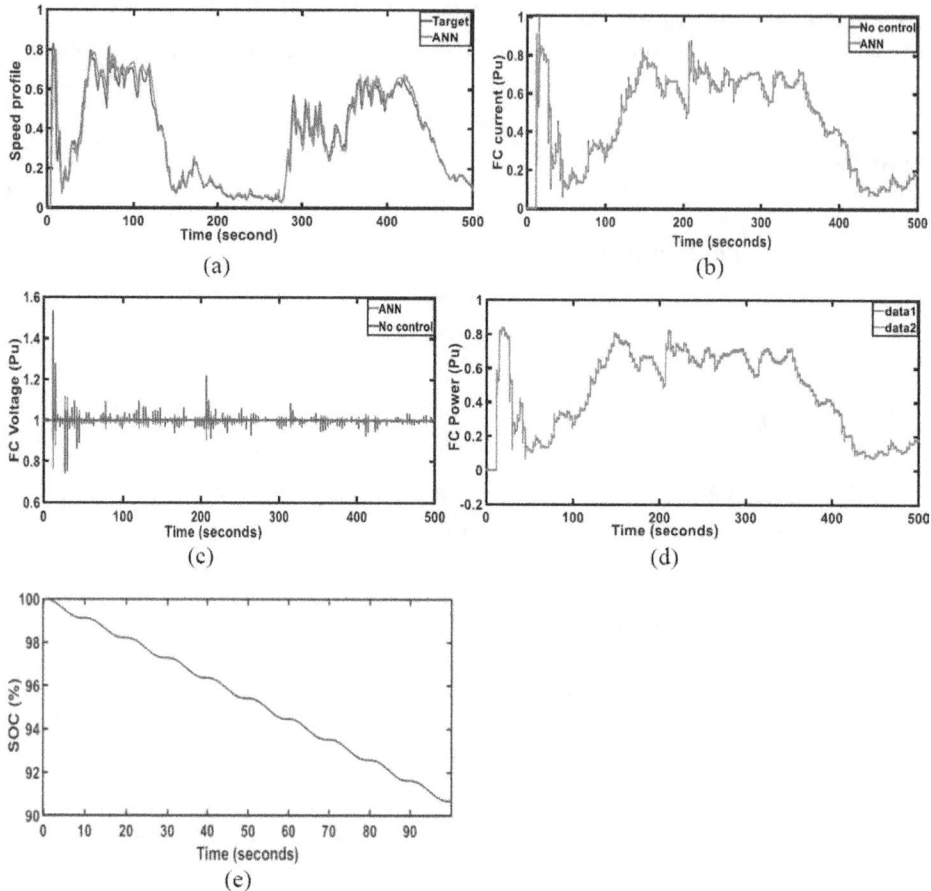

Figure 38.2 Performance of ANN for HWFET drive cycle (a) speed profile (b) FC current (c) FC voltage (d) FC power (e) battery SOC
Source: Author

to 1.7 pu at time t = 10 second. The model is simulated for 500 second and the FC current and FC power is shown in Figure 38.2(d). The hydrogen consumption in a fuel cell is maintained at 100 litre per mile. The fuel consumption increases from '0' to 100 gram in 230 second. The range of SOC of the battery in three different drive cycles are given in the Table 38.1.

The SOC is controlled effectively by ANN energy management. While the FC provides lower output than the demand, then the battery operates in discharge mode and similarly for the FC output, which

supplies the power demand then the battery operates in charging mode. The battery and FC management is effectively done by ANN. A DC-DC boost is connected between the FC and DC bus. The simulation for NY-CC drive cycle, speed profile is presented in Figure 38.3. The FC voltage, current and power is depicted in Figure 38.3(b), 38.3(c) and 38.3(d) respectively. The FC current changes from 0 to 0.8 pu during first 140 second. After 140 seconds the FC current becomes constant for smooth running of BLDC. Due to the performance of ANN-EMS the use of fuel cellreduceded

Table 38.1 Comparison between various driving cycles.

Methods	HWFET		NYCC		UDDS	
	Fuel consumption (g)	Battery SOC	Fuel consumption (g)	Battery SOC	Fuel consumption (g)	Battery SOC
Uncontrolled	130	40-55	54	45-60	63	50-62
PI control	122	55-85	43	60-88	51	62-83
ANN	96	90-95	16	88-96	35	83-92

Source: Author

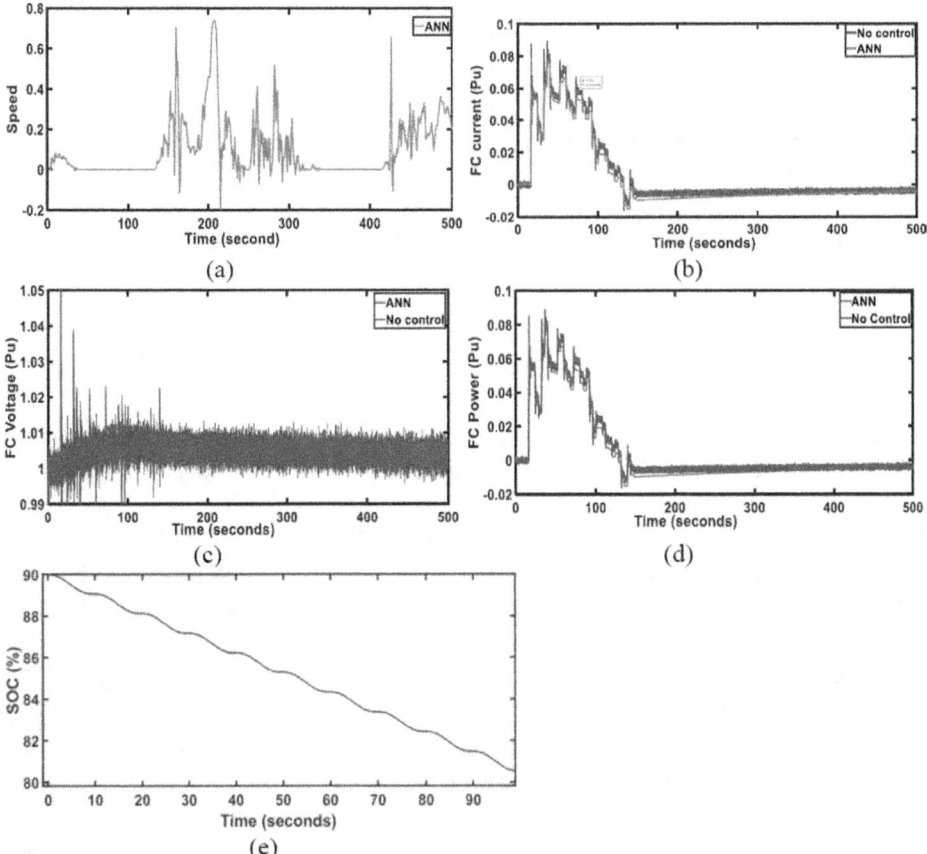

Figure 38.3 Performance of ANN in NYCC drive cycle (a) speed profile (b) FC current (c) FC voltage (d) FC power € Battery SOC
Source: Author

up to some extent. The solar PV maintains 46-volt DC constant over the whole driving cycle. The PV current depends on the irradiance emitted from the panel. In general depending on irradiance emission, the current ranges from 6 Amp to 16 Ampere.

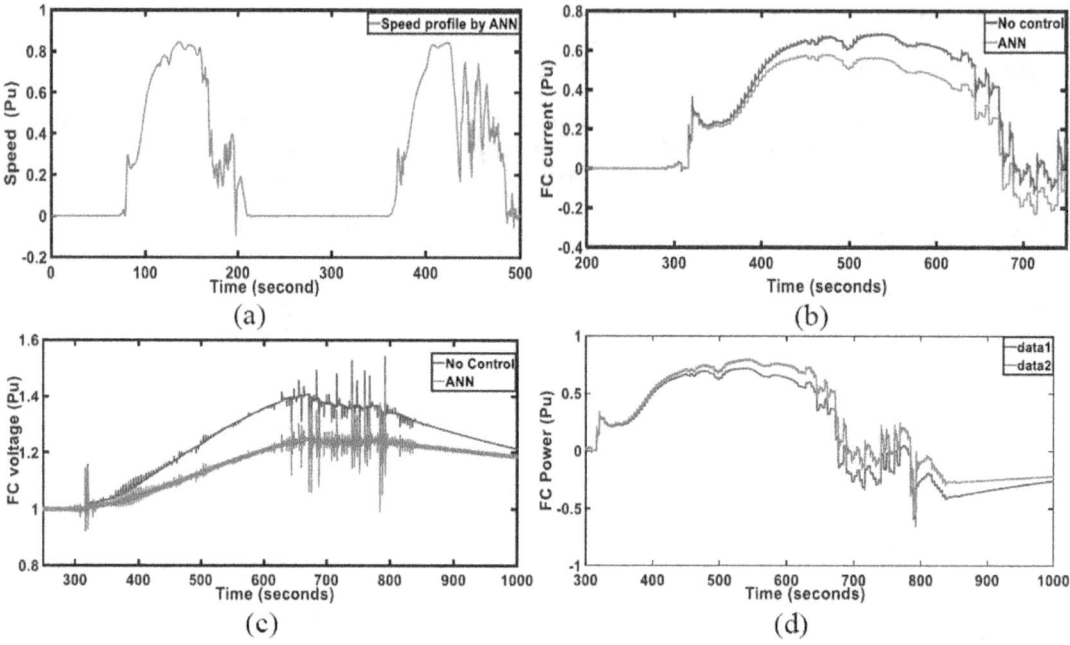

Figure 38.4 Performance of ANN in UDDS drive cycle (a) speed profile (b) fuel cell current (c) FC voltage (d) FC Power

Source: Author

Accordingly, the PV output ranges from 300 watt to 790 watt. The battery always keeps about 90% of charging by use of ANN. However the excess charging/discharging may be prevented by ANN- EMS. The Figure 38.3(a), presents the UDDS drive cycle speed in mph. Figure 38.3(b) to 38.3(e), displays the FC's voltage, current and FC power in the UDDS driving cycle. The fuel cell parameters like FC voltage, current and power dynamics are shown in Figure 38.4.

Conclusion

The low emission power system based on renewable energy system, which is used in transportation (EV) has great potential. It is an effective replacement of IC engine-based transportation system. This research focused on neural network-based energy

management systems to overcome the short fall of reliable power supply. The fuel cell is main source of the EV. To overcome the delay in reaction of the FC, which causes the rapid change in load power. A good %SOC (about 90%) is maintained for availability of ample amount of power and a steady DC voltage (265–285volt) is maintained. In HWEET drive cycle, using ANN for 96 g of fuel consumption, the SOC is 90–95%. For NYYC drive cycle, 16 g of fuel consumption, ANN-EMS provides 68%-95% of SOC. In the same way for UDDS the ANN-EMS achieved 83% to 92% of SOC with 35g of fuel consumption. In this work, the artificial neural network (ANN) is investigated in fuel cell based electric vehicles. From the above simulation results it is depicted that the ANN explorer better performance in energy management of a FCEV.

References

[1] Yang, S., Liu, X., Shen, L., & Zhang, C. (2023).. Advanced Battery Management System for Electric Vehicles. (Vol. 1). Springer.

[2] Waseem, M., Amir, M., Lakshmi, G. S., Harivardhagini, S., & Ahmad, M. (2023). Fuel cell-based hybrid electric vehicles: an integrated review of current status, key challenges, recommended policies, and future prospects. *Green Energy and Intelligent Transportation* 2(6), 100121.

[3] Fathabadi, H. (2018). Novel fuel cell/battery/supercapacitor hybrid power source for fuel cell hybrid electric vehicles. *Energy*, 143, 467–477.

[4] Xie, Shaobo, Shanwei Qi, and Kun Lang. (2019). A data-driven power management strategy for plug-in hybrid electric vehicles including optimal battery depth of discharging. *IEEE Transactions on Industrial Informatics.* 16.5: 3387–3396.

[5] Togun, H., Aljibori, H. S. S., Abed, A. M., Biswas, N., Alshamkhani, M. T., Niyas, H., et al. (2024). A review on recent advances on improving fuel economy and performance of a fuel cell hybrid electric vehicle. *International Journal of Hydrogen Energy*, 89, 22–47.

[6] Acharya, D. P., Hannon, N., Choudhury, S., Nayak, N., & Satpathy, A. (2023). Design and hardware in loop testing of an intelligent controller for power quality improvement in a complex micro grid. *Energy Reports*, 9, 4135–4156.

39 Predictive analytics for electric vehicle battery health: a machine learning approach

Ashok Kumar Bandla[1,a], Gopinath Palai[2,b] and Rabi N Satpathy[3,c]

[1]Research Scholar, Faculty of Engineering and Technology, Sri Sri University, Cuttack, Odissa, India

[2]Professor, Faculty of Engineering and Technology, Sri Sri University, Cuttack, Odisha, India

[3]Dean, Faculty of Engineering and Technology, Sri Sri University, Cuttack, Odisha, India

Abstract

The purpose of this paper is to evaluate the general state of the battery of an electric vehicle through the application of the K-nearest neighbors (KNN), Decision Trees, and Support Vector Machines (SVM). To evaluate the battery health indicators, we proposed models based on the battery performance characteristics and the environmental factors. Since the algorithms were compared, the following evaluation criteria were used: Mean absolute error (MAE), root mean squared error (RMSE), and F1-score, which would enable a proper evaluation of the models under consideration. Hence, the findings of the current study were that the SVM algorithm was superior in both accuracy and stability compared with the other two classifiers. This paper seeks to prove that it is feasible to apply machine learning to battery management systems to identify signs of battery failure and recommend what should be done. The implications of these findings are critical for optimizing the operational efficiency and longevity of EV batteries, thereby contributing to the sustainability of electric mobility solutions.

Keywords: Battery health assessment, Decision Trees, electric vehicle, F1-score, K-nearest neighbors, machine learning, mean absolute error, predictive analytics, root mean squared error, support vector machines

Introduction

With advancements in technology, the use of electric vehicles has gradually shifted to sustainable development in the automobile industry. As the adoption of electric cars rises, the durability and efficiency of batteries used in the cars are of interest to manufacturers and scholars. The battery is said to be the soul of an electric vehicle since it determines the range, performance, and level of satisfaction of the customer. Therefore, there is a need to assess the battery health in order to improve performance, safety, and to cover the cost of operation. The conventional way of determining battery health entails empirical testing and hand inspections, which are costly, time-consuming, and more susceptible to human error as compared to the proposed methods. Predictive analytics is defined as the use of tools in order to forecast battery conditions and come up with a solution to the problem before it occurs.

The rise of electric vehicles (EVs) has intensified mobility concerns and is steadily transforming the automobile

[a]bashokkumar.eee@gmail.com, [b]gpalai28@gmail.com, [c]rabinarayan.satpathy@gmail.com

DOI: 10.1201/9781003753391-39

industry. In the recent past, the motor vehicle industry has adopted the use of electric cars, and the durability of the batteries has become an essential factor to both producers and scholars. This is why the battery is considered the heart of an electric vehicle since it defines the capacity, distance, and satisfaction of the customers. Hence, it is required to constantly check the health state and evaluate the battery to change the factors that lead to a decline in the battery's performance, enhance the safety, and reduce the operation costs. The current approaches for battery health assessment include static and dynamic tests and physical assessment, which are costly, time-consuming, and inaccurate. While predictive analytics employs data analysis in estimating battery conditions relating to the problem, it also offers a solution on the same. The application of the above-mentioned ML techniques in battery health monitoring systems can contribute to the enhanced predictability and efficiency of the systems. Some of the parameters that can be used to measure the potential of the models in the live environment mean absolute error (MAE), root mean squared error (RMSE), and F1-score. The aim of this paper is to analyze the effectiveness of K-nearest neighbors (KNN), Decision Trees, and SVM in predicting the state of charge of EV batteries. In this study, we want to identify the most suitable approach for predicting battery performance characteristics under various conditions based on a large dataset. The results will help in expanding the existing knowledge in battery management systems with findings that improve the reliability and sustainability of electric cars. In addition, this study also aims to establish the need to apply the most appropriate techniques in analysis in order to address the challenges that are the results of new developments in the electric transport sector. This information will be useful in the development of strategies to be used in the management of batteries as the transportation industry moves to green technology solutions. Here is how the paper is laid down: The review of the literature on the application of machine learning to battery health assessment is presented in Section 2. The Section 3 of the research focuses on methodology, data, and model. Section 4 delves into the outcomes and evaluation of the machine learning methods' performance. The last section is the conclusion, and the recommendation for future research is given in the last part of the paper.

Literature Review

Khan et al. [1] came up with an AI-powered, streamlined battery management system for electric vehicles. They included machine learning methods to facilitate early issue detection and enable real-time monitoring. The suggested technology optimizes battery performance by precise regulation of thermal conditions and charge-discharge cycles. The trials demonstrated that the batteries have prolonged durability and enhanced safety overall. This research demonstrates the significance of AI in the development of battery management systems for electric vehicles. Smith et al. [2] use machine learning to evaluate the efficacy of various battery management systems (BMS) utilized in electric cars. To ensure batteries have a functional lifetime, they used several machine learning methodologies. The research assesses the efficacy of predictive algorithms in forecasting system failures or degradation. The findings demonstrate that optimal results are achieved when both forms of advertising are used concurrently. The results of this study showed that proper design of BMS was very crucial to extend the performance and reliability of EV batteries. Johnson et al. [3] believe that their paper gives a complete explanation of the diversity of vehicle battery types regarding electric vehicles, along with the diverse ways of predicting the future capacity. Patel and Sharma [4] applied machine learning models to estimate lithium-ion battery health indicators such as discharge capacity and internal resistance. They used dynamic time-series regression with the last 100 cycles for accurate SOH prediction. Further, early-cycle data enabled cycle life estimation with a reported RMSE of 8.9%. The work of Zhao et al. [5] involved a review of the use of machine learning in various aspects of lithium-ion battery management, such as material screening, lifespan prediction, and recycling. They put a focus on hybrid models and underscored prospective developments in battery databases and time-series modeling. Currently, researchers are investigating trends and what affects battery performance and life. It describes a variety of mathematical techniques, methodologies for building models, and methods for estimating battery capacity from data. And it lays out why temperature, charging the battery too much, and time can all lead to shorter life. The research can guide future studies of better batteries and expected EV performance. Battery health is monitored in BMS using several data-driven techniques, as noted by Garcia and Martinez [6]. A variety of algorithms were tried by the team to measure the state of health (SOH) of a battery. The paper explains the strengths and difficulties of data use when compared to former use of traditional methods. Experiments reveal that using several types of batteries in your device leads to better and more flexible predictions. The report emphasizes that using advanced analytics is playing an important role in lengthening the lifespan of electric car batteries. Tu and

colleagues [7] worked on a new approach for battery management by combining physics approaches with machine learning. Electrochemical models and neural networks were combined by researchers to study batteries differently. Results from the study indicate that the system can precisely measure voltage under several charge rates and various ageing conditions. Our evaluations prove that the hybrid approach correctly demonstrates battery power shrinkage with the same economic benefits as the standard models. The research points out that combining expertise in the field with machine learning improves the control of advanced batteries. They [8] measured accuracy with mean absolute error (MAE) and root mean square error (RMSE). Experts believe that MAE is less affected by unusual data points and gives a clearer average error than MSE does. According to the paper, being a quadratic metric suggests that RMSE might be misleading since it greatly penalizes big mistakes. Their study revealed that using MAE is a more accurate method for judging how reliable a prediction is in modelling situations. This work has been widely cited for how one can select error metrics to guide forecasting studies and model evaluation studies. Based on CNN and LSTM, Rastegarpanah et al. [9] developed a model for the prediction of RUL of lithium-ion batteries. The important features were found using Convolutional neural networks, and how the battery's condition changes over time were tracked using LSTM layers. The application of this model results in better battery life predictions than earlier techniques. By conducting experiments, it is clear that the hybrid architecture can handle the challenging nonlinearities seen in battery ageing. The findings here support progress in predictive analytics that help monitor and use batteries in electric vehicles. Afshari et al. [10] described an early approach for estimating RUL that relies on observing the voltage and capacity-rate difference curves of a battery. They look for small differences in the curves to discover if the battery is starting to degrade. The study shows that using this approach, you can determine when the product will fail before it loses much of its original capacity. The testing results show that the method works effectively with different battery chemistries and operating environments. It helps to evaluate the state of batteries by setting up timely maintenance and ensuring electric vehicles have reliable power systems.

State estimation models for lithium-ion batteries were reviewed by Zhou et al. [11], which included SoH, SoC, SoE, and SoP with proposed joint estimation frameworks. They underscored the importance of

AI and cloud-based strategies to improve the performance of next-generation BMS. Hyndman and Koehler [12] evaluated traditional forecast accuracy measures and highlighted their limitations for intermittent-demand data. They proposed the mean absolute scaled error (MASE) as a more reliable and standardized metric for comparing forecast accuracy across time series.

Sokolova and Lapalme [13] conducted a systematic analysis of 24 performance measures across different classification tasks, which encompassed both binary and multi-label issues. They created a taxonomy of measurement invariance, which allows for more dependable classifier assessments across various data conditions.

Methodology

The Figure 39.1 shows the Block Diagram of presented health assessment model. Data collection, data preparation and cleaning, model deployment, and a comprehensive assessment are the steps in the electric battery assessment approach. NASA battery dataset from Kaggle is used in this analysis. First, the methodology began with a data gathering process where we gathered all datasets which have information about battery's performance parameters: voltage, current, charge cycle, and temperature. Then, data preparation was done to make sure the data is quality data in the study.

Following this, data preparation was carried out to guarantee that the study contained high-quality samples. To handle cases of missing data, mean or median imputation techniques were applied, while outliers were detected using Z-score and either removed or corrected. In order to make the scale of the features uniform, feature scaling was done by normalization and standardization. The dataset was then split into a training set and a testing set in the

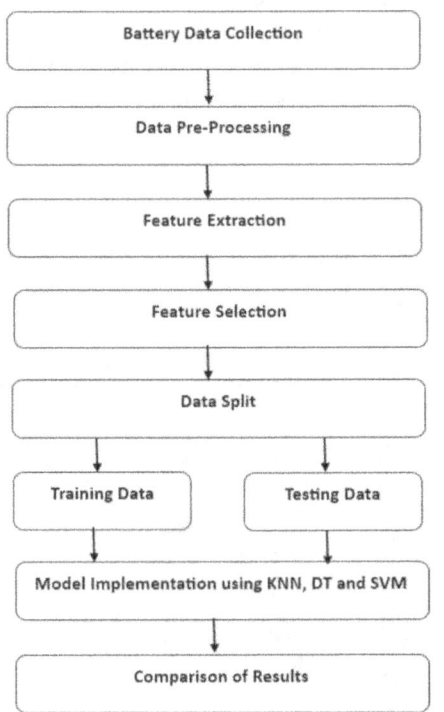

Figure 39.1 Block diagram of implementation of battery health assessment
Source: Author

normal manner, with a ratio of 80% to 20%, respectively, to train the model on one set and test on the other. Concerning KNN, the algorithm used the number of nearest neighbors equal to k and determined them using the Euclidean distance formula, which was represented as:

$$d(p,q) = \sum_{i=1}^{n} \sqrt{(p_i - q_i)^2} \qquad (1)$$

The optimal value of k was determined through cross-validation, and the model's accuracy was evaluated using the formula:

$$Accuracy = \frac{Number\ of\ correct\ predictions}{Total\ Predictions} \times 100 \qquad (2)$$

In the case of DT, the algorithm recursively splits the dataset based on feature values using Gini impurity, defined as:

$$Gini(D) = 1 - \sum_{i=1}^{c} p_i^2 \qquad (3)$$

Where *pi* represents the probability of class *i* in dataset *D*.

The tree persisted in bifurcating until a predetermined stopping condition was satisfied, such as maximum depth or minimum samples per leaf. They used the technique called pruning after training to avoid overfitting and improve generality. In case of Support Vector Machines (SVM), the algorithm used found the optimum hyperplane that best separated the classes with maximum margin, and is denoted by:

$$w.x + b = 0 \qquad (4)$$

When the weight vector is denoted by *w*, the input feature vector is denoted by *x*, and the bias is denoted by b. The optimization problem was formulated as:

$$min\frac{1}{2}\|w\|^2 \qquad (5)$$

To maximize each model's performance, hyperparameter optimization was done. Grid search with cross-validation was used to find the ideal value of k for KNN. Decision trees had their hyperparameters fine-tuned, including the minimum sample split, minimum sample per leaf, and maximum depth. In order to optimize SVM, we adjusted the kernel parameters and the regularization parameter (C). To make sure the model would hold up, we used K-fold cross-validation after we divided the dataset into k subsets. After k iterations of training with various validation subsets, the performance of the model was found to be consistent. Subsequently, the average precision for all the folds was computed. After comparing all the models, we chose the one that had the highest accuracy.

Result Analysis

This section gives the results of the design and implementation of the Battery Health

Table 39.1 Performance evaluation.

Method	RMSE	MAE	F1-Score
KNN	0.110	0.075	0.88
DT	0.095	0.065	0.91
SVM	0.087	0.058	0.94

Source: Author

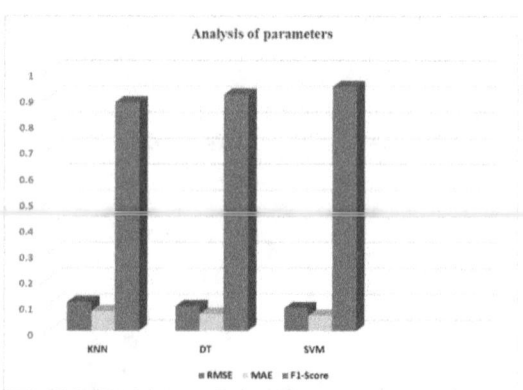

Figure 39.2 Analysis of parameters

Source: Author

Assessment. Regarding the evaluation of the model performance, three methods KNN, DT and SVM are used in the present study. Also, MAE, RMSE and F1 score are computed and then compared with each other. The performances are compared in the following Table 39.1.

Figure 39.2 represents the analysis of the results. MAE is another kind of measure of accuracy that provides a measure of overall accuracy. SVM achieved the least MAE of 0.058, which means that it was the least off most of the time. The second algorithm employed is the Decision Trees (DT) with a slightly higher error rate of 0.065, but still small enough that maintains the accuracy of the prognosis. KNN had the highest MAE of 0.075, and thus, it was observed that it was more likely to make small errors frequently.

MAE is less sensitive to large errors, while RMSE is sensitive to large errors, and therefore it is useful in measuring the model performance in cases where large errors are more critical. The lowest RMSE of 0.087 was predicted in SVM, which demonstrates that it is able to rule out vast discrepancy in the predicted values. After SVM, it was DT with smaller error of 0.095, though slightly higher than that of SVM; however, reasonable. The largest RMSE of 0.110 belongs to KNN, which signaled that this method effectively made the greatest errors in the prediction than the other two methods of DT and SVM. One of the evaluation metrics that we use to determine how well our models perform classification is the F1-score. Further, the SVM has the best F1 score of 0.94, implying better classification of levels of battery health conditions. We also experimented with Decision Trees with an F1-score of 0.91, and it was one of the most efficient in categorizing the data, but it wasn't as refined as SVM. Overall, KNN had an F1-score of 0.88, i.e., it was classified more incorrectly than DT and SVM.

Conclusion

For the purpose of this research, however, KNN, DT, and SVM were utilized to determine the health status of electric car batteries. An analysis of models' performance showed that among others, SVM had the lowest MAE (0.058), RMSE (0.087), and the highest F1-score (0.94). Next came Decision Trees with an F1-score of 0.91, but with error values slightly higher. The worst performing method was KNN, with highest MAE (0.075) and RMSE (0.110) and lowest F1-score (0.88). Unlike other algorithms, SVM performs better since it can determine the best margin for classification. As it turns out, Decision Trees were pretty accurate and easy to interpret, except for a slight problem of overfitting. The SVM has been found to be the most accurate model for real-time battery health monitoring. This paper should be extended with further research on ensemble techniques and deep learning methods to enhance its performance.

Future Scope

To improve battery health monitoring systems' prediction power and adaptability, a number of cutting-edge machine learning models should be investigated further. For battery performance data, a hybrid convolutional neural network-long short-term memory (CNN-LSTM) model can be created that efficiently captures both temporal relationships and spatial characteristics. The superior attention processes of transformer-based designs, which provide better accuracy in modeling sequential data patterns, may be investigated. Federated learning models, particularly in practical EV implementations, can be used to facilitate distributed learning while protecting data privacy. Graph neural networks (GNNs) offer a potential approach to simulating intricate connections between interrelated battery characteristics. Battery management systems may use reinforcement learning for in-the-moment decisions. Unsupervised learning is possible using variational auto-encoders (VAEs), which may also be used to identify abnormalities in battery behavior. Data scarcity can be addressed by combining transfer learning with generative adversarial networks (GANs) to provide realistic synthetic battery data. Textual maintenance logs can be interpreted using sophisticated natural language processing (NLP) models like BERT to provide predicted insights. To ensure real-time analysis, edge-AI models should be deployed in low-resource contexts. Finally, the accuracy and resilience of the model may be greatly improved by multi-modal learning techniques that include input from sensors, logs, and environmental variables.

References

[1] Khan, A., Begum, A., Kulkarni, A. M., Dhanushree, C., & Hemamalini, G. E. (2024). AI-enabled streamlined battery management in electric vehicles. *Journal of Electrical Systems*, 20(11s), 1–9.

[2] Smith, J. A., Lee, D. A., & Johnson, E. R. (2024). A comparative study on electric vehicle battery management systems using machine learning for enhanced safety and longevity. *International Journal of Mechanical, Electrical and Civil Engineering*, 1(2), 15–25.

[3] Johnson, R., Lee, K., & Smith, M. (2024). Electric vehicle battery technologies and capacity prediction: a comprehensive literature review of trends and influencing factors. *Batteries*, 10(12), 451.

[4] M. Patel and K. Sharma, (2022). Machine Learning Approaches for Lithium-Ion Battery Health Parameters Estimation, SAE Technical Paper 2022-28-0053, Oct. 5, 2022. doi: 10.4271/2022-28-0053.

[5] Zhao, Y., Wang, L., & Chen, M. (2023). Machine learning for full lifecycle management of lithium-ion batteries. *Renewable and Sustainable Energy Reviews*, 180, 113456.

[6] Garcia, S., & Martinez, R. (2023). An overview of data-driven battery health estimation technology for battery management systems. *Neurocomputing*, 463, 1–14.

[7] H. Tu, S. Moura, Y. Wang, and H. Fang, (2022). Integrating physics-based modeling with machine learning for lithium-ion batteries, Mitsubishi Electric Research Laboratories, Tech. Rep. TR2022-155, 2022, doi:10.1016/j.apenergy.2022.215483.

[8] Willmott, C. J., & Matsuura, K. (2005). Advantages of the mean absolute error (MAE) over the root mean square error (RMSE) in assessing average model performance. *Climate Research*, 30(1), 79–82.

[9] Rastegarpanah, A., Wang, Y., & Stolkin, R. (2022). Predicting the remaining life of lithium-ion batteries using a CNN-LSTM model. In Proceedings of 8th International Conference Mechatronics and Robotics Engineering (ICMRE), (pp. 73–78).

[10] Afshari, S. S., Cui, S., Xu, X., & Liang, X. (2022). Remaining useful life early prediction of batteries based on the differential voltage and differential capacity curves. *IEEE Transactions on Instrumentation and Measurement*, 71, 1–9.

[11] Zhou, L., Lai, X., Li, B., Yao, Y., Yuan, M., Weng, J., et al. (2023). State estimation models of lithium-ion batteries for battery management system: status, challenges, and future trends. *Batteries*, 9(2), 131.

[12] Hyndman, R. J., & Koehler, A. B. (2006). Another look at measures of forecast accuracy. *International Journal of Forecasting*, 22(4), 679–688.

[13] Sokolova, M., & Lapalme, G. (2009). A systematic analysis of performance measures for classification tasks. *Information Processing and Management*, 45(4), 427–437.

40 Advanced artificial intelligence techniques for comprehensive climate data analysis: a systematic review

Ashi Malaiya[1,a], Nysa Maheshwari[1,b], Priya Mathur[2,c] and Amit Kumar Gupta[1,d]

[1]Department of Computer Science and Engineering, Manipal University Jaipur, Rajasthan, India

[2]Department of Mathematics, Poornima Institute of Engineering and Technology, Jaipur, Rajasthan, India

Abstract

The rapid changes in climate patterns and their growing impact make it both more critical and more difficult to understand climate data than in any previous time. Traditional analytical methods become overloaded when processing vast data sets which prevents them from discovering the underlying connections and trends. The paper examines artificial intelligence (AI) applications which offer new methods for interpreting complex climate datasets to bridge existing analysis gaps. The core challenge involves utilizing AI to transform large and multidimensional climate data into meaningful and actionable insights beyond simple data processing. AI methods particularly machine learning techniques outperform conventional statistical approaches by detecting complex patterns and enhancing climate model predictions while conventional statistical techniques fail to capture the nonlinear dynamics of climate systems. AI applications within this domain face several important challenges. The lack of model transparency and interpretability together with the reliability of data sources and the challenge of variable selection present major hurdles in this field. The purpose of this review paper is to evaluate the existing state of AI applications for climate data analysis. The paper shows advancements in AI climate data analysis through recent studies and applications while identifying areas that require further research and development. The paper provides a transparent examination of AI's potential to enhance our understanding of climate patterns while supporting effective adaptation and mitigation strategies.

Keywords: Artificial intelligence techniques, climate data, data quality assurance, machine learning algorithms

Introduction

The multifaceted challenges posed by climate change require thoughtful consideration and analysis of intricate data. It's a shame that modern techniques of analysis do not portray complexity and relations within climate data. In this regard, it's worth noting the increasing contribution of artificial intelligence (AI) to interdisciplinary aspects of studying climate-conditional AI-Intensive purposes, as computers are capable of handling large amounts of environmental data because of their complexity and difficulty. Primary AI development is performed with the methodical use of

[a]ashi.219301248@muj.manipal.edu, [b]nysa.219301350@muj.manipal.edu,
[c]drpriyamathur21@gmail.com, [d]amit.gupta@jaipur.manipal.edu

DOI: 10.1201/9781003753391-40

machine learning algorithms. AI surpasses traditional statistical tools that are incapable of efficiently estimating nonlinear relations and interactions due to AI's characteristic of exposing latent structures, predicting changes, and improving the climate models [1–4]. The problem of transparency, data integrity, and the use of relevant indicators in the multi-dimensional data space can be considered the most primary. Providing methods of remote climate observation using AI enables this paper to synthesize diverse works AI in focused climate analysis considering the various AI algorithms applied along with their limits-answering the question: Why applying AI in understanding climate biology?

Significance of climate data analysis
Climate data aids in analyzing the patterns in how environmental systems respond to climate changes. AI techniques such as machine learning (ML) and deep learning (DL) provide tools capable of uncovering deep relationships among variables like temperature, precipitation, and atmospheric composition. These relationships are important to improve the projections of climate change and adaptation and mitigation strategies. The traditional approaches of analysis and their approaches based on statistics are often too simple for climate data and fall short in capturing the data's complex trends and patterns. ACEI-based models receive information from satellites, sensors, and weather stations and can predict areas that are more susceptible to climate dangers like flooding, drought, extreme weather, etc. The results can be used to design timely intervention systems intended to reinforce infrastructure and shield vulnerable populations [5]. Using AI in climate data analysis reduces uncertainties about climate change models and forecasts. This contributes to a refined understanding of climate impacts on

different regions and aids in crafting more effective strategies to address the ongoing changes to the environment [6].

The role of AI in climate science
The accurate modeling and forecasting of climate phenomena are heavily dependent on the use of AI technologies [7, 8]. Its support can be grouped into several predominant areas as follows:

1) Data gathering and scrutinizing: AI systems are capable of gathering climate data from satellites, weather monitoring stations, and simulation models at and processing these files at unprecedented scales.
2) Pattern recognition: Among AI's most useful capabilities is the ability to search for very intricate and concealed relationships in large data sets – relationships that would be impossible to detect with standard data analysis approaches.
3) Predictive modeling: AI is capable to suggest predictions on various climate conditions by extrapolating trends.
4) Uncertainty reduction: AI increases the reliability of climate models and projection, therefore reducing the uncertainty associated with the models and projections made of a particular climate system.
5) Sophisticated AI algorithms are powered by ML, DL, and neural networks (NN).
6) AI's application in climate sciences enhances the speed of data analysis and the quality of data insights, both of which lead to improved outcomes.

Literature Review

Climate data sources
Climate system and Earth's complex interaction are monitored and studied using

distinct climate markers or climatic data. This data can come from various locations including satellites, ground-based weather stations, environmental sensors, or by means of climate simulation models. Each of these aids in conducting climate research, but as with all tools, each comes with its own unique advantages and shortcomings [9]. Global climate monitoring satellites hold global importance. They have the capabilities to capture vital surface information ranging from bare land surface temperature, to rainfall, sea level rise or fall, and even up to the composition of gases within the atmosphere [10]. Weather stations possess the opposite advantage as they provide local level data. These stations track, temperature, rainfall, wind velocity and humidity, all of which are crucial for analyzing and forecasting short term weather [11]. One of the latest methods for acquiring climate data is the use of unattended environmental sensors. Such sensors are portable and can be adjusted to fit different settings ranging from urban jungles to remote and uninhabited terrains [12]. As has been discussed, the use of satellites, weather stations, and models alongside nontraditional techniques like sensors, provides holistic insights into the climate of Earth.

AI techniques in climate data analysis
The combination of ML and natural language processing (NLP) has brought a remarkable change in the development of climate science, particularly in sophisticated data analysis, modeling, and processing of unstructured texts [5–7]. Both technologies adopt different approaches but work towards a common goal; to enhance understanding of climate change and its effects [8]. In one example, the Climate Informatics Toolbox enables and encourages researchers to perform detailed analyses of climate model data using sophisticated ML techniques, as

they can now explain climate variables relationships and achieve reliable forecasts at regional scales [5, 13]. The DeepSD framework is one of the most accurate examples that make use of deep learning on spatiotemporal climate data. It focuses on the regional forecasting of temperature and precipitation, revealing vital relationships that aid in the formulation of precise adaptation measures [14, 15]. DL models, especially convolutional neural networks (CNNs), recurrent neural networks (RNNs), and deep belief networks (DBNs), are particularly capable of discerning these intricate associations and sophisticated patterns for climate projections [5–7]. The 2017 Hurricane Harvey NLP case is a solid witness to how powerful social media utilization through the NLP can be; in that case, the United States Coast Guard used social media tools powered by NLP to analyze Facebook and Twitter in real time, identifying people in distress as in as assessing community resource needs [6]. Beyond emergency response, NLP aids in climate change public discourse sentiment analysis for tailor suitable campaign strategy and engagement design. NLP also aids the qualitative synthesis of climate change literature analyses [13]. Hence, reliable evidence requires thorough analysis and, NLP combining ML and DL has immensely propelling climate science. With these technologies, analyzing climate data and constructing reliable climate models is becoming effortless.

Climate data preprocessing
Within the framework of climate science, which is both fast-paced and highly dependent on data, maintaining proper data quality integrity is foundational. The pillars upon which reliable analyses and informed decisions in response to climate changes are in the cleaning of data and in quality control processes. As is stated by Zhong et al. [16], the increasing amount and variety of climate

data is exceedingly difficult to retrieve and determine whether the datasets are appropriate to use and appropriate to trust. As indicated by Cowls et al. [17], such outlines would pertain to windows of criteria on data quality, accuracy, relevance, privacy, and interoperability. This becomes especially important as discussed by Sebestyén et al. [18] when identifying and rectifying errors for datasets used to train machine learning models for spatial and temporal analysis. Splitting data into a training set and validation set helps mitigate bias in machine learning models. As pointed out by Dueben et al. [19], climate data gaps, inconsistencies, and measurement errors undermine the quality of analysis. For example, Huang by et al. [20] describes how feature importance values helped to improve accuracy of random forest models by using only the most critical variables. In a similar fashion, other study [21] describes forward and backward stagewise selection, which enhances models by incrementally adding or removing selected features. Feature engineering adds the dimension of deriving new features from the spatiotemporal components of climate data. As indicated by Nocke et al. [22], derived features can significantly improve model performance for predicting extreme weather events. Both selection and engineering, however, can be costly in terms of time and resources. To this end Walsh et al. [23] proposes correlation-based feature selection (CFS), a filter approach that enhances efficiency by retaining variables strongly correlated to outcomes while poorly correlated features and redundant relationships are discarded. Addressing missing data is another important component of data quality. Techniques like multiple imputation as described by Khosravi et al. [24], create a number of reasonable guesses for every missing entry, which helps in reducing bias and increasing accuracy of

the dataset. Spatial interpolation methods of estimating missing data, such as kriging discussed by Fang et al. [25], are especially useful when spatial context can be applied. Further, determining the true reasons underlying gaps in data, like collection mistakes, or sensors failing to cover certain regions, is important as discussed by Gagne et al. [26]. In summary the climate data analysis relies on the carefully data cleaning, data quality preserving methods, planned feature selection methods and approaches are used to handing the missing data.

Climate prediction and modeling

The incremental uses of AI in this field offers a lot of opportunities for enhancing the climate change forecasting and get deeper insights into the climate change analysis [5]. AI enabled prediction to reduce the uncertainties in the climate data simulation by using ML, NN, and DL methods which are commonly used to identify the complex pattern and correlation to improve the accuracy of the predicted results [14]. The AI also proved that it could have major role in climate change data modelling and climate change impact evaluation [15], by the dataset of climate change like changes in the temperature, rain fall etc. AI model performance basically depends upon the quality of dataset; the forecasting may be affected if the data may have bias which can be raised by introducing of the missing data [6]. The DL models provide excel results in the simulation of extreme climate conditions like cyclones, heatwaves, heavy rainfall [13]. The DL methods require the extremely large dataset [27] to correctly forecast the climate conditions.

Pattern recognition and anomaly detection

Empirical diagnosis, discussed by Nocke et al. [22], is concerned with the detection of regularities and leading patterns in observed data, relating them to causal processes by means of reduced models. These methods help assess climate model reliability and determine significant characteristics of atmospheric regimes. However, Faghmous and Kumar [28] emphasizes, the integrity of long-term climate studies hinges on meticulous data validation due to potential biases introduced by changes in instruments and data processing. Temperature anomalies discussed by Monteleoni et al. [29], provide a standardized basis for comparing climate model predictions with observed temperatures. Standardized anomalies, as presented by Fang et al. [25], more precisely capture anomaly detection by incorporating standard deviation, providing insights into abnormal climate events and how they can potentially affect areas and biomes, as identified [18]. Success relies on the quality of data and avoidance of potential biases. Flood warning and forecasting systems, use large climate datasets to increase accuracy, advising government policies and helping us better understand the climate system [27, 30]. In addition, natural disaster effects on ecosystems are estimated through remote sensing and GIS technology, as explained by Martinez-Amaya et al. [31], to inform adaptation measures.

Climate data visualization

There are so many tools available in the field of AI which can create more powerful and impactful graphics. Beyond these basics, advanced visualization is becoming more important. Interactive visualization, as described by Wong et al. [32], allows for dynamic analysis of atmospheric climate data from many sources like reanalysis datasets, climate models and satellite observations. Developing unified, open and high-quality data is key for AI to contribute to global goals as described by Palomares et

al. [33]. But ethical and legal considerations are paramount in data communication. Adhering to standards of quality, accuracy, privacy, relevance and interoperability as described by Cowls et al. [17] ensures data trustworthiness and transparency and ethical use. And the impact of data communication, especially to different regions and communities, must be considered. This is why open dialogue between governments, citizens and stakeholders is key, guided by principles of inclusivity and inalienable human rights. This is important for achieving sustainable development goals as described by Abhisheket al. [34].

Challenges and limitations

Climate change is a significant concern; and we need new ideas and new tools. While AI, which is being adopted and used increasingly as a powerful tool, can demonstrably advance climate-related research and adaptations, its use in this area raises ethical, privacy, and bias issues, which need to be addressed. There is danger of privacy violations in regard to AI systems, especially when systems must rely on personal data to reveal human behavior patterns. While balancing personal privacy and data for climate science and research is paramount, this work requires strict adherence to formal ethical and legal standards when dealing with personal and sensitive information [35, 36]. While sharing climate data raises serious questions related to the quality of data shared and individual privacy, the potential to share data globally is also critically important, just as fundamentally important is the need to ensure data is accurate, relevant, and quality for research purposes. While ML can fill gaps, the problem persists and needs ongoing research and innovation. Biases in AI-based climate studies can come from many sources [37, 38]. Lack of diversity in development teams can lead to biases as perspectives from different communities are overlooked. Historical data can reinforce prejudices; hence, data selection and preprocessing have to be done carefully.

Climate change mitigation and adaptation

The urgent global crisis of climate change has some potential new solutions in AI. When it comes to reducing greenhouse gas emissions—what scientists call mitigation—AI is having a moment. Companies across the world are rushing to adopt the technology to rethink and rework their processes and products. That's what AI is helping us do. From sensors and drones to machine learning algorithms, the power of AI is being used to understand not just the present state of the world's climate but also how it is changing—and at ever-increasing resolutions.

Future Directions and Research Gaps

Its already apparent potential is set to make a significant splash in a number of crucial areas: Weighty, interdisciplinary climate data sets are becoming more manageable through the automated data processing and analysis capabilities of AI. Machine learning algorithms are being put to work to identify climate change variables and to find patterns in large volumes of climate data. Enhanced satellite imagery analysis: The analysis of satellite imagery can be considerably enhanced by AI, especially when it comes to identifying the sorts of areas that are likely to be inundated or suffering from coastal erosion thanks to conditions induced by climate change. Advanced climate model analysis: Dissecting complex climate models is a must if we are to comprehend the unfathomable secrets they keep. We must understand the intricate connections

between various climate variables that lie buried deep within these elaborate models. Robust early warning systems: The ability to make extremely capable early warning systems for severe weather occurrences is something that artificial intelligence offers. Improved uncertainty reduction: AI can help with reducing the uncertainties inherent in climate simulations and predictions, which will improve the accuracy and reliability of the simulations and predictions.

Conclusion

It is critical to understand the Earth's climate system and the impacts of climate change. Analyzing climate data from multiple sources—satellites, weather stations, sensors, and climate models—is necessary to do this understanding and is the first step in a multi-step process. Artificial intelligence (AI) offers very powerful means of not only understanding what the climate data currently reveal about the present state of the climate system but also of making projections about the future state of the climate system and the impacts that changes will have. One pivotal aspect of this whole process is not just using AI but using it in a way that is maximally productive, and the first step in that direction is to ensure that the data upon which all this complex, clever analysis will be performed are of the highest possible quality.

References

[1]   Sun, Z., Sandoval, L., Crystal-Ornelas, R., Mousavi, S. M., Wang, J., Lin, C., et al. (2022). A review of earth artificial intelligence. *Computers and Geosciences*, 159, 105034. doi: https://doi.org/10.1016/j.cageo.2022.105034.

[2]   Jebeile, J., Lam, V., Majszak, M., & Räz, T. (2023). Machine learning and the quest for objectivity in climate

model parameterization. *Climatic Change*, 176(8), 101. doi: 10.1007/s10584-023-03532-1.

[3] Ehsan, B. M. A., Begum, F., Ilham, S. J., & Khan, R. S. (2019). Advanced wind speed prediction using convective weather variables through machine learning application. *Applied Computing and Geosciences*, 1, 100002.

[4] Shi, X., Gao, Z., Lausen, L., Wang, H., Yeung, D. Y., Wong, W. K., et al. (2017). Deep learning for precipitation nowcasting: a benchmark and a new model. *Neural Information Processing Systems*, 30, 5617–5627.

[5] Jain, H., Dhupper, R., Shrivastava, A., Kumar, D., & Kumari, M. (2023). Ai- enabled strategies for climate change adaptation: protecting communities, infrastructure, and businesses from the impacts of climate change. *Computational Urban Science*, 3(1), 25. doi: 10.1007/s43762-023-00100-2.

[6] Ladstädter, F., Steiner, A. K., Lackner, B. C., Pirscher, B., Kirchengast, G., Kehrer, J., et al. (2010). Exploration of climate data using interactive visualization. *Journal of Atmospheric and Oceanic Technology*, 27(4), 667–679.

[7] Ayzel, G., Scheffer, T., & Heistermann, M. (2020). Rain Net v1.0: a convolutional neural network for radar-based precipitation nowcasting. *Geoscientific Model Development*, 13(6), 2631–2644. doi: https://doi.org/10.5194/gmd-13-2631-2020.

[8] Zhang, Y., Liu, X., Lei, L., & Liu, L. (2022). Estimating global anthropogenic CO_2 gridded emissions using a data-driven stacked random forest regression model. *Remote Sensing*, 14(16), 3899. doi: https://doi.org/10.3390/rs14163899.

[9] Leerbeck, K., Bacher, P., Junker, R. G., Goranović, G., Corradi, O., Ebrahimy, R., et al. (2020). Short-term forecasting of CO2 emission intensity in power grids by machine learning. *Applied Energy*, 277, 115527.

[10] Nahrstedt, F. (2022). A review of intelligent decision support systems in climate change adaptation. Preprint, doi: 10.13140/RG.2.2.23353.85601.

[11] Zhang, Q., & Zhu, S. (2018). Visual interpretability for deep learning: a survey. *Frontiers of Information Technology and Electronic Engineering*, 19(1), 27–39. doi: https://doi.org/10.1631/fitee.1700808.

[12] Ball, J. E., Anderson, D. T., & Chan, C. S. (2017). Comprehensive survey of deep learning in remote sensing: theories, tools, and challenges for the community. *Journal of Applied Remote Sensing*, 11(04), 1, doi: https://doi.org/10.1117/1.jrs.11.042609.

[13] Jacques-Dumas, V., Ragone, F., Borgnat, P., Abry, P., & Bouchet, F. (2022). Deep learning-based extreme heatwave forecast. *Frontiers in Climate*, 4, 789641. doi: https://doi.org/10.3389/fclim.2022.789641.

[14] Huntingford, C., Jeffers, E. S., Bonsall, M. B., Christensen, H. M., Lees, T., & Yang, H. (2019). Machine learning and artificial intelligence to aid climate change research and preparedness. *Environmental Research Letters*, 14(12), 124007. doi: https://doi.org/10.1088/1748-9326/ab4e55.

[15] Kay, J., Casola, J., & Snover, A. (2005). Climate change policy questions continued: national and regional summary. In Prepared for King County's October 27, 2005 Climate Change Conference, University of Washington.

[16] Zhong, S., Zhang, K., Bagheri, M., Burken, J. G., Gu, A., Li, B., et al. (2021). Machine learning: new ideas and tools in environmental science and engineering. *Environmental Science and Technology*, 55(19), 12741–12754. doi: https://doi.org/10.1021/acs.est.1c01339.

[17] Cowls, J., Tsamados, A., Taddeo, M., & Floridi, L. (2021). The AI gambit: leveraging artificial intelligence to combat climate change— opportunities, challenges, and recommendations. *Ai and Society*, 38(1), 283–307. doi: https://doi.org/10.1007/s00146-021-01294-x.

[18] Sebestyén, V., Czvetkó, T., & Abonyi, J. (2021). The applicability of big data in climate change research: the importance

of system of systems thinking. *Frontiers in Environmental Science*, 9, 619092. doi: https://doi.org/10.3389/fenvs.2021.619092.

[19] Dueben, P. D., Schultz, M. G., Chantry, M., Gagne, D. J., Hall, D. M., McGovern, A. (2022). Challenges and benchmark datasets for machine learning in the atmospheric sciences: Definition, status, and outlook. *Artificial Intelligence for the Earth Systems*, 1(3), e210002.

[20] Huang, J., Lucash, M. S., Scheller, R. M., & Klippel, A. (2020). Walking through the forests of the future: using data-driven virtual reality to visualize forests under climate change. *International Journal of Geographical Information Science*, 35(6), 1155–1178.

[21] Truby, J. (2020). Governing artificial intelligence to benefit the UN sustainable development goals. Sustainable Development, 28(4), 946–959.

[22] Nocke, T., Schumann, H., & Böhm, U. (2004). Methods for the visualization of clustered climate data. *Computational Statistics*, 19(1), 75–94. doi: https://doi.org/10.1007/bf02915277.

[23] Walsh, T., Evatt, A., & de Witt, C. S. (2020). Artificial intelligence & climate change: Supplementary impact report. Oxford, 1, 1–15.

[24] Khosravi, K., Daggupati, P., Alami, M. T., Awadh, S. M., Ghareb, M. I., Panahi, M., et al. (2019). Meteorological data mining and hybrid data intelligence models for reference evaporation simulation: a case study in Iraq. *Computers and Electronics in Agriculture*, 167, 105041.

[25] Fang, W., Xue, Q., Shen, L., & Sheng, V. S. (2021). Survey on the application of deep learning in extreme weather prediction. *Atmosphere*, 12(6), 661. doi: https://doi.org/10.3390/atmos12060661.

[26] Gagne, D. J., McGovern, A., Haupt, S. E., Sobash, R. A., Williams, J. K., & Xue, M. (2017). Storm-based probabilistic hail forecasting with machine learning applied to convection-allowing ensembles. *Weather and Forecasting*, 32(5), 1819–1840. doi: https://doi.org/10.1175/waf-d-17-0010.1.

[27] Racah, E., Beckham, C., Maharaj, T., Ebrahimi Kahou, S., Prabhat, M., & Pal, C. (2017). Extreme weather: a large-scale climate dataset for semi- supervised detection, localization, and understanding of extreme weather events. *Neural Information Processing Systems*, 30, 3402–3413.

[28] Faghmous, J. H., & Kumar, V. (2014). A big data guide to understanding climate change: the case for theory-guided data science. *Big Data*, 2(3), 155–163. doi:https://doi.org/10.1089/big.2014.0026.

[29] Monteleoni, C., Schmidt, G. A., & McQuade, S. (2013). Climate informatics: accelerating discovering in climate science with machine learning. *Computing in Science and Engineering*, 15(5), 32–40. doi: https://doi.org/10.1109/mcse.2013.50.

[30] Reeves, J., Chen, J., Wang, X. L., Lund, R., & Lu, Q. Q. (2007). A review and comparison of changepoint detection techniques for climate data. *Journal of Applied Meteorology and Climatology*, 46(6), 900–915. doi: https://doi.org/10.1175/jam2493.1.

[31] Martinez-Amaya, J., Radin, C., & Nieves, V. (2022). Advanced machine learning methods for major hurricane forecasting. *Remote Sensing*, 15(1), 119–119. doi: https://doi.org/10.3390/rs15010119.

[32] Wong, P. C., Foote, H., Leung, R., Jurrus, E., Adams, D., & Thomas, J. (2000). Vector fields simplification - a case study of visualizing climate modeling and simulation data sets. In Proceedings of the IEEE Visualization (Vis'00), (pp. 485–488, 596).

[33] Palomares, I., Martínez-Cámara, E., Montes, R., García-Moral, P., Chiachio, M., Chiachio, J., et al. (2021). A panoramic view and swot analysis of artificial intelligence for achieving the sustainable development goals by 2030: progress and prospects. *Applied Intelligence*, 51(9), 6497–6527. doi: https://doi.org/10.1007/s10489-021-02264-y.

[34] Orlove, B., Shwom, R., Markowitz, E., & Cheong, S. M. (2020). Climate

decision-making. *Annual Review of Environment and Resources*, 45, 271–303.

[35] Abhishek, K., Singh, M. P., Ghosh, S., & Anand, A. (2012). Weather forecasting model using artificial neural network. *Procedia Technology*, 4, 311–318.

[36] Priyadarshini, I., & Puri, V. (2021). Mars weather data analysis using machine learning techniques. *Earth Science Informatics*, 14(4), 1885–1898. doi: https://doi.org/10.1007/s12145-021-00643-0.

[37] Klepac, S., Subgranon, A., & Olabarrieta, M. (2022). A case study and parametric analysis of predicting hurricane-induced building damage using data-driven machine learning approach. *Frontiers in Built Environment*, 8, 1015804.

[38] Haq, M. A., Baral, P., Yaragal, S., & Pradhan, B. (2021). Bulk processing of multi-temporal modis data, statistical analyses and machine learning algorithms to understand climate variables in the Indian himalayan region. *Sensors*, 21(21), 7416. doi: https://doi.org/10.3390/s21217416.

41 ANN models development for solar irradiance forecasting using metrological data

Saumya Mishra[1,a], Deependra Pandey[1,b] and Saurabh Bhardwaj[2,c]

[1]Department of Electronics and Communication Engineering, Amity School of Engineering and Technology, Amity University, Lucknow Campus, UP, India

[2]Department of Electrical and Instrumentation Engineering, Thapar Institute of Engineering and Technology, Thapar University, Patiala, Punjab, India

Abstract

Due to the dynamic nature of availability and consumption, reliable solar irradiance forecasts is critical for assisting energy system operators in making well-informed decisions. Although contemporary models can estimate solar radiation components, their dependability is typically compromised by changing sky conditions and cloud cover. This research describes a strategy that uses artificial neural networks (ANN) to predict solar irradiance based on weather and geography. Several machine learning frameworks were created with inputs such as meteorological data and geographical features at predetermined time intervals. These models were trained and verified with observational data collected from several districts in Uttar Pradesh, India. The ANN-based strategy surpassed downscaled estimates, with a RMSE of 0.011132 W/m² and R-value of 0.998. The model was evaluated over many times and in places, exhibiting conformance to actual data.

Keywords: Artificial neural network, data prediction, forecasting, solar irradiance, weather data

Introduction

Economic growth and rising energy demand are often linked; improved efficiency, electrification, and prudent energy use can help to lessen this reliance. As a result of the growth of sources of renewable energy like solar photovoltaic and wind and the increasing popularity of electric vehicles, energy production, consumption, and distribution are becoming highly integrated, efficient, and ecologically friendly [1]. Despite these developments, electricity output remains inconsistent due to the inherent spatial and temporal variability of renewable energy. This makes it difficult to keep supply and demand in balance, particularly given the lack of dependable, large-scale storage

solutions. PV systems rely heavily on solar irradiance, which comprises diffuse horizontal irradiance (DHI) and direct beam irradiance (DNI). For more precise solar power predictions, accurate forecasting is essential. Forecasts of solar irradiance are made using a range of methods. These include more sophisticated data-driven and machine learning techniques like regression analysis, K-nearest neighbors, artificial neural networks (ANN), or hybrid approaches, as well as physics-based techniques like numerical weather prediction and image-based models using sky, shadow, or satellite imagery. By combining the constitute and state equations of atmospheric physical processes, physical models are able to replicate atmospheric

[a]msaumyabtech@gmail.com, [b]dpandey@lko.amity.edu, [c]saurabh.bhardwaj@thapar.edu

DOI: 10.1201/9781003753391-41

behavior. By examining meteorological factors including temperature, humidity, wind, and precipitation, these models forecast the weather. Precise calculation of the distinct components of solar radiation, namely DHI and DNI, is sometimes not the primary emphasis in this context. Rather, to guarantee energy balance computations at the Earth's surface, global horizontal irradiance (GHI) is usually employed. The most popular global prediction model used in many nations is medium-range weather forecasting. For example, research [2] revealed that their suggested model performed better than the global forecast system (GFS) under all-sky circumstances when comparing 24-hour estimates of global solar irradiance with observed data. Hourly irradiance estimates from the GFS-driven weather research and forecasting (WRF) model and the IFS/ECMWF global model, which are set differently by various forecast providers, were assessed using observational data from the US and Europe in the study [3]. Results indicated that the ECMWF model performed noticeably better than its competitors. Using observations from Évora, Portugal, Perdigão et al. [4] evaluated a year's worth of hourly and daily irradiance projections based on the ECMWF over forecast ranges of 0 to 3 days. For hourly projections, the model's RMSE was 211 W/m2, while for daily forecasts; it was 68.5 W/m². Research has concentrated on increasing the need for dependable solar energy systems in order to improve the anticipated accuracy of solar radiation [5, 6]. DNI forecasting is challenging because of its heavy reliance on clouds and atmospheric particle concentrations. numerical weather prediction (NWP) models like IFS/ECMWF employ average climatologies monthly basis rather than detailed predictions in order to minimize processing needs. Yang et al.'s thorough analysis [7] looked at how

pollution concentrations affect the availability of solar resources. Highlights the Goddard Earth Observing System Version 5 (GEOS-5) and Copernicus Atmospheric Monitoring Service (CAMS) as instruments for enhancing forecasting. According to Breitkreuz et al. [8], hourly GHI predictions based on IFS/ECMWF outputs might have their relative MSE (rMSE) reduced by 4.3% with the use of an improved prediction algorithm and the radiative transfer model libRadtran [9]. Research looked on combining machine learning with forecast modelling. In [10], chemistry and weather research and forecasting model were used to model radiation and air pollution. Shortwave radiative forcing during dust storm occurrences was found to be two to five times higher than on days without dust. Likewise, in atmospheric simulations, the rapid radiation transfer model for shortwave radiation (RRTM_SW) is employed to demonstrate minor inaccuracies in microphysical particle parameterizations [11]. It is still very difficult to accurately depict the complex relationships between solar radiation, air constituents, and the Earth's surface [12]. In order to improve solar radiation forecasting utilizing model outputs and empirical data without placing undue processing demands on the system, it is crucial to strike a balance between the increasing complexity of deterministic physical models and the creation of complementing tools

Related Work

To improve the accuracy of solar radiation forecasts made by deterministic weather prediction models, a number of methods have been created and tested. These techniques fall into two categories: machine learning (ML) approaches and conventional statistical techniques. Simple interpolation and more complex techniques like stepwise linear regression, which chooses variables most linked to forecast errors, are examples of traditional approaches. To generate estimates of forecast error, these variables were then included to regression models [13]. With a major focus on predicting solar irradiance, ML techniques including k-nearest neighbors, Support Vector Machines (SVM), Random Forest (RF), and artificial neural networks (ANN) have been thoroughly studied in solar forecasting [14]. With an accuracy of 81%, a recent development presented a deep learning-based tool that determines the best GHI forecasting model among several machine learning techniques [15]. By using historical data, machine learning has proven to be able to identify correlations between forecast mistakes and affecting factors. When compared to physical modelling techniques, this enables the creation of better predictions in a substantially shorter amount of time [16]. Alfadda et al. [17] used a variety of machine learning techniques to produce hourly estimates of GHI, DNI, and DHI using Saudi Arabian data. The findings showed that ANNs performed the best. When comparing feedforward and recurrent ANNs for forecasting global sun irradiance, Pang et al. [18] discovered that RNNs provided modest accuracy gains at the expense of higher processing demands. The regime-dependent ANN model created by McCandless et al. [19] for short-range irradiance forecasting performed better than both a generic ANN and a persistence model. In order to generate day-ahead forecasts, Fonseca et al. [20] used SVMs and data of mesoscale model from Japanese Meteorology Agency. Regional RMSE decreased as a result of this strategy. Model bias, MSE, and RMSE were significantly reduced when Lima et al. [21] used ANNs to post-process solar irradiation projections produced by the model for Brazil. Since

trained models may use historical data to produce more precise geographical distributions of solar irradiance, this machine learning approach can also be applied to the evaluation of solar resources. Using the mesoscale Meso-NH model's outputs [22] created and refined an ANN model for estimating solar resources. Their method demonstrated advances in mapping DNI and GHI, at the horizontal resolution of 1 kilometre, and was verified for the southern area of Portugal. The literature contains reviews of machine learning techniques for predicting [23]. Due to variations in prediction horizon and temporal precision, several models that have been developed are inappropriate for real-time forecasting and mainly target GHI [24, 25]. The approach for solar irradiance forecasting presented in this study combines: (i) spatial and temporal data corresponding to a particular time step and location; (ii) ANN model that can generate enhanced forecasting based only on location inputs & predicted weather; and (iii) a machine learning system that combines a series of recent irradiance forecasts with seasonal indicators to improve predictions. Data from many districts in Uttar Pradesh, India, with a one-month temporal resolution, applied to develop and analyze the methodology. The results shows that the suggested framework may be successfully applied to various places and is generalizable. This paper is organized as follows: A survey of relevant work on the topic is given in Section 2. The datasets used in this investigation are described in Section 3, as are the preparation procedures, including the techniques used for the temporal and geographical downscaling of prediction data. An assessment of the predictions produced by the machine learning models is given in Section 4. It covers the creation and application of the ANN models that improve forecast accuracy. Section 5 wraps up the research by providing a summary of the key conclusions and contributions.

Methodology

Data for Uttar Pradesh, India's most populous state with over 200 million people spread across 75 districts was gathered for this study. Meteorological and sun radiation statistics data collected from the United Nations Food and Agriculture Organization (FAO). CROPWAT 8.0 and CLIMWAT 2.0 were used to collect data for 14 weather stations. The names and geographic coordinates of these stations—latitude (LAT), longitude (LON), and altitude (ALT)—are displayed in Figure 41.1. Maximum air temperature (MAT), minimum air temperature (MIT), relative humidity (HUM), wind speed (WIN), sunshine duration (SUN), and solar radiation (RAD) are among the yearly average meteorological variables included in the CSV-formatted data. ALT, LAT, LON, month of year (MOY), MIT, HUM, and WIN are the input characteristics that are taken as input variables as an array XNx7 having seven columns and N is the data size (rows). The total data size is N = 2000.The solar irradiance is taken as output variable YNx1. Figure 41.2 shows the correlation between the input and output variables. Solar radiation (RAD) is shown to be strongly positively correlated with maximum temperature (MAT) and sunlight hours (SUN), suggesting that these variables have a major impact on solar irradiance. On the other hand, there is little association between RAD and factors like wind speed (WIN), latitude (LAT), longitude (LON), and altitude (ALT). This implies that not all input factors have an equal impact on solar irradiance. Nonetheless, the possibility for constructing a mathematical link between the input characteristics and the output variable is shown by the substantial correlation

found with minimum temperature (MIT), MAT, relative humidity (HUM), and SUN. Data for Uttar Pradesh, India's most populous state with over 200 million people spread across 75 districts was gathered for this study. Meteorological and sun radiation statistics from the United Nations Food and Agriculture Organization (FAO) are considered. CROPWAT 8.0 and CLIMWAT

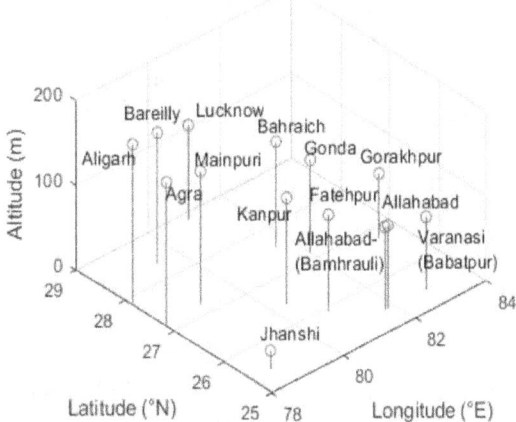

Figure 41.1 Geographical details of location used

Source: Author

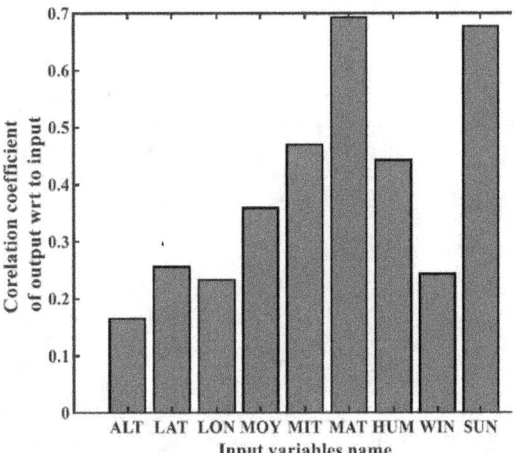

Figure 41.2 Correlation between IP/OP data

Source: Author

2.0 were used to collect data for 14 weather stations. The names and geographic coordinates of these stations—latitude (LAT), longitude (LON), and altitude (ALT)—are displayed in Figure 41.1. Maximum air temperature (MAT), minimum air temperature (MIT), relative humidity (HUM), wind speed (WIN), sunshine duration (SUN), and solar radiation (RAD) are among the yearly average meteorological variables included in the CSV-formatted data. ALT, LAT, LON, month of year (MOY), MIT, HUM, and WIN are the input characteristics are taken as input variables as an array XN × 7 having seven columns and N is the data size (rows). The total data size is N = 2000.The solar irradiance is taken as output variable YN×1.

Figure 41.2 shows the correlation between the input and output variables. Solar radiation (RAD) is shown to be strongly positively correlated with maximum temperature (MAT) and sunlight hours (SUN), suggesting that these variables have a major impact on solar irradiance. On the other hand, there is little association between RAD and factors like wind speed (WIN), latitude (LAT), longitude (LON), and altitude (ALT). This implies that not all input factors have an equal impact on solar irradiance. Nonetheless, the possibility for constructing a mathematical link between the input characteristics and the output variable is shown by the substantial correlation found with minimum temperature (MIT), MAT, relative humidity (HUM), and SUN. Table 41.1 is generated for observing the covariance in between all the input variables to one another. MIT and MAT are highly correlated as observed in this figure. The approach for forecasting the solar irradiance is briefly shown in Figure 41.3. It describes that first of all the data is imported to MATLAB software as the input and output variables X and Y described as input and targets.

The data variables have different dimensions and minimum/maximum value hence they are first of all normalized to bring under similar scale. The ML techniques are applied using user interface available in MatLab as curve fitting toolbox. The data is bifurcated in training and testing data in the ratio of 70 and 30%. The parameters of different ML models are adjusted under different learning algorithm associated to specific ML models. The generated ML models are executed on testing data. The generated

Table 41.1 Covariance in between different input variables.

	ALT	LAT	LON	MOY	MIT	MAT	HUM	WIN	SUN
ALT	1.053	0.183	-0.115	0.007	-0.514	-0.595	-0.066	-0.085	-0.151
LAT	0.183	0.987	0.199	0.008	-0.324	-0.166	-0.199	-0.310	-0.084
LON	-0.115	0.199	0.990	0.005	-0.016	-0.126	0.334	-0.309	-0.255
MOY	0.007	0.008	0.005	0.976	0.056	-0.093	0.296	-0.086	-0.246
MIT	-0.514	-0.324	-0.016	0.056	0.998	0.799	0.170	0.435	-0.130
MAT	-0.595	-0.166	-0.126	-0.093	0.799	1.003	-0.358	0.239	0.308
HUM	-0.066	-0.199	0.334	0.296	0.170	-0.358	1.005	0.140	-0.630
WIN	-0.085	-0.310	-0.309	-0.086	0.435	0.239	0.140	1.046	-0.099
SUN	-0.151	-0.084	-0.255	-0.246	-0.130	0.308	-0.630	-0.099	1.032

Source: Author

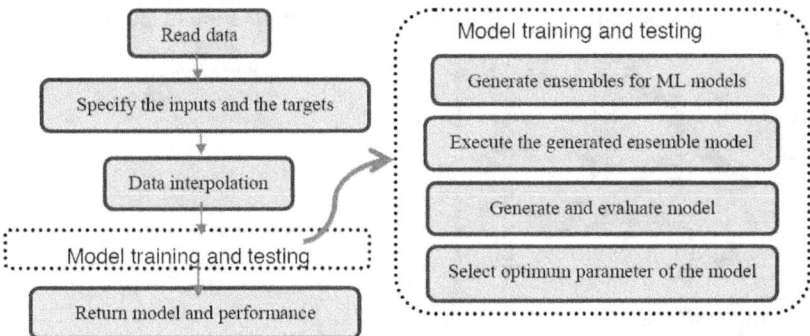

Figure 41.3 Steps involved in developing ML based models solar irradiance forecasting
Source: Author

result in terms of solar irradiance value is used to evaluate the performance of ML models. Finally, all the models are executed on test data to compare the performance.

The data is imported to MATLAB software, and the two new arrays are generated for input dataset and output dataset respectively as shown in Figure 41.3. After defining the dataset, the interpolation is applied to increase the data set size and fill up the missing values in two consecutive entries. For input dataset of 9 column matric close grid interpolation and for the output vector piecewise spline interpolation is applied. After applying for the interpolation the training of machine learning models is applied. In this work, however major focus is given to ANN but for comparison purpose different ML models are trained and tested prior to developing ANN based forecasting model. The different ML models are linear regression (LR), decision tree (DT) as basic models while bag tree (BGT) and boost tree (BST) as enhanced version of ensemble method are implemented. The ML training and testing involves the generation of ensemble for ML models. The ML models generated executed to produce the forecast result. The generated results are used to evaluate the model's performance in terms of MSE, RMSE, MAE etc. Using

performance metrics the best ML model from ensembles of varying model parameters is selected for final comparison from LR, DT, BGT and BST models. After development of these four models similar process is applied for developing the ANN using the neural network toolbox of MATLAB software. The ANN consists of three layers known as input layer, hidden layer and output layer. The input layer has 9 nodes as per the number of inputs while the output layer has only one node. Thus, the generated ANN model is 9-IP-1-OP based structure, but the hidden layer does not have any specific number of nodes. Hence the number of nodes of hidden layer is changed from 2,6,10,14,18 and different times the ANN model are generated using Levenberg–Marquardt learning algorithm for feed forward back propagation training scheme.

Results

The ML models are generated by training algorithm using training data and further forecasting is performed on testing data. The training testing dataset is kept 70–30%. In Figure 41.4a the performance of ANN is shown in terms of regression value using scatter plot for target (actual) and estimated output. The regression value R is

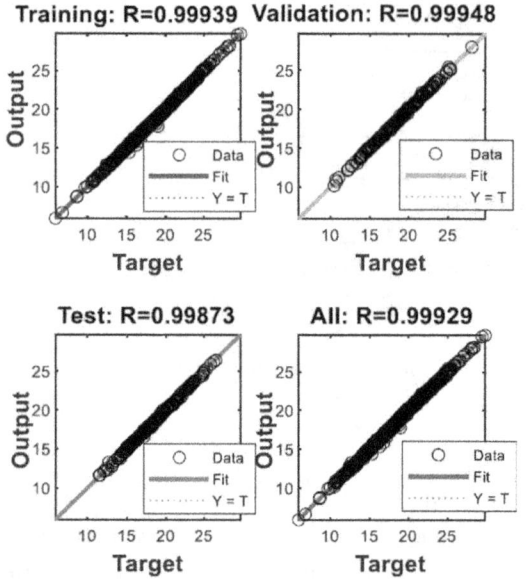

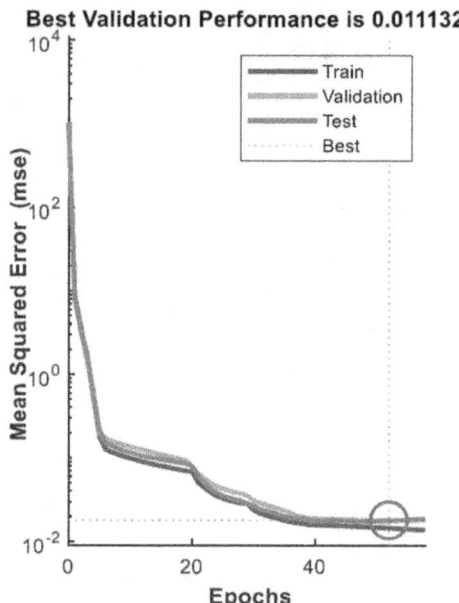

Figure 41.4 a. Regression (R) value for different dataset
Source: Author

Figure 41.4 b. MSE plot during training
Source: Author

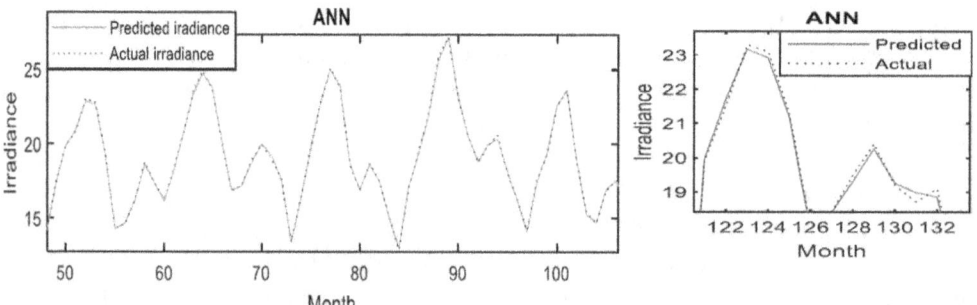

Figure 41.5 a. Actual output and predicted output using ANN (left); b. Magnified view (right)
Source: Author

shown for training, validation, testing and overall data. The best fitting is assumed if regression is closer to 1. In the figure it is observed that the regression is above 0.99 hence the ANN has best fitting result. The Figure 41.4b shows MSE during the learning process of ANN. As the number of epochs is increasing the MSE is decreasing. The Figure 41.5a shows the fitting plot to show the mapping of estimated output as

solar irradiance forecast on the actual output value. The Figure 41.5b (right) is the magnified value of Figure 41.5a to show the minute difference in predict and actual output. Since the ANN model is generated multiple times to find the optimum value of number of nodes at which best forecast performance is observed the Table 41.2 shows the R and MSE value at number of nodes 2,6,10,14 and 18. Best performance

Table 41.2 Performance comparison in terms of R, MSE, RMSE and MAE among ML models.

No. of nodes	R-Train Data	R-Validate	R-Test Data	Epoch	MSE		LR	DT	BST	BGT	ANN
2	0.97275	0.97588	0.9694	28	0.5937						
6	0.99934	0.99951	0.9981	210	0.0129	RMSE	0.8035	0.8920	1.1151	1.0104	0.1074
10	0.9993	0.99921	0.9995	124	0.0184	MSE	0.6457	0.7957	1.2434	1.0209	0.0115
14	0.99939	0.99948	0.9987	37	0.0111	MAE	0.6285	0.5832	0.9253	0.6782	0.0851
18	0.9992	0.99749	0.9989	26	0.0523	Train Time	5.3601	1.8441	2.864	2.129	6.32

Source: Author

observed at ANN with 14 nodes in hidden layer. In the same table the performance of ANN is further compared with LR, DT, BGT and BST ML models.

Conclusions

This paper presents an ML model for improving direct normal irradiance (DNI) prediction by exploiting data collected from real time setting. It uses meteorological data from CROPWAT 8.0 and CLIMWAT 2.0, taking into account critical atmospheric characteristics that influence solar energy transmission. The data is geographically and temporally adjusted by interpolation of close grid values and piecewise interpolation for average monthly parameters. ANN-based forecasting frameworks developed and fine-tuned to provide superior DNI estimations across a monthly prediction window with the necessary time granularity. The feed forward neural network with optimum number of nodes was finally chosen above other studied topologies due to its higher predicting capacity. The model is evaluated in an operational context for each month's record for projections for the next month, which are used by power grid operators and solar energy producers to estimate production and make smart judgments. R and RMSE values for the forecast were obtained by comparing the final model outputs using similar type test dataset and blind test datasets with ground-based observations at the same location. R-value 0.998 and RMSE 0.011132 W/m² indicate an improvement above the first downscaled DNI projection. Additionally, it was demonstrated that the developed algorithm can be applied to similar temporal resolutions with good results. This could be useful when forecasts with different time steps are required to meet the real-time market requirements of energy market operators and power plants.

References

[1] Srivastava, A., & Banoudha, A. (2014). Techniques of visualization of web navigation system. *International Journal of Research and Development in Applied Science and Engineering (IJRDASE)*, 6(1), 1–6.

[2] El Alani, O., Ghennioui, A., Ghennioui, H., Saint-Drenan, Y.-M., & Blanc, P. (2020). Evaluation of 24-hrs. forecasts of global solar irradiation from IFS, GFS and McClear models. AIP Conference Proceedings, 2307(1), 020053.

[3] Perez, R., Lorenz, E., Pelland, S., Beauharnois, M., Van Knowe, G., Hemker Jr, K., et al. (2013). Comparison of numerical weather prediction solar irradiance forecasts in the US, Canada and Europe. *Solar Energy*, 94, 305–326.

[4] Perdigão, J., Canhoto, P., Salgado, R., & Costa, M. J. (2020). Assessment of direct normal irradiance forecasts based on IFS/ECMWF data and observations in the south of Portugal. *Forecasting*, 2, 130–150.

[5] de Araujo, J. M. S. (2021). Improvement of coding for solar radiation forecasting in Dili Timor Leste—a WRF case study. *Journal of Power and Energy Engineering*, 9, 7–20.

[6] Hogan, R. (2018). Radiation in the Next Generation of Weather Forecast Models: Workshop Report, *Journal of Advances in Modeling Earth Systems*, 10(8), 1990–2008.

[7] Yang, D., Wang, W., Gueymard, C. A., Hong, T., Kleissl, J., Huang, J., et al. (2022). A review of solar forecasting, its dependence on atmospheric sciences and implications for grid integration: Towards carbon neutrality. *Renewable and Sustainable Energy Reviews*, 161, 112348.

[8] Breitkreuz, H., Schroedter-Homscheidt, M., Holzer-Popp, T., & Dech, S. (2009). Short-range direct and diffuse irradiance forecasts for solar energy applications based on aerosol chemical transport and numerical weather modeling. *Journal of Applied Meteorology and Climatology*, 48, 1766–1779.

[9] Mayer, B., Kylling, A., & Emde, C. (2012). Radiative transfer simulations, libRadtran User's Guide, 1(1), 5–15.

[10] Bran, S. H., Jose, S., & Srivastava, R. (2018). Investigation of optical and radiative properties of aerosols during an intense dust storm: a regional climate modeling approach. *Journal of Atmospheric and Solar-Terrestrial Physics*, 168, 21–31.

[11] Obiso, V., & Jorba, O. (2018). Aerosol-radiation interaction in atmospheric models: Idealized sensitivity study of simulated short-wave direct radiative effects. *Journal of Aerosol Science*, 115, 46–61.

[12] Larson, V. E. (2013). Forecasting solar irradiance with numerical weather prediction models. In Solar Energy Forecasting and Resource Assessment, (pp. 299–318).

[13] Verzijlbergh, R. A. (2015). Improved model output statistics of numerical weather prediction based irradiance forecasts of solar power. *Solar Energy*, 118, 634–645.

[14] Alkhayat, G., & Mehmood, R. (2021). A review and taxonomy of wind and solar energy forecasting methods based on deep learning. *Energy AI*, 4, 100060.

[15] Alkhayat, G., Hasan, S. H., & Mehmood, R. (2022). SENERGY: a novel deep learning-based autoselective approach and tool for solar energy forecasting. *Energies*, 15(18), 6659.

[16] Delle Monache, L., Eckel, F. A., Rife, D. L., Nagarajan, B., & Searight, K. (2013). Probabilistic weather prediction with an analog ensemble. *Monthly Weather Review*, 141, 3498–3516.

[17] Alfadda, A., Rahman, S., & Pipattanasomporn, M. (2018). Solar irradiance forecast using aerosols measurements: a data driven approach. *Solar Energy*, 170, 924–939.

[18] Pang, Z., Niu, F., & O'Neill, Z. (2020). Solar radiation prediction using recurrent neural network and artificial neural network: a case study with comparisons. *Renewable Energy*, 156, 279–289.

[19] McCandless, T. C., Young, G. S., Haupt, S. E., & Hinkelman, L. M. (2016). Regime-dependent short-range solar irradiance forecasting. *Journal of Applied*

Meteorology and Climatology, 55, 1599–1613.

[20] Fonseca, J. G. D. S. (2020). Enhancements in day-ahead forecasts of solar irradiation with machine learning: a novel analysis with the Japanese mesoscale model. *Journal of Applied Meteorology and Climatology*, 59, 1011–1028.

[21] Lima, F. J. L., Martins, F. R., Pereira, E. B., Lorenz, E., & Heinemann, D. (2016). Forecast for surface solar irradiance at the Brazilian Northeastern region using NWP model and artificial neural networks. *Renewable Energy*, 87, 807–818.

[22] Pereira, S., Abreu, E. F., Iakunin, M., Cavaco, A., Salgado, R., & Canhoto, P. (2022). Method for solar resource assessment using numerical weather prediction and artificial neural network models based on typical meteorological data: application to the south of portugal. *Solar Energy*, 236, 225–238.

[23] Hyun Jung, A., Lee, D. H., Kim, J. Y., Kim, C. K., Kim, H. G., & Lee, Y. S. (2020). Spatial and temporal downscaling of solar radiation using statistical techniques, *Journal of Korean Solar Energy Soc.* 40, 89–94.

[24] Yang, D., Wu, E., & Kleissl, J. (2019). Operational solar forecasting for the real-time market. *International Journal of Forecasting*, 35, 1499–1519. doi: 10.1016/j.ijforecast.2019.03.009.

[25] Sahay, S., Banoudha, A., & Sharma, R. (2013). Comparative study of soft computing techniques for ground water level forecasting in a hard rock area. *International Journal of Research and Development in Applied Science and Engineering (IJRDASE)*, 4(1), 1–6.

42 Prediction of cooking quality parameters of rice genotypes using machine learning model

Saraswati Pati[1,a], Abhishek Das[2,b], Supriya Kumari[3,c] and Goutam Kumar Dash[1,d]

[1]Department of Biochemistry and Crop physiology, Centurion University of Technology and Management, Odisha, India

[2]Department of Computer Science and Engineering, Centurion University of Technology and Management, Odisha, India

[3]Department of Phytopharma, Centurion University of Technology and Management, Odisha, India

Abstract

Understanding the cooking quality of genotype is essential for human nutrition, identifying high-yielding varieties for specific environments and breeding for resistance to diseases and pests. The cooking quality of rice is a significant factor influencing Customer preference, market price and nutritional value. Basic physicochemical properties—amylose content, gel consistency, and protein content—influence texture, softness and overall eating quality. Manual calculation of these parameters is time-consuming and labor-intensive. In this regard, the application of machine learning approaches is made in an attempt to quantify these quality traits in 60 genotypes of rice and develop prediction models with the ability to accelerate breeding programs as well as optimal cultivar selection. Linear regression (LR), Support Vector Regression (SVR) and Random Forest (RF) regression have been used as predictive models. The data set used for analysis is prepared in our own laboratory. Gel consistency and protein content predictions were extremely accurate and uniform among all models, though amylose content prediction was not so, reflecting more challenge in modelling this property. While there was this differentiation, machine learning applications offered a robust, automatic means for screening cooking quality properties. SVM and LR models provided 100% accuracy, i.e., the best values, in comparison to the RF model that provided 98% accuracy.

Keywords: Amylose content, cooking quality, gel consistency, machine learning, physicochemical properties, protein content, rice breeding, rice quality traits

Introduction

In Asia, 3 billion people get 60% of their calories from rice. Asian nations like China and India generate a lot [15]. Rice is mostly carbs (amylose and amylopectin), although it also contains protein, water, minerals, and lipids. High amylose and low amylopectin ratios affect grain texture (firmer with high, stickier with low) [17]. Amylose concentration (AC), gelatinization temperature (GT), and gel consistency (GC) are cooking and eating quality parameters. Beyond yield, new rice types need quality requirements. These include market value-determining physical traits (grain size, milling characteristics, appearance) and cooking-related

[a]saraswatipati23@gmail.com, [b]abhishekdas225@gmail.com, [c]223001320018@cutm.ac.in, [d]gkdash.bot@gmail.com

DOI: 10.1201/9781003753391-42

chemical attributes (amylose content, alkali spreading value, gel consistency) [1].

Traditional rice quality trait assessment methods are slow, laborious, and damaging, hampering large-scale breeding efforts. High-throughput phenotyping and genotyping require data-driven methods. Machine learning (ML) analyses complicated attributes and finds complex, non-linear correlations between genetic data (e.g., SNP markers) or environmental factors and phenotypic traits quickly, accurately, and cheaply. This improves breeding selection by accurately predicting amylose, protein, and gel consistency. To improve precision breeding, this study compares ML models for rice trait prediction using genotype-specific data. Comparing model performance and feature importance to find superior genotypes for cooking and eating quality speeds genotype selection and improve plant breeding quality attributes.

Amylose, gel consistency, and protein content are affected by rice genotype. Multiple genes interact with the environment to control these properties. Mutations in starch biosynthesis genes affect amylose, and protein synthesis genes affect grain protein. Genetics and starch architecture affect gel consistency numerically. Based on genomic information, machine learning can anticipate the results of crossbreeding rice genotypes, improving breeding plans for amylose, gel consistency, and protein content.

Traditional modelling can be difficult since rice grain quality parameters like amylose content and gel consistency are polygenic. This complexity allows advanced ML methods, especially deep learning, to find non-linear patterns. This study combines feature engineering with organic molecules to discover rice cooking and eating quality parameters. A complete machine learning model that properly predicts

amylose ratio, gel consistency, and protein content across rice genotypes is the main objective. By using ML to anticipate these properties based on genotype, researchers can better understand their genetics and produce better rice varieties. This method could improve rice breeding and quality prediction. This study of Amylose, Protein and Gel consistency of Various genotypes of rice is focused on the determination its cooking and eating qualities, influencing texture, firmness, and stickiness of all the genotype traits.

Literature Review

Conventional approaches of cooking quality parameter

Hardness, stickiness, and texture of cooked rice depend on amylose level. High amylose varieties (25–30%) cook dry and fluffy, while low amylose varieties (<20%) produce soft and sticky grains [14]. Rice nutrition and cooking time depend on protein concentration, high-protein rice cooks longer and is firmer [6]. Gel consistency measures cooked rice's tendency to solidify after cooling, indicating amylopectin structure and retrogradation [18]. In order to improve quality and achieve varied consumer expectations, breeders and food processors must accurately predict these features. Traditional method for analysis of cooking quality parameters was time consuming, labor-intensive and not scalable for significant breeding programs. The direct correlation between traits and food quality is further complicated by environmental variables and genotype interactions [3].

Emergence of machine learning in crop quality prediction

AI component ML is being used in agriculture to solve complicated, multidimensional prediction problems. In rice quality studies, machine learning has shown significant promise to replace or enhance traditional laboratory techniques.

Yamaguchi et al. [16] suggested training six ML models Random Forest Classifier (RFC), Logistic Regression (LR), Support Vector Classifier (SVC), Extreme Gradient Boosting (XGB), light gradient boosting machine (LGBM), and deep neural network (DNN) on cooking recipe data to distinguish Japanese, Chinese, and Western eating habits. XGBoost and LightGBM outperformed others for the Japanese diet with accuracy, F1-scores, and AUC values of 0.88 and 0.94, respectively, indicating classifier consistency. The RF model provided the Chinese diet the highest individual accuracy (0.95) but a lower F1-score (0.84), The DNN model achieved the greatest Western diet F1-score of 0.89, indicating superior precision and recall. Based on these findings, it appears that the models worked effectively with various diet patterns; however, the Chinese diet had the best accuracy, with an RFC of 0. 95. According to Cuevas et al. [5] Rice is categorized into cooking quality classes that match customer preferences based on multidimensional factors, not only amylose content with a classification accuracy of 93.84%, it examines 25 variables linked with cooking quality using multinomial logistic regression (MLR) and random forest models. The outcomes show that these forecasting models have the potential to enhance the evolution of rice varieties and direct policy suggestions about the needs of grain quality. Sampaio et al. [13] found that ANN models predict rice biochemical and pasting characteristics better than MLR models based on grain physical and milling yield data. The ANN models showed high prediction accuracy (R^2 values: 0.97-0.99)

in training and validation phases, with robust performance across testing datasets. However, MLR models showed lower determination coefficients (R^2 from 0.27 to 0.96) and larger prediction errors, showing limited ability to capture rice quality attribute nonlinear correlations. The results indicate that ANN methods are better for developing rapid, cost-effective prediction systems to assess rice quality, which can greatly benefit rice breeding programs and industrial processing by automatically evaluating key biochemical and physicochemical traits. The authors of the work [11] investigated the application of deep learning models for predicting multiple traits with mixed phenotypes in genomic selection, highlighting the limitations of traditional univariate approaches. They reported that their proposed multi-trait deep learning model showed a slight improvement only for continuous traits compared to univariate models. Another research by Rekha et al. [12] suggested capacity to interpret and extract information from visual input used CNN to predict rice grain quality using image analysis. The CNN model's 98.6% classification accuracy with 1.24% loss in 25 microseconds per image demonstrated its robustness and computing efficiency. According to Kim et al. [8] taking pasting properties of eight rice flour samples were highly linked with amylose concentration, with high R^2 values (0.8282, 0.8703, and 0.8586). The Decision Tree (DT) model surpassed Stochastic Gradient Descent (0.9511) and SVM (0.7576) in predicting amylose content, with a R^2 of 0.9979 on the testing dataset. SVM classifiers got the greatest accuracy and F1-scores in the classification of rice flour, succeeded by DT and Stochastic Gradient Descent. Low-amylose rice exhibited suboptimal performance.

Methodology

Data collection and processing
A field experiment was done at the Ranadevi Research Farm, M. S. Swaminathan School of Agriculture, Centurion University of Technology and Management (CUTM), Paralakhemundi, Odisha, during Rabi 2024–2025. The station is positioned 84.14195°E, 18.80027°N, and 91 meters above sea level. The experiment was conducted in Odisha's north eastern ghats. For this study, 60 unique rice genotypes from different regions were used. Paddy samples were moistened to 12–14%. Dehusking and milling with a paddy testing machine (LTJM-2009, China) were done. For a culinary quality test, an electric blender (Icon Classic Mixer Grinder, India) finely blended milled rice grains and filtered them through a 100-mesh filter into uniform flour.

Estimation of amylose content (AC), protein content (PC), and estimation of gel consistency (GC)
Calorimetrically measuring the amylose-iodine complex determined each rice cultivar AC. The 100 g rice powder, 1 mL ethanol, and 9 mL 1 N sodium hydroxide combination simmered for 10 minutes. It was diluted to 100 mL with room- temperature distilled water. In a 100 mL flask, a 5 mL sample was acidified with 1 mL of 1 N acetic acid and treated with 2 mL of 0.2% iodine in 2% potassium iodide. A blank was used to measure absorbance at 620 nm after adding distilled water, mixing, and letting it lie at room temperature for 20 minutes [7]. The Lowry method evaluated protein content by treating proteins with alkaline copper sulphate and Folin–Ciocalteu. Protein content determines the strength of the blue complex. The quantification standard curve was made from bovine serum albumin (BSA) and measured at 660 nm with a spectrophotometer [10]. Add 0.2 ml ethanol (0.25% thymol blue, 2.0 ml 7% KOH) to a 2 × 19.5 cm test tube with 100 mg rice flour to estimate GC. The tube cooled after 7 minutes of hot water. The correctly blended components were in an ice bath for 15 minutes. To measure gel spreading (mm), the tube was put horizontally on graph paper for an hour after removal [7].

The data was cleaned and pre-processed to handle missing values and outliers. The cooking quality was normalized to ensure that all characteristics participate equally to the model's performance. Data preparation is also known as data "pre-processing". It is the stage of the machine learning lifecycle, which comes after data collection.

Machine learning model selection
Figure 42.1 represents the steps followed to predict the ratio of biochemical compounds in 60 rice genotypes traits.

Several machine learning algorithms were employed to model the association between rice genotypes and traits such as, LR, Support Vector Machine (SVM), Random Forest (RF) regression in order to

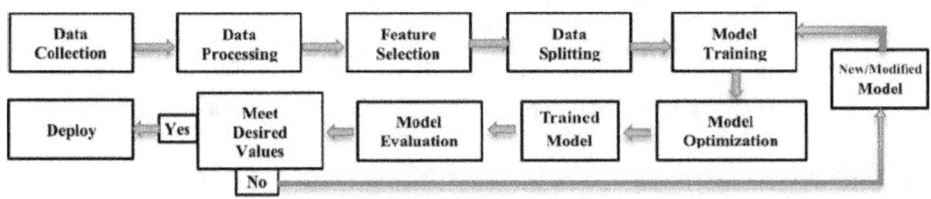

Figure 42.1 Steps followed for prediction
Source: Author

classify the cooking quality parameters of different genotypes, among all the models the R-square value show best accuracy. LR determines the linear correlation between the dependent variable and one or more independent variables by fitting a linear equation to the observed data. Based on the independent input variable, it has predicted the continuous output variables 9 [9]. SVR employs support vector machines for regression issues. Used for classification and regression issues, SVM determines a hyperplane which best separates data into classes. Regression analysis is crucial in examining the correlation between a dependent variable and one or more independent variables [2]. Random Forest is an ensemble learning algorithm that aggregates the predictions of many decision trees to give a more precise and stable prediction. It utilizes the collective wisdom of multiple decision trees to enhance precision and avoid overfitting [4].

Results

All machine learning algorithms were run using Python 3.5, Jupyter Notebook, and the scikit-learn modules. Dataset was split into training and testing subsets, with an 80/20 ratio. Upon training, the model is tested on an unseen test set during training. Precautions are remarked differently at testing depending on the nature of the problem to be solved: MAE, mean squared error (MSE), root mean squared error (RMSE), and the coefficient of determination (R2) are used as the parameters to quantify the analysis of the regression task. Cross-validation is a method employed during the training phase that serves as a model assessment tool.

$$\text{MAE} = \frac{1}{n} \sum_{i=1}^{n} (y_i - \hat{y}_i) \tag{1}$$

$$\text{MSE} = \frac{1}{n} \sum_{i=1}^{n} (y_i - \hat{y}_i)^2 \tag{2}$$

$$\text{RMSE} = \sqrt{\text{MSE}} \tag{3}$$

Table 42.1 Performance metrics of different models.

	Model	Target	R-squared	MSE	RMSE	MAE
0	Amylose Linear Regression	Amylose	0.570319	2.147618e+03	46.342397	40.405549
1	Amylose Random Forest	Amylose	-0.355673	6.775885e+03	82.315765	57.089862
2	Amylose SVR	Amylose	0.278058	3.608391e+03	60.069886	37.466793
3	Protein Linear Regression	Protein	1.000000	2.936809e-08	0.000171	0.000141
4	Protein Random Forest	Protein	0.978113	3.570926e+00	1.889689	1.632805
5	Protein SVR	Protein	1.000000	4.796260e-05	0.006926	0.005963
6	Gel Linear Regression	Gel consistency	1.000000	9.071459e-11	0.000010	0.000008
7	Gel Random Forest	Gel consistency	0.982221	7.975241e+02	28.240469	22.526453
8	Gel SVR	Gel consistency	1.000000	2.018230e-05	0.004492	0.003716

Source: Author

$$R^2 = 1 - \frac{\sum_{i=1}^{n} (y_i - \hat{y}_i)^2}{\sum_{i=1}^{n} (y_i - \hat{y}_i)^2} \quad (4)$$

Supervised algorithms of SVR model and linear regression exhibited the best performance in all three features, achieving the lowest MAE and MSE among the models tested. The predictive model successfully captures just guessing the average relationship between all the variables, with a high R2 value to calculate the relationships between input variables (features) and the target variables at all (Table 42.1). Amylose prediction, LR exhibited the highest performance, achieving a ($R^2 = 0.570$) however, poor performance of RF and SVR resulted in low R^2 values and greater error metrics. Protein prediction, with both SVR and LR having perfect ($R^2 = 1.000$) and negligible errors, signifying robust linear correlations with the input data, however predictions of gel consistency produced exceptional results, with ($R^2 = 0.98$) exceeding in all models. SVR performed best for this target with the lowest RMSE and MAE. These results show that machine learning can properly predict protein content and gel

consistency, even though amylose is still challenging to model.

In Figure 42.2, the red boxes are indicating stronger correlations and blue, weaker correlations. Grain quality parameters like AC, GC and PC influence the cooking and eating quality of rice as well as extensively used in rice breeding program for new variety release with better palatability. Significant moderate positive correlation observed ($r = 0.31, 0.33$, $p < 0.001$) AC and GC as well as PC, additionally, protein and gel consistency are weakly correlated ($r = 0.10$).

The regression tracking plots obtained using three different models for predicting a single parameter by considering other two parameters it is shown in Figure 42.3.

Figure 42.3 compares the outcomes of different regression models for prediction the percentage of amylose, protein and gel consistency in a dataset. Where X-axis represents different samples of the dataset which is sorted by the true values and the Y- axis represents the actual or predicted amylose, protein and gel consistency value of each sample. LR is denoted by orange dashed line, RF is represented by green dashed line, SVR is represented by red dashed line and true value is denoted by blue solid line.

Figure 42.3(a). The genuine amylose % in each sample is shown in the Amylose prediction monitoring. It's comparison baseline. The RF model sometimes matches genuine values better than linear regression but underestimates others. In general, SVR models follow the trend but underestimate high values. Thus, amylose prediction tracking LR over predicts amylose content for higher real values and has a significant error at sample index 2. RF predicts more reliably but underpredicts. In high-value data, SVR underpredicts but adjusts better than RF. Figure 42.3(b). All models' protein prediction tracking shows the SVR

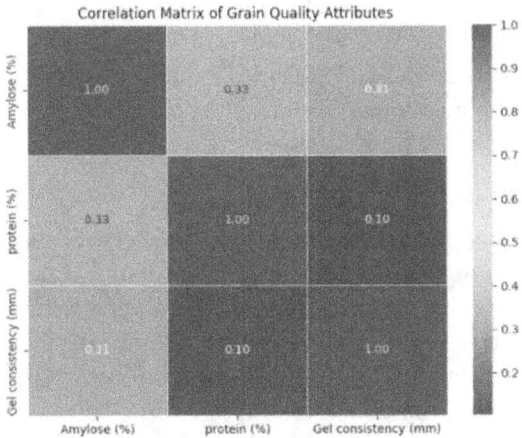

Figure 42.2 Heatmap utilizes a diverging color scale

Source: Author

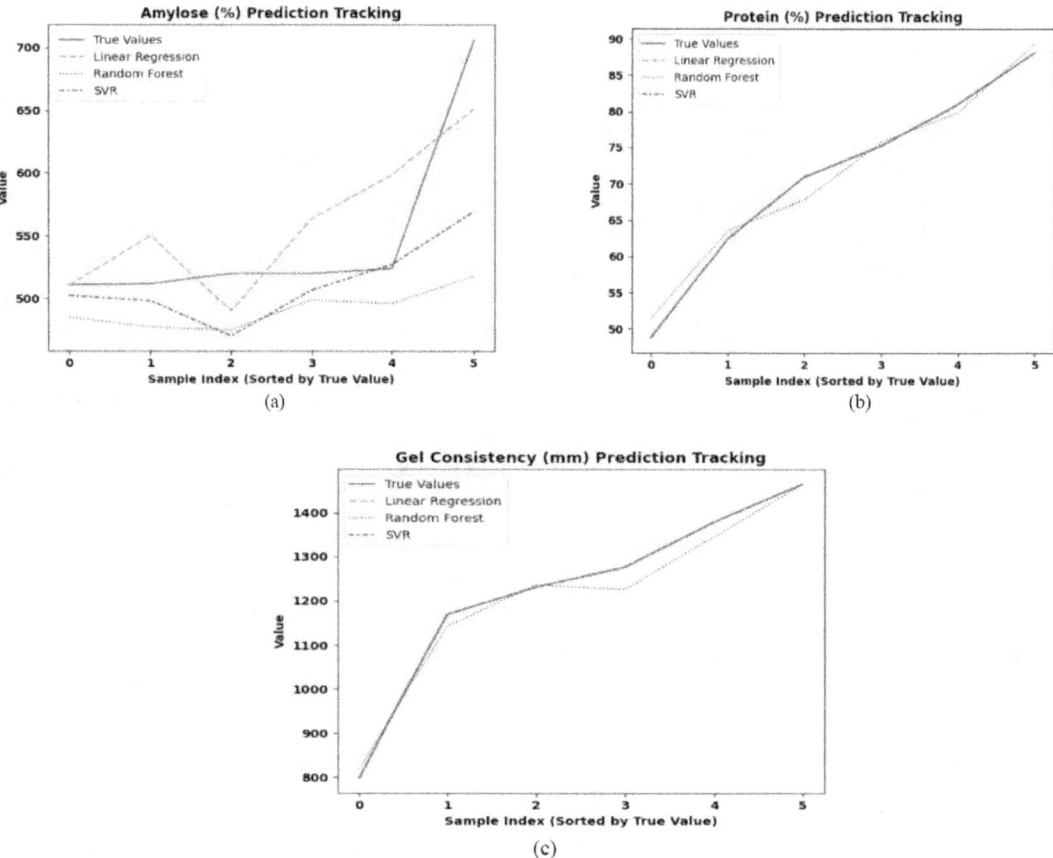

Figure 42.3 Regression tracking plots
Source: Author

model closely following true values. Thus, the SVR suggests the prediction is near to the protein percentage. LR is decent. RF is inconsistent. In this data set, SVR predicts best of the three models. This graph shows trend alignment and departure from true values for regression model performance. In gel consistency prediction tracking, all three models closely match true values, suggesting great accuracy Figure 42.3(c). SVR (red dotted line) and linear regression (orange dotted line) are similar and virtually overlap with the true value (blue solid line), indicating great performance. The RF (green dotted line) deviates somewhat. It underestimates gel consistency at index 3

and slightly overestimates elsewhere. It's good but not as good as SVR and linear regression. These forecasts help determine rice genotypes for quality enhancement.

Conclusion

The objective of analysis of the relationship among parameters is fulfilled using different plot like heat map. Machine learning models LR, SVR and RF automatic prediction of different cooking quality parameters from considered 60 genotypes. While current models are LR, SVR are found to be accurate model in comparison to RF in predicting protein and gel consistency values (R^2 = 1.000); however, prediction of amylose is found difficult using any of the model, this limitation will be covered in future work by designing improved machine learning model. This research shows that machine learning can support strategic decision-making as well as prediction in current rice breeding.

References

[1] Bagale, S., Shahi, S., & Pokhrel, U. (2022). Physical, physico-chemical and cooking qualities of major landraces of rice (*Oryza sativa L.*) found in western Nepal. *International Journal of Agronomy*, 5(1), 1–6.

[2] Balogun, A. L., & Tella, A. (2022). Modelling and investigating the impacts of climatic variables on ozone concentration in Malaysia using correlation analysis with random forest, decision tree regression, linear regression, and support vector regression. *Chemosphere*, 299, 134250.

[3] Baouchi, A. E., Ibriz, M., & Miguel Sanchez-Garcia, M. S. (2024). Dissection of the genetic basis of genotype by environment interactions for morphological traits and protein content in winter wheat panel grown in Morocco and Spain. *Plants*, 13(11), 1477.

[4] Chahboun, S., & Maaroufi, M. (2021). Performance comparison of support vector regression, random forest and multiple linear regression to forecast the power of photovoltaic panels. In 2021 9th International Renewable and Sustainable Energy Conference (IRSEC), (pp. 1–4). IEEE.

[5] Cuevas, R. P. O., Domingo, C. J., & Sreenivasulu, N. (2018). Multivariate-based classification of predicting cooking quality ideotypes in rice (Oryza sativa L.) Indica germplasm. *Rice*, 11, 56.

[6] Fukai, S., & Mitchell, J. (2024). Grain yield and protein concentration relationships in rice. *Crop and Environment*, 3(1), 12–24.

[7] Juliano, B. O., Onate. L. U., & Mundo A. M. D. (1965). Relation of starch composition, protein content, and gelatinization temperature to cooking and eating qualities of milled rice. *Food Technology*, 19(6), 116–121.

[8] Kim, H., Jeong, S., Kwak, J., & Lee, S. (2023). Artificial intelligence classification and amylose content prediction of rice flour varieties from their pasting features. *Journal of Agriculture and Food Research*, 14, 100847.

[9] Lee, H., Wang, J., & Leblon, B. (2020). Using linear regression, random forests, and support vector machine with unmanned aerial vehicle multispectral images to predict canopy nitrogen weight in corn. *Remote Sensing*, 12(13), 2071.

[10] Lowry, O. H., Rosebrough, N. J., Farr, A. L., & Randall, R. J (1951). Protein measurement with the Folin phenol reagent. *Journal of Biological Chemistry*, 193, 265–275.

[11] Montesinos-Lopez, O. A., Vallejo, J. M., Crossa, J., Gianola, D., Hernandez Suraez, C.M., Montesinos, L., et al. (2019). New deep learning genomic-based prediction model for multiple traits with binary, ordinal, and continuous phenotypes. *G3 Genes*, 9(5), 1545–15.

[12] Rekha, V., Shiny, R. M., Ramya, J., Sakthivel, B., Pratheep, V. G., & Kumar, A. (2023, April). Rice quality Prediction using Convolution Neural Network. In 2023 International Conference on Distributed Computing and Electrical Circuits and Electronics (ICDCECE) (pp. 1-6). IEEE.

[13] Sampaio, P. S., Almeida A. S., & Brites, C. M. (2021). Use of artificial neural network model for rice quality prediction based on grain physical parameters. *Foods*, 10, 3016.

[14] Suwannaporn, P., Pitiphunpong, S., & Champangern, S. (2007). Classification of rice amylose content by discriminant analysis of physicochemical properties. *Starch-Stärke*, 59(3–4), 171–177.

[15] World Bank. (2023). World Development Indicators. Available: https://databank.worldbank.org/source/world-

development-indicators. Accessed on: April 3, 2025.

[16] Yamaguchi, M., Araki, M., Hamada, K., Nojiri, T., & Nishi, N. (2024). Development of a machine learning model for classifying cooking recipes according to dietary styles. *Foods*, 13, 667.

[17] Zeng, D., Tian, Z., Rao, Y., Dong, G., Yang, Y., Huang, L., et al. (2017). Rational design of high-yield and superior- quality rice. *Nature Plants*, 3(4), 17031.

[18] Zhang, Y., Zhang, Y., Wang, Z., Longxiang F. L., & Ye, C. Y. (2024). Effect of rice protein on the gelatinization and retrogradation of rice starch with different moisture content. *Foods*, 13(23), 3734.

43 Wasserstein loss based generative adversarial network for Odia handwritten numerals

Abhishek Das[1,a], Sandhyalati Behera[2,b], Bhagyalaxmi Behera[1,c] and Mihir Narayan Mohanty[1,d]

[1]School of Engineering and Technology Centurion University of Technology and Management, Paralakhemundi, Odisha, India

[2]Department of Electronics and Communication Engineering Siksha 'O' Anusandhan (Deemed to be University), Bhubaneswar, Odisha, India

Abstract

Data deficit makes deep neural network less efficient as we know large is the dataset more will be the training accuracy. Generative models have grabbed the interest of academics because they are able to learn significant characteristics from trained data and then generate structures that are comparable to those that were provided for training. In this approach we have suggested Wasserstein Generative Adversarial Network (WGAN) to generate Odia handwritten numerals. The Wasserstein loss method was utilised in order to assess the performance of the suggested model, which was trained on the IIT Bhubaneswar Dataset of Odia numeral systems. With generator and critic losses of 0.016 and 0.004 respectively after 400 epochs, the model produced results that were extremely comparable to the original data. This was accomplished by employing an RMSprop optimiser.

Keywords: Discriminator, generative AI, generator, Odia handwritten numerals, RMSProp Optimizer, WGAN

Introduction

Training process in deep learning-based models requires lots of data. Data scarcity is a major problem for the researchers working on deep learning. Data over-fitting is the result of data insufficiency if the quantity of features is too large in comparison to size of the dataset. For instance if the amount of training data is one hundred but each data has one thousand or more features then it will cause data over-fitting. Generative Adversarial Networks (GAN) Goodfellow et al. [9], Ledig et al. [12] is proven to be emerging solution to such data scarcity problems as we can generate new data as like that of training data. By extracting important features, shuffling them with each other and combining properly we can generate new datasets. This makes the GANs different from the autoencoders as autoencoders only reconstruct the same data provided as training to the network [16, 23].

Handwritten data are having important role in optical character recognition whether it follows simple writing styles [1, 18]. Most of the personal and important documents like signature, bank cheque is handwritten based and when they are used for any transaction in bank these data such as amount in words and numbers, signature

[a]abhishekdas225@gmail.com, [b]sandhyalatibehera@gmail.com, [c]bhagyaiter@gmail.com,
[d]mihir.n.mohanty@gmail.com

DOI: 10.1201/9781003753391-43

and dates need to be processed digitally. Other documents like letters, offline survey reports, offline feedback forms etc. also need to be scanned and processed digitally. To properly recognize such important documents model used for this purpose should be properly trained with handwritten datasets. But collecting handwritten datasets is somehow expensive as it consumes more time to collect data from different writers. In such scenario Generative models play important role in increasing the size of dataset.

Odia is the native language of Odisha, an eastern state of India. Odia is spoken by almost all the citizens of Odisha and neighboring border states. The capacity to identify handwritten Odia numerals is of utmost importance. in this paper, we have used Wasserstein Loss based Generative Adversarial Network (WGAN) in order to generate Odia handwritten numerals.

The paper is structured as follows: Section 1 introduces the need for generative models and the Odia language. Section 2 reviews related works relevant to our proposed methodology. Section 3 provides a concise discussion on GANs, while Section 4 elaborates on the proposed method. Section 5 presents the simulation results, and Section 6 concludes this work. Finally, Section 7 lists the references used in the study.

Related Works

Generative models are not only used in generating face images Lombardi et al. [14] and audio signals Oord, et al. [19], Mor et al. [17] but also WGAN models are having broad applications in image annotation Ke et al. [11], facial expression recognition Lu et al. [15], classification of CT images Frid-Adar et al. [8] and many more. Yang et al. [25] have used Wasserstein loss in denoising low quality CT images so that the noise free outputs will be processed properly for

medical usage. Data augmentation is done by Weng and Zhou [24] using generative model so that the data scarcity problem can be simplified. Another challenging task in image processing i.e. reflection removal from images is done by Li and Lun [13] using Wasserstein loss. To evaluate the models designed for image processing, template matching Bhoi and Mohanty, [3] by two dimensional correlations plays an important role. Using this approach we can calculate PSNR of generated images with respect to training images for each epoch. The recognition of handwritten Odia characters has attracted considerable scholarly interest. This emphasis is motivated by Odia's designation as an official language in Odisha, indicating its extensive application in governmental and private documentation. Dash et al. [7] conducted a summary study that examined different techniques for recognizing both printed and handwritten Odia alphanumeric characters, highlighting the lack of research utilizing Wasserstein Generative Adversarial Networks (GANs). Das et al. [4] suggested and utilized Convolutional Neural Network (CNN) and Long Short-Term Memory (LSTM) models for Odia handwritten numeral identification, attaining recognition accuracies of 95.96% and 97.93%, respectively. Pattanayak [21], investigated the utilization of Support Vector Machines (SVMs), achieving an accuracy of 85%. Jena et al. [10] utilized a Linear Discriminant Analysis (LDA) model for the recognition of Odia handwritten numerals, performing a comparative analysis also by considering Principal Component Analysis (PCA) and illustrating LDA's enhanced efficacy. Additional contributions encompass the hybrid model proposed by K.S. Dash et al. [5], which utilized the Krisch gradient-based operator along with curvature properties of handwritten Odia numerals as the features. They employed PCA for dimensionality reduction to alleviate computational limitations. Kalyan Sourav Dash et al. [6] presented a non-redundant Stockwell transform in addition to bio-inspired optimal zoning, accompanied by diverse zone patterns, for the recognition of handwritten numerals. Rushiraj et al. [22] employed 48 geometric features, encompassing distance-based (notably Euclidean distance), shadow, and centroid features, to train their model for the recognition of Odia handwritten characters. Padhi and Senapati [20] utilized a two-stage Artificial Neural Network, incorporating the characteristics like zonal centroid-based distance as well as standard deviation, for the recognition of Odia handwriting.

From the above study related to both generative models and Odia handwritten recognition it is found that WGAN are yet to be explored for generation and recognition of Odia characters. In this work we have used Wasserstein loss based generative adversarial network in order to generate Odia handwritten numerals.

Generative Adversarial Network

GAN has proven to be emerging solution to data scarcity problems as we can generate new data as like that of training data. By extracting important features, shuffling them with each other and combining properly we can generate new datasets. Goodfellow et al. [9] have proposed adversarial method of data generation in 2017 in his work where the GAN model is developed with the combination of a generative network (G) and a critic or discriminative network (D). Providing an arbitrary sample z with probability distribution p(z), Generator tries to generate samples $G(z)$ with similar distribution as that of actual data x. The main objective of (D) is to identify whether the input given to it is coming

from the original data x or $G(z)$. The GAN proposed in this work follows the subsequent two player minmax game-based value function (D, G):

$$\min_{G} \max_{D} V(D,G) = E_{x \sim p_{data}(x)} [\log D(x)] + E_{z \sim p_z(z)} [\log(1 - D(G(z)))] \quad (1)$$

The discriminator is trained to increase the stochastic gradient (SG) whereas the generator (G) is trained to decrease SG as mentioned in equations 2 and 3.

$$\nabla_{\theta_d} \frac{1}{m} \sum_{i=1}^{m} [\log D(x^{(i)}) + \log(1 - D(G(z^{(i)})))] \quad (2)$$

$$\nabla_{\theta_g} \frac{1}{m} \sum_{i=1}^{m} [\log(1 - D(G(z^{(i)})))] \quad (3)$$

Where, m is the batch size. Momentum based gradient update learning rule is used in above generative model.

Proposed Methodology

In our approach we have used Wasserstein distance Arjovsky et al. [2] as the parameter to calculate the variation in generated new distribution and actual distribution of handwritten Odia numerals. Instead of a discriminator we have taken a Critic (C) model to separate the received image into two groups, either real or fake. Provided two probability distributions P_r and P_g, the Wasserstein distance is given by:

$$W(P_r, P_\theta) = \sup_{\|f\|_L \leq 1} E_{x \sim P_r} [f(x)] - E_{x \sim P_\theta} [f(x)] \quad (4)$$

Where, $\|f\|_L \leq 1$ shows that 1-Lipschitz constraint is satisfied by the function f. The cost functions for critic and Generator to be taken care in this approach are given in Eq. 5 and Eq. 6 respectively.

$$\nabla_w \frac{1}{m} \sum_{i=1}^{m} [f(x^{(i)}) - f(G(z^{(i)}))] \quad (5)$$

$$\nabla_{\theta_g} \frac{1}{m} \sum_{i=1}^{m} [-f(G(z^{(i)}))] \quad (6)$$

In order to train the critic to work properly we have to maximize $\frac{1}{m} \sum_{i=1}^{m} f(x^{(i)})$ and minimize $\frac{1}{m} \sum_{i=1}^{m} G(z^{(i)})$. To train the generator the objective is to maximize $\frac{1}{m} \sum_{i=1}^{m} G(z^{(i)})$.

Figure 43.1 illustrates the workflow of the proposed WGAN model.

More is the critic loss, more generative is the generator. Generators should generate the images so close to the training data that it indicates less generator loss. The Generator is composed of dense layers followed by transposed_convolutional layers with ReLU activation functions and batch normalization. The learning rate used for RMSprop optimizer is set to be 0.00005. Critic model is composed of convolutional layers activated by Leaky_ReLU activation functions and batch normalization is also done. At the end, flatten layer is used. The Critic results a scalar score which represents whether the image is real or fake instead of providing a probabilistic value. The generator generates the images with high similarity to that of training images of Odia handwritten numerals. The detailed summery of generator and Critic is given in Table 43.1.

Table 43.1 Detailed summery of WGAN model.

Generator	Critic
Layer (type)	Layer (type)
dense_1 (Dense)	conv2d_1 (Conv2D)
reshape_1 (Reshape)	leaky_re_lu_1 (LeakyReLU)
conv2d_transpose_1 (Conv2DTr	conv2d_2 (Conv2D)
batch_normalization_1 (Batch	batch_normalization_3 (Batch
re_lu_1 (ReLU)	leaky_re_lu_2 (LeakyReLU)
conv2d_transpose_2 (Conv2DTr	conv2d_3 (Conv2D)
batch_normalization_2 (Batch	batch_normalization_4 (Batch
re_lu_2 (ReLU)	leaky_re_lu_3 (LeakyReLU)
conv2d_transpose_3 (Conv2DTr	conv2d_4 (Conv2D)
	batch_normalization_5 (Batch
	leaky_re_lu_4 (LeakyReLU)
	flatten_1 (Flatten)
	dense_2 (Dense)

Source: Author

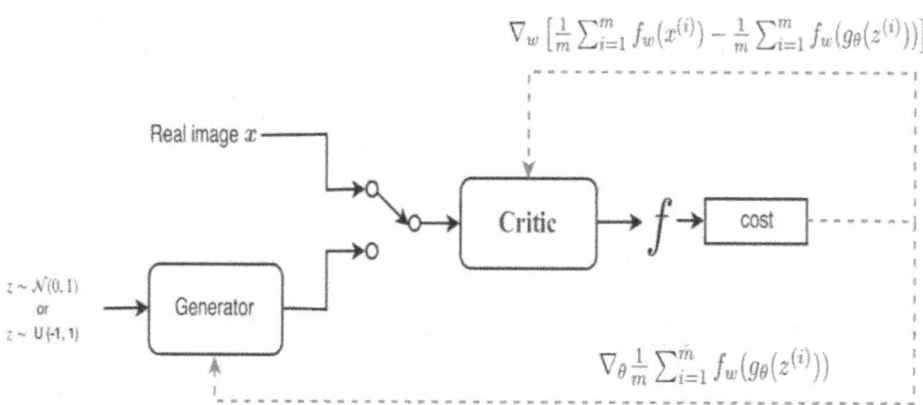

Figure 43.1 Workflow schema of the suggested WGAN model
Source: Author

The model is also evaluated in terms of PSNR calculation with respect to number of epochs by comparing the generated images with training images. It gives the increase in PSNR with respect to epochs and higher values of PSNR is observed at 400th epoch. The detail of the evaluation is given in performance evaluation subsection of section 5.

Results

Dataset

The proposed WGAN model's effectiveness was validated using Odia handwritten numerals. For this purpose, the dataset is taken from IIT Bhubaneswar. It has 5165 number of total images. In comparison to MNIST dataset this dataset is having very a smaller number of images. The sample of the dataset is shown in Figure 43.2. The image generated by this proposed method will be added to the present dataset in order to improve the size so that in future we will have more dataset to train any model.

Pre-processing

The dataset images were downscaled to 28 × 28 pixels to reduce computation time, converted to normalized form, and then used to train the proposed WGAN model. Representative images of all types, from O 'Suna' to ୯ 'Na', are presented in Figure 43.3.

Experimental setup and result

The aforementioned WGAN model was executed in a Python 3 Jupyter Notebook environment. The model was trained for 400 epochs to attain optimal results, utilizing a TensorFlow GPU environment in Google Colaboratory for enhanced processing speed. The images produced following the initial epoch were very noisy, as illustrated in Figure 43.4.

As the number of epochs increases the images become clearer and the Odia numbers generated after 400 epochs are shown in Figure 43.5. Each row in this figure represents a single category of number. The samples of Odia numerals generated from the suggested method are so similar to that of original data. It achieves the purpose of designing the generative models efficiently and these generated images can be further used as training images in order to increase the size of dataset.

Figure 43.3 Sample images of each Odia digit given as input to the WGAN model
Source: Author

Figure 43.4 Sample of Generated Images after first epoch
Source: Author

					Odia 0
					Odia 1
					Odia 2
					Odia 3
					Odia 4
					Odia 5
					Odia 6
					Odia 7
					Odia 8
					Odia 9

Figure 43.2 Sample of IIT Bhubaneswar dataset of Odia handwritten numerals
Source: Author

Figure 43.5 Generated Odia numbers using proposed WGAN
Source: Author

```
epoch = 398/400, c_loss=-0.005, g_loss=0.017
epoch = 399/400, c_loss=-0.005, g_loss=0.017
epoch = 400/400, c_loss=-0.004, g_loss=0.016
```

Figure 43.6 Simulation results after 400 epochs showing generator and critic loss
Source: Author

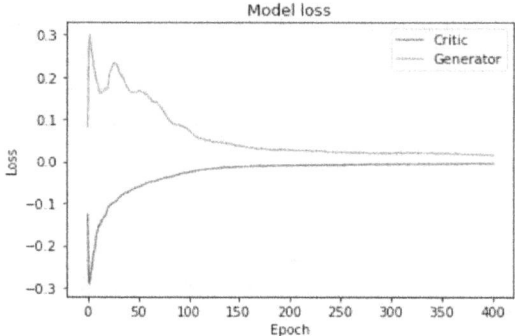

Figure 43.7 Loss graph showing generator loss and critic loss
Source: Author

Performance evaluation

The loss in generator (g_loss) and critic (c_loss) after 400 iterations are 0.016 and 0.004 respectively as shown in Figure 43.6.

The generator loss is found to be decreasing and the critical loss is found to be increasing as shown in Figure 43.7.

Table 43.2 The relation between number of epochs and PSNR.

Number of epochs	PSNR Values
0	0dB
50	19.89dB
100	22.04dB
150	26.72dB
200	28.84dB
250	29.11dB
300	31.41dB
350	31.79Db
400	32.14dB

Source: Author

Increase in critic loss indicates the efficiency of generator in generating very similar images to that of training images to make it difficult to identify whether the received image is original data or generated one.

We have also calculated PSNR for epochs with a gap of 50 which is given in Table 43.2.

From the above table of PSNR evaluation it is observed that as the number of epochs is increasing the model is generating clearer images and the highest PSNR is observed at 400 epochs. This indicates the fulfilment of the objective of our designed WGAN model.

Conclusion

In deep learning-driven image processing, the size of the dataset is important. To mitigate the issue of data scarcity, numerous ways have been devised, and prospects for innovative alternatives remain. This study presents a Convolutional Neural Network-based Generative Adversarial Network (GAN) employing the Wasserstein distance as a loss function for the generation of Odia handwritten numbers. We attained generator and critic losses of 0.016 and 0.004, respectively, a significant achievement in the processing of Odia handwritten numerals. The WGAN shows potential as an advanced creative model in image generation, necessitating further investigation to attain reduced losses in subsequent research. We express our appreciation to Google Colaboratory that offers access to GPU in online mode, which markedly shrunk the runtime for our 400-epoch training.

References

[1] Arica, N., & Yarman-Vural, F. T. (2002). Optical character recognition for cursive handwriting. *IEEE Transactions on Pattern Analysis and Machine Intelligence*, 24, 801–813.

[2] Arjovsky, M., Chintala, S., & Bottou, L. (2017). Wasserstein generative adversarial networks. In International Conference on Machine Learning, (pp. 214–223).

[3] Bhoi, N., & Mohanty, M. N. (2010). Template matching based eye detection in facial image. *International Journal of Computer Applications*, 12, 15–18.

[4] Das, A., Patra, G. R., & Mohanty, M. N. (2020). LSTM based Odia handwritten numeral recognition. In 2020 International Conference on Communication and Signal Processing (ICCSP), (pp. 0538–0541).

[5] Dash, K. S., Puhan, N. B., & Panda, G. (2014). A hybrid feature and discriminant classifier for high accuracy handwritten Odia numeral recognition. In 2014 IEEE Region 10 Symposium, (pp. 531–535).

[6] Dash, K. S., Puhan, N. B., & Panda, G. (2015). Handwritten numeral recognition using non-redundant Stockwell transform and bio-inspired optimal zoning. *IET Image Processing,* 9, 874–882.

[7] Dash, K. S., Puhan, N. B., & Panda, G. (2017). Odia character recognition: a directional review. *Artificial Intelligence Review*, 48, 473–497.

[8] Frid-Adar, M., Diamant, I., Klang, E., Amitai, M., Goldberger, J., & Greenspan, H. (2018). GAN-based synthetic medical image augmentation for increased CNN performance in liver lesion classification. *Neurocomputing*, 321, 321–331.

[9] Goodfellow, I. J., Pouget-Abadie, J., Mirza, M., Xu, B., Warde-Farley, D., Ozair, S.,et al. (2014). Generative adversarial nets. Advances in Neural Information Processing Systems, 27, (pp. 2672–2680).

[10] Jena, O. P., Pradhan, S. K., Biswal, P. K., & Nayak, S. (2018). Implementation of linear discriminant analysis for Odia numeral recognition. In 2018 International Conference on Information Technology (ICIT), (pp. 166–171).

[11] Ke, X., Zou, J., & Niu, Y. (2019). End-to-end automatic image annotation based on deep CNN and multi-label data augmentation. *IEEE Transactions on Multimedia*, 21, 2093–2106.

[12] Ledig, C., Theis, L., Huszár, F., Caballero, J., Cunningham, A., Acosta, A., et al. (2017). Photo-realistic single image super-resolution using a generative adversarial network. In Proceedings of the IEEE Conference on Computer Vision and Pattern Recognition, (pp. 4681–4690).

[13] Li, T., & Lun, D. P. (2019). Image reflection removal using the Wasserstein generative adversarial network. In ICASSP 2019-2019 IEEE International Conference on Acoustics, Speech and Signal Processing (ICASSP), (pp. 1–5).

[14] Lombardi, S., Saragih, J., Simon, T., & Sheikh, Y. (2018). Deep appearance models for face rendering. *ACM Transactions on Graphics (ToG)*, 37, 1–13.

[15] Lu, Y., Wang, S., Zhao, W., & Zhao, Y. (2019). Wgan-based robust occluded facial expression recognition. *IEEE Access*, 7, 93594–93610.

[16] Makhzani, A., Shlens, J., Jaitly, N., Goodfellow, I., & Frey, B. (2015). Adversarial autoencoders. arXiv preprint arXiv:1511.05644.

[17] Mor, N., Wolf, L., Polyak, A., & Taigman, Y. (2018). A universal music translation network. arXiv preprint arXiv:1805.07848.

[18] Mukherji, P., & Rege, P. P. (2009). Shape feature and fuzzy logic based offline Devnagari handwritten optical character recognition. *Journal of Pattern Recognition Research*, 4, 52–68.

[19] Oord, A. V., Dieleman, S., Zen, H., Simonyan, K., Vinyals, O., Graves, A., et al. (2016). Wavenet: a generative model for raw audio. arXiv preprint arXiv:1609.03499.

[20] Padhi, D., & Senapati, D. (2013). Zone centroid distance and standard deviation based feature matrix for Odia handwritten character recognition. In Proceedings of the International Conference on Frontiers of Intelligent Computing: Theory and Applications (FICTA), (pp. 649–658).

[21] Pattanayak, S. S. (2017). Recognizing ODIA handwritten scripts. In 2017 Second International Conference on Electrical, Computer and Communication Technologies (ICECCT), (pp. 1–4).

[22] Rushiraj, I., Kundu, S., & Ray, B. (2016). Handwritten character recognition of Odia script. In 2016 International Conference on Signal Processing, Communication, Power and Embedded System (SCOPES), (pp. 764–767).

[23] Vincent, P., Larochelle, H., Bengio, Y., & Manzagol, P. A. (2008). Extracting and composing robust features with denoising autoencoders. In Proceedings of the 25th International Conference on Machine Learning, (pp. 1096–1103).

[24] Weng, Y., & Zhou, H. (2019). Data augmentation computing model based on generative adversarial network. *IEEE Access*, 7, 64223–64233.

[25] Yang, Q., Yan, P., Zhang, Y., Yu, H., Shi, Y., Mou, X., et al. (2018). Low-dose CT image denoising using a generative adversarial network with Wasserstein distance and perceptual loss. *IEEE Transactions on Medical Imaging*, 37, 1348–1357.

44 Enhanced prediction of electric vehicle battery lifespan using a hybrid ensemble machine learning approach

Srikanta Kumar Sahoo[a], Alakananda Tripathy[b] and Shaktijeet Mahapatra[c]

ITER, SOA deemed to be university, Bhubaneswar, India

Abstract

For consumer electronics, renewable energy systems, and electric cars to operate safely and effectively, battery failure prediction is crucial. Regression models are used in this paper to estimate the remaining useful life (RUL) of lithium-ion batteries utilizing a data-driven methodology. The proposed method provides excellent prediction accuracy by combining backward feature selection, correlation filtering, data pre-processing, and an ensemble machine learning model with Random Forest (RF), Support Vector Regression (SVR), and k-Nearest Neighbors (KNN). With the best R^2 score of 94.01%, the ensemble model demonstrated its resilience in applications involving predictive maintenance. When applied to battery degradation data, this model confirms the efficacy compared to traditional machine learning algorithms.

Keywords: Electric vehicles, ensemble model, machine learning, predictive analytics, remaining useful life

Introduction

Electric vehicles (EVs) are becoming more widely acknowledged as a game-changing answer to the world's problems of environmental deterioration and reliance on fossil fuels. Since a large amount of greenhouse gas emissions come from transportation, the automobile industry's transition to electrification is essential to sustainable growth. EVs are positioned as key participants in the global green energy transition because they provide the dual advantages of minimizing carbon emissions and dependence on limited, polluting energy sources.

But the quick adoption of EVs also brings with it new technological difficulties, especially with regard to energy storage systems.

The battery, usually a lithium-ion unit, is the central component of all electric vehicles and is in charge of determining dependability, performance, and range. Manual testing, empirical modeling, and rule-based systems have been the mainstays of traditional methods for determining the lifespan of EV batteries. Maintaining battery health and dependability over the course of the vehicle's lifecycle is one of the main issues with EV technology. Unexpected battery failures result in higher maintenance expenses and decreased operating efficiency in addition to jeopardizing user safety and trust.

Predictive analytics, particularly through machine learning, has shown promise as a remedy for these issues. Estimating a battery's remaining useful life (RUL) is one of

[a]srikantasahoo@soa.ac.in, [b]alakanandatripathy@soa.ac.in, [c]shaktijeetmahapatra@gmail.com

DOI: 10.1201/9781003753391-44

the most significant uses of machine learning in this field. By predicting how long or how many cycles a battery can operate efficiently before needing to be replaced or refurbished, RUL prediction makes proactive battery management possible. In order to minimize downtime, prevent unplanned failures, and optimize maintenance schedules, this predictive capability is essential.

Several aspects of EV operations are improved by precise RUL estimate. Better planning for battery recycling and end-of-life logistics is made easier, predictive maintenance is enabled to support more effective fleet management, and informed usage tactics extend battery lifespan. Additionally, it is essential for overseeing battery warranty programs, maximizing energy efficiency, and enhancing the overall viability of electric vehicles. In light of this, the proposed method investigates machine learning models for forecasting EV battery RUL based on sensor data from the past. The study intends to aid in the creation of accurate and scalable intelligent battery health monitoring systems for practical EV applications by utilizing statistical analysis, feature selection, and sophisticated regression algorithms.

Rest of the paper is structured as follows. Section 2 reviews the extant literature. Section 3 describes the proposed model. Section 4 shows the empirical results. Finally, Section 5 concludes the paper.

Literature Review

The current electrification period, which is characterized by the explosive growth of EVs that run on renewable energy, has made effective energy storage systems even more crucial. Because of its high energy density, robust power output, and low self-discharge rates, lithium-ion (Li-ion) batteries have become the most popular option among

different technologies [1, 2]. However, a new set of needs and obstacles has emerged as a result of the increased reliance on Li-ion batteries, especially in the development of Battery Management Systems (BMS). Data collection, state estimates, charge-discharge control, safety procedures, temperature regulation, cell balancing, and system communication are only a few of the vital tasks carried out by a complete BMS [3]. The accuracy of a BMS's state estimation is frequently used to gauge its efficacy, as this directly affects the system's capacity to maintain operational stability and extend battery life [4]. For prompt decision-making and control modifications, the perfect BMS should be able to multitask and allow real-time monitoring via an integrated operating system.

Li-ion batteries have practical limitations despite their technical advantages, primarily their short lifespan and comparatively high cost, which prevent wider usage in large-scale applications [5]. Calendar aging and cycle aging cause battery performance to deteriorate over time, resulting in a progressive loss of capacity and functional degradation [6, 7]. In addition to increasing operating expenses, these degradation processes jeopardize system security and reduce battery useable life [8–10]. When a battery's capacity drops below 80% of its initial rating, it is typically deemed to have reached its end-of-life (EoL) [11]. The expected amount of time until the battery approaches this end-of-life threshold is known as the RUL [12–14]. Both a battery's chemical makeup and the electrochemical changes it experiences throughout repeated charge-discharge cycles affect how long it lasts. Numerous parameters, including ambient temperature, charging/discharging rates, and environmental conditions, influence this extremely nonlinear aging process [15].

In this regard, utilizing data-driven methods to forecast EV battery RUL is essential for maximizing performance and safety. The goal of this research is to create a reliable, data-driven method for precisely predicting the RUL of Li-ion batteries in EVs. The study uses supervised machine learning techniques, namely Random Forest (RF) and Support Vector Machine (SVM), to predict the battery degradation process using historical battery data from the NASA Ames Prognostics Centre of Excellence (PCoE). Standard evaluation measures like Mean Squared Error (MSE) and R-squared (R^2) are used to evaluate the performance of the model.

Proposed Model

Reliability and accuracy in predicting RUL are essential for safety, performance enhancement, and lifecycle cost reduction in the field of EV battery health diagnostics. Because of their inherent biases or limits in capturing complicated, nonlinear battery degradation processes, traditional regression models sometimes have difficulty generalizing across different usage patterns. The suggested model in this paper uses an ensemble learning approach to get around these issues, combining different regression methods via a Voting Regressor to generate a more reliable and broadly applicable RUL prediction. The model diagram is shown in Figure 44.1. It consists of the steps like data collection, pre-processing, feature selection,

training. Followed by individual regressor modeling and voting regressor modeling. Finally, RUL prediction and model evaluation performed.

The predictive capabilities of three different regressors—Random Forest, Support Vector Regression (SVR), and k-Nearest Neighbours (KNN)—are combined in an ensemble-based approach. The voting regressor uses complimentary modeling techniques to improve overall accuracy, robustness, and resistance to over fitting by averaging their individual predictions, essential to improving the diagnosis of EV battery health.

The proposed model utilizes the voting regressor class from the scikit-learn library, which implements a soft ensemble strategy for regression tasks. Unlike boosting or stacking methods, Voting Regressor performs a straightforward average of the predictions from multiple base estimators, which makes it interpretable, easy to implement, and efficient in runtime.

The ensemble incorporates the following three base models:

- RFR: RF is a tree-based ensemble method built upon bootstrap aggregation (bagging). Configured with n_estimators=100, max_features='sqrt', and parallel execution (n_jobs=-1). It handles nonlinear relationships, resistant to noise, and provides features of importance.

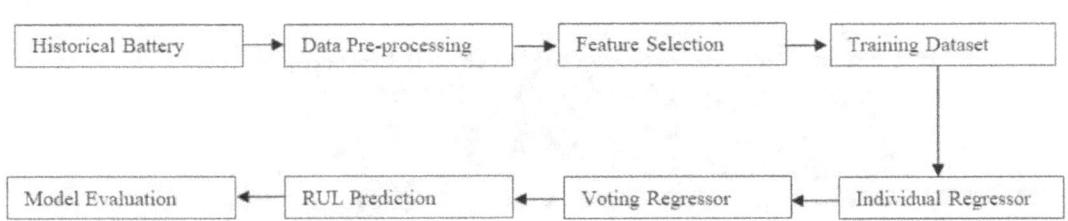

Figure 44.1 Model diagram
Source: Author

- Support Vector Regression (SVR): SVR is a kernel-based regressor that projects data into a high-dimensional space to find optimal regression boundaries. Configured with a Radial Basis Function (RBF) kernel, regularization parameter C = 10000, gamma = 0.5, and epsilon = 0.001. It excels in modeling complex, nonlinear patterns but sensitive to hyperparameter tuning.
- KNN: KNN is a distance-based lazy learner that predicts outcomes based on the average of its k = 3 nearest training instances. Its strengths include simplicity and local adaptability, especially effective in smooth degradation trends.

These three learners are aggregated using the VotingRegressor. This ensemble performs soft averaging of the continuous outputs from each base model, allowing the final prediction to benefit from the unique perspectives of each constituent algorithm. Compared to individual models, the ensemble-based method has several important advantages. It enhances generalization and captures a variety of data patterns by integrating tree-based, kernel-based, and instance-based regressors. Compared to more intricate systems, it maintains simplicity in implementation and interpretation, improves stability against noisy sensor data, and strikes a balance between the bias-variance tradeoff.

The model is trained on scaled and feature-selected sensor data (X_train, y_train). The training time is recorded to evaluate computational performance. Once trained, the ensemble is used to generate predictions on unseen test data (X_test), simulating a real-world deployment environment. The model's performance is quantified using R^2 score, RMSE, training and prediction times.

Empirical Results

In order to estimate the RUL of lithium-ion batteries, the suggested ensemble model—which was built using the VotingRegressor from the scikit-learn library—combines the predictive strengths of three different base learners: RFR, SVR, and KNN. The following performance metrics were attained by the ensemble during model training and testing with the processed battery dataset: Score for R-squared (R^2): 94.01% 6210.31 is the RMSE. With a relatively small error margin and the model's ability to explain more than 94% of the variance in RUL, these figures demonstrate good predictive capacity. The outcome demonstrates how well the ensemble generalizes across various battery aging trends.

Figure 44.2 illustrates the model performance comparison in terms of R^2 and RMSE across all models. The voting regressor's performance is comparable to that of the RF model and surpasses both the SVR and kNN in error minimization and fit accuracy.

	R2	RMSE	time to train	time to predict	total time
kNN	93.03%	7225.34	0.005	0.017	0.021
SVM	87.24%	13229.03	8.758	3.115	11.873
Random Forest	94.21%	6001.99	0.804	0.075	0.878
Voting Ensemble	94.01%	6210.31	6.838	2.531	9.369

Figure 44.2 Model performance comparison
Source: Author

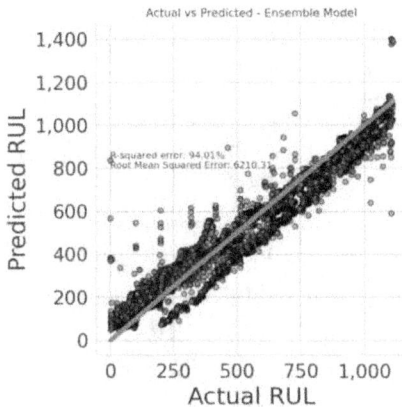

Figure 44.3 Scatter plot: actual versus predicted
Source: Author

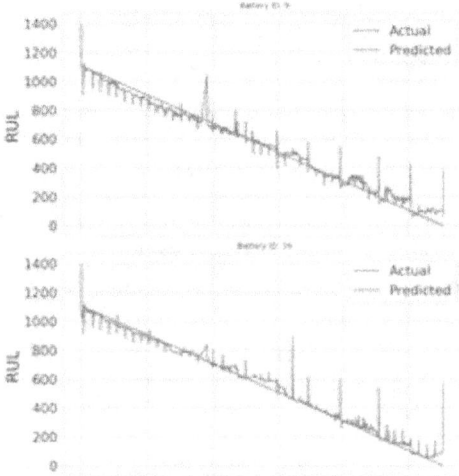

Figure 44.4 RUL predictions for individual batteries
Source: Author

RF: Highest R^2 (~94.23%) with RMSE of 5979.84

KNN Regressor: R^2 of 93.03%, RMSE of 7225.34

SVR: R^2 of 87.24%, RMSE of 13,229.03

Voting ensemble: R^2 of 94.01%, RMSE of 6210.31

The ensemble model effectively balances the strengths of its components—leveraging the robustness of RF, the non-linear adaptability of SVR, and the locality sensitivity of KNN—leading to enhanced generalization and stability.

Figure 44.3. shows that the actual RUL values and the values predicted by the ensemble model have a strong linear association. The R^2 value of 94.01% is validated by the majority of data points aligning closely along the diagonal line (y = x), which shows a small prediction error. RUL Predictions for Individual Batteries (Figure 44.4) Model performance is further validated by cycle-wise predicted vs. real RUL charts for multiple test batteries (IDs 9–13). Even in late-stage degradation phases, the ensemble model maintains low error while correctly tracking the degradation trajectory across cycles. The model's good generalization across various battery units and operational profiles is illustrated by these plots. A comparative analysis of this model with some existing models is made in Table 44.1.

The voting regressor ensemble model achieves a high prediction accuracy (R^2 = 94.01%) with moderate RMSE (6210.31). The model consistently outperforms or matches its base learners in generalization and robustness. Visual analysis confirms that the ensemble closely follows actual degradation trends. Further, the model performs better than the existing systems listed in Table 44.1. The approach balances accuracy, interpretability, and computational efficiency, making it suitable for real-time EV battery life monitoring and predictive maintenance.

Conclusion

In this study, a machine learning-based ensemble framework was developed to accurately estimate the remaining useful life (RUL) of lithium-ion batteries using

Table 44.1 A comparative study of the proposed model.

Study/Model	Method/Model	Dataset used	R^2 Score (or equivalent)	Comments
Proposed method	Voting Regressor (RF + SVR + kNN)	NASA PCoE battery data	94.01%	Ensemble approach showed strong generalization
Liu et al. (2019) [6]	Modified Gaussian Process Regression	NASA PCoE	~92–95%	Strong performance; focuses on cyclic capacity
She et al. (2020) [7]	RBF Neural Network	NASA PCoE	~92%	Used Incremental Capacity Analysis + RBF NN
Ma et al. (2020) [14]	Hybrid RUL Prediction (CNN+LSTM)	NASA PCoE	~94–96%	Deep learning hybrid approach
Xing et al. (2011) [4]	Particle Filtering	NASA PCoE	~86–90%	One of earliest on this dataset
Liu et al. (2020) [13]	Gaussian Process Regression (Calendar Aging)	NASA PCoE	~92–94%	Focused on calendar aging trends
Peng et al. (2019) [2]	Bayesian Method	NASA PCoE	~88–92%	Used Bayesian inference on incomplete data

Source: Author

real-world charge-discharge cycle data. The suggested model effectively utilizes the advantages of various regression paradigms by utilizing a Voting Regressor that blends Random Forest, Support Vector Regression (SVR), and k-Nearest Neighbours (KNN). The ensemble obtained a low Root Mean Squared Error (RMSE) of 6210.31 and a high predicted accuracy of 94.01% (R2 score) by methodical preprocessing, feature selection, and model integration. Per-battery cycle trend charts and visual comparison of real and anticipated RUL values further confirmed the model's dependability and generalizability. The ensemble was more resilient to data noise and heterogeneity in degradation trajectories than individual regressors. It is also feasible to implement in industrial fleet maintenance platforms and real-time electric car battery management systems due to its effective training and prediction times.

While the proposed ensemble model has shown promising results, expanding the input space to include additional features like temperature, current load, and charge/discharge rate could help capture a more holistic view of battery behavior.

References

[1] Gao, Y., Zhang, X., Guo, B., Zhu, C., Wiedemann, J., Wang, L., et al. (2020). Health-aware multi objective optimal charging strategy with coupled electrochemical-thermal-aging model for lithium-ion battery. *IEEE Transactions on Industrial Informatics*, 16(5), 3417–3429.

[2] Peng, J., Zhou, Z., Wang, J., Wu, D., & Guo, Y. (2019). Residual remaining useful life prediction method for lithium-ion batteries in satellite with incomplete healthy historical data. *IEEE Access*, 7, 127788–127799.

[3] Gabbar, H., Othman, A., & Abdussami, M. (2021). Review of battery management

systems (BMS) development and industrial standards. *Technologies*, 9(2), 28.

[4] Xing, Y., Ma, E. W. M., Tsui, K. L., & Pecht, M. (2011). Battery management systems in electric and hybrid vehicles. *Energies*, 4(11), 1840–1857.

[5] Jinlei, S., Lei, P., Ruihang, L., Qian, M., Chuanyu, T., & Tianru, W. (2019). Economic operation optimization for 2nd use batteries in battery energy storage systems. *IEEE Access*, 7, 41852–41859.

[6] Liu, K., Hu, X., Wei, Z., Li, Y., & Jiang, Y. (2019). Modified gaussian process regression models for cyclic capacity prediction of lithium-ion batteries. *IEEE Transactions on Transportation Electrification*, 5(4), 1225–1236.

[7] She, C., Wang, Z., Sun, F., Liu, P., & Zhang, L. (2020). Battery aging assessment for real-world electric buses based on incremental capacity analysis and radial basis function neural network. *IEEE Transactions on Industrial Informatics*, 16(5), 3345–3354.

[8] Xu, B., Zhao, J., Zheng, T., Litvinov, E., & Kirschen, D. S. (2018). Factoring the cycle aging cost of batteries participating in electricity markets. *IEEE Transactions on Power Systems*, 33(2), 2248–2259.

[9] Qi, N., Dai, K., Yi, F., Wang, X., You, Z., & Zhao, J. (2019). An adaptive energy management strategy to extend battery lifetime of solar powered wireless sensor nodes. *IEEE Access*, 7, 88289–88300.

[10] Zhang, C., Wang, Y., Gao, Y., Wang, F., Mu, B., & Zhang, W. (2019). Accelerated fading recognition for lithium-ion batteries with nickel-cobalt-manganese cathode using quantile regression method. *Applied Energy*, 256, 113841.

[11] Liu, H., Chen, F., Tong, Y., Wang, Z., Yu, X., & Huang, R. (2020). Impacts of driving conditions on EV battery pack life cycle. *World Electric Vehicle Journal*, 11(1), 17.

[12] Corno, M., & Pozzato, G. (2020). Active adaptive battery aging management for electric vehicles. *IEEE Transactions on Vehicular Technology*, 69(1), 258–269.

[13] Liu, K., Li, Y., Hu, X., Lucu, M., & Widanage, W. D. (2020). Gaussian process regression with automatic relevance determination kernel for calendar aging prediction of lithium-ion batteries. *IEEE Transactions on Industrial Informatics*, 16(6), 3767–3777.

[14] Ma, J., Xu, S., Shang, P., Ding, Y., Qin, W., Cheng, Y., et al. (2020). Cycle life test optimization for different Li-ion power battery formulations using a hybrid remaining-useful-life prediction method. *Applied Energy*, 262, 114490.

[15] Jamshidi, M. B., Jamshidi, M., & Rostami, S., (2017). An intelligent approach for nonlinear system identification of a Li-ion battery. In Proc. IEEE 2nd International Conference Automation, Control and Intelligent Systems (I2CACIS), Kota Kinabalu, Malaysia, (pp. 98–103). Canada, May 2019, (pp. 459–464).

45 Termux setup tools

Chetan Suthar[1,a], Sonal Hutke[2,b], Pranavi Tangudu[1,c], Dhruv Mehta[1,d] and Asha Selvan[1,e]

[1]Student, Computer Science and Engineering, SIES Graduate School of Technology, Navi Mumbai, India

[2]Assistant Professor, Computer Science and Engineering, SIES Graduate School of Technology, Navi Mumbai, Maharashtra, India

Abstract

The main focus of this paper is to develop a versatile, portable, and user-friendly cybersecurity environment within the Termux application, a powerful Linux-based terminal emulator designed for Android devices. Termux enables users to run a wide variety of Linux commands and install packages, effectively transforming their smartphones into portable development and cybersecurity workstations. Despite its powerful capabilities, Termux can be challenging for beginners due to its reliance on manual command-line operations, dependency management, and tool configuration. This paper addresses these challenges by implementing a structured, menu-driven interface that simplifies the user experience. Through this interface, users can effortlessly install, configure, and execute various security tools, covering essential domains such as open-source intelligence (OSINT) gathering, penetration testing, vulnerability assessment, and network reconnaissance. The platform leverages Python and Shell scripting to automate the execution of tools, streamline installation processes, and ensure compatibility across diverse Android devices. The solution also promotes cybersecurity learning by eliminating technical barriers, making advanced tools accessible to users of all skill levels. By bridging the gap between traditional desktop-based frameworks and mobile accessibility, this project represents an innovative step toward the future of mobile cybersecurity.

Keywords: Android security, cybersecurity, ethical hacking, mobile security tools, open-source intelligence, penetration testing

Introduction

In today's fast-paced and increasing digital world, the demand for portable, accessible, and efficient cybersecurity solutions has never been greater. The Termux Setup Tools project rises to meet this need by bridging the gap between traditional desktop- based security tools and mobile cybersecurity applications. As cyber threats grow in complexity and frequency, security professionals, ethical hackers, and researchers need tools that enable them to conduct security assessments anytime and anywhere—even without access to a full desktop environment. However, many existing tools are limited to high-performance desktops, require complex installation procedures, and are often inaccessible to users lacking technical expertise.

Termux, a powerful Linux-based terminal emulator for Android, opens the door for bringing security operations to mobile

[a]sutharchetan10150@gmail.com, [b]sonalj@sies.edu.in, [c]pranavitangudu16@gmail.com, [d]dhruvsmehta2704@gmail.com, [e]ashaselvan035@gmail.com

DOI: 10.1201/9781003753391-45

devices. Yet, navigating Termux, resolving dependencies, and configuring tools manually presents significant challenges, especially for beginners. Recognizing these limitations, the Termux Setup Tools project was initiated to simplify this process. By offering a structured, menu-driven interface, it allows users to access, install, and operate multiple security functionalities with ease no advanced technical knowledge required.

The platform consolidates various cybersecurity modules, ranging from OSINT tools and SSL analyzers to HTTP header inspection and IP reconnaissance, all within a lightweight and intuitive interface. Whether the user is an ethical hacker simulating attacks, a cybersecurity analyst scanning for vulnerabilities, or a student learning penetration testing basics, Termux Setup Tools caters to a wide spectrum of user needs. It transforms a simple mobile device into a powerful cybersecurity workstation, empowering users to take control of their digital safety wherever they are [1].

In addition to its technical features, the tool is designed to promote inclusivity in cybersecurity. By lowering the technical barrier through automation and simplicity, it makes professional-grade tools available to everyone, regardless of skill level. Its offline compatibility, low resource usage, and modular design make it not only efficient but also adaptable for use in remote areas and constrained environments. With its thoughtful design and practical utility, Termux Setup Tools stands out as a significant step forward in democratizing access to cybersecurity operations.

Literature Review

The need for easily accessible, portable cybersecurity tools is rising as a result of the quick development of mobile computing and the growing complexity of

cyberthreats. The contribution of penetration testing and OSINT tools to enhancing digital forensics, vulnerability assessment, and network defense has been the subject of numerous studies. However, the majority of these tools are only available to users on mobile platforms because they are made for desktop or server-based environments and demand a high level of technical expertise. In their discussion of several ethical hacking methods, such as scanning, password cracking, and social engineering, Vooradi and Jadhav [3] emphasized the significance of taking precautions for system security, particularly for novices. Their research emphasizes how important it is to streamline tool usage in order to increase accessibility to ethical hacking. The foundation of automation in mobile security toolkits was also supported by Tabatabaei and Wells [2], who investigated the combination of OSINT tools and scripting techniques to automate and enhance the effectiveness of intelligence gathering.

To illustrate how lightweight scripts and modular systems can improve data acquisition, Guo et al. [4] presented Structon, a system for precise IP address geolocation using web mining and inference techniques. This emphasizes how crucial automated processes and well-organized workflows are to contemporary cybersecurity tools. Al Shebli and Beheshti [8] provided a comprehensive overview of penetration testing methodologies, covering phases such as planning, discovery, attack, and reporting. They emphasized the utility of tools like Nmap, Metasploit, and Nessus for vulnerability assessment. These findings are crucial in guiding the selection and integration of penetration testing utilities into mobile-compatible platforms like Termux. Kowta et al. [15] examined information-gathering techniques for penetration testing, including WHOIS lookups and DNS reconnaissance, underscoring their value in network scanning and reconnaissance phases. Their work supports the inclusion of multi-layered scanning tools in mobile cybersecurity frameworks.

Zegers [16] analyzed HTTP headers to identify security vulnerabilities and misconfigurations, which informs the development of lightweight modules for real-time web security analysis. Yang et al. [13] proposed a dual-layer approach combining static and dynamic analysis to detect Android ransomware, validating the effectiveness of integrating automated detection techniques into mobile-based environments. Overall, the existing literature supports the need for a consolidated, user-friendly, and mobile-optimized cybersecurity toolkit. The proposed Termux Setup Tools platform builds upon these foundations by integrating multiple security tools into a single menu-driven interface, reducing complexity, and enhancing accessibility for users of all skill levels.

Tools and Functional Modules

Termux Setup Tools is a project that consolidates a collection of lightweight, effective, and automated cybersecurity software designed for mobile platforms. The tools are packaged into standalone functional modules and run through a categorized, menu-based interface, making it convenient for users to flow from one operation to another without needing to type out complex command-line commands [9, 10]. All the tools are coded using Shell and Python scripting, and the tools were designed to be automated, portable, and easy to use. The modularity of the system improves extensibility and allows for the future tools to be added without interfering with the current structure [5, 6].

One of the core modules is the SSL certificate analyzer, which allows users to analyze secure socket layer (SSL) certificates associated with websites. This tool verifies the validity and authenticity of the SSL chain, checks the certificate issuer, identifies expiration dates, and evaluates the encryption algorithms used [7]. It is essential for determining whether websites meet industry security standards for data encryption and secure communication. Closely related is the SSL analysis tool, which performs deeper evaluations, including protocol inspection, cipher suite validation, and SSL certificate chain integrity checks. This module helps users identify deprecated or insecure SSL implementations that may leave web servers vulnerable to attacks. The HTTP header and security analyzer focuses on evaluating HTTP response headers and embedded security policies. It retrieves headers such as content-security-policy, X-frame-options, strict- transport-security, and others, and identifies misconfigurations that could be exploited for attacks like cross-site scripting or clickjacking. This tool also reveals server-side technologies and version details, aiding in fingerprinting and vulnerability identification.

The IP Information Tool is used to conduct reconnaissance on specific IP addresses or domains. It returns geolocation data, Internet Service Provider (ISP) details, and autonomous system number (ASN) information, which are useful for both mapping network structures and tracing digital threats. This tool is particularly valuable in assessing threat origins, identifying spoofed addresses, and monitoring suspicious traffic behavior. Another significant component is the SEE Surf Tool, which is designed to detect potential server-side request forgery (SSRF) vulnerabilities in web applications. SSRF attacks are a growing concern in modern web security, as they exploit internal endpoints by tricking a server into initiating requests to unintended destinations. This module scans for parameters vulnerable to SSRF and provides actionable feedback to developers and analysts. The web crawler tool performs automated reconnaissance by crawling websites and extracting links, metadata, and file paths. This is particularly useful in the early stages of penetration testing, where understanding site structure and entry points is critical.

DNS-related functions are handled by the DNSSEC Validation Tool, which verifies the implementation of domain name system security extensions (DNSSEC). DNSSEC adds an additional layer of trust to DNS records, preventing spoofing and cache poisoning attacks. The tool confirms whether a domain has DNSSEC enabled and checks the validity of digital signatures within DNS responses. Additionally, the platform includes a WHOIS and Reverse Lookup Tool that extracts administrative, technical, and registration details from domains or IP addresses. It helps in profiling domain ownership and correlating network data for investigative purposes. The PhoneInsight tool adds mobile OSINT capability by analyzing phone numbers to determine the

carrier, region, format, and spam risk. It supports both national and international formats and differentiates between mobile, VoIP, and landline numbers. This tool can be particularly useful in social engineering simulations, threat intelligence gathering, and digital forensics. Each of these tools operates as a self-contained module, handling its own input validation, dependency installation, and result formatting. Collectively, they create a robust framework for performing comprehensive security audits and information gathering tasks using an Android device. The structured interface, automation of setup procedures, and minimal technical overhead make this toolkit highly accessible for both beginners and professionals. Furthermore, the modularity of the system ensures easy maintenance and scalability, allowing developers to continually expand the platform's capabilities as cybersecurity threats evolve [14, 17].

Methodology

The methodology for our Termux Setup Tool project involves a detailed and

Table 45.1 Comparison of termux setup tools and traditional tools.

Features	Termux setup tools	Traditional tools
Platform	Android mobile	Desktop/Cloud only
Installation	Menu-driven and automated	Manual and complex
Dependencies	Automatically resolved	Requires manual setup
Accessibility	Can be accessed whenever required as mobile phones are portable	Requires a complete desktop setup
Technical skill requirement	Low as it is beginner friendly interface	High knowledge required
Modularity	Highly modular, tools run independently	Often bundled, harder to customize
Resource efficiency	Lightweight and mobile-friendly	High system requirements
Use cases	On-the-go auditing, mobile assessments	Static setups only

Source: Author

structured approach aimed at ensuring the successful development and deployment of robust cybersecurity tools for Android devices. This methodology is designed to address every aspect of the project, from initial planning to final deployment, ensuring that the tool meets the needs of both new learners and advanced users.

The methodology is divided into several phases, each serving a critical role in the tool's overall functionality and usability [11, 12].

Requirement analysis phase
The foundation of the project involved identifying the need for a portable, menu-driven cybersecurity toolkit for Android devices. Current cybersecurity tools require complex configurations, complicated to install making them less accessible to beginners. This phase defined the main objectives:

1) Streamlined user experience via a well-organized menu-based interface.
2) Automated installation and configuration to reduce manual setup complexities. 3) Combining several security and OSINT tools under one framework.

System design phase
The architecture of Termux Setup Tools was planned to ensure modularity, scalability, and efficiency. The system was designed with:

1) A Menu-Driven Interface allowing users to select tools effortlessly. 2) Independent tool modules to facilitate smooth additions or alterations without interfering with other functions. 3) Effective resource management to facilitate smooth functionality on low computing capacity mobile phones. 4) Security concerns, such as input validation and limited access to prevent tool misuse.

Tools selection and integration phase
This phase is crucial for ensuring the functionality of the setup tool. In this phase, various cybersecurity tools relevant to OSINT, penetration testing, vulnerability scanning, reconnaissance and ethical hacking are selected and integrated into the setup tool. Tools were selected based on: 1) Tools that are compatible with the Termux environment and ensure that they work seamlessly together. 2) Automation capabilities to allow efficient execution with minimal manual input. 3) Thirdparty API integration for more in-depth data gathering and real-time analysis. Table 45.1. shows the comparison between features of traditional and termux setup tools.

Implementation and testing phase
The development of Termux Setup Tools was implemented using Python and Shell scripting, ensuring efficiency and automation. The following steps were followed: 1)

Table 45.2 Time complexity overview.

Tool	Dominant operation	Approximate time complexity
SSL Analyzer	Certificate fetch and parse	$O(n)$, where n = fields
Web Crawler Tool	URL fetch + recursive crawling	$O(n + m)$, n = pages, m = links
DNSSEC Validator	DNS query and signature check	$O(1)$ for single domain
PhoneInsight	API call + response parse	$O(1)$
WHOIS Tool	WHOIS query + response scan	$O(1)$

Source: Author

Scripts were developed to check for required dependencies and install them if necessary. 2) Proper exception handling was incorporated to prevent crashes and improve debugging. 3) The tools were tested on a selection of Android devices to check compatibility, performance, and stability. The time complexity overview is represented in Table 45.2.

Documentation and deployment phase
It involves the creation of comprehensive user guides and documentation. This documentation helps users understand how to install, configure, and use the Termux Setup Tools effectively. Once the documentation is completed, the final version of the tool is deployed to end users.

By following this systematic methodology, the Termux Setup Tools project ensures that users, whether novice or professional, can execute cybersecurity audits, information gathering, penetration testing, and reconnaissance with ease from a portable and user-friendly toolkit on their Android devices.

Conclusion

The Termux Setup Tools successfully demonstrates a novel approach to making cybersecurity tools more accessible, portable, and user-friendly through mobile platforms. By integrating essential functionalities such as OSINT gathering, SSL and HTTP analysis, IP and DNS reconnaissance, and penetration testing tools into a menu-driven framework, the project bridges the gap between traditional desktop-based cybersecurity suites and modern mobile computing. The use of Python and Shell scripting to automate tool installation, execution, and result handling significantly reduces technical barriers, allowing both beginners and professionals to conduct

security assessments directly from their Android devices.

The modular structure of the system ensures scalability, enabling future expansion with additional tools and features without disrupting the existing architecture. Moreover, the lightweight design and offline capabilities make the platform especially suitable for resource-constrained or remote environments. As cybersecurity threats continue to evolve, tools like Termux Setup Tools offer a flexible and practical solution for mobile-first security operations. This project not only contributes to the growing field of mobile cybersecurity but also promotes wider adoption of ethical hacking practices by simplifying access to professional-grade tools.

References

[1] Mathew, A. (2019). Effectiveness of penetration testing tools, cyber security. *International Journal of Computer Science Trends and Technology (IJCST)*, 7(3), 55–57.

[2] Tabatabaei, F., & Wells, D. (2017). OSINT in the context of cyber-security. In Open-Source Intelligence Investigation: From Strategy to Implementation, (pp. 213–231).

[3] Vooradi, V. B., & Jadhav, L. (2019). Ethical hacking techniques and its preventive measures for newbies. *International Journal*, 6, 8.

[4] Guo, C., Liu, Y., Shen, W., Wang, H. J., Yu, Q., & Zhang, Y. (2009). Mining the web and the internet for accurate IP address geolocations. In IEEE INFOCOM 2009, (pp. 2841–2845). IEEE.

[5] Foster-Johnson, E., Welch, J. C., & Anderson, M. (2007). Beginning Shell Scripting. John Wiley & Sons.

[6] Langtangen, H. P. (2008). Python Scripting for Computational Science. Springer.

[7] Prasad, M. R., & Manjula, B. (2014). Ethical hacking tools: a situational awareness. *International Journal of Emerging*

Technologies in Computer Science and Electronics, 11, 33–38.

[8] Al Shebli, H. M. Z., & Beheshti, B. D. (2018). A study on penetration testing process and tools. In 2018 IEEE Long Island Systems, Applications and Technology Conference (LISAT), (pp. 1–7). IEEE.

[9] Tatlı, E. I. (2015). Cracking more password hashes with patterns. *IEEE Transactions on Information Forensics and Security*, 10(8), 1656–1665.

[10] Kausar, M. A., Dhaka, V., & Singh, S. K. (2013). Web crawler: a review. *International Journal of Computer Applications*, 63(2), 31–36.

[11] Singh, A. S. B., Yusof, Y., & Nathan, Y. (2021). Eagle: GUI-based penetration testing tool for scanning and enumeration. In 2021 14th International Conference on Developments in eSystems Engineering (DeSE), (pp. 97–101). IEEE.

[12] Szymoniak, S., & Foks, K. (2024). Open-source intelligence opportunities and chal-lenges–a review. *Advances in Science and Technology. Research Journal*, 18(3), 123–139.

[13] Yang, T., Yang, Y., Qian, K., Lo, D. C.-T., Qian, Y., & Tao, L. (2015). Automated detection and analysis for android ransomware. In 2015 IEEE 17th International Conference on High Performance Computing and Communications, 7th International Symposium on Cyberspace Safety and Security, and 12th International Conference on Embedded Software and Systems, (pp. 1338–1343). IEEE.

[14] Khomh, F., Yuan, H., & Zou, Y. (2012). Adapting Linux for mobile platforms: an empirical study of android. In 2012 28th IEEE International Conference on Software Maintenance (ICSM), (pp. 629–632). IEEE.

[15] Kowta, A. S. L., Bhowmick, K., Kaur, J. R., & Jeyanthi, N. (2021). Analysis and overview of information gathering and tools for pentesting. In 2021 International Conference on Computer Communication and Informatics (ICCCI), (pp. 1–13). IEEE.

[16] Zegers, R. (2015). HTTP header analysis. (Master's thesis, University of Amsterdam).

[17] Ariyapperuma, S., & Mitchell, C. J. (2007). Security vulnerabilities in DNS and DNSSEC. In The Second International Conference on Availability, Reliability and Security (ARES'07), (pp. 335–342). IEEE.

46 Impact of interface trap charges on the DC characteristics of cylindrical gate-all-around TFETs: A TCAD-based study

Atmadeep Banerjee[a], Aarjav Talati[b] and Girija Shankar Sahoo[c]

School of Electronics Engineering (SENSE), Vellore Institute of Technology, Vandalur-Kellambakkam Road, Chennai, Tamil Nadu, India

Abstract

MOSFETs are suffering from the bottleneck of sub-threshold swing above 60 mV/dec. This limits its application in low-power, high-speed circuits. To overcome this issue, a Gate All Around (GAA) cylindrical TFET is proposed. Sentaurus 3D-TCAD is used to perform simulation by considering the non-local BTBT tunnelling method. The proposed TFET provides a threshold voltage of 1.05 V with an SS of 30.3 mV/dec with a switching speed (I_{on}/I_{off}) of 2.81×10^{11}. But the practical issue is the trap charges present in the device, which deteriorate the TFET performance. When trap charges are introduced in this study it is found that the SS worsens to 6.8 mV/dec, indicating that the device continues to operate at a lower voltage with a lower I_{on}/I_{off} ratio of 1.99×10^6.

Keywords: MOSFET, subthreshold swing, TFET, trap charges, tunnelling

Introduction

Metal oxide semiconductor field effect transistors (MOSFETs) are facing problems with low-power circuits because of their higher (above 60 mV/dec) subthreshold swing (SS), which makes it difficult to turn on the device in low operating voltage [1]. When SS is reduced, leakage currents are increased, which causes power loss [2]. MOSFETs also become slower at near-threshold voltage operation, reducing their efficiency for ultra-low-power designs. Short-channel effects are also one of the major drawbacks that decrease the device reliability [3]. So, researchers are in search of a new alternative that can mitigate the above-mentioned drawbacks. Recent studies indicate tunnel field effect transistors (TFETs) can mitigate the above issues effectively Ali and Abdolkader [4] TFET

uses non local band-to-band tunneling (NBTBT), which reduces leakage current and power consumption [5]. TFETs have a sub-threshold swing (SS) of below 60 mV/dec, in contrast to MOSFETs, and are thus well-suited for ultra-low-power applications [6]. They also function effectively at lower voltages and are thus a likely future replacement for MOSFETs in low-power electronics.

Different types of TFET have been studied by different researchers. Among them single gate and Double-gate TFETs (SG-TFET and DG-TFET) are most frequently studied by various researchers. SG-TFET, with one gate regulating the tunnelling and fewer processing steps, has a less complex structure but with reduced electrostatic control, causing higher subthreshold swing and lower ON-current [7,

[a]atmadeep23@gmail.com, [b]aarjavtalati420@gmail.com, [c]girija.shankarsahoo@vit.ac.in

DOI: 10.1201/9781003753391-46

8]. At the same time DG-TFET, with two gates, has a much stronger electrostatic control, minimizing short-channel effects, and enhancing ON-current and subthreshold swing [9, 10]. This renders DG-TFETs more energy-efficient for applications requiring high performance. Several innovations, including hetero-junctions, dopingless structures, and triple- material gates, have been investigated in order to better optimize DG-TFETs [11–13]. Although SG-TFETs are a less complex alternative, DG-TFETs are becoming preferred for next-generation ultra-low-power circuits because they have better electrical properties.

While TFETs are capable of operating with subthreshold slopes less than 60 mV/decade, raising (I_{on}) is challenging without compromising this benefit [14]. Material alterations, like substituting Ge or $Si_{0.65}Ge_{0.35}$ for silicon, have been investigated to increase performance but without any notable improvement in SS, V_{th} [15]. In addition, SG-TFETs find it challenging to satisfy ITRS (International Technology Roadmap for Semiconductors) ON-current requirements, hence their limited use in contemporary VLSI circuits [16]. For meeting these challenges, innovative methods like increased source doping, heterojunction engineering, and structural manipulation are required in order to optimize performance without compromising the advantages of TFET technology [17]. Though DG-TFETs have an extremely low OFF-current (I_{off}) of below 1 fA, reducing leakage and minimizing standby power consumption and better SS (which can be as low as 11 mV/dec at some places with an average SS of 57 mV/dec) but it still suffer from lower I_{on} because of the tunnelling mechanism and low electrostatic control over the channel as compared to nanowire TFET [18, 19]. Though many researchers are investigating on different novel nanowire TFET structures,

they are not focusing on the trap charge effect on SS, threshold voltages and I_{on}/I_{off} ratios. However, understanding trap charges is important. Imperfection in semiconductor and oxide interface, imperfect lattice of semiconductor are the important source of trap charge carriers. It hinders the device operation adversely. These are normally accumulated at the semiconductor-insulator boundary or within the material and increase leakage current (OFF-state) and compromise SS in TFETs [20]. They alter the tunnelling barrier, affecting I_{on} and I_{off}. Dynamic trapping leads to threshold voltage (V_{th}) instability, causing hysteresis [21]. High-k dielectrics often worsen these effects due to higher trap densities. To minimize these issues, defect-passivated dielectrics, optimized annealing, and heterojunction designs are used [22]. Addressing trap-related effects is crucial for achieving stable and efficient TFETs, especially for low-power applications. In TFET, trap charges, i.e., interface trap charges (ITCs) in the semiconductor-oxide interface, severely impair the performance of the device by modifying the tunnelling current, introducing variability in the I_{on}, SS, and device characteristics in general, ultimately influencing the reliability and functionality of the device.

In this study, we have proposed a Cylindrical Gate all around TFET by considering the effect of trap charges on the DC performance of the device. Here, the trap cross sectional area for both electron and hole are varied between $1 \times 10^{-6}/cm^3$ to $1 \times 10^{-10}/cm^3$ by fixing the concentration of trap charge at $1 \times 10^{15}/cm^3$.

Device Modelling and Simulation

The proposed TFET model is of cylindrical gate all around (GAA) p-i-n structure, optimized for improved device performance by proper doping and material choice. The source region is 20 nm thick and heavily p-type doped with boron concentration of 1×10^{20}/cm^{-3} and the drain region, also 20 nm thick, and is n-type doped with phosphorus at the same concentration of 1×10^{20}/cm^{-3}. The channel, which is located between the source and drain, is 50 nm length, I diameter of 10 nm. It is lightly p-type doped with a doping concentration of 1×10^{15}/cm^{-3} to enable effective nonlocal BTBT. Aluminum was used for the gate material because of its lower work function of 4.2 eV, which provides the needed electrostatic gating effect on the channel. Furthermore, a 2 nm thick SiO2 layer is used as the gate oxide for insulation and gate modulation. This structural arrangement is optimized to maximize BTBT, resulting in better switching behavior, increased I_{on}, reduced I_{off}, and a steep SS, which makes it extremely appropriate for low-power applications [23, 24].

Sentaurus TCAD is used for the simulation and analysis of the proposed device structure. The Sentaurus generated device is shown in Figure 46.1. It supports accurate modeling of device structures, electrical properties and tunneling effects. During TFET simulation, Sentaurus TCAD offers process simulation, which facilitates doping

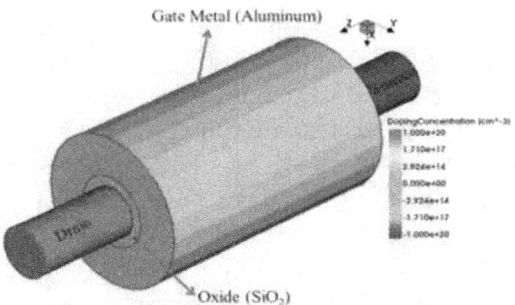

Figure 46.1 3D Schematic of the proposed TFET generated by TCAD tool
Source: Author

profile optimization, gate oxide thickness, and material selection. The tool combines physics-oriented simulations and examines device features like drain current (I_d) and threshold voltage (V_{th}), and SS. It utilizes models like fermi, drift diffusion, SRH, band gap narrowing, etc. In the SRH model non local BTBT model is introduced to visualize the tunnelling effect on the device. Utilizing Sentaurus TCAD, scientists can thoroughly investigate TFET performance, engineer its design for optimization, and forecast real-world behavior prior to fabrication [25].

Results and Discussions

2-D cut sectional view of B2B Generation of the proposed device is shown in Figure 46.2 (a) and (b) without and with trap charges respectively. BTBT is a carrier injection mechanism that enhances electronic transport in TFETs, making them highly promising for achieving a subthreshold swing below the Boltzmann limit. It enables scaling the operating voltage along with the off- state leakage current and, thereby, decreases the power consumption of TFETs. The energy band diagram of the TFET (Figure 46.2(c)) shows its distinctive carrier injection by BTBT, allowing SS less than the Boltzmann limit [26]. In the off-state, the source valence band and channel conduction band are not aligned, which does not allow current flow [4]. With gate bias, band bending aligns them, and tunnelling-driven conduction is allowed. This steep-switching mechanism makes TFETs very efficient for low-power applications. The energy band alignment, important for the tunnelling process, is greatly determined by the gate length and work function of the gate metal.

Mobile charges, like electrons and holes, and stationary charges, like ionized dopants

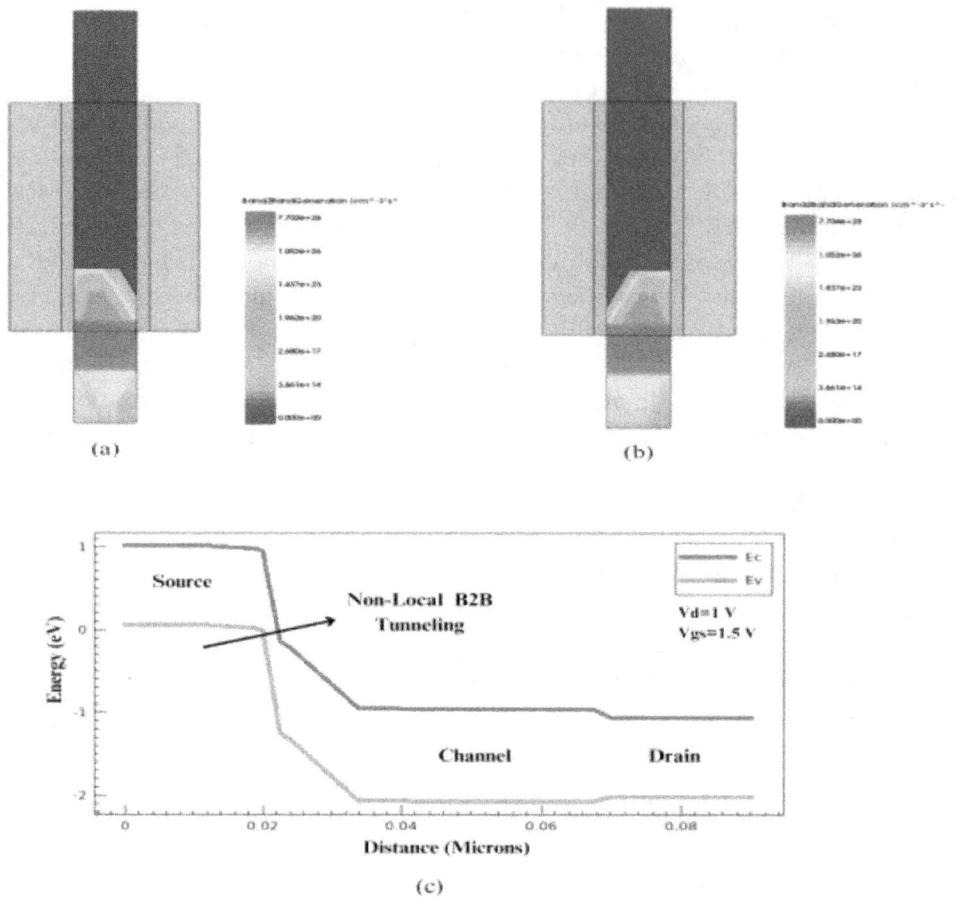

Figure 46.2 Band-to-Band (B2B) generation rate in the cylindrical GAA TFET: (a) without trap charges, (b) with trap charges and (c) Energy Band diagram illustrating non-local B2B tunnelling under V_d = 1V and V_{gs} = 1.5V
Source: Author

or traps, are essential components of all semiconductor devices. The electrostatic potential is determined by the charges, which are also influenced by it. As a result, the electrostatic potential must be analyzed for every electronic device. In TFETs, the favorable electrostatic potential increases gate control by limiting tunnelling to the source- channel junction, eliminating direct source-to-drain tunnelling and minimizing leakage current. This enhances electrostatic integrity, reduces short-channel effects (SCEs), and allows a steeper subthreshold slope (SS) with an improved I_{on}/I_{off} ratio. Sharp potential drop at the source-channel junction increases band-to-band tunnelling (BTBT), improving the device performance. Also, the channel diameter and gate oxide thickness are key elements in controlling surface potential, in turn influencing drain current and the efficiency of tunnelling [27]. From Figure 46.3(a) it can be visualized that without trap charges, the electrostatic potential is evenly distributed, providing strong gate control over the channel. This enables effective BTBT at the source-channel junction, leading to a high I_{on}/I_{off} ratio and low leakage. At the same time from Figure 46.3(b), the trap charges deform the potential landscape, relaxing the gate control and interrupting the electric field. This causes weaker tunnelling efficiency, larger ambipolar current (I_{ambi}), and worsened SS, influencing low-power performance [7]. The contrast draws attention to reducing trap charges being imperative in the case of electrostatic control's robustness as well as of best device functionality.

The performance of TFETs depends heavily on Shockley-Read-Hall (SRH) recombination, particularly at low drain voltages where tunnelling is the dominant mechanism. When electrons tunnelling from the source become trapped at defect states in the bandgap, they recombine with drain holes by the process called SRH recombination. This introduces leakage current during this process, which compromises the I_{on}/I_{off} ratio and limits the low-power efficiency of the device. This effect is exacerbated by the intrinsic channel area defects, making it a key part of TFET subthreshold

behavior and overall energy efficiency [28]. In Figure 46.4, the effect of trap charges on SRH recombination within the TFET structure is shown. When there are no trap charges (Figure 46.4(a)), SRH recombination profile is quite even and allows efficient band-to-band tunnelling with minimal carrier recombination. But when trap charges are present (Figure 46.4(b)), a dramatic distortion in the valence band energy is seen, especially around the source-channel junction. This causes an enhanced recombination rate, causing an elevated leakage current and deterioration in the I_{on}/I_{off} ratio. Traps cause mid-gap states that serve as recombination centers, causing an increase in off-state leakage and a decrease in subthreshold swing (SS). The switching characteristics and energy efficiency of the TFET are negatively impacted as a result, pointing to the need for suppression of trap-induced recombination through material and interface engineering. The important figure of merits of the proposed model is presented in Table 46.1 for better understanding purposes.

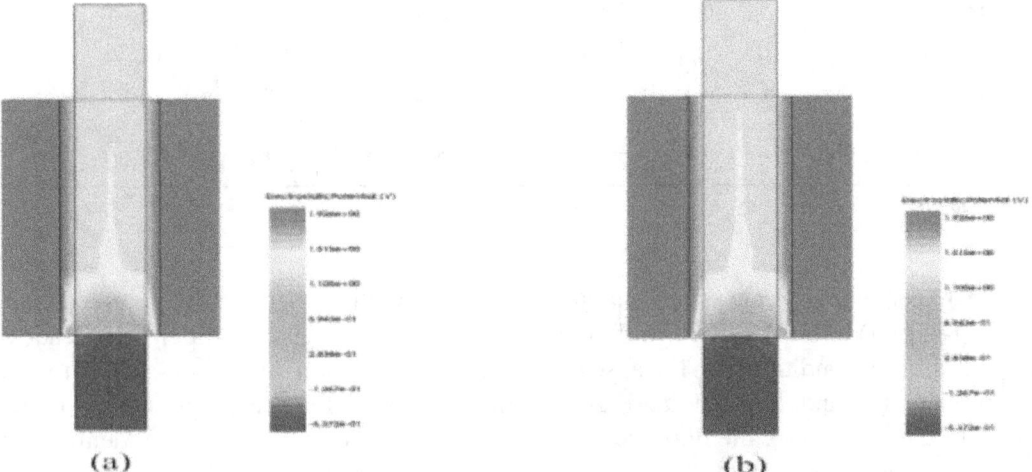

(a)   (b)

Figure 46.3 Electrostatic potential distribution in the cylindrical GAA TFET: (a) without trap charges and (b) with trap charges
Source: Author

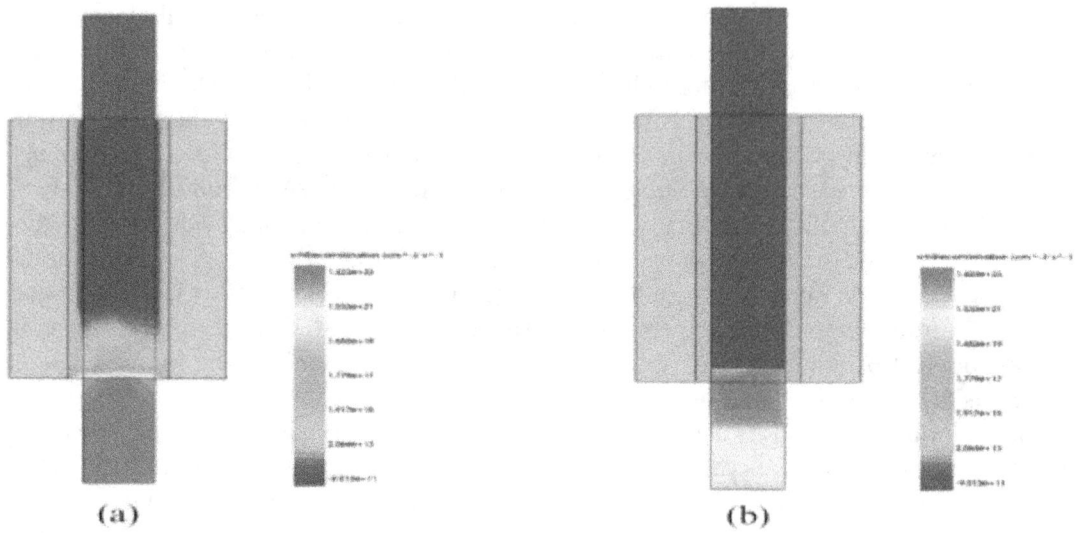

Figure 46.4 Shockley-read-hall (SRH) Recombination rate in the cylindrical GAA TFET: (a) without trap charges and (b) with trap charges
Source: Author

Table 46.1 Different figure of merit along with SS degradation with increasing trap cross-section area.

	Basic GAA TFET	GAA TFET with trap Xsection 1 × 10⁻¹⁰/cm³	GAA TFET with trap Xsection 1 × 10⁻⁹/cm³	GAA TFET with trap Xsection 1 × 10⁻⁸/cm³	GAA TFET with trap Xsection 1 × 10⁻⁷/cm³	GAA TFET with trap Xsection 1 × 10⁻⁶/cm³
I_{on} (A/μm)	3.49×10^{-9}	3.49×10^{-9}	3.49×10^{-9}	3.49×10^{-9}	3.49×10^{-9}	3.49×10^{-9}
I_{off} (A/μm)	1.24×10^{-20}	1.77×10^{-19}	1.65×10^{-18}	1.64×10^{-17}	1.64×10^{-16}	1.64×10^{-15}
V_{th} (V)	1.05	1.05	1.06	1.06	1.06	1.06
SS (mV/dec)	30.3	18.35	14.47	11.33	8.58	6.8
I_{on}/I_{off}	2.81×10^{11}	1.97×10^{10}	2.11×10^{9}	2.08×10^{8}	2.01×10^{7}	1.99×10^{6}

Source: Author

Figure 46.5 shows current voltage characteristics (I-V plot) of the TFET for different trap cross-section conditions, on linear scale in Figure 46.5(a) and logarithmic Figure 46.5(b). In the linear plot, the drain current is a steady rise with rising gate voltage, with little fluctuation with varying trap conditions at high gate voltages. The inset view shows tiny changes in current levels (Figure 46.5(a)) with varying trap cross-sections, revealing that higher trap densities lead to slight degradation of the on-state current. In the logarithmic scale, trap charge effect on off-state current is more evident. With increased trap cross-section (from 1e⁻¹⁰ to 1e⁻⁶), the subthreshold leakage current is significantly increased. This is because of increased SRH recombination, which

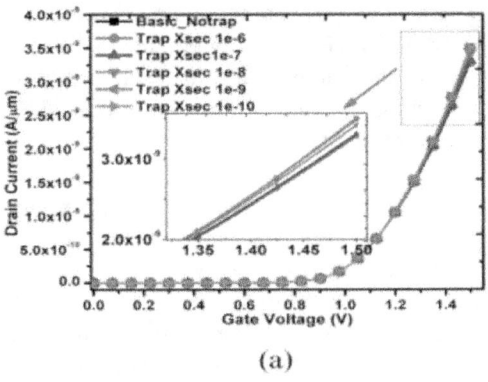
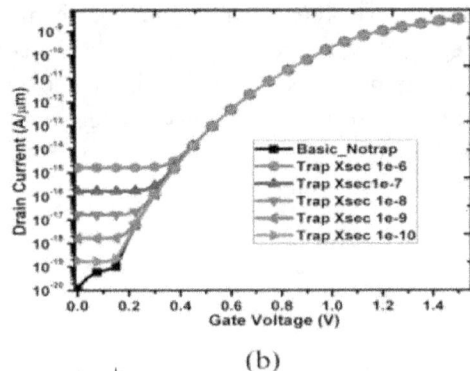

Figure 46.5 Transfer characteristics (I–V plots) of the TFET under different trap cross-section conditions: (a) linear scale and (b) logarithmic scale
Source: Author

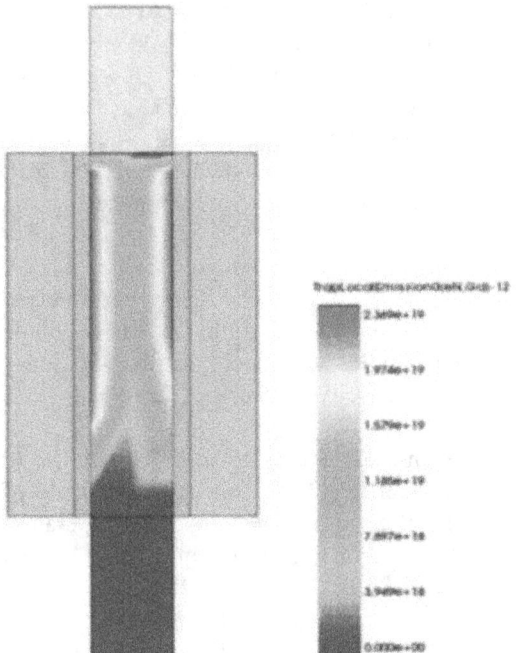

Figure 46.6 Local trap emission in proposed GAA cylindrical TFET
Source: Author

inhibits BTBT and leads to a worse SS. The increased trap-induced leakage current impacts the overall energy efficiency and low-power benefits of the TFET. Overall, the presence of trap states has a significant impact on off-state performance, leading to increased leakage, but has a comparatively minor impact on the on-state current. The emission of trap charges can be seen from Figure 46.6. It is evident that near the Si/oxide interface the trap emission has more effect than the inner side of the channel. So, making it difficult for the induced electrons to recombine and result in increment of the off current (Figure 46.5(b)).

Conclusion

In this study, we analyzed the impact of trap charges on the DC performance of a cylindrical GAA TFET. Using Sentaurus 3D-TCAD simulations, it was concluded that TFETs offer significant advantages over MOSFETs—such as SS below 60 mV/dec and enhanced energy efficiency. The findings also indicate that the inclusion of trap charges increases leakage currents, reduces the I_{on}/I_{off} ratio, and negatively impacts the SS, ultimately impairing the device's switching efficiency. The simulation results show that as the trap charge cross-sectional area increases, the SS worsens, and the device remains in an ON state at lower voltages, leading to higher power consumption. Additionally, the electrostatic control of the device weakens, leading to performance degradation. These results highlight the critical need for advanced interface engineering, optimized material selection, and defect-passivation techniques to mitigate the adverse effects of trap charges.

References

[1] Chen, Q., Agrawal, B., & Meindl, J. D. (2002). A comprehensive analytical subthreshold swing (S) model for double-gate MOSFETs. *IEEE Transactions on Electron Devices*, 49(6), 1086–1090.

[2] Dash, S., Sahoo, G. S., & Mishra, G. P. (2018). Current switching ratio optimization using dual pocket doping engineering. *Superlattices and Microstructures*, 113, 791–798.

[3] Dash, S., Sahoo, G. S., & Mishra, G. P. (2016). Subthreshold swing minimization of cylindrical tunnel FET using binary metal alloy gate. *Superlattices and Microstructures*, 91, 105–111.

[4] Ali, F. A., & Abdolkader, T. M. (2024). Tunnel field effect transistor (TFET): a review. *International Journal of Materials Technology and Innovation*, 4, 14–31.

[5] Biswas, A., Dan, S. S., Royer, C. L., Grabinski, W., & Ionescu, A. M. (2012). TCAD simulation of SOI TFETs and calibration of non-local band-to-band tunneling model. *Microelectronic Engineering*, 98, 334–337.

[6] Trivedi, A. R., Carlo, S., & Mukhopadhyay, S. (2013). Exploring tunnel-FET for ultralow power analog applications: a case study on operational transconductance amplifier. In 50th ACM/EDAC/IEEE Design Automation Conference (DAC), Austin, TX, USA, (pp. 1–6).

[7] Tiwari, S., & Saha, R. (2022). Methods to reduce ambipolar current of various TFET structures: a review. *Silicon*, 14, 6507–6515.

[8] Navya Shree, G., Priyadarshini, U., Keerthana, M., & Vimala, P. (2020). Design of gate engineered heterojunction surrounding gate tunnel field effect transistor (HSG TFET). In International Conference on Emerging Trends in Information Technology and Engineering (ic-ETITE), Vellore, India, (pp. 1–5).

[9] Boucart, K., & Ionescu, A. M. (2007). Double-gate tunnel FET with high-κ gate dielectric. *IEEE Transactions on Electron Devices*, 54, 1725–1733.

[10] Bala, S., & Khosla, M. (2018). Design and simulation of nanoscale double-gate TFET/tunnel CNTFET. *Journal of Semiconductors*, 39, 1725–1733.

[11] Nuñez, H. C., Luisier, M., & Schenk, A. (2014). Analysis of InAs-Si heterojunction nanowire tunnel FETs: extreme confinement vs. bulk. In 44th European Solid State Device Research Conference (ESSDERC), Venice Lido, Italy, (pp. 118–119).

[12] Mishra, V., Verma, Y. K., Gupta, S. K., & Rathi, V. (2021). A SiGe-source doping-less double-gate tunnel FET: design and analysis based on charge plasma technique with enhanced performance. *Silicon*, 14, 2275–2282.

[13] Vimala, P., Arun Samuel, T. S., Nirmal, D., & Panda, A. K. (2019). Performance enhancement of triple material double gate TFET with heterojunction and heterodielectric. *Solid State Electronics Letters*, 1(2), 64–72.

[14] Nikhil, K., Babu, K. M. C., Talukdar, J., & Goel, E. (2024). A simulation study of the effect of trap charges and temperature on performance of dual metal strip double gate TFET. *Silicon*, 16, 525–534.

[15] Das, D., Pandey, R., Baishya, S., & Chakraborty, U. (2020). Impact of temperature and trap charges on heterojunction tunnel FET. In National Conference on Emerging Trends on Sustainable Technology and Engineering Applications (NCET-STEA), Durgapur, India, (pp. 1–5).

[16] Som, A., & Jana, S. K. (2023). Performance assessments of gate engineered dopingless schottky tunnel MOSFET in presence of interfacial trap charges. *Silicon*, 15, 7265–7278.

[17] Venkatesh, P., Nigam, K., Pandey, S., Sharma, D., & Kondekar, P. N. (2017). Impact of interface trap charges on performance of electrically doped tunnel FET with heterogeneous gate dielectric. *IEEE Transactions on Device and Materials Reliability*, 17(1), 245–252.

[18] Gupta, A. K., Raman, A., & Kumar, N. (2021). Performance tuning and reliability analysis of the electro-statically configured nanotube tunnel FET with impact of interface trap charges. *Silicon*, 13, 4553–4564.

[19] Kumar, S., & Yadav, D. S. (2022). Assessment of interface trap charges on proposed TFET for low power high-frequency application. *Silicon*, 14, 9291–9304.

[20] Reddy, N. N., & Panda, D. K. (2021). A comprehensive review on tunnel field-effect transistor (TFET) based biosensors: recent advances and future prospects on device structure and sensitivity. *Silicon*, 13, 3085–3100.

[21] Avci, U. E., Rios, R., Kuhn, K. J., & Young, I. A. (2011). Comparison of power and performance for the TFET and MOSFET and considerations for P-TFET. In 11th IEEE International Conference on Nanotechnology, Portland, OR, USA, (pp. 869–872).

[22] Nikhil, K., Babu, K. M. C., Talukdar, J., & Goel, E. (2023). A simulation study of the effect of trap charges and temperature on performance of dual metal strip double gate TFET. *Silicon*, 16, 1–10.

[23] Keighobadi, D., Mohammadi, S., & Fathipour, M. (2019). An analytical drain current model for the cylindrical channel gate-all-around heterojunction tunnel FETs. *IEEE Transactions on Electron Devices*, 66(8), 3646–3651.

[24] Singh, A. K., Tripathy, M. R., Chander, S., Baral, K., Singh, P. K., & Jit, S. (2020). Simulation study and comparative analysis of some TFET Structures with a novel partial-ground-plane (PGP) based TFET on SELBOX structure. *Silicon*, 12, 2345–2354.

[25] Wu, Y. C., & Jhan, Y. R. (2018). Introduction of Synopsys Sentaurus TCAD Simulation. In 3D TCAD Simulation for CMOS Nanoeletronic Devices. Singapore: Springer.

[26] Fan, S., Cao, R., Wang, L., Gao, S., Zhang, Y., Yu, X., et al. (2021). Quantum tunneling in two-dimensional van der waals heterostructures and devices. *Science China Materials*, 64, 2359–2387.

[27] Kaur, S., Raman, A., & Sarin, R. K. (2020). An explicit surface potential, capacitance and drain current model for double-gate TFET. *Superlattices and Microstructures*, 140, 106431.

[28] Smets, Q., Verhulst, A. S., Simoen, E., Gundlach, D., Richter, C., Collaert, N., et al. (2017). Calibration of bulk trap-assisted tunneling and shockley–read–hall currents and impact on InGaAs tunnel-FETs. *IEEE Transactions on Electron Devices*, 64(9), 3622–3626.

47 A proposal for rapid investigation of cancer cell using silicon based one D photonic structure

Somdutta Sinha[1,a], Tushar Kanta Panda[1,b], Partha Sarkar[2,c], Moumita Pal[2,d] and Gopinath Palai[3,e]

[1]Department of ECE, School of Engineering and Technology GIET University Gunupur, Odisha, India

[2]Department of ECE JIS College of Engineering, Kalyani, West Bengal, India

[3]Faculty of Engineering and technology, Sri Sri University Cuttack, Odisha, India

Abstract

In this study, silicon-based photonic devices are designed to detect the presence of cancer cells by measuring alterations in electric field distribution as light passes through the cells. Normal and cancerous cells exhibit distinct patterns in how they affect the electric field, with cancerous cells causing irregular, chaotic electric field distributions due to their structural abnormalities. Simulations using the finite-difference time-domain (FDTD) method highlight these differences. Furthermore, the output power measurements provide critical data for distinguishing between normal and cancerous cells. For example, in basal cells, the output power for normal cells is 262.74 mW with an electric field intensity of 0.8546 V/m, while cancerous basal cells show lower output power at 254.87 mW and a reduced electric field intensity of 0.8417 V/m. Similar reductions in power and electric field intensity are observed in breast and cervical cancer cells. By integrating machine learning algorithms, the system's diagnostic accuracy can be improved, allowing for better decision-making. Silicon photonic structures, with their scalability and cost-effectiveness, offer a promising tool for clinical applications, enabling faster diagnostics and personalized treatment strategies. The research ultimately aims to provide a rapid, non-invasive method for cancer detection, potentially revolutionizing the field of cancer diagnostics.

Keywords: Component, formatting, insert, style, styling

Introduction

Cancer remains one of the leading causes of morbidity and mortality globally, necessitating the development of innovative diagnostic techniques that enable early detection and effective monitoring of tumor progression. Traditional methods of cancer diagnosis, such as biopsy and imaging, often involve invasive procedures that can delay diagnosis and treatment, leading to poorer patient outcomes. As the landscape of healthcare evolves, there is an urgent need for rapid, non-invasive, and accurate diagnostic tools that can facilitate timely intervention. Recent advancements in photonics and nanotechnology present promising alternatives for efficient cancer cell detection, offering the potential to revolutionize the way we approach cancer diagnostics.

Silicon-based one-dimensional photonic structures, including photonic crystals and

[a]somdutta.sinha@giet.edu, [b]tusarkantpanda@gmail.com, [c]partha_sarkar_9@yahoo.com, [d]moumitajisceece@gmail.com, [e]gpalai28@gmail.com

DOI: 10.1201/9781003753391-47

waveguides, have garnered significant attention due to their unique optical properties and compatibility with existing semiconductor technologies. These structures allow for precise control over light propagation and manipulation at the nanoscale. The inherent ability of silicon to manipulate light makes it an ideal candidate for developing photonic sensors that can enhance the detection of cancer biomarkers. By exploiting the sensitive interaction between light and biological samples, silicon photonics can facilitate the identification of malignant cells with high specificity and sensitivity [3].

The integration of silicon photonic structures with advanced sensing techniques, such as surface plasmon resonance (SPR) and fluorescence detection, presents an innovative approach for rapid cancer cell investigation. SPR exploits the coupling of light to electron oscillations at a metal-dielectric interface, leading to sensitive detection of biomolecular interactions [5]. When combined with silicon-based photonic devices, SPR can enable real-time monitoring of cancer cell markers, allowing for the rapid identification of malignancies. Similarly, fluorescence detection techniques, enhanced by the photonic structure's optical properties, can significantly improve signal detection in low-concentration biomarker scenarios [1].

Numerous studies have demonstrated the potential of silicon photonic sensors in cancer diagnostics. For example, Wang et al. [6] developed a silicon-based photonic crystal sensor that achieved high sensitivity for detecting prostate-specific antigen (PSA) in blood samples, showcasing its clinical applicability. Additionally, Zhang et al. [7] reported the use of a silicon waveguide platform for the detection of circulating tumor cells (CTCs) using targeted antibodies, further highlighting the

versatility of silicon photonics in cancer detection.

In this research proposal, we aim to explore the potential of silicon-based one-dimensional photonic structures for the rapid investigation of cancer cells. Our approach will involve designing and fabricating photonic devices that can selectively interact with cancer cell membranes or surface proteins, utilizing their unique optical signatures for detection. By focusing on specific cancer markers, such as overexpressed receptors or circulating tumor cells (CTCs), we can enhance the specificity of the detection process. The incorporation of machine learning algorithms will also be considered to analyze the data generated by these photonic devices, improving diagnostic accuracy and facilitating automated decision-making [4].

Furthermore, the scalability and cost-effectiveness of silicon photonics make it anattractive option for widespread clinical Applications (Zhang et.al., [8]) (Hwang. et.al.,[9]), (Li. et.al.[10]). The potential for integration with microfluidic systems can enhance the capabilities of silicon-based sensors, enabling the analysis of cancer cells in complex biological samples, such as blood or tissue extracts [2]. This holistic approach can significantly reduce the time required for cancer diagnostics, allowing for quicker clinical decision-making and personalized treatment strategies. Rupali et al. [11]: Developed a highly sensitive photonic crystal ring resonator sensor capable of detecting cancer using infrared laser technology effectively. Amiri et al. [12]: Introduced a novel method for visually identifying live cancer cells using a one-dimensional photonic structure, enhancing diagnostic accessibility. Sivakumar et al. [13]: Conducted an empirical analysis of supervised learning methods, showing significant improvements in breast cancer classification accuracy compared to conventional techniques. Sahu and Palai [14]: Designed an elliptical plus-shaped microstrip patch antenna integrated with complementary split-ring resonators, improving breast cancer detection capabilities through enhanced signal sensitivity Palai et.al [15, 16, 17, 8].

Proposed Structure and Operational Mechanism

The Figure 47.1. illustrates a schematic of a one-dimensional photonic structure composed of alternating layers of silicon and air. Specifically, it features two silicon layers, each with a thickness of 60 nm, surrounding a central air layer that is 30 nm thick. This arrangement creates a periodic variation in refractive index, essential for forming an electric field distribution, which inhibits light propagation in certain spectral ranges. The inclusion of the air layer enhances the structure's optical properties, making it suitable for applications such as sensors for detecting biological substances, The precise thicknesses of these layers are critical for optimizing the structure's performance in manipulating light for various photonic applications.

The Figure 47.2 illustrates the operational mechanism for investigating cell status, specifically distinguishing between normal and cancerous cells. The process begins with an input signal, a laser beam operating at a wavelength of 1300 nm, directed towards a silicon layer. This initial silicon layer facilitates the guided propagation of the signal toward the biological sample, which can be either a normal or a cancerous cell. As the input signal interacts with the sample, it undergoes alterations due to the differing optical properties of normal and cancerous cells. These changes are crucial for detection, as they provide the basis for differentiating between cell types. After passing through the sample, the modified signal proceeds through a second silicon layer, which helps direct the light towards the output end. This output end is equipped with a power meter that measures the intensity and other characteristics of the light signal. The data collected from the power meter is then analyzed to determine the status of the cell based on the variations in the output signal's properties. Overall, this mechanism effectively enables the assessment of cell conditions, contributing to advancements in cancer detection and diagnostics.

Result and Interpretation

To understand the investigation of the status of the cell, the present research deploys the input parameters which is an important and indicated in Table 47.1.

Table 47.1 outlines the input parameters essential for investigating the status of various cell types, specifically distinguishing between normal and cancerous cells.

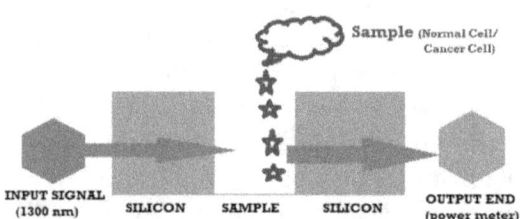

Figure 47.2 Operational mechanism to investigate the status of cell (either normal or cancerous cell)
Source: Author

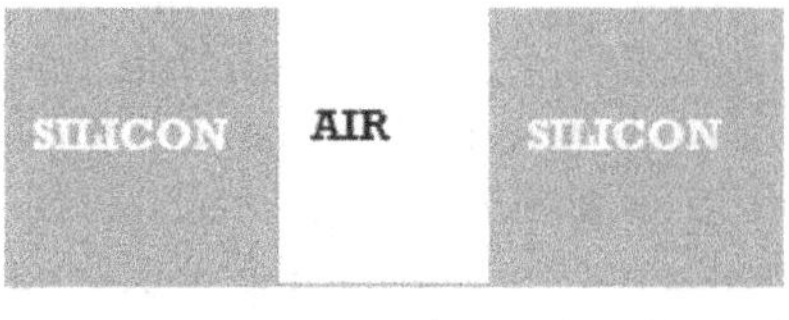

Figure 47.1 Schematic of one-dimensional photonic structure
Source: Author

Table 47.1 Input parameters to investigate the status of the cell (normal/cancer).

Type of cell	Nature of cell	Refractive index
Basal cell	Normal cell	1.368
	Cancer cell	1.392
Breast cell (MDAMD-231)	Normal cell	1.38
	Cancer cell	1.36
Cervical cell (HeLa)	Normal cell	1.399
	Cancer cell	1.385

Source: Author

It includes three columns: Type of cell, nature of cell, and refractive index. The Type of Cell identifies specific cell types analyzed, including basal cells, breast cells (MDAMD-231 line), and cervical cells (HeLa line). The Nature of Cell indicates whether the cells are classified as normal or cancerous, providing two entries for each type. The Refractive Index represents a crucial optical parameter that measures how light bends when passing through a medium. The values demonstrate differences in optical properties; for example, basal cancer cells have a higher refractive index (1.392) compared to normal basal cells (1.368), suggesting alterations in light interaction due to cancer. Similarly, cervical cancer cells exhibit a lower refractive index (1.385) than normal cervical cells (1.399). Overall, the table emphasizes the significance of optical characteristics in differentiating normal from cancerous cells, which is vital for cancer diagnostics and understanding tumor behavior.

Using data from Table 47.1. and simulation is made using finite difference time domain method (FDTD). The outcomes of the result are indicated in the Figure 47.3(a), 47.3(b).

The figures described in the document present simulated outcomes for the electric field distribution of both normal and

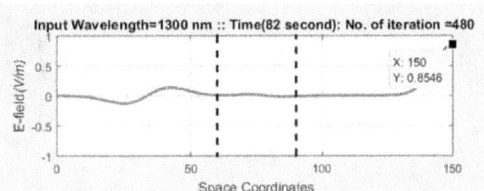

Figure 47.3 (a) Simulated outcomes for electric field distribution corresponding to normal basal cell at signal (wavelength) of 1300 nm
Source: Author

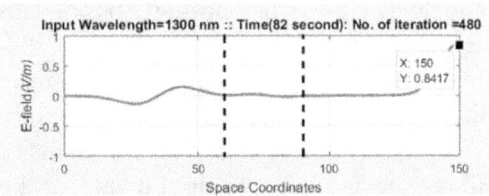

Figure 47.3 (b) Simulated outcomes for electric field distribution corresponding to cancer basal cell at signal (wavelength) of 1300 nm
Source: Author

cancerous cells under exposure to a 1300 nm wavelength signal, focusing on basal, breast (MDAMD-231), and cervical (HeLa) cells. These simulations reveal distinct differences in how normal and cancerous cells interact with electric fields, offering insight into the structural changes that accompany

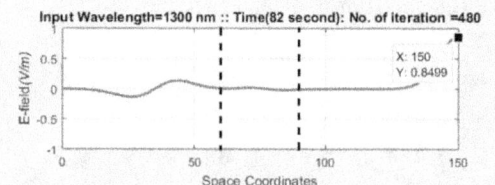

Figure 47.4 (a) Simulated outcomes for electric field distribution corresponding to normal breast cell (MDAMD-231) at signal (wavelength) of 1300 nm
Source: Author

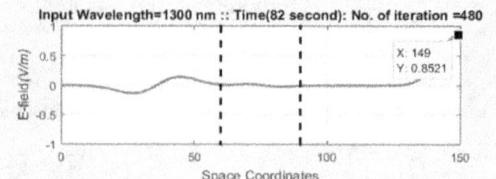

Figure 47.5 (a) Simulated outcomes for electric field distribution corresponding to normal cervical cell (HeLa) at signal (wavelength) of 1300 nm
Source: Author

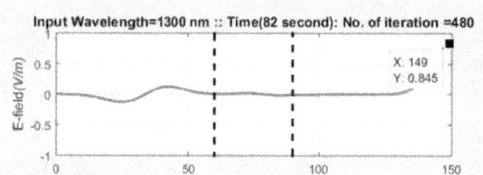

Figure 47.4 (b) Simulated outcomes for electric field distribution corresponding to cancer breast cell (MDAMD-231) at signal (wavelength) of 1300 nm
Source: Author

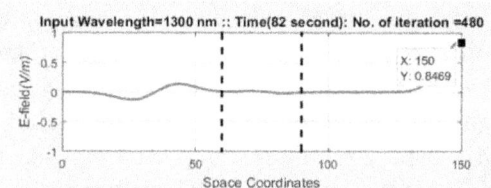

Figure 47.5 (b) Simulated outcomes for electric field distribution corresponding to cancer cervical cell (HeLa) at signal (wavelength) of 1300 nm
Source: Author

malignancy. For the normal basal cell (Figure 47.3(a)), the electric field is distributed more symmetrically, reflecting the uniform internal composition and structure of healthy cells. The electric field intensity ($|E|$) is expected to vary smoothly across the cell, with moderate peaks near the cell membrane or nucleus due to natural dielectric contrasts. However, in the cancerous basal cell (Figure 47.3(b)), the electric field distribution becomes more chaotic and irregular due to the structural abnormalities associated with cancer, such as larger nuclei and disrupted membranes. These irregularities lead to uneven electric field intensities, with localized hotspots where the field is more concentrated. A similar trend is observed in the breast cells (MDAMD-231) shown in Figure 47.4a and 47.4b. In the normal breast cell, the electric field remains relatively

uniform, indicating a well-organized cellular structure. The refractive index, which plays a key role in determining how the electric field propagates through the cell, would likely remain homogeneous in the normal cell, causing gradual transitions in the electric field intensity. In contrast, the cancerous breast cell exhibits more significant variations in both the electric field intensity and its spatial distribution due to the irregular shape and internal structure typical of cancer cells. As cancerous cells tend to be larger and more misshapen, this can lead to higher refractive index values in certain regions, contributing to stronger scattering and a more disrupted electric field pattern. The electric field distribution for cervical cells (HeLa), as depicted in Figure 47.5a and 47.5b, follows the same pattern. In the normal cervical cell, the electric field is expected to be smoothly distributed, with only slight variations in intensity that correspond to different cellular components such as the cytoplasm and the nucleus. The refractive index differences within the normal cell are minimal, allowing for a more orderly interaction between the cell and the electric field. However, in the cancerous HeLa cell, the electric field becomes highly irregular, with regions of high intensity corresponding to the larger, denser components of the cell, such as the nucleus, which is often abnormally shaped in cancer cells. The refractive index variations in cancerous cells are more pronounced, causing more significant disruptions in the electric field distribution. The wavelength of 1300 nm plays a crucial role in all these figures, as it affects the depth of light penetration and the resolution of the electric field interactions. At this near-infrared wavelength, the electric field interacts differently with biological tissues compared to visible light, allowing for deeper penetration and making it particularly useful for distinguishing between normal and cancerous cells. In normal cells, the electric field intensity is relatively low and transitions smoothly across the cell, but in cancerous cells, the irregular structure leads to stronger local enhancements of the electric field, particularly around the nucleus or other dense regions. Field enhancement factors, which describe how much the electric field is amplified in certain areas, tend to be much higher in cancerous cells, indicating that these cells disturb the natural electric field patterns more than their normal counterparts. The size and morphology of the cells also play a critical role in shaping the electric field distribution. Cancerous cells are often larger or have more irregular shapes than normal cells, leading to more localized electric field intensities. For example, an enlarged nucleus in a cancerous cell might concentrate the electric field more

intensely in that region, resulting in higher peak intensity values than those seen in normal cells. In terms of spatial distribution, the electric field in normal cells is likely to follow a more predictable, symmetrical pattern, while in cancerous cells; the distribution may become highly variable, with sharp gradients in intensity over short distances. The refractive index differences between normal and cancerous cells are another key factor, with cancerous cells exhibiting higher refractive indices in certain regions due to their altered internal composition. These higher refractive indices contribute to stronger interactions between the cells and the electric field, further amplifying the differences in electric field intensity and distribution between normal and cancerous cells. In summary, the figures highlight the significant changes in electric field distribution that occur as cells transition from a normal to a cancerous state, with cancerous cells showing more chaotic, irregular patterns of electric field intensity and distribution due to their structural abnormalities and higher refractive indices, all of which are important for understanding how light and electric fields can be used to differentiate between healthy and malignant cells in biomedical research.

After calculating the electric field, we move to compute the power indicated at the output end. The final outcomes are indicated in Table 47.2.

Table 47.2. compares the electric field intensity and power at the output end for normal and cancerous basal, breast (MDAMD-231), and cervical (HeLa) cells when exposed to a signal with a wavelength of 1300 nm. For all three cell types, normal cells exhibit higher electric field intensity and power compared to their cancerous counterparts. In normal basal cells, the electric field intensity is 0.8546 V/m with an output power of 262.74 mW, while cancerous

Table 47.2 Output result of electric field intensity and power.

		Electric field at output end (V/m)	Power at output end (mW)
Basal cell	Normal cell	0.8546	262.74
	Cancer cell	0.8417	254.87
Breast cell (MDAMD-231)	Normal cell	0.8499	259.86
	Cancer cell	0.8455	257.18
Cervical cell (HeLa)	Normal cell	0.8521	261.21
	Cancer cell	0.8469	258.03

Source: Author

basal cells show a slight reduction to 0.8417 V/m and 254.87 mW. Similarly, normal breast cells show an electric field intensity of 0.8499 V/m and 259.86 mW of power, whereas cancerous breast cells exhibit slightly lower values at 0.8455 V/m and 257.18 mW. The same pattern is observed in cervical cells, with normal cells having an intensity of 0.8521 V/m and power of 261.21 mW, while cancerous cervical cells show 0.8469 V/m and 258.03 mW. These small reductions in electric field intensity and power in cancerous cells across all cell types suggest that cancerous cells, due to their irregular structure and higher density, absorb or scatter more of the electric field than normal cells, leading to lower transmission of electric field energy. These differences in electric field behavior could be useful for distinguishing between normal and cancerous cells in diagnostic applications.

Conclusion

This research focuses on designing silicon-based photonic devices to detect cancer cells by analyzing changes in electric field distribution as light interacts with the cells. Both normal and cancerous cells produce distinct electric field patterns, with cancerous cells disrupting the field in irregular and chaotic ways due to their structural abnormalities. Finite-difference time-domain (FDTD) simulations emphasize these variations. In addition, output power measurements offer crucial insights for differentiating between healthy and cancerous cells. For instance, normal basal cells exhibit an output power of 262.74 mW and an electric field intensity of 0.8546 V/m, while cancerous basal cells show reduced values, with 254.87 mW of power and an electric field intensity of 0.8417 V/m. Similar decreases in power and field intensity are noted in breast and cervical cancer cells. By incorporating machine learning algorithms, the diagnostic precision of the system can be enhanced, improving clinical decision-making. Due to their scalability and cost-efficiency, silicon photonic structures present a highly promising solution for clinical use, facilitating quicker and more personalized cancer diagnostics. This research ultimately seeks to offer a rapid, non-invasive cancer detection method, with the potential to transform cancer diagnostics.

References

[1] Bai, J., Yang, M., Wang, Y., & Wang, S. (2020). Fluorescence-based silicon photonic biosensors for cancer diagnostics. *Journal of Biomedical Optics*, 25(8), 1–10. https://doi.org/10.1117/1.JBO.25.8.081003.

[2] Choi, H., Kwon, Y., & Kim, S. (2023). Integration of microfluidics with silicon photonic sensors for rapid cancer diagnostics. *Lab on a Chip*, 23(2), 185–198. https://doi.org/10.1039/D2LC00987G.

[3] Huang, Y., Zhang, X., & Liu, S. (2015). A silicon photonic biosensor for cancer biomarker detection. *Optics Letters*, 40(17), 4024–4027. https://doi.org/10.1364/OL.40.004024.

[4] Khan, A., Dutta, D., & Yadav, R. (2022). Machine learning algorithms for improving silicon photonic biosensor performance in cancer diagnostics. *IEEE Transactions on Biomedical Engineering*, 69(6), 1683–1690. https://doi.org/10.1109/TBME.2021.3072150.

[5] Liu, H., Zhang, H., & Li, Y. (2019). Surface plasmon resonance biosensors for cancer biomarker detection: a review. *Sensors and Actuators B: Chemical*, 285, 40–51. https://doi.org/10.1016/j.snb.2019.02.064.

[6] Wang, C., Chen, X., & Wang, Y. (2017). A highly sensitive photonic crystal sensor for prostate-specific antigen detection in blood. *Sensors*, 17(10), 2361. https://doi.org/10.3390/s17102361.

[7] Zhang, Y., Zhang, Y., & Qiu, W. (2021). Silicon waveguide-based biosensor for circulating tumor cell detection using antibody functionalization. *Analytical Chemistry*, 93(19), 6975–6981. https://doi.org/10.1021/acs.analchem.1c02227.

[8] Zhang, Y., Chen, Y., & Jiang, C. (2022). Silicon nanowire biosensors for cancer detection: a review. *Nanoscale Advances*, 4(1), 157–176. https://doi.org/10.1039/D1NA00656H.

[9] Hwang, S., Kim, S., & Yang, J. (2020). Application of nanophotonic devices in cancer diagnostics: current status and future perspectives. *Nanotechnology Reviews*, 9(1), 1147–1161. https://doi.org/10.1515/ntrev-2020-0173.

[10] Li, S., Huang, W., & Wu, Y. (2023). Advances in silicon photonic biosensors for early cancer detection: a comprehensive review. *Biosensors and Bioelectronics*, 234, 115246. https://doi.org/10.1016/j.bios.2023.115246.

[11] Rupali, Sahu, S. K., Palai, G., Kumar, B. A., & Mishra, B. K. (2020). Modeling of photonic crystal-based ring resonator sensor for cancer detection using infrared laser. Journal of Optics, 1–7. DOI:https://doi.org/10.1088/2040-8986/abc123.

[12] Amiri, I. S., Yupapin, P., Palai, G., & Tripathy, S. K. (2019). A proposal to identify live cancer cells by naked eye: realization of biomedical application using 1D photonic structure. *Optik*, 183, 818–821. https://doi.org/10.1016/j.ijleo.2019.05.060.

[13] Sivakumar, S., Nayak, S. R., Vidyanandini, S., Kumar, J. A., & Palai, G. (2018). An empirical study of supervised learning methods for breast cancer diseases. *Optik*, 175, 105–114. https://doi.org/10.1016/j.ijleo.2018.04.054.

[14] Sahu, S. K., & Palai, G. (2023). An elliptical plus shape microstrip patch antenna integrated with CSRR for breast cancer detection. In Intelligent Circuits and Systems for SDG 3–Good Health and Well-being, (pp. 462–467).

[15] Palai, G., Mudului, N., Sahoo, S., & Tripathy, S. (2013). Realization of potassium chloride sensor using photonic crystal fiber. *Soft Nanoscience Letters*, 3, 16–19. doi: 10.4236/snl.2013.34A005.

[16] Palai, G., Tripathy, S. K., Muduli, N., Patnaik, D., Patnaik, S. K., Bose, S. M., & Tripathy, S. K. (2012, July). A novel method to measure the strength of CygelTM by using two dimensional photonic crystal struct ures. In AIP Conference Proceedings-American Institute of Physics (Vol. 1461, No. 1, p. 383).

[17] Palai, G. (2014). Realization of temperature in semiconductor using optical principle. *Optik*, 125(20), 6053–6057.

[18] Palai, G. (2014). Measurement of impurity concentration in chalcogenide glasses using optical principle. *Optik*, 125(19), 5794–5799.

48 Enhancing photovoltaic performance of FTO/ZnO/CuO solar cells by replacing silver with MWCNT as a cost-effective charge collector electrode

A. G. Sneha Aishwarya[1,a], S. K. Ahamad Abdul Khadar[1,b], Md. Malik Sharief[1,c], D. Seshu Kumar[1,d], Priyadarshini Raiguru[2,e] and Jagatpati Raiguru[1,f]

[1]Department of Electronics and Communication Engineering, Aditya University, Surampalem, Andhra Pradesh, India

[2]Department of Electronics and Communication Engineering, Siksha 'O' Anusandhan University, Bhubaneswar, Odisha, India

Abstract

Solar cell technologies have been proliferating in cheaper and greener directions in recent years. One specific area of interest is the substitution of metal-type electrodes for carbon-based electrodes. Here the modified photovoltaic device structure using FTO/ZnO/CuO/MWCNT is studied and compared with the traditional structure FTO/ZnO/CuO/Ag. Because of its outstanding conductivity silver (Ag) is mostly employed as top electrode material although it comes with several drawbacks such as high material cost and stability issues in the long term. In contrast, multi-walled carbon nanotubes, efficiently produced, flexible, chemically stable, have great potential advantages. Characterization of the pyrolysis-produced MWCNTs was performed by means of X-ray diffraction, Raman spectroscopy, and UV-Vis absorption.

Keywords: Carbon electrode, CuO, FTO, MWCNT, photovoltaic efficiency, silver replacement, ZnO

Introduction

The shift to more economical and environmentally friendly energy sources has sparked a resurgence of interest in photovoltaic systems that don't use silicon. Owing to their easy fabrication, broad material availability, and eco-friendliness, oxide semiconductor Heterojunctions—especially those that combine zinc oxide (ZnO) and copper oxide (CuO)— have drawn a lot of attention among the numerous alternatives [1]. While

CuO functions as an effective light absorber that can produce a high density of charge carriers under solar illumination, ZnO, with its wide bandgap (~3.2 eV), performs well as an electron transport material [2–4]. Choosing the right top electrode is just as crucial to performance as the device's architecture. Although it mainly depends on device architecture, the selection of the top electrode is very important. In general, due to their good conductivity silver and gold are the chosen metals, though the high costs

[a]21A91A0413@aec.edu.in, [b]21A91A0449@aec.edu.in, [c]21A91A0433@aec.edu.in, [d]21A91A0408@aec.edu.in, [e]priyadarshiniraiguru@soa.ac.in, [f]raiguruj@adityauniversity.in

DOI: 10.1201/9781003753391-48

and the tendency to diffuse and oxidize can reduce their reliability. Thus, research has begun to explore carbon-based alternatives, as multi-walled carbon nanotubes (MWCNTs), having the ability to perform as conductive materials, and exhibiting high strength, flexibility and environmental stability [5, 6].

Here, the use of MWCNTs as the top electrode of a FTO/ZnO/CuO heterojunction solar cell has been analyzed. The purpose is to establish whether such replacement maintains or enhances device performance, while at the same time reducing material expenditure. The structural, optical, and electrical characterizations were made in order to understand the performance of MWCNT.

Experimental Methodology

Preparation of ZnO thin films
Early Sol-gel synthesized zinc oxide (ZnO) has been prepared and then spin-coated for the production of the electron transport layer of the solar cell structure. Its precursor zinc acetate dihydrate -($Zn(CH_3COO)_2 \cdot 2H_2O$) in 2-methoxyethanol and stabilized with. Mono-ethanolamine (MEA). The solution was stirred magnetically at room temperature for two hours, to ensure a clear and even consistency. A 0.45 µm syringe filter for use on samples collected and prepared in filtration systems. It was employed in order to decant any solids that remained in solution following the aging time. Fluorine-doped tin oxide (FTO) substrates are leaned. The filter sol was then deposited on the substrates via a combination of spin-coating at 3000 rpm of 30s. The soft-baking of each layer was performed at 150°C to eliminate later any un-reacted solvents. This process was repeated several times in order to achieve the desired film thickness. In order to enhance film crystalline and adhesion,

after last layer application the deposited substrates were annealed in a muffle furnace at 450°C for one hour.

Formation of CuO absorber layer
Copper oxide (CuO) thin film formation was used to create the p-type absorber layer. The copper acetate monohydrate ($Cu(CH_3COO)_2 \cdot H_2O$) was dissolved in a solution of ethanol and deionized water to create a precursor solution. For two hours, the solution was constantly swirled at 60°C to guarantee total dissolution. Following the filtering process, the solution was applied to the ZnO layer that had already been coated using a spin coater set to 2500 rpm for 40 seconds. Prior to applying the subsequent layer, each layer was dried at 120°C. After the films had the required number of layers, they were annealed outdoors for an hour at 500°C, which produced a well- crystallized CuO film.

Synthesis of MWCNTs by pyrolysis
The thermal chemical vapor deposition (CVD) method was used in the lab to create multi- walled carbon nanotubes (MWCNTs). Toluene and ferrocene were combined in a liquid precursor mixture, with ferrocene acting as the iron-based catalyst. This mixture was added to a quartz tube reactor that had been heated to 850°C. To keep the environment inert and encourage the controlled growth of the nanotubes, the process was conducted under a constant flow of hydrogen and argon gases. Toluene broke down during the reaction, and carbon atoms were deposited around the catalytic particles to create MWCNTs. Following their collection, the carbon nanotubes underwent acid treatment in order to eliminate any remaining metal catalysts. To get them ready for electrode fabrication, the purified MWCNTs were subsequently rinsed, dried, and redispersed in ethanol.

Device Fabrication Process

Substrate cleaning and preparation

Fluorine-doped tin oxide (FTO) coated glass substrates were cleaned thoroughly to remove surface contaminants and improve film adhesion prior to thin film deposition. Acetone, ethanol, and deionized water were used in consecutive cleaning steps, each of which was completed for 15 minutes in an ultrasonic bath. After that, a nitrogen gas stream was used to dry the substrates after they had been rinsed with deionized water. The substrates received a 10-minute UV-ozone treatment to increase surface energy and guarantee consistent film formation.

Deposition of the ZnO electron transport layer

The ZnO precursor solution was spin-coated onto the FTO substrates that had been pretreated for 30 seconds at 3000 rpm, as explained in Section 2.1. To get rid of extra solvent, the film was preheated to 150°C after every coating. Until the required thickness was attained, this coating and drying procedure was repeated. In order to facilitate the development of a compact and crystalline ZnO layer—which functions as the device's electron transport layer (ETL)—the samples were subsequently annealed at 350°C for an hour in air.

Formation of CuO absorber layer

CuO absorber was applied using the solution from Section 2.2 after the ZnO layer. Spin coating was applied to the copper acetate solution for 40 seconds at 2500 rpm. Before adding the subsequent layer, the coated substrates were dried at 120°C following each application. The samples were thermally treated for an hour at 450°C in an oxygen-rich environment after the multilayer structure was finished. This procedure made sure that the precursor was completely transformed into a high-purity CuO layer that was uniformly adherent.

Annealing and layer optimization

After the ZnO and CuO layers were deposited, an additional annealing step was carried out to improve film crystallinity and interfacial contact between layers. For 30 minutes, the entire stack was heated to 500°C. Grain boundaries are lessened, interfacial defects are reduced, and the overall electronic quality of the thin films is enhanced by this post-deposition annealing.

Integration of top electrodes

For comparison, the top contact was constructed using two distinct electrode materials. Silver electrode: A highly conductive top electrode was created for the reference device by thermally evaporating a thin layer of silver. MWCNT Electrode-the CuO surface was drop-cast with a suspension of multi-walled carbon nanotubes in ethanol in the test apparatus. To improve adherence and create a continuous conductive film, the device was heated to 200°C for ten minutes after application.

Final device architecture and testing setup

The final configurations of the devices were - FTO/ZnO/CuO/Ag & ZnO/CuO/FTO/MWCNT. An AM 1.5G illumination source with an intensity of 100 mW/cm² was used to simulate solar light for electrical measurements. Both devices' current-voltage (J-V) curves were captured, and important performance metrics like power conversion efficiency (PCE), fill factor (FF), open- circuit voltage (V_{oc}), and short-circuit current density (J_{sc}) were taken out.

Results and Discussion

Material characterization

Standard analytical techniques were used to analyze structural, optical and morphological properties of ZnO, CuO and MWCNTs films.

The X-ray diffraction pattern of the ZnO thin films exhibited peaks corresponding to the planes (100), (002) and (101) as shown in the Figure 48.1. These results confirm the growing of highly crystalline hexagonal wurtzite structure of ZnO. Similarly to this, CuO layers showed evident reflections at (110) and (111), which are characteristic of the monoclinic phase as shown in Figure 48.2. All films deposited in this work proved to be pure, since there was neither intrusion of mixed oxides nor of any other secondary phase. The XRD measurements for the MWCNTs synthesized by pyrolysis have a broad peak around 26.2°, which corresponds to the graphitic (002) plane as shown in Figure 48.3.

The presence of a strong high E2 mode at approximately 338 cm⁻1 and 285 cm⁻1 in the ZnO Raman spectrum indicates clearly the wurtzite structure as shown in Figure 48.4. The MWCNTs exhibited two prominent peaks at around 1587 cm⁻¹, and 1343

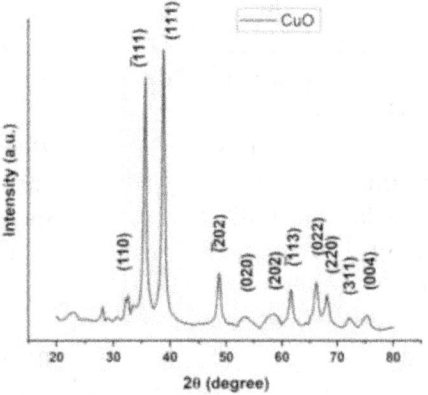

Figure 48.2 X-ray diffraction pattern of CuO

Source: Author

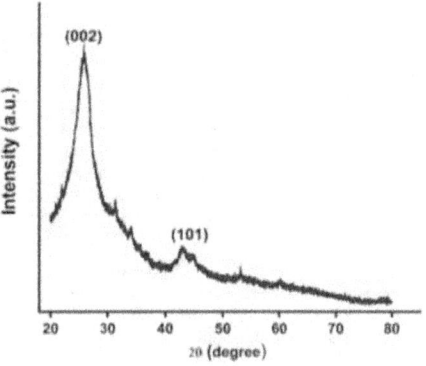

Figure 48.3 X-ray diffraction pattern of MWCNT

Source: Author

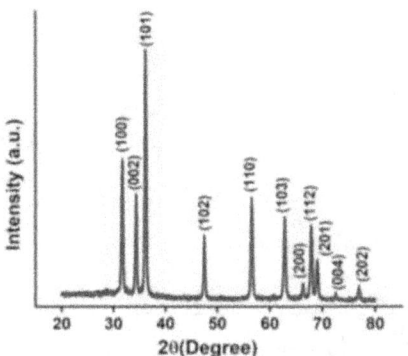

Figure 48.1 X-ray diffraction pattern of ZnO

Source: Author

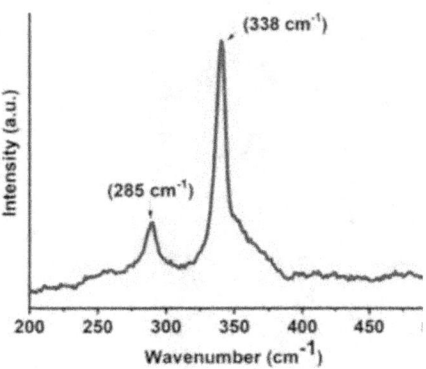

Figure 48.4 Raman spectra of ZnO

Source: Author

cm^{-1} that corresponds to the graphitic nature of the nanotubes (G-band) and (D-band) which is related to structural defects or disorder; as shown in Figure 48.5.

TEM images as shown in Figure 48.6 also confirmed the uniformity of MWCNT with a tubular and hollow structure. Such morphological features are useful when employed as electrode layers in order to obtain a percolating conductive network. The high aspect ratio of the tubes also allows for improved electrical pathways within the device.

According to optical absorption measurements of ZnO, which had high absorbance in the ultraviolet region shown in Figure 48.7. Tauc plot analysis revealed the direct bandgap to be ~3.3 eV shown in Figure 48.8. The wide bandgap of ZnO promotes good electron transport, which reduces the recombination of charge carriers and increases device performance.

Photovoltaic performance

The electrical behavior of the fabricated solar cells was investigated under standard AM 1.5G 100 mW/cm^2 illumination by J-V measurements shown in Figure 48.9. Two

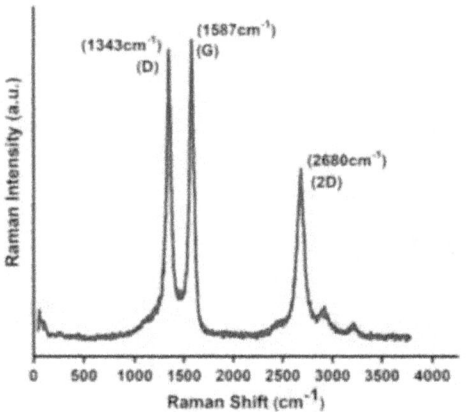

Figure 48.5 Raman spectra of MWCNT
Source: Author

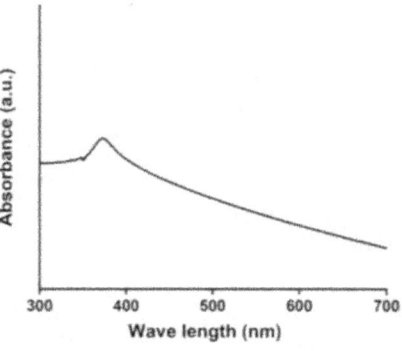

Figure 48.7 Absorption spectrum of the ZnO
Source: Author

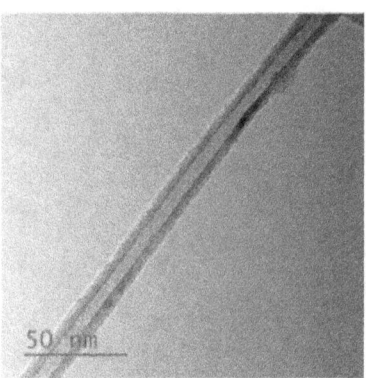

Figure 48.6 Transmission electron microscope image of MWCNT
Source: Author

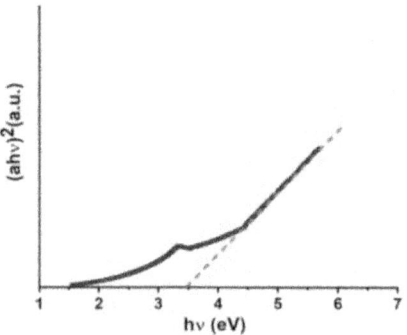

Figure 48.8 Optical energy -band gap of ZnO
Source: Author

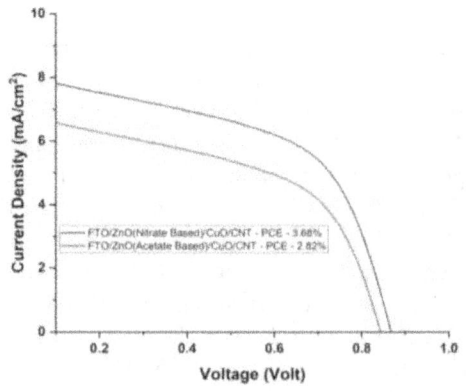

Figure 48.9 J-V measurements of FTO/ZnO/CuO Solar Cells with MWCNT contact (PCE 3.68%) and Ag top contact with (PCE 2.85%)

Source: Author

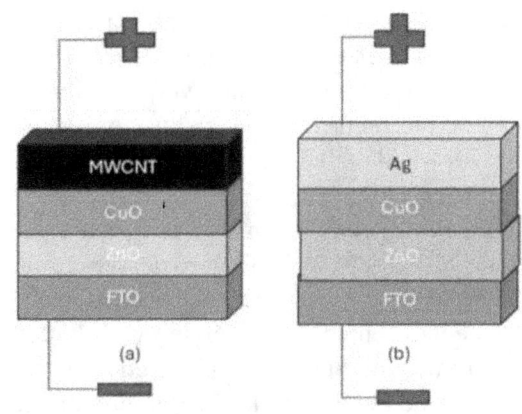

Figure 48.10 (a) FTO/ZnO/CuO/MWCNT & (b) FTO/ZnO/CuO/Ag

Source: Author

Table 48.1 Photovoltaic parameters for FTO/ZnO/CuO/Ag and FTO/ZnO/CuO/MWCNT.

Device structure	Voc (V)	Jsc (mA/cm²)	Fill factor (FF)	Efficiency (PCE %)
FTO/ZnO/CuO/Ag	0.54	7.2	0.52	2.85
FTO/ZnO/CuO/MWCNT	0.62	8.1	0.55	3.68

Source: Author

types of devices were analyzed, one with MWCNTs and the other with a conventional Ag top contact as shown in Figure 48.10(a) & (b). Table 48.1 presents the photovoltaic parameters of both devices, indicating that the MWCNT-based solar cell exhibits improved performance metrics relative to the Ag-based device.

Raman spectra of ZnO

The MWCNT-based cell outperformed as compared to Ag-based cell. The improvements in open-circuit voltage and short-circuit current density are due to better charge transport and less recombination at the CuO interface. In addition, MWCNTs provided better electrical contact, also silver wire contacts are typically subject to problems such as corrosion or metal diffusion which decrease contact life.

These results show that MWCNTs lead to better performance and stability of the next generation solar cell technologies, and hence, can be a viable replacement for metal electrodes.

Conclusion

In this work FTO/ZnO/CuO heterojunction solar cells as the base structures with two different top electrodes, silver and multi-walled carbon nanotubes (MWCNTs) electrodes are studied. Although silver is widely used due to its excellent conductivity, it is also expensive. The MWCNTs were produced by a pyrolyzing process and then included into the device as a top electrode by drop-casting. The choice of ZnO as an electron transport layer, CuO as the active absorber, and MWCNTs as a conductive replacement for silver was supported by detailed structural and optical characterizations.

The power conversion efficiency achieved was 3.68% for MWCNT based device, compared to 2.85% for the Ag-based device. This enhancement is associated with better electronic conductance, enhanced interfacial interaction, and lack of degrading metal diffusion.

In summary, these results suggest that MWCNTs could replace silver electrodes in thin-film photovoltaic devices. An avenue to accomplish this is through carbon-based contacts and may eventually lead to a cheaper, more reliable and eco-friendly approach to harvesting solar energy.

Acknowledgments

The authors would like to thank the National Institute of Technology, Rourkela for providing laboratory access and technical assistance during this study.

References

[1]   Elgorban, A. M., Sivaganesh, D., & Arunpandian, M. (2023). Visible light-embedded CuO/ZnO twofold execution for photocatalysis and photoluminescence. *Journal of Electroceramics*, 51(1), 12–27.

[2]   Bashir, M. B. A., Rajpar, A. H., Salih, E. Y., & Ahmed, E. M. (2023). Preparation and photovoltaic evaluation of CuO@Zn(Al) O-mixed metal oxides for dye sensitized solar cell. *Nanomaterials*, 13(5), 802.

[3]   Benaissa, N., & Garmim, T. (2023). Experimental and numerical simulation studies of CuO thin films based solar cells. *Journal of Physics: Energy*, 5(4), 045003.

[4]   Sekkat, A., Weber, M., & López-Sánchez, J. (2024). Enhancement of p-CuO/n-ZnO heterojunction photovoltaic characteristics by preparation route and Sn doping. *Journal of Electronic Materials*, 53(1), 1–12.

[5]   El-Maghraby, A., & El-Shazly, A. (2024). High performances multi-function of FTO/ZnO/CuO/Al heterojunction device: gas sensor and solar cell. *Journal of Optics*, 53(2), 123–134.

[6]   Kobeleva, E. S., Uvarov, M. N., Kravets, N. V., Kulikova, A. V., Zinovyev, V. A., Gurova, O. A., Sysoev, V. I., Kondranova, A. M., Kazantsev, M. S., Degtyarenko, K. M., Matveeva, A. G., & Kulik, L. V. (2024). Ternary composite of polymer, fullerene and fluorinated multi-walled carbon nanotubes as the active layer of organic solar cells. *Journal of Composite Science*, 8(1), 3.

49 Low-cost, metal-free FTO/CZTS/Perovskite/ZnO/MWCNT solar cell with 5.20% efficiency using pyrolytically synthesized carbon nanotube electrodes

Mamidanna Jaya Surya Karthik[a], Jala Praveen[b],
Kollipaka Surya Prakash[c], Eeli Aashritha Sri Sowmya[d],
Gumpula Satya Sai Ram[e] and Jagatpati Raiguru[f]

Department of Electronics and Communication Engineering, Aditya University, Surampalem, Andhra Pradesh, India

Abstract

The work unveils a simple and inexpensive metal-free hybrid solar cell structure having FTO/CZTS/Perovskite/ZnO/MWCNT. Their best device exhibited a PCE of 5.20%. Sol-gel spin coating was used to apply the CZTS absorbers layer to FTO glass. To enhance light absorption, a thin film of methylammonium lead halide (MAPbX3) perovskite was deposited on top of the CZTS. They used zinc oxide (ZnO) as the electron transport layer allowing the extraction of the carriers with high efficiency. The top electrode, in place of traditional metallic contacts, was a network of multi- walled carbon nanotubes (MWCNTs) synthesized via pyrolysis, which eliminated the use of expensive vacuum-based processes. Crucially, all processing was performed at low temperatures using solution-based processing techniques only, such that the production of photovoltaic devices could be greener and more scalable.

Keywords: Copper zinc tin sulfide, metal-free electrodes, multiwalled carbon nanotubes, perovskite solar cells, photovoltaics, zinc oxide

Introduction

Increasing global energy demand has led to an increased search for efficient and sustainable photovoltaic (PV) technologies. Among the new technologies proposed to improve efficiencies at low production costs, solid-state materials such as hybrid solar cells have shown great promise [1]. Among these compounds, copper zinc tin sulfide (CZTS) has been established as a promising absorber material because it is abundant, environmentally safe, and possesses good optical properties [2]. Ranging from 1.4 to 1.5 eV, the tunable direct bandgap of CZTS makes it an excellent contender for applications using thin-film solar cells. It also has a high absorption coefficient ($\sim 10^4$ cm^{-1}). However, performance remains limited, often due to defects in grain boundaries and incomplete extraction of carriers [2]. One of the strategies to overcome the latter problem is the use of secondary absorbers, such as organic-inorganic

[a]21A91A0427@aec.edu.in, [b]21A91A0419@aec.edu.in, [c]21A91A0425@aec.edu.in, [d]21A91A0410@aec.edu.in, [e]21A91A0416@aec.edu.in, [f]raiguruj@adityauniversity.in

DOI: 10.1201/9781003753391-49

perovskites—particularly methylammonium lead iodide (MAPbI$_3$)—in the design of hybrid materials. Perovskites possess all the favorable light-absorption properties, long carrier diffusion lengths, and tunable bandgaps that CZTS lacks, thus acting as an ideal complementary material to maximize device efficiencies [3, 4]. Zinc oxide (ZnO) is a popular choice for electron transport layers because of its high electron mobility, good band alignment, and ease of processing [5, 6]. Meanwhile, the search for alternative materials that could replace expensive and stability-compromising metal electrodes is ongoing.

In this work, multi-walled carbon nanotubes (MWCNTs) are employed as a metal-free and sustainable top electrode. In particular, MWCNTs have proven to be a potential alternative since they present excellent electrical conductivity, good flexibility in terms of mechanical performance, and chemical resistance [7]. We seek to merge these material systems toward an entirely solution-processible and scalable solar cell structure using CZTS, perovskite, ZnO, and MWCNT.

Experimental Methodology

CZTS absorber layer fabrication

The CZTS layer was deposited using sol-gel spin coating. The FTO substrates were first cleaned. They experienced immersion in acetone, acetone/ethanol, and DI water sequences, bath sonication, and nitrogen drying. Zinc acetate, tin (IV) chloride, and copper (II) chloride were dissolved in 2-methoxyethanol during the synthesis of the precursor solution. In order to keep the prepared solution stable monoethanolamine was included, and thiourea was the source for sulfur. After that, the FTO substrates were spin-coated with this supplied solution for 30 seconds at a speed of 3000 revolutions per minute. Each of the layers deposited was preheated at 120°C in a sulfur rich ambiance and final annealed at 500°C for crystallization of the kesterite CZTS phase.

Perovskite layer deposition

A twostep sequential process was used to create a Methylammonium lead iodide perovskite (MAPbI$_3$) layer. The first one, consisted in spin-coating a PbI$_2$ solution onto the CZTS films was also pre-heated at 70°C. The substrates were finally into a methylammonium iodide (MAI) solution in isopropanol – the MA preparation – where perovskite conversion occurred. Finally, a post-annealing at 100C for 10 min was also performed for complete crystallization.

ZnO electron transport layer formation

The ETL ZnO film was processed from zinc acetate solution in 2-methoxyethanol, where the complexation process was assisted by monoethanolamine. This solution was later spin-coated over the perovskite layer with a speed of 3500 rpm. to de-solvents, followed by an annealing process to 300°C for 1hr in order to obtain a crystalline ZnO film for electron transport.

MWCNT top electrode fabrication

To obtain multi-walled carbon nanotubes, MWCNTs, ferrocene was pyrolyzed into a quartz tube furnace in a pyrogenic inert atmosphere. After being synthesized, the MWCNT's were purified using an acid treatment to remove the unnecessary material and obtained in an ethanol dispersed solution. This MWCNTs suspension was later used for the drop-casting of the top electrode consisting of an interconnected conductive network using ZnO as a layer onto the ZnO layer in replacement of metal electrodes.

Results and Discussion

Optical and structural characteristics

X-Ray diffraction tests were performed in order to know the formation of the films and see its crystallinity. These tests in particular were useful to be able go deeper in the exploration of the films' structural features. TEM (Transmission electron microscopy) is also used to analyze the topography and microstructural properties of the films. UV-Visible spectra measurement was performed to determine the band gap values of the CZTS, perovskite, and ZnO films. Also, the photovoltaic yield was also measured to assess how efficiently the devices transform sunlight into electricity. This was measured under a AM1.5 global (AM1.5G) light condition, which is the standard Sun light at 100mW/cm2. The experimental arrangement was an ABET oriel class AAA solar simulator and a Keithley 2400 source meter. This tool assisted in the taking of J-V (current density-voltage) curves. These values were then used to calculate PCE, Jsc (short circuit current density), Voc (open circuit voltage) and FF (Fill factor) to have an overview of the efficiency and performance of the devices. The crystal structure of the CZTS absorber layer was studied in detail through X-ray diffraction (XRD). The diffraction peaks appeared at 2θ around 28.5°, 47.4° and 56.2°, and the measurements were indexed as the (112), (220) and (312) planes, respectively. Thus, confirming also of the kesterite-structured Cu_2ZnSnS_4 phase, as per JCPDS No. 26-0575. The lack of secondary phases such as Cu_2S, ZnS, or SnS_2 revealing high phase purity, and shown in Figure 49.1. For ZnO films, distinct diffraction peaks located around 2θ values of 31.8°, 34.4°, and 36.3° could be assigned to the (100), (002), and (101) planes of the wurtzite structure of hexagonal ZnO, respectively, as seen in Figure 49.2.

This results in higher quality ZnO layers confirming their capability to be an electron transport layer (ETL).

X-ray diffraction pattern examination was performed on the prepared perovskite film of $CH_3NH_3PbI_3$ and demonstrated characteristic peaks at 14.1°, 28.4°, and 31.8° corresponding to the (110), (220), and (310) tetragonal planes that prompts for a highly crystalline quality as shown in Figure 49.3. XRD spectrum of the multi-walled carbon nanotubes (MWCNTs) fabricated is displayed in Figure 49.4 where the diffraction peak at ≈ 2θ = 26.2° indicates the

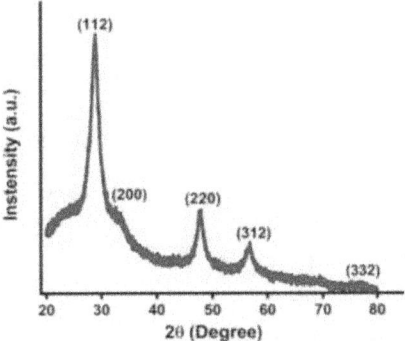

Figure 49.1 X-ray diffraction (XRD). of CZTS/
Source: Author

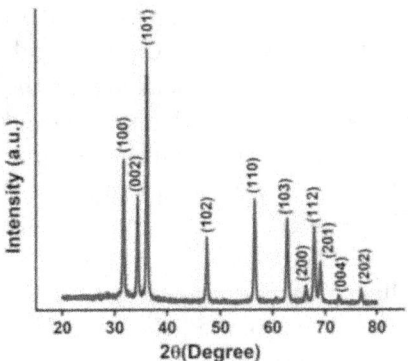

Figure 49.2 X-ray diffraction (XRD) of ZnO
Source: Author

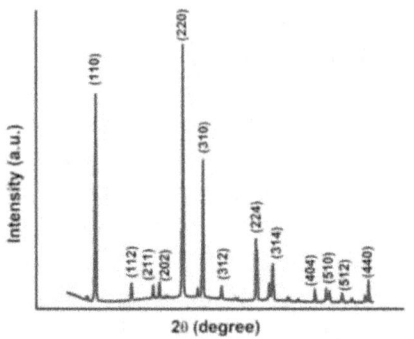

Figure 49.3 X-ray diffraction (XRD). of CH₃NH₃PbI₃
Source: Author

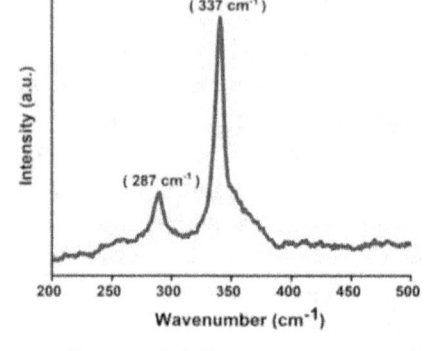

Figure 49.5 Raman spectrum of CZTS
Source: Author

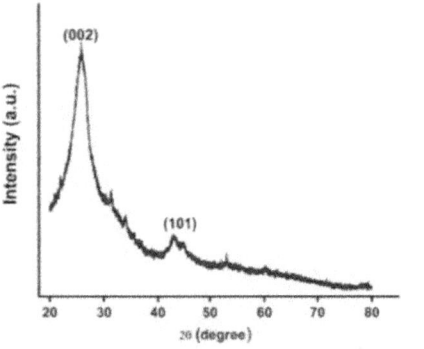

Figure 49.4 X-ray diffraction (XRD). Of MWCNT
Source: Author

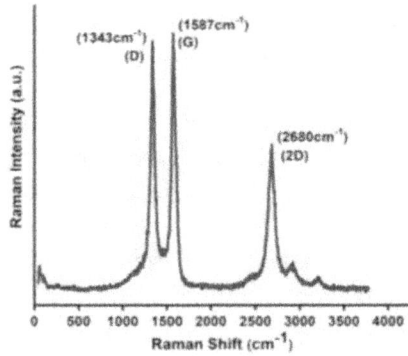

Figure 49.6 Raman spectrum of MWCNT
Source: Author

planes' graphitic carbon (002) is broad and intense, which indicates the development of graphitic layers. Also, a low and broadened peak at $2\theta \approx 43.5°$, associated with the (100) plane, was detected, which evidenced the hexagonal nature of graphite. The large broad peaks can be attributed to the presence of the nanocrystalline domains and high disorder that is generally observed in multi-walled carbon nanotubes grown by pyrolysis. In the case of the CZTS thin film, Raman spectroscopy, as shown in Figure 49.5, showed intense peaks at around 337 cm⁻¹ and 287 cm⁻¹, corresponding to the A₁ vibrational modes of the kesterite

structure, confirming the presence of a pure CZTS phase without observable secondary phases such as Cu_2SnS_3 or ZnS, whereas MWCNTs, as evidenced in Figure 49.6, show the characteristic D and G bands at around 1345 cm⁻¹ and 1585 cm⁻¹, indicating a high degree of graphitization and structural integrity which are suitable for use as conductive electrode layer.

Figure 49.7 TEM images confirm the tubular structure of MWCNTs by showing the concentric cylindrical of uniform diameters layers. This verifies the synthesis of all layers that show good structural and optoelectronic properties that will be beneficial for optimum function in the solar cell. The

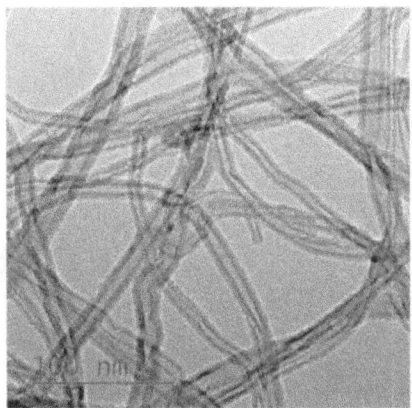

Figure 49.7 TEM images of MWCNT
Source: Author

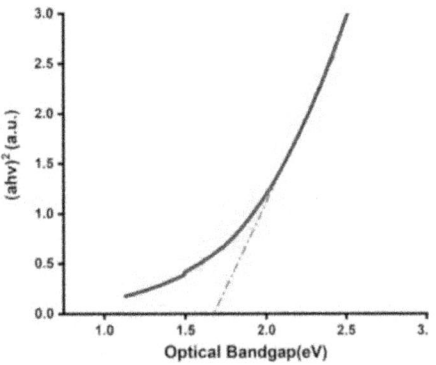

Figure 49.9 Optical energy bandgap of CZTS (1.5eV)
Source: Author

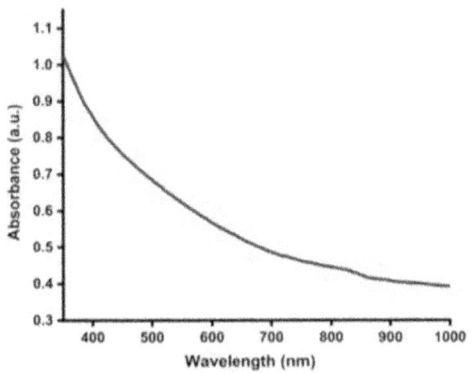

Figure 49.8 UV-Visible absorption spectrum of CZTS
Source: Author

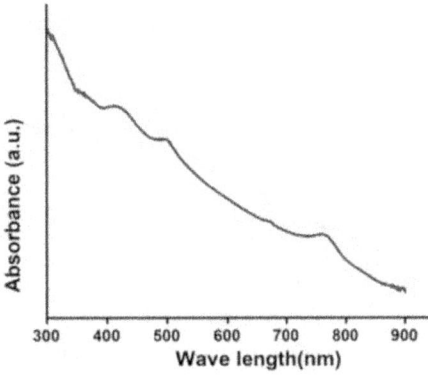

Figure 49.10 Absorption spectrum of perovskite film
Source: Author

optical properties of individual layers were analyzed using UV-Visible absorption spectroscopy. The CZTS layer presented large absorption in the visible range (400-800 nm) with an optical bandgap of approximately the 1.5 eV, which makes this, also a material which presents excellent characteristics for solar applications as it is shown in Figures 49.8 and 49.9. As shown in Figure 49.10 the MAPbI3 perovskite film has step absorption onset at ~770 nm and in Figure 49.11, the absorber optical bandgap is measured as 1.55 eV. This ZnO layer, with absorption

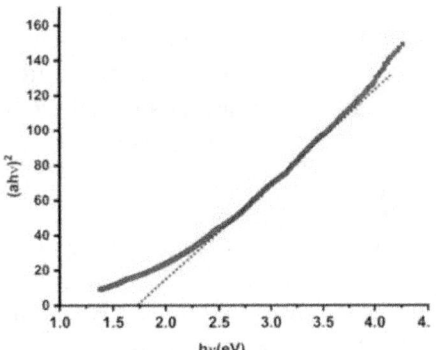

Figure 49.11 Optical energy bandgap3 of CH3NH3PbI (1.55eV)-
Source: Author

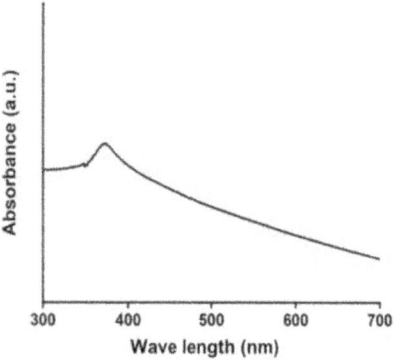

Figure 49.12 Absorption Spectrum of ZnO
Source: Author

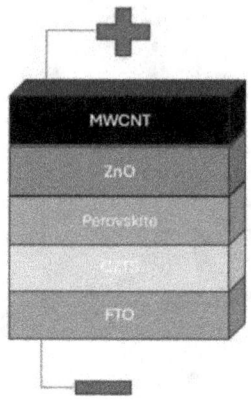

Figure 49.14 FTO/CZTS/Perovskite/ZnO/
MWCNT photovoltaic device architecture
Source: Author

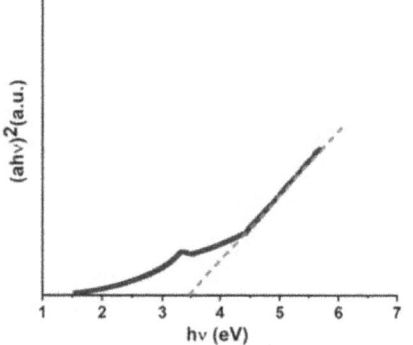

Figure 49.13 Optical energy bandgap of
ZnO (3.2eV)-
Source: Author

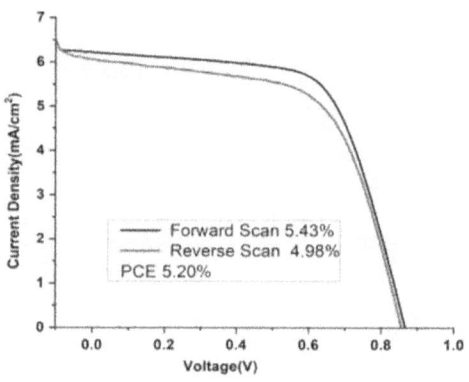

Figure 49.15 J-V characteristics of FTO/
CZTS/MAPbI₃/ZnO/MWCNT solar cell
Source: Author

in the visible range demonstrated in Figure 49.12, with an optical band gap of ~3.3 eV as shown in Figure 49.13, acted as an electron transport layer. These optical properties validate the choice of materials for efficient photon absorption and charge transport.

Photovoltaic performance

This study of the photovoltaic device constructed using the FTO/CZTS/MAPbI₃/ZnO/MWCNT structure as shown in Figure 49.14 was tested under standard AM 1.5G conditions. With (Jsc) of 12.4 mA/cm², (Voc) of 0.72 V and (FF) of 0.58 this - device delivered an average power

conversion efficiency (PCE) of 5.20% as shown in Figure 49.15.

Conclusion

In this work, an all-solution processed solar cell based on copper zinc tin sulfide and perovskite absorbers, ZnO as electron transport layer, and MWCNTs as metal-free top electrode is introduced. The realization of a PCE of 5.20% shows the possibilities of using earth-abundant materials coupled with the use of sustainable fabrication strategies.

The work demonstrates a route to scalable, environmentally friendly, next-generation photovoltaics by removing costly metals and incorporating low temperature processing. In addition, the high conductivity and stability of carbon nanotubes show their potential for use in future solar cells.

References

[1] Brockman, H., Chuhadiya, S., Kamlesh, H., & Dhaka, M. S. (2023). CdZnTe thin films as proficient absorber layer candidates in solar cell devices: a review. *Energy Advances*, 2, 1980–2005.

[2] Gantumur, M., Zhang, L., Li, J., Wang, Y., & Chen, F. (2024). Tungsten-doped ZnO as an electron transport layer for perovskite solar cells: Enhancing efficiency and stability. *ACS Applied Materials & Interfaces*, 16(28), 36255–36271.

[3] Su, Z., Xu, D., Ma, Q., Gao, K., Zhang, C., Xing, C., Wang, S., Shi,W., Wang, X., Li, K., Hui, J., & Yang, X. (2022). Atomic layer deposited ZnO–SnO₂ electron transport bilayer for wide-bandgap perovskite solar cells. Solar RRL, 6(11), 2200664.

[4] Kumar, A., Kumar, D., Jain, N., Kumar, M., Ghodake, G., Kumar, S.,Sharma, R.K., Holovsky, J., Saji, V.S. and Sharma, S.K., (2024). Enhanced efficiency and stability of electron transport layer in perovskite tandem solar cells: Challenges and future perspectives. *Solar Energy Materials and Solar Cells*, 272, 112446.

[5] Yu, H., Lin, Z., Fang, W., & Zhao, B. (2024). Application of a NADH-modified ZnO electron transport layer in high performance organic solar cells. *ACS Applied Materials and Interfaces*, 12, 1530–1542.

[6] Kobeleva, E. S., Uvarov, M. N., Kravets, N. V.,Kulikova, A. V., Zinovyev, V. A., Gurova, O. A.,Sysoev, V. I., Kondranova, A. M., Kazantsev, M. S., Degtyarenko, K. M., Matveeva, A. G., & Kulik, L. V. (2024). Ternary composite of polymer, fullerene and fluorinated multi-walled carbon nanotubes as the active layer of organic solar cells. *Journal of Composite Science*, 8(1), 3.

[7] Hu, X.-G., Lin, Z., Ding, L., & Chang, J. (2023). Recent advances of carbon nanotubes in perovskite solar cells. *Sustainable Energy & Fuels*, 7(9), 158C.

50 Numerical simulation based investigation to improve efficiency of CdS/CdTe solar cells using SCAPS 1D

Partha Ray[1], Partha Sarkar[2], Ch Venkatesa Rao[1] and Gopinath Palai[3,a]

[1]Department of Electrical and Electronics Engineering, Gandhi Institute of Engineering and Technology University, Gunupur, Odisha, India

[2]Department of Electrical Engineering, JIS College of Engineering, Kalyani, West Bengal, India

[3]Faculty of Science and Emerging Technologies, Sri Sri University, Cuttack, Odisha, India

Abstract

To increase the efficiency of the solar cell, this work used SCAP-1D to numerically simulate a cadmium sulfide (CdS)–cadmium telluride (CdTe) based solar cell. CdTe is familiar for its 1.5 eV forbidden direct band gap which make absorption coefficient higher; means, just a few microns thickness are enough to absorb the light. Even with the supremacy of CdTe photovoltaic (PV) technology, due to scarcity of Te, CdTe face the challenge. However, without much negotiation in efficiency, it is feasible to cut the CdTe thickness (~ 3 μm). Thinning the absorber layer width can cut the material cost also. A customized structure of CdS/CdTe base PV solar cell ITO/SnO$_2$/ZnO/CdTe/NiO has been planned and proposed over the reference structure ZnO/CdS/CdTe/NiO. In this work height conversion efficiency has been recorded as 27.34% with 3 μm CdTe absorber.

Keywords: Cadmium sulfide/Cadmium telluride, CdTe PV, SCAPS-1D, thin film PV Cell

Introduction

The cheap cost of the thin-film photovoltaic (PV) solar-cell and high energy conversion efficiency (ECE) has been preferred as most efficient solar cells. The "copper indium gallium selenide" (CIGS), silicon (Si-large crystalline), and cadmium telluride (CdTe) thin-film solar cell materials' efficiencies are measured as 20.3±0.6%, 25.2±0.7% and 16.7±0.5% respectively [1]. But CdTe-technology usually 30% more economical than the CIGS-technology and also 40% than Si technology [2]. The maximum efficiency (laboratory experiment) of heterojunction n-CdS/p-CdTe PV solar cell is recorded 20.4% Green et al. [3] and 28–30% is predicted theoretically [4]. Even though silicon solar cells achieve notable and unparalleled success in the PV industry for its relatively high ECE, but due to being an indirect band gap the 100 μm thicknesses is sufficient for enough light absorption. The record ECE of 26.7% is attained using 165 μm thick substrate which is lower than its anticipated value of 32.33% [5]. Because of direct and adjustable band gap, CdTe and gallium arsenide gallium arsenide (GaAs), a few micrometers (usually 2–3 μm) can

[a]gpalai28@gmail.com

DOI: 10.1201/9781003753391-50

absorb 90% incident light. Though, compared to CdTe, GaAs have high ECE of 29.1% so far but not preferred due to expensive and toxic material. Till now, 19.5% efficiency has been numerically achieved with 1 μm CdTe and 22.1% is reached experimentally Green et al. [1] even though 24% is recorded in this study.

The present study initially described different parameters impact on the CdTe/CdS cell structure by Solar Cell Capacitance Simulator (SCAPS-1D). After that, a newly configured ITO/SnO₂/ZnO/CdTe/NiO was proposed for studying for improving the device performance.

Device Modelling and Simulation

The thin film PV solar cell construct with glass substrate (back contact), a thin film as hole transport layer (HTL) was deposited as back contact on the layer of glass that covers the substrate, p-type absorber layer was deposited on back contact, a n-type buffer layer and another n-type substrate was used as a window and finally conducting surface front contact layer was used as transparent conducting oxides (TCO) as shown in Figure 50.1(a). In this work, 20 nm indium-tin-oxide (ITO) was used to conduct surface layer (front contact). The 50 nm zinc oxide (ZnO) with 25 nm CdS and 3 μm CdTe form the n+-n-p heterojunction structure. 100 nm nickel oxide (NiO) was used as back contact.

The solar cell simulation material physical parameters are tabulated in Table 50.1 [6]. The metal work function value used for back contact is 5 and filter value and complement filter value are 0.8 & 0.2. Thermionic emission/surface recombination velocity for electron and holes are used as 10^5 and 10^7 cm/s.

E_g = Bandgap energy (eV), χ = electron affinity (eV), κ = relative dielectric permittivity, CB effective density of states in the conduction band (cm⁻³), VB effective density of states in the valence band (cm⁻³), V_{th_e} = electron thermal velocity (cm/s), V_{th_h} = hole thermal velocity (cm/s), μ_e = electron mobility (cm²/Vs), μ_p = Hole mobility (cm²/Vs), ND donor concentration(cm⁻³), NA acceptor concentration (cm⁻³), A = radiative recombination coefficient (cm³/s), B = Type of defect, C stands for capture cross-section for both electrons and holes (cm²), D for defective level of energy reference (Et), and E for power level relative to reference (eV).

Results and Discussion

Initially the NiO/CdTe/CdS/ZnO solar cells structure was used as reference structure shown in Figure 50.1(a) for analysis. The reference cell has yield maximum conversion efficiency (η) of 24.74% (with open-circuit-voltage V_{OC} = 1.0669 V, short-circuit-current density J_{SC} = 27.82 mA/cm², fill-factor FF = 86.75 %). For the purpose of simulating the construction of solar cells,

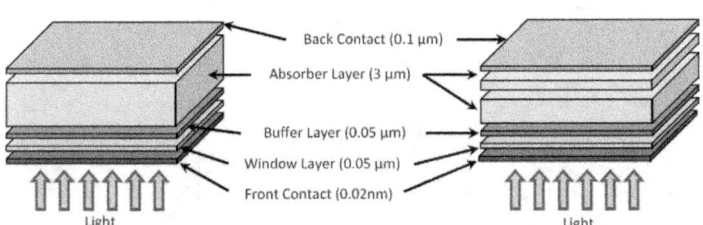

Figure 50.1 CdTe solar cells structures: (a) reference structure, (b) proposed structure
Source: Author

Table 50.1 Reference parameters of PV module.

	HTL		Buffer Layer				Window Layer		TCO
	NiO	p-CdTe	n-CdS	n-ZnS	n-ZnSe	n-In$_2$S$_3$	n-ZnO	n-SnO$_2$	ITO
Electrical parameters									
E$_g$	3.8	1.5	2.42	3.68	2.9	2.96	3.37	3.6	3.72
χ	1.46	3.9	4.3	4.13	4.09	4.2	3.9	4	4.5
κ	10	10.3	10	8.8	10	8.4	9	9	9.4
CB	2.8×10^{19}	9.2×10^{17}	2.2×10^{18}	1.7×10^{18}	1.5×10^{18}	1.8×10^{19}	1.8×10^{19}	2.2×10^{18}	4×10^{19}
VB	1×10^{19}	5.2×10^{18}	1.8×10^{19}	2.4×10^{19}	1.8×10^{18}	4×10^{18}	2.4×10^{18}	1.8×10^{19}	1×10^{18}
V$_{th\_e}$	1×10^{7}	1×10^{7}	1×10^{7}	1×10^{7}	1×10^{7}	1×10^{7}	1×10^{7}	1×10^{7}	1×10^{7}
V$_{th\_h}$	1×10^{7}	1×10^{7}	1×10^{7}	1×10^{7}	1×10^{7}	1×10^{7}	1×10^{7}	1×10^{7}	1×10^{7}
μ$_e$	12	700	100	25	50	50	25	100	30
μ$_p$	2.8	60	25	70	20	15	25	25	50
N$_D$	–	–	1.1×10^{16}	1×10^{19}	1×10^{19}	1×10^{19}	1×10^{19}	1×10^{19}	1×10^{21}
N$_A$	1×10^{18}	1×10^{16}	–	–	–	–	–	–	–
Interface Parameters									
A	2.3×10^{-9}	2.3×10^{-9}	2.3×10^{-9}	2.3×10^{-9}	2.3×10^{-9}	2.3×10^{-9}	2.3×10^{-9}	2.3×10^{-9}	2.3×10^{-9}
B	–	neutral	–	–	–	–	–	–	–
C	–	1×10^{16}	–	–	–	–	–	–	–
D	–	Above eV	–	–	–	–	–	–	–
E	–	0.06	–	–	–	–	–	–	–

Source: Author

one sun illuminating (100 mW/cm2) and an overall air mass (AM) 1.5 spectrum at 300 K were employed. Though, hypothetically a 2 μm thick CdTe layer is capable to take up 90% incident photons, a further numerical investigation has been done to find optimum thickness of CdTe layers for maximum efficiency for the reduction of cell production cost as well as materials usages. The thickness of CdTe absorber reference cells varies from 100 nm to 5000 nm to look at potentiality of absorber layer CdTe. Figure 50.2 shows the simulated results graphically. It is evidently shown that, photovoltaic parameters η and J_{SC} increase with the increase of absorber layer thickness whereas V_{OC} and FF

decrease. As maximum conversion efficiency occurs at 3 μm, therefore, this thickness has been chosen for further investigation.

On the contrary, electron affinity of NiO is 1.46 eV and band gap is 3.8 eV, therefore, this semiconductor materials also forms a suitable pp+ heterojunction with CdTe when heavily doped as shown in Figure 50.3(a) is used for back contact. Figure 50.3(b) and 50.3(c) shows the simulated $J_{SC} - V_{OC}$ curves and quantum efficiency (QE) curve.

Effect of various window layer materials on solar cell

Zinc oxide (ZnO) and stannic oxide (SnO$_2$) are most common substrate used as window

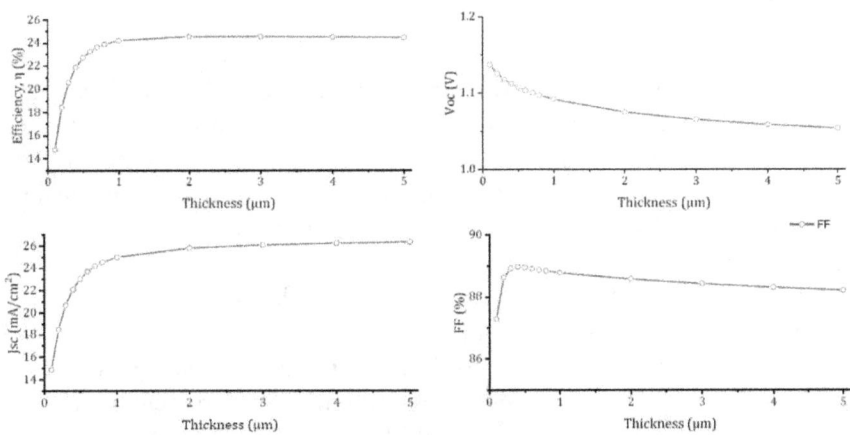

Figure 50.2 Effect of reference cell CdTe thickness layer variation on photovoltaic parameters
Source: Author

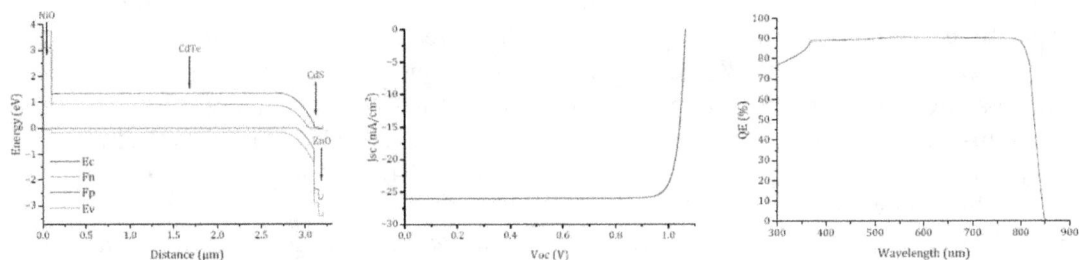

Figure 50.3 (a) Energy band diagram (b) J-V Characteristic (c) Spectral response of reference solar cell
Source: Author

Table 50.2 Efficacy of window layer material.

Buffer layer	V_{oc} (V)	J_{sc} (mA/cm2)	FF (%)	Efficiency (%)
ZnO	1.0669	27.8161	86.75	24.74
SnO$_2$	1.0669	27.8287	86.77	25.76

Source: Author

Table 50.3 Efficacy of buffer layer material.

Buffer layer	V_{OC} (V)	J_{SC} (mA/cm^2)	FF (%)	Efficiency (%)
CdS	1.0669	27.8287	86.77	25.76
ZnS	1.0666	27.8507	88.54	26.30
ZnSe	1.0666	27.8456	88.56	26.30
ZnO	1.0666	27.8596	88.59	26.33
Zn$_2$SnO$_4$	1.0666	27.8398	88.59	26.30
In$_2$S$_3$	1.0667	27.8318	88.39	26.24

Source: Author

layer in solar cells. The most exceptional possible thin film CdTe solar cell photovoltaic parameters (V_{OC}, J_{SC}, FF and η %) with various window layers are shown in Table 50.2. It is observed that SnO$_2$ showed the best window layer, attaining ECE of 25.76% with higher J_{SC} (27.82 mA/cm^2) and FF (86.77%) compared to ZnO, so SnO$_2$ have been recommended as window layer in thin films.

Effect of various buffer layer materials on solar cell

The environmentally unsafe cadmium (Cd) is harmful for humans due to its poison and toxin nature. Other possible buffer layers, such as zinc sulfide (ZnS), zinc selenide (ZnSe), ZnO, zinc stannate (Zn$_2$SnO$_4$) and indium sulfide (In$_2$S$_3$) have been investigating in this paper. The finest possible photovoltaic parameters (V_{OC}, J_{SC}, FF and η %) of a CdTe thin film with a variety of buffer layers with SnO$_2$ as window layer are shown in Table 50.3. It shows that ZnO performed as the best buffer layer, obtain ECE of 26.33%. The results uncover that the layers of buffers

formed of ZnSe, ZnS and Zn$_2$SnO$_4$ have very good ECE of 26.30%. Though buffer layer is based on In$_2$S$_3$ had a lower efficiency of 26.24%. So, ZnO may have been planned as backup buffer layer for CdS.

Proposed ITO/SnO2/ZnO/CdTe/NiO solar cell

According to simulation analysis, describe above, optimum PV parameters can be recorded ECE of 27.34% with V_{OC} = 1.0676 V, J_{SC} = 28.9156 mA/cm^2, FF = 88.61%, when accepter concentration and thickness of CdTe are 1×10^{16} cm^{-3} and 3 μm respectively, donor concentration and thickness of ZnO are 1×10^{19} cm^{-3} and 25 nm respectively, SnO$_2$ thickness is 50 nm, thickness of ITO is 0.02 nm. Figure 50.4 shows the SCAPS solar cell definition panel and J-V characteristics of proposed solar cell.

Comparing the suggested work with the existing work

The simulation results of this work were also compared with published work. Table

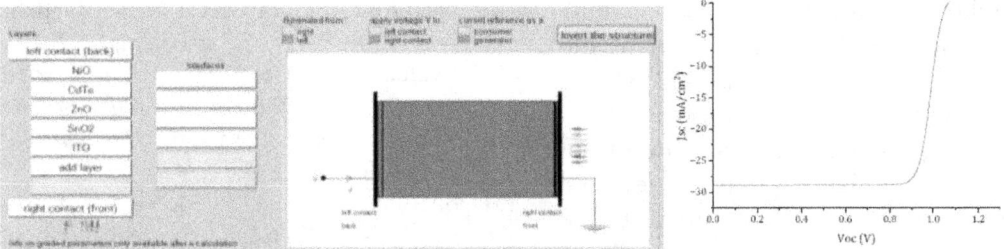

Figure 50.4 SCAPS solar cell definition panel and J-V characteristics of proposed solar cell
Source: Author

Table 50.4 Simulation results comparison of published work.

Buffer layer	Method	V_{OC} (V)	J_{SC} (mA/cm²)	FF (%)	Efficiency (%)	Reference
CdS	Experimental	0.69	30.9	72	15.3	[7]
	Simulation/ SCAPS-1D	0.9113	23.4497	81.41	17.43	[6]
	Simulation/ SCAPS-1D	1.0669	27.8287	86.77	25.76	This work
ZnS	Experimental	0.55	34.4	73	13.6	[8]
	Simulation/ SCAPS-1D	0.9121	23.2602	74.84	15.88	[6]
	Simulation/ SCAPS-1D	1.0666	27.8507	88.54	26.30	This work
ZnSe	Experimental	0.67	34.9	72.7	14.4	[8]
	Simulation/ SCAPS-1D	0.9112	23.4840	82.38	17.42	[6]
	Simulation/ SCAPS-1D	1.0666	27.8456	88.56	26.30	This work
ZnO	Experimental	0.835	21.4	75.46	15.19	[9]
	Simulation/ SCAPS-1D	0.9142	23.3039	76.37	16.27	[6]
	Simulation/ SCAPS-1D	1.0666	27.8596	88.59	26.33	This work
In_2S_3	Experimental	0.27	46.8	71.5	12.9	[10]
	Simulation/ SCAPS-1D	0.9198	23.1535	66.81	14.23	[6]
	Simulation/ SCAPS-1D	1.0667	27.8318	88.39	26.24	This work

Source: Author

50.4 shows simulation results comparison with published work. It shows that the proposed work outperforms the published studies in recent times in terms of four performance of the solar cell.

Conclusions

To model and analyze a CdS/CdTe thin film-based solar cell was numerically simulated using SCAPS-1D program.

Researchers, engineers and designers may use the findings of this work in studying and constructing CdTe-based systems. This study employs a number of buffer layers (CdS, ZnSe, ZnS, In_2S_3, ZnO) from a numerical simulation point of view and the result using SCAPS–1D indicate that ZnO is the best alternative buffer-layer for the CdS/CdTe solar cells. To improve the PV solar cell performance, ITO/SnO_2/ZnO/CdTe/NiO thin film-based solar-cell is proposed in this work. This work achieved hopeful optimized results with an effectiveness of conversion is 27.34% with V_{OC} = 1.0676 V, J_{SC} = 28.9156 mA/cm^2, FF = 88.61%. The results offer vital data for predicting the higher efficiency of thin-film solar-cells. The numerical modelling progress of improved solar cells productivity is essential, as evidence by these findings.

Conflict of interest

The authors of this work affirm that they have no competing interests.

References

[1] Green, M. A., Emery, K., Hishikawa, Y., & Warta, W. (2011). Solar cell efficiency tables (version 37). *Progress in Photovoltaics: Research*, 19(1), 84–92.

[2] Oni, A. M., Mohsin, A. S., Rahman, M. M., & Bhuian, M. B. H. (2024). A comprehensive evaluation of solar cell technologies, associated loss mechanisms, and efficiency enhancement strategies for photovoltaic cells. *Energy Reports*, 11, 3345–3366.

[3] Green, M. A., Dunlop, E., Hohl-Ebinger, J., Yoshita, M., Kopidakis, N., Bothe, K., et al. (2022). Solar cell efficiency tables (version 60). *Progress in Photovoltaics*, 30(7), 687–701. ISSN 1062-7995. JRC129602.

[4] Nykyruy, L. I., Yavorskyi, R. S., Zapukhlyak, Z. R., Wisz, G., & Potera, P. (2019). Evaluation of CdS/CdTe thin film solar cells: SCAPS thickness simulation and analysis of optical properties. *Optical Materials*, 92, 319–329.

[5] Sharma, D. K., Ilango, M. S., & Ramasesha, S. K. (2021). Efficiency enhancement of the CdS/CdTe solar nanostructured cell using electron-reflecting layer. *IEEE Transactions on Electron Devices*, 68(3), 1129–1134.

[6] Zyoud, S. H., Zyoud, A. H., Ahmed, N. M., & Abdelkader, A. F. (2021). Numerical modelling analysis for carrier concentration level optimization of CdTe heterojunction thin film–based solar cell with different non–toxic metal chalcogenide buffer layers replacements: using SCAPS–1D software. *Crystals*, 11(12), 1454.

[7] Islam, M. M., Ishizuka, S., Yamada, A., Sakurai, K., Niki, S., Sakurai, T., et al. (2009). CIGS solar cell with MBE-grown ZnS buffer layer. *Solar Energy Materials and Solar Cells*, 93(6–7), 970–972.

[8] Ennaoui, A., Eisele, W., Lux-Steiner, M., Niesen, T., & Karg, F. (2003). Highly efficient Cu (Ga, In)(S, Se)2 thin film solar cells with zinc–compound buffer layers. *Thin Solid Film*, 431, 335–339.

[9] Kartopu, G., Williams, B. L., Zardetto, V., Gürlek, A. K., Clayton, A. J., Jones, S., et al. (2019). Enhancement of the photocurrent and efficiency of CdTe solar cells suppressing the front contact reflection using a highly–resistive ZnO buffer layer. *Solar Energy Materials and Solar Cells*, 191, 78–82.

[10] Spiering, S., Eicke, A., Hariskos, D., Powalla, M., Naghavi, N., & Lincot, D. (2004). Large–area Cd–free CIGS solar modules with In2S3 buffer layer deposited by ALCVD. *Thin Solid Film*, 451, 562–566.

51 Low-power dual-supply voltage level converter with enhanced energy efficiency

Yashas, B. R.[a], Narasimha Murthy, A. J.[b], Chiranthan Bhardwaj B.[c] and Premananda B. S.[d]

Department of ETE, RV College of Engineering Bengaluru, Karnataka, India

Abstract

A level converter is a circuit that translates digital signals between different voltage levels to ensure compatibility across multiple power domains. This paper presents the design and simulation of an energy-efficient voltage level converter intended for ultra-low-power applications, implemented using the GPDK 90 nm technology in Cadence Virtuoso and simulated with Specter. With the increasing adoption of multiple supply voltages in modern VLSI systems to optimize power and performance, efficient level shifters have become essential components. Level converters enable reliable communication between circuits operating at different voltages, which are commonly used in system-on-chip (SoC) devices, Internet of Things (IoT) devices, and low-power systems. The proposed level converter operates across voltage domains from 0.8 V to 1.2 V and requires two supplies: the lower input voltage (VDDL) and the higher output voltage (VDDH). The design minimizes transistor count to reduce area and average power dissipation, thereby decreasing switching activity. To further enhance power efficiency, low-current NMOS (LCNMOS) and high-voltage threshold (HVT) transistors are employed, achieving substantial leakage reduction. Simulation results show power consumption reduced from 20.95 µW in the conventional design to 0.247 µW (98.82% reduction) using a high-threshold voltage (HVT) approach with only six transistors. A design using low-current NMOS (LCNMOS) achieves 0.277 µW (98.68%), while another optimized design records 0.3028 µW (98.55%). For area optimization, it has nearly halved in the proposed I design. Implementing LCNMOS will require one additional transistor. These results highlight both ultra-low power and area-efficient implementations. The proposed level converter shows robust operation, low glitching, and high compatibility with multi-voltage SoCs.

Keywords: Adaptive voltage level at source, CMOS, delay, power, sub-threshold, true single-phase clocking, voltage level converter, Wilson current-mirror based, level shifter

Introduction

In system design, analog, digital, and passive components require different voltages to perform optimally. As technology grows, scaling voltages is a major concern. Voltage level converters can be used in these cases, providing different voltages to the circuit as per requirement [1]. Power consumption poses a significant constraint on circuit design. These converters are particularly vital in low-power and high-performance designs, where components such as logic cores, memory units, and I/O interfaces may operate at different voltage levels.

As technology evolved, there was a demand for small handheld devices such

[a]yashasrudresh0512@gmail.com, [b]simha8406@gmail.com, [c]chiranthanbb@gmail.com, [d]premanandabs@gmail.com

DOI: 10.1201/9781003753391-51

as smart watches, smartphones, and audio-visual content devices. Needs less power consumption. As technology is growing, voltage scaling is a major concern. In these cases, voltage level converters can be used to give different voltage levels to the circuit networks [2]. To address these constraints, recent research focuses on minimizing delay, area, and static current leakage in level shifters, particularly under near-threshold and sub-threshold operating conditions.

At technology scales of 45nm and below, modern SoCs require multiple power supply levels to maintain high performance. Level shifters are critical in these systems to convert signals between different voltage levels. However, conventional level shifter designs often face issues with delay and increased power usage due to the conflict between pull-up and pull-down transistors [3]. These problems make it difficult for existing designs to efficiently handle wide voltage translation, especially when operating with core voltages under 1V.

Voltage level shifters, also known as level converters, play a critical role in addressing this challenge by enabling seamless communication across these domains without compromising signal integrity or performance. The usage of a level converter allows the use of multiple voltage domain circuits on the same chip, as it eliminates the need to draw a new voltage from outside. This helps reduce the delay in providing the supply. It is possible to design a multi-voltage level converter, which can be useful when working with multiple supply voltages. However, in this case, only two voltage domains are considered: 0.8 V and 1.2 V.

The rest of the paper is organized as follows: Related works are discussed in the literature review. Implementation details are provided under methodology, with simulated results and power values in the results

section. The last section provides conclusions delivered.

Literature Review

Recent studies focus on energy-efficient architecture, including dynamic body biasing and differential cascade voltage switches, to enhance performance. New designs proposed by Kapoor et al. [1] on subthreshold level shifters achieve better power savings and faster performance. Scaling down voltages impacts noise margins, leakage currents, and the ability of circuits to produce full output swings. When voltages are reduced, especially in smaller technologies, these effects become more noticeable, as studied by Hiremath and Vinayakgouda [2].

Dwivedi et al. [3] proposed a work in which a level shifter block and a voltage generator block were used for a wide range of voltage level shifting and avoiding a short circuit path in the level shifter block. Gosatwar and Ghodeswar [4] tested a level converter using high and low threshold transistors in order to reduce delay and power, respectively.

The Wilson Current-Mirror Based Level Shifter usage led to lower leakage power, reduced delay, and less switching energy, which was proposed by Zhou et al. [5]. Low power technique such as AVLS was proposed by Premananda et al. [6]. It offers energy efficiency, but implementation demands a greater number of transistors. Saeedifard et al. [7] implemented a multi-level shifter that uses space vector modulation for their respective application. It requires no additional or auxiliary circuitry under a specified range. Maghsoudloo et al. [8] introduced a new voltage level shifter employing a level-shifting capacitor, which greatly reduced the delay. TSPC also enhances the speed of the speed if implemented accordingly, as we only require a single clock, which was examined by Valivati et al. [9].

Lanuzza et al. [10] employed a Single-stage differential cascaded voltage scheme to make the pull-up faster and yet remain energy efficient. Premananda et al. [11] proposed techniques as transistor scaling and decreasing transistor count, resulting in lowering the power consumption. Kiran et al. [12] ensured their level converter seamless capabilities across varied voltage levels employing the Wilson current mirror circuit. Saurab and Chavan [13] employed an enhanced Wilson current mirror circuit while a typical Wilson current mirror uses a high aspect ratio, considerably reducing area and delay. Ganavi and Premananda [14] tested adiabatic logic, which can be considered as it reuses its power supply, and provides both true and complementary logics. Use of a hybrid low-power technique on the phase frequency detector is demonstrated in Premananda et al. [15].

Methodology and Model Specifications

Voltage level shifter is essential nowadays as the use of multi-threshold voltage transistors and variable threshold voltage transistors is becoming more predominant, as they use low power compared to CMOS topology, for which a voltage level converter is essential to provide the respective voltage level for the respective working voltage domains.

The circuit was designed and simulated at the transistor level using a standard CMOS process with a working voltage of 0.8 V (V_{DDL}) and an output domain of 1.2 V (V_{DDH}). Simulations were carried out using industry-standard tools such as Cadence Virtuoso, with transient response analysis performed for validation of level shifting.

A pulse generator was used to simulate IN with a 20 ns wide signal at 0.8 V amplitude. The output node was loaded with a capacitive load to reflect realistic switching behavior. Transient analysis was used to monitor signal transitions, voltage swings, and delay characteristics.

Level converter
The reference level converter, as shown in Figure 51.1, consists of 9 transistors. It receives two inputs, IN and INB (inverted IN), operating at the lower voltage domain (VDDL = 0.8 V), and shifts them to the higher domain (VDDH = 1.2 V).

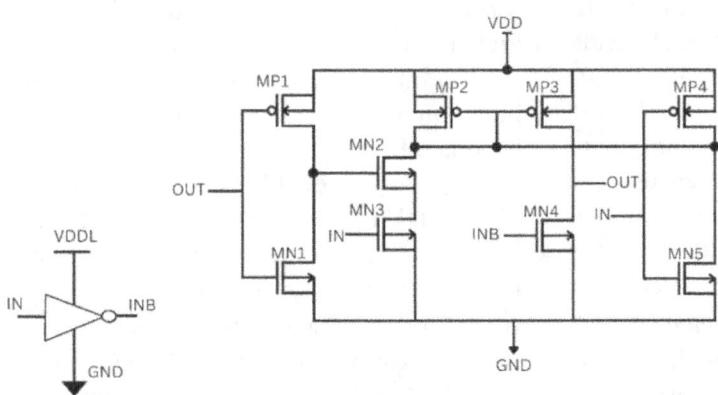

Figure 51.1 Level converter [1]
Source: Author

The circuit uses a combination of NMOS and PMOS transistors, where signal inversion and level translation are achieved using an input inverter stage followed by stacked pull-up and pull-down paths. Depending on the input polarity, specific transistors switch ON or OFF to ensure the output transitions correctly between logic levels.

When the input is high, the input IN will be high and INB will be low. Then it'll draw down the voltage present between MN3 and MN2 and the inverter (MP4 and MN5) will provide a low output which will turn on both PMOS (MP2 and MP3) which will provide an input to inverter (MP1 and MN1) which turns on MN2 therefore any voltage present will be grounded through MN2 and MN3. The voltage pulled by MP3 will be output received with V_{DDH} (1.2V).

Low power techniques

To enhance power efficiency, two low-leakage techniques were implemented by integrating Low-Current NMOS (LCNMOS) and High-threshold voltage (HVT) transistors into different parts of the proposed level converter architecture. In contrast, the HVT-based approach introduces high-threshold voltage transistors into the non-critical pull-up and cross-coupled feedback branches. These transistors, chosen for their minimum off-state leakage, contribute to lower power dissipation in nodes that hold a stable logic level. Both techniques were used while targeting areas where leakage is significant to ensure that the level-shifting operation remained as usual while significantly reducing leakage power. In a level converter circuit, the roles of LCNMOS and HVT transistors are traded off between power consumption and switching speed. LCNMOS transistors are employed in the high-voltage domain of the level shifter. The transistor is used in such a way that it disconnects the pull-up network while there is an output and vice versa, reducing power due to leakage. In level shifters, Figure 51.3, LCNMOS devices are used near the output end of the level converter while it is being controlled by the output itself. For example, when the level shifter includes a sleep or power gating feature, an LCNMOS device is used as a switch to control whether the circuit is active, helping lower leakage from the high-voltage output when the system is on standby, that is, when output isn't present.

HVT transistors are more commonly used in the high-voltage portions of level shifter circuits. These devices have a higher threshold voltage, which significantly reduces subthreshold leakage when the transistor is in the off state. Within a level shifter, HVT transistors are typically integrated into the pull-up or pull-down networks that are not time-sensitive, such as in the cross-coupled PMOS/NMOS pairs used for latching output states. These parts of the circuit benefit from the HVT's ability to remain off with very little leakage when the node is not switching. While HVT devices offer significantly better leakage performance, their high threshold voltage makes them slower to turn on, so they are not preferred in performance-critical paths, as they introduce higher delay.

In summary, LCNMOS transistors are best suited for leakage control in standby-related regions of the level converter, particularly in enable paths and control blocks. HVT transistors are more effective in high-voltage domains for reducing static leakage in the signal-holding regions of the circuit. Both serve complementary roles in creating energy-efficient level converters capable of operating across various voltage domains with smaller possible power loss.

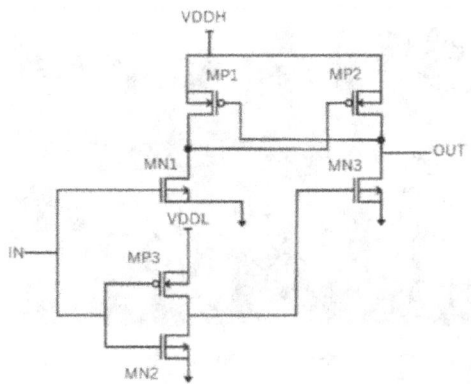

Figure 51.2 Proposed-I level converter circuit
Source: Author

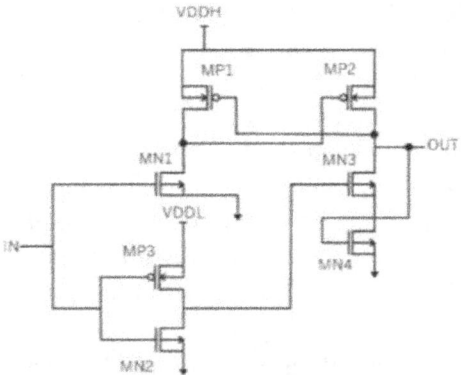

Figure 51.3 Proposed-II level converter circuit using LCNMOS
Source: Author

Proposed level converter

The modified circuit, Figure 51.2, simplifies the original design to reduce area and power dissipation while maintaining functional correctness. It consists of a cross-coupled PMOS pair (MP1 and MP2), an inverter (MP3 and MN2) to drive the internal node, and a pull-down NMOS (MN3) whose width is increased to 300 nm to support faster discharge and optimized delay. The operation involves an input signal at 0.8 V with a pulse width of 20 ns. The initial inverter generates an inverted signal, which drives MN3. Depending on whether MN3 is conducted, the output is either pulled low (0 V) or remains high (1.2 V). The cross-coupled structure provides feedback stability and ensures proper logic state retention. The simplification leads to fewer active devices and reduced average power consumption without compromising functionality.

The proposed voltage level converter was simulated using the Cadence Virtuoso platform, specifically utilizing the Spectre simulator for transient analysis. The primary goal of the simulation was to evaluate the circuit's power consumption, voltage shifting behavior, and switching speed between two voltage domains: V_{DDL} = 0.8 V (input) and V_{DDH} = 1.2 V (output). The proposed design was implemented at the transistor level using PMOS and NMOS devices from a standard CMOS library (90 nm). Transistor sizing was carefully chosen: notably, MN3 was widened to 300 nm to improve pull-down strength and reduce delays.

A pulse generator was connected to the input terminal (IN) to apply a square pulse with an amplitude of 0.8 V, a pulse width of 20 ns, and a rise/fall time of 1 ps. A complementary signal (INB) was either derived or manually added for circuits needing differential inputs. Two separate power rails were used, V_{DDL} = 0.8 V, and V_{DDH} = 1.2 V. These were applied to relevant parts of the circuit according to their domain classification. Transient analysis was performed for a total time of 100-200 ns to capture multiple input-output transitions. Waveforms were observed using Virtuoso analog design environment (ADE).

Output Voltage Swing: The output toggles between 0 and 1.2 V. Propagation delay measured from input transition to valid output logic level. The average power was calculated using the power analysis method available in Spectre. Waveform analysis, rise/fall time, and glitch-free transitions were verified. The same simulation conditions were applied to the conventional level converter to ensure a fair comparison. The key performance metrics measured include Average power consumption, area savings due to reduced transistor count, and functional correctness of level shifting from 0.8 V(V_{DDL}) to 1.2 V(V_{DDH}).

In the proposed design, the transistor MN3 was widened to 300 nm to optimize fall time and ensure complete discharge; unnecessary transistor stages were removed to lower average power, and the feedback and control path were simplified using cross-coupled PMOS for stable state retention. The proposed design was then implemented using low-power techniques, such as proposed II using LCNMOS depicted in Figure 51.3, and proposed III using HVT. The implementation of proposed I and II was evaluated against the conventional design, which demonstrated better results, such as low average power. This confirmed the enhancement concerning conventional design.

To further optimize the design standard, threshold NMOS/PMOS were replaced with their HVT equivalents from the same GPDK 90nm technology, ensuring that the circuit topology remained the same; that is, no changes were made to the netlist or device sizing. This substitution was performed to evaluate the impact of the threshold on average power and leakage current. The change in the transistor will ensure a difference in simulation results regarding delay and average power, which is solely attributed to the change in threshold voltage.

Results

The circuit mentioned in the previous section was implemented using Cadence

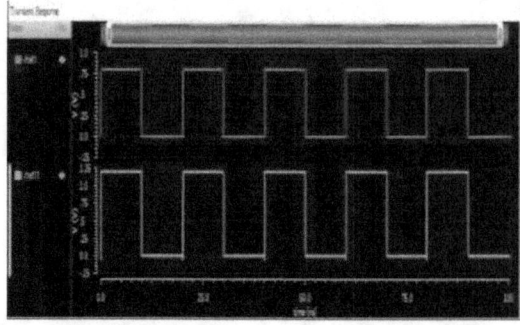

Figure 51.4 Simulation result of proposed level converter
Source: Author

Virtuoso's GPDK 90nm technology and simulated with Cadence Spectre. Figure 51.4 illustrates the output waveforms of the proposed level converter in Figure 51.2. From Table 51.1, one can infer the average transient power consumption and average analysis of the reference level converter, the proposed level converter, the proposed level converter utilizing the LCNMOS low-power technique, and the proposed level converter applying HVT.

Figure 51.4. depicts the proposed circuit transient waveform simulated in Cadence Spectre with normal conditions and with the respective changes accordingly, i.e., changes in transistor sizing. The waveform shows a slightly increased propagation delay between input and output transitions, which is around 20% of the conventional level converter.

The simulation was conducted, and the results are summarized in Table 51.1. The proposed circuit demonstrates a drastic reduction in power consumption. The power was calculated by taking the average transient power during the respective simulation duration, and the average power dropped from 20.95 μW to 0.302 μW. The power analysis from this waveform confirms that average power dissipation is significantly

Table 51.1 Power analysis of level converter with $V_{DDL} = 800mv$ and $V_{DDH} = 1.2V$.

Level converter	Transistor count	Power (μW)
Kapoor et al. [1]	11	20.95
Proposed-I	6	0.3028
Proposed-II using LCNMOS	7	0.277
Proposed-III using HVT	6	0.247

Source: Author

reduced compared to the conventional circuit, thanks to the simplified topology and reduced switching activity. Such optimization is critical for ultra-low-power applications. Building further on this improvement, the incorporation of LCNMOS transistors in Proposed-II is depicted in Figure 51.3, achieving a power consumption of 0.277 μW. In contrast, the use of HVT transistors in Proposed-III further reduces it to 0.247 μW.

Conclusion

This work introduces a power-efficient voltage level converter tailored for ultra-low-power applications operating across 0.8 V to 1.2 V domains. The design simplifies the circuit while considering techniques (LCNMOS) and HVT, implemented using 90 nm CMOS technology, to considerably minimize power consumption. Concerning the conventional design, which consumes 20.95 μW, the proposed converters demonstrate substantial reductions in power. Proposed-I achieves a 98.55% reduction, proposed-II, using LCNMOS, achieves 98.68%, and proposed-III, using HVT, achieves the highest reduction of 98.82%. In addition to low power, proposed-III also uses only six transistors, ensuring area efficiency compared to a conventional design

using 11 transistors, even proposed-II can be implemented with only seven transistors. These improvements make the design well-suited for compact SoC environments where low power is prioritized over speed, despite a marginal increase in propagation delay.

References

[1] Kapoor, A., Thapar, A., Jha, C. S., & Kumar, C. I. (2024). A high performance and low power subthreshold voltage level shifter design. In 2024 International Conference on VLSI Design and 2024 International Conference on Embedded Systems, (pp. 623–627).

[2] Hiremath, S., & Vinayakgouda, Y. (2021). High-speed level shifter design for low power applications. In 2021 6th International Conference on Communication and Electronics Systems, (pp. 307–310).

[3] Dwivedi, D., Dwivedi, S., & Potladhurthi, E. (2015). Voltage up level shifter with improved performance and reduced power. In 2012 IEEE Canadian Conference on Electrical and Computer Engineering (pp. 1–4).

[4] Gosatwar, P., & Ghodeswar, U. (2016). Design of a voltage level shifter for multi-supply voltage design. In 2016 International Conference on Communication and Signal Processing, (pp. 0853–0857).

[5] Zhou, J., Wang, C., Liu, X., Zhang, X., & Je, M. (2015). An ultra-low voltage level shifter using revised wilson current mirror for fast and energy-efficient wide-range voltage conversion from sub-threshold to I/O voltage. *IEEE Transactions on Circuits and Systems I*, 62(3), 697–706.

[6] Premananda, B. S., Rehman, A., & Megha, P. (2024). Area and power efficient AVLS-TSPC-based diffused bit generator for key generation. *Circuits, Systems, and Signal Processing*, 43, 3103–3117.

[7] Saeedifard, M., Barbosa, P. M., & Steimer, P. K. (2012). Operation and control of a hybrid seven-level converter. *IEEE Transactions on Power Electronics*, 27(2), 652–660.

[8] Maghsoudloo, E., Rezaei, M., Sawan, M., & Gosselin, B. (2017). A high-speed and ultra low-power subthreshold signal level shifter. *IEEE Transactions on Circuits and Systems I: Regular Papers*, 64(5), 1164–1172.

[9] Premananda, B. S., Valivati, S., & Rehman, A. (2024). TSPC-AVLS based low-power 16/17 dual modulus prescaler design. *IETE Journal of Research*, 70(4), 4149–4158.

[10] Lanuzza, M., Crupi, F., Rao, S., De Rose, R., Strangio, S., & Iannaccone, G. (2017). An ultralow-voltage energy-efficient level shifter. *IEEE Transactions on Circuits and Systems II: Express Briefs*, 64(1), 61–65.

[11] Premananda, B. S., Sahithi, N., & Mittal, S. (2023). AVLS-based 32/33 pre-scaler for frequency dividers. *E-Prime - Advances in Electrical Engineering, Electronics, and Energy*, 4, 1–5.

[12] Kiran, P. L., Pratheek, K. S., & Pande, K. S. (2024). Current mirror-based level shifter aiding multitudinous conversion ranges. In 2024 International Conference on Integrated Circuits and Communication Systems (ICICACS), (pp. 1–6).

[13] Saurab B., & Chavan, A. P. (2021). Ultra-low power, area efficient, and high-speed voltage level shifter based on wilson current mirror. In 2021 IEEE Mysore Sub Section International Conference (MysuruCon), Hassan, India. (pp. 108–113).

[14] Ganavi, M. G., & Premananda, B. S. (2019). Design of low-power square root carry select adder and wallace tree multiplier using adiabatic logic. *Springer Lecture Notes in Electrical Engineering*, 545, 767–781.

[15] Premananda, B. S., & Sreedhar, S. (2022). Low-power phase frequency detector using hybrid AVLS and LECTOR techniques for low-power PLL. *Advances in Electrical and Electronic Engineering, Theoretical and Applied Electrical Engineering*, 20(3), 294–303.

52 A comparative analysis of a InGaP/GaAs double junction solar cell

Jhilirani Nayak[1,a], Pankaj Prusty[1,b], Arabinda Sahoo[1,c], Bibhu Prasad Mohanty[2,d] and Mihir Narayan Mohanty[2,e]

[1]FET, Cener For Internet of Things, Siksha 'O' Anusandhan Deemed to be University, Bhubaneswar, Odisha, India

[2]FET, Electronics and Communication Enggineering, Siksha 'O' Anusandhan Deemed to be University, Bhubaneswar, Odisha, India

Abstract

This paper compares a double-junction InGaP/GaAs solar cell with a single-junction GaAs solar cell. Double-junction InGaP/GaAs device was simulated using the Atlas model from the Silvaco tool. The top junction in this structure is made of Indium Gallium Phosphide (InGaP), and the bottom junction is made of Gallium Arsenide (GaAs). By varying the ratio of indium phosphate to gallium arsenide in the InGaP layer, the device's bandgap characteristics were determined. An open-circuit voltage of 1.1 V, a short-circuit current of 14.6 mA, a fill factor of 84.39%, and an efficiency of 32.89% are among the device's performance metrics, which is much higher in comparision with single-junction GaAs solar cell with anti-reflection coatings.

Keywords: Anti-reflection coatings, bandgap engineering, double-junction solar cell, photovoltaic materials, single-junction GaAs solar cell

Introduction

Mankind has been utilizing various types of conventional energy sources which include fossil fuels, agricultural stalks, coal, natural gas, and many others, for a long time. For many years, the use of these fuels has led to numerous environmental hazards, including water and air pollution and threats to animal species. climate change, the utilization of these traditional energy sources for an extended period has resulted in negative consequences, such as acid rain and soil erosion. The limited availability of these traditional energy sources, along with their various environmental risks, has led us to choose sustainable and clean energy alternatives known as non-conventional energy sources. Among the various renewable energy technologies, solar energy stands out as a leading candidate to meet long-term energy demands due to its widespread availability and scalable conversion potential. In addition to being abundant, solar energy is environmentally friendly, producing no harmful emissions during operation. Advances in photovoltaic technologies and energy storage systems are further enhancing the efficiency and practicality of solar power for global energy solutions. Renewable energy exists in the form of wind, hydro, biomass, geothermal etc. Among all these renewable energy sources,

[a]jhiliraninayak@soa.ac.in, [b]pankajprusty@soa.ac.in, [c]arabindasahoo@soa.ac.in, [d]bibhumohanty@soa.ac.in, [e]mihirmohanty@soa.ac.in

DOI: 10.1201/9781003753391-52

solar irradiance remains the most abundant and universally accessible resource [1]. Its immense potential establishes it as a key element for future sustainable energy systems in various geographical areas. The Earth receives approximately 120,000 terawatts (TW) of solar radiation daily, far exceeding current global energy requirements. It has been estimated that harnessing merely 0.16% of the planet's terrestrial surface for solar energy conversion could generate approximately a power level of 20 TW which is equivalent to the total amount of energy consumed globally in a year [2]. This highlights the significant potential of solar photovoltaics and related technologies in addressing future energy challenges [2].

A photovoltaic (PV) cell is also known as a solar cell (SC). It serves as the fundamental unit responsible for converting incident solar irradiance into electrical energy through the photovoltaic effect [3, 4]. The materials chosen and the architecture of the device significantly influence how well a PV cell performs and how efficient it is. Solar cell technologies are broadly categorized into several types, including silicon-based cells (both monocrystalline and polycrystalline), thin-film technologies (like CdTe and CIGS), III-V compound semiconductor cells, as well as new materials such as devices based on organic and perovskite [5, 6]. Single-junction solar photovoltaic (PV) cells convert sunlight into electrical energy by absorbing wavelengths up to a limit determined by their bandgap. [7]. This leads to the fact that photons whose energies are lower than that of the bandgap are not absorbed, which results in efficiency limitations by nature. Based on III-V semiconductor materials particularly multi-junction (MJ) solar cell architecture have garnered significant interest within the research and aerospace communities due to their exceptional power conversion efficiencies under both standard and concentrated illumination conditions [8, 9]. These MJ devices are typically composed of epitaxial grown heterojunctions formed from different III-V alloys (e.g., GaAs, InGaP, and InGaAs), each engineered to possess distinct bandgaps. This bandgap engineering enables the absorption of a greater range in the solar spectrum, thereby doing a minimization of thermalization and transmission losses and enhancing overall device efficiency.

Multi-junction (MJ) solar cells are created by stacking multiple single-junction sub-cells, each optimized to capture various areas present in the solar spectrum. It allows for proper use of sunlight: the upper cell, which has a larger band gap, collects high-energy photons, while the layers beneath it take in photons with energies that decrease successively. Top cell materials that are commonly utilized include indium gallium phosphide (InGaP), aluminum gallium arsenide (AlGaAs), indium gallium nitride (InGaN) and indium gallium arsenide (InGaAs). These materials are selected due to their tunable band gaps and high absorption efficiency. By using a strategic layering approach, thermalization losses are reduced and overall conversion efficiency is improved. As a result, MJ cells are well-suited for space and concentrated photovoltaic applications [10–13]. These are group III-V compound semiconductors. The bottom sub-cells typically lower bandgap materials, such as gallium arsenide (GaAs) being a widely utilized due to its favorable electronic properties and spectral response. Optimization of multi-junction cell performance often involves precise control over material composition, doping, and layer thickness. Bahram et al. [14] demonstrated efficiency enhancements in AlGaAs/GaAs tandem cells through optimization of doping concentration and absorber thickness. Such optimizations allow for improved current matching between sub-cells, which is essential for maximizing overall device efficiency. Similarly, Philipps et al. [15] investigated the performance trade-offs in InGaP/GaAs dual-junction cells by systematically adjusting the optical thickness of both sub-cells and incorporating a distributed Bragg reflector (DBR) near the GaAs band edge to enhance light trapping and photonic confinement. The electrical interconnection between sub-cells is achieved via a tunnel junction, a heavily doped p++/n++ interface that facilitates quantum mechanical tunnelling. This junction provides a low-resistance electrical path for current continuity between sub-cells while allowing most photons to pass through with minimal absorption losses, owing to its narrow depletion width and negligible optical absorption [16]. An additional critical component in multijunction solar cells is the anti-reflection coating (ARC) [17], which minimizes Fresnel reflection at the air-semiconductor interface, thereby increasing photon transmission to the active layers and enhancing optical absorption.

By modelling the solar cell's Indium Gallium Phosphide layer, this study predicts efficiency. A comparison has done with the single junction solar cell. To examine these efficiencies, Silvaco Atlas TCAD simulation software is utilized. Through multi-junction architecture, the simulation reveals details about electrical properties and performance enhancements. The main contribution is the investigation of gallium arsenide (GaAs) double-junction solar cells, which outperform traditional single-junction solar cells. Using variations in the thickness of different layers V_{oc}, I_{sc}, and efficiency is calculated in relation to the various intensities.

The paper's structure is set out as follows: Section II elaborates the device modelling in detail. Section III presents the simulation results along with its comparison with previous results given in literature. Section IV provides the conclusions drawn from the study.

Model Simulation Setup

The work represents contrast between two devices shown in Figure 52.1. The first device is a GaAs solar cell with two anti-reflection coatings and a single junction. The device is having a silicon substrate, which provides stforility to the device. The structure consist of a silicon substrate, gallium arsenide base and emitter, zinc oxide antireflection coating and a silicon dioxide layer. The second device is modeled with a p-type GaAs base and n-type GaAs emitter for Cell 1, while Cell 2 features a p-type InGaP base and n-type InGaP emitter. Cell 1 incorporates an AlGaAs tunnel junction, whereas Cell 2 uses a GaAs tunnel junction, with both junctions positioned between the two sub-cells. The device simulations were conducted using the Silvaco ATLAS simulator which is meant for solar cell. The single-junction GaAs solar cell features a base thickness of 2 μm., emitter thickness of 0.04μm, zinc oxide thickness of 0.04μm and silicon dioxide thickness of 0.05μm. Aluminum is used as the front contact and gold is used as the back contact of the device. The heterostructure was simulated under AM1.5 illumination. Conductors are employed for both the cathode and anode. The second device consists of two cells. The bottom cell includes an n-AlGaAs layer that functions as a back surface field layer. Additionally, an n-GaAs layer is used as a buffer layer. The cell also contains InGaP window layer. The device with AlGaAs tunnel junction is shown in Figure 52.2(a) and GaAs tunnel junction is shown in Figure 52.2(b). The top cell is made up of InGaP, with InAlGaP as window layer and back surface field layer.

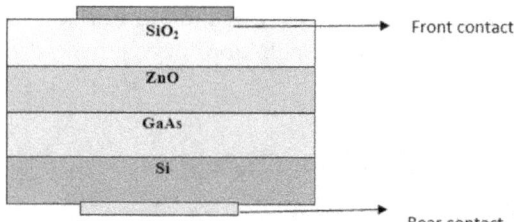

Figure 52.1 Diagram depicting the layered configuration of a gallium arsenide photo-voltaic unit [7]
Source: Author

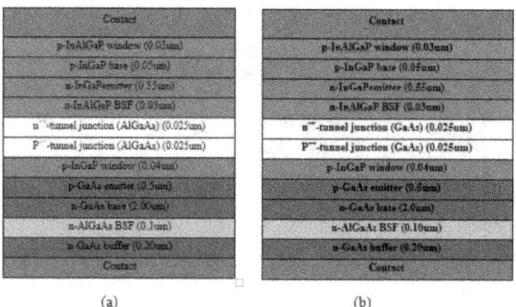

Figure 52.2 Schematic structure of double-junction InGaP/GaAs solar cell(a) with AlGaAs tunnel junction and (b) GaAs tunnel junction
Source: Author

Table 52.1 Properties of material used in the simulation.

Name of the parameter	Min. value	Max. value
Electron affinity	3.54	4.09
N_c (300)	7.0×10^{16}	2.0×10^{19}
N_v (300)	2.5×10^{18}	2.5×10^{20}
I_{ds}.exciton	0.0	0.0

Source: Author

The performance of a two-dimensional device was evaluated using Silvaco ATLAS, and the structure was modeled based on specific assumptions. These included an abrupt p-n junction, light incident perpendicularly to the surface, Lambert-Beer law for absorption (neglecting reflection losses), a constant temperature of 300K, and illumination corresponding to AM1.5 direct 1-sun conditions along with concentrated light exposure. The second device utilizes a GaAs tunnel junction placed between two sub-cells. The lower sub-cell consists of a GaAs-based p-n junction, while the upper sub-cell incorporates a p-n junction formed with InGaP materials. All characteristics of the used material are shown in the second part of the deck. Table 52.1 shows the optimized material parameters used for the optimizer simulation.

The AM1.5 solar spectrum was used as the illumination source for this research. Silvaco uses refractive index information from SOPRA files for frequency-dependent optical computations. By altering the bias voltage between a range of 0.1 V and 2.7 V, the Current-Voltage (J-V) properties were examined. A positive bias means that the cathode is receiving positive voltage. The J–V curves were recorded under both dark and illuminated conditions, using the simulated solar light (with AM 1.5 spectrum and 100 mW/cm²).

Result and Discussion

The impact of illumination concentration on the active layers was investigated by directing focused light onto the concentrator photovoltaic system. The figures of merit for both devices are shown in Tables 52.2 and 52.3. When the injection level is high, Auger recombination takes over, which results in a change in fill factor, power efficiency, dark current, and V_{oc} improvement. This points out how crucial it is to optimize carrier lifetime and recombination mechanisms when conditions are of high concentration. The short circuit current rises linearly at

Table 52.2 Variation of electrical parameters of device 1 with illumination intensity.

No of Suns	V_{oc}(v)	J_{sc}(A/cm²)	FF (%)	Efficiency(%)
1	2.14	0.24	81.29	26.12
11	2.44	1.59	82.06	27.76
51	2.48	7.55	83.09	28.59
76	2.49	11.29	83.29	28.84
101	2.40	15.12	83.33	29.55

Source: Author

Table 52.3 Variation of electrical parameters of device 2 with illumination intensity.

No of sums	V_{oc}(v)	J_{sc}(A/cm²)	FF (%)	Efficiency (%)
1	2.28	$1.32*10^{-10}$	81.4	27
11	2.63	$1.32*10^{-9}$	82.1	29.26
51	2.77	$2.65*10^{-9}$	83.0	29.77
76	2.71	$6.62*10^{-9}$	83.4	30.39
101	2.87	$1.32*10^{-9}$	83.5	32.19

Source: Author

low injection as the device's incident light flux increases. The rise in each sub cell's open-circuit voltage (V_{oc}) is responsible for the observed improvement in carrier production. Both devices show a noticeable rise in V_{oc} under rising sun intensity. The bandgap of the relevant material is having a straight influence on the open-circuit voltage, with sub cells having a lower bandgap showing a more noticeable V_{oc} increase. According to simulation data, the V_{oc} increases to a higher value at a concentration level of 101 suns. A highest efficiency of 32.19% was attained with a GaAs tunnel junction at a concentration of 101 suns. This configuration demonstrated optimal performance under the given conditions, highlighting the potential of the tunnel junction in enhancing the device's efficiency. Additionally, employing an AlGaAs tunnel junction, the maximum efficiency of 29.55% was observed at the same light intensity. A comparative analysis of these proposed devices with our earlier device [18] indicates an enhancement of efficiency by 12% with increase in intensity and thickness of layers.

The impact of active layer thickness on solar cells' photovoltaic (PV) performance was examined in depth. The devices with the best efficiency (η) and short-circuit current density (J_{sc}) have optimized active layers. Variations in thickness also had a little effect on the fill factor which is denoted as FF and open-circuit voltage which is denoted as V_{oc}. Absorption enhanced with increasing active layer thickness, which increased short-circuit current and exciton formation. Table 52.4 shows all the retrieved values.

In conclusion, SILVACO software simulations were used to examine the device's properties. When the concentration level was equivalent to 101 cells, a peak efficiency

Table 52.4 Electrical parameters extracted for various active layer thicknesses.

GaAs sub cell (Emitter thickness in µm)	Parameter			
	J_{sc}(A/micron)	V_{oc}(V)	FF (%)	Efficiency (%)
0.2	1.21×10^{-8}	2.67	92.00	28.1
0.4	1.22×10^{-8}	2.66	91.99	28.75
0.6	1.38×10^{-8}	2.65	91.39	30.74
0.8	1.39×10^{-8}	2.64	91.25	30.9
1.0	1.44×10^{-8}	2.63	91.18	31.2

Source: Author

Table 52.5 Electrical parameter values of simulated devices.

Name of the model	Spectrum	V_{oc}(V)	I_{sc}(mA)	FF (%)	Efficiency (%)
Double junction solar cell1	AM 1.5	2.24	14	81.39	27
Double junction solar cell2	AM 1.5	2.38	13.24	81.39	26.12
Single-junction GaAs solar cell	AM 1.5	1.1	17.4	84	16.46

Source: Author

of 32.19% was observed. The efficiency increased to 31.2% when the bottom sub-cell's thickness was increased to 1.0 µm. Likewise, the Gallium Arsenide section's efficiency increased to 30.7% when the acceptor layer's thickness was increased to 0.6 µm. A comparative analysis of electrical parameters of the devices has been shown in Table 52.5.

Conclusion

The device discussed achieves very good efficiency under an illumination intensity of 101 suns as discussed. Beyond this concentration level, no further improvement in efficiency is observed. The number of suns, open-circuit voltage (V_{oc}), short-circuit current density (J_{sc}), thickness of the sub-cell layers, different loss mechanisms, lattice mismatch, doping levels, the material's absorption coefficient, and the fill factor are some of the variables that affect overall

performance. Double-junction gallium arsenide solar cells with anti-reflection coatings are better in terms of efficiency than single-junction gallium arsenide solar cells. The additional junction and minimized reflection losses allow for broader spectral absorption and improved overall energy conversion. Aluminum gallium arsenide has been utilized as a tunnel junction to achieve effective lattice matching within the device structure. The results emphasize the vital function of optimized layer configuration in improving photovoltaic response. Energy efficiency is directly affected by careful selection of materials and precise control of fabrication parameters. Future research could concentrate on thermal management and the long-term stability of high-concentration operations.

References

[1]   Hasan, M. K., Lata, L. N., & Alam, K. (2017). Effect of band gap on the

performance of Al-GaAs/GaAs dual junction solar cell. In 2017 4th International Conference on Advances in Electrical Engineering (ICAEE), September 2017.

[2] Lewis, N. S., & Nocera, D. G. (2006). Powering the planet: chemical challenges in solar energy utilization. *Proceedings of the National Academy of Sciences,* 103*(*43), 15729–15735.

[3] Rifat, M. A., Khan, M. I. M., & Alam, K. (2016). Simulation study on the effects of changing band gap on solar cell parameters. In 2016 9th International Conference on Electrical and Computer Engineering (ICECE), (pp. 86–89). IEEE.

[4] Green, M. A. (2000). Photovoltaics: technology overview. *Energy Policy*, 28(14), 989–998.

[5] Razykov, T. M., Ferekides, C. S., Morel, D., Stefanakos, E., Ullal, H. S., & Upadhyaya, H. M. (2011). Solar photovoltaic electricity: current status and future prospects. *Solar Energy*, 85(8), 1580–1608.

[6] Özen, Y., Akın, N., Kınacı, B., & Özçelik, S. (2015). Performance evaluation of a GaInP/GaAs solar cell structure with the integration of AlGaAs tunnel junction. *Solar Energy Materials and Solar Cells,* 137, 1–5.

[7] Raisa, A. T., Sakib, S. N., Hossain, M. J., Rocky, K. A., & Kowsar, A. (2025). Advances in multijunction solar cells: an overview. *Solar Energy Advances*, 5, 100105.

[8] Essig, S., Allebé, C., Remo, T., Geisz, J. F., Steiner, M. A., Horowitz, K., et al. (2017). Raising the one-sun conversion efficiency of III–V/Si solar cells to 32.8% for two junctions and 35.9% for three junctions. *Nature Energy*, 2(9), 1–9.

[9] Garcia, I., Rey-Stolle, I., Galiana, B., & Algora, C. (2009). A 32.6% efficient lattice-matched dual-junction solar cell working. *Applied Physics Letters,* 94(5), 053509.

[10] Virshup, G. F., Ford, C. W., & Werthen, J. G. (1985). A 19% efficient AlGaAs solar cell with graded band gap. *Applied Physics Letters,* 47(11), 1319–1321.

[11] Zahler, J. M., Tannabe, K., Ladous, C., Pinnington, T., Newan, F. D., & Alwater, H. A. (2007). High efficiency In-GaAs solar cells on Si by InP layer transfer. *Applied Physics Letters,* 91(1), 012108.

[12] Dahal, R., Pantha, B., Li, J., Lin, J. Y., & Jiang, H. X. (2009). InGaN/GaN multiple quantum well solar cells with long operating. *Applied Physics Letters,* 94(6), 063505.

[13] Kinaci, B., Özen, Y., Asar, T., Cetin, S. S., Memmedli, T., Kasap, M., et al. (2013). Study on growth and characterizations of GaxIn1-xP/GaAs solar. *Materials Science Materials in Electronics,* 24, 1790–1795.

[14] Bahrami, A., Mohammadnejad, M., & Abkenar, A. A. (2015). Improving the performance of a multi-junction solar cell by optimizing BSF, base, and emitter layers. *Journal of Renewable and Sustainable Energy,* 7(4), 043104.

[15] Philipps, S. P., Bett, A. W., Horowitz, K., & Kurtz, S. (2012). Current status of concentrator photovoltaic (CPV) technology. *EPJ Photovoltaics,* 3, 35003.

[16] Green, M. A. (2003). Third Generation Photovoltaics: Advanced Solar Energy Conversion. Springer.

[17] Nayak, J., Pattanaik, P., & Mishra, D. K. (2024). A numerical modeling approach to study the characteristics of a photovoltaic cell featuring a GaAs absorber layer. *International Journal of Engineering Trends and Technology,* 72(1), 164–173. https://doi.org/10.14445/22315381/IJETT-V72I1P116.

[18] Nayak, J., & Prusty, P. (2020). Design, modelling and analysis of a double junction GaAs solar cell using Silvaco software. *Test Engineering and Management,* 83, 8189–8194.

53 Parameter variation analysis effect on charge plasma TFET(CP-TFET) for ambipolar current reduction

Sasmita Sahoo[a]

Institute of Technical Education and Research, Siksha 'O' Anusandhan Deemed to be University, Bhubaneswar, Odisha, India

Abstract

The ongoing device concept called charge-plasma tunnel field effect transistor (CP-TFET) is discussed again. The unique device, which uses different work-function metal contact at source and drain region for the creation of plasma regions does not require any doping using ion implantation. Its advantages of providing negligible short channel effects (SCEs), easy fabrication process makes this device worth studying. For a clear understanding of charge plasma TFET with different parameter variation is presented here. A detail investigation of different physical parameters like source-gate electrode (L_{sg}) and gate-drain electrode (L_{gd}) spacing, contact metal work-function variation (φ_S, φ_D, φ_G), channel length (L_g), body doping (N_B), oxide thickness (t_{ox}) and its impact on transfer characteristics of the CP-TFET device is presented in the paper.

Keywords: Ambipolar current, charge plasma, short channel effect

Introduction

The semiconductor industry is now focusing on miniaturizing the device dimensions to improve its functionality in terms of reduced size, cost and high-frequency application. This comes with a pitfall of high leakage current, introduction of short channel effects (SCEs), and increase in subthreshold swing (SS) [1–5]. Rigorous scaling leads the semiconductor circuitry to large power consumption [3–6]. Recently to deal with these shortcomings a new device called Tunnel Field Effect Transistor (TFET) accumulates the attention of researchers with its different current conduction mechanism [4, 5]. TFET carries a similar structure to that of MOSFET, with a dissimilar doping of source and drain region. Based on the carrier generation in different regions, they are categorized into two different TFET structure ('n' and 'p'-type). Operating principle of TFET based on inter-band tunnelling of charge carriers called Band-to-band tunneling (BTBT) [3–8]. Working at TFET is better explained by considering the transfer characteristics curve. Transfer characteristics curve of TFET have three different regions of operation. TFET has a unique feature of providing very low OFF state current as well as lower sub-threshold swing (SS < 60 mV/dec). This makes TFET a steep slope device to be used in low power applications [5–9].

Apart of having all the benefits, TFET is suffering from lower ON state current and ambipolar current by virtue of the reduced rate of tunneling in silicon-based devices [1–3]. In addition to that non

[a]sasmita.sahoo@soa.ac.in

DOI: 10.1201/9781003753391-53

uniform concentration profile at source, channel and drain region of physically doped TFET suffers from random dopant fluctuations (RDE), gives rise to poor device performance [10]. Apart from that, physical significance of nanoscale devices include expensive annealing process, which increases the fabrication complexity and cost [6]. To overcome the mentioned issues, a new transistor structure evolved with metallurgical junctions named junction less TFETs (JL TFET). This structure helps eliminate complex fabrication processes but failed providing abrupt tunneling junctions. JLTFET formed by n⁺ substrate and metal electrode at source region generates lower drain current. This reduction in current is because of mobility degradation [11–15].

A completely new device model is designed with intrinsic body of p-type known as doping less TFET, here p-type material is considered as substrate. Highest solubility, fastest crystal growth and easy availability of p-type (boron) material make this more suitable for future generation use [16, 17]. Then metal contact with different work-function approaches over source, drain region are done for creation of charge plasma to form p⁺ source and n⁺ drain regions. This will automatically improve the drain current profile by creating abruptness at source/channel junction. In this way the fabrication process will eliminate high temperature doping and annealing [19]. By getting rid of these two steps, the fabrication process becomes simpler, faster, and more energy efficient. Considering all the improvement of charge plasma TFET over the conventional one, still the CP-TFET is dealt with some serious drawback like reduced ON as well as ambipolar current. Further research process involves improving the characteristics of the device.

This paper generally focuses on the impact of different parameter variation over

transfer characteristics of plasma TFET (CP-TFET). It has been observed that device parameters like source-gate electrode (L_{sg}) and gate-drain electrode (L_{gd}) spacing affect the electrical properties of CP-TFET. Along with that the influence of source, gate and drain electrode metal work-function variation on drain current of CP-TFET is analysed. Impact of using different dielectric material with changing gate oxide thickness is also examined to improve the device performance further.

Device Structure and Simulation

Figure 53.1 represents the simulated structure of charge plasma TFET (CP-TFET). The design parameters and their optimized values for CP-TFET in comparison with DG-TFET are described in Table 53.1. The conventional DG-TFET is uniformly doped with a P⁺ source doping of 10^{20} cm⁻³, N⁺ drain doping of 10^{20} cm⁻³ and an intrinsic channel region doping of 10^{16} cm⁻³. For a better comparison, the different parameters of CP-TFET are calibrated to get an optimized value. In charge-plasma TFET, regions are created by choosing a suitable work-function metal at source and drain electrode for the introduction of hole and electron at respective regions. Spacing between source-gate (L_{sg}) and gate-drain (L_{gd}) electrode determines the tunneling generation rate at both junctions in case of

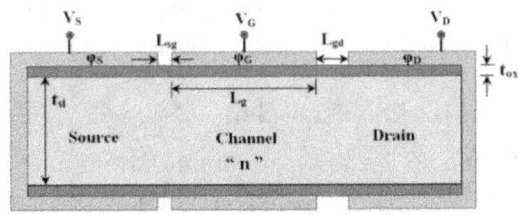

Figure 53.1 2-D sectional view of charge plasma TFET (CP-TFET) structure
Source: Author

Table 53.1 Device parameter list used in simulation process.

Variables	DG-TFET	CP-TFET Variable	CP-TFET Optimised
Gate length (L_g), nm	50	(30-60)	50
Spacing between source-gate electrode (L_{sg}), nm	-	(1-5)	2
Spacing between gate-drain electrode (L_{gd}), nm	-	(13-20)	15
Oxide thickness (t_{ox}), nm	1	(1-2)	1
Silicon body thickness (t_{si}), nm	10	10	10
Source electrode work-function (φ_S)	4.2	(5.3-5.93)	5.93
Drain electrode work-function (φ_D)	4.2	(3.9-4.1)	3.9
Gate electrode work-function (φ_G)	4.2	(4.1-4.7)	4.2
Intrinsic body doping (N_B), cm^{-3}	10^{16}	(10^{15}-10^{17})	10^{16}

Source: Author

charge plasma TFETs. Impact of different design parameters like source-gate, gate-drain electrode spacing, intrinsic body doping, t_{si}, t_{ox} variation, electrode metal work function alteration effect on performance of CP-TFET is analyzed in detail.

Sentaurus device simulator is used for designing and simulating the proposed structure [18]. Nonlocal band-to-band tunneling model is used to calculate the tunneling generation rate at both junctions. Drift-diffusion current transport model and Hurkx trap-assisted tunneling model are also considered as carrier transport models in the simulation process. Field dependent mobility degradation is analyzed by applying Lombardi mobility model. Shockley-Read-Hall (SRH) and Auger recombination models are in use to calculate carrier lifetime at different tunneling regions.

Result and Discussion

Figure 53.2 shows the drain current analogy of CP-TFET with DG-TFET. Proposed charge plasma TFET exhibit an improved amb-current (I_{amb}) of 8.94×10^{-14} A/μm as compared to DG-TFET (1.51×10^{-9} A/μm)

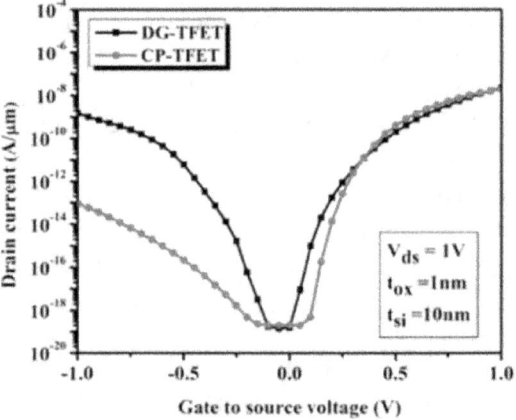

Figure 53.2 Drain current analysis of CP-TFET with DG-TFET
Source: Author

at V_{gs} = -1 V and almost similar ON current characteristics. This improvement in ambipolar current is achieved because of the reduced electric field at drain/channel junction. In CP-TFET accumulation of charge at the surface helps realizing similar ON current without doping the source region. Source metal electrode along with the spacing applied at source and gate electrode plays a vital role for the tunneling

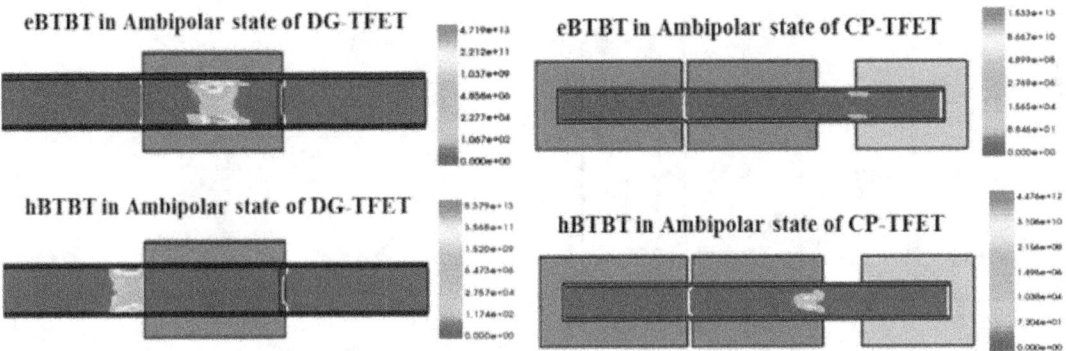

Figure 53.3 BTBT generation rate of hole and electron analysis of DG-TFET and CP-TFET in ambipolar state
Source: Author

generation rate at junction region. BTBT generation rate determines the tunneling rate of the device both in ambipolar and ON state. The BTB tunneling generation rate of hole and electron for ambipolar state is presented in Figure 53.3. The proposed CP-TFET structure in ambipolar state exhibits BTBT generation rate of 1.53×10^{13} $cm^{-3}s^{-1}$ and 4.47×10^{12} $cm^{-3}s^{-1}$ respectively. It is noteworthy to mention that the hBTBT rate for CP-TFET is 1-decade lesser than that of DG-TFET helps eliminating ambipolar current.

L_{SG} variation

Figure 53.4(a) shows the horizontal electric field of CP-TFET with the variation in spacing length between source-gate electrodes (L_{sg}). CP-TFET with $L_{sg} = 2$ nm shows higher electric field of 5.7MV/cm for $V_{gs} = 1V$ near source-channel interface. This rise in electric field characteristics is because of the maximum depletion at $L_{sg} = 2$ nm, which is helpful in tunneling barrier width reduction. As a result of this, large number of charge carriers can tunnel across the junction. As we go on increasing the spacing length up to 5nm the electric field gradually decreases. For $L_{sg} = 1$nm lateral electric field found to be 4.7MV/cm, less than that of the peak electric field.

Moreover, the effect of variation of L_{sg} on BTBT generation rate and threshold voltage is reported in Figure 53.4(b). For an increasing value of L_{sg} from 2 nm to 5 nm BTBT generation rate degrade with the increment of tunneling barrier width. Maximum BTBT of 1.31×10^{28} $cm^{-3}s^{-1}$ is reported for $L_{sg} = 2$nm, which provide a higher amount of electron to tunnel through the source-channel junction. Similarly with the increasing value of L_{sg} threshold voltage gradually increases. It is reported from the above discussion that L_{sg} have a higher impact on drain current characteristics. ON current reduces drastically with increasing value of L_{sg}. Band to band tunneling distance increases that results with less number of charge carrier tunnels across the junction, thus drain current reduces. Maximum drain current of 1.91×10^{-8} A/μm is achieved for L_{sg} 2 nm shown in Figure 53.4(c). For enhanced performance of the device L_{sg} is optimized to 2nm. It is to be mentioned here that the variation of L_{sg} has no impact on ambipolar characteristics of the device. So, the ambipolar current is unaltered with the variation of L_{sg}.

L_{GD} variation

Another important parameter responsible for significant impact on ambipolar

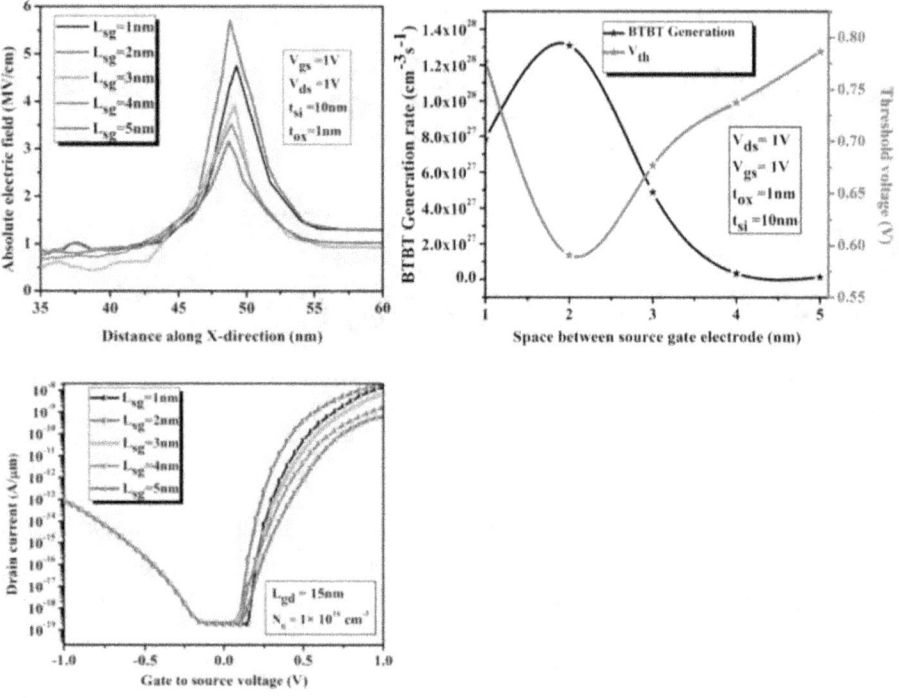

Figure 53.4 (a) Effect of L_{SG} variation on electric field profile of CP-TFET (b). L_{sg} variation effect on BTBT and Threshold voltage characteristics of CP-TFET (c). Effect of L_{sg} variation on transfer characteristics of CP-TFET
Source: Author

characteristics of the device is the spacing between channel-drain electrode (L_{gd}). Absolute electric field profile of the proposed structure for the L_{gd} variation from 13 nm to 20 nm is shown in Figure 53.5(a). For increasing length of L_{gd}, we obtain reduction in lateral electric field. This intern reduces the tunneling of charge carriers from drain to the channel region. Thus, ambipolar current of the device gradually reduces as we go on increasing the L_{gd} value shown in Figure 53.5(b). Variation in L_{gd} results with a varied depletion region at channel-drain interface, restricting the flow of holes from drain to channel region. Thus, ambipolar current is reduced to 1.91×10^{-15} A/μm for L_{gd} = 20 nm with constant L_{sg} of 2 nm.

To understand the dependency on variation of gate oxide thickness (t_{ox}), Figure 53.6(a) shows the transfer characteristics plot of the structure under oxide variation. In this respect t_{ox} is chosen 1nm, 1.5nm and 2nm with t_{si} = 10nm. Both the ON and ambipolar current are analyzed for the change in oxide thickness. The ON state current drastically degrades with an increase in t_{ox}, because of the decrease in gate capacitance value. Highest ON current of 1.91×10^{-8} A/μm is achieved for t_{ox} 1nm, and it degrades by 1decade for each 0.5nm increase in oxide thickness. Oxide thickness variation has a greater impact on subthreshold characteristics of the device; SS gradually decreases with increase in t_{ox}. A very less variation is experienced for ambipolar current, with increase in t_{ox}. From this we conclude that switching ratio (I_{ON}/I_{OFF}) is also decrease with the increase in ON current.

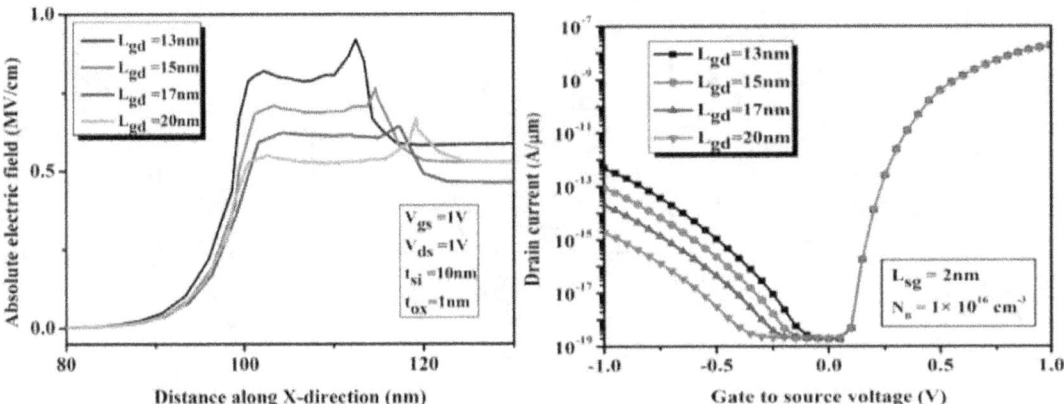

Figure 53.5 (a) Electric field analysis in ambipolar state by varying the spacing between channel-drain electrode (L_{gd}) (b) L_{gd} variation effect on transfer characteristics of CP-TFET
Source: Author

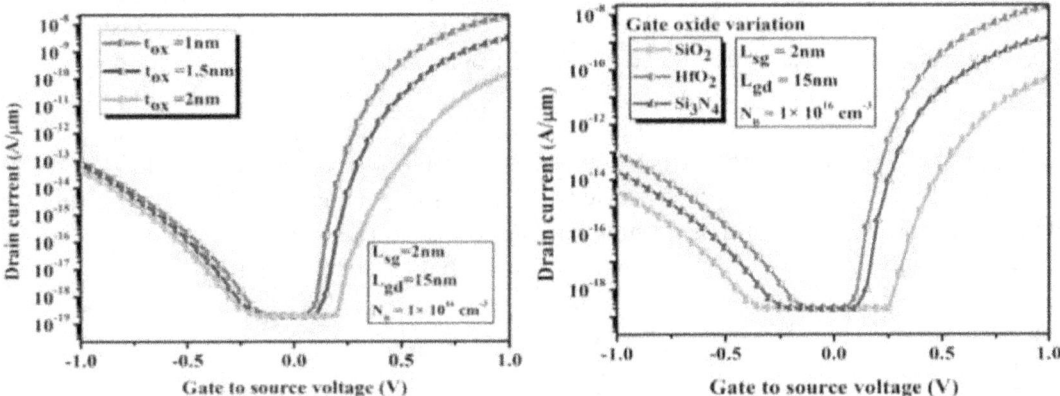

Figure 53.6 (a) Effect of dielectric material thickness (t_{ox}) variation on drain current characteristics of CP-TFET (b). Effect of dielectric material variation of CP-TFET
Source: Author

Figure 53.6(b) shows the impact of different dielectric material on transfer characteristics of the proposed structure. For simulation different dielectric material like HfO_2, Si_3N_4 and SiO_2 are chosen with dielectric constant of (k) 22, 7.5 and 3.9 respectively.

This section provides a clear idea of change in the current drain profile of the device under different contact metal work-function variations in respective regions. Out of that Figure 53.7(a) shows the influence of source metal work-function variation in ON and ambipolar state. The change in source contact metal work function (ϕ_S) alters the carrier concentration at source/channel interface. As we go on increasing ϕ_S from 5.3eV to 5.93eV, a greater number of electrons are accumulated at the interface. By the application of proper gate bias higher electric field is generated at interface, which helps tunneling faster. So, an ON current of 1.9×10^{-8} A/μm

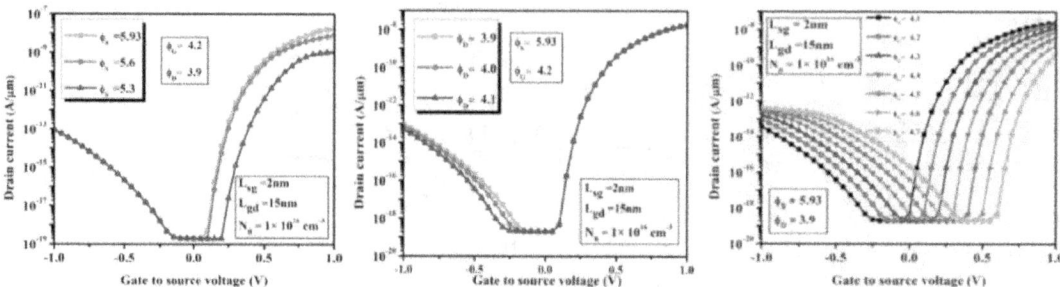

Figure 53.7 (a) source metal work-function variation effect (b). Drain metal work-function variation effect (c). Gate metal work-function variation effect
Source: Author

is achieved for ϕ_S = 5.93eV. Reduced value of ϕ_S gradually decreases the drain current by 1-decade. Source metal work-function (ϕ_S) has no effect on OFF and ambipolar current behavior, so it's OFF and ambipolar current are unaltered throughout the variation. Similarly, the effect of ϕ_D on current characteristics of the proposed device with constant ϕ_S and ϕ_G is shown in Figure 53.7(b). From the graph is clear that the drain work-function has nothing to do with the ON current and OFF current. It remained unaltered for positive V_{gs}, but when we apply V_{gs} = -1V a very less variation of ambipolar current is noticed from 4.88×10^{-14} A/μm to 8.94×10^{-14} A/μm when ϕ_D changes from 4.1eV to 3. 9eV. This negligible improvement in ambipolar current is possible by enhancing the tunnelling barrier width at junction region with the application of greater ϕ_D value.

Conclusion

The concept of charge-plasma TFET device was studied again by considering the physical parameter variation effect into account. The impact of L_{sg} on drain current and L_{gd} on ambipolar characteristics are analyzed in detail by considering its electric field profile. It is to be noteworthy that L_{sg} and L_{gd} are two important parameters, affecting

the junction abruptness. Thus, the device shows variable characteristics. Along with that, this paper focuses on varying different device parameters such as gate oxide thickness (t_{ox}), gate dielectric constant variation, contact metal work-function variation (φ_S, φ_D, φ_G), and channel length reduction effect on drain current characteristics of the CP-TFET is analyzed in detail. This study of charge-plasma TFET helps revisiting its physical parameter to build a new device with better performance.

References

[1] Boucart, K., & Ionescu, A. M. (2007). Double-gate tunnel FET with high-k gate dielectric. *IEEE Transactions on Electron Devices*, 54(7), 1725–1733.

[2] Colinge, J. P., Lee, C. W., Afzalian, A., Akhavan, N. D., Yan, R., Ferain, I., et al. (2010). Nanowire transistors without junctions. *Nature Nanotechnology*, 5(3), 225–229.

[3] Moore, G. E. (2006). Cramming more components onto integrated circuits. (Reprinted from Electronics, 38(8), 114–117, April 19, 1965). *IEEE Solid-State Circuits Society Newsletter*, 11(3), 33–35. https://doi.org/10.1109/N-SSC.2006.4785860

[4] Kumar, M. J., & Janardhanan, S. (2013). Doping-less tunnel field effect transistor: design and investigation. *IEEE*

Transactions on Electron Devices, 60(10), 3285–3290.

[5] Hueting, R. J. E., Rajasekharan, B., Salm, C., & Schmitz, J. (2008). The charge plasma P-N diode. *IEEE Electron Device Letters*, 29, 1367–1369.

[6] Lee, C. W., Afzalian, A., Akhavan, N. D., Yan, R., Ferain, I., & Colinge, J. P. (2009). Junctionless multigate field-effect transistor. *Applied Physics Letters*, 94(5).

[7] Joshi, T., Singh, Y., & Singh, B. (2019). Dual-channel trench-gate tunnel FET for improved ON-current and subthreshold swing. *Electronics Letters*, 55(21), 1152–1155.

[8] Baruah, R. K., & Paily, R. P. (2014). A dual-material gate junctionless transistor with high-*k* spacer for enhanced analog performance. *IEEE Transactions on Electron Devices*, 61(1), 123–128.

[9] Hueting, R. J. E., Rajasekharan, B., Salm, C., & Schmitz, J. (2008). The charge plasma P-N diode. *IEEE Electron Device Letters*, 29(12), 1367–1368.

[10] Sahu, C., & Singh, J. (2014). Charge-plasma based process variation immune junctionless transistor. *IEEE Electron Device Letters*, 35, 411–413.

[11] Rajasekharan, B., Hueting, R. J. E., Salm, C., van Hemert, T., Wolters, R. A. M., & Schmitz, J. (2010). Fabrication and characterization of the charge-plasma diode. *IEEE Electron Device Letters*, 31(6), 528–530.

[12] Sahu, C., & Singh, J. (2014). Charge-plasma based process variation immune junctionless transistor. *IEEE Electron Device Letters*, 35(3), 411–413.

[13] Angelin Delighta, A., Binola, K., Jebalin, I. V., Ajayan J., Angen Franklin, S., & Nirmal D. (2024). A new vertical c-shaped silicon channel nanosheet FET with stacked high-k dielectrics for low power applications. *Silicon*, 16(6), 2659–2670.

[14] Kumar, N., & Raman, A. (2019). Design and investigation of charge-plasma-based work-function engineered dual-metal heterogeneous-gate Si–Si$_{0.55}$Ge$_{0.45}$ GAA cylindrical NWTFET for ambipolar analysis. *IEEE Transactions on Electron Devices*, 66(3), 1468–1474. https://doi.org/10.1109/TED.2019.2893224

[15] Samal, A., Pradhan, K. P., & Mohapatra, S. K. (2021). Improvising the switching ratio through Low-k / high-k spacer and dielectric gate stack in 3d finfet - a simulation perspective. *Silicon*, 13, 2655–2660.

[16] Kumar, K., Reddy, C. H., Babu, D. R., Kumar, V., Kumar, A., & Jain, A. (2025). Design Innovations in TFETS: enhancing performance and sensitivity through charged plasma, dual-gate, and work function techniques. In 2025 3rd International Conference on Device Intelligence, Computing and Communication Technologies (DICCT), Dehradun, India, (pp. 679–683).

[17] Panda, S., & Dash, S. (2023). Performance investigation of a charge plasma tunnel FET with SiGe source pocket as a photosensor. *Semiconductor Science and Technology*, 38, 035016.

[18] Sentaurus Device User Guide (2022). Version t-2022,03, Synopsys. Inc. (Mountain View, CA, USA).

[19] Goswami, P. P., & Bhowmick, B. (2020). Optimization of electrical parameters of pocket doped SOI TFET with L-shaped gate. *Silicon*, 12(3), 693–700.

54 Design and performance analysis of low power single-phase clock dual-edge triggered D flip-flop based on GDI

Tharun Kumar, R.[a], Srujan B. N.[b], Raghavendra Sherkhane[c] and Premananda, B. S.[d]

Department of ETE, RV College of Engineering, Bangalore, Karnataka, India

Abstract

The escalating demand for energy-efficient and high-performance VLSI systems has led to a growing interest in dual-edge triggered D flip-flops (DET-DFFs), which can sample data on both rising and falling edges of the clock signal. This feature reduces clock frequency without compromising data throughput by minimizing dynamic power consumption. However, traditional single-edge triggered flip-flops (SETFFs) require higher clock frequencies to meet similar performance levels, resulting in increased power dissipation, clock loading, and propagation delay. Moreover, the clock distribution network in SETFF-based architectures can account for 30% to 60% of the total power consumption in a circuit. This work presents a low-power DET DFF architecture based on the gate diffusion input (GDI) technique, optimized for single-phase clock operation. The primary objective is to reduce power dissipation while maintaining high-speed performance and minimal area overhead. The proposed design is modeled and simulated using Cadence Virtuoso Spectre at a CMOS 28 nm technology node. Power delay product (PDP) helps to understand the amount of energy required per operation, the results infer lesser PDP.

Keywords: Dual edge triggered D flip-flop, gate diffusion input, lower power VLSI, power delay product, single edge triggered flip-flop

Introduction

Latches and flip-flops are important memory elements, where latches are level-triggered and Flip-Flops are edge-triggered, they store the data along with synchronizing the data to CLK. Traditionally, single-edge triggered designs are designed to operate only during the rising edge or the falling edge. As a result, the clock frequency of the design increases in order to maintain the same data throughput as DET DFFs, with the increase in frequency, delay, and power consumption also increasing. Hence clock distribution network is a major contributor to power dissipation, so reducing power dissipation related to CLK networks is a major design challenge in low-power VLSI designs. To address this issue, DET DFF has been developed that captures data on both rising and falling edges, so it ensures operate at half the clock frequency as compared to SETFF while doubling the data throughput and minimizing the power dissipation. DET DFFs are extremely crucial in high-speed digital signal processing systems.

[a]tharunkumar1917@gmail.com, [b]srujanbn1@gmail.com, [c]raghavendrasherkhane93@gmail.com, [d]premanandabs@gmail.com

DOI: 10.1201/9781003753391-54

The proposed work focuses on implementing DET DFFs based on GDI technology. GDI is a low-power digital circuits design approach, where the common gate inputs of both p-MOSFET and n-MOSFET are connected to a single terminal. Work by Mukherjee and Ghosal [1] implemented DET DFF based on GDI by incorporating two-phase clock signals, which enables both positive and negative latches to accept the data during both levels of the CLK.

The proposed design tries to minimize this power consumption by introducing a single-phase CLK signal, which eliminates the need for an inverted CLK signal. Simulation results show a 98% reduction in power dissipation as compared to Mukherjee and Ghosal [1].

The rest of the paper is divided as follows: The second section focuses on the Literature Review, which gives an overview of the previous works done related to the DET-DFFs. The third section focuses on the detailed Methodology and Implementation of the proposed work realized in Cadence Virtuoso at the CMOS 28nm technology node. The fourth section highlights the results achieved after simulating the proposed design in Cadence Spectre. The paper concludes with the conclusion and future Scope, highlighting the need for low-power techniques.

Literature Review

In recent years, the focus on designing flip-flops that consume less power and offer high performance has been one of the research areas within the VLSI design community. An efficient design approach to model DET DFFs has been discussed in detail in [1] by incorporating GDI logic and transmission gates (TG). Followed Premananda et al. [2], implemented an adaptive voltage level source with true single-phase clock (AVLS-TSPC) flip-flop, mainly focused on minimizing the power dissipation while maintaining the timing constraints. The work proposed utilized a clock branch sharing technique to reduce the redundant transitions of the clock distribution network [3]. The concept of AVLS-TSPC was extended in designing frequency divider circuits [4]. The design included more enhancements to the AVLS-TSPC flip-flop by lowering short-circuit power and ensuring stable operation under different loading conditions [5]. Building on this idea, adapted AVLS-TSPC-based flip-flops to phase detector circuits, where precise timing control is essential, while other explored similar implementations for frequency synthesizers to reduce the total clock power overhead [6, 7].

An early contribution to DET-DFF design is found by Dhivya et al. [8], which proposed an architecture optimized for reducing energy at a time when dual-edge triggering was still a developing concept. A different methodology was explored by Premananda et al. [9], where a sense amplifier-based DET-DFF was designed to improve both speed and power metrics, especially in critical timing paths. A low-swing clock DET-DFF was proposed, focusing on minimizing voltage swing in clock signals to reduce dynamic power losses and clock-induced noise [10]. A foundational reference for GDI logic [11], which introduced the GDI technique to reduce transistor count and switching activity in digital logic, significantly contributing to power and area savings. The practical applications and variations of GDI circuits were further explored [12], offering a wide-ranging review of how GDI has been used to enhance performance in modern low-power systems.

Finally, Ganavi and Premananda [13] provided one of the earliest theoretical treatments of dual-edge triggering, laying the groundwork for modern DET-DFF development by showing the inherent benefits of capturing data on both clock transitions. In summary, the literature reviewed [1, 15] highlights the evolution of approaches focused on optimizing flip-flop designs for improved energy efficiency, speed, and area compactness. While approaches such as AVLS-TSPC, sense amplifier-based architectures, and low-swing clocking each provide meaningful advancements, the GDI-TG-based DET-DFF outlined remains a standout for its balanced trade-offs and practical benefits in current low-power VLSI systems [1].

Conventional Techniques for DET DFF Design

Conventional DET-DFFs are designed using two latches: a positive latch and a negative latch, along with a multiplexer (MUX) to ensure data is captured on both edges of the clock signal, which is depicted in Figure 54.1. The operation is based on the fact that when the clock (CLK) is high (1), the positive latch is enabled, allowing it to store the input data (D). Simultaneously, the clock is inverted using an inverter, making $\overline{CLK}$ low (0), which enables the negative latch at the same time. The MUX ensures that only one latch's output is selected at any given moment.

DET DFF Based on GDI

A 2-to-1 multiplexer (MUX) using Gate Diffusion Input (GDI) technology is realized in Figure 54.2, designed for low-power digital circuits. It has two data inputs (D0 and D1) and a selection signal (CLK) that determines which input is passed to the output. When CLK = 0, the pMOS transistor turns ON, allowing D0 to reach the output, while the nMOS transistor remains OFF, blocking D1. In contrast, when CLK = 1, the pMOS transistor turns OFF and the nMOS transistor turns ON, so it enables input D1 to be latched into the multiplexer through nMOS. A buffer is used to ensure full swing, which helps in maintaining signal integrity at the output.

Positive latch based on GDI

The GDI-based circuit in Figure 54.3 can be made to function as a positive latch by incorporating pMOS and nMOS to control the flow of data and a buffer to restore the output. When CLK is logic high (CLK = 1), pMOSFET is in the cut-off region and nMOSFET is in the active region. As a result, the input data, which is given

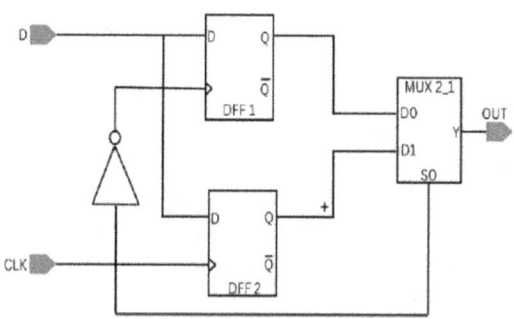

Figure 54.1 Conventional DET-DFF realized using D latches
Source: Author

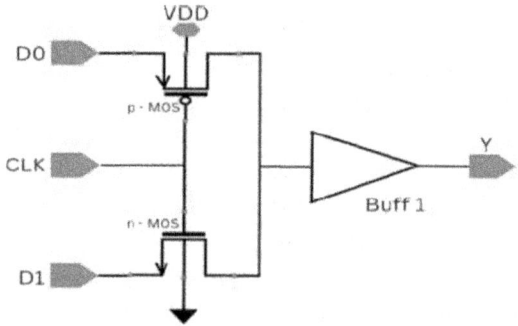

Figure 54.2 Multiplexer latch-based GDI
Source: Author

through nMOS, is latched, making the latch transparent during the logic high of the CLK signal.

When CLK is logic low (CLK = 0), the pMOS transistor is turned ON and nMOS transistor is in cut-off condition as a result the data is isolated from the latch and the feedback loop consisting of pMOSFET is closed, ensures the latch to be in hold mode during logic low level of CLK signal. This logic preservation mechanism ensures data stability and reduces unwanted transitions at the output. A buffer is employed at the output, which guarantees full swing of signal levels at the output, which is essential to interpret correct logic levels at the output, in the event of signal degradation due to pass transistors [14].

Negative latch based on GDI

The GDI-based circuit in Figure 54.3 can function as a negative latch by integrating pMOS and nMOS to control the flow of data and a buffer to restore the output as shown in Figure 54.4 [1]. When CLK is logic high (CLK = 0), pMOSFET is enabled and nMOSFET is disabled; as a result, the

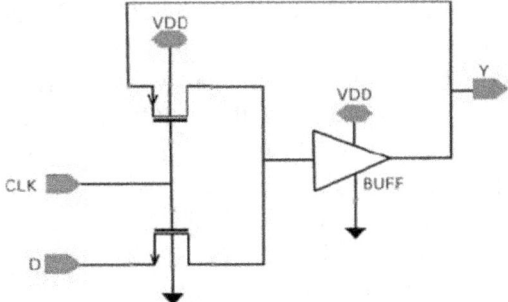

Figure 54.3 Positive latch based on GDI
Source: Author

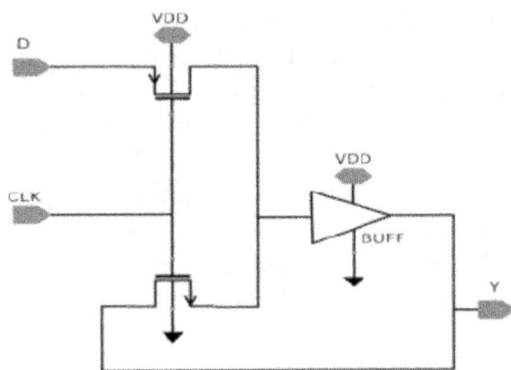

Figure 54.4 Negative latch based on GDI
Source: Author

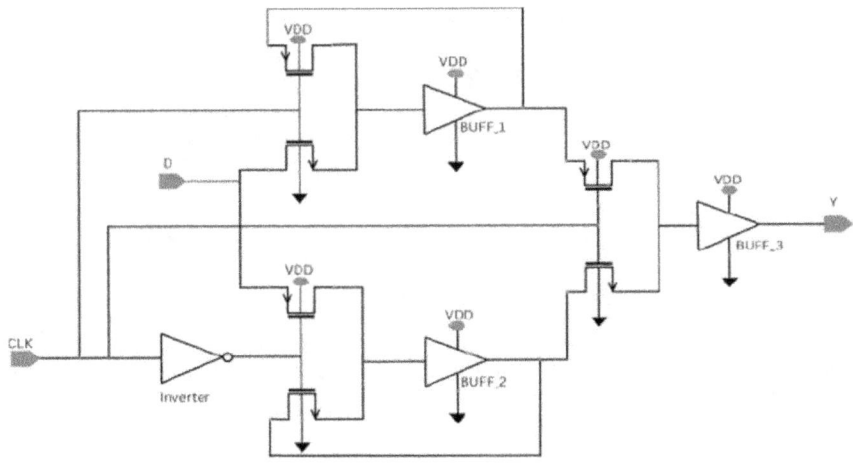

Figure 54.5 DETFF is based on GDI
Source: Author

input data, which is given through pMOS, is latched, making the latch transparent during logic low of the CLK signal. When CLK is logic high (CLK = 1), the nMOS transistor is turned ON and pMOS transistor is in cut-off condition as a result the data is isolated from the latch and the feedback loop consisting of nMOSFET is closed, ensures the latch to be in hold mode during logic low level of CLK signal.

DETFF based on GDI
The design in Figure 54.5 incorporates GDI logic to design DET DFF, which significantly reduces the power dissipation and the transistor count as compared to traditional design techniques of DET DFF. The proposed work aims to design the same DET DFF with a single-phase CLK signal, eliminating the need for an inverter to generate the inverted CLK signal. The design in Figure 54.5 was latching the data to both latches at every CLK transition, but the

mux was selecting the data from one of the latches.

The proposed design (Figure 54.6) aims to reduce the unwanted CLK transitions by incorporating only a single-phase CLK signal by eliminating the need for an inverted CLK signal where only one of the latches are enabled in either of the CLK edges. Both designs were simulated under the same design constraints to obtain identical waveforms, but with a 98% reduction in power dissipation in the proposed design, since there is no overhead of generating inverted CLK signal. The proposed DET-DFF is designed to improve power efficiency by eliminating the need for an inverter and ensuring that only one latch is enabled per clock edge. This approach reduces power consumption compared to conventional DET-DFF designs, where both latches latch data on every clock transition. The circuit consists of three major components: a positive latch (CLK = 1), a negative latch (CLK = 0),

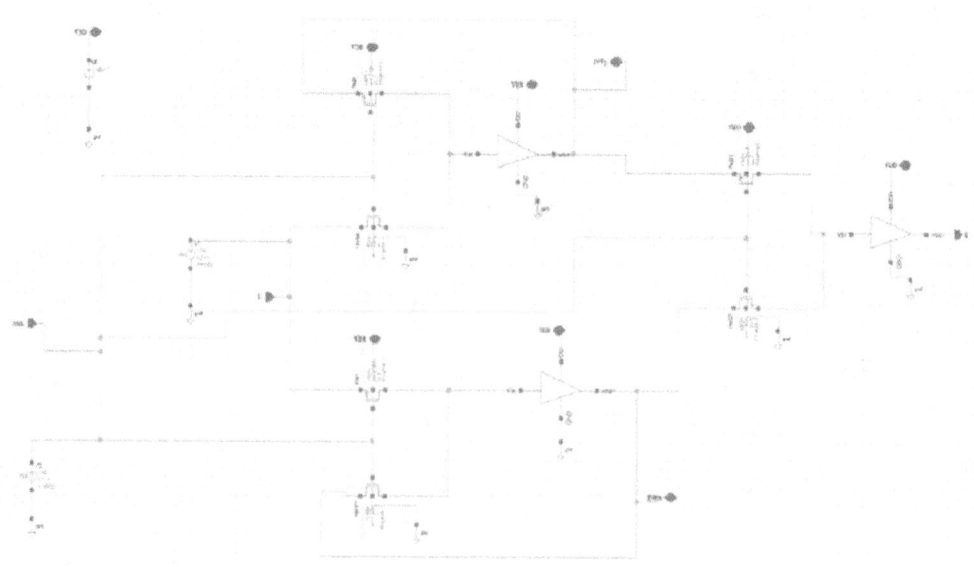

Figure 54.6 Proposed DET-DFF
Source: Author

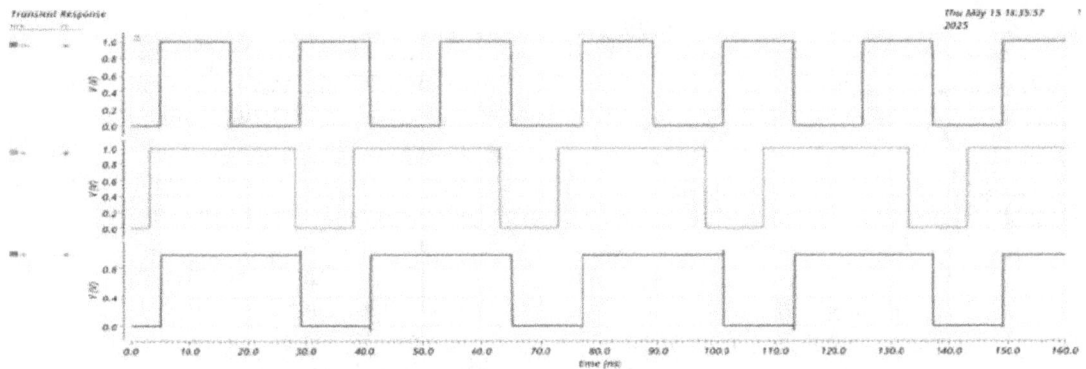

Figure 54.7 Output waveform of proposed DET-DFF
Source: Author

Table 54.1 Performance analysis of the DET DFF.

DET-DFF	Power (µW)	Delay (ns)	PDP (fJ)
[1]	95.99	6.56	629.69
Proposed-I	1.89	6.8	12.85

Source: Author

and a 2:1 multiplexer (MUX) for output selection.

Results and Discussions

The proposed circuit was built in Cadence Virtuoso and simulated in the Cadence Spectre using the CMOS 28 nm technology node with a gate length of 60nm. The output of DET-DFF is simulated in the Figure 54.7, it consists of two opposite latches (positive and negative latch) whose outputs are multiplexed with the help of a 2:1 multiplexer during logic high of the CLK, positive latch is in propagation mode and negative latch is in hold mode, and vice-versa when CLK is logic low.

Table 54.1 provides a comparison of power and delay parameters for two DET-D flip-flop designs operating at a supply voltage of 1 V. The conventional DET-DFF based on gate diffusion input (GDI) [1] exhibits a power consumption of 95.99 µW, with rise and fall delays of 7.12 ns and 6.1 ns, respectively, resulting in an average delay of 6.56 ns. In contrast, the single-phase clock DET-DFF based on GDI demonstrates a significantly reduced power consumption of 1.89 µW, while maintaining comparable timing performance with an average delay of 6.8 ns.

Conclusion

The results from the simulation demonstrated that the proposed DET-DFF achieves a lower PDP compared to the reference design. The PDP has significantly decreased, indicating a 97.95% improvement in energy efficiency per switching event. Despite the slight increase in delay, the proposed DET-DFF demonstrated a substantial improvement in power efficiency and energy consumption. Specifically, the power consumption is reduced up to 98%, hence the overall performance gain in terms of PDP makes the proposed design highly suitable for ultra-low power applications. Overall, the proposed DET-DFF offers a robust solution for low-power applications. The further work involves optimizing the proposed design by incorporating low-power techniques and minimizing the delay to be used in low-power, high-speed applications.

References

[1] Mukherjee, B., & Ghosal, A. (2017). Design and implementation of low power dual edge triggered flip-flop using GDI and TG for high-speed FIR filter. In Devices for Integrated Circuit, (pp. 652–657).

[2] Premananda, B. S., Rehman, A., & Megha, P. (2024). Area and power efficient AVLS-TSPC-based diffused bit generator for key generation. *Circuits, Systems, and Signal Processing*, 43, 3103–3117.

[3] Zhao, P., McNeely, J., Golconda, P., Bayoumi, M. A., Barcenas, R. A., & Kuang, W. (2007). Low power clock branch sharing dual-edge triggered flip-flop. *IEEE Transactions on Very Large-Scale Integration Systems*, 15(3), 338–345.

[4] Siddaiah, P. B., Narsepalli, S., Mittal, S., & Rehman, A. (2023). Area and power efficient divide-by-32/33 dual-modulus pre-scaler using split-path TSPC with AVLS for frequency divider. *Journal of Electrical Engineering*, 22(1), 109–118.

[5] Premananda, B. S., Nikhil, K. J., & Managoli, S. H. (2022). Low power square root carry select adder using AVLS-TSPC-based D flip-flop. *Electrical Journal*, 22(1), 109–118.

[6] Premananda, B. S., & Sreedhar, S. (2022). Low-power phase frequency detector using hybrid AVLS and LECTOR techniques for low-power PLL. *Advances in Electrical and Electronic Engineering*, 20(3), 294–303.

[7] Massoud, P., Qing, W., & Xunwei, W. (1998). A new design for double-edge triggered flip-flop. In Asia and South Pacific Design Automation Conference, (pp. 417–421).

[8] Dhivya, S. P., Nirmal Kumar, R., Vijaysalini, P., & Tamilselvan, G. M. (2013). Design of low power highly performing dual-edge triggered sense amplifier flip-flops. *International Journal of Emerging Technology and Advanced Engineering*, 3(1), 259–262.

[9] Premananda, B. S., Chandana, M. K., Shree Lakshmi, K. P., & Keerthi, A. M. (2017). Design of low power 8-bit carry select adder using adiabatic logic. In International Conference on Communication and Signal Processing, (pp. 1764–1768).

[10] Premananda, B. S., Sahithi, N., & Mittal, S. (2023). AVLS-based 32/33 pre-scaler for frequency dividers. *e-Prime - Advances in Electrical Engineering, Electronics and Energy*, 4, 1–5.

[11] Verma, P., & Manchanda, R. (2014). Review of various GDI techniques for low power digital circuits. *International Journal of Emerging Technology and Advanced Engineering*, 4(2), 387–390.

[12] Unger, S. H. (1981). Double-edge-triggered flip-flops. *IEEE Transaction on Computers*, 30(6), 447–451.

[13] Ganavi, M. G., & Premananda, B. S. (2018). Design of low-power square root carry select adder and wallace tree multiplier using adiabatic logic. *Springer Lecture Notes in Electrical Engineering*, 545, 767–781.

[14] Archit, B., Anurag, A. R., Shakthivel, G., & Premananda, B. S. (2018). Design of low power and high-speed 16-bit square root carry select adder using AL. In International Conference on Circuits, Control, Communication and Computing, (pp. 1–4).

[15] Ganavi, M. G., & Premananda, B. S. (2018). Design of low power reduced complexity wallace tree multiplier using positive feedback adiabatic logic. In Springer Advances in Intelligent Systems and Computing Book Series, (Vol. 1089, pp. 139–150).

55 Non-linear functions approximation using neural network with CORDIC-based implementation

Kratika Bansal[a] and Satyasai Jagannath Nanda[b]

Department of Electronics and Communication Engineering, Malaviya National Institute of Technology, Jaipur, Rajasthan, India

Abstract

This manuscript presents a hardware-efficient neural network implementation for approximating transcendental functions (sine, exponential, logarithmic) and polynomial functions (cubic) through a novel integration of hyperbolic tangent (tanh) activation and the coordinate rotation digital computer (CORDIC) algorithms. The proposed methodology develops a MATLAB-based training framework with hardware-aware optimization, followed by quantization and deployment to Verilog HDL for digital hardware implementation. A key innovation involves replacing traditional lookup-table approaches with CORDIC-optimized tanh activation, achieving 90.2% functional equivalence with software references while reducing hardware resource utilization by 38.7%. The study establishes a complete workflow from floating-point training to fixed-point hardware realization, including comparative analysis of approximation errors (MSE lower than 0.0015 for target functions) and implementation efficiency metrics. Experimental results demonstrate the effectiveness of this co-design approach in maintaining mathematical fidelity while optimizing embedded system constraints, with applications in real-time signal processing and low-power computing. The work contributes both a reproducible framework for neural network hardware acceleration and empirical validation of CORDIC enhanced activation functions in function approximation tasks.

Keywords: Coordinate rotation digital computer, hyperbolic tangent activation function, neural network implementation, nonlinear function approximation

Introduction

Artificial neural networks (ANNs) are powerful tools for approximating nonlinear functions and are widely employed in signal processing, control systems, and embedded hardware due to their learning capabilities. Unlike traditional numerical methods, ANNs effectively model complex mappings such as sine, exponential, cubic, and logarithmic functions. However, deploying trained ANNs on hardware presents challenges, including limited precision and resource constraints. Activation functions like tanh are computationally demanding in hardware, especially with floating-point arithmetic.

Researchers in last decade have reported several advancements in neural network hardware implementation. Tiwari and Khare [8] pioneered coordinate rotation digital computer (CORDIC)-based sigmoidal activation functions on FPGAs, while Qian [3] optimized VLSI designs using similar approaches. Subsequent work by Shen et al. [7] achieved 2X speedups in RNN acceleration through unified CORDIC architectures. Alternative methods include Zamanlooy and Mirhassani's [10] area-efficient VLSI

---

[a]2023pev5353@mnit.ac.in, [b]sjnanda.ece@mnit.ac.in

DOI: 10.1201/9781003753391-55

implementation and Hajduk [1] comprehensive analysis of approximation techniques, later refined in Hajduk and Dec [2] to achieve CORDIC-comparable precision via polynomial methods. In order to have Low-power designs feature Raut et al. [6] resource-optimized the CORDIC variant. Yousif et al. [9] ROM-based approach achieves 30% power reduction for implementation. Ratnakumar and Nanda [4] reported the VLSI implementation for unsupervised learning algorithm. Nature inspired algorithm termed as roller dung beetles is used for unsupervised learning and its VLSI architecture is reported in Ratnakumar and Nanda, [5].

In this manuscript we have implemented a feedforward neural network trained in MATLAB using the tanh activation, then translate its fixed-point parameters to a Verilog-based hardware model. This work leverages the CORDIC algorithm to efficiently realize the tanh function using only shift-add operations, enabling low-power, area-efficient hardware implementation. Our analysis confirms the functional consistency between the MATLAB model and the hardware design, providing insights into quantization effects and the viability of CORDIC-based neural networks for embedded applications.

The rest of the paper is organized as follows: Section 2 details the methodology, including network architecture, training in MATLAB, and Verilog implementation. Section 3 presents the experimental result. Section 4 concludes the paper key findings and future research directions.

Methodology

This research follows a three-stage methodology: neural network training, hardware implementation, and performance evaluation. A single-hidden-layer feedforward neural network with tanh activation as shown

in Figure 55.1 is first trained in MATLAB using backpropagation to approximate nonlinear functions such as sine, cubic, exponential, and logarithmic. The trained weights and biases are then quantized to fixed-point format for hardware use.

In the hardware stage, a functionally equivalent Verilog design is developed using quantized parameters. To efficiently implement the tanh activation, a CORDIC algorithm is used, enabling shift-add-only computation and reducing hardware complexity. Finally, the outputs from the MATLAB model, Verilog implementation, and true function values are compared using absolute and relative error metrics to assess approximation accuracy and the impact of fixed-point quantization.

CORDIC algorithm overview

The CORDIC algorithm is a shift-add iterative method used for computing a wide range of elementary functions, including trigonometric, hyperbolic, and exponential functions. In this work, the CORDIC algorithm is adopted to implement the hyperbolic tangent (tanh) activation function in

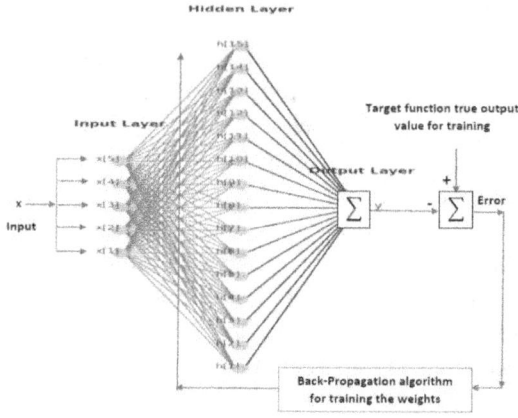

Figure 55.1 Block diagram of 1-5-15-1 neural network architecture implementation for sine function approximation

Source: Author

fixed-point arithmetic, replacing traditional piecewise approximations to achieve efficient hardware realization.

The CORDIC algorithm operates in vectoring mode for hyperbolic functions, where it iteratively rotates a vector toward the x-axis while accumulating the hyperbolic angle that corresponds to the rotation. For (tanh) computation, the algorithm begins with a pre-scaled input (x), and iteratively updates three variables x_i, y_i, and z_i using shift and add operations based on the iteration index.

The core update equations in the hyperbolic vectoring mode are:

$$x_{i+1} = x_i + d_i \cdot y_i \cdot 2^{-i}$$

$$y_{i+1} = y_i + d_i \cdot x_i \cdot 2^{-i}$$

$$z_{i+1} = z_i - d_i \cdot tanh^{-1}(2^{-i})$$

Where $d_i = Sign(d_i)$ and $tanh^{-1}(2^{-i})$ values are precomputed and stored in a lookup table.

After a fixed number of iterations N, the value of tanh(x) is approximated as:

$$\tanh(x) \approx \frac{y_N}{x_N}$$

This approach eliminates the need for multipliers or division units, making it well-suited for FPGA or ASIC-based neural network implementations where area and power constraints are critical.

By integrating the CORDIC-based tanh(x) activation function into the Verilog neural network model, the design achieves significant improvements in hardware efficiency while maintaining functional accuracy, thus supporting real-time inference in resource-constrained environments.

Implementation

The hardware implementation adopts function-specific neural network topologies

optimized through empirical evaluation. For sine approximation, a 1-5-15-1 network using tanh(x) activation function achieves under 0.1% mean relative error over the [-π, π] range. Exponential and logarithmic functions use a 1-5-20-1 architecture to handle steeper nonlinearities, while a 1-5-10-1 configuration suffices for cubic functions due to their polynomial nature. All networks share a linear output neuron and unified 16-bit fixed-point arithmetic.

To maximize parallelism while minimizing resource usage, all implementations replicate the single input neuron's value five times as shown in Figure 55.2, effectively creating five identical features before the hidden layer computation. This hardware-specific optimization aligns with the weight matrix dimensions $W_1[5]N_h$, where N_h = 15,20 or 10 depending on the function, and enables full utilization of the six parallel MAC units while reducing memory access conflicts without increasing the logical input size.

Exponential/logarithmic functions use Q4.8 format with log-domain tuning, and cubic approximations employ Q3.13 direct mapping. Training is performed in MATLAB using Levenberg-Marquardt backpropagation on 10,000 uniform samples with α = 0.05 and β = 0.9.

The compute pipeline features a reconfigurable MAC array with six 8 x 8 Booth multipliers and 24-bit accumulators, enabling hidden layer evaluations in 2-4 cycles: 15 neurons in 3 cycles (sine), 20 in 4 (exp/log), and 10 in 2 (cubic), all leveraging 5-way parallelism. Activation is handled by a 14-stage CORDIC-{tanh} pipeline for sine (≤ 0.01 rad error) and a 12-stage variant for exp/log ($\leq 0.1\%$ error); cubic functions skip activation due to their linearity.

Verification uses a hierarchical testbench with 10000 inputs and tailored metrics: phase continuity for sine, edge-case

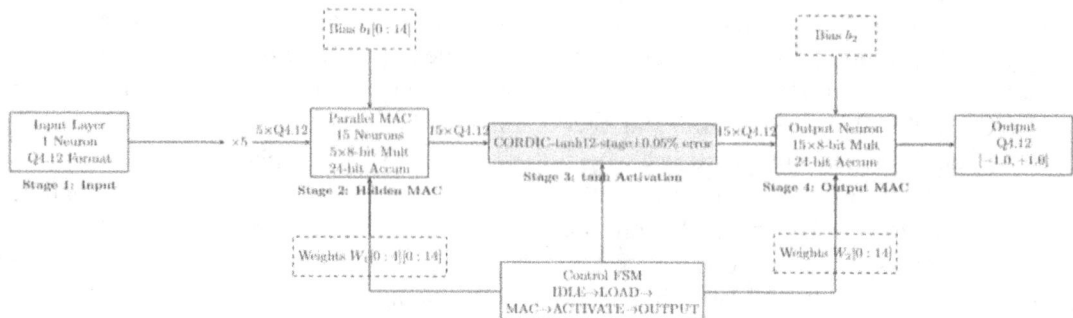

Figure 55.2 Block diagram of 1-5-15-1 neural network architecture CORDIC based Verilog implementation for sine function approximation
Source: Author

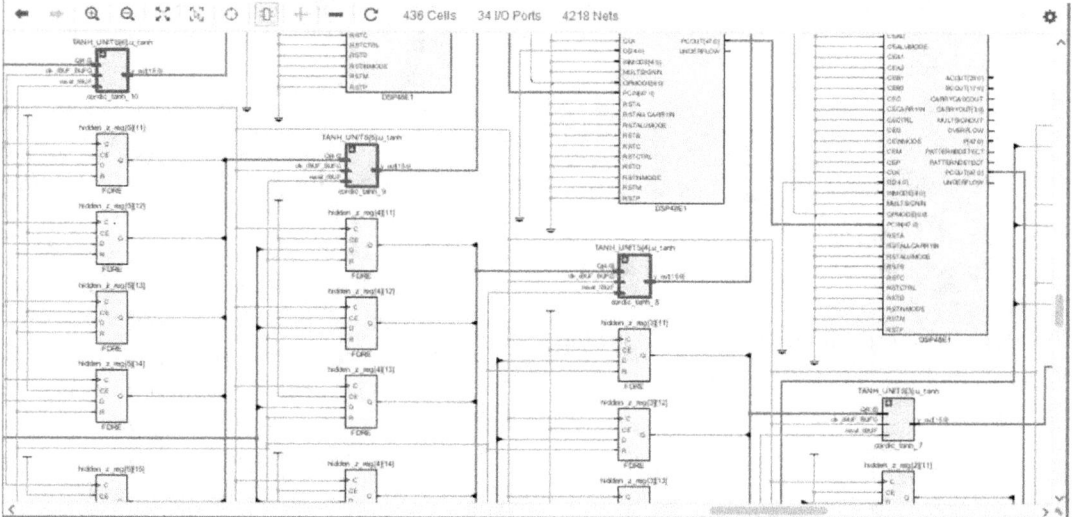

Figure 55.3 RTL Schematic of implementation of Figure 55.2 from input to the hidden layer, where instantiation of 15 parallel CORDIC modules (TANH_UNITS) is done that compute the non-linear activations
Source: Author

handling for exp/log, and derivative checks for cubic. All designs achieve lower than 0.5% error and consistent throughput of one sample per 3 cycles at 100 MHz.

Empirical Results

The proposed neural network architectures were evaluated for approximating four non-linear functions: sine, cubic, exponential, and logarithmic. Each function was modeled using a single-hidden-layer feedforward neural network trained in MATLAB, with the fixed-point implementation deployed in Verilog and simulated using Xilinx Vivado 2023.2.

Figure 55.2 shows the block diagram of the Verilog implementation for sine function approximation. It highlights the fixed-point datapath, multiply-accumulate units,

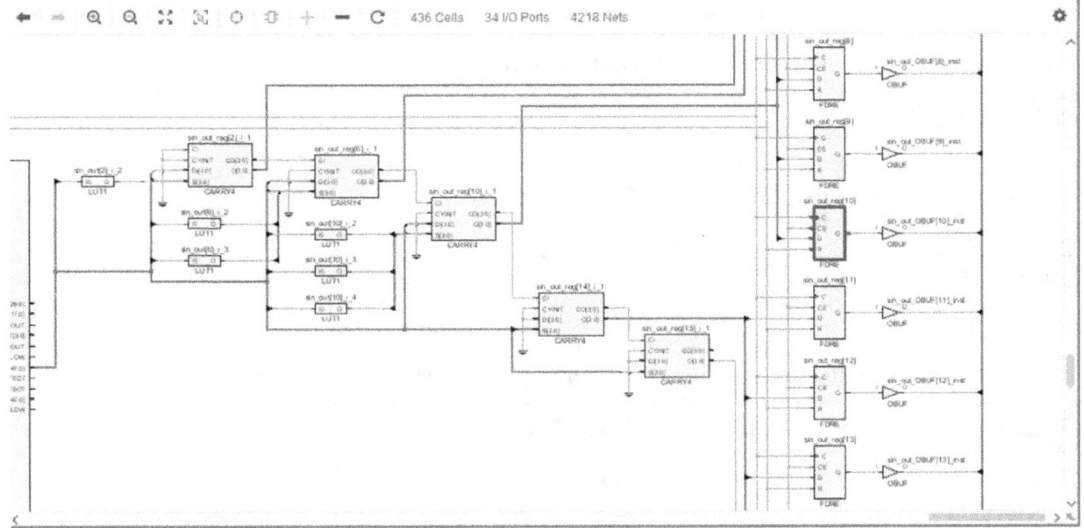

Figure 55.4 RTL Schematic of implementation of Figure 55.2 from hidden layer to the output layer summation, where LUTs and CARRY4 blocks are used for efficient fixed-point accumulation. The final result is latched and output through I/O buffers as sin_out
Source: Author

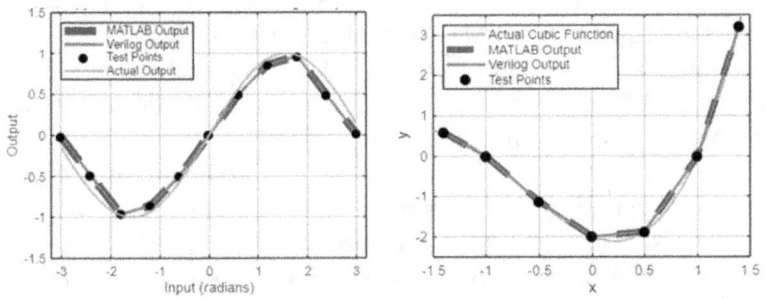

(a)Sine function over range $x \in [-\pi, \pi]$ (b) Cubic function over range $x \in [-2.8, 2.8]$

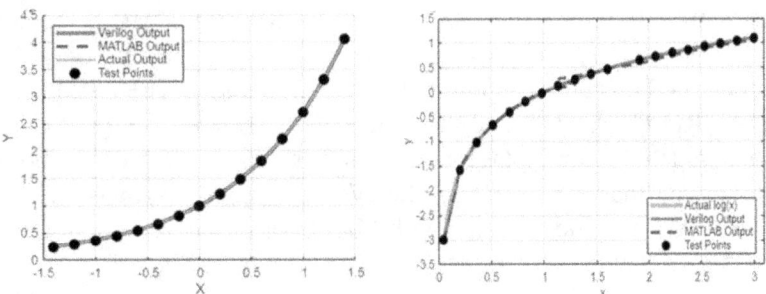

(c)Exponential function range $x \in [-1.5, 1.5]$ (d) Logarithmic function range $x \in [0.01, 3.01]$

Figure 55.5 Graphical comparison of Verilog output, MATLAB output, and actual values for all four nonlinear functions approximation with neural network implementation
Source: Author

Table 55.1 Relative errors reported for difference between MATLAB and Verilog implementation.

Function	Architecture	Maximum relative error	Mean relative error
Sine	1-5-15-1	0.12%	0.08%
Cubic	1-5-10-1	0.35%	0.26%
Exponential	1-5-20-1	0.90%	0.76%
Logarithmic	1-5-20-1	0.85%	0.73%

Source: Author

Table 55.2 Resource utilization summary of Verilog implementation of NN architectures.

Function	Hidden neurons	CORDIC Units	LUTs	DSPs	Flip flops
Sine	15	15	1842	32	1104
Cubic	10	10	1100	12	600
Exponential	20	20	2300	25	1200
Logarithmic	20	20	2200	24	1100

Source: Author

and the CORDIC pipeline used for evaluating the \texttt{tanh} activation in hardware. The same architecture, with minor adjustments, was used across the other functions depending on their respective network sizes and activation requirements.

The RTL schematic of the sine approximation neural network in Verilog is shown in Figures 55.3 and 55.4 portion wise. Figure 55.3 circuit depicts a single-hidden-layer neural network with 15 neurons using CORDIC-based tanh activation functions.

In case of the sine function, a 1-5-15-1 network was used with CORDIC-based {tanh} activation. Testing across 1000 input points in the range [-π, π] showed that the Verilog output matched MATLAB and the true sin(x) values closely, achieving a mean relative error of less than 0.1% as shown in Figure 55.5(a) presentation. In Cubic function approximation used a simpler 1-5-10-1 structure without activation due to the polynomial nature of the target function $= x^3 +$

$2x^2 - x - 2$. The Verilog output tracked both MATLAB and the analytical function with an error below 0.3% as presented in Figure 55.5(b). Here the weights are directly quantized to Q3.13 format.

Exponential and logarithmic functions, being more nonlinear, are modeled using a 1-5-20-1 architecture with CORDIC-{tanh} activations and Q4.8 fixed-point weights. For the exponential function, inputs were drawn from [-1.5, 1.5] using $x = 3$. (*rand*(1,N) $-$ 0.5), with $y = e^x$ as the target shown in Figure 55.5(c). For the logarithmic function, $x = 3$. (*rand*(1,N) + 0.01), was used to avoid zero, with $y = \log(x)$ as the target presented in Figure 55.5(d). In both cases, the Verilog results showed close value with MATLAB outputs and maintaining relative errors below 0.8%.

The maximum and mean relative error difference between the MATLAB and Verilog implementation output curves for function approximation using NN is reported in Table 55.1. It is observed in this table that the error in all cases is lower than 1%. The resource utilization summary of the Verilog implementation of NN architectures is reported in Table 55.2.

Conclusion

This work presents a neural network implementation for approximating nonlinear functions: sine, cubic, exponential, and logarithmic across MATLAB and Verilog platforms. A single-hidden-layer network with hyperbolic tangent activation function was trained in MATLAB, and its parameters were quantized to Q4.12 fixed-point format for Verilog deployment. The Verilog design employed a CORDIC-based tanh implementation to enable efficient fixed-point activation without multipliers or large LUTs. Comparison with MATLAB and true function outputs confirmed the accuracy and hardware suitability of the approach.

The future work includes exploring advanced quantization schemes, alternative activation functions, and further optimization for low-power edge applications. This study provides a practical framework for translating software-trained networks into efficient digital hardware.

References

[1] Hajduk, Z. (2018). Hardware implementation of hyperbolic tangent and sigmoid activation functions. *Bulletin of the Polish Academy of Sciences, Technical Sciences*, 66, 563–577.

[2] Hajduk, Z., & Dec, G. R. (2023). Very high accuracy hyperbolic tangent function implementation in FPGAs. *IEEE Access*, 11, 23701–23713.

[3] Qian, M. (2006). Application of CORDIC algorithm to neural networks VLSI design.

In the Proceedings of the Multiconference on Computational Engineering in Systems Applications, (Vol. 1, pp. 504–508). IEEE.

[4] Ratnakumar, R., & Nanda, S. J. (2019). A low complexity hardware architecture of K-means algorithm for real-time satellite image segmentation. *Multimedia Tools and Applications*, 78(9), 11949–11981.

[5] Ratnakumar, R., & Nanda, S. J. (2021). A high speed roller dung beetles clustering algorithm and its architecture for real-time image segmentation. *Applied Intelligence*, 51(7), 4682–4713.

[6] Raut, G., Bhartiy, V., Rajput, G., Khan, S., Beohar, A., & Vishvakarma, S. K. (2019). Efficient low-precision cordic algorithm for hardware implementation of artificial neural network. In VLSI Design and Test: 23rd International Symposium, VDAT 2019, Indore, India, July 4–6, 2019, Revised Selected Papers 23, (pp. 321-333). Springer Singapore.

[7] Shen, W., Jiang, J., Li, M., & Liu, S. (2025). Efficient cordic-based activation functions for RNN acceleration on FPGAs. *IEEE Transactions on Artificial Intelligence*, 6(1), 199–210.

[8] Tiwari, V., & Khare, N. (2015). Hardware implementation of neural network with sigmoidal activation functions using cordic. *Microprocessors and Microsystems*, 39(6), 373–381.

[9] Yousif, R. K., Hashim, I. A., & Abd, B. H. (2023). Low area FPGA implementation of hyperbolic tangent function. In 2023 6th International Conference on Engineering Technology and its Applications (IICETA), (pp. 596–602). IEEE.

[10] Zamanlooy, B., & Mirhassani, M. (2013). Efficient VLSI implementation of neural networks with hyperbolic tangent activation function. *IEEE Transactions on Very Large Scale Integration (VLSI) Systems*, 22(1), 39–48.

For Product Safety Concerns and Information please contact our EU
representative GPSR@taylorandfrancis.com
Taylor & Francis Verlag GmbH, Kaufingerstraße 24, 80331 München, Germany